Juni K...
11/03

P9-BZL-963

THE BACK DOOR GUIDE TO
SHORT-TERM
JOB ADVENTURES

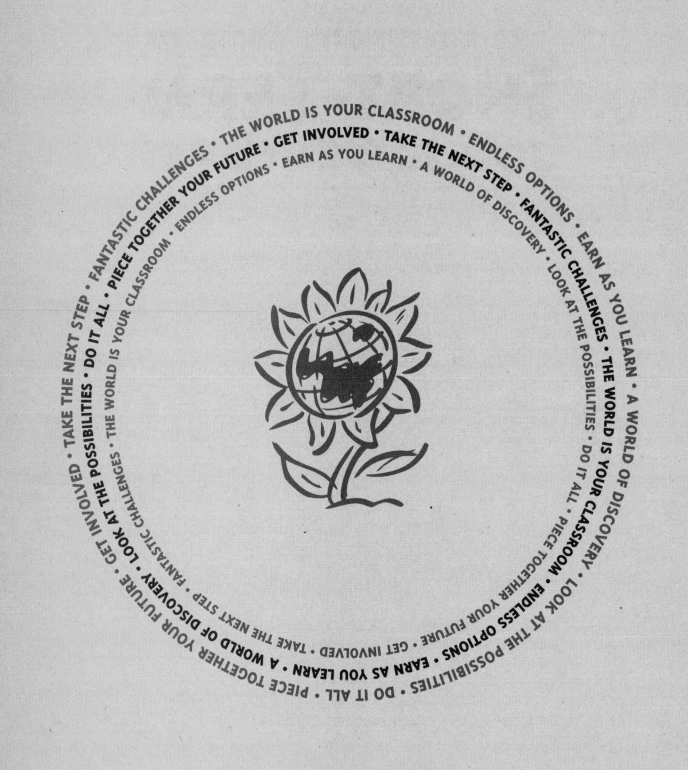

THE BACK DOOR GUIDE TO

SHORT-TERM

JOB ADVENTURES

INTERNSHIPS, EXTRAORDINARY EXPERIENCES, SEASONAL JOBS, VOLUNTEERING, WORK ABROAD

BY MICHAEL LANDES

TEN SPEED PRESS
BERKELEY · TORONTO

DEDICATION

To my mom and dad, who not only opened my eyes to so many things
while growing up but who also provided me with the tools
I needed to develop into the person I am today.
I feel very fortunate—it's comforting to know that someone
encourages and has faith in your abilities no matter what.

Text copyright © 2002 by Michael Landes

All rights reserved. No part of this book may be reproduced in any form, except
brief excerpts for the purpose of review, without written permission of the publisher.

A Kirsty Melville Book

Ten Speed Press
P.O. Box 7123
Berkeley, California 94707
www.tenspeed.com

Distributed in Australia by Simon and Schuster Australia, in Canada by Ten Speed Press Canada, in New Zealand by Southern
Publishers Group, in South Africa by Real Books, in Southeast Asia by Berkeley Books, and in the United Kingdom and Europe
by Airlift Book Company.

Library of Congress Cataloging-in-Publication Data

Landes, Michael.
  The back door guide to short-term job adventures / by Michael
Landes.— 3rd ed.
     p. cm.
Includes bibliographical references and index.
  ISBN 1-58008-449-4 (pbk.)
 1. Job hunting. 2. Interns. 3. Volunteers. I. Title: Short-term job
adventures. II. Title.

HF5382.7 .L352 2002
 650.14—dc21

                          2002010605

Cover design by Catherine Jacobes
Text design by Linda Davis

Front cover photographs of mountain biker, rock climber, and paint brushes courtesy of Photo Disc. Front cover photographs of
castle and man doing yoga courtesy of Digital Vision. Front cover photograph of sailing ship courtesy of Chris Bowser. Back
cover photograph of conservation workers courtesy of Vermont Youth Conservation Corps. Back cover photograph of kayaker
courtesy of Jake Mills. Back cover photograph of volunteers repairing stairs courtesy of Marya Dumont.

First printing of this edition, 2002
Printed in the United States

1 2 3 4 5 6 7 8 9 10—05 04 03 02 01

CONTENTS

Remember when you thought about "what I want to be when I grow up?" Not there now? Well, think about it again, because you still have plenty of options to choose from. At first glance, you may think this book is solely an encyclopedia of unique short-term job opportunities. Undoubtedly, this may be the most alluring ingredient—especially since there are roughly 350 pages worth of life-changing opportunities. However, I don't believe that a book of opportunities makes much sense without first questioning your existence and your purpose—you know, the *who, what, where, how,* and *why*. That's why the first three sections of your guide—the self-help component—focus solely on the philosophies that will help to bring happiness, meaning, passion, and lifelong learning. And that's exciting stuff.

Start by doing what's necessary, then what's possible . . . and suddenly you are doing the impossible.
—Saint Francis

So what is the secret to discovering your passion, achieving your dream career, pursuing a lifelong interest, or just doing something different (whether or not it relates to your career)? Simply ask yourself, "Does the opportunity have heart?" If not, what could you do that does? In other words, begin your journey by doing things that naturally harmonize with your values, skills, abilities, and God-given talents. Create a vision—your game plan for your *personal path* through life, then map out how you'll get there. If you haven't found out already, you'll learn that the things you do right now affect who you will become in the future.

Although "discovering your passion" and "achieving your dream career" sound like far-fetched and highfalutin goals, remember that every journey starts with one step. Think about your path step by step. Yes, it's a long process, but it will also be filled with exploration, adventure, and fulfillment that you can feel with each step, knowing you're on your way. It's also important to realize that every new path you take is an opportunity to create, learn, grow, and stretch while exploring life's possibilities—whether or not it leads to a dream career.

When you try something new, your mind, body, and soul stretch and never go back to their original shape. Opening the back door to your future is really about growing and gravitating toward something that brings meaning to your life. Each experience will move you in new directions that you never imagined before you came up with the idea. You'll also find that these experiences are shaping your life—pushing and pulling you in different directions—until eventually you find something that really rocks your world. Just like getting on a train and picking up momentum—your life will gain momentum and get better and better.

OPENING THE BACK DOOR TO YOUR FUTURE

You must not let your life run in the ordinary way; do something that nobody else has done, something that will dazzle the world. Show that God's creative principle works in you. —PARAMAHANSA YOGANANDA

Look at your current situation. Does it fit in with your vision? If not, change it! (Again, the best place to start is with the heart.) And don't be afraid to do what feels natural for you, even if these things sound totally far out. If it interests you and excites you and attracts you, it's a pretty good bet. Societal norms dictate many people's lives. Creating your own path means becoming a pioneer and explorer, discovering new places, exploring new ideas, meeting new people, and, most of all, uncovering the unique gifts that you were born with. Since no one blatantly tells us what these gifts are, we have to challenge ourselves to bring them out. Fortunately, you'll find that these gifts always direct you to your place in the world.

It's also about finding your *zone space*. Do you know that feeling—the zone you get into when everything feels right? Some figure out their zone space right away, others take a lifetime to get there, and, unfortunately, many give up when success is just around the corner (so please, please don't give up!). It may take a lot work on your part, but you can carve out the path that's right for you. You'll know it right away. It will be a path with heart and it will energize your existence on earth.

In a recent short-term job adventure as an apprentice with Michaela Farm (see page 259), I learned about the art of farming—just one of many experiences that are tucked away on my life's list of things to accomplish (have you created yours?). While at the farm, I participated in a series of classes focusing on the spiritual component of farming and life (just one of the benefits of a short-term job adventure!). One class of particular interest centered on the influences from St. Francis—insights that have resonated with my very own work. Read through the following insights and see what each means to you (I've also included corresponding feature stories throughout your guide for further understanding):

- To find your calling, put silence in your life.
  (Food for the Soul, page 235)

- Open yourself up to who you really are.
  (Open Yourself Up to the Possibilities, page 65)

- Let go, so something greater can come forth.
  (Open Letter to a Friend, page 14)

- Understand your path of conversion—the natural growth that takes place when you stay on your path; no matter how hard it may become. (Finding a Place in the World, page 368)

- Keep developing your gifts one step at a time. This work will take you (and keep you) on the right path.
  (In Search of a Mission—A Deeper Calling, page 310)

My hope is that the many "voices" that speak to you throughout the pages of your guide will not only encourage you to find your place in the world, but also allow you to realize that life is truly a miraculous event.

In 1996 a dream of mine finally came to fruition—the creation of the very guidebook you're holding. Much has changed since these early roots; however, the heart of your guide has not—it's still a tool that can change lives. That's why your guidebook goes beyond a directory of different opportunities to explore. It features seven unique components to make the most of your new journey: three sections of self-help material (so you can discover who you are and what you want to do); seven sections of program listings (full of organizations that provide job opportunities season-after-season and year-after-year); five indexes (so you quickly locate the material you need); over 250 inspirational quotes peppered throughout (I suggest pulling out your favorites and posting them on the walls of your home); hundreds of recommended resources, books, and websites (for further research); feature stories from experts in the field (you'll really enjoy these!); and over eighty photos (so you can begin to visualize your dreams!). Most of all I have worked very hard at making the content playful, inspirational, and fun-to-read—with a design that's fresh and engaging.

You will recognize your own path when you come upon it, because you will suddenly have all the energy and imagination you will ever need.
—Jerry Gillies

With each new edition, every word, fact, philosophy, program, resource, quote, and visual is looked at with discriminating eyes—and dramatic changes occur. Just as I'm growing and learning and exploring, so does the book. Writing, carefully researching, updating, and revising a guidebook involves an enormous amount of information gathering and exacting attention to the nitty-gritty. Each year I'm presented with new programs, new resources, new ideas, new stories, and new quotes. In the process of writing and updating this book, I am fortunate to be able to communicate with thousands of people and programs. However, the real joy of my work is the process of going "under cover"—actually visiting the programs in your guide; then writing from these experiences. I encourage you to do the same. Visit a prospective organization whenever possible prior to inking the deal. This small adventure will not only impress the hiring team, but will allow you make a sound decision based on the big picture (and if it doesn't work out, think of all the learning that took place!).

AT THE HEART OF YOUR GUIDE

The people who get on in the world are the people who get up and look for the circumstances they want and if they can't find them, make them. —GEORGE BERNARD SHAW

This book evolves by my gathering of information, talking with people, showing up at their back door, and finding out what really goes on. One thing leads to the next. You can do the same. Beyond my own research, *Back Door* readers have proved to be a valuable asset by providing me with the realities of working for a particular program. Any comments I receive from readers on their experiences, I try to integrate into the respective listing. Many times you'll find a direct quote at the bottom of the listing that captures readers' experiences.

Whatever the way I've uncovered the information, every fact is verified with the program directors prior to inclusion in the guide. The updating process (which I do both through mail, email, and phone) also serves as my weeding-out process. The challenge is to sift through all the important stuff and present you with a unique blend of information and inspiration. I spend thousands and thousands of hours writing and rewriting each listing so that it conveys the spirit and soul of each adventure. My formative years taught me that you should do a job to the best of your ability or not do it all. I hope that you will find that my work reflects this very philosophy.

A CALLING UNIQUE TO ME

As I reflect on a handful of experiences in my lifetime—learning to "think different" as an intern at Apple Computer; counseling and inspiring college students about the importance of internships at a university; venturing to Europe on a solo backpacking and cycling adventure; experiencing the beauty of Yellowstone National Park while working as a recreation manager; connecting more with the earth as an apprentice at a farm, or teaching elementary school children—I've realized that every experience, no matter how unrelated they were, has made me the person I am today. By looking at the world with curious eyes and exploring what's on the other side of the mountain, I now can see this incredible place we live in from many perspectives. Amazingly, I've seen my calling in life develop through this extraordinary sojourn that I've experienced. Fortunately, I can now share my insights, fumbles, adventures, and philosophies with you through this book (which I'm very thankful for).

With over twelve years of experience in the career and life-planning field (and considered an internship guru in job adventure circles), Michael Landes believes there is room for every person to "find their place in the world" and meaning in their work. At age thirty-seven (and a kid at heart), Landes has worked in literally hundreds of short-term job experiences over the course of his life. Currently he is inspiring, encouraging, and teaching elementary school kids in New York while developing his website, Backdoorjobs.com.

CONNECTING WITH THE AUTHOR

Simply stated, I'd love to hear from you. Your adventurous (and not-so-adventurous) tales, experiences, suggestions, and feedback help to fuel my passion and make each edition better than the last. Since my journeys take me to different locales throughout the year, the best way to contact me is through email. Send me a note at mlandes@backdoorjobs.com or visit my companion website at www.backdoorjobs.com.

Happy adventures!

It's a funny thing about life; if you refuse to accept anything but the best, you very often get it. —W. SOMERSET MAUGHAM

The amazing journey of creating your guidebook has boiled down to two key ingredients—people and place—ingredients that have colored every aspect of my writing. The very nature of this guidebook has allowed me to transplant myself to many new environments; however, this component has also challenged me in many ways. Leading an adventurous life is definitely invigorating, but I have also been challenged with the balancing transition and stability. This means creating a home base that I could find comfort in and an environment that would allow me to explore and take part in all the world has to offer—a factor that you must look at very carefully as you begin your own adventurous pursuits. As I began revising and rewriting the pages of this third edition, I've been very fortunate to have dear friends and family who have helped me to balance this sense of place.

Reach for the highest
Strive for the best . . .
Live day by day
And to God leave the rest.

Beyond the sense of place that was created and nurtured, it was my connections with an amazing group of people (my "back door" team) that helped my words come alive. I feel very blessed for the following people who have influenced and added their gifts to this book: Mike and Dorrie Williams, Scott Lewis, Craig Dunkin, Bri-Guy Kean, and Sunny Sue (for her constant support and inspiration, invaluable suggestions, and constant stream of incredible quotes).

My team of contributing writers: Jill Baxter, Bill Borrie, Patrick Combs, Michele Gran, Elizabeth Kruempelmann, David Lyman, Cori Stennett, and Catharine Sutherland, along with the many readers who have sent me their insider tips.

All the program directors and staff members who year-after-year provide me with information and invaluable insights about their short-term job opportunities.

My talented team at Ten Speed Press who amazingly turned my words into this beautiful book: Jean Bloomquist for her unbelievably thorough copyedit, Linda Davis for the creative design of every page in your guide, Catherine Jacobes for her incredible cover design, Jasmine Star for her careful proofread and attention to detail, Jacinta Monniere, Jon Haug, and Chloe Nelson for keying in corrections, Ken DellaPenta for his exceptional job on the indexes, and finally, my editor, Carrie Rodrigues, for putting her magical touches on the entire project.

And finally, many many thanks go to each of you for believing in and supporting all my hard work. Thank you for keeping my passion alive!

ACKNOWLEDGMENTS

The Climb

A small boy heard the mountain speak,
"There are secrets on my highest peak;
but beware, my boy, the passing of time.
Wait not too long to start the climb."

So quickly come and go the years,
and a young man stands below—with fears.
"Come on—come on," the mountain cussed.
"Time presses on—on, climb you must."

Now he's busied in middle-aged prime,
and maybe tomorrow he'll take the climb.
Now is too soon—it's raining today;
Gone all gone—years are eaten away.

An old man looks up—still feeling the lure.
Yet, he'll suffer the pain—not climb for the cure.
The hair is white—the step is slow.
And it's safer and warmer to stay here below.

So all too soon the secrets are buried,
along with him and regrets he carried.
And it's not for loss of secrets he'd cried,
But rather because he'd never tried.

—PHYLLIS TRUSSIER

1

For those who already know they want to excavate an archaeological dig in Peru or teach kids about the wonders of the Atlantic Ocean and don't need to do extensive soul searching, taking a peek at this section can't hurt. Finding yourself, deciding what brings meaning to your life, and determining your destiny all take time. This section will give you some creative ideas about the bigger picture in life and start your climb off on the right foot.

This section will help you to:

- Uncover who you are and what naturally motivates you.

- Find balance in your life.

- Map out the big picture of your life.

- Understand the power of people and place.

- Begin the decision-making process.

BEGINNING
THE CLIMB

How can you get very far,

If you don't know who you are?

How can you do what you ought,

If you don't know what you've got?

And if you don't know which to do

Of all the things in front of you,

Then what you'll have when you
    are through

Is just a mess without a clue

Of all the best that can come true

If you know what and which and who.

—Winnie the Pooh

We could all use an emptying out of identity every now and then. Considering who we are not, we may find the surprising revelation of who we are.

—Thomas Moore

Everyone has his own specific vocation or mission in life to carry out a concrete assignment which demands fulfillment. Therein he cannot be replaced, nor can his life be repeated. Thus, everyone's task is as unique as is his specific opportunity to implement it.

—Viktor Frankl

WHO ARE YOU? . . . .

If you want to become an extraordinary, happy, fulfilled, and balanced person, it's time to stop being nebulous. Now is the time to take inventory of your talents, your personal quirks, and the careers that might resonate with your skills and abilities. With the work you are about to engage in, you will gain the ability to promote your uniqueness with passion and vigor when the time comes. Think of your life as a long, never-ending pathway stretching out ahead of you, with many pathways leading off to either side. The path you are on now represents the lifestyle you are now living (whether it be good or challenging); the offshoots from this pathway represent new directions you might take—new jobs, new places to live, new relationships, and new experiences. However, in giving yourself many options, you'll always come to a signpost on the road presenting you with two or three (or four . . .) attractive possibilities. Which one should you take? Which one in the short run will help you with your long-term goals? Of course, some of these paths might have huge doors in front of them, and to get through these doors, you must do certain things before they swing open for you. A particular door might need a certain skill, a degree, a well-connected friend or family member, a unique personal characteristic, or a past experience as a key. So, let's start from the beginning and uncover the unique you.

SETTING THE STAGE . . . .

Have you ever been to a play? If not, make plans to see a production for the sheer enjoyment of it. Now, take a few minutes and ponder all the things that went into the play's production: the directors, producers, writers, cast, set designers, musicians, costuming, acting, rehearsals, development, fund-raising, program design, publicity, and so forth. It's amazing to think of all the steps necessary to create one production. Have you thought about what will make your very own "production" incredible? Have you thought about the things you want to (or may want to) accomplish to create an incredible story for yourself? Are you the director and author of your story, or are you letting societal norms or others dictate or shape your story? Are you actively taking the time to develop your plot and create the things that are the most important? Think of all the players who are involved in your story: the scenery, the things that happen on a daily basis, the decisions that are made, the highs and the lows.

I dare you to think differently and to take your potential seriously. It's time to call on all your resources—to stretch them and challenge them. It's time to trade in your days of getting by and begin to work toward a life that brings fulfillment in everything you do. Today is the day. This journey must begin with an understanding of what's happening in your life right now—behind the scenes and on center stage. A powerful way to visualize the big picture of your life is by explicitly writing out all the important details—the fabric that will give you something to work with and something to act upon.

> It's very important to fall in love with what you're doing. To be able to get out of bed and do what you love for the rest of your day is beyond words. It'll keep you around for a long time.
>
> —GEORGE BURNS

MAKE TIME THIS WEEK TO ANSWER THE FOLLOWING QUESTIONS (or begin a journal!):

- What kind of person do you want to be?
- What (and whom) do you gravitate toward naturally?
- What are your values?
- What are your unique qualities?
- What are your likes and dislikes?
- What are five skills you enjoy using?
- What three words best describe you?
- What are your dreams and fears?
- Where do you need improvement?
- What do your friends say you are good at?
- Whom do you admire?
- What traits of those you admire would you make your own?
- Putting money aside, what job would give you the most satisfaction?
- If you could begin any hobby, what would that be?

Working through these questions (and additional ones you might have) will set the tone for the events and experiences that are now taking shape. You might also uncover some very interesting facts about yourself. But don't be alarmed if you don't. You might just need to think, explore, and do more. Once you begin to understand who you are and what is unfolding in your life, it will be easier to set goals, make decisions, and push past any barriers that might come your way. If you don't know yourself and the tools you have to work with, you'll certainly have a "mess without a clue" (as Pooh suggests). It's important not to overlook this important step in your journey.

I can play the piano. I speak two languages. I can juggle. I love teaching kids about the wonders of the world. I hate snakes. I love frogs. I'm a so-so painter. I love thunderstorms and crazy weather. I'm afraid of not having enough money, going into debt, or being dependent on my parents or another person. I'm a pretty good baker. I'm a rotten city driver and really don't care for big cities. I really want to be a writer, photographer, teacher, and speaker! I'm not very organized. I love Italian music and food. A lot of money is not important to me. I want to travel in my work. I enjoy helping others out. I want to be settled somewhere. I just want to goof off for a couple of months. I'd like to try living on a boat or on a remote island. One day I'd like to have my own business—maybe open a coffee shop. I want to work on an organic farm in another country. I like a lot of change and stimulation. I've always wanted to visit every national park in the U.S. (and even work at one!).

I've learned that everyone wants to live on top of the mountain, but all the happiness and growth occurs while you're climbing it. —ANDY ROONEY

THE BALANCING ACT . . . .

As you uncover who you are, it's equally important to strive for balance in all you do. This means stimulating your mind, exercising your body, viewing the world as an integrated whole, and understanding that life is not a series of random, meaningless events. When you strive to reach this balance in your life, you'll harmonize your actions with the way life is and make the will of nature your own. Remember, it's not what you do once in a while that will shape your life, it's what you do on a consistent basis. Make the time each day to work on the whole you!

MENTALLY

Becoming mentally active means becoming aware of the world around you. Every relationship, experience, mishap, or good fortune in your life is making an impact on who you become. The information you take into your mind, whether it be from a conversation with a stranger, news on television, concepts you learned from a workshop, or an idea from a book, is a continual process. Although some experiences are beyond your control, you must realize that you have the ability to influence what you decide to take into your mind or not. Are the turmoil and mishaps from the evening news helping to shape your life or detracting from it? Are the people you interact with on a daily basis adding a positive component to your life or inhibiting it? Since we generally find ourselves in other people and events, it's important to be aware of these associations.

What, then, are ways to include positive stimuli in your mind? For instance, make a list of friends and colleagues who make you feel more alive, happier, and more positive about life. Make it a point to spend more time with these people. Pay close attention to the book recommendations I have made throughout your guide (as well as recommendations from other friends). The words found in books will help you to think better and to become a more discerning and reflective person. Books will help you exercise the mind—learn a new skill, uncover new places to explore, be introduced to a new philosophy, and open your world to new concepts and ideas that will help to shape your life. In addition to reading the words of others, you might decide to create your own. I've had an ongoing journal for most of my life, which has included my thoughts, insights, experiences, or lessons I've learned. I generally carry my journal everywhere I go—you never know when a great idea might come your way! My journal has also served as the basis for much of the writing that has been included in your guide.

Tips on Reaching Your Goals

- Memorize your favorite motivating phrases in your guide and say them everyday!

- Make little signs (or huge obnoxious ones that demand your attention) that point toward what you want in your life and put them all over your home. These will serve as reminders of where you want your life to go. Don't take them down until you have actually succeeded in your efforts.

- If you can verbalize your top goals without having to sit down and think about them, you're closer to reaching them than you realize.

The importance of the whole—the balance of the mind, body, and spirit—is essential for anyone who wants to make a personal commitment to self-exploration and growth. Explore your options at various retreat centers found in the Food for the Soul section on page 235.

Nurture your mind with great thoughts, for you will never go any higher than you think.

—BENJAMIN DISRAELI

Keeping a Journal

Make time in your life to reflect upon your experiences. You don't have to start a new job or partake in a new experience to begin. Start today! Journals can help you discover new ideas, take action on these ideas, sort out difficulties with others, invent new ways of seeing things, plan new adventures, and help you to relive your experiences later in life. Books with blank pages seem to work the best. It's up to you to fill them with pictures, inspiring quotes, collages, or whatever is on your mind. You might just find the answers you were looking for.

The best of all things is to learn. Money can be lost or stolen, health and strength may fail, but what you have committed to your mind is yours forever.

—LOUIS L'AMOUR

PHYSICALLY

All right, put your guide down and give me fifty—fifty push-ups, that is. Being physically balanced means making a commitment to taking care of your body. For one, this means adding positive behaviors that promote good health, as well as strengthening habits you've already created for yourself. It also means making a commitment to exercise every day. You'll find that when you look and feel your best, you tend to be a happier person, with more confidence propelling everything you do.

For some it will take breaking old habits and starting out fresh. Changing habits is especially hard at first, because it requires determined efforts and time to make the changes stick. If you are just beginning your journey with exercise, walking is truly the best activity because it provides you with a complete workout. My preference is to walk in beautiful surroundings during the morning hours (there is something magical about the world waking up). I either walk with a companion to converse with, or by myself so I can be alone with my thoughts and nature. Begin with ten minutes each day; then gradually increase the duration so that you are walking at least thirty to forty minutes per day. Daily stretching, which improves the flexibility of your body, is another healthful component to include in your exercise program. The more flexible your body is, the better it can meet the demands of life. You might also explore yoga as a formal way of stretching your body (and mind). Yoga helps to tone every muscle in your body and will assist in balancing all parts of your body, along with helping you to relax.

Make exercise a daily ritual and vary it every so often so you find

If you stuff yourself full of poems, essays, plays, stories, novels, films, comic strips, magazines, and music, you automatically explode every morning like Old Faithful. I have never had a dry spell in my life, mainly because I feed myself well, to the point of bursting. I wake early and hear my morning voices leaping around in my head like jumping beans. I get out of bed to trap them before they escape.

—RAY BRADBURY

Spend at least ten minutes a day meditating on how you can become a better person.

You are today where your thoughts have brought you; you will be tomorrow where your thoughts take you. —JAMES ALLEN

We are what we repeatedly do. Excellence, then, is not an act, but a habit.

—ARISTOTLE

Before you indulge in your next meal, take a moment and feel gratitude for the food you are about to eat. This will help to raise your spiritual awareness and provide a firmer sense of your dependence on other living things.

it refreshing and invigorating. Those who are more active can find a variety of pursuits that can help get the heart going, along with sweating out all the daily toxins of life. If you're not a fan of active sports, such as mountain biking, sea kayaking, or surfing, joining a fitness center will provide varied activities to keep your routine fresh. I especially like the energy that comes from step aerobics or a spinning class, or the spiritual connection that yoga provides. One key to exercise is making time for it, but the most important key is listening to your body. It will tell you if you've had too much or too little, so don't overdo. Sometimes curling up with a good book is all you really need to recharge your batteries. So listen. Getting sufficient sleep and relaxation is just as important as pushing your body.

Along with your exercise prescription, healthy eating habits are just as important. Those who are creating and eating well-balanced and healthful meals that include whole grains, fresh vegetables and fruits, fish, and minimal amounts of meats, are off to a great start. It's especially beneficial to seek out people whose lifestyle promotes healthier eating habits, as you are more apt to mirror their habits. What you take into your body will largely affect how you feel throughout the day. It takes time to figure out your balance. Because we need food to sustain us, it's exciting to explore the possibilities that will not only bring ample energy to all we do, but will also enhance and protect our healing abilities. Those of you who work hard at maintaining a proper diet, daily exercise, and proper relaxation will find an energy that will invigorate everything you do.

Walking is the best exercise. Habituate yourself to walk very far.

—THOMAS JEFFERSON

Optimum Health. It's about creating healthy habits for eating, exercising, breathing, using your mind, and nourishing your spirit. It's about wholeness and balance. It's about making health choices on a daily basis that allow you to meet the demands of living without being overwhelmed. Holistic guru Dr. Andrew Weil, with his book *Eight Weeks to Optimum Health* (Fawcett Books, $13.95), provides a week-by-week program that will help shape and strengthen behaviors for becoming naturally healthy throughout your life. To explore other resources and advice from Dr. Weil, check out his companion website at www.drweil.com.

EATING WITH WELLNESS IN MIND

It's true—you are what you eat. This also means that what you take in affects how you feel, both emotionally and physically. Obviously a diet rich in sweets and soda (or alcohol and nicotine) encourages mood swings, while one filled with truckloads of fresh fruit will make you feel so good that you will be sitting around giggling and playing with your toes! Hey, give it a try. . . . It's important to understand how your body works and what it needs to foster an energized you. As you embark on your road to wellness, it's important to understand how the body deals with food. Stephen Seipel, a vegetarian and former intern at Michaela Farm (page 259), shares his secrets (but realize you must uncover what works best for you!):

The body normally follows three basic cycles:

1. Appropriation (eating) noon to 8 P.M.

2. Assimilation (digesting/metabolizing) 8 P.M. to 4 A.M.

3. Elimination (excreting) 4 A.M. to noon

Looking at these three phases will help you to understand why it's best to stay away from anything heavy or processed for breakfast. The body is trying to get rid of what it ate the day before, so the most you should have before noon is just a piece or two of juicy fruit, such as an apple, pear, grapes, and/or a big glass of freshly squeezed orange juice.

After the noon hour, focus on raw foods, as the body is still in the elimination phase. Some fresh fruit, salad, nuts, alfalfa sprouts combined with radish, or freshly made juice (especially carrot juice) is best!

For dinner, a baked sweet potato, brown rice, steamed veggies, rice and beans, and a huge salad are good starting points for an energized you! Digestion of food takes more energy than any other activity that we do. This is why it's best to eat cooked foods at the end of the day, when all the work is finished, so that the body is not making competing energy demands.

SPIRITUALLY

The point of bringing a spiritual perspective into your life is a simple reminder that you are more than just your physical body. I also believe it's accepting in childlike faith that a Supreme Being exists. I was born and raised Catholic, so my parents provided a solid foundation in my spiritual growth. It was not until college that I questioned just about everything—especially my existence and the meaning of life. I took classes on Buddhism and existentialism, and began exploring different types of organized religions. After years of agonizing over this area in my life, I realized it didn't really matter what everyone called this Being from above, so long as I reaffirmed that he did exist and that I needed to live my life with this knowledge. Life didn't really get any easier with this knowledge; however, my existence has become more meaningful, more magical, and more heartfelt by nourishing this spiritual side.

The way we spiritually connect to the world will be different for each person, but once you find this connection, everyday problems

Building a deeper life of spirituality often begins with the development of a personal prayer life. *Beginning to Pray* by Anthony Bloom (Paulist Press, $6.95) offers practical guidelines on the power of prayer for people at all spiritual levels.

Don't be weary in prayer; keep at it; watch for God's answers and remember to be thankful when they come. —COLOSSIANS 4:2

Slow me down, God, and inspire me to send my roots down deep into the soil of life's enduring values, so I may grow toward the stars and unfold my destiny.

—WILFRED PETERSON

The secret to enjoying life to to be thankful for what each day brings.

of life (when we feel helpless, confused, or resentful) become more tolerable, and everyday occurrences become more purposeful. Nourishing your spirituality might include reading inspirational quotes, immersing yourself in nature, listening to the rhythms of a particular song, bringing fresh flowers into your home, lighting candles and being silent, praying, meditating, or listening to a sermon each Sunday. Whatever you do to get in touch with your core, it's very important to view the world as an integrated whole and live your life with faith. Religious leader David McKay taught, "The greatest battles of life are fought out daily in the silent chambers of the soul." Once you deal with these inward battles (and realize you cannot anticipate or control events), you will find that life is not a series of random, meaningless episodes. Set aside a small part of your day to spiritually connect and become familiar with the complexities of your inner life.

EMOTIONALLY

Life is continually filled with emotions tied to daily occurrences in your life. What happens in these everyday situations can also affect the way you feel. Staying emotionally balanced is the ability to be secure enough within yourself to handle life's ups and downs and not allow these things to control your life. Realize some things are within your control and others are not. You always have a choice about the content and integrity of your own life; however, external events and circumstances are beyond your control. When things don't go as you planned or people don't react the way you had hoped, you have the choice to allow feelings of hurt, anger, and inner turmoil to spread throughout your body or not.

You also have the choice to fill yourself with thoughts and actions that make you feel inspired, happy, excited, passionate, magical, energized, and enthusiastic. Positive results generally follow positive actions. Even though you may find yourself in challenging or difficult situations, these occurrences, approached with positive eyes, all help to make you a stronger and happier person. Tom Dennard, in his book *Discovering Life's Trails,* puts it this way: "We all have a tendency to want to label events in our lives as being good or bad because that's how we perceive them at the time. But bad can blend into good and good can blend into bad. We need to alter our perception of life's happenings as being good or bad and realize that every occurrence is necessary to make us who we are."

As you begin to understand your emotions, I encourage you to enjoy life's simple pleasures: compliment a stranger, hug a friend, laugh hysterically, scream at the top of your lungs, cry until the tears run dry. Remember you're human; do what you need to balance your emotions.

Often people attempt to live their lives backwards: they try to have more things, or more money, in order to do more of what they want so that they will be happier. The way it actually works is the reverse. You must first be who you really are, then, do what you need to do, in order to have what you want.

—MARGARET YOUNG

Dreams

Listen to yourself and listen through your dreams. Dreams can help you understand your inner workings, solve life's problems, and see what your unconscious mind is working on at the moment. Dreams can point you in the right direction, whether you are lost or on the right track. You'll also find that your unconscious mind loves to guide you and answer questions you're not ready to ask your conscious mind.

If you can dream it, you can do it.

—WALT DISNEY

BRINGING IT ALL TOGETHER. . . .

Now that you have a better picture of who you are, your desires, and how to maintain balance in all you do, it's time to focus on your needs. The most basic of human needs are food, shelter, and the ability to make enough income to meet your financial obligations. Once these essentials have been fulfilled, you can take strides to include more in your life—the path of self-actualization. Everyone will have different levels of each need as well as different ways to meet them. Up to this point, much of the focus has been on your wants. Wants are, well, anything. If you can figure out what you really want to do and what your basic needs are, you can be creative and resourceful about meeting both of them.

CREATE A HAPPY BOX

Find an old shoe box and fill it with your favorite quotes. When you're feeling dispirited, pull one out at random and see what words of wisdom will help to inspire you, change your way of thinking, and move you in a new direction.

A happy person is not one with a certain set of circumstances, but rather a person with a certain set of attitudes. —HUGH DOWNS

MASLOW'S HIERARCHY OF NEEDS

SELF-ACTUALIZATION:
Step 5: Beauty, Truth,
Goodness, Aliveness, Individuality,
Perfection, Necessity, Completion, Creativity,
Simplicity, Playfulness, Self-Sufficiency, Significance

GROWTH NEEDS:
Step 4: Self-Esteem, Status, Ego, A Feeling of Importance
Step 3: Belonging, Companionship, Love
Step 2: Safety, Security, Risk Avoidance

BASIC NEEDS:
Step 1: Health and the Preservation of Life, Air and Water, Food, Shelter, Sleep, Sex, Clothing

EXPLORE SIMPLICITY

To explore simplicity involves thinking about how your actions affect the earth, yourself, and others in this world. Simplifying your lifestyle is a continual process of choosing to focus on what is most important mentally, physically, emotionally, and spiritually. This may mean learning to become more self-reliant (such as planting your own garden or learning a new skill), seeking out entertainment that involves creativity and community growth, cooking from scratch to minimize waste, or volunteering your skills for a cause that helps to make the world a better place. The process of simplifying enables you to reexamine your wants and needs, and to shed the burdens of the unnecessary. You might also be pleasantly surprised that happiness goes beyond the material things in life.

PEOPLE AND PLACE. . . . .

Your connections with people and places, which have provided a definition of who you are, are now changing. Change requires a release of these connections. The times of transition—changing jobs, changing eating habits, changing partners, changing where you live—all require you to give something up in order to gain. Definitely not an easy process! When you hold onto what used to be, it inevitably blurs your reasons for change in the first place. The only way you can grow is by pushing past your old way of thinking to create the things that are important to you.

Living simply need not translate into becoming poor, but rather making the wisest use of time and resources to live a richer and more joyful life. *The Simple Living Guide* by Janet Luhrs (Broadway Books, $21.95) brings all the key elements together—from money, working, and travel to exercising, housing, and health—and is rich in resources and real-life examples to help you explore the possibilities of a simpler lifestyle.

THE HUMAN CONNECTION

Once you've focused on what is important, whether this means becoming a more balanced person or turning your dream job into a reality, that "fire in your belly" will take hold and bring energy and enthusiasm to everything you do. The things you thought you could not do become visions of the past. Undoubtedly you will have periods of discouragement or times when progress appears to be at a standstill. To push past these fleeting moments, it is important to seek out people, teachers, and mentors who will not only encourage you but who will also enable you to develop your initial enthusiasm over the long haul.

I believe in the old adage—when the student is ready, the teacher will come. Of course, this does not mean that someone will appear at your back door or your phone will magically ring with your teacher ready to guide you. However, it does mean that your commitment, your hard work, and your enthusiasm toward your passion will promote this ability to uncover people who will take your passions to a

The people I consider successful are so because of how they handle their responsibilities to other people, how they approach the future—people that have a full sense of the value of their lives and what they want to do with it.

—RALPH FIENNES

LESSONS FROM GEESE
(based on the work of Milton Olson)

Fact: As each goose flaps its wings, it creates an uplift for the bird that follows. By flying in a V formation, the whole flock adds 72 percent greater flying range than if each bird flew alone.

Lesson: People who share a common direction and sense of community can get where they are going quicker and easier because they are traveling on the thrust of one another.

Fact: When a goose falls out of formation, it suddenly feels the drag and resistance of flying alone. It quickly moves back into the formation to take advantage of the lifting power of the bird immediately in front of it.

Lesson: If we have as much sense as a goose, we stay in formation with those headed where we want to go. We are willing to accept their help and give our help to others.

Fact: When the lead goose tires, it rotates back in the formation and another goose flies to the point position.

Lesson: It pays to take turns doing the hard tasks and sharing leadership. As with geese, people are interdependent on each other's skills, capabilities, and unique arrangement of gifts, talents, and resources.

Fact: The geese flying in formation honk to encourage those up front to keep up the speed.

Lesson: We need to make sure our honking is encouraging. In groups where there is encouragement, the production is greater. The power of encouragement (to stand by one's heart or core values and encourage the heart and core values of others) is the quality of honking we seek.

Each day comes to me with both hands full of possibilities, and in its brief course I discern all the verities and realities of my existence: the bliss of growth, the glory of action, the spirit of beauty. —HELEN KELLER

During your life, everything you do and everyone you meet rubs off in some way. Some bit of everything you experience stays with everyone you've ever known, and nothing is lost. That's what's eternal, these little specks of experience in a great and enormous river that has no end.

—HARRIET DOERR

If you always do what you've always done, you'll always get what you've always got.

—LARRY WILSON

If we are always arriving and departing, it is also true that we are eternally anchored. One's destination is never a place, but rather a new way of looking at things.

—HENRY MILLER

Just as it is important to find a career that brings meaning to life, it is also important to find a home with heart. *House As a Mirror of Self* by Clare Cooper Marcus (Conari Press, $16.95) explores the deeper meaning of home and the complex connections that each of us creates with our surroundings.

new level. For instance, when I made the decision to write this book, I began calling other like-minded authors who could provide me with insights from their journeys. Over a period of a couple years, I soon developed a network of people that I could bounce ideas off and share my enthusiasm with, and people who would keep me focused when I had lost momentum or felt discouraged. With their support and words of wisdom, I have been able to grow in ways I never thought imaginable when I first started out. The key to developing relationships such as these was putting myself out there, with the realization that some people would be willing to help and others would not. It's those who did that have made all the difference in the world.

CREATING A SENSE OF PLACE

long with the importance of people, our surroundings also shape our thoughts, emotions, and actions. We need places that support, rather than fragment our lives. Many times your growth is limited by sitting around in your old haunts, which promotes the way things used to be. Again, it's important to break past these associations, so you may respond to the positive stimulation of new things and places, which, in turn, promotes new directions and possibilities. When you are in an environment that offers few distractions and allows you to experience things you weren't sure you could do, it's much easier to figure out what matters and what doesn't, and to make the necessary changes in your life.

On the other hand, the current home environment that many of you have created often provides structure, a connection to family and friends, and familiar surroundings. There is also a certain aspect of yourself that resides in this place and that needs to be embraced. But, like it or not, we all have to leave home to find ourselves. The self you may be seeking is not "out there" in the literal sense but always within; often it reveals itself through your journey. To leave is to grow through adventure, risk taking, and excitement. Understand

that a "coming home" can also provide you with stability and strength. As you stumble in your quest for self-discovery and growth, you will find that leaving and staying are necessary components. The secret is to heed the wisdom that emanates from your soul and find the balance between each path.

MAKING CHOICES . . . .

As you begin to take action in your new beginning, you will be faced with many choices that will lay the foundation for your adventure and how you live your life. When you face the difficulties of making conscious choices, you will grow stronger, more capable, and more responsible to yourself. Choices are never easy; however, with a little planning, you can map out a tentative course of action, realizing that the outcome may or may not work. By understanding that either a positive or a negative outcome may result, you'll save yourself a lot of grief when unforeseen or unwanted consequences follow. That's why choices must first begin with a commitment attached to your choices. Tentative efforts always lead to tentative outcomes. Consider the real nature of your aspirations, begin making decisions based on these aspirations, then fully give yourself to these endeavors. It's only when you fully commit that the world responds in magical ways.

Autobiography in Five Short Chapters
by Portia Nelson

ONE
I walk down the street. There is a deep hole in the sidewalk. I fall in. I am lost. I am helpless. It isn't my fault. It takes forever to find a way out.

TWO
I walk down the same street. There is a deep hole in the sidewalk. I pretend I don't see it. I fall in again. I can't believe I am in the same place. But it isn't my fault. It still takes a long time to get out.

THREE
I walk down the same street. There is a deep hole in the sidewalk. I see it is there. I still fall in. It's a habit. My eyes are open. I know where I am. It is my fault. I get out immediately.

FOUR
I walk down the same street. There is a deep hole in the sidewalk. I walk around it.

FIVE
I walk down another street.

Why is it that some people thrive in the hustle and bustle of city life or choose to find comfort in the quiet of the countryside? *In The Power of Place* (HarperPerennial, $13), Winifred Gallagher takes a hard look at how our physical place can delight us, deprive us, alter our moods, confine us, or influence everything we do. Revealing the complexities between people and the places in which they live, work, and enjoy, this book is highly recommended for those searching for a place that brings a sense of home.

We are a product of the choices we make, not the circumstances that we face. —ROGER CRAWFORD

OPEN LETTER TO A FRIEND

My friend:

Your life is now. I tell you this from the bottom of my heart. It is not what you did yesterday. It is not what you will do tomorrow or in your future. It is now. Today is your opportunity to live the real life. Today is your time to get out of the swamp of the status quo. You need to be different on purpose:

- Don't sit around your house and watch TV.
- Don't sell your soul for a great benefits package.
- Don't buy things to have a cooler image.
- Don't hang around with people aiming low in their lives.
- Don't chase money and stuff.
- Don't let the majority shape you.

You are a great-spirited person; it shows in your ambitions and dreams. However, you are not taking your potential seriously. You're trading invaluable days for mere "good times" and "getting-by," because you're letting your fears get the best of you. You fear the time is not right, the resources aren't there, you don't have what it takes. And now, your fear is slowing you down like an anchor that slips overboard and drags along the bottom.

The only fear you need is the fear that you might continue living a life much smaller than your spirit and awake someday to find yourself a shell of a person, a product of a hundred small mediocre choices. Or worse yet, you might die unexpectedly tomorrow, next week, or next month with your music still in you. Your life is now. Your life is now, or never.

- You can't choose money over your real dreams, without a negative consequence on your spirit.
- You can't keep putting your true talents on hold, without ending up talentless.
- You can't keep putting off your big move without, bit by bit, killing off your desire to make a move.

- You can't go on trading away your true power for comfort, without someday ending up weak.

Call on your tremendous mental and physical resources. They want to be stretched, exercised, and challenged. They demand to be used to their full capacity. Your reward for doing so will be greatness and excellence.

Let me be blunt, in hopes of making my true point: Everyday you do not commit yourself to greatness, you are falling asleep, allowing yourself to suffocate on an atmosphere of mediocrity. Is the spirit-killing atmosphere I reference real? You only need to look at the newspaper or TV to know we are surrounded by negativity that cares little about inspiring greatness. We are often exposed to people who care nothing about being different, trying harder, or aiming higher. And you are barraged by a constant stream of products and services and efforts where average makes the grade. Yes indeed, you live in an atmosphere of mediocrity, and like poison gas it will dull you, bore you, disillusion you, and lessen you if you don't wake up and do something about it.

My friend, your life is now. Make the best of it.

Sincerely,

Patrick

Patrick Combs with his
daughter Alyssa.

—CONTRIBUTED BY PATRICK COMBS, who is an internationally known as a best-selling author, an Internet columnist, and a television personality for PBS's Career Advantage. After paying his way through college by managing a rock band, he became one of the youngest managers at Levi Strauss & Co. At twenty-six, he walked away from corporate America to help students succeed. While supporting himself by testing video games, he became a published author and a fixture on the college speaking circuit. His book, *Major in Success: Make College Easier, Fire Up Your Dreams, & Get a Very Cool Job,* has sold over 100,000 copies and was given a "Best Book" award by the New York Public Library. Patrick lives in San Diego with his wife and daughter. For more inspirational insights from Patrick, explore the Goodthink.com website or contact him at pcombs@goodthink.com.

2

Each path is only one of a million paths. Therefore, you must always keep in mind that a path is only a path. If you feel that you must now follow it, you need not stay with it under any circumstances. Any path is only a path. There is no affront to yourself or others in dropping it if that is what your heart tells you to do. But your decision to keep on the path or to leave it must be free of fear and ambition. I warn you—look at every path closely and deliberately. Try it as many times as you think necessary. Then ask yourself and yourself alone one question. It is this— does this path have a heart? If it does, then the path is good. If it doesn't, it is of no use.

—CARLOS CASTANEDA,
The Teachings of Don Juan

This section will help you to:

- Explore your options and gather information.
- Be successful in getting the right job based on your passions.
- Fund your adventure and think about money.
- Make the most of your short-term job adventure.

The work you have done in Section 1—understanding who you are, accepting yourself at every level, becoming your best, and uncovering what motivates you—has provided the foundation and structure for building your path. With this foundation, you will be able to uncover your passions more easily and make choices that affect the bigger picture of your life. This process takes time and will undoubtedly change as your life evolves. This section is about putting your ideas into action, knocking on the right doors, and making your dreams a reality.

YOUR PATH

THE TOP TEN SECRETS TO ACHIEVING YOUR DREAM CAREER

10. What would you attempt to do if you knew you could not fail?

9. "Whatever you can do, or dream you can, begin it. Boldness has genius, power, and magic in it. Begin it now."—ATTRIBUTED TO JOHANN VON GOETHE

8. Plan ahead! It wasn't raining when Noah built the ark.

7. Don't spend a lifetime exploring possibilities and do nothing. Action requires courage.

6. Don't put all your eggs in one basket. Always have an alternate plan.

5. To get what you want in life, you've got to ask others for help.

4. The shortest route to your life's work is not necessarily a straight line.

3. "Never let the fear of striking out get in your way."
—BABE RUTH

2. "Perseverance is a great element of success. If you only knock long enough and loud enough at the gate, you are sure to wake up somebody."
—HENRY WADSWORTH LONGFELLOW

1. "Never, never, never give up!"—WINSTON CHURCHILL

A wise man will make more opportunities than he finds.

—FRANCIS BACON

Never look down to test the ground before taking your next step. Only he who keeps his eye fixed on the far horizon will find the right road.

—DAG HAMMARSKJÖLD

GATHERING INFORMATION AND TAKING THE NEXT STEP . . . .

Profound joy of the heart is like a magnet that indicates the path of life. One has to follow it, even though one enters into a way full of difficulties.

—MOTHER TERESA

You have options—and lots of them! What will it be for you? Interning at an environmental education center? Seasonal work at Yellowstone? Leading raft trips on the jungle rivers of Costa Rica? Inspiring kids at a summer camp? Becoming an apprentice at an organic farm? Playing the life of a cowboy at a dude ranch? Preparing for a career in theatre? Helping those with mental illness? Patrolling a remote island wilderness in Alaska by kayak? Raising the sails on a fifty-foot schooner every day? Playing the role of a historic resident at a living history museum?

In the path of life, don't try to cover your footsteps. Instead look back on them to see where you have grown. —COLT WYNN

Don't follow the path. Go where there is no path and begin the trail. When you start a new trail equipped with courage, strength, and conviction, the only thing that can stop you is you!

—RUBY BRIDGES

Attention college students and alumni: don't forget to take advantage of your career services office. Besides being filled with hundreds of resources and job opportunities to explore, you'll also get to bounce ideas off professional counselors at no cost!

You will never change your life until you change something you do daily.

—MIKE MURDOCK

Enter phase two of your journey—gathering information and connecting with the right people. If you haven't done so already, take the time to read through your entire guide and highlight programs, resources, and ideas that will assist you with your dream. And that's just for starters. Realize that this book is only one of many, many resources that will help you along on your journey. A recommended book or web link just might turn into hundreds of other leads for you. Don't cut any corners at this stage. Make an investment in every resource that piques your interest. Join an association, attend their national conference, and connect with like-minded people in your field. By immersing yourself completely in this information-gathering stage, you will be able make sound decisions on the direction of your life.

Collecting information also means talking to anybody and everybody who might help you to see more clearly and present you with ideas to fuel your fire. Think of all the possibilities: family and friends, career counselors and professors, colleagues, and even strangers. One of the best ways to get more information about a career that you are exploring is to talk to someone who is actually in the job you desire. For instance, if you want to write a book, talk to authors; if you want to be a raft guide, talk to raft guides; if you want to work for the Peace Corps, talk to volunteers. Find role models who are acting in ways you are gravitating toward; then, make time in your day to talk to these people.

YOUR CHALLENGE

This week I challenge you to seek out one person who might help you in your pursuits. For those who are extroverts, this might be a simple task; however, for others, pushing yourself out of your comfort zone can be quite a daunting exercise. Enter risk taking. Risking is about moving from the fear of the unknown to the excitement of what is about to happen. Without risks, you'd never move away from home, find a great job, make a new friend, or fall in love. By learning how to take small risks, you'll begin to feel more comfortable about asking for anything that you want to help you in your journey.

So where do you start? You might begin your efforts by calling a friend who's participated in a life-changing work experience and asking what steps he took. Or, depending on your situation, you might make an appointment with a career counselor at school or through work and pick her brain. These initial strides will help to broaden your comfort zone, so you will be able to approach just about anyone. The worst-case scenario in asking for help is rejection. This just means you made contact with the wrong person, so you move on to the next person until you find someone who will help.

CONNECTIONS..................

After you have uncovered specific organizations throughout your guide or through your conversations with people that appear to be strong work possibilities, narrow down your prospective leads to about ten (so you don't get overwhelmed at first). Out of this ten, pick the one program that interests you the least, and call them for more information. This call serves as your training ground, allowing you to get all your phone-talk kinks worked out prior to conversing with the program that is on top of your list. With time, you will feel more comfortable and confident about talking with program directors and asking the right questions.

Your guide includes contact names for many of the programs listed, so be sure to ask for this person; however, sometimes you'll find that the contact has changed. Don't let that throw you off. Generally, someone will just transfer you to the right person; other times you'll have to explain who and what you're after. Eventually, you will talk to the right person.

This initial call is the first impression you will make on both the program director and the organization, so make sure it is a good one. Something that happens in this conversation just may be the link that eventually gets you the job. Some program contacts are receptive to talking; others don't have the time. At this point, you are mainly gathering information and promoting your enthusiasm as a potential candidate. During your conversation, you might ask for program brochures and an application, inquire about upcoming deadlines or the number of applicants that are hired, and uncover what they are specifically looking for in a candidate. Most of the information can be gathered through your guide and the organization's website, but it's also a good idea to verify any specific facts with the person you are talking to (largely because the nitty-gritty details can change from year to year).

> Never be scared to ask. Ask and keep asking. Communicate your needs to others. Call people out of the blue. Take people to lunch. Open yourself up to others. You'll find success is usually a team effort. Asking is powerful. It can work magic. It sure isn't easy and it doesn't work every time. It will, however, if you persist. So ask, and it shall be given to you!

> Go around asking a lot of damn fool questions and taking chances. Only through curiosity can we discover opportunities, and only by risking can we take advantage of them.
>
> —CLARENCE BIRDSEYE

Send short, handwritten thank-you notes to all who help you in your quest. Not only will you realize at a later point how important these people were in getting you where you are today, this small note of appreciation can also lead to lifelong connections and friendships with exciting possibilities.

Thank You!

Half the time you won't speak to a real person; you'll talk to their voice mail. Be prepared. If you stumble here, there's no way to erase what you've said. Prior to calling, it is a good idea to loosely script out what you want to say. It might go something like this: "Hello, my name is Brian Kean and I read in *The Back Door Guide to Short-Term Job Adventures* that you offer a summer internship program. Could you please send me an informational brochure and application?" At this point, give your mailing address, email address, and phone number. It's also important to speak slowly and clearly, and spell out any words that are difficult to understand. Remember, someone is writing down your message to get you the information you need. Conclude with any enthusiasm you may have about the possibility of joining their program.

Many of you will request information through a simple email note. Although email seems to be the most efficient way to get the information you need, many programs are generally bogged down by all the notes they receive in a day's time. So be patient in receiving a response. Prior to clicking on your send button, be sure you have crafted a professionally written letter that has been spell-checked, grammar-checked, and proofread several times. Remember, you are not emailing a friend to say hello. Think of this note as your initial cover letter to the program, which means putting effort into what you write. Although email serves as an easy way to communicate, keep in mind that it also lacks the human ingredient. Anytime I want to make an impression on a new client or am seeking out a new work assignment, I either call the person over the phone or schedule a meeting in person. Never overlook the power of the human connection.

STAYING ORGANIZED

What works best for you? Whether it be with index cards or through your computer, you need to keep track of all the information you'll be collecting. For starters, create a "Notes Log" of all your correspondence. Write down everything: from the date of your initial phone call to the details of your conversation. This is especially beneficial if you are applying to a handful of programs—your log will keep you focused on the needs of each. Make notes of important dates: deadlines, dates to make follow-up phone calls, or when you need to send off a thank-you letter. I also jot down personal tidbits about the person after talking with them. These tidbits serve as great conversation starters the next time you talk with the person, as they generally are surprised you remembered something so personal.

THE APPLICATION PROCESS . . . .

Once you receive the program's application packet in the mail, act upon it right away. Many times positions are filled as soon as applications have been reviewed. "The early bird gets the worm" saying generally holds true when applying for seasonal-type jobs. Although each program wants the best person for a specific job, many directors are concerned about filling the position before it is too late.

You'll also find that putting together your application seems to take longer than you anticipate, especially if the program has a four-page form to fill out and desires a couple of short essays and three letters of recommendation (along with a personalized cover letter and your updated resume). Yes, many programs ask a lot from you, but this is their first opportunity to weed out candidates who haven't taken this step seriously. Keep in mind the payoff for all your hard work: the possibility of working with a program that will forever change your life. Whatever you're asked to do in the application process, be sure that your skills, interests, and abilities are very apparent in the packet you send them.

YOUR RESUME AND COVER LETTER

Your resume might be the most important document to assist you in your job search. The resume is your marketing brochure and selling tool—information that will hopefully paint a very clear picture of your talents and abilities. What kind of person are you? What kind of skills do you have? What are some of your life experiences? What do you do in your spare time? What hobbies do you have? What are some major things that you have accomplished? If you've done your homework in Section 1, answering these questions will come easily and naturally.

The best resumes are those that are filled with the entire you. Along with your academic record and work experiences, be sure to include your skills, accomplishments, volunteer service, and any other unique attributes that make you stand out. I even put my favorite quote at the bottom of my resume.

As you create and develop your resume, it's very helpful if a team of people looks it over for ideas, spelling errors, and areas you could improve on. If at all possible, have a career counselor or program director provide you with feedback; otherwise, there are plenty of resume books that are filled with great ideas. No matter what advice is given, the beauty of creating your resume is that anything goes—you get to make all final decisions!

Set your resume aside for a few days before you come back to it for revisions. This will give you time to work on a personalized cover

Don't just randomly apply to every job you're remotely qualified for or interested in. Put together a list of all the aspects of your ideal job, taking into account your personality, skills you enjoy using, what's important to you, the work environment, and your talents. Then go after it with complete determination and optimism. You have the power to make it happen!

Before sending off your completed application, make a copy of it. In case it gets lost in the mail, you'll have a spare copy. This will also serve as your master for doing other applications.

Originality is not doing something no one else has ever done, but doing what has been done countless times with new life, new breath. —MARIE CHAPIAN

Good hiring managers always smell a form letter before you lick the stamp. Bring out your inner child and make it personal!

letter (also known as a letter of interest or intent). Many people think that cover letters are the same as a Post-it note that says: "Hey, check this out—I'd really like to work for you!" Unfortunately, you'll find these cover letters lying in the bottom of recycle bins. Your cover letter is the icing on the cake and is just possibly as important as the resume itself. It serves as an expansion of your resume and answers these key questions: what you are applying for, why you want to work for this particular organization, examples of your skills and abilities (as they relate to the job opportunity), and why they should hire you.

Your cover letter also describes your *potential* to the employer. Let your personality shine in your writing. You might not have all the necessary skills, but your cover letter can demonstrate that you're trainable for the job. Remember, many applicants aren't necessarily hired based on skill, but more so for enthusiasm and energy. Job-specific skills and responsibilities, in general, can always be taught.

LETTERS OF RECOMMENDATION

Unless you've planned ahead and already have copies of letters of recommendation from former bosses, professors, or colleagues, this task might take some work on your part. First off, I need to emphasize how important it is to develop relationships with your professors or people who might serve as mentors in your career development. This means reaching out to others, asking for help, and seeing what develops and what doesn't. These people will serve as allies in all you do, especially when it comes to developing your future.

For those who haven't developed a network of support and "sideline cheerleaders," it's best to ask former bosses, teachers, or anyone who can provide a sincere impression of your talents and abilities. Query your list of possible candidates to see who is comfortable in sharing with others about your skills and abilities. To help the person in writing your letter, provide them with information about the program, the position you are applying for, and strengths that should be highlighted. Another nice touch is to provide them with a postage-paid envelope, so they can either send it to you or directly to the employer. After all is said and done, be sure to thank these people who have taken time out of their lives to help you along in your path. A handwritten letter always makes a nice touch.

Even though a program might not ask for letters of recommendation, include them anyway. They will make your application packet stand out.

FOLLOW-UP

Although each step in getting your dream job is important in itself, following up on your application might make the difference in who gets the job and who does not. One to three weeks after sending in your application materials, pleasantly surprise your contact with a phone call. In this phone call, verify that they have received your application, and at the same time, ask if there is anything else you can provide as well as any other questions that concern you. Once again, promote your enthusiasm about the program and job prior to ending your conversation.

YOUR INTERVIEW

Congratulations! Once you've made it this far, all your preliminary hard work has paid off (and impressed the hiring team). The interview, the final step of landing the job, is where you get to show off what you're all about and how you'll make a difference in their program. Whether you are interviewing in person or over the phone, it's best to prepare a loose script prior to your interview. Your script should include various trigger words that will help your brain connect your thoughts. These words are simply reminders of items (skills, unique stories, and strengths) you need to cover as you talk about yourself and the position. Moreover, if the work you want to do is really something you believe in, the feeling of enthusiasm will come across naturally.

To grapple with any uneasiness prior to your interview, I suggest working with a friend who can act as your interviewer. Come up with a list of typical interview-type questions and challenge yourself to answer them out loud. By speaking out your answers, you are connecting your thoughts and ideas with actual words and stories. With practice, you'll be able to answer any question that comes your way. Remember, your goal is to paint a very real and sincere picture of who you are, what skills you have obtained over the years, and your potential for future growth. You should have the ability to talk about anything mentioned in your resume, along with supporting examples. If a question ever catches you off guard, don't be afraid to pause while you think about the question posed—silence many times works to your advantage. Those who have successful interviews are those who have done plenty of preparation and anticipate what questions the interviewer might ask. Just like anything, the more you interview, the better you will become.

Whether you are fresh out of college or are trying to put together a resume at age seventy, Yana Parker will assist you with all the details in her book, *Resume Catalog: 200 Damn Good Examples* (Ten Speed Press, $16.95). Yana's collage of resume ideas and inspiring advice will help you craft a resume that will not only paint a clear picture of your talents and abilities but also help you land more interviews. The book's website is "damn good" too (www.damngood.com).

Think of the Hansens as your personal cover letter coaches. Their book, *Dynamic Cover Letters* (Ten Speed Press, $12.95), now in its third edition, will guide people of all ages and experiences through a step-by-step process of crafting an irresistible cover letter for any situation. The Quintessential Careers companion website (www.quintcareers.com) includes heaps of career resource links, ranging from job-hunting sites and career articles to cover letter and resume sites.

Far away, there in the sunshine are my highest aspirations. I may not reach them, but I can look up and see their beauty. Believe in them and try to follow where they lead. —LOUISA MAY ALCOTT

That which we persist in doing becomes easier—not that the nature of the task has changed, but our ability to do so has increased.

—RALPH WALDO EMERSON

THOSE PESKY INTERVIEW QUESTIONS

You never know what will be asked of you in your interview; however, these questions and ideas will help you to prepare for anything asked of you:

- How would you describe yourself to someone who didn't know you?
- What qualities do you most admire (and dislike) about yourself?
- Explain your creative side.
- Describe yourself in one word.
- Give three specific examples of your strengths.
- What things come easily to you? What's more difficult?
- What have you learned about yourself in the last year?
- What's important to you in life?
- Describe a role model in your life.
- If you could get two famous people (past or present) to work with you, who would they be and why?
- Write five reasons why you shouldn't be hired. Come up with rebuttals for each and memorize them. Alternately, come up with five specific reasons why you should be hired.

Practice interviewing in front of your cat, dog, or goldfish. Pets are always a supportive audience and will definitely build your confidence. (Be sure to thank your critter with a treat or two!)

Your interview also serves as your time to ask those all-so-important questions that will help you make decisions about your future. Just as your prospective employer is studying everything about you during the interview, you should be doing the same. You're both sizing each other up to see if you are compatible for a budding work relationship. Think of it in the same light as dating. Here are some key questions that you want to ask of your prospective employer:

- **What investment will the program make in directing and enhancing your natural learning process in exchange for your work and energy?**
  On-the-job training is inherent in every position that you will be considering; however, the amount of training you will receive is an important consideration—especially if this is your first job in the field. Those that offer intensive training programs, informal and formal discussions, workshops, seminars, or lectures as part of your learning experience should make a big impact on your decision-making process.

- **What staff members will you be working with and what are their backgrounds?**
  The permanent staff will serve as your mentors, your teachers, and your guides. These people will also help you network in the field and connect you to possibilities that will enhance your career. You must decide whether you'll get the guidance you need given the staffing arrangement that exists.

- **What are the criteria for hiring short-term staff members?**
  You'll find that your peers will provide some of the best sources of inspiration, learning, sharing, and friendship during your experience. Will your peers be likely to have a level of schooling and experience that will ensure that you are surrounded by a strong support group?

- **What kind of living conditions will be provided?**
  A nice benefit for short-term work opportunities is that many offer room and board as part of your compensation package. If not, be sure to ask what type of housing assistance they provide, if any. Don't be the person that arrives at their new job only to find out that they will be sharing a room with three others and eating meals that don't do much for a healthy lifestyle. Will you have a private room? Will you share a bathroom? What types of meals are served? Are there kitchen facilities available for your use? Whatever is important to you, find out these important details.

- **What kind of experience did past interns have with the program?**
  I always suggest talking candidly to others who have participated in the program to get their impression of the experience. You'll find that many programs also provide the names and phone numbers of past participants, so be sure to ask. In addition to talking with former participants, you might find it to your advantage to schedule an on-site interview (if one isn't provided), so you can talk with various staff members and interns who are currently working there, along with getting a feel for your work environment.

- **What kind of job opportunities will exist after completion of your assignment?**
  The beauty of a short-term work opportunity is that it can naturally evolve into a lifelong career with the organization. Many times the permanent staff is made up of former interns. It's important to see if there will be opportunities for future growth within the organization along with any career assistance that will be provided upon conclusion of your experience.

You have a unique message to deliver, a unique song to sing, a unique act of love to bestow. This message, this song, and this act of love have been entrusted exclusively to the one and only you.

—JOHN POWELL

If a man is called to be a street sweeper, he should sweep streets even as Michelangelo painted, or Beethoven composed music, or Shakespeare wrote poetry. He should sweep streets so well that all the hosts of heaven and earth will pause to say, here lived a great street sweeper who did his job well.

—MARTIN LUTHER KING, JR.

Ask, and it shall be given to you; seek, and ye shall find; knock, and it shall be opened unto you. —MATTHEW 7:7

Life is not easy for any of us. But what of that? We must have perseverance and above all confidence in ourselves. We must believe that we are gifted for something, and that this thing, at whatever cost, must be attained.

—MARIE CURIE

If you're not rejected ten times a day, you're not trying hard enough.

—ANTHONY COLEMAN

Everyone has a talent. What is rare is the courage to follow that talent to the dark place where it leads.

—ERICA JONG

ASK AND YOU SHALL RECEIVE!

If you have gathered enough information during your interview to make a sound decision about joining their program, be sure to tell them so. Many applicants leave this open-ended as their interview comes to a close, allowing the recruiter to make his or her own judgment. If you feel that you can make an impact on their program, and that they offer an experience that will enhance your talents and abilities, let them know! Most often, you won't get a job offer on the spot, but your enthusiasm will definitely leave an impression.

After you've had a chance to digest your interview, take the time to send a handwritten letter to the person who interviewed you (once again). Reiterate your enthusiasm for the program (and position), expand on anything that you felt was left open-ended in the interview, and again, let them know that you want the job. Often, recruiters interview a handful of super applicants for only one position. Your persistence will often help influence their decision to hire you!

REJECTION SHOCK

After all the hard work, time, and energy that you put into landing what you thought was the ideal job, there may be a time the mail brings a thin letter that states (in so many nice words) that you will not be offered a position. Enthusiasm and excitement quickly turn to feelings of failure. Nobody likes rejection; however, you must realize that this component will be part of your life no matter how hard you try. In fact, what has been thought of as a failure often turns into a blessing in disguise, even though it's not very apparent at the time. It's like falling off your bike for the first time. You simply get on it and try again. Life is constantly like this—especially for those who are willing to risk and go after what they truly believe in.

That's why it's very important not to put all your eggs in one basket. It's easier to set yourself up for success by opening yourself up to many opportunities. By applying to many programs that pique your interest, you are bound to receive an offer or two—many times, more than you anticipated!

APPROACH YOUR LIFE WITH A LONG-HAUL MENTALITY

As I'm sure you are well aware, it takes time for careers, opportunities, and relationships to develop in your life. There is a process to everything you do. Again, try to think of what you are doing right now as your never-ending journey.

A long-haul mentality approach will help you understand that the things you do now entirely affect the opportunities that are presented in your future. Overnight success is rare (and is usually because of the hard work that led up to that point). Don't rush the process. Each step in your journey takes time.

Those who have planted a vegetable garden or have spent time on a farm know that there are certain steps that are necessary to turn a seed into something that is life sustaining. Mother Nature will also challenge this process every step of the way. That's why life should be approached with a long-haul mentality. Enjoy every good and challenging step along the way. Good things come to people who work hard to get what they're after. You might not see the results today or next week or even a month from now, but they'll hit you when you least expect it, and you'll be very happy to know that all your hard work has paid off.

SKEPTICS

Watch out for skeptics who want to divert you from your destiny. Cling to what you know in your heart is best.

If I had thought about it, I wouldn't have done the experiment. The literature was full of examples that said you can't do this.
—Spencer Silver, originator of Post-it notepads

Guitar music is on the way out.
—Decca Records turning down the Beatles in 1962

TV won't hold on to any market it captures after the first six months. People will soon tire of staring at a box every night.
—Darryl Zanuck, head of 20th Century Fox, 1946

Everything that can be invented has been invented.
—Charles Duell, Office of Patents Commissioner, 1899

Louis Pasteur's theory of germs is ridiculous fiction.
—Pierre Pachet, Professor of Physiology, 1872

Don't forget Columbus who was looking for India, or the fact that Edison knew 1,800 ways not to build a light bulb. It was Mark Twain who once said, "Let us be thankful for the fools—but for them the rest of us could not succeed!" Although many will like you to fail (misery loves company), don't you ever give up. You'll find that success is generally just around the corner.

DON'T QUIT

When things go wrong, as they sometimes will; when the road you're trudging seems all uphill; when the funds are low and the debts are high, and you want to smile, but you have to sigh; when care is pressing you down a bit—rest if you must but don't you quit.

Life is queer with its twists and turns, as every one of us sometimes learns; and many a fellow turns about when he might have won had he stuck it out. Don't give up though the pace seems slow—you may succeed with another blow.

Often the goal is nearer than it seems to a faint and faltering man; often the struggler has given up when he might have captured the victor's cup; and he learned too late when the night came down, how close he was to the golden crown.

Success is failure turned inside out— the silver tint of the clouds of doubt; and you never can tell how close you are. It may be near when it seems afar; so stick to the fight when you're hardest hit—it's when things seem worst that you mustn't quit.

The greatest mistake you can make in life is to be continually fearing that you will make one. —ELBERT HUBBARD

DON'T TRAVEL DOWN THAT BIG RIVER IN EGYPT

I was raised to sense what someone wanted me to be and be that kind of person. It took me a long time not to judge myself through someone else's eyes.

—SALLY FIELD

The college years—a time of exploration, excitement, discovery, and learning. Should I study architecture or maybe engage in the field of psychology? Like many of us navigating through this period in our life, Craig Dunkin was presented with a handful of tough questions—questions he had to answer without much direction. At that age, who really is aware of what we want our life to develop into? Unfortunately, most of us opt for the easy route, allowing the hand of society to push us in certain directions, instead of making the big decisions for ourselves. Craig was really interested in sports broadcasting; however, smart people go to law school, so that's what he did.

Twelve years later, Craig sits in his office at a very reputable law firm in Los Angeles. He's very successful and makes good money, but on this day, mindless lawyer tasks are par for the course. Then, the epiphany hit: "There is more to life than what I'm doing." This thought consumed him for the rest of the day. The "Inner Craig" whispered, "What are you doing practicing law? What are you working toward?" This day changed his life.

While still acting as a lawyer, Craig decided to take a class at a local community college on sports broadcasting. A professor soon became his mentor, helping him to answer many of the tough questions he ignored in college. With excitement and passion as his guides, Craig spent the next few years revitalizing his inborn talents. He spent his evenings and weekends at any sporting event he had time to experience. However, he didn't sit there like any other ordinary fan, he was there on a mission. Positioning himself in the centerfield bleachers or away from the crowds, a sports broadcaster was soon born.

Using a microphone and tape recorder as his tools of the trade, he began giving play-by-play action of the games. Although he did not actually engage an audience on the details of the event (except for a few fans sitting near him), these demo tapes soon doubled as a key component of his sports broadcasting portfolio. Shortly thereafter, he began scouting out ball teams to expose his talents to the world. "I called every minor league baseball team across the nation and asked if they needed a broadcaster. If they said 'yes' or 'maybe,' I sent those tapes."

Months (which seemed like years) went by until he finally got a break from a ball team in the South who thought he had potential. A deal was made, and this ex-California lawyer made his way to the small town of Clarksville, Tennessee.

Although he would spend extra time on weekends and at night figuring out the small details that make a ball game exciting, the extra work became a labor of love, rather than just laboring (as he had done as a lawyer). "That's what drew

me to it all. This was my chance to be really good at something." He looks back at all his lawyer years as "floating down that big river in Egypt." Confused by what he meant, he continued, "You know, the Nile?" You see, the Nile was a constant reminder that he had been living in a world of denial—denial of what he really felt and wanted to do with his life.

Craig's thoughtful advice for anyone looking to make sense of their career is this: "If you don't like being a lawyer, but it allows you to have season tickets to the opera or a beautiful home on five acres—and that's what brings meaning to your life—then so be it. But if that's not enough for you, then why do it? You have to figure out what's important and then fill that aspect in your life. No matter how difficult it is to get into something, don't let that stop you. If you feel you are a talented actor, go do that. But, most importantly, just don't visit that river out in Egypt."

The significant problems we face cannot be solved at the same level of thinking we were at when we created them. —ALBERT EINSTEIN

MONEY AND FUNDING YOUR ADVENTURE. . . . .

Once you realize that your self-worth has nothing to do with your net worth, money will not be the only source of richness and fulfillment in your life. Obviously a lack of money can constrain us from doing the things we really want to do, especially if we're burdened by school loans, credit card debts, or making just enough to meet our daily financial obligations. Those in this situation will learn to become resourceful; there is always another way to make your dreams come alive, no matter the roadblocks that lay ahead. Once you've committed to a goal, whether it be working as a seasonal employee at a national park, starting a business, participating in a service learning adventure, or funding an experience abroad, opportunities will start taking shape. By broadcasting your intentions to the world, the world usually responds back in amazing ways (and if it doesn't, this might tell you that you've walked down the wrong path or perhaps you just need to try a little harder).

So how do you survive in the world while funding your passion in life? Although some of the ideas below might seem ludicrous, being resourceful and creative will help you create a livelihood that will blossom over time.

One of the main reasons wealth makes people unhappy is that it gives them too much control over what they experience. They try to translate their own fantasies into reality instead of tasting what reality itself has to offer.

—PHILIP SLATER

SELL LEMONADE!

Many of us had the chance to become young entrepreneurs as we grew up—selling lemonade, mowing lawns, washing cars—experiences that taught us the value of money. Apply this same philosophy to your current situation. What skill do you have that could benefit others, and at the same time, bring in some extra cash? Are you a budding artist? Perhaps a local business in town might need your help in designing a few brochures for a fee. Or possibly the local health club wouldn't mind offering you a membership in their club for your creativity? How about writing an article in your field of expertise and finding a website willing to publish the content for its readers? (Even though you might not get paid, this is a great way to attract attention to yourself). Whatever your goal, bartering your unique skills will definitely help in funding your passion.

We are very short on people who know how to do anything. So please don't set out to make money. Set out to make something and hope you get rich in the process.

—ANDY ROONEY

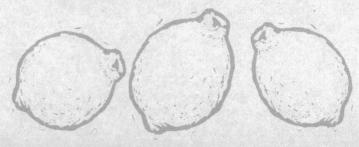

TEMP JOBS

This is a great way to provide structure in your life while searching out what really matters, and at the same time, keeping a steady stream of money to meet your financial obligations. Many people have developed a complete lifestyle engaged in temporary work because of the diversity in job assignments and varied time commitments. You'll also find that more and more temp agencies are offering health insurance and other services, which are benefits you don't want to overlook. Once you've built a reputation with a few organizations who like your work, many turn mundane work assignments into challenging work projects. Often this leads into permanent or consulting work that pays more and provides more freedom. Temp agencies abound in urban and suburban areas. Kelly Services (www.kellyservices.com) and Manpower (www.manpower.com) are two agencies that you might check out as you explore this option.

SUBSTITUTE TEACHING

If you have a college degree and like children, substitute teaching in an elementary, middle, or high school is a perfect in-between job—and just possibly, the start of a new career. Not only does it pay fairly well and offer a flexible schedule, you'll learn just as much from the children as they will from you. It's also a chance to work on your speaking skills and connect more with people in your community.

POSSESSION DOWNSIZING

Most of us have garages or closets filled with possessions that have been sitting around for years—these make up all the key ingredients in conducting a profitable garage sale. The old adage of "one man's trash is another man's treasure" can bring you enough money to make a dent in your fund-raising efforts. A successful garage sale takes planning on your part: all your items should be priced, an ad should go in the local paper, and huge signs should be put up around the neighborhood the night before. I even conduct a pre-garage-sale for neighbors and friends the night before. Many people who know you are fund-raising to support your passion might even provide a monetary donation. Whatever the case, it's a good way to clear out clutter and make some extra cash on the side.

The man who does not work for the love of work but only for money is not likely to make money nor find much fun in life.

—CHARLES SCHWAB

Spreading the "frugal gospel," Amy Dacyczyn's *The Complete Tightwad Gazette* (Random House, $19.99) includes 900 pages worth of sensible advice, recipes, tips, tricks, and strategies to save money.

The pessimist sees difficulty in every opportunity. The optimist sees opportunity in every difficulty. —WINSTON CHURCHILL

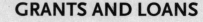

GRANTS AND LOANS

Many seeking to participate in worthy causes can raise money through philanthropic groups (like Kiwanis), campus/alumni groups, community organizations, civic/religious groups, local businesses, colleagues, or even your current coworkers. There are also plenty of grants that major nonprofits give out each year. (Check out your library's reference area for books that cover grant possibilities.) In addition, don't be afraid to ask your family for help. A small loan might be the helping hand you need until you get on your feet.

SPARKLETT'S JUG THEORY

Find yourself an old Sparklett's jug at your local thrift store. Set it somewhere in your house and start dropping in your spare change. I find that it's more exciting if you attach a goal to the money you're saving prior to putting in your first coin.

DO WITHOUT

Simply stated, live within your means. The next time you go shopping, ask yourself, "Do I really need this?" More than likely, you don't. Remember the financial goal you've set up for yourself and don't stray from that path.

MAKING THE MOST OF YOUR EXPERIENCE . . . .

The day will come when you've packed your car and your short-term job adventure begins. It will undoubtedly bring you a wealth of experience, a firmer sense of who you are and where your career is going, and a supportive network of friends and colleagues in the field. Before you rush off, here are some ideas to help you make the most of your new adventure:

- Make alliances with the administrative support team right away. That's right, secretaries are the eyes and ears of the organization and can really enhance your experience. Smile, sincerely get to know them, make friends with them, and ask for their helping hand.

- Doesn't it feel good when someone remembers your name? Make an effort to learn people's names right away. This is a

Life is change.
Growth is optional.
Choose wisely.

—KAREN KAISER CLARK

great first step at building relationships and paying your coworkers a subtle compliment. Practice by repeating a person's name several times in conversation and associating the name with their expressions or appearance.

- Be prepared to work in areas not related to your main responsibility, have a "can do" attitude, and chip in wherever needed. Look at every job you're given as an opportunity to learn more about the field you've chosen and a chance to contribute to the overall success of the program.

- Make it a goal to acquire as many skills, in as many areas, as you can. Attend every class and seminar that is offered and immerse yourself in every aspect of the program.

- Hard work is not the only key to success—enjoy yourself and have fun!

- Enthusiasm and a positive spirit are contagious—bring these traits with you to work every day. Not only will your coworkers appreciate your "happy" energy, your supervisor will undoubtedly take note and give you more responsibilities. On the same note, stay clear from the troublemakers—you'll find out who they are right away. Don't allow their negativity, complaining, or disrespect of others become your reality. Rise above and always focus on the positive—it will carry you far!

- Throughout the course of your adventure, talk to fellow staff members about their careers and lives. You'll be surprised at how much your peers enjoy giving advice and sharing their story with you. It's also flattering (to most) to be asked one's opinion—another person's insights might help you make better decisions in your life and further develop your career.

- Show a sincere interest in others and try to develop as many friendships as possible. Not only is it important to create a support group for yourself, you never know when a newfound alliance will have the opportunity to help you with your path at a future point!

- Finally, follow those hunches, take risks, be flexible, make plans, bend with life's twists and turns, and look at each day as an exciting learning adventure that you can make happen!

Work is about daily meaning as well as daily bread. For recognition as well as cash; for astonishment rather than torpor; in short, for a sort of life rather than a Monday through Friday sort of dying. . . . We have a right to ask of work that it include meaning, recognition, astonishment, and life.

—STUDS TERKEL

Happiness is like a butterfly. The more you chase it, the more it will elude you. But if you turn your attention to other things, it comes and softly sits on your shoulder.

As you venture down the path of life, keep these tips in your back pocket:

Find your own retreat (and use it often).

Give support, encouragement, and praise to others; and learn to accept them in return.

Change your routine often and your tasks when you can.

Focus on a good thing that happened during your day.

Be creative and try new approaches.

Use the "buddy system" regularly as a source of support, assurance, and redirection.

Surprise someone with something.

Find the child inside.

Laugh, play, and smile.

Be gentle with yourself and do the best job you can do.

Purchase a book that you've been meaning to get; then lose yourself completely in the words.

Reflect on the gifts you've been given from "Above." Write about this awareness.

Think different.

See how many colors you can incorporate into a meal.

Think of something you're grateful for, then call or write to thank the person responsible.

Treat yourself to a massage or a day at a spa. Feel the beauty in your life as you fall asleep.

Tape a favorite quote to your computer. Read it every day this week.

Say something nice to a person you've never met. See what happens.

Create a list of places you want to visit, things you want to do, and people you want to meet. See how many you can cross off your list this year.

Fill the pages of your life with wonder and imperfection.

Choose a job you love and you will never have to work a day in your life.

—CONFUCIUS

 s you begin to map out the big picture of your life (and turn your inspiration into action!), you'll definitely need some tools to help you navigate through the twists and turns of your adventures. Fortunately, for every idea you have, there's a resource that can provide you with the information and enlightenment to build upon your dreams. To help you in "finding your way," this section offers reviews of my favorite books, publications, resources, and websites that have helped supercharge, guide, invigorate, and shape my career and life—and I know many of these will do the same for you!

This section will also help you to:

- Understand how the listings are organized
- Land a job in the U.S. (if you're an international applicant!)

FINDING YOUR WAY

SAMPLE LISTING

ANGELIC ORGANICS

Organic Farming • Illinois • 3–7 Months
www.angelicorganics.com

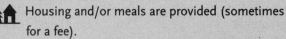

FOR THOSE WHO haven't worked on a farm before, Angelic Organics describes it this way: "It's chaotic, messy, unpredictable, tiring, low-paying, uncomfortable, and unforgiving in ways that probably go beyond your normal understanding of these words (we love what we do, but we want people to know that farm life is not a pastoral paradise)." At Angelic Organics, interns will practice the hands-on work of organic and biodynamic farming for their Community Supported Agriculture (CSA) program: everything from planting and harvesting to packing and creating a beautiful presentation for CSA shareholders. The experience begins with a four-day training beginning mid-April, and includes informal discussions, seminars, conferences, and visits to other farms throughout the course of the internship. Benefits include a $300 monthly stipend ($500 for those with at least one year of experience), shared furnished housing and meals, and staples and produce from the garden. Call for their internship booklet, which contains application materials and articles on farming practices. The best time to apply is late fall/early winter and it's highly suggested that you visit the farm for a couple days to a week on a trial basis. International applicants are accepted on a three-month or less basis.

For More Information:
John Peterson, General Manager
Angelic Organics
1547 Rockton Rd.
Caledonia, IL 61011-9572
(815) 389-2746 • (815) 389-3106 (fax)
csa@angelicorganics.com

USING YOUR GUIDE . . . .

With so many short-term opportunities presented throughout the pages of your guide, the challenge may well be in picking one to do. To ease this challenge, each section introduction provides an overview of what's tucked inside. This introductory material also includes information on a variety of opportunities in the section, along with special stories and other insights that you don't want to miss. Each section concludes with my recommendations on other resources—books, newsletters, web links, associations—for further exploration.

UNDERSTANDING THE LISTINGS

Each listing is visually laid out in the same fashion, so at first glance you can get the bigger picture of the program. The header information includes important facts about the program—the category (or "buzzword") it represents, the specific state or country where you will work, and the time commitment that is needed from you. These three elements also make up three of the five indexes found at the end of your guide. Note that when an organization has its work assignments evenly spread throughout many states, it is listed as U.S. On the same note, if the program covers many regions throughout the world, it is listed as Worldwide. The header information also contains up to four icons that represent compensation or fees, if housing is offered or provided, and eligibility requirements.

KEY TO ICONS

💰 Compensation is provided.

♥ Volunteer opportunity.

🏠 Housing and/or meals are provided (sometimes for a fee).

🎓 The program is geared specifically for college students or recent graduates. Listings without this icon generally indicate that anyone over the age of eighteen is eligible to apply. Further details can be found in the listing!

🌐 International applicants are also eligible to apply (see opposite page).

INSIDE INFORMATION FOR INTERNATIONAL APPLICANTS. . . . .

I f you're from the U.S. and want to work overseas, head on over to the Opportunities Abroad section on page 348 for all sorts of ideas, requirements, and unique programs and resources. Otherwise, if you don't reside in the U.S., you'll want to pay close attention to programs with a "globe" icon noted with their listing. This icon denotes the program hires international applicants; however, this doesn't always mean the organization will help you with all the details or pay for the proper working visa to legally work in the U.S. Your first move is to contact EACH organization that piques your interest and obtain more information about international applicant requirements. You'll find that some programs will help with the visa process, while others will refer you to many of the exchange programs mentioned below. As I'm sure you are aware, obtaining a visa is a little tougher than it used to be. Here are your options:

- The F-1 Visa allows students to work while enrolled in school in the U.S., as well as for a period of fourteen months after graduation, for what is often referred to as "practical training."

- The J-1 Exchange Visitor's Visa allows internationals to enter the U.S. for cultural exchange work and travel for a specific period of time (generally from four months to two years). Applicants that fall under the J-1 status generally include students, teachers, scholars, camp counselors, au pairs, and participants in summer travel/work programs.

- The H-2B is strictly for seasonal/temporary work in the U.S. for up to one year. With this option, applicants must have a job offer from a U.S. employer, although the visa is not guaranteed until it is approved by INS (Immigration and Naturalization Service) and a consulate. Many ski resorts (see page 129) offer a limited number of H-2B Visas each year, otherwise they are hard to come by. Check out the Immigration Services of America at www.isaunited.com for more information and ideas.

FINDING OUT MORE

Bunac.org

Camp Counselors USA (www.ccusa.com)

CouncilExchanges.org

Interexchange.com

International Student Travel Confederation (www.istc.org)

Visanow.com

WorkExperienceUSA.com

Vacation Work (www.vactionwork.co.uk) publishes a handful of unique "short-term work" publications for those who reside outside the U.S.

RECOMMENDED BOOKS, RESOURCES, AND WEBSITES . . . .

There is more treasure in books than in all the pirates' loot on Treasure Island . . .and best of all, you can enjoy these riches every day of your life. —Walt Disney

I am truly amazed at all the resources that people are continually creating to help us with our very own journey (thank goodness they have taken the time to share their secrets with the world!). Whether you need a resource to enrich your soul, a book to offer a fresh perspective, or, perhaps, a website that offers a directory of great job resources, the following area is a compilation of my favorites. Any books that I have reviewed can also be found at the bookshop on my companion website at **Backdoorjobs.com** (with direct links to Amazon.com). Additional topic-specific resources can also be found at the end of each section of your guide. Read through and see what resources might help in shaping your life!

BOOKS TO ENRICH THE SOUL

Treat yourself to a mind-stretching book or two that will certainly change the way you look at life.

Santiago, a shepherd boy searching for his treasure, teaches us about listening to our heart, acting upon the omens strewn along life's path, and realizing one's destiny is a person's only real obligation. Full of adventure, magic, and wisdom, *The Alchemist* by Paulo Coelho (HarperSanFrancisco, $13) shares with us that the possibility of having a dream come true is what makes life interesting!

Richard Bode's lifelong love affair with sailing provides a vivid metaphor on living life to the fullest. *First You Have to Row a Little Boat* (Warner Books, $10) is a wonderful book that teaches us to maneuver with patience around the obstacles we encounter in our own passage through life.

Shamanic teacher and healer Don Miguel Ruiz offers a different way to approach his book, *The Four Agreements* (Amber-Allen Publishing, $12.95). First off, read the book as quickly as possible to understand the flow and spirit; then read it again more slowly. Second, begin practicing the agreements: Be impeccable with your word. Don't take anything personally. Don't make assumptions. Always do your best. Finally, share these principles with those that you interact with on a daily basis. I'll leave it to you to see what transformation takes place!

What would it be like if we were each given a life assignment? *The Giver* by Lois Lowry (Laurel Leaf, $6.50) provides a somewhat eerie look at the way we might live someday. The story takes place in a

You can become blind by seeing each day as a similar one. Each day is a different one, each day brings a miracle of its own. It's just a matter of paying attention to this miracle.

—PAULO COELHO

I come now, at the late juncture of my life, to this sudden realization: I have no destination, no real destination in the literal sense. The destination, the place toward which my life is tending, is the journey itself and not the final stopping place. How I get there is more important than whether I arrive, although I know I will arrive.

—RICHARD BODE

utopian community where there is no hunger, no disease, no pollution, no fear—until a twelve-year-old boy rebels against the choices that have been denied him.

Hope for the Flowers . . . (Paulist Press, $14.95, splurge for the hardcover.) The rush to get to the top will take new meaning after you read this touching and thought-provoking story about two caterpillars. Author Trina Paulus challenges us to believe in the butterfly inside.

"I command that you be happy in the world, as long as you live!" What if someone demanded that of you? And is it really possible? A wonderful story (and quick read), Richard Bach's **Illusions: The Adventures of a Reluctant Messiah** (Dell, $6.99), takes you on a journey that just possibly answers the question of why we exist. And if you like **Illusions,** you'll also want to read **Jonathan Livingston Seagull** (Avon, $6.50), a unique fable about a bird's journey of freedom and flight. Through the eyes of Jonathan, you'll learn that there's much more to life than searching for food and flying with the flock. Both these classics can be found at most used bookstores across the country.

While lying in a hospital bed some ten years ago, a dear friend of mine gave me a small book called **The Little Prince** by Antoine de Saint-Exupéry (Harcourt Brace, $18, splurge for the hardcover). Within a few hours my entire perspective of life changed—yours will too, as "what is essential is invisible to the eye." Also check out the animated "claymation" video, which is superb!

Dr. Seuss opens the door to all the exciting possibilities that lie ahead and earnestly warns of the potential pitfalls. You'll find **Oh, the Places You'll Go!** (Random House, $17, splurge for the hardcover) to be the perfect send-off for your new adventure.

Benjamin Hoff's **The Tao of Pooh** (Viking Press, $11.95) is the perfect read for anyone wanting to learn the basic principles of Taoism, but through the eyes of the beloved character Winnie the Pooh, who "wanders around asking silly questions, making up songs, and going through all kinds of adventures, without ever accumulating any amount of intellectual knowledge or losing his simpleminded sort of happiness." Maybe Pooh has something, huh?

FRESH PERSPECTIVES

*These resources will help you to look at yourself
in a whole new way.*

How do I live a happy, meaningful, and flourishing life? How can I be both a noble and effective person? Answering these fundamental questions was the single-minded passion of Epictetus, the revered philosopher who was born a slave about A.D. 55 in the eastern out-

The important thing is to strive toward a goal that is not immediately visible. That goal is not the concern of the mind, but of the spirit.

—ANTOINE DE SAINT-EXUPÉRY

I like nonsense, it wakes up the brain cells. Fantasy is a necessary ingredient in living; it's a way of looking at life through the wrong end of a telescope. Which is what I do, and that enables you to laugh at life's realities.

—DR. SEUSS

Everything has its own place and function. That applies to people, although many don't seem to realize it, stuck as they are in the wrong job, the wrong marriage, or the wrong house. When you know and respect your own Inner Nature, you know where you belong. You also know where you don't belong.

—BENJAMIN HOFF

FIVE TRUTHS ABOUT FEAR
by Susan Jeffers

1. The fear will never go away as long as I continue to grow.

2. The only way to get rid of the fear of doing something is to go out and do it.

3. The only way to feel better about myself is to go out and do it.

4. Not only am I going to experience fear whenever I'm on unfamiliar territory, but so is everyone else.

5. Pushing through fear is less frightening than living with the underlying fear that comes from a feeling of helplessness.

If you go around doing your thing without expectation, then you already have everything you need. If you receive something in return, you take it with open arms. It should always come as a surprise. But if you expect a response and it comes, it's a bore. Cease expecting and you have all things.

—LEO BUSCAGLIA

reaches of the Roman Empire. Both of his works, *The Art of Living* and *A Manual for Living,* a condensed version (Harper San Francisco, $16.95/$9), provide a day-by-day, down-to-earth life of virtue.

Most people don't fully appreciate the fact that no matter who you are, if you want something in life, you've got to learn to ask for it. *Ask for the Moon—and Get It* by Percy Ross focuses on this most neglected secret to success and happiness. (Find this one in used bookstores.)

"Excitement wears orange socks, faith lives in the same apartment building as doubt. . . . " *The Book of Qualities* by Ruth Gendler (HarperCollins, $12) challenges you to look at your emotions and unique character in new and inspiring ways.

Do you need a whack on the side of the head . . . or maybe just a kick in the pants? Then indulge in Roger von Oech's **Creative Whack Pack** (U.S. Games Systems, $16), a deck of cards (sixty-four in all!); each provides a brief story, hint, or insight that will keep your mind spinning for days to come.

How many times have you talked yourself out of something because of self-sabotaging fears? *Feel the Fear and Do It Anyway* by Susan Jeffers (Fawcett Books, $14) will teach you to push past the negative chatter in your head, risk a little every day, and turn every decision into a "no-lose" situation.

Wouldn't it be nice to live a happier, more successful, and more peaceful life? *Happiness Is a Choice* (Fawcett Books, $10.95) is about believing in ourselves, having a positive attitude, and being hopeful about the events that shape our lives. And after reading Barry Kaufman's book, you might also want to take part in one of the many educational programs he (and his happy staff) offer through the Option Institute (see their listing on page 242). Whether you want to improve the quality of your life or overcome a challenging adversity, the program will help you actively explore a new way to live your life.

Based on the Myers-Briggs personality test, *Lifetypes* by Sandra Krebs Hirsh and Jean Kummerow (Warner Books, $13.95) gives you the tools to develop a psychological self-portrait. After completing a series of questions (which is great fun with a group of friends), your "lifetype" emerges. The book then provides you with examples of each personality type as it relates to careers, relationships, and recreational activities that you should choose or avoid—and how to get the most out of your life by gaining a better understanding of yourself.

Leo Buscaglia has to be one of my all-time favorite authors. His writings teach us to be human—to be who we are and what we feel, and how we can learn to be loving individuals and get the most out of life through love. Known for getting his students to hug trees (and each other) at the University of Southern California while teaching a class on love, Dr. Buscaglia will guide you to new levels of happiness (on this fantastic journey we're all on). *Love* and *Living, Loving, and Learning* (Fawcett Books, $11/$12) are my favorites.

How is it that we can find meaning in life when confronted with a hopeless situation? This is the very premise in Dr. Viktor Frankl's reflective and inspiring writings. Born out of the years he spent as a prisoner in concentration camps—and what kept him going, *Man's Search for Meaning* (Washington Square Press, $6.99) explores the basis of human potential and how we can rise above any situation that causes suffering.

Self-doubt and negative thoughts seems to be the most devastating handicaps for many. But it doesn't have to be this way—and *The Power of Positive Thinking* (Ballantine Books, $12) will help you to climb above those old habits and unleash your true potential. Dr. Vincent Peale offers powerful tips, prayerful exercises, and "filling your mind full of God" each day to positively master those challenges of everyday living. For positive thinking tune-ups, turn to *Guideposts* (www.dailyguideposts.com) or get in touch with The Peale Center for Positive Thinking at (845) 855-5000.

What would your life be like if you never took risks? You'd never find a great job, make a new friend, fall in love, or . . . ! If you're having trouble making crucial choices in your life—moving from the fear of the unknown to the excitement of what is about to be—then read David Viscott's *Risking*. (Find this one in used bookstores.) In addition, Dr. Viscott has many other books that center around emotional resilience.

Stroll down the path of life with SARK and learn about her 250 jobs, how to relax about money, making friends with freedom and uncertainty, living juicy, drawing on the walls, and making your life an adventure. SARK's *Inspiration Sandwich* (Celestial Arts, $14.95) will inspire your creative freedom, and *Living Juicy: Daily Morsels for Your Creative Soul* (Celestial Arts, $15.95) will challenge the way you look at your life and bring a refreshing new approach to "daily meditation." Camp SARK, her companion website (www.campsark.com), provides all the details—including some of her latest books. For those who need a quick dose of inspiration, call her Inspiration Hotline at (415) 546-3742 for a three-minute recorded message.

Work, love, friendship, spirituality, living fully . . . how do we make sense of life's daily challenges as friends, parents, or leading a balanced lifestyle and achieving our best? *Touchstones: A Book of Daily Meditations for Men* by David Spohn and *Each Day a New Beginning: Daily Meditations for Women* by Karen Casey (Hazelden, each $12) are great companions to begin each day with a thought-provoking meditation, helping you to ignite new possibilities and strengthen you on your path.

> Everything can be taken from us but one thing: the last of our human freedoms—to choose one's attitude in any given set of circumstances, to choose one's own way.
>
> —VIKTOR FRANKL

> The greatest power we have is the power of choice. It's an actual fact that if you've been moping in unhappiness, you can choose to be joyous instead and, by effort, lift yourself into joy. If you tend to be fearful, you can overcome that misery by choosing to have courage. Even in darkest grief you have a choice. The whole trend and quality of anyone's life is determined in the long run by the choices that are made.
>
> —NORMAN VINCENT PEALE

Joy increases as you give it, and diminishes as you try to keep it for yourself. In giving it, you will accumulate a deposit of joy greater than you ever believed possible. —NORMAN VINCENT PEALE

POSITIVE STEPS TO CAREER CHANGE

If you need some career insights from the experts, you've come to the right place!

Inspiration, self-improvement, and motivation. Need some? With Josh Hinds behind the inspiration wheel, **Getmotivation.com** will provide you with ideas and insights on leading a more successful, fulfilling life. Sign up for the inspiration a day—a daily newsletter including motivational quotes, an inspiring story, and engaging commentary by Josh.

Your dream job doesn't have to be just a dream. There are millions of fulfilling and interesting jobs out there for folks that don't seem to fit the norm. Being different, unconventional, and hard-to-categorize can be a big asset if you know how to use it. After all, do you really want to do what everybody else does? *The Career Guide for Creative and Unconventional People* by Carol Eikleberry (Ten Speed Press, $11.95) gives you a boost to make your dreams a reality.

Career counselor Rick Jarow challenges each of us "to create a life work that will reflect our own nature, and to develop the courage and wisdom to bring it into form." *Creating the Work You Love* (Inner Traditions, $14.95) offers a step-by-step and self-reflective process based on the seven chakras (the body's energy centers) that will challenge you to move past the daily struggles of life and push toward making your life a work of art. Also, visit Rick's "anticareer" website at **www.anticareer.com** for more spirited words.

Unfortunately, many of us look at money as an end, rather than as a means. Marsha Sinetar's *Do What You Love, the Money Will Follow* (Dell, $13.95) will help you realize that if you do what brings meaning to your life, you'll pleasantly find that you'll have all the riches in the world. The book is filled with inspirational examples of people who have pursued what they love, rather than just the making of money. A must for those who are in jobs for the wrong reason or need a push in the right direction.

"Whether our gift is baking bread, assessing environmental hazards, teaching children, or powerhouse investing, it's never going to be enough to just dabble a little here and a little there. If you wish for full satisfaction, you must give yourself completely to this work, 100 percent." Complete with hands-on exercises, *How Much Joy Can You Stand?* by Suzanne Falter-Barns (Ballantine Wellspring, $12) helps fuel, free, excite, and encourage the small dreams we keep like secrets and never do anything about. Her companion website, **www.howmuchjoy.com,** might also reignite a few creative sparks.

Is your life and career a little foggy? Barbara Sher—motivational specialist, therapist, and career counselor—has a handful of books to help you lift this fog, gain momentum, and get your life on the right path. *Live the Life You Love* (Dell, $11.95) provides ten step-by-step lessons to create a meaningful, rewarding life, with exercises that are actually quite fun. *I Could Do Anything If I Only Knew What It Was* (Dell, $13.95) explores the basic fact that each of us really does know what we want. Through creative exercises once again and fresh perspectives, Sher will definitely help you to create your own luck, push past the fears of success, and make your dreams come alive. Check out www.barbarasher.com for an overview of all her books, including more about the author, events, and to sign up for her e-newsletter.

If you are looking for that perfect job but aren't sure how to find it, *The Pathfinder* (Fireside, $14) will help you dispel those feelings of uncertainty and make a career direction your reality. Through extensive exercises such as goal setting, list making, self-tests, and other diagnostic tools, author Nicholas Lore shows you how to live a life you love, how to get there from here, and how to design your future career.

If you've been dreaming of embarking on a life-transforming journey, one that will take you away from the office for a while, *Six Months Off* by Hope Dlugozima and James Scott (Henry Holt, $14) can help you take your fantasies off the shelf and transform them into reality. The authors talked to more than two hundred sabbatical-takers who'd actually gathered the gumption to take time off of work and make their vagabond dreams come true.

The 7 Habits of Highly Effective People by Stephen Covey (Simon and Schuster, $14) provides a step-by-step pathway for living principles that give us the security to adapt to change, and the wisdom and power to take advantage of the opportunities that change creates.

If you're going through a transition, whether it be a breakup, career change, or ending something, and are unsure about your next step, I highly recommend *Transitions* (Perseus Press, $16). William Bridges takes you through the three stages of transition: Endings (that difficult process of letting go of an old situation), the Neutral Zone (that seemingly unproductive and confusing nowhere of in-betweenness), and the New Beginning (launching forth again in a new situation). To guide you through this transitional path, see his companion website at www.wmbridges.com.

What Color Is Your Parachute? (Ten Speed Press, $16.95) Just the title of this book intrigues me. After reading it from cover to cover (and working through a dozen of Richard Bolles's flower exercises), I realized that it should be required reading for anyone who wants to successfully carve out their own career niche. Revised and updated annually, *Parachute* (a metaphor coined by the author when he was referring to career transitions back in the late 1960s) is about taking chances, gaining confidence, and making changes in your career and life. Complete with exercises on self-assessment and career planning, it is perhaps most valuable to those who are securely employed but unhappy with what they're doing. As a companion for his wit, words, and wisdom, Richard Bolles has also crafted a magnificent website—**JobHuntersBible.com**, replete with many, many job finding and career links and advice.

It's incredibly easy to get caught up in an activity trap, in the busy-ness of life, to work harder and harder at climbing the ladder of success only to discover it's leaning against the wrong wall. Thus every step we take just gets us to the wrong place faster. We may be very busy, we may be very efficient, but we also will be truly effective only when we begin with the end in mind.

—STEPHEN COVEY

Though we might think God will yell out our mission in life from some mountain top, we find ourselves in the valley, where God softly speaks "take one step at a time," even when you don't see where it all is leading or where your mission is going. The path of life and the moments of decision. . . Take the one that leads to more gratitude, more kindness, more love in the world.

—RICHARD BOLLES
(from the book *How to Find Your Mission in Life*)

Most successful new businesspeople do not start out in life thinking that this is what they want to do. Their idea springs from a deep immersion in some occupation, hobby, or other pursuit, spurred by something missing in the world.

—PAUL HAWKEN

Are you "navigating" through your first year in college? **First Year Focus** (www.abacon.com/firstyearfocus) provides support, information, and tips that will help get you on the right path. Included are some great ideas on internships and careers.

BECOMING YOUR OWN BOSS

If you're ready to start that business you've always dreamed of doing, these books will fuel your fire!

Do you have the urge to strike out on your own and develop a career path that just might have the greatest job satisfaction and personal development? Let Paul Hawken show you the way. *Growing a Business* (Fireside, $12) provides straight talk on what works and what doesn't, and why. You'll also learn that being in business is not about making money. It is a way to become who you are.

For some reason, we have been brainwashed with the fact that the more we work, the better off we become. *The Joy of Not Working* (Ten Speed Press, $14.95) teaches us how we can create a paradise away from the workplace—and develop our world of leisure (while making a living). Ernie Zelinski's down-to-earth writing is filled with great stories, cartoons, quotes, and plenty of exercises—all of which provide insights on how to get that zest back into your life and become excited about everything you do.

Got the urge to throw in the towel at what you're currently doing and become joyfully jobless? Barbara Winters's book, *Making a Living without a Job* (Bantam Books, $13.95), is for anyone who has always dreamed of becoming their own boss (and creating the work they love). She'll take you on a step-by-step journey that integrates the things you like to do with the things you're good at doing. She also self-publishes *Winning Ways,* a brilliant bimonthly newsletter (six issues per year for $33), which is designed to share creative ideas about successful self-employment, along with thoughts on personal development. By the way, if you're ready to become an entrepreneurial gypsy, she also teaches a unique seminar entitled "How to Support Your Wanderlust" in various locales throughout the country. You can reach Barbara at babswinter@hotmail.com or by calling (952) 835-5647.

CAMPUS CROWD

Whether you're in high school, or college, or are a student of life, these resources will jump start your journey!

Are you in the search for a college education that will support your values while providing you with the tools to make a better world? Miriam Weinstein's *Making a Difference College and Graduate Guide* (New Society Publishers, $19.95) profiles hundreds of alternative and innovative colleges that range from sustainable development and earth literacy to experiential-based international programs. To fund your new vision in life, Weinstein also offers information on college scholarships, fellowships, and other funding options in her companion guide—***Making a Difference Scholarships for a Better World*** ($15.95). More information can be found at www.making-a-difference.com.

If you are searching out a path to greatness, you definitely want to check out what Patrick Combs has to say. Geared mainly to the college crowd, although helpful to people of all ages, ***Major in Success*** (Ten Speed Press, $12.95) will walk you through an inspirational journey, helping you to take a fresh look at your life and explore how to uncover your dream job. Once you've absorbed the information in his book, turn to his website at www.goodthink.com for more motivation, inspiration, and life-changing stories. (In fact, you can read one on page 148.) *Good Thinking Hot Tips* can also be received through email by signing up on the Web.

A practical and inspirational collection of profiles of more than thirty students, ***Taking Time Off*** by Colin Hall and Ron Lieber (Noonday Press, $10) demonstrates how taking time off gives you a chance to explore career interests, gain practical experience, and develop a new perspective on your studies.

Are you craving real-world experiences and learning opportunities beyond the standard fare in high school? Then come explore the possibilities presented in Rebecca Greene's ***The Teenagers' Guide to School Outside the Box*** (Free Spirit Publishing, $15.95), and you'll definitely be armed with the tools to plot out your own alternative learning adventure. For other books that promote positive self-esteem in teens (written by experts in the field), check out Free Spirit on the Web at www.freespirit.com.

If you're just about to graduate from high school and are off to college just because "that's what you're supposed to do," ***The UnCollege Alternative*** (ReganBooks, $14.95) might change your mind or, at least, provide a better direction. College is definitely one path to a great career; however, it can also become an expensive and unnecessary delay, according to Danielle Wood. She presents chapter after chapter of options and alternatives—from "busting the blue collar myth" to careers in alternative medicine.

UNIQUE JOB SITES AND RESOURCES

To explore some of the best job and career links on the Web—from cool jobs to international internships—check out **About.com's Guide to Job Searching (www.jobsearch.about.com),** hosted by career guru Alison Doyle. Along with spotlight articles and hundreds of hot job-seeking tips, be sure to sign up for her weekly newsletter, which includes information on upcoming features and updates to the website.

Ever wanted to learn more about being a marine biologist or a screenwriter? With **GetThatGig.com,** you can find heaps of information and links in a very informative and playful way. Targeted to high school students looking for a cool summer job or internship or those in college about to make their first career decision, twenty categories highlight a variety of interesting and unique programs with additional links, resources, and stories to kick-start your career.

The important thing is not to stop questioning. Curiosity has its own reason for existing. One cannot help but be in awe when he contemplates the mysteries of eternity, of life, of the marvelous structure of reality. It is enough if one tries merely to comprehend a little of this mystery every day. Never lose a holy curiosity.

—ALBERT EINSTEIN

We read books to find out who we are. What other people, real or imaginary, do, think, and feel is an essential guide to our understanding of what we ourselves are and may become. —URSULA K. LEGUIN

45

For endless career and job link opportunities, all the major search engines on the Web have career directories that are sure to give you more ideas. My favorite is **Google.com.** Try typing in "Adventure Jobs" and see what listings appear.

The higher you climb . . .
The more that you see.

The more that you see . . .
The less that you know.

The less that you know . . .
The more that you yearn.

The more that you yearn . . .
The higher you climb.

The farther you reach . . .
The more that you touch.

The more that you touch . . .
The fuller you feel.

The fuller you feel . . .
The less that you need.

The less that you need . . .
The farther you reach.

—DAN FOGELBERG

The **Aboutjobs.com** network provides a variety of job venues—including summer, resort, overseas, and intern jobs—for the adventure seeker, complete with a database searchable by location or keyword.

What's it like to be a postal worker, a McDonald's team player, or a clown? **AboutMyJob.com** provides a place for ordinary people to share their stories of exciting and not-so-exciting jobs and places. You definitely can't believe everything you read, but it just may help you decide whether you should learn to cope better with your current situation or head out to greener pastures!

Published six times a year, *Career Opportunities News* is filled with interesting career tidbits, ranging from free and inexpensive career materials and book reviews to feature stories that cover everything from internships to education and work. This sixteen-page, advertising-free publication runs $40 per year. Contact Ferguson Publishing at (800) 306-9941 or by visiting their website at www.fergpubco.com.

If you were to start from scratch on finding a job on the Internet, you might start with **Rileyguide.com.** It's filled with link upon link of job resources, listings, and information guides. The site's "webmistress," Margaret Dikel, is also the author of the *Guide to Internet Job Searching* (McGraw Hill, $14.95), which is published every other year. The guidebook offers expert advice and information for bulletin boards, recruiter information, job listings, discussion groups, resume-posting services—if it's career-related, you'll find the links in this book.

For heaps of career resource links, job-hunting sites, career articles, cover letter and resume advice, explore the gems found in **Quintessential Careers** (www.quintcareers.com). Be sure to sign up for *QuintZine,* their biweekly newsletter filled with career advice, job information, and the latest website news.

An adventurous lifestyle means to grow through excitement, challenge, and risk taking. It's about learning to look at the world through curious eyes—to wonder what's on the other side of the mountain—and allowing wanderlust to become your guide. The intimacy of your adventurous pursuits will allow you to see, hear, taste, and smell more intensely. You'll work hard and you'll play hard; however, by exploring your options in this section, you'll learn that work and play become the same thing. Push past your doubts and fears and let your journey to adventure begin!

I learned early that the richness of life is adventure. Adventure calls on all faculties of mind and spirit. It develops self-reliance and independence. Life then teems with excitement. But you are not ready for adventure unless you are rid of fear. For fear confines you and limits your scope. You stay tethered by strings of doubt and indecision and have only a small and narrow world to explore.

—WILLIAM O. DOUGLAS

Unique Opportunities to Explore in This Section:

- Looking for excitement, risk, unique experiences, education, and fun? Learn what an expert river guide has to say about the outdoor adventure field, her experiences, and why she loves her job so much in this special "day-in-a-life" story. And if this story sends chills up your back, you'll want to explore the details for a handful of river outfitters who are awaiting your job application (page 48).

- Is it true that the more risk you take, the more you can open yourself up to new adventures? Find out how Michael and Dorrie Williams left their Corporate America jobs and experienced an adventure of a lifetime by pedaling their bikes across America. This special cycling section also features seasonal employment opportunities with some of the best biking adventure programs in the U.S. (page 65).

- Experience the four pillars of self-reliance, fitness, craftsmanship, and compassion taught at Outward Bound, by participating in one of their rugged adventure programs or becoming a seasonal staff member at one of their five wilderness schools (page 82).

- Road Trip USA? If you're about to hit the road for a cross-country adventure and are looking for a budget-conscious housing option with a spirited twist, staying at a youth hostel might be your answer. Read more about hostel-style travel and your working options in this special section (page 95).

Photo Credit: Alaska Wildland Adventures

A seasonal raft guide with Alaska Wildland Adventures (page 56) leads a trip in the Kenai Peninsula.

ADVENTURE CAREERS

PLAYING FOR A LIVING:

A River Guide's Perspective on the Outdoor Adventure Field

There is no denying that outdoor adventure has come into its own. I still remember the days when people would look at me sideways with that "you are a bright girl, don't you think you should have a real job" look on their faces when I told them that I was an adventure tourism guide. But these days the responses are very different indeed. Now, a little light shines in their eyes and they ask me which rivers I have guided and if I can give them any advice in planning their next trip. How things change.

Adventure travel and ecotourism form one of the world's fastest growing tourism sectors, with outdoor adventure programming at the heart of this growth. Consumers of these programs are looking for excitement, a level of risk, unique experiences, education, and fun. With the growth of the industry

has also come a need for professionals to be on the front line to deliver these programs—and a well-qualified professional is a sought-after commodity worldwide in adventure travel. Many colleges and universities have keyed into this need and are now offering excellent programs that provide students with a solid foundation in the outdoor adventure tourism industry. Although employers value post-secondary education, most programs do not hire solely on industry-recognized skills certification. It is the combination of attitude, knowledge, skills certification, and experience that will make you marketable in this field.

I always tell people starting out in this industry that what I do, I do because I love it, and what I get paid for is having the judgment and decision-making skills necessary to lead a successful trip. By that I mean, your goal as a river guide is to make sure people have a great time—that they are fed amazing food, hit all the big rapids, and learn things about the new places they have visited. But I am more than a river hostess: I have years of experience behind every decision I make; I have specialized training in rescue and wilderness medicine; I have studied the places I work in and respect the inherent risks of my working environment; I have planned every detail of the trip beforehand and drawn up contingency plans; and I understand both the strengths of my group and my own limitations.

This is not a job for everyone. It is not for people who do not want to take responsibility. This is a job for leaders—which doesn't mean someone who is a control freak. It is someone who is well organized, cares about people, and puts group and guest needs ahead of their own. It is someone who is flexible, has a sense of humor, and is so passionate about what they do that their professionalism and pride in their work shows through in their every action. Though I cannot remember who said it, the words ring in my ears: A good leader is one who, at the end of the day and when all the goals have been met, will have the group say, "we did it ourselves." Many times I have guided trips with corporate executives who have told me that if ever I get tired of "playing for a living" I would be welcome in their human resources depart-

ment or in a managerial position. Needless to say, I have never taken any of them up on their offers.

I have now been "playing for a living" for over ten years and I am not prepared to quit any time soon. Why would I? I love my office, the casual dress (and the need not to worry about how my hair looks), all the wild and wonderful places of the earth that I get to experience, the fabulous people I meet, and the new inspirations that come forth each day because of the variety of my job.

A typical day may involve waking up in some spectacular place, making coffee, and packing your gear before anyone else is out of their tents. After breakfast, perhaps a hike or a paddle on the river—and if you see something wonderful, you stop and check it out. Maybe it's a herd of caribou or young golden eagles in their nest; maybe it's a stream that meanders to a waterfall just perfect for swimming under; or perhaps it's the artwork of a people who traveled the same way thousands of years before you.

All day long you play, you discover, and you explore the places around you. You learn, you teach, and you soothe your tired and happy body with a soak in a natural hot spring. It is hard work, but you will truly love your job. You're also guaranteed to hear these words from almost every one of your guests at one time or another: "Boy, it must be great to get paid for what you do!" and you will heave a big sigh and say "yeah . . . it is."

—CONTRIBUTED BY JILL BAXTER, who has been a working professional in the outdoor adventure industry for over ten years, with teaching at the heart of her passion. She has guided extended river expeditions from the awe-inspiring Grand Canyon of the Colorado River to the legendary Nahanni River in Canada's Northwest Territories. Currently she is the owner/operator of Bear Creek Outdoor Centre (www.bearcreekoutdoor.com), located near Canada's capital city of Ottawa. Bear Creek runs a ten-week intensive summer leadership training and certification in outdoor adventure, with activities including white-water canoeing, kayaking, rafting, mountain biking, climbing, wilderness first aid, swift-water rescue, riverboarding, leadership development, team building, and a wilderness canoe expedition. Contact Jill at jill@bearcreekoutdoor.com or by calling (888) 453-5099.

Every job should be looked at as an education and an adventure. The satisfaction must come from your work. —RICHARD BOLLES

RIVER OUTFITTERS

If you want to play for a living on the white waters of North America, here's a handful of outfitters that specialize in river guiding. Unless you're an experienced guide, it will be necessary to participate in a pre-season certificate training workshop in the spring. No need to worry, because most outfitters offer this training for a fee—and some at no cost! In addition to becoming a river guide, many outfitters hire base-camp staff, cooks, and drivers.

ADVENTURE CONNECTION

River Outfitter • California • Seasonal
www.raftcalifornia.com

ADVENTURE CONNECTION WAS created by a dedicated group of river enthusiasts who saw how river trips had the power to change lives. After working for, and with, some of California's finest professional river outfitters, they knew they could offer something different—a little more luxury, a tastier menu, a slightly higher-class trip—and still have competitive prices. They are now one of California's largest outfitters in the Mother Lode area.

What You'll Be Doing: An annual white-water rafting workshop is offered each spring where Adventure Connection hires guides from among its best students (the course costs $800). A low student-to-instructor ratio is maintained in order to provide each participant with the best opportunity to develop their skills. Since Adventure Connection's hiring varies from year to year, the course also helps workshop participants apply to all outfitters in the area. Canoe and kayak instruction is also offered.

Perks and Rewards: Pay varies by the river and the experience of the guide. Trip guides are paid by the day, generally $60 to $100 per day. Guides also receive generous tips, free meals and camping facilities, use of equipment for private trips, and a chance to work in the great outdoors.

The Essentials: Those with great attitudes and good social skills make the best candidates. Applicants for guide positions with no prior experience should enroll in the company's annual river-guide school.

Your First Move: Call for application materials (which are due by March 1). Prospective candidates should attend the white-water rafting workshop, generally held in early April of each year.

For More Information:
Nate Rangel, President
Adventure Connection
P.O. Box 475
Coloma, CA 95613
(800) 556-6060 • (530) 626-7385 • (530) 626-9268 (fax)
getwet@raftcalifornia.com

BIG BEND RIVER TOURS

River Outfitter • Texas • 1–6 Months
www.bigbendrivertours.com

TUCKED AWAY IN A remote corner of southwestern Texas lies a colorful, majestic, and sparsely populated area called Big Bend. The river gave this piece of Texas its name by bending like an elbow while cradling the desert, sheer-walled canyons, deep gorges, and Chisos mountains. The river is also home to Big Bend River Tours, offering year-round adventures by paddle, oar, foot, or jeep. Seasonal guides lead groups on rafting, canoeing, hiking, and interpretive tours throughout the region and into Mexico. Guides must complete a training program (usually one week for experienced guides; three months for trainees)

River guides set up base camp on the spectacular Rio Grande with Big Bend River Tours.

before leading trips. All applicants must be CPR and first-aid certified as well as hardworking and willing to go the extra mile. Pay is on a per-trip basis, with camping available at the boathouse. New trainees must commit to six months, while experienced guides must commit to a minimum of one month. Call, write, or email for an information packet and application.

For More Information:
Jan Forté, General Manager
Big Bend River Tours
P.O. Box 317
Terlingua, TX 79852
(800) 545-4240 • (915) 371-3033 • (915) 371-3034 (fax)
employment@bigbendrivertours.com

CHUCK RICHARDS' WHITEWATER

River Outfitter • California • Summer
www.chuckrichards.com

HERE'S RAFTING SOUTHERN CALIFORNIA style—blazing hot days, balmy starlit evenings, sizzling barbecues, great grins, no bugs, and no goosebumps. Raft guides will take adventure seekers on the Kern River, which provides class three to class five rapids. In order to be a summer guide, applicants need to participate in three to five successive weekends of training in March and April (for a fee of $350). Along with lodging in their bunkhouse, guides receive $55 to $70 per day (plus tips).

For More Information:
Chuck Richards, President
Chuck Richards' Whitewater
Box W.W. Whitewater
Lake Isabella, CA 93240
(760) 379-4444 • (760) 379-4685 (fax)
chuckww@lightspeed.net

DENALI RAFT ADVENTURES

River Outfitter • Alaska • Seasonal
www.denaliraftadventures.com

DENALI RAFT ADVENTURES offers two- and four-hour, full-day, and overnight raft trips on the mighty Nenana River, which forms the eastern border of Denali National Park. The season runs from mid-May through mid-September, and seasonal staff work as reservations

clerks, bus drivers, and river guides. Dormitory-style rooms run $70 per month, and everyone gets a room-mate. Ideal applicants are those who enjoy the outdoors and are punctual, friendly, outgoing, hardworking, energetic, enthusiastic, and guest oriented. Send a cover letter and resume to begin the application process.

For More Information:
Jim and Val Raisis, Directors
Denali Raft Adventures
Drawer 190
Denali Park, AK 99755
(888) 683-2234 • (907) 683-2234 • (907) 683-1281 (fax)
denraft@mtaonline.net

EPLEY'S WHITEWATER ADVENTURES

River Outfitter • Idaho • Summer
www.epleys.com

LEADING GREAT ADVENTURES since 1962, Epley's provides half- to five-day river float trips on the lower Salmon River. In addition to leading float trips, guides also get involved with maintenance of equipment, buildings, and grounds; food preparation; and kitchen cleanup. The all-expense-paid training period begins June 1. Upon proper certification, Epley's will obtain a guide license for guides at a cost of $105. Guides then work a six-day workweek and finish up about August 31. Beginning pay starts at $750 per month, plus room and board, free laundry service, and medical benefits. Guides live in group quarters with a bathroom, beds, refrigerator, and living room. They also have a VCR, trampoline, and basketball hoop for after-work entertainment. Candidates must be at least eighteen years of age; completed applications must be turned in by February 1.

For More Information:
Ted Epley, Owner/Operator
Epley's Whitewater Adventures
P.O. Box 987
McCall, ID 83638
(800) 233-1813 • (208) 634-5173 • (208) 634-5270 (fax)
epleys@micron.net

We are looking for guides who have high morals, a willing-to-learn attitude, who work well with people, and don't drink alcohol or smoke.

FOUR CORNERS RAFTING

River Outfitter • Colorado • Summer
www.fourcornersrafting.com

COLORADO'S ARKANSAS RIVER is home to the most popular mild-to-wild raft trips in the country. Since 1976, Four Corners has been operating white-water rafting and float-fishing trips. Guides run mostly half- and one-day trips on various stretches of the Arkansas River (primarily class three and some class four and five white water), teaching paddlers about the local history, geology, plants, and animals.

Commitment: Applicants must be able to start guide training in mid-May, followed by additional training on a local river until competent. Some guides are ready in late May; most, the first week of June.

Perks and Rewards: First-season guides can expect $1,800 to $2,000, plus $400 to $800 in tips (more for experienced guides). Benefits include use of equipment on days off, discounts on river gear and clothing, and for extended river trips, the opportunity to learn to kayak. Housing can be difficult to find, although they keep an eye out for you. Four Corners leases campsites or spaces in large, lockable tents for $50 to $150 per month.

The Essentials: Applicants must be at least eighteen, have first-aid and CPR certification, and be comfortable in water, a good swimmer, personable, well groomed, and able to work in hot, wet, or cold weather. Any river training or experience you can get on your own or in other guide schools, a higher level first-aid certification, and ability to stay past mid-August help. Most guides are educators, college students or graduates, or ski personnel.

Your First Move: Call for application materials or visit their website. After a screening process and reference check, selected candidates are invited for the training trip (usually six days on the Dolores River in southwestern Colorado). Training is $300, with half refunded if you stay the whole season. Hiring is done after the six-day training trip. There is no guarantee you will be hired if you are selected to go on the training trip.

For More Information:
Jim Sampson, President
Four Corners Rafting
P.O. Box 219
Nathrop, CO 81236
(800) 332-7238 • (719) 395-4137 • (719) 395-4130 (fax)
info@fourcornersrafting.com

Get on a river with an outdoor club or check out nearby guide-training schools. Contact us early and do your paperwork correctly and neatly. Be complete and make sure your references have current contact information.

MAD RIVER BOAT TRIPS

River Outfitter • Wyoming • Summer
www.mad-river.com

ARE YOU READY to experience the adrenaline-filled rush of the Big Kahuna while checking out panoramic views of the Grand Tetons? As the largest white water and scenic rafting company in Jackson Hole, Mad River Boat Trips offers some of the wildest white-water on the Snake River—and you could be a part of the adventure! Each summer, both experienced and novice river guides are hired. Those without experience must complete a week-long course (for a fee) at Mad River that begins mid-May; however, this doesn't mean you'll get hired. Generally only four are selected from their guide school, but don't let this deter you: the skills you'll learn will be invaluable for other guide opportunities. In addition to river-guide positions, Mad River hires river cooks (steak and trout BBQs are the norm), reservationists (over thirty thousand people book river trips each year), and shuttle drivers. Guides and cooks are paid per trip, while reservationists and shuttle drivers are paid per hour. Beyond the qualifications needed for each position, applicants must meet the minimum age requirements: eighteen for guides/reservationists; twenty-three for cooks/shuttle drivers. Applications are available online or call for further information.

For More Information:
Operations Manager
Mad River Boat Trips
P.O. Box 10940
Jackson, WY 83002
(800) 458-7238 • (307) 733-6203

OUTDOOR ADVENTURE RIVER SPECIALISTS

River Outfitter • California • Seasonal
www.oars.com

OUTDOOR ADVENTURE RIVER SPECIALISTS, also known as OARS, has been recognized worldwide as the industry model for river outfitters. They operate river trips on over twenty-five rivers in the western U.S., as well as on Canadian and international waters. Choose the challenge of class five rapids or gentler trips with an "oar" option, meaning the guide does all the rowing while guests sit back and enjoy the ride. Internships are available in marketing, customer service, interpretation, and Internet development. Pay is $200 per week, with basic housing. Free trips are also available during days off.

For More Information:
Greg MacDonald, General Manager
Outdoor Adventure River Specialists
P.O. Box 67
Angels Camp, CA 95222
(800) 346-6277 • (209) 736-4677 • (209) 736-2902 (fax)
gregm@oars.com

RIVER ODYSSEYS WEST

River Outfitter • Idaho/Montana • Summer
www.rowinc.com

RIVER ODYSSEYS WEST, commonly known as ROW, leads wilderness rafting and walking trips in Idaho, Oregon, and Montana, as well as voyageur canoe trips, rafting adventures, and yachting and barge trips throughout the world. With the chance to run spectacular rapids, sleep under the stars, meet interesting people, make new friends, and be surrounded by nature's beauty, being a river guide is a dream job for many. But make no mistake about it, being a river guide is hard work and physically demanding.

What You'll Be Doing: If you don't have any previous white-water or guiding experience, but want to experience a great summer in the outdoors, becoming a swamper or river jester (ROW's term for guide assistants) may be your ticket. Swampers travel in cargo boats ahead of the river group to set up camp and greet the guests. In addition to swamper duties, river jesters lead family activities and games geared toward learning about nature.

Guide positions are the most sought after at ROW. Those who have experience will lead one- to six-day white-water trips on the rivers of northern and central Idaho. Some trips paddle through deep gorges; others through beautiful valleys.

Commitment: Bear in mind that guiding is physically demanding work with long hours. During the peak season in July and August, guides may be asked to work six days a week.

Perks and Rewards: Meals, housing, and a daily wage are provided for all.

The Essentials: The ideal candidate has great people skills and previous river guiding and natural/cultural history interpretation experience. Those who play a musical instrument for campfire entertainment are also preferred.

Your First Move: Initial contact is preferred through email.

For More Information:
Peter Grubb, Owner
River Odysseys West
P.O. Box 579
Coeur d'Alene, ID 83816-0579
(800) 451-6034 • (208) 765-0841 • (208) 667-6506 (fax)
info@rowinc.com

> Any guide who has little or no white-water experience and is seeking employment for our two-month Clark Fork season is required to attend our guide school in late June. In this five-day clinic, experienced guides will demonstrate the camping, food preparation, and organizational and rafting techniques that we use on our trips. By the end of the clinic, our goal is to have you ready to guide. We do not necessarily seek people who have previous experience; rather we seek those with strong people skills, intelligence, humor, organizational aptitude, attention to detail, and a strong work ethic. Cost for this five-day clinic, including instruction and meals, is $350.

A man without a goal is like a ship without a rudder. —THOMAS CARLYLE

RIVER OUTFITTERS

RIVER OUTFITTERS

USA RAFT

River Outfitter • West Virginia • Seasonal
www.usaraft.com

WITH OPTIONS RANGING from a world-class raft trip (the ultimate white-water thrill) to a family introductory trip, USA Raft offers adventures on eight rivers in North Carolina, Tennessee, and West Virginia from March through November. Seasonal job openings at various outposts include river guides, store personnel, bus drivers, and other support staff. On-the-job training is provided for all positions with the exception of river guides, who must participate in specialized training for a fee (which doesn't guarantee employment). Beginning in March, experienced trainers will teach basic river-guiding skills, hydrology, rescue techniques, and the dynamics of a raft trip, including people skills. The minimum age for all positions is eighteen, except for bus drivers, who must be at least twenty-five. Current job openings can be found online using their searchable job bank database.

For More Information:
Staffing Director
USA Raft
P.O. Box 277
Rowlesburg, WV 26425
(800) 872-7238 • (304) 454-2475 • (304) 454-2472 (fax)
raft@usaraft.com

WILDWATER LTD.

River Outfitter • Carolinas/Tennessee • Seasonal
www.wildwaterrafting.com

BEGINNING AT THE base of Whitesides Mountain in North Carolina and flowing along the Sumter and Chattahoochee National Forests to the border of South Carolina and Georgia, the Chattooga River is definitely one of the wildest and most beautiful white-water rivers in the country. The Chattooga is also home to Wildwater Ltd., the oldest outfitter on the river. In addition to white-water rafting on three other rivers in the Carolinas and Tennessee, Wildwater offers canoe and kayak clinics, raft and rail excursions, team-building retreats, and a variety of lodging facilities.

What You'll Be Doing: With two offices and four rafting centers, Wildwater has plenty of seasonal work opportunities to explore. Guide and trip leader positions are the most numerous and the most sought after; however, if you love people (and don't have the desire to play in water all day), you might consider a land-based position. Reservations personnel take that first phone call from guests (and also provide that first impression of Wildwater); front desk/retail management staff are the first smiling faces guests see while assisting in the retail shop; marketing staff are responsible for the entire marketing effort in the local area; transportation drivers keep guests coming and going; and food service team members prepare and serve meals to guests and employees.

Commitment: The white-water season runs from March through October; and consequently, preference is given to those who can work the entire season (however, opportunities do exist for the summer months, their busiest time).

Perks and Rewards: In addition to competitive wages, free staff housing (bunkhouse and dorm-style), and meal options (for a small fee) at some locations, you can also expect a lot of benefits: unlimited river trips, complimentary tickets and lodging discounts for family/friends, pro deals with various equipment vendors—and working with like-minded and adventurous people.

The Essentials: Since guests and seasonal staff are Wildwater's lifeblood, applicants who are willing to go out of their way to meet or exceed expectations (and have a positive attitude, good work ethic, and friendly personality) are always at the top of the hiring list. Previous experience is not necessary, but can be helpful in obtaining the position you want. Guides must be eighteen years of age, certified in first aid and CPR, and be able to participate in the guide school during the spring. Guide training is unpaid, but is also provided at no cost (except for food and supplies).

For More Information:
Staffing Director
Wildwater Ltd.
P.O. Box 309
Long Creek, SC 29658
(800) 451-9972 • (864) 451-9972 • (864) 647-5361 (fax)
wwltd@carol.net

ADVENTURE PURSUITS

Adventure Education • USA/Canada • Summer
www.apadventures.com

ADVENTURE PURSUITS OFFERS wilderness adventure programs throughout the U.S. and Canada for young adults who desire an active and challenging outdoor experience. Personal achievement, teamwork, challenge, and fun are the underlying goals for each adventure. Groups work together to surpass individual expectations, whether it be climbing a 14,000-foot peak, negotiating a challenging section of white-water rapids, or sharing a great day's experiences with new friends around an evening campfire.

What You'll Be Doing: Trip leaders, sharing responsibility with a coleader of the opposite sex, are responsible for up to thirteen teenage students. Leaders must be willing and prepared to sacrifice personal goals, if necessary, in response to the students' needs, and similarly, must be willing and able to adapt previous experiences to the goals of Adventure Pursuits. Unpaid internships are also available year-round in administrative support, marketing, and promotion (a great way to get your foot in the door).

Commitment: Trip leaders are typically hired for the entire duration of the season, which runs mid-June through late August. The position requires continuous duties for as long as twenty-eight days without time off. Time off varies from two to four days between trips.

Perks and Rewards: Pay begins at a daily wage of $36 for first-year leaders, along with in-depth training, room and board, and pro deals for outdoor gear.

The Essentials: Applicants must be at least twenty-one, certified in wilderness first aid, be physically and mentally able to lead extended trips in wilderness environments, and be able to hike, climb, bike, raft, kayak, and participate in and/or lead all activities on assigned trips. The average age of staff members and trip leaders is twenty-six.

For More Information:
Farley Kautz, Program Director
Adventure Pursuits
31160 Broken Talon Trail
Oak Creek, CO 80467
(970) 736-0043 • (970) 736-0043 (fax)
humanresources@apadventures.com

We are looking for mature young adults with a proven ability to combine backcountry and teaching skills with solid experience working with teenagers.

ADVENTURES CROSS-COUNTRY

Adventure Education • Worldwide • Summer
www.adventurescrosscountry.com

IMAGINE BACKPACKING THROUGH Yosemite, sea kayaking in the San Juan Islands, sailing the Kona Coast of Hawaii, rafting jungle rivers in Costa Rica, or scuba diving the Great Barrier Reef in Australia. With Adventures Cross-Country, teenagers have the opportunity to participate in mentally and physically challenging wilderness adventure travel programs in unique places in the western United States, New England, and abroad in Australia, British Columbia, Costa Rica, France, Italy, Spain, and Switzerland.

What You'll Be Doing: Guides lead a group of up to thirteen teenagers, with a coleader of the opposite sex, through a rigorous wilderness trip, with activities that may include backpacking, rock climbing, mountain biking, rafting, kayaking, mountaineering, and scuba diving. The trips are both mentally and physically challenging for guides and participants, with adventures ranging from fifteen to forty days (twenty-four hours a day).

Commitment: Guides must be available starting in mid-June, and typically finish their assignments sometime between mid-July and late August.

Perks and Rewards: Wages for first year staff members range from $920 to $1,550 depending on the number and length of trips led. In addition, leaders enjoy the added benefits of available pro deals from well-known companies and a discounted Wilderness First Responder (WFR) course, as well as a weeklong staff training at the beginning of the summer season. All leader living and travel expenses are provided while working.

The Essentials: Applicants must be at least twenty-one years of age, possess strong wilderness/backpacking skills, and have experience working with teenagers, along with current certification in WFR. (For those who are not WFR certified, a WFR course is offered in early June.)

THE BACK DOOR GUIDE TO SHORT-TERM JOB ADVENTURES

A safari guide with Alaska Wildland Adventures spots an eagle (or could it be a moose, bear, or caribou?) with participants on a mountain adventure.

Those who are charismatic, fun, flexible, and easygoing will thrive in this environment.

Your First Move: Leader details and applications can be obtained online. If Web access is not available, an application may be requested via phone or email.

For More Information:
Jason Metzler, Staffing Coordinator
Adventures Cross-Country
242 Redwood Hwy.
Mill Valley, CA 94941
(800) 767-2722 • (415) 332-5075, ext. 230
(415) 332-2130 (fax)
employment@adventurescrosscountry.com

ALASKA HERITAGE TOURS

Adventure Travel • Alaska • Seasonal
www.ahtours.com

PROVIDING A SPECIAL niche in Alaska tourism, Alaska Heritage Tours (AHT)—under the umbrella of CIRI Alaska Tourism—is one of twelve Alaska-based regional corporations established by Congress and solely owned and operated by Alaskan natives. Specializing in "soft" adventure tours that focus on the native heritage of south-central Alaska, AHT hires over five hundred seasonal employees from May through September. Positions

are available in food and beverage, guest services, retail, housekeeping, landscaping, train and driver guides, tour boat deckhands, and business operations. Lodge- and land-based positions are paid hourly, with the average workweek ranging between forty to sixty hours; while marine positions aboard the tour boats are based on a daily wage, with schedules that range from eight to ten hours a day. In addition to shared housing (at $3 to $5 per day), staff members receive complimentary passes on all tour boats and discounted rates at the lodges. Applications are available online.

For More Information:
Recruitment
Alaska Heritage Tours
2525 C St., Suite 405
Anchorage, AK 99503
(877) 258-6877 • (907) 265-4500 • (907) 263-5559 (fax)
info@ahtours.com

ALASKA WILDLAND ADVENTURES

Ecotourism • Alaska • Seasonal
www.awasummerjobs.com

ALASKA. FROM EAGLES and caribou to the midnight sun and northern lights. Yes, now is the time to share your spirit of adventure and the outdoors this summer with

Photo Credit: Alaska Wildland Adventures

Alaska Wildland Adventures. Whether you'll lead a small group of adults on natural history safaris or on a rafting or fishing adventure, this is ecotourism-based travel at its best—and a summer you will never forget! In addition to the more adventurous seasonal employment opportunities available, don't overlook all their other unique positions, which range from safari drivers to cooks. Salaries range from $800 to $1,600 per month (plus gratuities). Tent housing is provided along with a payroll deduction for meals. Most positions run from mid-May through mid-September. Send a resume and cover letter requesting an application. Hiring begins in December.

For More Information:
Catherine McDermott, Program Director
Alaska Wildland Adventures
P.O. Box 389
Girdwood, AK 99587
(800) 334-8730 • (907) 783-2928 • (907) 783-2130 (fax)
summerjobs@alaska-wildland.com

AMERICAN TRAILS WEST

Adventure Travel • USA/Canada/Europe • Summer
www.americantrailswest.com

FROM THE NATURAL beauty of national parks to the energy of major cities, teens can take to the road with American Trails West (ATW) during the summer months (with three-, four-, five-, and six-week itineraries). With destinations across the U.S., Canada, and western Europe, it's not all sight-seeing—every trip provides ample time for recreation, nightlife, sports, and outdoor adventuring. These fun-filled adventures are orchestrated by ATW directors and a team of counselors, who are responsible for supervising the group (from seven to ten campers) and assisting with all the logistics of travel and activities. In addition to an exciting summer, counselors receive an all-expense paid trip along with a stipend for each week spent working with the campers. Applicants must be at least twenty-one years of age, have a valid driver's license, and be able to participate in a five-day orientation in the Pocono Mountains. An application can be filled out online or call for further information.

For More Information:
Staffing Director
American Trails West
92 Middle Neck Rd.
Great Neck, NY 11021
(800) 645-6260 • (516) 487-2800 • (516) 487-2855 (fax)
info@americantrailswest.com

THE APPALACHIAN MOUNTAIN TEEN PROJECT

Youth Development • New Hampshire •
5–10 Months

THE PURPOSE OF the Appalachian Mountain Teen Project is to offer support to rural teens and their families as they face critical life transitions, along with building strong and resilient communities, families, and individuals. Activities include a wide range of outdoor adventure programs (from canoeing to ropes-course activities), vocational trips, education and community mentoring, community service, and cross-cultural experiences. Interns assist with program planning, community organizing, trip leadership, and fund-raising, and plan and execute projects of their own. Counseling opportunities and classroom experiences are also possible. Most of the experience involves working directly with youth ages twelve to eighteen. A small stipend is generally offered. The Teen Project will also assist in locating housing, and all outdoor clothing and equipment may be borrowed from the program. Most interns have been graduate-level students in related fields.

For More Information:
Donna San Antonio, Ed.D., Program Director
The Appalachian Mountain Teen Project
P.O. Box 1597
Wolfeboro, NH 03894
(603) 569-5510 • (603) 569-5510 (fax)
sanantdo@gse.harvard.edu

> *In our program, you won't hang off the highest cliffs, speed down the fastest zip line, or paddle the biggest waves . . . but you might develop the deepest relationships and see the widest connections in appreciative, small-town communities.*

Avoiding danger is no safer in the long run than outright exposure.
Life is either a daring adventure or nothing. —HELEN KELLER

BOMBARD BALLOON ADVENTURES

Ballooning • Europe • Seasonal
www.bombardsociety.com/jobs

BOMBARD BALLOON ADVENTURES engages guests in hot-air ballooning adventures throughout Europe each May through October. Along with balloon pilots, chefs, and guides, the ground crew facilitates all the details of each ballooning adventure—from preparing each trip to mapping out and retrieving the balloon once it has landed (and it's noted that there is a lot of driving over the course of a workday). Applicants must have a clean driving record and, for those who reside outside of Europe, must have a valid work permit prior to application. (See InterExchange on page 372 or the Council Exchanges on page 360 for more information on obtaining a work permit.) While fluency is not required, working knowledge of spoken French, Italian, and/or German is definitely helpful. Benefits include a small wage along with lodging and meals. Send a resume, a copy of your driver's license, dates of availability, and your height and weight.

For More Information:
Mike Lincicome, Staffing Director
Bombard Balloon Adventures
Château de Laborde
21200 Beaune, France
(011) 33 380 26 63 30
mike@bombardsociety.com

BOOJUM INSTITUTE FOR EXPERIENTIAL EDUCATION

Experiential Education • California • 4 Months
www.boojum.org

BOOJUM INSTITUTE is a nonprofit educational organization whose mission is to promote self-discovery, constructive interaction with others, and a deeper understanding of nature through experiential, adventure, and environmental education. The institute primarily serves students from sixth grade through college, but also provides programs for youth-at-risk. A full challenge-course program is offered, along with backpacking, ropes courses, rock climbing, canoeing, hiking, and sea kayaking.

Your Surroundings: You'll have the opportunity to travel to some of the most remote and beautiful areas of the southwestern United States, including Joshua Tree National Park, the Sierra Nevada Mountains, Lake Mead National Recreational Area, Yosemite National Park, and Point Reyes National Seashore.

What You'll Be Doing: Boojum instructors provide facilitation and instruction in outdoor skills, natural history, environmental awareness, challenge-course activities, and life skills in order to "unlock potential, promote self-discovery, and inspire growth" in their students. The internship program is designed to expose participants to program operations behind the scenes, including logistics, training and support, the development of learning and teaching curricula, as well as the delivery and evaluation of field programs. All staff kick off the season with intensive training that includes familiarization with team challenge courses, experiential education techniques, natural history overviews, and group process and facilitation skills.

Commitment: Positions are available from March through June and August through November. Instructors can expect to work weekends and some holidays depending on course load.

Perks and Rewards: Instructors start at $65 per day, with paid prep days before every course (along with housing between courses); interns receive a stipend of $150 per month, comfortable housing, and expenses paid while in the field. There are preseason training opportunities for WFR or AMGA Top Rope certification for a fee.

The Essentials: All applicants must be at least twenty-one years old, hold current WFR (Wilderness First Responder) and CPR certification, and have an excellent driving record. At least one year of leadership experience in the outdoor education field is required, and a college degree/experience is preferred. Instructors should have balanced proficiency in communication and technical skills (including minimum impact techniques, rock climbing, canoeing, kayaking, backpacking, and backcountry travel and navigation).

Your First Move: The first step is to email or telephone the program director to discuss your goals and time line. An application, cover letter, resume, and references are required.

For More Information:
Jeff Skinner, Program Director
Boojum Institute for Experiential Education
P.O. Box 687
Idyllwild, CA 92549
(877) 659-6250 • (909) 659-6250, ext. 19
(909) 659-6251 (fax)
employment@boojum.org

These are base-level positions with room for advancement. We are looking for folks who are open, honest, have a sense of humor, and good self-assessment skills. Please contact us well in advance as we hire early for upcoming seasons.

BOSTON UNIVERSITY SARGENT CENTER FOR OUTDOOR EDUCATION

Outdoor Education • New Hampshire • 3–9 Months
www.bu.edu/outdoor

INTENSIVE STAFF TRAINING. Extensive work experience. Community living. Recreation wonderland. Professional contacts in the field. Future long-term employment opportunities. These benefits form the foundation for seasonal teaching internship opportunities at Boston University Sargent Center and their residential outdoor education program. Interns will learn how to create compelling lesson plans, then instruct groups of ten to twelve students (primarily grades five through eight) in all aspects of environmental education, outdoor skills, and adventure challenge. Benefits include a weekly stipend of $150 to $190, room in two spacious housing facilities, meals, Internet and outdoor equipment access, and temporary health and accident insurance. Applicants must be at least eighteen years of age and comfortable working long hours outdoors. A college degree in a related field is preferred, as is experience working with children. Three-, six-, and nine-month positions are available (however, nine-month applicants are preferred). Check out their website for other short-term opportunities, including summer positions at their adventure camp.

For More Information:
Diane Silver, School Program Coordinator
Boston University Sargent Center for
Outdoor Education
36 Sargent Camp Rd.
Hancock, NH 03449
(603) 525-3311, ext. 18 • (603) 525-4151 (fax)
school_program@busc.mv.com

BRADFORD WOODS OUTDOOR CENTER

Adventure Education/Therapeutic Recreation • Indiana • Seasonal
www.bradwoods.org

BRADFORD WOODS, INDIANA UNIVERSITY's premier outdoor center, provides residential environmental education for school-age children as well as challenge education and adventure experiences that focus on personal growth and leadership development. The campus is also home to a variety of summer residential camping programs that serve children and adults with disabilities. Each year, Bradford Woods hires over one hundred seasonal staff members from all over the world. During the fall and spring, staff members are cross-trained in environmental education, therapeutic programs, and adventure recreation. They then facilitate day, residential, and wilderness adventure recreation and leadership programs that include lake activities, team and high ropes courses, caving, canoeing, backpacking, and wilderness trips. Summer camp opportunities include activities coordinator, counselors, instructors/assistants, and interns, with activities including adventure challenge, creative arts, nature, outdoor living skills, recreation, and waterfront programming. Stipends range from $50 to $220 per week, along with room and board, wilderness first-aid course and certification, and use of facilities and equipment. All candidates must be at least eighteen years old with a background in the outdoor education/adventure field and CPR and first-aid certified. Applications are available online as are email addresses of staff directors for each job position.

For More Information:
Staffing Coordinator
Bradford Woods Outdoor Center
5040 State Road 67 North
Martinsville, IN 46151
(765) 342-2915 • (765) 349-1086 (fax)

BRECKENRIDGE OUTDOOR EDUCATION CENTER

Outdoor Education/Therapeutic Recreation • Colorado • 4–6 Months
www.boec.org

SINCE 1976, BRECKENRIDGE Outdoor Education Center (BOEC) has offered quality outdoor adventure expeditions and trips, therapeutic adventure programs, team building and leadership development, and adaptive-skiing experiences to people of all abilities, including those with disabilities and special needs. The center's goal is to provide students and guests with the opportunity to learn new skills, experience natural areas, challenge themselves, and work together to enhance the health and self-confidence necessary to expand their full potential.

What You'll Be Doing: Because BOEC courses rely primarily on interns, the internship program offers its participants the chance to play an integral role in empowering people of all abilities through outdoor experiences. A unique aspect of the BOEC internship is that it gives the interns an unlimited amount of responsibility. After an intense monthlong training, winter interns become an integral part of the Adaptive Ski Program, with duties first as assistant instructors, and quickly advancing to primary instructors for people with various disabilities and special needs, along with facilitating wilderness courses. The life of a winter intern is not all skiing, as many days are also spent doing administrative duties at the ski office. Summer interns participate in a three-week intensive training, then become staff members of the Wilderness Program. Responsibilities include planning, implementing, facilitating, and evaluating one- to ten-day courses that are held at the BOEC wilderness site or in a mobile format (camping, canoeing, or rafting trips away from BOEC). Participants on these programs range from children with traumatic brain injuries, epilepsy, or cancer, to adjudicated or "high-risk" youth.

Commitment: Applicants must commit to working full-time for an entire season. The winter season runs from early November to May 1, and the summer season from mid-May to mid-September. Expect few days off and long workdays.

Perks and Rewards: A monthly stipend of $50 is provided, along with meals and housing in rustic and peaceful cabins. Perks include a ski pass during the winter, and of course, the invaluable training and great experience that come from participation in the internship. Interns are able to trade some of their time and wilderness expertise for membership at the Breckenridge Recreation Center, which has an indoor climbing wall and track, hot tubs, swimming pools, and workout equipment.

The Essentials: Group facilitation and strong supervisory skills are important. Other qualities, such as flexibility, willingness to work long hours, and the ability to live harmoniously with others in a community setting are just as important. However, they have hired interns with a limited experiential education background, basing their decisions largely on the applicant's commitment, good attitude, and enthusiasm for the BOEC and its mission. Applicants must be over twenty-one years of age and have advanced first-aid and CPR certification.

Your First Move: Applications can be found on BOEC's website. Along with a completed application, a cover letter, resume, and one letter of reference are needed. Application deadlines: summer—March 1; winter—September 1.

For More Information:
Robyn Graber, Internship Coordinator
Breckenridge Outdoor Education Center
P.O. Box 697
Breckenridge, CO 80424
(800) 383-2632 • (970) 453-0146 • (970) 453-4676 (fax)
internship@boec.org

BROADREACH

Adventure Education • Worldwide • Summer
www.gobroadreach.com

TREK SNOW-CAPPED Andes Mountains. Become an accomplished sailor in Tobago. Scuba-explore the exotic French island of St. Barts. Unlock the secrets of the marine world with a professional marine biologist. These are just some of the summer "learn by doing" programs that Broadreach provides for teenagers between the ages of thirteen and eighteen. Each program has its own blend of discoveries and challenges, designed to take advantage of the unique character and opportunities of the region, while focusing on individual success and group dynamics.

What You'll Be Doing: Each summer a unique team of highly qualified leaders is formed who lead, teach, role model, care for, inspire, and educate small groups in places all over the world. Whether working as an open water scuba instructor, sailing master, wilderness leader (hiking, climbing, rappelling, rafting, and sea kayaking), or marine biologist, Broadreach leaders must have a special understanding of group dynamics, leadership, and teamwork. Because of the nature of Broadreach programs, instructors are often expected to handle course leadership, instruction, logistics, course paperwork, and bookkeeping as well as the mundane details. In addition to leader positions, a variety of program support staff positions and internships are available.

Commitment: The summer kicks off with an intensive one-week training in early June (although many leaders come the week before for a required Wilderness First Responder certification course). There is limited time off between programs; the workload is demanding and the days are long.

Perks and Rewards: Along with a salary based on experience, program length, and responsibilities, benefits include round-trip air travel (for staff training and program location), meals, and accommodations.

The Essentials: Along with the necessary hard skills (i.e., sailing, sea kayaking, and so on) required for each trip, staff members must be at least twenty-one years of age, college graduates, certified Wilderness First Responders, experienced working with teens and leading groups, and possess flexibility, solid communication skills, and a healthy respect for the views and opinions of others.

Your First Move: It's best to explore job descriptions and qualifications online, then call for further information and an application.

For More Information:
Staffing Director
Broadreach
P.O. Box 27076
Raleigh, NC 27611
(888) 833-1907 • (919) 833-1907 • (919) 833-2129 (fax)
staffinquiry@gobroadreach.com

CANADIAN BORDER OUTFITTERS

Canoe Outfitter • Minnesota • Summer
www.canoetrip.com

CANADIAN BORDER OUTFITTERS—located where the air is clear, lakes are deep, fishing is excellent, hiking trails are well marked, and wildlife is abundant—is a full-service wilderness canoe trip outfitter located in the northeast corner of Minnesota, just a few miles from the Ontario border. Most staff are hired not to work in one specific

job but rather in an area of the business. Assignments may include work in the pack house, restaurant, or store, or in cleaning/maintenance, dock/canoe handling, or wilderness instruction. While the canoe outfitting season is short (May through September), there is a great deal of site maintenance, ordering, customer service, and marketing that goes on during the whole year. Six permanent staff work year-round, while fifteen to twenty staff members work seasonally during the summer months. Hourly wages range from $5.75 to $6.50. Limited lodging is available for staff at the base on Moose Lake, and some choose to rent apartments in the Ely area, share expenses, and commute to Moose Lake. Meals can be purchased at the base camp at a discount. Applications are available online; the hiring process involves two job interviews in person or over the phone, along with reference checks.

For More Information:
Deb Florer, Owner
Canadian Border Outfitters
14635 Canadian Border Rd.
Ely, MN 55731
(800) 247-7530 • (218) 365-5847 • (218) 365-5847 (fax)
cbo@cbo-ely.com

CHALLENGE ALASKA

Therapeutic Recreation • Alaska • 10–12 Weeks
www.challenge.ak.org

PROVIDING SPORTS AND recreational therapy opportunities to Alaskans with disabilities, Challenge Alaska believes that everyone, regardless of ability, should have an equal opportunity to engage in diverse recreational activities. Exhilarating physical recreation is a crucial aspect of early rehabilitation and lifelong well-being, an important track to improved mobility, increased self-confidence, and development of specific skills. These benefits, in turn, promote employment opportunities, social integration, spiritual peace, and physical independence. Activities include sea kayaking, fishing, camping, rafting, skiing, waterskiing, wheelchair racing, and a variety of other events. Interns assist in recreation, special events, volunteer coordination, administration, resource development, newsletter production, and database operations. A ten- to twelve-week commitment from June through October is needed. Experience and/or a desire to work with special populations is a must! Benefits include a $50 per week stipend and some assistance with food.

For More Information:
Heather Plucinski, Internship/Volunteer Director
Challenge Alaska
3350 Commercial Dr., Suite 208
Anchorage, AK 99501
(888) 430-2738 • (907) 344-7399 • (907) 344-7349 (fax)
challenge.alaska@acsalaska.net

CLEARWATER

Sailing • New York • 1 Week–4 Months
www.clearwater.org

Photo Credit: Chris Bowser

Sailing apprentices and their classroom of waves aboard Clearwater's flagship sloop.

WITH THE MISSION to protect and restore the Hudson River (and its tributaries and related waterways), Clearwater conducts environmental education, advocacy programs, and celebrations—simple reminders that the vitality of the region is tied to the health of the environment. The sloop *Clearwater* (a magnificent 106-foot replica of boats that sailed the Hudson over one hundred years ago), serves as its classroom of waves, providing unique programs on ecology, history, awareness, and teamwork to nearly twenty thousand adults and children every year.

What You'll Be Doing: Crew for the sloop is made up of six paid professionals, including first and second mates, a third mate (deckhand), a bosun (who does odd jobs), an engineer, and a cook. Two sailing apprentices, one education intern, and six volunteers also join the crew each week. After intensive training by professional educators, everyone will participate in all aspects of the sloop, including sailing, educational activities, and maintenance (woodworking, engineering, and finish work), with the opportunity to contribute your own special talents to the overall effort.

Commitment: The sailing season begins in early April and ends in early November, although positions are available year-round. Crew positions run four months; education assistants—one to two months; sailing apprentices— one month; and interns/volunteers—at least one week. Between the months of November and March, there are also opportunities for winter crew who are interested in maintenance (woodworking, engineering, and finish work).

Perks and Rewards: All crew, apprentices, and interns receive room and board. Crew salaries range from $180 to $360 per week, while apprentices and interns receive a stipend of $50 per week ($75 per week during the winter). Weekly volunteers first must become Clearwater members ($35 per year) and also contribute a small fee for food. The living quarters are rustic, featuring open bunks, no showers (although some docks have facilities), composting, and unique toilets.

The Essentials: Candidates must be sixteen years or older, and willing and able to work outdoors eight to ten hours per day. Strength and sailing skill are not as important as coordination, common sense, and an enthusiasm for learning. The ability to deal intelligently with the sloop's hundreds of passengers and casual visitors, and to live and work cooperatively in a close and sometimes stressful environment, is critical.

Your First Move: Call for application materials and current deadlines. It's recommended you volunteer for one week to see what it's like before you commit to other positions.

For More Information:
Samantha Heyman, Captain
Clearwater
Hudson River Sloop
112 Market St.
Poughkeepsie, NY 12601-4095
(845) 454-7673, ext. 114 • (845) 454-7953 (fax)
office@clearwater.org

Photo Credit: Clipper Cruise Line

The yacht-like Clipper Odyssey travels to the remote corners of the Pacific.

CLIPPER CRUISE LINE

Sailing • Worldwide • 1 Year
www.clippercruise.com

CLIPPER CRUISE LINE's fleet of small ships leads passengers and crew on several itineraries throughout the world. Like many birds, their ships are migratory and follow the sun—northbound in the summer and southbound in the winter. Each ship is equipped with a motorized inflatable landing craft that can be launched in minutes for spontaneous landings on small islands and deserted beaches. Onboard crew members begin their assignments in entry-level positions, which include housekeepers/servers, galley assistants, or deckhands. Applicants must commit for one year, be at least twenty-one years of age, pass a pre-employment drug screen and merchant marine physical, have U.S. citizenship, be friendly and outgoing, and have the stamina to work long hours—seventy-two to seventy-five hours per week! In addition to a salary and tips, crew members receive room (in shared crew cabins with private bath), meals, transportation to and from the ship, and a full-benefit medical package. This is a unique opportunity to travel to places around the world while saving money. A generous bonus is also awarded at the completion of twelve months of service. Applications are available online or call for more information.

For More Information:
Captain Scott Will, Global HR Services
Clipper Cruise Line
7711 Bonhomme Ave.

St. Louis, MO 63105
(800) 325-1933 • (314) 727-2929 • (314) 721-1412 (fax)
employment.global@nwship.com

CONTIKI HOLIDAYS

Tour Guide • USA • Summer
www.contiki.com

IN 1961, A YOUNG New Zealander named John Anderson arrived in London to tour Europe. He didn't want to go alone and didn't have much money, so he put a deposit on a minibus and gathered a group of travelers who spent twelve weeks exploring Europe. At the end of the trip, John tried to sell the minibus but no one wanted it. So in spring of 1962, he advertised his Europe tour again. This time, he was able to fit two trips into the summer season and doubled his business. Over thirty years later, Contiki has become the world's largest travel company for eighteen to thirty-five year olds, taking participants on adventurous trips to all corners of the world. Note that Contiki in the U.S. only runs tours in North America.

What You'll Be Doing: Tour managers with Contiki conduct city tours, give historical and practical information talks, and organize each day of a tour, including stops en route, meals, and excursions. Coach drivers work with a tour manager on most tours and are responsible for driving motor coaches seating up to fifty-three passengers.

Commitment: Tours, which all depart from Anaheim, range in duration from three to twenty-three days and

You can be anything you want to be, do anything you set out to accomplish if you hold to that desire with singleness of purpose. —ABE LINCOLN

generally are conducted May through October. Tour managers are responsible for their clients twenty-four hours per day.

Perks and Rewards: Tour managers receive $355 per week, while drivers receive $66 to $73 per day depending on the duration of the tour. Accommodations, food, and some expenses are covered while on tour; however, the biggest perk is the places you'll go!

The Essentials: It's preferred that tour manager applicants have a college degree, a couple years of work experience, knowledge of U.S. history and geography, and a great personality. Mandatory training for tour managers begins mid-March with a tour manager training school. (A fee is charged, although it is reimbursed after four successful tours.) Drivers can be trained at any time to receive their Class B Commercial driver's license, free of charge. This particular office runs North American tours only and legal U.S. working status is required.

Your First Move: Applications are accepted beginning in November. Interviews are generally conducted mid-January through March.

For More Information:
Kelly Camps, Operations Manager
Contiki Holidays
801 E. Katella Ave., 3rd Floor
Anaheim, CA 92805
(800) 266-8454 • (714) 740-0808 • (714) 740-1715 (fax)
kcamps@contiki.com

CRUISE WEST AND ALASKA SIGHTSEEING

Sailing • Alaska • 3–7 Months
www.cruisewest.com

....

UP-CLOSE, CASUAL, and personal. That's what Cruise West delivers for guests onboard their fleet of small ships—the largest holding just 114 guests—and that's where the work of their sea crew truly shines. Whether you'll be leading nature walks in the wilds of Alaska, bringing iced tea to a guest on the shores of Mexico, or performing in the "No-Talent" night onboard a British Columbia bound ship, your job is to ensure a perfect vacation for each guest. Having fun may be at the cornerstone of your job, but there's also a lot of hard work. The pace is quick, the hours are long, and you can't go home at the end of the day. All vessel positions (from galley assistants to deck-

hands) work on a "rotation schedule." This means you'll be scheduled to work on board from four to six weeks at a time, with a daily shift of ten to fourteen hours. During this period, you'll receive meals, shared crew quarters (with up to four other crew members), and competitive pay and gratuities. After each rotation, a time-off period of two weeks is provided (although you'll be responsible for your own room and board). Applicants must be at least eighteen years of age and most positions require a commitment from March through September. Mid-season openings in May, June, and July are possible, as are a limited number of year-round positions. Applications are available online.

For More Information:
Gabriella Vetsch, Employment Specialist
Cruise West and Alaska Sightseeing
People Care and Development
2401 Fourth Ave., Suite 700
Seattle, WA 98121-1438
(888) 842-8029 • (206) 733-5676 • (206) 733-5654 (fax)
resume@cruisewest.com

If working onboard one of Cruise West's small ships is not for you, you might consider seasonal opportunities with their land-tour division. Tour guides/drivers will greet guests, handle luggage, and conduct sightseeing/narrative tours that explore the gold country of Fairbanks, the Mendenhall Glacier in Juneau, wildlife and wilderness experiences in Denali National Park, the mountain town of Ketchikan (a place only accessible by ship or plane), or the fishing village of Petersburg. In addition, guest service representatives provide guests with general information and orientation to the local area. The majority of positions typically begin in May and end in early September. (Plan on working in excess of fourteen hours per day.) All guides go through a comprehensive paid training program in early April. For more information on these positions, email akjobs@cruisewest.com.

CYCLING ADVENTURES
Open Yourself Up to the Possibilities

It's those who take the risk and make that "left-hand turn in the road" who get the most from life.

—MICHAEL WILLIAMS

Michael and Dorrie Williams were living the American Dream—well-paying corporate jobs, benefits, a beautiful two-story home, security, and all the possessions that a lifestyle like this can bring. Yet there was a downside to the world the Williamses created for themselves. They were married to their jobs, Uncle Sam was taking most of their loot, and another snow-filled winter in Philadelphia wasn't helping their mental state. All they could think of was a week's vacation that would recharge their batteries.

However, their plan for a one-week vacation soon turned into two weeks, and then kept lengthening the more they talked about it. "We got to thinking. Why are we living this sort of lifestyle? What were we really working toward? What would we do if we put all our responsibilities aside?" Finally, it was an overnight decision. An overwhelming realization consumed them. Now was the time for them to walk away from the things that society dictated as being the right things to do. Their decision? To adventure around the U.S. on their bikes for not a week or two—but a whole year.

That night they talked about their trip. The next morning they worked out the details. Just like that. They soon broke the news of the new direction in their life to coworkers, family, and friends. At the same time, they started sifting through the material possessions in their home, soon to be peddled off

Michael and Dorrie Williams conquer the top of their third pass across the perilous Rockies on their bike adventure across America.

Be not the slave of your own past. Plunge into the sublime seas, dive deep, and swim far, so you shall come back with self-respect, with new power, with an advanced experience, that shall explain and overlook the old. —RALPH WALDO EMERSON

and turned into funds for their trip. "It was the biggest garage sale we ever had. We sold everything except for the things that meant the world to us (and a couple bikes)."

What about security? What about money? What about the future? "That's why a lot of people don't want to make a change. They're scared about starting over, that they're not going to find a job again." Quite the contrary for Michael and Dorrie—"There will always be jobs out there. If you want something bad enough, you'll get it eventually."

And the adventure began! They hopped on their bikes and took off across America—from the hills of Kentucky, through the flatlands of the Midwest (milking a few cows along the way), across the perilous Rockies (conquering the tops of three mountain passes), all the way to the Pacific Ocean. To help them on their 3,700-mile journey, they used maps and guides purchased through the Adventure Cycling Association (page 70), which provided information on hostels, campgrounds, bike shops, where to get food, and distances between landmarks on the Trans-America Bike Trail.

The trip wasn't about covering a certain distance each day for the Williamses. Their philosophy: open yourself up to the experience and other people, and let anything happen; then deal with it, learn from it, and experience it as it comes to you. "We knew nothing about what to expect, and that's why we had such a great time. Without setting up a structure or any restrictions, you won't set yourself up for a letdown. Some days we rode just a few miles because we loved where we were or the company we were with." The key—the more risk they took, the more they opened themselves up to new adventures.

What do you do when you finish a cycling adventure like this? Michael and Dorrie found themselves back in the small college town where they first met and created jobs that resonate with the simple things that are most important to them. Their trappings are fewer, and they live on less, but they live more happily and at a better pace. "It's nice to plant some roots, have a circle of friends, and balance adventure with the grounding we've created."

It's amazing how much more mental a long journey on a bicycle is than physical! It can be a group journey, but there is plenty of time on one's own, pedaling away. There's a lot of time to think and grow and look into yourself.

—Sarah Wagoner

re you thinking about creating your own cycling adventure? Not only can you pedal anywhere in the world, you might also consider leading others on a cycling trip by working seasonally for a bike adventure organization. Here's a handful of programs based in the U.S. that offer riding adventures and other work opportunities that will take you to all corners of the earth:

BACKROADS

Active Travel • Worldwide • Seasonal
www.backroads.com

....

BACKROADS OFFERS MORE than 150 different types of active-travel vacations, including bicycling, walking, hiking, and multisport journeys in more than eighty-five destinations around the world. Traveling actively means traveling under your own power and at your own pace—not watching the world go by from behind the window of a car or tour bus. It means getting out there by foot, bicycle, water, or ski—seeing, touching, feeling, and experiencing. It means trying out the native greetings, meeting the locals, making new friends, and having a whole lot of fun.

What You'll Be Doing: As a leader, you're the catalyst for a fun, interesting, safe, and personally rewarding experience for your guests. This means being able to think on your feet and display total confidence when unusual situations arise. It also means displaying infinite compassion and patience at all times, and maintaining a positive attitude and sense of humor. You'll become involved in every aspect of the adventure, ensuring that all equipment is in optimal working condition; buying and preparing food; delivering luggage at each night's accommodations; acting as a representative at hotels, restaurants, campgrounds, and with the general public; and keeping accurate financial records and complete written reports.

Perks and Rewards: First-year leaders receive $55 per day for hotel trips and $73 per day for camping trips, plus gourmet meals, accommodations in some of the best inns or campgrounds the region has to offer, and transportation costs. The pay scale and benefits increase in recognition of each year's experience. Backroads requests that you be at least a temporary resident of the Bay Area during the trip-leading season. All leaders are flown to and from trips out of either San Francisco or Oakland airports. If you are not living in the area, you are responsible for getting yourself to the Bay Area prior to your flight. All leaders are expected to attend events at Backroads' Berkeley headquarters to launch the summer season in April and celebrate its end in October.

The Essentials: The staff is composed of high-energy individuals with varied backgrounds who enjoy people, travel, and the outdoors. To become a leader, candidates must be a minimum of twenty-one years of age, have a valid driver's license, and an excellent driving record. The ideal candidate is a master problem-solver, effective public speaker, chef, area expert, translator (on trips to Europe), skilled driver, meticulous record keeper, a motivating force in group dynamics while being sensitive to individual needs, and in great physical shape. Foreign applicants must be citizens of the European Community.

Your First Move: Write to request a detailed application packet or call the Backroads Job Hotline at (510) 527-1889, extension 560, for voice-recorded information twenty-four hours a day. Leader applications are evaluated starting in January with interviews conducted from February through April. The application deadline is April 1; however, it is to your advantage to submit your application as early as possible.

For More Information:
Leader Applications—BDG
Backroads
801 Cedar St.
Berkeley, CA 94710-1800
(800) 462-2848 • (510) 527-1889, ext. 560
(510) 527-1444 (fax)
humanresources@backroads.com

BIKE-AID

Cycling • USA • 2 Months
www.bikeaid.org

....

A UNIQUE PROGRAM of JustAct (www.justact.org), Bike-Aid is a vibrant, innovative cycling adventure that combines physical challenge, community interaction, education, leadership, fund-raising, and community service in the empowering experience of a lifetime. With departures from San Francisco and Seattle beginning in mid-June, eighty individuals from around the world will cycle to Washington, D.C., over a two-month period. Cyclists will raise $1 for every mile ridden, totaling $3,600 (and Bike-Aid will provide an endless source of creative ideas to help with your efforts). Three scholarships are

CYCLING ADVENTURES

CYCLING ADVENTURES

also offered for those who are able to spend time organizing the ride during the spring prior to participation. Overnight lodging is donated by community organizations, schools, and individuals, and will include some camping. Beginners to prize-winning racers have participated in Bike-Aid, and riders from the ages of sixteen to sixty have met the challenge. It is not a race, and it encourages the participation of people from all backgrounds, ages, and abilities. Cyclists are advised to apply by March 31 to save on registration fees.

For More Information:
Laura McNeill, Program Director
Bike-Aid
JustAct—Youth Action for Global Justice
333 Valencia St., Suite 101
San Francisco, CA 94103-3547
(800) 743-3808 • (415) 431-4204, ext. 203
(415) 431-5953 (fax)
bikeaid@justact.org

> *Bike-Aid satisfied my quest
> for community. My interests lay in the cause—
> promoting environmental solutions—rather than
> in the physical challenge of the ride itself.
> To me, the group dynamics were more of a
> challenge than the actual pedaling.
> Each of us is part of the solution:
> it takes too much wasted energy to
> blame others for things that don't work
> right in our world.*
>
> —ALONA JASIK, participant

BIKES NOT BOMBS

Youth Development • Massachusetts • Seasonal
www.bikesnotbombs.org

BIKES NOT BOMBS is a nonprofit organization working for alternative transportation and community development. The group operates the Bicycle Recycling and Youth Training Center near Boston and promotes environmental education, meaningful employment, and safe sustainable communities in places as far as the Dominican Republic, Haiti, and Nicaragua. Thousands of bicycles and tons (literally!) of bicycle parts and tools have been sent overseas to help groups do everything from start a small cargo bike

manufacturing facility to cooperatively run a bike shop and training center. Volunteers—including experienced, bilingual mechanics, administrative and outreach interns, and fieldwork organizers for international efforts—are needed to fill a variety of roles in Massachusetts. Send a cover letter and resume to begin the application process.

For More Information:
Outreach Coordinator
Bikes Not Bombs
59 Amory St., Suite 103
Roxbury, MA 02119
(617) 442-0004 • (617) 445-2439 (fax)
mail@bikesnotbombs.org

CICLISMO CLASSICO

Cycling • Italy/USA • Seasonal
www.ciclismoclassico.com

EXPERIENCE ITALY'S HIDDEN treasures by pedaling, walking, or skiing with Ciclismo Classico. These cultural adventures offer educational and dreamy itineraries that celebrate the Italian landscape, art, language, music, folklore, and its beloved cuisine. As cultural liaisons, bicycling and walking leaders take small groups on nine- to fifteen-day tours from April through October. Leaders engage participants in musical evenings, Italian lessons, wine tastings, cooking demonstrations, and other authentic

Bicycle leaders with Ciclismo Classico engage participants in Italy's hidden treasures.

Photo Credit: Lauren Hefferon

experiences with their extensive network of Italian friends and families. For those that want to experience the U.S. before heading on over to Italy, Ciclismo now offers adventure trips throughout New England. Applicants must be at least twenty-three years of age, fluent in Italian (for Italy tours), and have travel and group-leader experience, bike-mechanic skills, and boundless energy. Benefits include all trip expenses, along with a $400 (and up) per week salary plus bonuses and tips. Call or email for an application packet.

For More Information:
Lauren Hefferon, Director and Founder
Ciclismo Classico
30 Marathon St.
Arlington, MA 02474
(800) 866-7314 • (781) 646-3377 • (781) 641-1512 (fax)
sim@ciclismoclassico.com

SOCKEYE CYCLE

Cycling • Alaska • Summer
www.cyclealaska.com

LOCATED AT THE upper end of the Tongass National Forest (covering sixteen million acres), Sockeye Cycle offers cycling adventures along local roads and trails that are home to grizzly bears, moose, mountain goats, black-tailed deer, and bald eagles. From May through the end of September, Sockeye hires a variety of seasonal employees, including guides, bicycle mechanics, managers, and photographer/retailers. At minimum, applicants must be twenty-three years old with a clean driving record. Wages run from $9 to $12 per hour, plus tips. Limited employee housing is available and returning staff have first priority. Applications are available online or send off your resume and cover letter. Interviews begin in January with positions filled by April 1.

For More Information:
Thomas Ely, President
Sockeye Cycle
P.O. Box 829
Haines, AK 99827-0829
(907) 766-2869 • (907) 766-2851 (fax)
sockeye@cyclealaska.com

STUDENT HOSTELING PROGRAM

Cycling • USA/Canada/Europe • Summer
www.biketrips.com

SINCE 1969, THE Student Hosteling Program (SHP) has been offering one- to nine-week teenage bicycle touring trips through the countrysides and cultural centers of the U.S., Canada, and Europe. SHP trips provide adventure, fun, outdoor education, and the opportunity for emotional growth, while providing one of the safest and most wholesome youth environments available. Their groups are small, usually eight to twelve participants and two to three leaders, making possible a close and rewarding group experience. SHP groups travel by bicycle, at their own pace and close to the land, using public and private transportation when necessary. Groups live simply, using campsites, hostels, and other modest facilities. In the countryside, groups buy food at local markets and cook their own meals.

What You'll Be Doing: Senior leaders and assistant leaders conduct bicycling tours for students, grades seven through twelve. Prior to becoming a leader, participants will complete a five-day training course to find out which age groups and types of trips are a good fit. From there, leaders receive further training for their particular trip during a four-day preparation and orientation period just before their trip departure date. Leaders are known to be firm in matters of safety, respect for others, and the SHP rule structure, and also have the warmth, the humor, and the enthusiasm to provide a rewarding group experience.

Commitment: The minimum leadership time commitment is four weeks. Employment begins in late June for part or all of the summer.

Perks and Rewards: Senior leaders earn $728 to $1,932 depending upon the length of the work period; assistant leaders earn from $520 to $1,380. In addition, all trip-related expenses are paid.

CYCLING

The Essentials: Senior leaders must be at least twenty-one years of age (the average is about twenty-five) and are typically teachers, graduate students, and college seniors. Assistants must be at least eighteen years old and are usually college sophomores and juniors. Many are former SHP trip participants. All leaders must hold a valid Red Cross first-aid certificate and many have advanced first-aid training as well. Most importantly, the leader's personality is the most critical element in making a trip work.

Your First Move: After a lengthy screening process, leaders are selected to complete one of the five-day training courses in Massachusetts before being assigned a trip.

For More Information:
Ted Lefkowitz, Program Director
Student Hosteling Program
1356 Ashfield Rd.
P.O. Box 419
Conway, MA 01341
(800) 343-6132 • (413) 369-4275 • (413) 369-4257 (fax)
shpbike@aol.com

RECOMMENDED RESOURCES

The Adventure Cycling Association

(www.adventurecycling.org) is America's largest non-profit recreational bicycling organization. Since 1973 they have been helping their members use their bicycles for adventure, exploration, and discovery. They publish detailed bike maps for over twenty-five thousand miles of scenic backroads and mountain trails in North America, which allow you to travel cross-country without ever seeing an interstate highway. The maps include information on bicycling conditions, local history, and services that cyclists need (such as location of bike shops, campgrounds, motels, and grocery stores). Membership ($30 per year; students/seniors—$24) provides discounts on all sorts of resources, and includes *Adventure Cyclist* (their member-only magazine published nine times a year) and *The Cyclist's Yellow Pages,* its annual guide to bicycle maps, books, routes, and organizations (which is also available online).

For those who want to lead tours of their own, you may considering taking part in Adventure Cycling's three-day leadership training course, designed to teach the fundamentals of leading a self-contained bicycle expedition. There's a fee of $400 and training takes place in various spots throughout the U.S. from January through May. For more information contact the Adventure Cycling Association, P.O. Box 8308, Missoula, MT 59807-8308; (800) 755-2453, info@adventurecycling.org.

The International Bicycle Fund

(www.ibike.org) is dedicated to promoting sustainable transport and international understanding, with major areas of activity including nonmotorized urban planning, economic development, bike safety education, and responsible travel and cycle tourism. In addition, they provide cross-cultural, educational bicycle tours that allow Westerners to learn more about Africa, Asia, Cuba, Ecuador, and the U.S. at a person-to-person level not usually available to tourists. Itineraries highlight the cultural, historical, economic, and physical diversity of the area. Tours are generally two and four weeks long with costs ranging from $900 to $1,290, not including airfare. Unpaid internships are also available at their office in Seattle, Washington, with a majority of the work focused on grant writing, fund-raising, administration, and supporting bicycle advocacy organizations around the world. Call for the free newsletter, *IBF News* (or check it out at www.ibike.org/ibfnews.htm), which includes information on grassroots cycling programs all over the world. For more information contact the International Bicycle Fund, 4887 Columbia Dr., South, Seattle, WA 98108-1919; (206) 767-0848, ibike@ibike.org.

DEISHU EXPEDITIONS

Kayak Outfitter • Alaska • Summer
www.seakayaks.com

DEISHU EXPEDITIONS DRAWS its name from the Tlingit Indian word for the cove on which the modern town of Haines sits in Southeast Alaska. To the Tlingits, *Deishu* meant the "end of the Portage Trail," or "place where the boats are put back in the water." Keeping in this same tradition, Deishu Expeditions gets people back on the water through wilderness, educational, and instructional kayak adventures.

What You'll Be Doing: From the last week of April through the end of September, as many as a dozen first-year guides paddle with groups in some of the most beautiful spots in the world. Put simply, the guide position is an extremely challenging one and involves lots of hard, physical labor. With dynamic paddle destinations and groups of up to forty-eight people, guides often end up moving literally tons of kayaks and gear several times in a day. Though the rigging and derigging of gear can be taxing, the skills one can learn and the experiences one can have with people and wildlife while on the water can be life altering. A good guide will use his or her excitement, enthusiasm, and knowledge to bring clients to a level of understanding and appreciation for their surroundings.

Perks and Rewards: First-year guides earn $9 to $10 per hour depending upon experience and whether they have their own kayak and gear. Housing is not included; however, Deishu will help with inexpensive or free living arrangements. Off time can be spent in the friendly and unique town of Haines (population 2,500), climbing nearby peaks, exploring the rich river valleys, mountain biking, fishing for any of the five Pacific salmon species that run up local rivers, and, well, more river kayaking!

The Essentials: Candidates should have advanced paddle skills (including braces and rolls) along with certification in Wilderness First Responder and advanced CPR. Preference is given to paddlers who own their own expedition sea kayaks and gear (including VHF radio), those with extensive paddle and backcountry experiences, and those who have a personal interest in and knowledge of marine wildlife and ecology. Ideally, applicants should be at least twenty-four years of age to qualify for Deishu's automobile insurance.

Your First Move: Send a resume (that includes both work and outdoor experience and skills) as well as reference names and contact numbers from your last four to five employers and a recent photo.

For More Information:
Ned Rozbicki, Owner
Deishu Expeditions
425 Beach Rd., Box 1406
Haines, AK 99827
(800) 552-9257 • (907) 766-2427 • (907) 766-2423 (fax)
paddle@seakayaks.com

ECKERD YOUTH ALTERNATIVES

Therapeutic Camp/Wilderness Adventure • East Coast • 2 Years
www.eckerd.org

FRESH AIR. OPEN SPACES. Miles of blue sky above. You won't find them in a corporate cubicle. But as a youth counselor at an Eckerd Youth Alternatives (EYA) wilderness camp, the whole outdoors is your office. In fact, you'll live year-round in one of the most beautiful natural locations in the eastern U.S. (camps are spread out over eighteen sites in Florida, Georgia, North Carolina, Tennessee, Vermont, Rhode Island, and New Hampshire). Hike the Appalachians. Canoe the Suwannee. Sleep under the stars. Develop personal relationships. And help at-risk kids get back on track. It's an adventure that can change their lives—and yours—forever.

What You'll Be Doing: Over a two-year period, wilderness youth counselors supervise a group of ten to twelve at-risk youth twenty-four hours a day. Daily activities involve the construction and maintenance of the group's common living area. Additional activities vary, but can include leading the children in hiking, backpacking, low and high ropes work, playing outdoor games and planning and preparing events such as cook outs and canoe trips. All activities are frameworks for problem solving and developing basic life skills.

Perks and Rewards: The starting salary is $20,000 per year (with the opportunity to receive up to four pay increases and two promotions over a two-year period). Extensive paid training, along with room, board, relocation assistance, and comprehensive health benefits are provided.

The Essentials: All candidates must be at least twenty-one years of age and some state contracts require a four-year degree. Child-care experience, paid or volunteer, is preferred, as well as diverse outdoor experiences and an interest in athletics and physical game activities. All non–U.S. citizen candidates must be eligible to work in the U.S. without needing sponsorship.

Your First Move: Applications are available online or call for more information.

For More Information:
Career Advisor
Eckerd Youth Alternatives
100 N. Starcrest Dr.
Clearwater, FL 33758
(800) 222-1473 • (727) 461-4387 (fax)
recruiting@eckerd.org

ENVIRONMENTAL TRAVELING COMPANIONS

Therapeutic Recreation • California • Seasonal
www.etctrips.org

FOUNDED IN 1971, Environmental Traveling Companions (ETC) is a nonprofit organization which provides outdoor adventure and environmental education experiences for people with special needs and disadvantaged youth. The populations they serve are diverse—many of their participants have visual and hearing impairments, physical and/or developmental disabilities, and some are disadvantaged, inner-city youths. ETC's primary goal is to provide access to the wilderness to people of all abilities and to promote self-esteem, self-sufficiency, and a greater appreciation for the environment. Annually, they serve over two thousand participants in three outdoor programs, which include white-water rafting, sea kayaking, and nordic skiing, with destinations primarily in Northern California.

What You'll Be Doing: White-water rafting field interns assist and/or guide white-water rafting trips and outdoor activities and games as well as aid in logistical planning, coordination of volunteers, program development, maintenance of the site, and repair of equipment. White-water guide school takes place in early spring and is mandatory for prospective interns without solid class three rafting skills. Nordic ski-guide interns live in the beautiful Sierra Nevada Mountains and lead adaptive ski trips for people with special needs. Interns aid in trip coordination and logistics, maintenance of the site and equipment, and program development. Mandatory intern guide training takes place in mid-January. Sea-kayak office and field interns work in the San Francisco headquarters and guide one- to two-day sea kayak trips on San Francisco Bay.

ETC also has salaried, short-term management and administration positions (call for details on these).

Commitment: Positions are offered seasonally throughout the year (from thirty to forty hours per week), with the exception of sea kayak positions, which are only available from April through October, twenty-forty hours per week.

Perks and Rewards: Interns benefits include a small stipend of $200 per month, room, partial board, and rafting, skiing, and sea-kayaking privileges. One of the biggest perks is the intensive training each intern receives. Training focuses on instruction in their specialty, disability and diversity awareness, working with special populations, and outdoor leadership skills. Management position wages range from $1,000 to $1,700 per month, along with room and partial board.

The Essentials: Applicants must have a desire to develop leadership skills; be enthusiastic about wilderness adventure; be comfortable in the outdoors; be a self-starter and able to work independently; enjoy working with people; and be CPR/first-aid certified. Experience in desired positions and work with special populations is preferred but not necessary. ETC guides represent a diversity of cultures, abilities, and backgrounds—including teachers, engineers, counselors, carpenters, lawyers, and university interns.

Your First Move: Write or call for application details. Deadlines: Nordic Skiing Program—October 15th; Rafting/Sea Kayaking Programs—February 28th.

For More Information:
Sue Judson, Office Manager
Environmental Traveling Companions
Fort Mason Center, Building C
San Francisco, CA 94123
(415) 474-7662, ext. 10 • (415) 474-3919 (fax)
info@etctrips.org

The over four hundred volunteer-guide pool makes up an incredibly enthusiastic, eclectic, and fun community. Once introduced, most folks get sucked into the ETC whirlpool and stay involved for years to come!

FOUR CORNERS SCHOOL OF OUTDOOR EDUCATION

Adventure Travel • Utah • 3–6 Months
www.sw-adventures.org

HERE IN THE rugged terrain of the "four corners" where Arizona, Colorado, New Mexico, and Utah meet, participants join Four Corners School of Outdoor Education on unique educational vacations. Programs are by foot, van, and raft, and explore areas such as wilderness advocacy, archaeology, and research with the Bureau of Land Management, National Park Service, and U.S. Forest Service. The school's goal is low-impact adventures with a very healthy dose of education.

What You'll Be Doing: Internships vary with the season, program content, special projects, and office load. Four Corners School is very conscious about maintaining a balance between office work and fieldwork. Special skills may be put to use, such as public relations, computer programming, painting, and carpentry.

Commitment: Internships generally run in three sessions, with start dates in March, mid-June, and mid-August.

Perks and Rewards: A small stipend is provided. Interns are also in the unique position to go on a number of outdoor field programs, which generally last five days. Their programs are so diverse that one week you may be out backpacking, the next on the San Juan River. You'll also have access to their world-class experts.

The Essentials: Applicants must be at least eighteen years of age. No area of interest supersedes another, but some prior knowledge of the outdoors is very helpful.

Your First Move: Call for application materials (which must be received by January 15.) Phone interviews will be conducted.

For More Information:
Janet Ross, Executive Director
Four Corners School of Outdoor Education
Southwest Ed-Ventures
P.O. Box 1029
Monticello, UT 84535
(800) 525-4456 • (435) 587-2156 • (435) 587-2193 (fax)
fcs@sanjuan.net

> We like applicants who are excited about the outdoors and make good ambassadors for the school. Our participants like friendly, knowledgeable people. We all have to work hard, so it helps to have an intern who doesn't mind the work. It doesn't hurt to know about the office environment, as duties will include some office times.

GRAY LINE OF ALASKA

Tour Guide • Washington/Alaska • Summer
www.graylineofalaska.com

ALASKA IS DEFINITELY the last frontier—an outdoor enthusiast's paradise and playground for Gray Line of Alaska's motor-coach tours. Gray Line is a subsidiary of Holland American Line–Westours, which operates cruise ships, dayboats, Westmark Hotels throughout Alaska and the Yukon, and the McKinley Explorer glass-domed railcars on the Alaska Railroad (running between Anchorage and Fairbanks through Denali National Park).

What You'll Be Doing: Becoming one of their summer guides doesn't mean you'll merely be a chauffeur; rather, you'll learn and develop informative and entertaining tour narratives in order to provide an enjoyable vacation experience for their passengers. Yes, drivers must be willing to go that "extra mile" to meet the needs of their passengers. Note that seasonal opportunities also exist with McKinley Rail and with Holland America on day boats (call for details).

Commitment: Guides must be able to attend a ten-week training program that starts in early February or March at one of the training locations in the lower forty-eight or Alaska. After training is complete, guides must be able to commit to a one-hundred-day contract working in Alaska during the summer. Guides average fifty to fifty-five hours per week, with daily workloads varying between six and thirteen hours, depending on the tour assignment.

Perks and Rewards: During the training period, guides receive minimum wage. First-year drivers generally make $6,000 to $8,000, plus gratuities. Gray Line also has a bonus program in which drivers can earn up to 12 percent of their total wages for the season. Housing varies with each location.

The Essentials: Guides must be self-confident, have the ability to speak well, present a professional image, and maintain a responsible attitude. All applicants must be twenty-one years of age, with no more than one moving violation on driving records in the last three years. Those who love working with and around people, are able to go with the flow, and have a work hard/play hard mentality will thrive in this program.

Your First Move: Submit application materials by the end of January. An audition and interview is required.

For More Information:
Manager of Training
Gray Line of Alaska
300 Elliott Ave., West
Seattle, WA 98119
(800) 976-3840 • (206) 281-0559

GREENBRIER RIVER OUTDOOR ADVENTURES

Adventure Education • West Virginia • 2–12 Weeks
www.groa.com

GREENBRIER RIVER OUTDOOR ADVENTURES offers a wide variety of programs for young people between the ages of ten and seventeen. Programs are based on the development of self-esteem and leadership through adventure, challenge, and small-group experiences, including community service projects. Everything—playing, cooking, eating, and sleeping—is done outdoors. While not a survival program, a large part of the program is learning how to live comfortably outdoors while taking time to enjoy the experience.

Your Surroundings: The base camp is located on a 250-acre site, nestled in the West Virginian mountains of the Monongahela National Forest, home to top-rated rock climbing and mountain biking along with white-water rafting, caving, and backpacking. Their New England programs explore the White Mountain National Forest, Acadia National Park, and other beautiful areas of northern New England.

What You'll Be Doing: Staff members kick off the summer by participating in a weeklong intensive training session in West Virginia. Group leaders and activity instructors along with interns provide supervision (and general safety) of participants, oversee program logistics and itinerary, teach outdoor living skills and adventure activities, and facilitate and develop group dynamics.

Commitment: Since some staff members might be looking for a full summer of employment (June through August) while others are only interested in leading programs for just a few weeks, positions are available from two to twelve weeks (with most positions available from six to twelve weeks).

Perks and Rewards: A competitive salary is provided along with room and board. Pro deals are also available on outdoor clothing and equipment.

The Essentials: Intern applicants must be at least nineteen years old, while seasonal staff must be at least twenty-one. All candidates must have certificates in CPR, first aid, and water safety. A sincere interest in working with youth in the outdoors, experience in the field, and competency in outdoor living are traits found in their staff.

Your First Move: Printable applications can be found online; otherwise, send your resume and a cover letter requesting an application

For More Information:
Matthew Tate, Program Director
Greenbrier River Outdoor Adventures
P.O. Box 160
Bartow, WV 24920-0160
(800) 600-4752 • (304) 456-5191 • (304) 456-3121 (fax)
groa@groa.com

HULBERT OUTDOOR CENTER

Experiential Education • Vermont • 3–11 Months
www.alohafoundation.org/hulbert

ESTABLISHED IN 1978, the Hulbert Outdoor Center is a nonprofit educational institution that serves six thousand participants annually through programs designed to foster personal growth, self-reliance, cooperation, confidence, and a sense of community in people of all ages. Year-round programs range from school programs, wilderness trips, Elderhostel experiences, and a unique leadership training program that includes certifications in everything from Wilderness First Responder and Backcountry Search and Rescue to lifeguard training and the ACA Canoe Instructor's Course (which are available to staff members!).

Your Surroundings: The Center is located in Vermont's Upper Connecticut River Valley on the shores of Lake Morey, surrounded by over five hundred acres of young forests, bluffs, and rolling countryside. Recreation opportunities include miles of mountain biking, hiking, backcountry skiing, and access to developed ski areas and water sports.

What You'll Be Doing: Hulbert provides unique opportunities that combine elements of wilderness travel, outdoor skill development, teamwork, sensitivity to the environment, and personal growth experiences. The prime responsibility of school program staff is to work with middle-school-aged children in programs emphasizing team building, the ropes course, natural history, and other curriculum areas. Trip leaders guide extended wilderness experiences for groups of eight to ten participants.

Commitment: During the summer, a three-month commitment is ideal; trip staff are contracted per course. During the spring and fall a five-month commitment is necessary, and some positions have the option of continuing on for nine or eleven months.

Perks and Rewards: Dependent upon experience, wages begin at $45 to $55 per day, along with room and board included and paid staff training. Trip staff are contracted per trip.

The Essentials: Applicants must be at least twenty-one years of age and have a bachelor's degree, certification in first aid and CPR (WFR or higher preferred), a valid driver's license, the ability to work long hours in the outdoors, and a demonstrated experience teaching (preferably in the experiential education field).

Your First Move: Send a cover letter and resume. An application packet will be mailed upon receipt.

For More Information:
Greg Auch, Wilderness Trips Director
Hulbert Outdoor Center, The Aloha Foundation
2968 Lake Morey Rd.
Fairlee, VT 05045-9400
(802) 333-3405, ext. 121 • (802) 333-3404 (fax)
greg_auch@alohafoundation.org

The staff at Hulbert form a unique community of educators that values dedication, creative problem solving, and hard work. In the course of our work, we put in long hours and fill diverse roles. Throughout, in work and in the residential environment, we strive to create and to maintain a positive sense of community.

HIOBS-SOUTHERN PROGRAMS

Wilderness Education • Florida • 3 Months
www.members.tripod.com/outward.bound

THE HURRICANE ISLAND Outward Bound School's (HIOBS) Southern Programs offers the Outward Bound experience and philosophy to both delinquent and at-risk youth throughout Florida. The U.S. Department of Justice reported HIOBS as one of the five most successful programs in the nation. The program serves over one thousand youths per year and is a leader in community service.

What You'll Be Doing: The Southern Programs have six programs located throughout Florida, with each program teaching the four pillars of Outward Bound (self-reliance, craftsmanship, physical fitness, and compassion) to young adults between the ages of twelve and eighteen. Programs are either exclusively wilderness based or a combination of wilderness and residential programming. Courses range from 20 to 180 days, and all programs work with teams of instructors and teachers. The internship experience includes an eleven-day orientation/expedition along with up to two and a half months of experiential work in two program areas. Interns will undertake lots of draining, exhausting, feel-good work, which will train them to become wilderness instructors.

Commitment: The Adolescent Instructor Practicum ends when participants attain a recommendation as an assistant instructor for HIOBS, which can take one- to two-months. Seasonal and full-time work is available following the program.

Perks and Rewards: There is a cost of $250 per participant for the orientation, which includes all food and lodging for ten days. During the internship, a daily stipend of $15 to $35, food, lodging, and travel between bases is provided. Interns also have access to HIOBS staff trainings and pro-deal purchases.

The Essentials: At the minimum, applicants must be at least twenty-one years of age and have current CPR and first aid certification. Preference is given to those who have participated in an Outward Bound course as a student, experience working with teenagers, and have an enthusiasm and interest to impact young adults.

Your First Move: The application process (including an online application) can be viewed on their website. It's noted that applicants should be patient after submitting their materials; however, feel free to be persistent!

For More Information:
Alyse Ostreicher, Staff Developer/Recruiter
HIOBS—Southern Programs
Adolescent Instructor Practicum
177 Salem Ct.
Tallahassee, FL 32301
(850) 414-8816 • (850) 922-6721 (fax)
flrecruit@hurricaneisland.org

INTERLOCKEN CENTER FOR EXPERIENTIAL LEARNING

Adventure Travel • New Hampshire • Summer
www.interlocken.org

SINCE 1961, MORE than ten thousand young people have explored the world Interlocken-style. Whether participants join the residential summer camp in New Hampshire or a travel- or community-service program throughout the world, Interlocken campers and students learn by doing. They enrich their lives with lasting friendships, new skills, self-discoveries, and increased environmental and cultural awareness.

What You'll Be Doing: The International Summer Camp is a creative community of 180 boys and girls (ages nine to fifteen) and 60 staff members from all over the world. Counselor opportunities abound at Interlocken—from outdoor adventures and land sports to dance, woodworking, and gardening. Travel leaders take to the road with small groups of twelve to sixteen students and explore new and unusual environments, learn new skills, and challenge themselves physically and intellectually. These programs focus on a traveling theatre performance show, adventure/wilderness, coastal environmental studies, cycling, horsemanship, leadership training, and community service in the U.S. and abroad.

Commitment: Camp counselors must make a ten-week commitment beginning in early June; travel leaders can opt for either the three- or six-week program.

Perks and Rewards: Camp position wages range from $1,300 to $2,200 for the summer; while travel leader wages range from $1,500 to $3,125. All staff members receive room, board, pro-deal purchases, and extensive training.

The Essentials: Summer-camp applicants must be at least twenty years of age and have finished one year of college as well as have experience teaching children and expertise in one of the many activities Interlocken provides. Travel-leader applicants must be at least twenty-four years of age, with expertise in teaching theatre, visual arts, outdoor adventure, language (French or Spanish), or environmental education, along with the ability to work with small groups of teenagers.

Your First Move: Send resume and cover letter requesting staff application packet (or you can download an application online). It's best to apply by January.

For More Information:
Staff Coordinator
Interlocken Center for Experiential Learning
R.R. 2, Box 165
Hillsboro, NH 03244
(603) 478-3166, ext. 20 • (603) 478-5260 (fax)
mail@interlocken.org

INTERNATIONAL FIELD STUDIES

Sailing/Education • The Bahamas • 1 Year+
www.intlfieldstudies.com

INTERNATIONAL FIELD STUDIES (IFS) is a nonprofit organization that operates Forfar Field Station and a sailing program on Andros Island in the Bahamas (where you can find the world's third-largest barrier reef).

What You'll Be Doing: Staff at the field station educate and lead high school- and college-age groups in natural science activities and perform routine maintenance on boats, vehicles, and the facility. As a captain or first mate in the sailing program, staff live on the boat (and are responsible for maintaining it), as well as running trips and sailing.

Commitment: A minimum one-year commitment is required.

Perks and Rewards: Benefits include a monthly stipend beginning at $200, along with meals, rustic housing on the beach or onboard sailboats, travel between Florida and the Bahamas, educational courses, permits, training, licenses in scuba and outboards, four weeks' paid vacation, and two complimentary one-week trips to the station for family members.

The Essentials: Applicants must be able to withstand bugs, heat, and the lack of a U.S.–style civilization. Especially needed are applicants who are great with people from all walks of life, hardworking, eager to learn, self-motivated, positive, patient, and flexible. Mechanical aptitude and a knowledge and love of nature are also highly desirable.

Your First Move: Download an application from their website, then send completed application, a resume, and letter of intent either through regular mail or email. Selected applicants will be scheduled for an interview week in the Bahamas. The only way IFS can get serious applicants is to charge $595 for the interview week (which will be reimbursed after a year of service).

For More Information:
Special Projects Coordinator
International Field Studies
709 College Ave.
Columbus, OH 43209
(800) 962-3805 • (614) 235-4646 • (614) 235-9744 (fax)
employment@intlfieldstudies.com

KIEVE AFFECTIVE EDUCATION

Experiential Education • Maine • 4–10 Months
www.kieve.org

KIEVE'S LEADERSHIP DECISIONS Institute (LDI), a leader in adventure-based, experiential education and prevention, works with over 13,000 students each year from over 120 school systems all over Maine and New England. Throughout the spring and fall seasons, middle school students travel to their camp facility on Damariscotta Lake and spend up to five days working on skills in teamwork, conflict resolution, relationships, communication, decision making, leadership, and positive risk-taking. During the winter months, Kieve staff travel to schools to deliver outreach programs based on the same curriculum.

What You'll Be Doing: Ten-month interns are integrated closely into all aspects of the Kieve programming, including classroom management, curriculum development, peer mediation, conflict resolution, and adventure-based instruction. During the fall and spring programs, most of the time is spent on-site. The schedule guarantees a mix of observation, one-on-one and group discussion, and, as the intern's experience grows, in-class facilitation. During the winter months, interns have the opportunity to accompany and assist the teaching staff in delivering outreach programs at schools. Seasonal Peer Resident Overseers (PROs) responsibilities include organizing and supervising students during out-of-class time along with supervision of a cabin of fifteen boys or girls, operation of the ropes course and climbing wall, waterfront and other recreational activities, and performing in an interactive theatre skit.

Commitment: The ten-month intern program generally runs from late August until early June. Seasonal PRO positions are available either during the spring (February through mid-June) or the fall (late August through early December). Kieve is flexible with start and end dates.

Perks and Rewards: Ten-month interns will receive a stipend of $8,000 (with health benefits available), while seasonal employees receive $150 per week. Benefits include housing in cabins, meals, laundry facilities, computer and Internet access, a health club membership, access to their recreational building, and a spectacular waterfront location.

The Essentials: Intern applicants must be college graduates seriously considering a career in education who feel they would benefit from a year of hands-on training; at the minimum, seasonal employees must be at least eighteen years of age. All staff must be compassionate, caring people with lots of energy to work within a residential program.

Your First Move: Call or email for additional information. Applications are accepted continually throughout the year.

For More Information:
Gretchen Rand, Staffing Coordinator
Kieve Affective Education
Leadership Decisions Institute
P.O. Box 169
Nobleboro, ME 04555
(207) 563-6212 • (207) 563-5833 (fax)
ldi@kieve.org

LINDBLAD EXPEDITIONS

Sailing • USA/Canada/Mexico • 6 Months
www.expeditions.com

KNOWN FOR THEIR expedition travel voyages, Lindblad Expeditions places a strong emphasis on in-depth exploration and discovery, where passengers (and the crew) learn about the environment, ecology, and natural history of a region through lectures, slide presentations, and guided walks. The vessels are small (just 152 feet in length), so the twenty-two crew members and seventy passengers are able to travel where the big ships cannot. Destinations include the Sea of Cortez and Baja California, the Columbia and Snake Rivers (Oregon/Washington), British Columbia, and southeast Alaska. Most shipboard staff work year-round; however, stewards and deckhands can work over a six-month period. The work is demanding—averaging twelve hours a day—but time off is often filled with the chance to go hiking, snorkeling, kayaking, whale watching, or attending beach BBQs. Crew members earn on average $2,000 per month and receive room and board. Along with an adventurous spirit and outgoing personality, applicants must be at least eighteen years of age. On the basis of your cover letter and resume, applications are sent to those who they feel are a good match.

For More Information:
Employment Department
Lindblad Expeditions
1415 Western Ave., Suite 700
Seattle, WA 98101
(206) 382-9594 (fax)
crewus@expeditions.com

LONGACRE EXPEDITIONS

Adventure Travel • Worldwide • Summer
www.longacreexpeditions.com

EACH SUMMER LONGACRE EXPEDITIONS leaders and groups of ten to sixteen teenagers bicycle, backpack, rock climb, kayak, mountaineer, white-water raft, snowboard, snorkel, scuba dive, explore caves, and canoe across miles of the most beautiful territory in North and Central America as well as Iceland. Trips focus on group living, wilderness skills, cooperation, independence, and fun.

What You'll Be Doing: Trip leaders and assistants coordinate different trips that emphasize different ability levels—from basic "kid" trips to challenging courses for teenagers. Besides leadership positions, there are other jobs that are just as essential, including base camp cook, kitchen assistant, nurses, and various specialists. All staffers are required to attend an eight- to nine-day staff training period, which begins around June 15.

Commitment: Seasonal staff have various work schedules to choose from, including leading a trip for four weeks, then acting as support staff for two to five additional weeks; working a two- to six-week trip; or arriving a few weeks early to help open the base camp before staff week, as well as scouting new routes and campsites.

Perks and Rewards: Adventure leaders are paid $46 and up per day; base camp staff is paid $1,050 to $2,500 depending on position and length of contract; and staffers who hold current certificates in EMT or WEMT are compen-

sated an additional $100. There is no compensation for the staff training period; however, room and board are supplied. Perks include pro-deal purchases.

The Essentials: Applicants must be twenty-one years of age, have a good driving record, and have certification in first aid, a water-safety course, and CPR. Common traits include ability to communicate and be comfortable with teenagers, competence in a variety of outdoor activities, great physical condition, the ability to embrace Longacre's trip-leading philosophy, and commitment to the group. Staffers come from all over the country and are often graduate students or college juniors/seniors who have taken a few years off to take a job or tour the world. Others are teachers who see the summer as an opportunity to be with kids in a non-classroom setting. Still others join Longacre each year, coming from seasonal positions at ski resorts, environmental centers, and other wilderness programs.

Your First Move: Applications must be received by June 15. A personal interview is highly recommended.

For More Information:
Meredith Schuler, Program Director
Longacre Expeditions
4030 Middle Ridge Rd.
Newport, PA 17074
(800) 433-0127 • (717) 567-6790 • (717) 567-3955 (fax)
longacre@longacreexpeditions.com

MINIWANCA EDUCATION CENTER

Experiential Education • Michigan • 5–12 Months
www.ayf.com

THE AMERICAN YOUTH FOUNDATION is a nonprofit organization founded in 1925 to help young people and those who serve young people achieve their personal best, lead balanced lives, and serve others. Programs include a residential summer camp, a Four-Trails Adventure program, and a high-school leadership conference, along with year-round outreach programs to serve communities that house their sites and programs. Interns at the Miniwanca Education Center assist in the facilitation of outdoor education, team building, leadership development, and service-learning programs for a variety of populations over a semester or full year. Interns will also gain training and experience facilitating the low and high ropes course and climbing tower, and be given the opportunity to create and complete an individual project. Intern periods run mid-August through December and mid-January through early June, and many interns start or end with summer-camp positions. Applicants must have experience working with youth programs, an ability to laugh easily, a positive attitude, and a willingness to put 110 percent energy into the program. A monthly stipend of $500 is provided, along with room, partial board, and medical insurance. Applications are available online.

For More Information:
Adam Russell, Outreach Program Coordinator
Miniwanca Education Center
American Youth Foundation
8845 W. Garfield Rd.
Shelby, MI 49455
(231) 861-2262, ext. 1111 • (231) 861-5244 (fax)
adam.russell@ayf.com

THE MOUNTAIN INSTITUTE

**Environmental Education • West Virginia •
1 Week–8 Months**
www.mountain.org

SINCE THE EARLY seventies, the Mountain Institute has been running environmental education programming to a variety of schools and students, private organizations, and universities, with courses that highlight physical, emotional, and intellectual challenges, as well as discovery, growth, and the learning of new outdoor skills. Many programs work with twelve to fifteen students in an extended, field-based setting, either at their four-hundred-acre Spruce Knob facility or in yurts (a circular domed tent of skins or felt stretched over a collapsible lattice framework). Since programs are taught experientially, participants and the field staff can't help but wander into group dynamics and leadership.

What You'll Be Doing: The course instructor team works together to create a dynamic, educational week utilizing the surrounding landscape, with programming that covers the general topics of ecology, mountain geology, and biodiversity. Interns assist the staff with the delivery of all educational programs, including group handling, logistical planning and preparation, and field skills instruction.

Commitment: Course-instructor positions are seasonal and on a contract basis for each course, which are concentrated from mid-April to June and mid-September to mid-October. There are a limited number of opportuni-

ties in the summer, with the majority of staff working in the spring and fall. Interns generally work during the spring through fall for ten consecutive weeks. During the winter months, internships are administration focused.

Perks and Rewards: Field-staff wages start at $65 per day along with meals and tent housing. Interns are provided with room and board at the Mountain Center campus and receive $100 per week.

The Essentials: Field staff must be at least twenty-one years of age and have experience working with youth in the outdoors. CPR and WFR certifications are required. (However, the Institute hosts a WFR-CPR training in the spring for those that don't have current certification.) Interns must be at least nineteen years old with an interest in working for an environmentally-friendly nonprofit organization.

Your First Move: Send a resume, references, and a cover letter explaining why you would like to work for the institute.

For More Information:
Matthew Tate, Program Officer
The Mountain Institute
HC 75, Box 24
Circleville, WV 26804
(800) 874-3050 • (304) 567-2632 • (304) 567-2666 (fax)
learning@mountain.org

MUSIKER DISCOVERY PROGRAMS

**Educational Travel • USA/Canada/Europe •
Summer**
www.summerfun.com

MUSIKER TOURS OFFERS traveling programs for middle/high school students that last from four to seven weeks during the summer months in the U.S., Canada, and Europe. In addition, students have the option to participate in the Musiker Summer Discovery program, a pre-college enrichment program at seven university campuses—including UCLA, UC Santa Barbara, University of Michigan, University of Connecticut, Georgetown University, University of Vermont, and Cambridge University in the U.K. Tour counselors supervise, counsel, accompany, live with, and act as role models for teenagers; Summer Discovery counselors assist students with their academics, supervise residence-hall living, and accompany students on excursions off-campus. With the "one dorm, one community" philosophy, all staff members are essentially responsible for every student on the program; however, each counselor will be directly responsible for groups of six to fifteen students, depending on the program. A stipend of $200 per week is provided for Summer Discovery counselors ($100 per week for tour counselors), along with room, meals, and air transportation to and from your home city. Applicants must be twenty-one years of age, hold a U.S. driver's license, and have an abundance of energy. After submitting an application (which can be found online), call one week after to arrange a personal interview.

For More Information:
Personnel Department
Musiker Discovery Programs
1326 Old Northern Blvd.
Roslyn, NY 11576
(800) 645-6611 • (516) 621-3939 • (516) 625-3438 (fax)
staff@summerfun.com

NATIONAL OUTDOOR LEADERSHIP SCHOOL

Wilderness Adventures • Worldwide • 1–3 Months
www.nols.edu

🏕️ 🌍

THE NATIONAL OUTDOOR Leadership School (commonly known as NOLS) is an educational organization with its roots in extended wilderness expeditions—believing that long stays in wild places are vital to understanding both the natural world and ourselves. Courses take students away from the distractions of civilization and into the mountains, deserts, and oceans to learn the skills they need to run their own expeditions. NOLS graduates are leaders who have an understanding of environmental ethics, a sense of teamwork, an appreciation of natural history, and overall competence and good judgment. NOLS operates nine branch schools in Alaska, the Pacific Northwest, the Rocky Mountains, the Southwest, Teton Valley, Mexico, and the Yukon in North America, as well as in Kenya and Patagonia (Chile).

What You'll Be Doing: Prior to working at NOLS as a seasonal staff member or instructor, it's virtually necessary to have participated in a NOLS course. Most folks select their course by either concentrating on location or skills. Terrain, weather, expedition length, and specialized skills vary, but every course includes a core curriculum emphasizing leadership through the development of judgment and decision-making skills. Your choice will depend on

Photo Credit: Deborah Sussex

Instructor and students line up boats in the Yukon Territory, home of the NOLS canoe program.

your interests, experience, and time constraints. Course types include mountaineering, wilderness backpacking, ocean (sea kayaking and sailing), river (kayaking, rafting, and canoeing), winter (backcountry skiing and dogsledding), semester (a variety of skills over three months), outdoor educators (for practicing or potential outdoor educators), and shorter courses for people twenty-five years and older.

Once you've graduated, there are over one hundred temporary and seasonal positions at NOLS that you may consider. These include everything from managers to kitchen workers. In addition, there are over five hundred active NOLS instructors throughout the world. New instructors generally work only two summer courses during their first two years at the school (with 50 percent of the work available in the summer).

Commitment: Most courses run thirty days; however, there are ten-day courses and ninety-day semester courses.

Perks and Rewards: For participation in a NOLS course, fees range from $750 to $8,300 depending on the location and the length of the educational expedition. Pay for seasonal employment is usually entry level with benefits varying from branch to branch.

The Essentials: Successful students come willing to learn and develop leadership skills and wilderness ethics. Prior outdoor experience is not a prerequisite for most NOLS courses, although being in good shape and having a positive attitude and the desire to learn wilderness skills in locations of incredible beauty are musts.

Your First Move: For more information on employment opportunities, contact the Human Resources Director, or for participating in a NOLS course, call or send an email note to admissions@nols.edu.

For More Information:
Human Resources Director
National Outdoor Leadership School
284 Lincoln St.
Lander, WY 82520-2848
(307) 332-5300 • (307) 332-1220 (fax)
human_resources@nols.edu

OUTDOORS WISCONSIN LEADERSHIP SCHOOL

Adventure/Environmental Education • Wisconsin • 3–10 Months
www.augeowms.org

ENTER THE DYNAMIC field of experiential learning with the Outdoors Wisconsin Leadership School (OWLS) and the Outdoor Environmental Education program (OEE), one of the largest adventure/environmental education programs in the Midwest. Thousands of participants have experienced a program at OWLS and OEE as a means of achieving personal and team growth in areas such as leadership, communication, creativity, trust building, and problem solving. You, too, may find the Lake Geneva Campus to be the ideal spot for learning and personal growth.

What You'll Be Doing: Adventure education instructors and interns facilitate team building and leadership development programs for high schools, colleges, and adult groups. The curriculum includes trust building, group initiatives, high and low ropes courses, team and individual climbing elements, and off-campus rock climbing. Outdoor environmental education instructors and interns develop and teach classes to K-8 students in natural awareness, wetlands, lake study, astronomy, and the weather, as well as coordinate school-group programming. Outdoor/guest recreation interns lead activities, including sports, games, natural awareness, and orienteering, and coordinate conference groups. Other seasonal positions range from arts and crafts teachers and lifeguards to bakers and groundskeepers.

Commitment: Adventure education internships and seasonal positions are available from March through November; outdoor environmental education positions run September through early June; and outdoor/guest recreation positions are available during the summer and winter.

Perks and Rewards: Wages vary from $250 to $350 per week (depending on experience and position), along with room, board, and supplemental health insurance.

Staff members live on a beautiful, lakefront campus in comfortable, rustic cabins that include showers, toilet facilities, and single beds with linens. No more than two people share a room, and single rooms are assigned whenever possible. Wholesome and nutritious meals are served family- or buffet-style in their spacious dining room. Recreational facilities, including a waterfront, tennis courts, golf course, and cross-country skiing, are available during time off.

The Essentials: For instructor positions, applicants should be college graduates with degrees in education or recreation with experience teaching in the outdoors. Interns should have at least college-senior status, with coursework in related areas and experience working with people. A high energy-level, good communication skills, and a strong commitment to creating powerful recreational and learning experiences for others are the most important qualifications for all positions.

Your First Move: Send a cover letter, resume, and names and addresses of three references within four to six months of start date.

For More Information:
Cathy Coster, Associate Director, Adventure Education
Outdoors Wisconsin Leadership School
Aurora University—Lake Geneva Campus
P.O. Box 210
Williams Bay, WI 53191-0210
(262) 245-5531, ext. 8544 • (262) 245-8549 (fax)
owls@idcnet.com
For outdoor environmental education positions,
contact Sharon Wuttke, Associate Director, at
gwprogrm@idcnet.com.

To achieve the marvelous, you must do the unthinkable . . . the answer will hit,
like a big psychic orgasm, if you listen to your dreams. They never lie. —E. JEAN CARROLL

THE OUTWARD BOUND EXPERIENCE

In wildness is the preservation of the world.
—HENRY DAVID THOREAU

Outward Bound is a growing federation of Outward Bound schools and centers in twenty-six countries. In the U.S., five wilderness schools make up the Outward Bound USA system. Since the first U.S. school was established in 1961, over four hundred thousand people have participated in their programs. Many people who sign up for Outward Bound see the experience as a sabbatical of sorts—a time to get away from the routine, assess their current situation, and set new goals. Well over a million people of all ages and backgrounds have benefited from Outward Bound around the world.

Outward Bound courses are designed to help people develop confidence, compassion, an appreciation for service to others, and a lasting relationship with the natural environment. Outward Bound is not a survival school. They do offer, however, a rugged adventure in the wilderness during which you will receive unparalleled training in wilderness skills. They provide a unique, rigorous curriculum, in which you will learn by doing and put your learning to the test daily. The four pillars of self-reliance, fitness, craftsmanship, and compassion are central to the Outward Bound experience.

Outward Bound will challenge you, both individually and as a member of a team, by taking you into

Photo Credit: Terry Moore

unfamiliar territory and allowing you to apply your newfound knowledge and skills. Sometimes you may fail in your efforts. Facing failure and learning to overcome it through reasonable, responsible action is an essential part of the Outward Bound experience. Teammates and instructors provide the emotional support for you to try and, if you fail, to try again. Perseverance is the basis for the Outward Bound motto, "to serve, to strive, and not to yield."

WORKING FOR OUTWARD BOUND

Many factors influence the quality and success of a group's Outward Bound experience, but none is more important than the quality of the staff. Staff members are sensitive, highly skilled, energetic outdoor leaders who are committed to the Outward Bound philosophy. The majority of staff are educators who are also mountaineers, climbers, and paddlers with solid life experience. Some work year-round; others only work two or three courses per year and work the rest of the year in education or other professions. Above all, staff members possess one important outdoor skill—good judgment, or the ability to make sound, safe decisions under challenging circumstances.

Positions include instructional staff, support staff, and volunteer positions. All staff receive room and board and are paid on a per diem basis. The pay generally ranges from $40 to $125 per day (but varies with school and position) with generous discounts on outdoor equipment and clothing. Most of the schools also have programs for corporate clientele. Facilitators are recruited to deliver these programs, some of which are classroom based, while others are more wilderness oriented.

As a whole, Outward Bound does not offer a formal internship program. Occasionally an internship position is created for the "right" person who applies for the assistant instructor position and doesn't have all the necessary skills to assume the responsibilities of the position. Taking a course prior to working for Outward Bound is strongly encouraged and may be required, depending on the program to which you are applying. Wilderness Schools that have internship opportunities are noted below.

Photo Credit: Jake Mills

A kayaker learns about the four pillars of self-reliance, fitness, craftsmanship, and compassion taught at Outward Bound.

▶ HEADQUARTERS

Outward Bound USA
100 Mystery Point Rd.
Garrison, NY 10524-9757
(888) 882-6863 • (845) 424-4000
www.obusa.org

WILDERNESS SCHOOLS

COLORADO OUTWARD BOUND SCHOOL

KNOWN FOR BEING the first Outward Bound School in the U.S., premier mountaineers, white-water boaters, desert "rats," and sea kayakers teach students the skills to tackle the rugged challenges of backcountry travel (with a focus on personal development through exceptional wilderness education) in Colorado, Utah, New Mexico, Baja California, and Alaska.

For More Information:
Jill Lawrence, Staffing Director
Colorado Outward Bound School
910 Jackson St.
Golden, CO 80401
(800) 477-2627 (press 5)
jillla@cobs.edu • www.cobs.org/jobs

HURRICANE ISLAND OUTWARD BOUND SCHOOL

ESTABLISHED INITIALLY AS Outward Bound's landmark sailing program, the school now includes canoeing, backpacking, sea kayaking, rock climbing, winter programs, and a schooner, along with corporate, urban, and educational programs that provide initiatives and ropes/challenge-course activities as well as expeditions. Seasonal opportunities are available in Maine and Maryland;

When we are motivated by goals that have deep meaning, by dreams that need completion, by pure love that needs expressing, then we truly live life. —GREG ANDERSON

OUTWARD BOUND

Florida offers year-round opportunities working with at-risk and adjudicated youth, as well as a three-month internship program. See Hurricane Island's Southern Program on page 75 for details.

For More Information:
Josie Howard, Human Resources Specialist
Hurricane Island Outward Bound School
75 Mechanic St.
Rockland, ME 04841
(800) 643-4462 • (207) 594-5548, ext. 388
employment@hurricaneisland.org •
www.hiobs.org/employment

NORTH CAROLINA OUTWARD BOUND SCHOOL

SINCE ITS BEGINNINGS in the rugged mountains of Appalachia, the school has expanded its programming to the North Carolina Outer Banks, Florida Ten Thousand Islands, Exumas Bahamas, and Chilean Andes. Students choose from a range of activities that include rock climbing, mountaineering, white-water paddling, sea kayaking, mountain biking, and backpacking. The classic Outward Bound Course is a twenty-one- to twenty-eight-day multiactivity course, although courses range in length from four to seventy-eight days.

Experienced wilderness instructors are hired to deliver challenging, adventure-based courses aimed at skill development and individual growth. People with experience rock climbing, white-water canoeing, sea kayaking, or mountain biking are hired to oversee the operation of these program activities. Logistics staff and cooks work to keep the base camps running, while providing support to instructors. The selection of new applicants begins in November, with most contracts offered in February or March. Most people work for the majority of the summer in their first season, with opportunities for additional off-season work that becomes available in late summer.

North Carolina Outward Bound also offers a variety of training programs for people interested in getting into the outdoor field. These courses include the Outward Bound Instructor Course, Outdoor Leader Course, Whitewater Skills Training, Sea Kayak Skills Training, and Wilderness First Responder Certification.

For More Information:
Dave Hus, Director of Staffing and Staff Development
North Carolina Outward Bound School
2582 Riceville Rd.
Asheville, NC 28805
(800) 850-7823 • (828) 299-3366, ext. 142
staffing@ncobs.org • www.ncobs.org/jobs

PACIFIC CREST OUTWARD BOUND SCHOOL

WHETHER IT'S WHITE-WATER rafting, alpine mountaineering, sailing, sea kayaking, or other exciting adventures, participants engage in adventures along the Pacific Crest Trail amid glaciers, canyons, rivers, and peaks. Only expert staff members are hired with Pacific Crest.

For More Information:
Staffing Coordinator
Pacific Crest Outward Bound School
0110 SW Bancroft St.
Portland, OR 97239
(800) 547-3312 • (503) 243-1993
www.pcobs.org

VOYAGEUR OUTWARD BOUND SCHOOL

FROM THE REMOTE wilderness of Minnesota and Manitoba to the deserts and white waters of Texas and the Big Sky country of Montana, border-to-border adventures abound with Voyageur. With course areas in four states, Canada, and Mexico, Voyageur was also the first school to run women's, youth, and Life Career Renewal courses. Internships, which are offered in most of their program areas, begin with a training expedition in the given course with a senior staff trainer. Interns are then involved in a variety of course support roles including rock climbing, ropes course, driving, logistics and general base-camp maintenance. Great training, room, board, a weekly stipend, and pro-deal purchases are offered. Positions vary in length from five to nine weeks (generally from May through August) and are base-camp focused. Assistant instructor and logistics staff openings are also available for those with a strong base of experience. Although positions are available in the fall, winter, and spring, these positions are generally filled by their summer pool (translation: work for them in the summer first!). All applicants must be at least twenty-one and very excited about working with youth and at-risk populations.

For More Information:
Staffing Director
Voyageur Outward Bound School
101 E. Chapman St.
Ely, MN 55731
(800) 321-4453 • 218-365-7790
staffing@vobs.com • www.vobs.org

OUTWARD BOUND

BEYOND THE UNITED STATES

COSTA RICA RAINFOREST OUTWARD BOUND SCHOOL

Costa Rica Outward Bound has various staff and administration positions available throughout the year, including field instructor, surf instructor, student administrator, marketing positions, and webmaster. Candidates must have general outdoor education/leadership experiences or knowledge, and make a commitment of eight to twelve months depending on position (although shorter-term possibilities may be available). Spanish fluency is definitely a plus. Send your resume and philosophy statement to begin the application process. As a nonprofit foundation, they are able to obtain volunteer visas for foreign staff. This type of visa prevents them from paying volunteers a salary; however, it does allow the school to cover airfare, room, board, and a cash stipend. Health insurance is provided under the ISIC card that is purchased for all foreign staff.

For More Information:
Staffing Director
Costa Rica Rainforest Outward Bound School
SJO 829, Box 025216
Miami, FL 33102-5216
(506) 777-1222
In Costa Rica: CRROBS, P.O. Box 243,
Quepos, Costa Rica
info@crrobs.org • www.crrobs.org/employment

PUTNEY STUDENT TRAVEL

Educational Travel • Worldwide • Summer
www.goputney.com

Slovakia. The Caribbean. Tanzania. Costa Rica. The U.S. Yes, these are just a few of the locales you might venture off to this summer as an adventure travel guide for Putney Student Travel. Providing unusual education opportunities for small groups of secondary-school students, Putney trip leaders focus either on adventure-travel, language-learning, or community-service trips over a four- to six-week period during the summer months. Applicants must be energetic, fun, creative, active, knowledgeable about the area they are visiting, and excited about spending time with high school students.

Proficiency in the language of the host country is required (French, Spanish, Italian, Czech/Slovak, or Swahili). There are no foreign language requirements for trips to the Caribbean and the U.S. Leaders will receive a stipend along with all their expenses paid (including round-trip airfare, room, and board). If you are excited about the prospect of helping students learn about a different culture this summer, send a resume (with the phone numbers and/or email addresses of three references) and a cover letter which addresses the following topics: language proficiency; travel experience and/or knowledge of host country; experience in leadership/organization, working with teenagers, and community service (if applicable); and personal strengths and/or skills that make you an exceptional leader.

For More Information:
Paul Campbell, Leadership Coordinator
Putney Student Travel
345 Hickory Ridge Rd.
Putney, VT 05346
(802) 387-5885 • (802) 387-4276 (fax)
paul@goputney.com

In addition to Putney's travel guide opportunities, they also recruit qualified instructors and residential staff for their summer Excel program at campuses in the U.S., Europe, and Cuba. These nontraditional enrichment programs provide high school students with insights into college life in an informal campus environment while fostering a balance of personal and intellectual growth. Salaries are competitive and all living expenses are paid.
For more information on the Excel program, contact Tim Weed at tim@goputney.com.

REACHOUT EXPEDITIONS

Wilderness Adventure/Ministry • Washington • Seasonal
www.reachoutexpeditions.org

Are you interested in and committed to helping lead youth and adults closer to Christ? Do you enjoy spending time adventuring in the outdoors? Do you have a heart for service? Are you willing to work long hours and go the extra mile for others? If so, Reachout may have a job for you. Reachout has been leading life-changing wilderness adventures since 1979, an alternative for kids who are looking for something real, whether they realize it or not.

What You'll Be Doing: There are three ways you can get plugged into Reachout on a short-term basis: Resource staff are trained to become raft guides or rock-climbing instructors by Reachout and run programs for kids. In general, they are semi-local volunteers who help out on weekends (mostly) during the busy spring and summer seasons; summer staff work and live on-site and minister full-time for three to four months with sixteen other summer staffers from all over the world; finally, three interns become involved in projects such as helping out during the winter season, lending a hand in the rafting department, or assisting the adventure combo coordinator.

Perks and Rewards: Summer staffers are provided with room and board by host families. Beyond that, summer staff may choose to raise support, like a home-based missionary.

The Essentials: Although Reachout offers programs requiring technical wilderness skills, extensive wilderness training is not a prerequisite. Maturity, a commitment to Christ, a heart for youth, self-motivation, and a willingness to serve are most important.

Your First Move: Application materials are available for download online.

For More Information:
Paul Spence, Director
Reachout Expeditions
P.O. Box 464
Anacortes, WA 98221
(800) 697-3847 • (360) 293-3788 • (360) 293-8297 (fax)
rewinfo@yd.org

THE ROAD LESS TRAVELED

Wilderness Adventure • USA/Australia/ British Columbia/Costa Rica/Nepal • Summer
www.theroadlesstraveled.com

THE ROAD LESS TRAVELED coordinates summer wilderness adventure, cultural awareness, and environmental education programs for teenagers. Participants venture to unique and culturally rich spots in New England, as well as the north and southwest regions of the U.S. (including Alaska), Australia, British Columbia, Costa Rica, and

Nepal. Trip leaders begin their summer with ten days of staff training in Larkspur, Colorado; they then guide and engage participants in backpacking, ice and snow mountaineering, rock climbing, kayaking, white-water rafting, and desert hiking. Candidates must be at least twenty-one years of age, WFR or WEMT certified, have experience in working with teenagers, and have solid wilderness skills. Along with a per-day-rate salary (dependent upon experience), benefits include all living expenses during time of employment, full payment of WFR, WEMT, or EMT recertification (or $300 toward upgrade certification) upon successful completion of employment, pro-purchase deals for gear and clothing, and the opportunity to work with world renown and expert guides. Send off a cover letter and resume via fax, mail, or email to begin the application process. A personal interview and references are required.

For More Information:
Jim Stein, Director
The Road Less Traveled
2331 N. Elston Ave.
Chicago, IL 60614-2907
(800) 939-9839 • (773) 342-5200 • (773) 342-5703 (fax)
rlt1road@aol.com

SAIL CARIBBEAN

Sailing/Diving • The Caribbean • Summer
www.sailcaribbean.com

VOYAGING THROUGHOUT THE British Virgin, Leeward, and Windward Islands in the Caribbean, Sail Caribbean leads groups of teenagers from around the globe on sailing and diving adventures. Students develop leadership skills and self-confidence by taking turns reading charts, hauling in the sails, chopping vegetables, or just getting to know one another aboard fifty-one-foot sailboats with teens of their own age group. Summer staff opportunities include captains, mates, or scuba instructors with activities that range from instruction of curriculum and shipboard life to land activities and group dynamics. Applicants must have extensive sailing or diving credentials along with a strong background in working with teenagers. One full week of intensive training is provided in leadership skills, teaching methods, and safety techniques specific to Sail Caribbean. Benefits include a salary, room and board, and, of course, life in the Caribbean.

For More Information:
Michael Liese, Director
Sail Caribbean
79 Church St.
Northport, NY 11768
(800) 321-0994 • (631) 754-2202 • (631) 754-3362 (fax)
info@sailcaribbean.com

SAN JUAN SAFARIS

Ecotourism • Washington • Summer
www.sanjuansafaris.com

DESTINATION SAN JUAN ISLANDS—a spectacular area of Washington where you might catch a glimpse of wild orca whales, see bald eagles soaring high overhead, or watch sea lions frolicking in a cove. That is, if you have the right guide. San Juan Safaris exposes small groups to wildlife through boating and sea kayaking tours where participants not only get up close to wildlife, but also gain a deeper understanding and appreciation for the habitat. Whether giving talks as a whale-watching naturalist, leading sea kayak lessons for guests, or working the docks or appointment desk, those who are hard working, responsible, drug-free, and outdoorsy thrive in this environment. Wages range from $8 to $12 per hour (plus tips!), along with a season-end bonus based on $2 per every hour worked. At the minimum, applicants must have a strong ecological awareness and first-aid certification, and be able to work long days. Send off a cover letter and resume to begin the application process.

For More Information:
Colleen Johansen, Seasonal Employment Director
San Juan Safaris
P.O. Box 2749
Friday Harbor, WA 98250
(800) 450-6858 • (360) 378-1323 • (360) 378-6546 (fax)
fun@sanjuansafaris.com

SEMESTER AT SEA

Educational Travel • Worldwide • 3–4 Months
www.semesteratsea.com

WITH SEMESTER AT SEA, you'll watch twenty-foot waves hit the bow of your "campus" (the *SS Universe Explorer*), live with Chinese students in a dorm at the University of Beijing, stay at an "untouchable" village in India, walk the crowded byways of Istanbul's four-hundred-year-old covered markets, learn about the life of the Masai while on safari in Kenya, attend an Afro-Venezuelan drum workshop, or study tropical rain forests while canoeing down the Amazon River. These international field experiences, coupled with a stimulating on-board classroom environment, make Semester at Sea an exceptional opportunity for learning for both staff and participants alike.

What You'll Be Doing: Staff positions are available as administrative assistant, assistant dean, AV/media coordinator (and assistant), bursar (financial operations), director of student life, field office coordinator (and assistant), information technology coordinator, librarian (and assistant), mental health professional, nurse, photographer, physician, resident staff, secretary, security officer, and senior adult coordinator. In addition to regularly assigned duties, you'll be an integral part of the shipboard community, participating in all aspects of the program as your shipboard work schedule permits, as well as serving on a limited number of in-port duty assignments, which may include serving as a trip leader for some of the field practicums.

Commitment: Spring voyages depart from the Bahamas in late January and return mid-May in Seattle; summer voyages depart from Greece in early June and return mid-August in Greece; and fall voyages depart from Vancouver, Washington, in mid-September and return just before Christmas in Miami.

Perks and Rewards: A small stipend of $1,500 to $4,000 is provided along with room and board while on the ship. In addition, a $700 travel allowance is offered to help defray the cost of travel to/from the ports of embarkation/debarkation. Staff members are responsible for the cost of a passport, required visas (approximately $80 for U.S. citizens), and any required inoculations. Note that a spouse and/or dependent children may be able to accompany staff on the voyage for a fee of $1,850.

The Essentials: The ideal applicants are those who support the concept of academic and personal enrichment through travel and education. Maximum flexibility, cooperation, and adaptability are essential traits of all applicants.

Your First Move: Visit their website to view the most current information (and to download an application), or call for an application packet. Applying for a single, specific voyage and expecting to be hired is not realistic. While personally it might be the best time for an individual's own needs, applicants are rarely hired right away. For most positions, there are between forty and sixty

If you wait to do everything until you're sure it's right, you'll probably never do much of anything. —WIN BORDEN

applications on file; thus, competition is very high. Some applicants wait several years before receiving an interview and applications remain active for three years. Application deadlines: spring voyages—March 1; summer—October 1; and fall—January 1.

For More Information:
Staff Selection
Semester at Sea
University of Pittsburgh
811 William Pitt Union
Pittsburgh, PA 15260
(800) 854-0195 • (412) 648-7490 • (412) 648-2298 (fax)
shipboard@sas.ise.pitt.edu

SOUND EXPERIENCE

Sailing • Washington • 1–7 Months
www.soundexp.org

SOUND EXPERIENCE IS a nonprofit organization providing hands-on environmental education and leadership experiences for youth and adults. On exciting voyages aboard the historic schooner *Adventuress,* participants learn about the majesty and vulnerability of the Puget Sound and the San Juan Islands region.

What You'll Be Doing: During the months of March through October, Sound Experience hires ten to fifteen seasonal staff and selects up to twenty-four volunteer interns (for one month or longer) for the year. All staff and interns are given a thorough orientation to the ship and the responsibilities of working with youth, facilitating the Sound Experience program, and care for the shipboard community. Seasonal staff positions include first mate, second mate/educator, engineer, program director, environmental educator/deckhands, environmental educator interns, and galley coordinator. Volunteer interns will work in watches, team-teach, work in the galley, and participate in all areas of ship board operations.

Perks and Rewards: Salaries between $400 and $1,200 per month are provided for staff members. All staff members receive meals, lodging, and eight days off per month.

The Essentials: Priority is given to those who have proven experiences on tall ships, facilitating environmental education, and/or the ability to work with youth from diverse backgrounds. Teaching skills are strongly reviewed. All staff and interns must have a food-handlers permit and current first-aid and CPR certification; some positions

have other special requirements. Interns must be at least eighteen years old and be interested in pursuing a career related to environmental education or teaching.

Your First Move: Applications are available online, or call/email for more information.

For More Information:
Staffing Coordinator
Sound Experience
2310 Washington St.
Port Townsend, WA 98368
(360) 379-0438 • (360) 379-0439 (fax)
employment@soundexp.org

TOUCH OF NATURE ENVIRONMENTAL CENTER

Wilderness Education • Illinois • Seasonal
www.pso.siu.edu/tonec

SINCE 1969, Touch of Nature's wilderness programs have provided outdoor education and recreation experiences for a wide variety of groups. Through wilderness settings, initiative courses, and adventure activities, the Spectrum Wilderness Program helps participants achieve self-confidence, self-reliance, cooperation, trust, and appreciation of the outdoors. Interns work and learn in most aspects of outdoor adventure programming, including backpacking, initiative courses, rock climbing, caving, and canoeing, including a thirty-day wilderness course with youth-at-risk. A monthly stipend along with basic living quarters is provided. College graduates (or those nearing completion) who have experience working with youth-at-risk and wilderness training (including first-aid and CPR certifications) are encouraged to apply. This program works with a very challenging population in a wilderness setting. A strong desire to work with youth-at-risk is important.

For More Information:
Lisa Wait, Spectrum Wilderness Program Coordinator
Touch of Nature Environmental Center
Southern Illinois University
Mail Code 6888
Carbondale, IL 62901-6888
(618) 453-1121 • (618) 453-1188 (fax)
tonec@siu.edu

TRAILMARK OUTDOOR ADVENTURES

Adventure Education • USA • Summer
www.trailmark.com

THROUGHOUT NEW ENGLAND, the Mid-Atlantic, Colorado, the Northern Rockies, and the Pacific Northwest, Trailmark runs summer adventure-travel trips for teens ages ten to seventeen—programs that foster a genuine family-like atmosphere. Three-leader teams will guide twelve to eighteen participants in activities that encompass rafting, biking, backpacking, caving, horse packing, climbing, mountaineering, snowboarding, sailing, sea kayaking, and canoeing over a one- to four-week period. Well before the Trailmark summer begins, leaders participate in an intensive pre-camp training session, to prepare and review the summer's activities and itineraries, as well as teen-counseling issues. All leaders, who average twenty-five years of age, must have first-aid, CPR, and safety training. Many have been trained at Outward Bound and National Outdoor Leadership School (NOLS). A staff application can be downloaded online.

For More Information:
Rusty and Donna Pedersen, Directors
Trailmark Outdoor Adventures
16 Schuyler Rd.
Nyack, NY 10960
(800) 229-0262 • (888) 666-8562 (job hotline)
(845) 358-0262 • (845) 348-0437 (fax)
staff@trailmark.com

> *Trip leaders are experienced, talented, high-energy, and supportive. We only select leaders who have extensive experience, and the sensitivity and maturity to handle the needs of teenagers.*

TREK AMERICA AMERICAN ADVENTURES

Adventure Travel • USA/Canada/Mexico • Summer
www.trekamerica.com or
www.americanadventures.com

WITH OVER SEVENTY itineraries, Trek America/AmeriCan Adventures offers active, small-group camping tours to foreign travelers (usually between the ages of eighteen and thirty-five) that cover most of North America, including Canada, Alaska, and Mexico.

What You'll Be Doing: Tour leaders take their group in fifteen-passenger vehicles to national parks, cities, small towns, and everything in between. In a day's work, leaders must be prepared for driving, organizing activities, providing briefings and commentary, and leading a safe and enjoyable holiday for their passengers.

Commitment: First-year leaders can normally expect to work from April through mid-September; longer seasons are possible in subsequent years. Each tour lasts one to six weeks, with a two- to three-day break between each trip.

Perks and Rewards: The base pay for first-year leaders is $1,100 per month, and all accommodation is provided during the season. The biggest perk, perhaps, is meeting interesting people from around the world and participating in a variety of adventure activities ranging from jeep tours to water sports on a complimentary basis.

The Essentials: Applicants must be at least twenty-three with a clean driving record. The best applicants are outgoing, adventurous, and flexible, and have a considerable knowledge of North American history, geography, and culture. Knowledge of a foreign language is helpful, but not required. Leaders must participate in a three-week training process before leading any tours. While training, half wages are paid and all accommodations are provided.

Your First Move: Call for application materials. Applications are accepted throughout the winter, spring, and early summer. Training takes place from April until the end of July with various start dates.

For More Information:
Tour Leader Recruitment
Trek America/AmeriCan Adventures
Premiere International
P.O. Box 1338
Gardena, CA 90249
(800) 345-8777 • (310) 719-9877 • (310) 719-1478 (fax)
personnel@premiereops.com

Success isn't something you chase. It's something you have to put forth the effort for constantly. Then maybe it'll come when you least expect it. —MICHAEL JORDAN

U.S. ADAPTIVE RECREATION CENTER

Therapeutic Recreation • California • Seasonal
www.usarc.org

THE U.S. ADAPTIVE Recreation Center provides outdoor recreation opportunities to physically and cognitively challenged individuals. People with disabilities can now learn how to snow ski and water-ski safely and well. Adaptive teaching techniques and equipment can overcome almost any disability—physical or mental. Adaptive ski instruction is available all season, with the summer program focusing on waterskiing, sailing, fishing, canoeing, and kayaking. Volunteers may work as instructors or support staff, or participate in fund-raising activities. Summer volunteers are trained in adaptive waterskiing and water-safety procedures, adaptive camping, fishing, canoeing, and kayaking. All volunteers receive a complimentary ski pass.

For More Information:
Kelle Malkewitz, Executive Director
U.S. Adaptive Recreation Center
P.O. Box 2897
Big Bear Lake, CA 92315-2897
(909) 584-0269 • (909) 585-6805 (fax)
mail@usarc.org

U.S. NAVY MWR TRAINING BRANCH

Recreation • Worldwide • 3 Months
www.mwr.navy.mil/mwrprgms/intern.html

THE MORALE, WELFARE, and Recreation (MWR) Division of the United States Navy provides a variety of recreational/leisure programs and services to the worldwide Navy community of sailors, their families, military reservists, and retired personnel. With the goal of offering programs that contribute to the "retention, readiness, and mental, physical, and emotional well-being of their sailors," MWR operates in twenty-four states in the U.S. and in thirteen countries abroad (including Bahrain, Italy, Iceland, Japan, Korea, and Spain). Students in their senior year of college (or grad students) have the opportunity to participate in the MWR's intern program, with programs focusing on aquatics, child care and develop-

ment, food and beverage, recreation, young adult programs, sports and fitness, and teen/youth activities. Applicants must have programming experience (paid or volunteer), be earning credit for an internship, have basic first-aid and CPR certification, be mature and independent, and be an American citizen. Programs are offered for three months starting in January, May, and September. Housing and a weekly stipend of $150 to $250 is provided, and overseas interns also receive round-trip airfare. Application materials and a complete listing of opportunities can be found online.

For More Information:
Rick Harwell, Intern Program Manager
U.S. Navy MWR Training Branch
5720 Integrity Dr. (P654G)
Millington, TN 38055-6540
(901) 874-2497 • (901) 874-6847 (fax)
rick.harwell@persnet.navy.mil

U.S. OLYMPIC COMMITTEE

Sports • California/Colorado/New York • 13–21 Weeks
www.usolympicteam.com

THE U.S. OLYMPIC Committee is a nonprofit organization dedicated to providing opportunities for American athletes as well as preparing and training those athletes for challenges that range from domestic competitions to the Olympic Games.

What You'll Be Doing: The internship program is designed to provide a quality work experience and a unique opportunity for exposure to the Olympic movement and spirit in the U.S. The program offers internships in the divisions or areas of accounting, broadcasting, computer science, journalism, marketing, sports administration, and sport science (strength and conditioning). The majority of internships are at their headquarters in Colorado Springs; however, interns also might work at Lake Placid, New York, or Chula Vista, California.

Commitment: Internships are available each season, from thirteen to twenty-one weeks.

Perks and Rewards: A weekly stipend is provided, along with housing at Olympic Training Centers (where the athletes live) on a double-occupancy basis and meals at the athletes' dining hall. The complex in Colorado Springs is an athlete's paradise—gyms, weight room, pool, and recreational facilities.

Combining outdoor adventure with community service, a VISIONS Service Adventures team works with locals on a construction project in Peru.

The Essentials: Applicants must be enrolled in an undergraduate or graduate program and have completed at least two years of college before the start of their internship. Most who get accepted into the program have a GPA of 3.0 or higher and have good writing skills. Work experience, volunteer experience, and college extracurricular activities are seriously considered in the selection process. Internships are very competitive.

Your First Move: Operating twenty hours a day, the USOC Intern Information Line (at extension 2597) provides the latest information on internships. This is also a great way to have an application packet mailed to you. Applications must be received by these dates: winter/spring—October 1; summer—February 15; and fall—June 1. You will be notified four to eight weeks after submitting your application.

For More Information:
Student Intern Program
U.S. Olympic Committee
One Olympic Plaza
Colorado Springs, CO 80909-5760
(719) 632-5551, ext. 2597 • (719) 578-4817 (fax)
internprog@usoc.org

VISIONS SERVICE ADVENTURES

Service Adventures • Worldwide • 6–10 Weeks
www.visionsadventure.com

VISIONS SERVICE ADVENTURES offers teens a summer experience in Australia, the British Virgin Islands, Dominica, the Dominican Republic, Guadeloupe, Peru, Sea Islands, and in the U.S. (Alaska, Montana, and the Sea Islands in South Carolina). A VISIONS summer integrates community service (generally construction based), outdoor exploration and adventure, cross-cultural living, and learning (including language immersion and a homestay in selected sites) in coed residential programs of up to twenty-five high school students and six staff. Students and staff live in schools or other local buildings in the heart of each host community.

What You'll Be Doing: Serving as mentors, summer trip leaders and specialists supervise groups of teens in a residential-living setting and during community-service projects. Leaders also teach participants building techniques, basic carpentry or masonry skills, and outdoor activities such as backpacking, rock climbing, and rafting. In addition, leaders introduce participants to cross-cultural activities and experiences.

To know what you prefer instead of humbly saying Amen to what the world tells you ought to prefer, is to have kept your soul alive. —ROBERT LOUIS STEVENSON

Commitment: Staff positions are available for either six or ten weeks during the summer months.

Perks and Rewards: Stipends for staff positions start at $220 per week (dependent on position and experience) and also include room, meals, and travel to/from the program site.

The Essentials: All staff applicants must be at least twenty-two years old, have strong interpersonal skills, a safe driving record, current Wilderness First Aid and CPR certification, experience leading or teaching teenagers, and flexibility and a sense of humor. Carpentry and masonry skills and/or advanced first-aid certification are also desired for some positions. The Peru and Dominican Republic sites require fluency in Spanish; Guadeloupe requires French fluency.

Your First Move: Send application (which can be down-loaded from their website), cover letter, and resume (including three work references). Applications are accepted starting in October for the following season.

For More Information:
Joanne Pinaire and Teena Mills, Directors
VISIONS Service Adventures
P.O. Box 220
Newport, PA 17074-0220
(800) 813-9283 • (717) 567-7313 • (717) 567-7853 (fax)
visions@pa.net

VISIONS typically employs teachers, graduate students and Ph.D. candidates, returned Peace Corps volunteers, and experiential outdoor educators.

WHITE PASS AND YUKON ROUTE RAILROAD

Train • Alaska • Summer
www.whitepassrailroad.com

ALL ABOARD! Born in the scramble of the 1898 Gold Rush, the White Pass & Yukon Route (WP&YR) remains a rare nugget in the annals of railroad history. Prior to its golden beginnings, a mountain range—huge and looming—stood between a prospector and his fortune. But with a will, there's always a way; and soon enough, construction began on a narrow gauge railroad—an

Photo Credit: Christian Racich

With snow-capped mountain peaks in the background, summer staff aboard the White Pass Railroad have the opportunity to view and explore some of Alaska's incredible terrain.

engineering marvel that traverses some of the world's most breathtaking terrain. Through the years, the WP&YR has enjoyed a rich and colorful history; and today, modern-day "prospectors" get to enjoy an unforgettable trip through gold-rush history with the help of the WP&YR summer team. By far, becoming a tour guide is the most interesting of positions (unless you don't enjoy making an entertaining presentation to over five hundred people). Other positions include gift shop clerks, baristas (can you make a "triple dry cap?"), stockers, shuttle drivers, and ticket agents. Along with competitive wages, reasonably priced housing is provided. Applicants must be available for work from May 1 through late September. Applications are available online or call for more information.

For More Information:
Beth Cline, Assistant Manager
White Pass & Yukon Route Railroad
P.O. Box 435
Skagway, AK 99840-0435
(800) 343-7373 • (907) 983-2217 • (907) 983-2734 (fax)
beth@whitepass.net

WILDERNESS INQUIRY

Adventure Travel • Worldwide • 3–5 Months
www.wildernessinquiry.org

WILDERNESS INQUIRY is a nonprofit organization that focuses on getting individuals of all ages, backgrounds, and abilities to experience the natural world in destinations throughout the world. Whether by canoe, sea kayak, dogsled, horse pack, or backpack, trips are integrated to include lots of different folks. It's the unique mix of people and places that makes each trip a unique experience.

What You'll Be Doing: Trail leaders and assistant leaders are responsible for organizing and leading trips primarily throughout North America, with the chance to travel to Costa Rica or Australia. Rigorous adventures are par for the course, with groups usually traveling five to twenty miles per day. Over the course of a single trip, trail leaders may fill the roles of pack horse, teacher, rehabilitation specialist, folksinger, chef, personal-relationship counselor, storyteller, attendant, disciplinarian, dishwasher, and bush doctor. Canoe workshop staff either teach the basics of canoeing at community festivals across Minnesota and Wisconsin and/or lead three-hour Mississippi River trips. Internships are also available in outdoor recreation and experiential education, outreach and public relations, training, and fund-raising and development.

Commitment: Trip-leader positions are seasonal, from December through April, and June through September; canoe workshop staff must make a time commitment ranging from three to twenty days per month; and internships are offered year-round, from twenty to forty hours per week for a minimum of six weeks.

Perks and Rewards: Depending on the position, staff members can earn anywhere from $35 on up to $140 per day, along with meals while working and staff housing between trips. Full-timers also receive full benefits. The best perk has to be the opportunity to participate in outdoor adventures in locations around the globe.

The Essentials: Individuals with previous experience in working with people with disabilities and the outdoors is desired. Leaders and canoe staff must have all certifications (Wilderness First Responder, Lifeguard Training, CPR, and current driver's license) and be sensitive, responsible, have good judgment, a sense of humor, and be competent in providing training on all aspects of wilderness travel and living.

Your First Move: Send a resume, cover letter, three references, and application. Application materials are available for download (in PDF format) through their website.

For More Information:
Julie Green, Associate Program Director
Wilderness Inquiry
808 14th Ave. SE
Minneapolis, MN 55414-1516
(800) 728-0719 • (612) 676-9400 • (612) 676-9401 (fax)
juliegreen@wildernessinquiry.org

WILDERNESS VENTURES

Wilderness Travel • Worldwide • Summer
www.wildernessventures.com

SINCE THE EARLY seventies, Wilderness Ventures has been leading multi-environmental wilderness travel adventures for students between the ages of thirteen and twenty. Each summer, team leaders hit the road and take groups of up to twenty students on backpacking, climbing, canoeing, rafting, biking, mountaineering, kayaking, and service-projects trips to places all across the U.S. and as far away as Australia, Costa Rica, and Europe. Responsibilities include teaching outdoor skills, cultural history, minimum-impact camping, environmental awareness, outdoor education, and natural history. Applicants should have experience and an interest in the outdoors, but it is even more important to value working with teenagers. If your goal is to climb the Grand Teton, this is not the job for you. Your goal should be helping teenagers get up the Grand Teton, and helping them to learn about themselves and others at the same time. All applicants must be at least twenty-one and have valid CPR and first-aid certification (Wilderness First Reponder Certification is strongly encouraged). A nice wage and all trip expenses are provided. Applications can be downloaded from their website or send off your resume to begin the application process.

That is what learning is. You suddenly understand something you've understood all your life, but in a new way. —DORIS LESSING

93

For More Information:
Maury Wray, Personnel Coordinator
Wilderness Ventures
P.O. Box 2768
Jackson Hole, WY 83001
(800) 533-2281 • (307) 733-2122 • (307) 739-1934 (fax)
maury@wildernessventures.com

THE WORLD OUTDOORS

Adventure Travel • Worldwide • Seasonal
www.theworldoutdoors.com

Since 1988, World Outdoors has been offering high-quality services to individuals seeking adventure in the the outdoors along with learning the skills necessary to enjoy these activities. Sampler and multisport adventures combine hiking, sea kayaking, rock climbing, canyoneering, white-water rafting, horseback riding, or mountain biking all over the Rockies and the Southwest, as well as escapes to Alaska, Hawaii, Canada, Mexico, Belize, Costa Rica, Dominican Republic, Cuba, Australia, and New Zealand.

What You'll Be Doing: Tour leaders guide groups in backcountry biking, hiking, and multisport adventures, which feature both inn-to-inn and camping retreats over a six- to eight-day period. Yes, this means you might pedal along the shores of glacier-fed lakes, hike through an ancient rain forest, paddle the white water of a raging river, and sea kayak among sea lions all in the same trip! Internships are also available for those who are interested in the programming aspects of their activities.

Commitment: In-depth guide training is held each April. Most leaders spend two to four weeks per month on tour, with time off between trips, through October. A first-year leader can expect to work six to ten trips.

Perks and Rewards: Tour-leader wages begin at $50 per day, along with room and board during each trip. Tips from guests can also be expected, ranging from $200 to $400 per trip. All staff are expected to find their own living arrangements between trips.

The Essentials: Work as a tour leader is exciting and demanding. Those who have excellent people skills, thorough regional knowledge, and thrive in social situations fit the basic profile of their guides. Applicants must be at least twenty-five years old and, at a minimum, have Wilderness First Responder or equivalent certification. Leaders must also provide their own mountain bikes, helmets, first-aid kits, bike racks, and other personal gear (which can also be purchased through a discount program).

For More Information:
Jeff Martin, Director of Operations
The World Outdoors
2840 Wilderness Place
Boulder, CO 80301
(800) 488-8483 • (303) 413-0938 • (303) 413-0926 (fax)
jeffdmartin@earthlink.com

WYMAN CENTER

Experiential Education • Missouri • Seasonal
www.wymancenter.org

Known for being the oldest continuously operating youth camp west of the Mississippi (for over one hundred years), Wyman is an innovative experiential education center serving youth and adults from diverse backgrounds. Programs focus on youth development, environmental awareness, group dynamics, diversity, and enhancing self-esteem. Throughout the year, seasonal staff members instruct and facilitate groups in adventure, environmental, and life-skills programs. Along with extensive training, a $250 per week stipend, housing, and meals are provided. Applicants must be at least eighteen years of age and have interest in and experience working with children, excellent communication and leadership skills, flexibility, a strong work ethic, and a healthy sense of humor. Past staff members have said Wyman offers great training, a wonderful learning experience, and very rewarding work.

For More Information:
Cheryl Riley, Vice President Camping Services
Wyman Center
600 Kiwanis Dr.
Eureka, MO 63025
(636) 938-5245 • (636) 938-5289 (fax)
info@wymancenter.org

HOSTEL-STYLE ADVENTURES

Suppose that the thoughtful young people of all countries could be provided with suitable meeting places where they could get to know each other. That could and must be the role of our youth hostels, not only in Germany, but throughout the world, building a bridge of peace from nation to nation.

—RICHARD SCHIRRMANN, **father of the hosteling movement**

Short of camping on the roadside, hostels are by far the least expensive places to rest your weary head for the night, with costs ranging from $5 to $40 per night. The six thousand hostels scattered across the globe vary widely, from lighthouses, tree forts, and home hostels to ranch bunkhouses, Victorian buildings, mountain huts, and medieval castles—each with a personality and charm of its own.

One thing is certain about hostels: they are usually crammed with other budget-conscious folks and happy wanderers who are looking for the same things that you are—adventure and excitement. Many hostels are dormitory-style and separated by gender, while others offer private rooms (for a few dollars more) for those traveling together or if you desire a good night's rest. Hostels generally supply a bed and a blanket; you just need to bring your own sleepsack (or sleeping bag). Many provide do-it-yourself kitchens, lockers, laundry facilities, and common areas to discuss global events with people from the world over.

Hosteling is perhaps best described as traveling cheaply with an adventurous spirit. You see the world from a perspective that the average tourist will never see. You meet local people, learn customs, eat local food, and often have opportunities to do things you never imagined. Budget hotels, pensions (family-owned inns), university dorms, and bed-and-breakfasts provide alternatives to hostels for the same or slightly higher costs.

FINDING OUT MORE

Been there, done that? If you've explored the world hostel-style, you can now share your enthusiasm with others by volunteering at one of the many hostels throughout the U.S. with the help of Hostelling International–American Youth Hostels (HI-AYH). Positions range from travel workshop presenters and information center specialists to community service leaders and event hosts. If you have a skill, there's a good chance they'll have a position for you. Beyond meeting fellow volunteers and hostelers from around the world, you can accrue hours toward free hostel overnights, free memberships, and travel service discounts. The national office has a searchable database of current opportunities. Visit www.hiayh.org/programs/volunteer.htm or contact Hostelling International–American Youth Hostels, 733 15th St., NW, Suite 840, Washington, D.C. 20005; (202) 783-6161, volunteer@hiayh.org, www.hiayh.org.

The word hostel does not describe a place; it describes an attitude, a philosophy, a coming together of culturally diverse people sharing the wonders, high and low, of the traveling adventure.

—JANET THOMAS, **author of**
At Home in Hostel Territory
(Alaska Northwest Books; $12.95)

You gain strength, courage, and confidence by every experience in which you really stop to look fear in the face. —ELEANOR ROOSEVELT

HOSTEL-STYLE ADVENTURES

An investment in HI-AYH membership will help get you connected to the hosteling movement. A one-year membership card is $25, which includes a complimentary guide to HI-AYH hostels in Canada and the U.S., plus newsletters from a regional office. The membership also allows members to receive discounts while staying at HI-AYH sponsored hostels.

Many travelers have also turned their short stay at a hostel into a three- to six-month experience by working for HI-AYH. For instance, the Malta Youth Hostels Association operates a year-round work camp and focuses on helping people who come in need of shelter. Volunteers, aged sixteen to thirty, may receive free lodging and breakfast for two weeks to three months in exchange for three hours of work per day on various projects including hostel maintenance and administration. To apply, send three international reply coupons (which you can get at a local post office) or $2, and detailed information and an application form will be sent to you. Your completed application should be sent at least three months prior to your arrival date. Malta Youth Hostels Association Workcamp, 17, Triq Tal-Borg, Pawla, PLA 06, Malta; (011) 356-693957, myha@keyworld.net.

For a moment we smile, striving to pull down barriers quickly. Strangers becoming friends, we only have a small amount of time. Tomorrow . . . you go north, I go south. Adventures in travel, seeking new experiences. This moment is special. Our lives were meant to touch, to share. My life is richer because I have met you. There have been so many people like you in the youth hostels of the world.

—REDWOOD NATIONAL PARK
YOUTH HOSTEL JOURNAL

GATHERING MORE INFO

Everything you ever wanted to know about hosteling and the hostel movement can be found at **Hostels.com.** Along with advice, stories, budget travel resources, and a backpacker bookstore, visitors can search for information on any hostel in the world.

Are you headed to Canada? **Backpackers Hostels Canada** (www.backpackers.ca) provides links to hostels, retreat centers, campgrounds, guest houses, college residences, and hostel farms throughout North America (including the U.S. and Mexico). Accommodations generally run about $17CAN to $22CAN per person.

A must for information on cheap places to sleep in the U.S. and Canada is Jim Williams's *The Hostel Handbook* (www.hostelhandbook.com). This guide provides contact information and prices for more than six hundred Hostelling International hostels, independent hostels, and backpacker's bungalows. The information is extremely fresh, with a new edition of this pocket-sized guide released early every year (usually in March). A lifelong traveler and incredible cook, the author keeps busy by running his own hostel, the Sugar Hill International House, in New York City (which is conveniently located off the A-train express near 145th Street). If you do stay at his hostel, be sure to ask about the "six barstool" Texas Star, which serves up great food at 1950s prices. His handbook is available at independent hostels, book-stores, or by sending a check or money order for $5 (which includes shipping) directly to the author: Jim Williams, 722 St. Nicholas Ave., New York, NY 10031; (212) 926-7030, infohostel@aol.com.

From hostels that provide a real family spirit to those you might want to bypass altogether, **Hostels USA** (Globe Pequot Press, $15.95) details more than three hundred hostels throughout the country. With a new edition released every other year, this comprehensive and witty guide provides engaging descriptions, stories, and guest comments that will assist everyone from the "serious" hosteler to those who might want a romantic getaway. Author Paul Karr also has an entourage of other hostel guides that will take you beyond North America. Titles include hostel reviews for Austria/Switzerland, Belgium/Netherlands/Luxembourg, Canada, Europe, France/Italy, Germany, Ireland, or the United Kingdom (with the option of purchasing the book in PDF format for some titles).

When Tom Dennard takes a vacation from his day-to-day life, he makes the best of it in adventures that address the testing of self and self-discovery. Stories in his book, **Discovering Life's Trails: Adventures in Living** (Rainbow Books, $14.95), illustrate how he has managed to accommodate the realities of everyday life but still follow his dreams. The final chapter is a letter to his daughter (to share with her sons), which offers sixteen short essays addressing love, learning, and living. His own extensive travel experience around the globe introduced him to hosteling, which prompted his desire to build a hostel of his own, A Hostel in the Forest, where guests check in at a geodesic dome and can sleep in a bunkhouse or a private tree-house suite. To get your

own copy of his book or to learn more about staying at his hostel, call (912) 264-9738 or write A Hostel in the Forest, P.O. Box 1496, Brunswick, GA 31521; www.foresthostel.com.

BEYOND HOSTELS

If you ever imagined stepping into a simpler lifestyle, without the worry of rent or making a living, you might check out the opportunities listed in **The Caretaker Gazette** (www.caretaker.org). This unique bimonthly newsletter lists more than 130 caretaker and house-sitting positions throughout the U.S. and as far away as Australia or Costa Rica, at properties including estates, farms, ranches, resort homes, or even a private island. Yes, that's over eight hundred opportunities per year! Duties range from general house and property upkeep to land restoration, cooking, and organic farming. Caretakers are provided with free housing and some positions include meals and salaries. A one-year subscription is available for $29. Visit the Gazette online or call (715) 426-5500.

For a longer-term hiatus to rejuvenate the soul, you might consider spending some time at a retreat center. Work-study programs are offered at a variety of eco-villages, monasteries, yoga institutes, and Zen centers throughout the world. Explore your options in the "Food for the Soul" section on page 235.

Growth means change and change involves risks, stepping from the known to the unknown. —GEORGE SHINN

RECOMMENDED RESOURCES. . . . .

The Alaska Wilderness Recreation and Tourism Association (www.awrta.org) serves as the statewide wilderness guide and ecotourism professional organization. For $10, they will provide you with the *Alaska Adventure Source Book,* a gold mine of resources for any mountain, naturalist, rafting, paddling, or ski guide who is interested in work in Alaska. For more information contact the Alaska Wilderness Recreation and Tourism Association, 2207 Spenard Rd., Suite 201, Anchorage, AK 99503; (907) 258-3171, info@awrta.org.

The Association for Experiential Education (AEE) is a great way to begin your journey in experiential/outdoor education, and their website (www.aee.org) will fill you in with all the details. You'll learn about the benefits of becoming a member ($55 for students) or how to get involved in their next regional or international conference (a great way to network). In addition, AEE's Jobs Clearinghouse Online will provide you with information on hundreds of current seasonal, internship, and career jobs in the field. AEE can also be reached by calling (303) 440-8844.

If you are an aspiring outdoor enthusiast, **The Outdoor Network** (www.outdoornetwork.com) is a great starting point to explore the possibilities. Their website features the "Outdoor JobNet" which lists hundreds of internship and job opportunities in the field (and you can post your resume for free). Subscribe to their e-newsletter to catch the latest industry news, conferences, and jobs, or become a member and receive their forty-page quarterly newsletter. The Outdoor Network also relies on college interns (in part) to assist with various functions that keep its office up and running on a daily basis. Volunteer internships typically last from two to three months, with perks

including free outdoor gear, expenses paid for travel, and participation in outdoor industry conferences and trade shows. For more information contact the Outdoor Network, P.O. Box 1928, Boulder, CO 80306-1928; (800) 688-6387, editor@outdoornetwork.com.

Sailors and aspiring sailors can choose from over two hundred **American Sailing Association** schools, sailing clubs, and charter companies throughout North America and the Caribbean (all of which are listed on their website www.american-sailing.com). In addition, many of these sailing schools offer weeklong courses and noninstructional trips to exotic locations throughout the world. For more information contact the American Sailing Association, 13922 Marquesas Way, Marina del Rey, CA 90292-6000; (310) 822-7171, info@american-sailing.com.

If you're on a starboard tack and the wind veers, will you get lifted or headed? You'll learn the answer to this question, plus much more, by enrolling in **Offshore's Learn to Sail Program.** This program offers some invaluable experiences and unexpected lessons on the ABCs of sailing. When you finish this course, you should be able to day sail a sailboat of up to thirty feet without an instructor or paid skipper. The curriculum is based on seeing it, hearing it, and then going out and doing it. School locations include New Jersey, New York, Connecticut, Rhode Island, Florida, Illinois, and Tortola in the Caribbean. For more information contact the Offshore Sailing School, 16731 McGregor Blvd., Fort Myers, FL 33908; (800) 221-4326, sail@offshore-sailing.com, www.offshore-sailing.com.

Getting paid for what you love to do is the common theme within the pages of this section. Whether you are guiding kids at a summer camp, teaching adults how to ski at a resort, or strumming your guitar at the nightly campfire of a dude ranch, this section will provide you with insights and options on taking part in unique opportunities in unique places.

The luckiest people in the world are those who get to do all year round what they most like to do during their summer vacation.

—MARK TWAIN

Unique Opportunities to Explore in This Section:

- Are you ready to feel like a kid again—but with a lot more responsibility? Thousands of camp counselors travel to unique places each summer to share their skills, talents, and zest for life while mentoring, inspiring, and teaching kids in the pursuit of adventure and fun. Whether teaching surf classes (page 150) or academic and personal growth skills (page 147), or, perhaps leading global awareness workshops (page 121) or making musical instruments (page 112), you'll have plenty of exciting programs to explore in this section.

- Participation in meditation, yoga, and a Native American pipe and sweat-lodge ceremony are just a few of the unique opportunities that lie within a special place called Hidden Creek Ranch (page 118).

- Come explore the wonders of the Florida Keys, a place once inhabited by Indians and pirates, and minutes from the only living coral reef in North America. Instructors and camp counselors at Seacamp help participants gain a better understanding of the natural features of the ocean and its ecosystems, along with instructing them in activities ranging from sailing to scuba (page 128).

- Are you looking for a winter filled with glades, half-pipes, parks, bowls, and cruisers? What's that, you ask? Yes, skiers and snowboarders have a jargon of their own—just one of the many things you'll learn by working at a ski resort. This special section profiles forty of the best ski resorts along with all the details of the work, the rewards, and landing the job (page 129)!

Photo Credit: Eagle's Nest Foundation

99

Fresh air, mountain music, laughter, love, and unique learning experiences abound at Eagle's Nest Camp (page 112). This summer counselor demonstrates the art of raku firing to a camper at the natural arts arena.

CAMPS, RANCHES, AND RESORTS

ACADEMIC STUDY ASSOCIATES

Education • USA/England/France/Spain • Summer
www.asaprograms.com

ACADEMIC STUDY ASSOCIATES (ASA) offers innovative and challenging summer programs for middle- and high-school students. College-prep programs are offered at University of Massachusetts at Amherst, Emory University (in Georgia), UC Berkeley, and Oxford University (in England), along with study-abroad programs in Barcelona, Nice, and Oxford. Resident advisors live with a group of six to twelve students (depending on the program) and are responsible for their general well-being along with helping them prepare for the responsibilities of college. Extracurricular programming includes athletics, crafts, discussion groups, dances, cultural events, and literary magazine production. The ideal candidates are energetic, enthusiastic, and multitalented upperclassmen in college. Previous leadership experience and/or residence-life experience is strongly recommended. A weekly stipend of $300, along with room, board, and a travel stipend (for programs outside the U.S.) is provided. Those with teaching experience should inquire about short-term faculty openings. Applications are available online and personal interviews are held throughout the country.

For More Information:
Summer Staff Opportunities
Academic Study Associates
10 New King St.
White Plains, NY 10604
(800) 752-2250 • (914) 686-7730 • (914) 686-7740 (fax)
summerstaff@asaprograms.com

AMELIA ISLAND PLANTATION

Resort • Florida • 16 Weeks
www.aipfl.com

NOTED FOR THEIR environmentally conscious development, Amelia Island Plantation is known in Florida for being the greenest resort. This 1,350-acre gated resort and residential community offers miles of sandy beach in a preserved natural setting, along with many amenities. Internships have been offered at the resort for over twenty years, with many former interns now in various management positions (including the internship coordinator)!

What You'll Be Doing: Internships are offered in a variety of resort areas, including aquatics, social recreation, culinary education, corporate recreation, golf and tennis, environmental interpretation, marketing, recreation rental and retail, and turf management.

Commitment: Internships are offered throughout the year (spring, summer, and fall), and a sixteen-week minimum commitment is preferred (although some interns stay as long as forty-eight weeks).

Perks and Rewards: A housing stipend of $225 per week and two meals per workday are provided for most positions. Other positions receive an hourly wage in lieu of the stipend and meals. Other perks include assistance in locating housing, extensive training, and use of the amenities at discounted rates.

The Essentials: The resort recruits juniors and seniors, who must be receiving academic credit, at universities and colleges. Previous related experience (paid or unpaid) is a plus and a clean driving record is a requirement to even be considered for many areas. In addition, all candidates must be fluent in conversational English and provide their own transportation.

Your First Move: Applicants can request information through email or by calling. Be sure to indicate your area of interest and the semester you are required to intern so that the appropriate information may be sent. It's best to apply at least two months before the start date.

For More Information:
Barbara Ross, Internship Coordinator
Amelia Island Plantation
P.O. Box 3000
Amelia Island, FL 32035-3000
(904) 277-5904 • (904) 491-4345 (fax)
intern@aipfl.com

AMERICAN CAMPING ASSOCIATION— NEW YORK SECTION

Camp • New York • Summer
www.acampjob4u.org

Do YOU NEED a quick and easy way to get in touch with over three hundred summer camps on the East Coast? Well, look no further than the American Camping Association—New York Section, who will assist you with finding the perfect summer job. Member camps (from New York to Maine) are looking for both young and older

BEAVER RUN RESORT

Resort • Colorado • Seasonal
www.beaverrun.com

WITH SKIING AT Breckenridge Ski Resort out your back door during the winter months and hiking, mountain biking, fly-fishing, white-water rafting, and outdoor music festivals during the summer, Beaver Run Resort is the perfect destination for the outdoor enthusiast. A variety of hospitality, guest services, and lodging positions as well as college internships are offered seasonally. Wages start at $8.50 per hour and limited employee housing in shared and fully furnished apartments (two to three people per room) is available for $300 to $350 per month, per person. The latest openings, along with application materials, can be found through their website. Applicants are encouraged to stop in for a personal interview.

For More Information:
Personnel Director
Beaver Run Resort
P.O. Box 2115
Breckenridge, CO 80424-2115
(800) 288-1282, ext. 8737 • (970) 453-8737
(970) 453-9351 (fax)
work@beaverrun.com

BRUSH RANCH CAMPS

Camp • New Mexico • Summer
www.brushranchcamps.com

WITH TWO PRIVATE properties surrounded by the Santa Fe National Forest, Brush Ranch Camps offers a unique combination of arts, sports, and outdoor programs for children and teens. The original ranch consists of almost two hundred acres with the Pecos River running right through the middle of the property. Facilities include everything from a pottery studio and dance pavilion to a ropes challenge course and archery range. A variety of summer seasonal positions are offered, including counselors (with activities that range from nature study to fencing), trip leaders/facilitators, resource coordinator, office assistant, maintenance staff, and cooks. The base pay starts at $160 per week along with room and board. Applicants must be dedicated, fun loving, and at least nineteen years of age. Call or email for an application packet.

Challenging campers to make it the top of a climbing wall is just one of the many activities for an American Camping Association summer staff member.

adults (at least eighteen years of age) to work as general counselors, activity specialists, outdoor-adventure leaders, and support staff—opportunities that will definitely help you develop your leadership skills while making a difference in the lives of our youth. Room, board, and a salary are always provided for residential-camp positions (day-camp applicants must live within commuting distance; thus room and board is not provided). Positions begin around mid-June and last for eight to ten weeks, but don't delay; it's never too early to apply!

For More Information:
Robin Katz, Director of Camp Staffing Services
American Camping Association—New York Section
1375 Broadway, 4th Floor
New York, NY 10018
(800) 777-2267 • (212) 391-5208 • (212) 391-5207 (fax)
robin@aca-ny.org

For More Information:
Tamara Osburn, Staffing Director
Brush Ranch Camps
P.O. Box 5759
Santa Fe, NM 87502-5759
(800) 722-2843 • (505) 757-8821 • (505) 757-8822 (fax)
brc@nmfiber.com

C LAZY U RANCH

Guest Ranch • Colorado • Seasonal
www.clazyu.com

AT C LAZY U RANCH, there's still plenty of room to stretch out. Time to relax. A range to ride. Mountains to explore. Fish to catch. All simple pleasures to experience.

What You'll Be Doing: Working at C Lazy U is a great opportunity for folks who want hands-on experience in a resort setting. A large seasonal staff is hired each summer and winter with positions including wranglers, counselors (kid wranglers), housekeepers, kitchen help, waitstaff, bartenders, ranch hands, gardeners, and office help (the winter season adds on a cross-country ski instructor).

Commitment: The summer season runs from mid-May through mid-October, although the core season is from late May through Labor Day. The winter season is a short one month from mid-December to mid-January (an ideal time for college students looking for work during their holiday break).

Perks and Rewards: Compensation consists of a base pay of $800 per month, along with meals and bunkhouse-style housing (with two to four people per room). The biggest perk is joining guests in activities and entertainment during time off.

The Essentials: Good people skills are a must for all positions. Those who are enthusiastic, considerate, and genuinely friendly as well as hard workers and service-minded make the best staff members. Self-starters who can work with minimum supervision are also an asset. Counselor positions and wranglers must have riding experience. At minimum, applicants must be at least eighteen years of age and preference is given to those who can work at least through Labor Day for summer employment.

Your First Move: Applications are accepted for summer jobs beginning January 1; for winter, starting September 1. It's noted that you should give careful consideration to the dates of availability you list, which is instrumental in the decision-making process. You'll find applications on the Web.

Experience the American West with C Lazy U Ranch, where the lifestyle of the American cowboy lingers.

Photo Credit: C Lazy U Ranch

For More Information:
Tim Hennen, Guest Services Manager
C Lazy U Ranch
P.O. Box 379
Granby, CO 80446
(970) 887-3344 • (970) 887-3917 (fax)
ranch@clazyu.com

CAMP CHATUGA

Camp • South Carolina • Summer
www.campchatuga.com

CAMP CHATUGA IS a small, independent camp for boys and girls from six to sixteen, with a focus on developing their potential intellectually, emotionally, spiritually, and physically in a fun and relaxed natural environment. A job at Chatuga is not a summer vacation—it is work. It is mentally and physically exhausting, but unbelievably rewarding. Can you live without alcohol, tobacco, perfect hair, privacy, a Walkman, air-conditioning, a VCR, a predictable schedule, and lots of money? If you answered yes, then this may be the job for you. Nine-week summer positions include counselor, nanny, dining hall supervisor, waterfront supervisor, horseback supervisor, outdoor-program supervisor, health supervisor, health lodge counselor, mechanic, and maintenance crew. Pre-camp training helps staff members earn or renew certifications. Staff members receive $165 per week, plus free room and board. Salaries go up based on education, experience, and certifications. Other perks include free trips, laundry, and a staff T-shirt.

For More Information:
Kelly Moxley, Personnel Director
Camp Chatuga
291 Camp Chatuga Rd.
Mountain Rest, SC 29664
(864) 638-3728 • (864) 638-0898 (fax)
mail@campchatuga.com

CAMP COURAGE

Therapeutic Camp • Minnesota • 3 or 9 Months
www.couragecamps.org

CAMP COURAGE IS a residential environmental and outdoor education center with most of the teaching done outside! Students in the fourth through eighth grades will learn how to survive in the woods, predict the weather, canoe, and snowshoe, as well as gain an understanding of topics such as which critters live in the pond or what feed birds prefer. During the summer months, the camp becomes a barrier-free residential camp for people of all ages with a physical disability.

What You'll Be Doing: Environmental education staff prepare the camp and provide teaching and hosting for the various school groups. Duties include teaching environmental education and outdoor recreation classes, assisting with program development, and working on a special project. Once per month seasonal staff work with the respite program to gain experience working with special populations.

Commitment: Positions are available for three months during each season of the year or for nine months beginning each September.

Perks and Rewards: Room, board, and a monthly living allowance are provided.

The Essentials: Applicants must have at least two years of college, with classes in the natural sciences, recreation, or education fields. Consistent and appropriate leadership of children is vital, as are good communication skills. A qualified individual must be able to enthusiastically lead outdoor activities one day, then clean cabins or help in the kitchen the next.

For More Information:
Environmental Education Coordinator
Camp Courage
8046 83rd St., NW
Maple Lake, MN 55358
(320) 963-3121 • (320) 963-3698 (fax)
eecccourage@yahoo.com

CAMP COURAGEOUS OF IOWA

Therapeutic Camp • Iowa • 1–4 Months
www.campcourageous.org

CAMP COURAGEOUS OF Iowa, surrounded by hundreds of acres of state and county land, is a year-round camp founded on the belief that children and adults with disabilities have the right to opportunities found in the world around them. Campers with mental and physical disabilities, hearing and visual impairments, autism, brain injuries, and other distinct groups are served. Counselors supervise the health, well-being, and personal care of groups of campers and ensure that they have a

*It is good to realize that if love and peace can prevail on earth, and if we can teach our children to honor nature's gifts, the joys and beauties of the outdoors will be here forever. —*JIMMY CARTER

successful and enjoyable time. Activity specialists develop and implement everything from canoeing, camping, crafts, and nature activities to rock climbing, rappelling, caving, and the high- and low-ropes course. Full-time positions are offered from one to four months throughout the year, and the hours are long (generally sixty to eighty hours per week). Interns and volunteers receive a salary of $100 per month; seasonal staff receive $230 per week; and year-round staff receive up to $330 per week. All receive room and board. Candidates should have flexibility and patience. A genuine desire to give your time, energy, and enthusiasm to others is a must.

For More Information:
Jeanne Muellerleile, Camp Director
Camp Courageous of Iowa
12007 190th St.
P.O. Box 418
Monticello, IA 52310-0418
(319) 465-5916, ext. 206 • (319) 465-5919 (fax)
jmuellerleile@campcourageous.org

Working with children and adults with disabilities is an experience you will never forget.

CAMP HIGH ROCKS

Boys' Camp • North Carolina • Summer
www.highrocks.com

Camp High Rocks is a relatively small boys' camp with a staff-to-camper ratio of approximately one to three, insuring a high degree of individual attention for each boy. Activities include hiking, backpacking, mountain biking, rock climbing, English horseback riding, and water activities (from swimming to an extensive river canoeing and kayaking program). Counselors must have completed one year of college, be competent in their teaching field, and have an understanding of and interest in children. An extensive counselor training program is offered to staff before the camp begins. Counselor salaries range from $1,800 to $2,700 for the nine-week season, depending on qualifications. Room, board, laundry, and a two-day Wilderness Medical Associates Wilderness First Aid course are provided.

For More Information:
Hank Birdsong, Camp Director
Camp High Rocks
P.O. Box 210
Cedar Mountain, NC 28718-0210
(828) 885-2153 • (828) 884-4612 (fax)
staffinfo@highrocks.com

CAMP HIGHLAND OUTDOOR SCIENCE SCHOOL

Science School • California • Seasonal
www.camphighland.net

Camp Highland Outdoor Science School is an innovative residential grade-school science program in the foothills of the San Bernardino Mountains, just fifty miles from Joshua Tree National Park. During the spring and fall, outdoor education field/cabin instructors have the opportunity to teach over twenty classes, including archaeology, botany, ecology (wildlife, forest, mountain, and desert), entomology, canoeing, climbing, archery, ropes course, team building, and outdoor living skills. Summer staff members continue teaching the environmental curriculum, while providing additional recreational opportunities in horseback riding, water activities, and an adventure-trip program. Wages start at $45 per day, plus room and board. To begin the application process, send a resume, cover letter, and three references.

For More Information:
Director
Camp Highland Outdoor Science School
10600 Highland Springs Ave.
Cherry Valley, CA 92223
(909) 572-2020 • (909) 845-8090 (fax)
info@camphighland.net

CAMP LA JOLLA

Fitness Camp • California • Summer
www.camplajolla.com

Camp La Jolla is dedicated to providing preteens and teens, as well as women of all ages, with a nationally acclaimed fitness and weight-loss program. Just a short walk from the sandy beaches of the Pacific Ocean, programs are held on the beautiful campus of UC San Diego, with boundless recreational and educational opportunities. Live-in resident counselors—who also serve as teachers, parents, disciplinarians, brothers/sisters, and best friends to campers—provide sports and physical fitness activities (from aerobics to surfing) as well as nutrition education, behavior modification, field trips, and evening programs. A salary of $100 to $150 per week is provided, along with room and board. Applications are available online.

For More Information:
Nancy Lenhart, Founder and Executive Director
Camp La Jolla
176 C Ave.
Coronado, CA 92118
(800) 825-8746 • (619) 435-7990 • (619) 435-8188 (fax)
camplj@aol.com

CAMP SEALTH

Ocean-Based Camp • Washington • Seasonal
www.campfirecpsc.org

LOCATED ON AN island in the Puget Sound, Camp Sealth is a year-round resident camp that operates environmental education programs for school groups during the spring and fall along with a summer camp for youth ages six to seventeen. During the fall and spring environmental-education specialists plan and lead activities and lessons that enable students to explore and learn about the natural environment. A challenge course, team building, and group living are also important parts of this unique program. A variety of camp staff—from counselors and program specialists to rovers and program coordinators—are hired during the summer months. A wage of $140 to $250 per week is provided along with room and board. If you are an energetic, team-oriented, and child-focused person with a variety of skills, talents, and drive, Camp Sealth may have a place for you! Details and applications are available online.

For More Information:
Camp Director/Staff Applications
Camp Sealth
14500 S.W. Camp Sealth Rd.
Vashon Island, WA 98070-8222
(206) 463-3174, ext. 34 • (206) 463-6936 (fax)
campstaff@campfirecpsc.org

CANOE ISLAND FRENCH CAMP

Camp/French Language • Washington • Summer
www.rockisland.com/~canoe

A LITTLE BIT of France on a secluded island in the Pacific Northwest? Yes, French themes are at the heart of Canoe Island, where campers are able to learn about the language, history, and culture of France—everything from French cooking and language classes to fencing and art history. With Canoe Island's unique location in the San Juan Islands, afternoons are filled with sailing, canoeing, kayaking, and swimming. Because of the camp's small size (approximately forty campers in grades three through nine), the eighteen summer staff members can focus more on each individual, inspiring them to learn and experience a slower pace of life. Each staff member also wears many "chapeaux," working as counselors, French teachers, and outdoor-activity instructors. A $250-per-week salary is provided, along with lodging and meals (where "passez-moi le pain!" is the only way to ask for the bread). Lodging on days off is also provided in private, waterfront accommodations. Obviously language proficiency in French and English is required; applications are accepted December through March.

For More Information:
Richard Carter, Director
Canoe Island French Camp
P.O. Box 370
Orcas Island, WA 98280-0370
(360) 468-2329 • (360) 468-3027 (fax)
canoe@rockisland.com

CATALINA ISLAND CAMPS

Ocean-Based Camp • California • Summer
www.catalinaislandcamps.com

LOCATED ON THE remote west end of Catalina Island, Catalina Island Camps (CIC) offers a unique island experience for boys and girls entering third to tenth grade. While many camps allow campers to choose their own activities, the backbone of the CIC experience is group-centered, which allows campers to benefit from living and playing with the same group of peers.

What You'll Be Doing: First and foremost, the job as a CIC counselor is an opportunity to have a lasting positive impact on the lives of children twenty-four hours per day, while helping them to develop an appreciation of the natural environment. A big part of the job is encouraging campers to try new things and to help push them beyond their comfort level (with the goal of helping them to overcome fears and increase their self-respect). Positions include boys' and girls' counselors, waterfront specialists (sailing, waterskiing, and skin diving), land specialists (from ropes course instructors to outdoor-cooking specialists), and administrative and leadership positions.

Perks and Rewards: Salaries range from $160 to $175 per week, and a $25 per week completion bonus is also added to the final paycheck. Housing and meals are shared with the campers, so privacy will be minimal. The cabins are rustic one-room, single-wall structures with canvas covers over the windows.

The Essentials: Successful counselors are dynamic, energetic, and patient people who thrive on being outdoors and recognize that children need support and encouragement to be responsible adults. Candidates must be at least nineteen years of age, have CPR/first-aid certification (and lifeguard certification for waterfront specialists), and be available for the entire season (approximately mid-June through the third week of August).

Your First Move: CIC hires staff on a rolling basis, so the earlier you apply the better. Applications are available online.

For More Information:
Tom and Maria Horner, Camp Directors
Catalina Island Camps
P.O. Box 94146
Pasadena, CA 91109
(800) 696-2267 • (626) 296-4040 • (626) 794-1401 (fax)
jobs@catalinaislandcamps.com

CCUSA-WORK EXPERIENCE DOWN UNDER

Educational Travel • Australia/New Zealand • 3 Months
www.ccusa.com

CCUSA/WORK EXPERIENCE DOWN UNDER (WEDU) offers the opportunity for independent and adventurous Americans between the ages of eighteen and thirty to work and travel in Australia and New Zealand (with work ranging from ski resorts to the hospitality field). WEDU will provide you with a highly coveted four-month visa

(sponsored by the Australian Government for Special Programs) that allows you to work up to three months, with the option of staying an additional three months on a tourist visa. Finding the work and the job is up to each applicant; however, WEDU provides you with the tools to get you on your feet, including job search assistance, an airport pickup, and two nights lodging. Fees start at $365.

For More Information:
Program Director
CCUSA/Work Experience Down Under
2330 Marineship Way, Suite 250
Sausalito, CA 94965
(800) 999-2267 • (415) 339-2728 • (415) 329-2744 (fax)
info@ccusa.com

CENTER FOR TALENTED YOUTH

Education • USA • Summer
www.jhu.edu/gifted/jobs

THE CENTER FOR Talented Youth at Johns Hopkins University is a comprehensive, university-based initiative that promotes the academic ability of children and youth throughout the world. Each summer, the center holds residential and commuter programs that provide the opportunity for participants to take rigorous courses in the humanities (music/art, history, social sciences/philosophy, history/politics, language, and writing) and math/science (lab science, computer science, and mathematics). Residential programs are offered at sixteen sites around the country and held on beautiful college campuses in California, Maryland/Washington, D.C., Massachusetts, New York, Pennsylvania, and Rhode Island.

What You'll Be Doing: This is a wonderful opportunity to work with unique and highly able youngsters in a dynamic setting. Positions include instructional (instructors, teaching assistants, laboratory assistants, and program assistants), residential assistants (similar to a college residential assistant), and administrative (residential program assistants, health assistants, site nurses, office managers, academic counselors, academic deans, dean of residential life, and site directors).

Commitment: Applicants must commit to two three-week sessions, beginning in late June and ending in early August.

Perks and Rewards: The starting salary for instructors ranges from $1,800 to $2,800 per three-week session while instructional assistants earn $900 and residential assistants earn $1,000. All staff members receive a private room in a college dormitory and meals.

The Essentials: Applicants are generally in college or are recent graduates. All candidates must be creative, energetic, and dynamic, and have the desire to work with children in an academic setting.

Your First Move: Candidates whose application materials are completed by the end of January will be considered first. Some openings occur late in the hiring process, so qualified candidates are encouraged to submit and/or complete their application files through June.

For More Information:
Summer Programs Employment
Center for Talented Youth
The Johns Hopkins University
2701 N. Charles St.
Baltimore, MD 21218
(410) 516-0053 • (410) 516-0093 (fax)
ctysummer@jhu.edu

CHINGACHGOOK YMCA OUTDOOR CENTER AND CAMP

Outdoor Education • New York • 3–9 Months
www.chingachgook.org

CHINGACHGOOK (pronounced chin-ja-cook), located on spectacular Lake George in the New York Adirondacks, provides year-round programs for over thirteen thousand children and young adults each year. More than 150 interns and seasonal staff keep things hopping at its outdoor-education school and summer camp, where they teach environmental, recreational, and outdoor education as well as lead teen adventure trips (which focus on hiking, canoeing, rock climbing, mountaineering, rafting, ice climbing, kayaking, and camping). Most positions are available from March through November with various time commitments. Stipends begin at $190 per week, along with room, board, and extensive training. Preferred applicants are at least twenty-one years of age with experience in the outdoor-adventure field. Send resume, cover letter, and three references (with contact information).

For More Information:
Kenis Sweet, Outdoor Education Director
Chingachgook YMCA Outdoor Center and Camp
1872 Pilot Knob Rd.

Kattskill Bay, NY 12844
(518) 656-9462, ext. 14 • (518) 656-9362 (fax)
ksweet@cdymca.org

CHRISTODORA-MANICE EDUCATION CENTER

Wilderness Education • New York • 3–12 Months
www.christodora.org

COORDINATING CAMPING PROGRAMS since 1908, Christodora provides challenging and rewarding environmental learning experiences to motivate urban youths who generally come from economically or experientially disadvantaged families in New York City. The center is a small, high-quality residential center in the Berkshire Mountains, with a strong emphasis on environmental education and adventure programs.

What You'll Be Doing: Field teachers educate and facilitate the growth, understanding, and development of students (ages eleven to eighteen) in program areas such as environmental sciences, wilderness, group initiatives, and leadership training. This might also include supervision of overnight trips and wilderness expeditions. Outdoor-education interns assist field teachers in program areas while developing skills to teach their own lessons in a supervised setting. Wilderness-leadership interns supervise and co-lead six- to nineteen-day courses with field teachers. Interns working through AmeriCorps will spend three months teaching environmental education in New York City and six months in Massachusetts teaching at the Manice Education Center.

Perks and Rewards: Field teachers receive a minimum stipend of $300 per week, while interns receive a minimum of $170 per week. Room, board, equipment discounts, and insurance coverage are also provided. There is an AmeriCorps educational award for a nine-to twelve-month commitment.

The Essentials: Field-teacher applicants must have a college degree; outdoor-education interns must have completed one year of college; and wilderness-leadership positions require a minimum of two years of college. All candidates must have a strong interest in the wilderness, interpretation, and experiential education. CPR, first-aid, and lifeguard certifications are preferred.

Your First Move: Submit resume, cover letter, and three references.

If you take any activity, any art, any discipline, any skill, take it and push it as far as it will go, push it beyond where it has ever been before, push it to the wildest edge of edges, then you force it into the realm of magic —TOM ROBBINS

107

For More Information:
Program Director
Christodora—Manice Education Center
One East 53rd St., 14th Floor
New York, NY 10022
(212) 371-5225 • (212) 371-2111 (fax)
christodora@prodigy.net

CLEARWATER CANOE OUTFITTERS AND LODGE

Lodge • Minnesota • Summer
www.canoebwca.com

THE MAIN LODGE of Clearwater Canoe Outfitters and Lodge was completed in 1926 and is listed on the National Register of Historic Places. The largest remaining whole-log structure in northeastern Minnesota, it has retained the look and feel of the pioneer days. A few secluded cabins and bed-and-breakfast rooms in the lodge itself offer an alternative to camping. The business prides itself on its wilderness-preservation ethic and consists of six to eight staff members. Seasonal positions include front desk, housekeeping, waterfront, maintenance, cook, naturalist, and outfitting packer. (Most staff work in more than one position.) A salary along with room and board are provided.

For More Information:
Marti and Bob Marchino, Directors
Clearwater Canoe Outfitters and Lodge
774 Clearwater Rd.
Grand Marais, MN 55604
(800) 527-0554 • (218) 388-2254 • (218) 388-2254 (fax)
info@canoebwca.com

CLUB MED

Adventure Travel • USA/Mexico/The Bahamas/
The Caribbean • 6 Months
www.clubmedjobs.com

KNOWN FOR ITS great locations, interesting architecture, and carefree lifestyle, Club Med is the pioneer of the all-inclusive resort, attracting thousands of adventurous singles and families each year. Be it snorkeling, indulging in a gourmet meal, or being entertained, the "voice of Club Med" is their team of ten thousand GOs (gentils organisateurs)—those "young, bouncy, and good look-ing" men and women from all around the world who do everything they can to make their enthusiasm contagious to the flock of GMs (gentils membres)—the guests!

What You'll Be Doing: Each year Club Med recruits over thirty-five hundred new GOs in all areas of expertise. GOs work hard giving sports instruction, being sociable, leading group activities and tours, or putting on evening entertainment. Basically, from the moment the GMs arrive until their farewell cocktail party, their Club Med experience is defined by the GOs they meet along the way.

Commitment: GOs must commit to at least six months; the summer season starts in May and the winter season begins in November.

Perks and Rewards: You don't work at Club Med to become a millionaire, but rather to explore a different lifestyle—and to have some fun! Still, you should be able to save most of your salary since Club Med covers almost all your expenses, including transportation from your home to the village, room and board (GOs are generally lodged two to a room), health-care coverage, and full use of the village's amenities.

The Essentials: In order to qualify for a job, you'll need a lot of energy and a love of entertaining. Ideal applicants have knowledge of a second language and must speak English.

Your First Move: All applicants must complete an online application. A few common-sense tips: pay careful attention to the qualifications requested (language requirements, degrees, experience, and availability) and, most importantly, be sure you communicate all your enthusiasm and energy in the interview.

For More Information:
GO Recruiter
Club Med
75 Valencia Ave., 12th Floor
Coral Gables, FL 33134
(888) 233-0362 • (305) 925-9217 • (305) 925-9305 (fax)
resumes@clubmed.com

COFFEE CREEK RANCH

Guest Ranch • California • Seasonal
www.coffeecreekranch.com

LOCATED ON 367 acres surrounded by national forest and the Trinity Alps Wilderness Area in Northern California, Coffee Creek Ranch guests experience trout fishing, hiking, riding, kayaking, wilderness pack trips, nordic skiing, health-spa use, gold panning, and use of the rifle range. Seasonal staff members are needed in the office, the front desk, accounting, and the kitchen (including prep chefs and bakers). Pay depends upon the position and season chosen, but generally runs $850 to $1,100 per month. Room, board, and use of the facilities at the ranch (including the exercise room and hot tub) are provided.

For More Information:
Alicia and Shane Ryan, Owners
Coffee Creek Ranch
HC2, Box 4940
Trinity Center, CA 96091-9502
(800) 624-4480 • (530) 266-3343 • (530) 266-3597 (fax)

The more versatile you are the better. We are looking for a person that never says, "Not my job!"

THE COLLEGE SETTLEMENT OF PHILADELPHIA

Camp • Pennsylvania • Seasonal
www.collegesettlement.org

THE COLLEGE SETTLEMENT of Philadelphia operates a day and resident summer camp and a residential outdoor school, mostly for seven- to fourteen-year-olds from economically disadvantaged families. Many of these children live in difficult situations and face challenging problems in their daily lives. The Teen Adventure Program offers a once-in-a-lifetime chance for urban youth to experience the thrill of camping, hiking, and adventuring on the East Coast. Summer adventure-trip leaders plan custom trips and activities and take their groups by van to West Virginia and various locations in New England (from the Blue Ridge Mountains to Cape Cod); summer camp staff—from counselors to activity leaders—teach and share experiences with children in a fun and caring environment; and spring and fall teacher/naturalists teach science and team-building activities. Summer wages start at $3,000 for the season ($225 per week for spring/fall staff), along with a $100 stipend, meals, and housing. Applicants should have experience in outdoor pursuits (climbing, backpacking, rafting, or kayaking preferred), be enthusiastic, work well with others, and have a sense of fun mixed with a great dose of common sense. Those who are open-minded and enjoy making a difference in others' lives are strongly encouraged to apply.

For More Information:
Andrew Fielding, Program Director
The College Settlement of Philadelphia
600 Witmer Rd.
Horsham, PA 19044
(215) 542-7974 • (215) 542-7457 (fax)
camps@i-bob.com

THE COLORADO MOUNTAIN RANCH

Camp • Colorado • Summer
www.coloradomountainranch.com

OWNED AND OPERATED by the Walker family since 1947, The Colorado Mountain Ranch provides a warm, friendly environment where individual growth and learning occur through confidence-building activities in an active outdoor setting. Adventurous programming abounds at the ranch, where campers can participate in everything from a challenge ropes course to Western horseback riding, hiking, and camping.

Your Surroundings: Nestled in the pine and aspen forests and wildflower meadows of Colorado's Rocky Mountains, the ranch encompasses 180 acres at an elevation of 8,500 feet. The camp is bordered on the east by the mining town of Gold Hill, and to the west, Roosevelt National Forest rises to the magnificent snowcapped peaks of the Continental Divide. Days are generally sunny and warm, nights are cool, and the air is usually crisp and clear.

What You'll Be Doing: Summer seasonal staff are instrumental in creating and implementing every aspect of ranch programs, activities, facility use, food service, and maintenance. Every job (ranging from activity instructors to wranglers) involves inspiring and guiding campers, participating enthusiastically in all daily activities, and embracing the Native American philosophy of respect for self, others, and nature.

Commitment: Staff training begins in early June, with camp finishing in mid-August. Only those who are available for the entire season will be considered.

Perks and Rewards: Depending on the position, first-year staff members will earn $1,500 to $1,800 per season, along with meals, housing, leadership training, and future personnel references. Living with others and working together as a team, staff members will grow in love and understanding of themselves, each other, and life. The mountain climate and setting are also perfect for a full range of healthful, outdoor activities, from swimming and hiking to camping and playing in the high-country snowfields.

The Essentials: Applicants must be at least eighteen and have completed high school, and are selected on the basis of abilities, enthusiasm, creativity, reliability, sincerity, sensitivity, and a commitment to guiding others toward their full potential.

Your First Move: Applications can be downloaded from their website. Once you have submitted your application materials, you are encouraged to call for a personal telephone interview.

For More Information:
Lynn, Gail, and Mike Walker, Owners
The Colorado Mountain Ranch
10063 Gold Hill Rd.
Boulder, CO 80302-9770
(800) 267-9573 • (303) 442-4557 • (303) 417-9114 (fax)
office@coloradomountainranch.com

*The Ranch is a song; it is a song
of happiness, of love, of peace, and of
understanding. It is a song that had a
beginning, but that can never die for too many
people have heard this song.
The intertwining of the melodies will continue
until the song has become a part of everyone
who has come here. That song will go out
from here in the hearts and minds
of those who know it and spread itself
and become a part of all it touches.
Let your song reflect that
which you are and will become here,
and carry it with you when you leave.*

COLORADO TRAILS RANCH

Guest Ranch • Colorado • Summer
www.coloradotrails.com

BEAUTIFUL MOUNTAIN SCENERY, hard work, and lots of fun are just a few of the elements that guest ranch staff experience every summer at Colorado Trails Ranch. Crew positions include chef, riding guide, housekeeping, server, floater, counselor, maintenance, and sports/utility staff. If you have a ready smile, are willing to work hard, love the outdoors, and enjoy working with people, the ranch may have a job for you. A weekly wage (plus bonus) is provided along with room and board.

For More Information:
John Loftis, Manager
Colorado Trails Ranch
12161 Country Road 240
Durango, CO 81301-6306
(800) 323-3833 • (970) 247-5055 • (970) 385-7372 (fax)
info@coloradotrails.com

COLVIG SILVER CAMPS

Camp • Colorado • Summer
www.colvigsilvercamps.com

LOCATED IN THE San Juan Mountains of southwest Colorado, Colvig Silver Camps (CSC) is a residential, wilderness-oriented summer camp serving children seven to seventeen years of age. The camp is a short drive or hike from high alpine regions (14,000-foot peaks), desert canyon areas (including Anasazi ruins), low alpine regions, mountain lakes and streams, raging rivers, and ponderosa pine forests. Their program is unique in that they offer a mix of traditional summer activities along with overnight backcountry wilderness trips.

What You'll Be Doing: This summer you could lead a climb up a 14,000-foot peak or a moonlight exploration of a desert canyon . . . or teach someone how to fish a mountain lake, raft a river, or set up camp in a ponderosa pine forest . . . and that's just for starters! Here's a quick overview of the possibilities: program coordinators organize and implement the camp's daily schedule; counselors are responsible for planning and leading in-camp activities and wilderness trips as well as living with a group of four to six campers; arts-and-crafts coordinators develop crafts programs for all age levels; wranglers are responsible for planning and teaching Western-style riding and tack care; the climbing coordinator supervises, plans, and instructs all climbing wall and natural rock-climbing activities; and the expedition coordinator packs food and equipment for all expedition trips leaving camp.

Commitment: The season begins in early June (with mandatory staff training) and continues through mid-August.

Perks and Rewards: A salary of $1,000 to $1,625 is provided, along with room, board, laundry, training, and wilderness first-aid certification for head counselors.

The Essentials: Ideally, applicants must have completed one year of college and have first-aid and CPR certifications.

Your First Move: Visit their website for detailed job descriptions and an online application. After your application is received, they follow up on your references, then schedule an on-site or phone interview. Positions are filled on a first-come, first-served basis.

For More Information:
Amie Podolsky and Andrew Notbohm
Program Directors
Colvig Silver Camps
9665 Florida Rd.
Durango, CO 81301
(800) 858-2850 • (970) 247-2564 • (970) 247-2547 (fax)
colvigsilvercamps@compuserve.com

I have been intimately associated with Colvig Silver Camps for seven years. I saw it in your book and just wanted to let you know that I think it is a wonderful place to work. I was a camper there for five years beginning when I was eleven; and later went back to work there as a counselor for two years. This camp was my initial introduction to outdoor recreation and obviously had some pretty amazing influences on me, being that I now want to pursue a career in that field.

*—AMIE PODOLSKY,
camper, summer staff,
and now program director CSC*

COULTER LAKE GUEST RANCH

Guest Ranch • Colorado • Seasonal
www.guestranches.com/coulterlake

LOCATED ON THE scenic western slopes of the Rockies, with a sparkling lake for swimming, fishing, and boating, Coulter Lake Guest Ranch has eight cabins scattered

Photo Credit: Colvig Silver Camps

With the help of summer staff members at Colvig Silver Camps, "outposters" take on a leadership role for expeditions through mountains, rivers, lakes, deserts, and canyons in the Rockies.

along the lakefront, among the aspen trees. Seasonal positions, which are available throughout the year, include housekeepers, food and beverage staff, wranglers/trail guides, and maintenance staff. Staff members receive $100 or more per week, along with a tip pool, housing, meals, necessities, laundry, and horseback riding. Coulter Lake prefers a healthy, wholesome, active, organized, responsible, and tactful person. To begin the application process, send a resume and cover letter describing job desired and a brief rundown on experience. A snapshot is appreciated. Phone interviews are conducted after your materials are received.

For More Information:
Jill McAlice, Manager
Coulter Lake Guest Ranch
80 County Road 273
Rifle, CO 81650
(800) 858-3046 • (970) 625-1473
coulter@sopris.net

CYBERCAMPS

Computer Camp • USA • Summer
www.cybercamps.com

ATTENTION COMPUTER NERDS: do you have a passion for teaching and technology? Then you might want to consider a summer with Cybercamps. It's all the fun of a traditional camp, but without all the mosquitoes (that's not to say camp programmers never find "bugs!"). As a division of Giant Campus, Cybercamps is a progressive, innovative company that provides experience-based learning for boys and girls, ages seven to sixteen, at colleges and universities across the country. Summer staff—including camp directors, assistant directors, and computer camp counselors—provide hands-on learning and exposure to cutting-edge technologies, including web design, 3D animation, robotics, game design, programming, and digital arts. Both day and residential camp experiences are offered and vary by location. The average salary is $300 per week along with meals. For residential locations, housing may be available; if not, Cybercamps does their best to help out. Applicants must be at least eighteen years old, have the knack for working with children, and know how to work in a team environment. A solid knowledge in web-page design, programming, design software, robotics, hardware, 3D animation, or network maintenance is essential. Applications can be found online.

For More Information:
Kat Fitzgerald, Director of Staffing
Cybercamps
Giant Campus
720 Olive Way, Suite 1800
Seattle, WA 98101
(888) 904-2267
summerjobs@cybercamps.net

DROWSY WATER RANCH

Guest Ranch • Colorado • Summer
www.drowsywater.com

NOTHING LESS THAN real down-home hospitality amid unforgettable mountain scenery—that's what you'll find at the Fosha family's home and 600-acre working ranch called Drowsy Water—where the guests experience a true western ranch experience. Each week fifty-five guests come to the ranch to "play" with the Foshas and seasonal staff who are there to feed them, house them, and entertain them. Summer positions include housekeeping, food servers, cooks, office workers, children's program counselors, and wranglers. Along with meeting people from all over the world, staff members will receive a monthly salary, room, meals, and gratuities. Applications can be obtained online.

For More Information:
Ken and Randy Sue Fosha, Summer Staffing
Drowsy Water Ranch
P. O. Box 147
Granby, CO 80446-0147
(800) 845-2292 • (970) 725-3456 • (970) 725-3611 (fax)
dwrken@aol.com

EAGLE'S NEST FOUNDATION

Outdoor Education • North Carolina • Seasonal
www.enf.org

WITH THE MISSION of promoting the natural world and the betterment of human character, Eagle's Nest Foundation coordinates a children's summer camp (celebrating more than seventy-five years) and the Outdoor Academy of the Southern Appalachians, a semester school for tenth graders. This school-away-from-school focuses on environmental education, regional studies, and the arts, and centers students and faculty in a close community life.

Photo Credit: Eagle's Nest Foundation

Summer instructors at Eagle's Nest Camp get their bearings prior to leading a group of campers on a three-week adventure along the Appalachian Trail.

Pure and simple, the Eagle's Nest Foundation is about teaching and nurturing.

Your Surroundings: Nestled at the base of the Shining Rock escarpment (in Pisgah National Forest), Eagle's Nest is situated on 180 acres of wooded land, where there are many places to rock climb, white-water paddle, and soak up the culture of the southern Appalachians. Evenings are cool; summer days are warm.

What You'll Be Doing: There are two facets to Eagle's Nest staffing opportunities: (1) Summer camp staff members teach activities in the arts, music, and drama (batik, West African drum and dance, pottery, musical instrument making, and raku—not your everyday arts and crafts classes!), wilderness (white-water canoeing on a handful of rivers, rock climbing, and backpacking), and athletics (emphasizing skill and teamwork, not competition). Staff members also double as trip leaders, where they develop, plan, and set goals for the courses; then they take teenagers on intense wilderness experiences, such as hiking on the Appalachian Trail, mountain biking the Continental Divide Trail in Montana, service and cultural-exchange projects in Mexico, and paddling the chilly waters of northern Ontario. (2) Outdoor Academy teachers emphasize a broad spectrum of knowledge, skills, and attitudes in a college preparatory curriculum of English, history, natural science, fine arts, foreign languages, and mathematics. The program combines classroom activities inside and out, with experiential learning as its strength.

Commitment: The summer camp season runs approximately three months, while the Outdoor Academy season lasts from mid-August through mid-May. Some Outdoor Academy faculty members work the entire year, with the option of taking the summer off and returning in the fall.

The hours are long but very rewarding, as the staff works with kids who are eager to learn and do. Camp staff members have one twenty-four-hour day off per week and at least two hours off per day; faculty time off varies.

Perks and Rewards: A $170 to $300 per week salary, plus room and board from the whole-foods kitchen (which includes meals for vegetarians and vegans) is provided for the camp staff; Outdoor Academy benefits include year-round housing, full medical benefits, and a salary commensurate with experience. Fresh air, mountain music, laughter, and love abound at Eagle's Nest, and most thrive and live vivaciously in this community-empowering environment.

The Essentials: Applicants with experience in outdoor and experiential education and who have a strong desire to teach and play in the outdoors are desired. A high energy-level and creativity are a must.

Your First Move: Call (or email) for a staff application.

For More Information:
Paige Lester-Niles, Associate Camp Director
Eagle's Nest Foundation
633 Summit St.
Winston-Salem, NC 27101
(336) 761-1040 • (828) 877-4349 (summer)
page@enf.org

Being responsible to the community is at the heart of life at ENF. Consequently, attitude is the most important attribute at Eagle's Nest, that is, a willingness to be a jack-of-all-trades, have patience and love of children, a sense of goodwill and support of others, and a desire to develop one's own potential. It is a place that allows one to reap his or her own rewards.

EBNER CAMPS

Camp • Connecticut • Summer
www.awosting.com

EBNER CAMPS RUNS two children's resident summer camps: Awosting Camp for boys (the oldest private boys' program in the country) and Chinqueka Camp for girls. Summer camp counselors have the shared responsibility of running a group cabin as co-counselors as well as

We must be willing to get rid of the life we've planned, so as to have the life that is waiting for us. —JOSEPH CAMPBELL

working as instructors in selected activity areas. Teaching positions range from ceramics and photography to martial arts and canoeing (and everything in between). The season kicks off with a five-day intensive orientation period in mid-June and continues for eight weeks. Along with a salary that ranges from $1,200 to $1,800, staff perks include free lodging, meals, a uniform shirt, laundry, a complimentary suntan, and a busload of memories. A bonus of 10 percent of contract salary is given for a "job well done!" and there is a guaranteed gratuity amount of at least $500. Candidates must have some basic skill in one of the camp's teaching positions, and a knowledge of other languages is helpful when dealing with campers and staff that originate from all over the world. To begin the application process, send a cover letter and resume. There is a late April deadline; however, it's best to apply in January or February.

For More Information:
Buzz Ebner, Director
Ebner Camps
Route 202
Bantam, CT 06750
(800) 662-2677 • (860) 485-9566 • (860) 485-1681 (fax)
buzz@awosting.com

ELK MOUNTAIN RANCH

Guest Ranch • Colorado • Summer
www.elkmtn.com

SITTING AT ALMOST 10,000 feet, Elk Mountain Ranch is situated in the midst of the San Isabel National Forest in a remote and secluded setting (and in years past, the ranch was a mill site for a mining camp). For those that have a ready smile, are honest and willing to work long hard hours, love the outdoors, and enjoy working with people, Elk Mountain might be a great fit! Fourteen staff members are hired for the summer season, with positions including cooks, housekeeping/waitstaff, a children's counselor, wrangler, and maintenance (general ranch-hand work). Each staff member is given specific job duties and is also expected to help out wherever and whenever needed, six days per week. Along with a monthly wage and tips, modest shared housing, meals, and laundry facilities are provided. Staff also have the chance to participate in evening activities, including hayrides, square dancing, volleyball, games, and social events. Applicants must be at least eighteen years of age and willing to live on the ranch. Availability to work from mid-May to the end of August (with some positions that

extend through the end of September) is an important hiring criteria. Applications are available online.

For More Information:
Sue Murphy, Treasurer
Elk Mountain Ranch
P.O. Box 910
Buena Vista, CO 81211
(800) 432-8812 • (719) 539-4430
info@elkmtn.com

FAIRVIEW LAKE YMCA CAMPS

Environmental Education • New Jersey • 3–4 Months
www.fairviewlake.org

FAIRVIEW LAKE YMCA Camps provide environmental education and conference programming for students in first through twelfth grades. The camps' mission is to improve the quality of life in the community by fostering healthful living, developing responsible leaders and citizens, strengthening the family, promoting the equality of all persons, protecting the environment, and utilizing community members and organizations to solve contemporary problems.

Your Surroundings: Located on six hundred acres of mountains and forests, the camps offer miles of trails for hiking, a 110-acre lake, athletic fields, a lighted tennis and basketball complex, cross-country skiing, boating, and canoeing.

What You'll Be Doing: Intern responsibilities include participation in staff training; planning and teaching environmental lessons on a variety of subjects that range from aquatic ecology to survival skills; providing instruction on the Action Socialization Experience Course; leading evening activities; assisting at dining hall orientation and meal service when needed; assisting housekeeping and office staff; providing environmental education and recreational programming and services to conference groups; and completion of a project chosen in consultation with the director.

Commitment: Internships are available beginning in March, June, and September for three to four months.

Perks and Rewards: Interns are paid a stipend of $200 per week, plus room and board. Staff housing includes a semiprivate room with a kitchen/living room complex.

The Essentials: Lifeguard training, first-aid, and CPR certifications preferred, but training may be provided by the camp. People are considered based on their love of the outdoors, the desire to influence young minds, and flexibility of their work schedule.

Your First Move: Submit resume and cover letter.

For More Information:
Christina Henriksen
Environmental Education Director
Fairview Lake YMCA Camps
1035 Fairview Lake Rd.
Newton, NJ 07860
(973) 383-9282 • (973) 383-6386 (fax)
fairviewlake@nac.net

FARM AND WILDERNESS FOUNDATION

Farm Camp • Vermont • 11 Weeks •
www.fandw.org

FARM AND WILDERNESS is a nonprofit educational organization that operates five residential camps for children (ages nine to seventeen), a day camp, a family camp in late August, outdoor education programs in the spring through winter, a retreat center, and a spring and fall work crew. The essence of Farm and Wilderness can be found in the Quaker values of simplicity, honesty, self-reliance, and respect for all persons. These values are woven into the fabric of the Farm and Wilderness community, creating an environment where people develop a deep regard for one another and explore a style of life that is simple, rugged, and exciting.

What You'll Be Doing: Each year, nearly three hundred staff members are hired for seasonal work (250 of them in the summer). Jobs include camp counselors and administrators, carpenters, cooks, drivers, farmers, gardeners, maintenance workers, nurses, outdoor educators, special-event coordinators, and trip leaders. There are no sharp lines between work and play in the camps, because a cooperative group spirit enriches all the experiences of swimming and hiking, building and farming, dancing and music, crafts and cooking, and sharing thoughts and emotions.

Perks and Rewards: Salaries range from $900 to $5,500, plus room and board, for a season (approximately eleven weeks of work) depending on the position.

The Essentials: The staff is made up of "doers." They have backpacked in the Sierras, run food drives for the homeless, worked to clean up the environment, promoted the

concept of world peace, played in bands, built houses, operated farms, and climbed the Himalayas. In any given year, more than half are returning for another season.

Your First Move: Applications can be found online or call/email for more information.

For More Information:
Gavin Boyles, Staffing Coordinator
Farm and Wilderness Foundation
263 Farm and Wilderness Rd.
Plymouth, VT 05056
(802) 422-3761, ext. 228 • (802) 422-8660 (fax)
staffinginfo@fandw.org

THE FRESH AIR FUND

Camp • New York • Summer
www.freshair.org

THE FRESH AIR FUND provides New York City youngsters with completely free camping programs—with fun away from the hot and noisy streets of the city as its priority. Serving boys and girls between eight and fifteen years old, the fund operates five camps on a 3,000-acre preserve filled with forests, fields, lakes, and streams. In natural and rustic surroundings, campers learn to respect the environment and its wildlife. In addition, all activities are designed to provide challenges, build self-esteem, develop leadership and social skills, stimulate sharing and trust, encourage openness and cooperation, and create a sense of community.

What You'll Be Doing: During the summer months (from mid-June through mid-August) Fresh Air hires general counselors, program staff (who focus on everything from photography and wood shop to drama and outdoor living skills), waterfront staff, ropes-course facilitators, farm staff, and nutritionists. Staff members at Fresh Air are important people in the eyes of boys and girls who have just been introduced to a new and exciting world. They'll act as guides and role models, teach new skills, answer questions about unfamiliar sights and sounds, and help plan days filled with fun and discovery.

Perks and Rewards: Along with a seasonal wage ranging from $1,700 to $2,500, meals and housing are provided. A travel allowance is also provided for those who are traveling over three hundred miles to the camp.

The Essentials: Applicants must be at least eighteen years of age, have completed their freshman year of college, and have previous experience with children. The most

Photo Credit: Jerry Speier

Staff members at Fresh Air are important role models to boys and girls who have just been introduced to a new and exciting world.

admirable quality is a sincere motivation to work with inner-city children.

Your First Move: Their website covers specific details, along with a downloadable application. Additional questions can be directed to the camping assistant by phone or email.

For More Information:
Thomas Karger, Deputy Executive Director
The Fresh Air Fund
633 Third Ave., 14th Floor
New York, NY 10017
(800) 367-0003 • (212) 897-8979 • (212) 681-0147 (fax)
freshair@freshair.org

FRIENDSHIP VENTURES

Therapeutic Camp • Minnesota/USA • Seasonal
www.friendshipventures.org

ENRICHING THE LIVES of children and adults with developmental disabilities (from challenging behaviors to medical conditions), Friendship Ventures offers a variety of programs, including a camp during the summer months along with weekend respite care, adult travel programs (with destinations throughout the entire U.S.), and

Team Quest (a team-building/adventure challenge course) throughout the year. In addition to twenty-six core staff members, over 250 seasonal and on-call employees—including nurses, dieticians, travel leaders and guides, counselors, challenge-course facilitators and interns, and specialists in nature, aquatic activities, music, and art—work together to create an environment in which participants can relax, learn, have fun, and gain self-confidence and independence. Most resident camp staff members are required to live on site and receive a weekly salary, housing, and meals. For camp positions, a minimum commitment of two weeks is required, and additional pay is offered for working four weeks or more. Leaders and guides are hired throughout the year, while adventure-trip staff work during the summer months. Challenge-course facilitators are part-time, on-call positions, while intern positions are available for an eight-week period in April/May or September/October. Write, call, or email for more information.

For More Information:
Laurie Tschetter, Program Director
Friendship Ventures
10509 108th St., NW
Annandale, MN 55302
(800) 450-8376 • (952) 852-0101 • (952) 852-0123 (fax)
jobs@friendshipventures.org

GENESEE VALLEY OUTDOOR LEARNING CENTER

Experiential Education • Maryland • 3–9 Months
www.geneseevalley.org

. . . .

LOCATED ON A 350-ACRE farm, Genesee Valley Outdoor Learning Center (GVOLC) is host to one of the East Coast's largest ropes course, and specializes in youth development, outdoor education, environmental studies, and team-building retreats. During the spring and fall seasons, a majority of programs last for one day. Facilitators are challenged by various participants, including school groups, college organizations, community groups, at-risk youth, emotionally disturbed youth, and corporate groups. The summer season expands beyond the one day programs, and includes four different adventure camps for seven- to fifteen-year-olds.

What You'll Be Doing: GVOLC hires ropes-course facilitators and interns during the spring through fall and counselors-in-training for the summer. Interns participate in a two-week training program where they will learn theory, facilitation, and technical skills then cofacilitate groups before doing solo facilitating. Ongoing training in ropes course maintenance and administration is also provided. Counselors-in-training get involved in activities including environmental studies, outdoor skills, canoeing, rock climbing, introductory ropes course, swimming, arts and crafts, fishing, farm life, and gardening.

Perks and Rewards: Wages vary with the length of contract and experience (usually around $180 to $250 per week); health insurance assistance and a contributory retirement plan are also provided. All staff live in rustic, dormitory-style housing and enjoy meals together with vegetarian and meat options. GVOLC also fosters a strong, supportive community where your safety, individuality, growth, and happiness are important.

The Essentials: Instructors and interns must be at least eighteen years of age as well as interested in and dedicated to the experiential education field. Those who are flexible, committed to excellence, willing to take the initiative, team players, and sensitive toward others' needs will thrive here.

Your First Move: Send a resume and cover letter to begin the application process.

For More Information:
Marcia Denmark, Internship Coordinator
Genesee Valley Outdoor Learning Center
1717 Rayville Rd.
Parkton, MD 21120
(410) 343-0101 • (410) 343-1451 (fax)
info@geneseevalley.org

GUIDED DISCOVERIES

Science Camp • California • Summer
www.guideddiscoveries.org

. . . .

FOUNDED IN 1978, Guided Discoveries is a nonprofit outdoor educational organization providing hands-on science learning experiences for public and private schools. Based on discovery, adventure, and an environmentally conscious approach to learning, eight- to seventeen-year-olds have the opportunity to participate in the Catalina Island Marine Institute program, which focuses on marine science and island ecology on Catalina Island, or Astrocamp, which focuses on astronomy and space technology in the San Jacinto Mountains near Idyllwild. Summer positions include counselors, marine science instructors, scuba and sail staff, and astronomy instructors. While most staff work during the summer months, transitioning into the year-round program in the fall is a possibility. All staff receive a weekly salary, plus room and board. Teaching experience with youth, flexibility, and the ability to work with others as a team and to live in a rural setting are desired. Certificates in first aid, CPR, and lifeguard training are the norm.
Call for an application packet.

For More Information:
Ross Turner, Executive Director
Guided Discoveries
Catalina Sea Camp/Astrocamp
P.O. Box 1360
Claremont, CA 91711
(800) 645-1423 • (909) 625-6194 • (909) 625-7305 (fax)
info@guideddiscoveries.org

We look for employees who take pride in their work and are capable of thriving in a residential situation. The work can be hectic and difficult, but it is highly rewarding. Because the mountains and the ocean are such integral parts of the facilities, our employees often bring a love for the outdoors with them, or they quickly develop one.

A wise man will make more opportunities than he finds. —FRANCIS BACON

GUNFLINT LODGE AND NORTHWOODS OUTFITTERS

Canoe Outfitter • Minnesota • Seasonal
www.gunflint.com

GUNFLINT LODGE IS a seasonal canoe outfitter and fishing resort outfitter (without TV or radio reception) and is surrounded by over one million acres of wilderness in the Superior National Forest. Guests come from all over the country to relax in the north-woods atmosphere, fish, swim, canoe, and explore. Seasonal winter and summer opportunities may include activities leader, baker, trail guides, food and beverage staff, front desk, dock staff, dog musher, wilderness canoe guide, general helpers, and housekeepers. Resort and outfitting work means long, hard, and sometimes irregular hours. Although you may be hired for a specific position, there are times when you may be called upon to fulfill other job duties. Most positions pay $1,065 per month and recreational equipment is available for use in off-hours. Bunkhouse-style accommodations (with shared kitchen facilities) are available for $115 per month, as are a few employee trailer sites with full hook-ups. Gunflint hires approximately fifty-five employees during the summer and thirty-five during the winter, with staff members ranging in age from eighteen to seventy. Applications can be printed online.

For More Information:
Sandy Halteman, Assistant Manager
Gunflint Lodge and Northwoods Outfitters
143 S. Gunflint Lake
Grand Marais, MN 55604
(800) 328-3325 • (218) 388-2294 • (218) 388-9429 (fax)
hro@gunflint.com

GWYNN VALLEY

Farm Camp • North Carolina • Summer
www.gwynnvalley.com

AT THE HEART of Gwynn Valley Camp is the philosophy that every individual can make a difference in the world. Campers (kindergarten through eighth grade) and staff alike are encouraged to get back to basics, connect with the land and the simple joys of childhood, and honor the spiritual component—that hope and belief in things beyond the individual. The camp is set upon 350 acres of mountains, streams, fields, and woods, with a full working farm and 1890s grist mill. The majority of food is produced on the farm and prepared and served from their whole foods kitchen.

What You'll Be Doing: Summer opportunities include cabin counselors, activity heads, and program assistants as well as kitchen, housekeeping, and laundry staff. Whether it's playing a game of soccer, harvesting vegetables, searching for salamanders, hiking to an overnight campsite, making wheel-churned ice cream, writing and performing an original play, or learning from a new friend, the staff challenges each child to grow and thrive in an atmosphere of tolerance and trust.

Commitment: Positions are available for a seven- or ten-week period beginning in early June.

Perks and Rewards: A base salary of $190 to $230 per week is provided along with room, board, laundry facilities, staff training, and access to the camp's physician as well as pro deals to those that qualify.

The Essentials: Applicants must be at least nineteen years old, enthusiastic, filled with energy, certified in CPR and first aid, and have the desire to work with young children. Staff come from all over the world.

Your First Move: Call/email for application materials. The majority of interviewing is done in the winter and early spring.

For More Information:
Staffing Director
Gwynn Valley
1080 Island Ford Rd.
Brevard, NC 28712
(828) 885-2900 • (828) 885-2413 (fax)
mail@gwynnvalley.com

HIDDEN CREEK RANCH

Guest Ranch • Idaho • Seasonal
www.hiddencreek.com

YOU'LL FIND THAT horses, cowboys, and the Western American ranching traditions are front and center in many of the activities at Hidden Creek Ranch; however, they have a different philosophy on the dude ranch experience. Native American undertones resonate through all their unique offerings, whether it's participation in the holistic education program, a pipe and sweat lodge ceremony, the team-building challenge course, or the

Photo Credit: Chris Hollo

Whether working as a wrangler, baker, or counselor, each staff member at Hidden Creek Ranch is cross-trained in all aspects of ranch operation.

nature-awareness course for children. Hidden Creek Ranch is about celebrating life, being fully alive, and connecting with Mother Earth.

What You'll Be Doing: When you begin working at Hidden Creek Ranch, you become an integral part of the ranch family. Whether working as a wrangler, kids' wrangler or counselor, baker or chef, waitstaff, housekeeper, maintenance staff, or massage therapist, you will have only one responsibility: to truly make each guest feel at home. To ensure that the staff has a frequent change of scenery, everyone will be cross-trained to help in other aspects of the ranch operation. Besides your main job, you might also be helping in the kitchen; serving the meals and caring for the guests; assisting in some outdoor cooking; helping in the care of the animals; helping unload and stack the hay; providing airport transportation; and doing general errands and maintenance.

Commitment: The guest season starts in the middle of April and ends in September. Some positions start as early as February or begin as late as June, although you must be available to work June through August.

Perks and Rewards: Along with a base salary, all staff will earn a bonus for successfully completing their contract. Benefits include three all-you-can-eat gourmet meals per day and housing in Wrangler's Haven (which Hidden Creek boasts is "the finest employee housing in the business"). Everything is provided, including fully furnished rooms (shared with one other person), laundry, recreation room, and satellite television—a place that certainly will provide that home-away-from-home feeling.

The Essentials: Applicants must be at least eighteen years of age and have current standard first-aid and CPR certi-

fication. International applicants must have a valid work visa and English-language fluency.

Your First Move: Send a resume and cover letter, denoting your earliest start and finish dates. An application, which you can submit through email, is also available online. It is advised to get your application in as early as possible (over eight hundred are received each year); the hiring process begins in November.

For More Information:
Cindy Loe, Human Resources
Hidden Creek Ranch
7600 E. Blue Lake Rd.
Harrison, ID 83833
(800) 446-3833 • (208) 689-3209 • (208) 689-9115 (fax)
jobs@hiddencreek.com

HIDDEN VALLEY CAMP

Camp • Maine • Summer
www.hiddenvalleycamp.com

NESTLED IN A valley near the coast, with a beautiful lake, rolling hills, and old farmhouses, Hidden Valley is an "amazingly creative community of children and adults." The camp offers a well-rounded blend of both artistic and outdoor-adventure programming—everything from pottery, stained glass, batik, and photography to organic gardening, horseback riding, the challenge course, and outdoor-living experiences. Creativity is definitely at the heart of the staff and campers alike.

What You'll Be Doing: Teaching a child to throw a mug. Greeting a camper at the top of the climbing wall for the first time. Hiking up Tipi Hill to paint wildflowers. Llama trekking to a picnic. That's right, summer staff are the role models that help campers explore, take risks, make choices, and have lots of fun. The staff is broken into two areas: cabin counselors/instructors and noncabin professional staff. Up to four counselors care for their children (ages eight to thirteen), provide teaching in various areas and plan events for the community. Established professional artists share their talents in one particular teaching area.

Commitment: Counselors kick off the summer with two weeks of staff training in early June (are you ready to challenge yourself on the zip line in the high ropes course?); then participate in two four-week sessions through mid-August. Professional artist staff usually stay for one four-week session.

Perks and Rewards: A salary, housing, healthy meals (rumor has it there is a lobster banquet), and generous off-time is provided. Whether you want to grab a sundae at the Superscoop, climb Mount Katahdin, or canoe at sunrise, there are plenty of off-time activities to complement your work experience. Those anticipating a career working with children will find Hidden Valley a supportive learning environment with many opportunities to develop strengths and recognize limitations.

The Essentials: Energetic, thoughtful people who have experience working with children make the best candidates.

Your First Move: Applications are available online or call/email for materials.

For More Information:
Gi Reed, Program Director
Hidden Valley Camp
Freedom, ME 04941
(800) 922-6737 • (207) 342-5177 • (207) 342-5685 (fax)
summer@hiddenvalleycamp.com

THE HOME RANCH

Guest Ranch • Colorado • Seasonal
www.homeranch.com

THE CALL OF the West has always been strong in the hearts of Americans. No matter if they were raised on the romantic tales of Zane Grey, thrilled by the heroics of matinee idols like Roy Rogers, or laughed at the antics depicted in *City Slickers,* it is a safe bet that people of every generation have longed for the opportunity to ride the range and conquer the mountains. Working at The Home Ranch is a chance to heed that "call," if only for a little while. The 1,500-acre ranch accommodates over forty-two guests per week, with activities including wilderness hikes, horseback riding, or fly-fishing on the Elk River in the summer, and cross-country skiing, snowshoeing, and downhill skiing in the winter. Seasonal staff positions include children's counselors, kitchen helpers, cooks, dishwashers, waitstaff, housekeepers, front desk and maintenance personnel, hiking guides, fly-fishing instructors, and wranglers. All positions are offered with a graduated salary starting at $900 per month, plus room, board, and laundry facilities. The summer season runs from May through October, and the winter season extends from December through March. Applications are available online.

For More Information:
Will Hardly, Manager
The Home Ranch
P.O. Box 822
Clark, CO 80428
(970) 879-1780 • (970) 879-1795 (fax)
info@homeranch.com

HORIZON CAMPS

Camp • East Coast • Summer
www.horizoncamps.com

HORIZON CAMPS CONSIST of five unique camps that work together to celebrate the growth and development of children. Both Camp Echo Lake and Southwoods are located in the heart of the Adirondack Mountains; Kamp Kohut is located on magnificent Lake Thompson in Maine; Indian Head Camp is found in the Endless Mountains of northeast Pennsylvania; and Twin Creeks is set in the Allegheny Mountains of West Virginia. All are in rustic, wooded settings with hundreds of acres to enjoy.

What You'll Be Doing: Being a camp counselor is a demanding and often a difficult job. Counselors live, work, eat, sleep, and play with campers nearly all day, every day. Cabin specialists spend a majority of their time with their group of campers and benefit from a variety of activities throughout the course of a day. Activity specialists also live with campers, but their daytime focus is on a specific activity area. Additionally, there are some positions that allow staff members to become a "jack-of-all-trades."

Commitment: Depending on the camp and position, the camp season runs from approximately mid-June to mid-August, which includes a five-day orientation.

Perks and Rewards: All staff receive an unforgettable, powerful experience with children, along with a salary, shared housing in wood-frame cabins, meals, and travel.

The Essentials: Those who will thrive at Horizon Camps have high energy, are hardworking, and are committed to working with children. The average age of the staff is twenty-one; some are college students, some are teachers, others have graduated and are looking for a fulfilling way to spend a summer. At minimum, one year of college is required.

Your First Move: Applications are accepted from November through May, although early applications are encouraged (as positions fill quickly).

For More Information:
Staff Recruiter
Horizon Camps
3 West Main St.
Elmsford, NY 10523
(800) 544-5448 • (914) 345-2086 • (914) 345-2120 (fax)
staff@horizoncamps.com

If you are looking for a quiet, relaxed, "laid-back" environment, that's not what you'll find at our camps. However, if you are looking for a great life experience and a superb resume-building opportunity, a summer with Horizon might just be for you.

HUNEWILL GUEST RANCH

Guest Ranch • California • Seasonal
www.hunewillranch.com

HUNEWILL RANCH IS situated in Bridgeport Valley, California, in the heart of the eastern Sierras, at 6,500 feet. Directly behind the ranch are snow-covered crags that mark the boundary of Yosemite National Park. Staff members come back year after year to work hard and meet vacationers from all over the world while spending free time in the Sierras, breathing fresh, clean air. Seasonal staff, who must be at least eighteen years of age, are hired to work from the end of May to early October, with duties that may include maintenance, child care, work in the kitchen, cleaning cabins, or wrangling. Applicants must be wholesome, robust, and cheerful employees who are willing to pitch in where needed. Benefits include a wage of $5.75 to $7 per hour (plus any tips), housing in employee cabins, and meals for a nominal fee (no cooking facilities are available in the cabins). Send a cover letter and resume to begin the application process.

For More Information:
Betsy Hunewill Elliott, Personnel Director
Hunewill Guest Ranch
200 Hunewill Ln.
Wellington, NV 89444
(775) 465-2201 • (760) 932-7710 (Summer)
(775) 465-2056 (fax)
hunewillranch@tele-net.net

LAKE MANCOS RANCH

Guest Ranch • Colorado • Summer
www.lakemancosranch.com

SADDLE UP HORSEBACK and get in touch with nature in the heart of Mesa Verde country! Located thirty-five miles west of Durango, Lake Mancos Ranch promotes a true family atmosphere for its guests. To many, a guest-ranch job sounds exciting and arouses images of cowboys riding the range, rodeos, and fireside sing alongs. Yes, they have the cowboys, but working on a guest ranch is not glamorous—there are meals to cook, beds to make, toilets to scrub, floors to mop, yards to mow, and plumbing to unclog. Staff members are hired for specific assignments, including kitchen assistants, recreation counselors, dining-room servers, maids, wranglers, and maintenance staff, but also share in chores related to community living. The summer season starts the first weekend of June and runs through September and most staff arrive mid-May and stay through the end of August. Along with a weekly wage, dormitory-style housing (one to two roommates) and meals are provided. Before considering Lake Mancos Ranch, applicants must be willing to put in long hours with great enthusiasm (and be at least eighteen years of age). Application materials are available online.

For More Information:
Todd Sehnert, Summer Staffing
Lake Mancos Ranch
42688 CR "N"
Mancos, CO 81328
(800) 325-9462 • (970) 533-1190 • (970) 533-7858 (fax)
tsehnert@fone.net

LEGACY INTERNATIONAL GLOBAL YOUTH VILLAGE

Global Camp • Virginia • Summer
www.globalyouthvillage.org

EVERY SUMMER SINCE 1979, a dynamic learning environment has been created at Legacy's Global Youth Village that emphasizes experiential learning and challenges young people and staff to turn cross-cultural theory and skills into practical action. Each person contributes his or her own thread of education, thought, personality, and dreams to Legacy. Legacy's aim is to transform the legacy of prejudice, fear, confusion, and misunderstanding into a legacy of hope and to help future generations realize their capabilities.

What You'll Be Doing: Summer staff live and work with people from all over the world, while developing a deeper understanding of community development issues, discovering the broader implications of daily actions and choices, and exploring the complexity of political and social situations. Very different from an academic environment, this experience is an intensive and fulfilling learning opportunity that requires active, responsible participation. A ten-day preprogram training enhances the diverse skills and perspectives represented within the staff team. The Global Youth Village experience offers a hodgepodge of staff positions—from leadership instructors and global-awareness trainers to lifeguards, art staff, counselors, and food-service staff.

Commitment: The program extends from early July through early August, with most positions involving a six-and-a-half-day workweek (including twenty-four-hour on-site responsibility as live-in cabin counselors).

Perks and Rewards: Benefits include a stipend (between $900 to $1,200 for the season depending on the position), housing, meals, and laundry service. Accommodations are in cabins with youth and/or other staff. In addition, Legacy offers a healthful rural environment including a whole-foods, vegetarian diet.

The Essentials: Whether you are finishing college or in graduate school, the Global Youth Village experience offers an amazing learning opportunity. All applicants must have previous youth work experience, be at least twenty-one years of age, and seek to enhance professional youth work or teaching experience. In addition, the applicant should have some previous experience of immersion in a culture different from his or her own, whether it be abroad or within one's own country. Smoking and alcohol use are not allowed during the term of employment.

Your First Move: Visit their website for details on the experience, a listing of available positions, and an online application. It is suggested you contact Legacy by April 1 at the very latest.

For More Information:
Leila Baz, Staff Director
Legacy International—Global Youth Village
1020 Legacy Dr.
Bedford, VA 24523
(540) 297-5982 • (540) 297-1860 (fax)
staff@legacyintl.org

We look for people who are really excited about the program and show the flexibility and maturity to work in an intense, multicultural setting with lots of challenges. An ability to work in a close team is essential! With these qualities, we'll sometimes overlook a person's lack of experience just because of their openness, idealism, and excitement, and we'll train them.

LIFE ADVENTURE CAMP

Therapeutic Camp • Kentucky • Summer
www.lifeadventurecamp.org

SPONSORED BY THE United Way, Life Adventure Camp is a primitive wilderness camp concerned primarily with providing a successful and positive camping experience for children with emotional and behavioral problems. The program is designed around decentralized camping; campers and staff live in small groups (consisting of eight to ten campers and three counselors) in a primitive outdoor setting.

Your Surroundings: The campsite is located sixty miles southeast of Lexington on five hundred acres of rugged, undeveloped land in Estill County. The land is densely forested and offers wildlife, creeks, caves, rock outcroppings, and other natural areas for exploring.

What You'll Be Doing: After an extensive two-week training (which includes safe crisis/behavior management), camp staff provide opportunities and activities that enhance a positive self-concept; provide a group living setting that encourages and teaches appropriate social-interaction skills among peers and adults; and teach basic and advanced low-impact camping skills, with the hope of increasing each camper's awareness and appreciation for the natural environment. There are no permanent facilities at the campsite; thus, campers and staff must build their campsites, using natural materials and plastic tarps. This is the perfect opportunity for anyone wanting to lead outdoor programs or work with children.

Commitment: The season begins in mid-May and continues through early August.

Perks and Rewards: A stipend of $1,600 to $2,600 is provided, along with room and board. Housing is provided in Lexington during in-town staff training sessions and during time off between sessions for those staff members who do not live in the Lexington area. First-aid and CPR certifications will be provided at no cost.

The Essentials: Applicants must be at least nineteen years of age, and those with experience working or volunteering with children and seeking a career in social work, counseling, or outdoor education are preferred.

Your First Move: Call for application materials. All staff members are generally hired by April.

For More Information:
Brother Wolf, Program Director
Life Adventure Camp
1122 Oak Hill Dr.
Lexington, KY 40505
(859) 252-4733 • (859) 225-5115 (fax)
lac@lifeadventurecamp.org

We are looking for open-minded men and women who want to learn to live a simple lifestyle and share this with children. People who are excited about living in the woods, cooking meals over a fire, exploring caves and creeks, and being with children will thrive in our program.

THE LIGHTHOUSE INN

Lighthouse • Massachusetts • Summer
www.lighthouseinn.com

SITUATED ALONG THE shore of Nantucket Sound in Cape Cod, the Lighthouse Inn provides seclusion, relaxation, and fun for family vacationers from mid-May through mid-October. Providing all the guest and hospitality services are the inn's team of seasonal staff. Positions are available in food and beverage (from servers to chefs), the front office (from children's program staff to front desk workers), and in housekeeping. Along with a weekly wage, housing is provided for those who can work through mid-October. Applications are available online and a personal interview is required.

For More Information:
Staffing Director
The Lighthouse Inn
1 Lighthouse Inn Rd.
P.O. Box 128

West Dennis, MA 02670
(508) 398-2244 • (508) 398-5658 (fax)
inquire@lighthouseinn.com

MOHONK MOUNTAIN HOUSE

Resort • New York • Seasonal
www.mohonkjobs.com

ONE OF THE last of the great nineteenth-century Victorian castles, Mohonk Mountain House is surrounded by thousands of acres of unspoiled forest and winding trails (with trail signs that read "Slowly and Quietly Please.") This is the essence of Mohonk (which means "lake in the sky")—a unique setting for relaxation and renewal of the body, mind, and spirit in a beautiful natural surroundings. Family-owned since 1869, the resort grounds feature gardens, a greenhouse, picnic areas, a museum, stables, sports facilities, and an observation point known as Sky Top Tower. Seasonal and year-round staff members (with the majority of positions extending from April or May through mid-November) have the opportunity to work in all resort areas, including food and beverage, conference services, hotel operations, personnel, properties, retail, and guest services. Along with an hourly wage, there is limited dormitory-style housing available for a modest fee, which includes three meals per day. The resort also prides itself on offering use of the facilities and activities and encourages employees to participate in scheduled events. All applicants must be at least eighteen years of age and a personal interview is required for all positions. For more info on the resort itself, visit www.mohonk.com.

For More Information:
Personnel Director
Mohonk Mountain House
1000 Mountain Rest Rd.
New Paltz, NY 12561
(845) 256-2089 • (845) 256-2049 (fax)

MOUNTAIN TRAIL OUTDOOR SCHOOL

Outdoor Education • North Carolina • Seasonal
www.kanuga.org

MOUNTAIN TRAIL OUTDOOR SCHOOL is the outdoor education wing of Kanuga Conference Center, a nonprofit conference and retreat center affiliated with the Episcopal

Church. Kanuga also offers residential summer camp programs for youth and adults. Mountain Trail is set among a 1,400-acre area of the beautiful Blue Ridge Mountains with many scenic vistas and an endangered species on the property. After a training period, instructors and interns are responsible for teaching natural history classes, environmental awareness, new games and initiatives, adventure activities, low and high ropes, rock climbing, and assisting with program development. Wages start at $200 per week, plus room and board. The program runs February to May and August to December, with several separate summer camp programs available from June through August. Prior experience with children, nature studies, and the outdoors are key assets for prospective applicants. It's best to send in all application materials by December 31.

For More Information:
Paul Bockoven, Outdoor Education Director
Mountain Trail Outdoor School
Kanuga Conference Center
P.O. Box 250
Hendersonville, NC 28793-0250
(828) 692-9136 • (828) 696-3589 (fax)
mtos@kanuga.org

NATURE CAMPS, INC.

Camp • Maryland • Summer
www.naturecamps.com

WITH A BACK-TO-NATURE philosophy, Nature Camps, Inc. gets children (ages five to sixteen) into 285 acres of woods, fields, and streams in a real and personal way, while providing an atmosphere of adventure and creative expression. With the big outdoors as the teacher, camp staff provide the knowledge and supervision, and help campers make choices, become self-directed, and take responsibility for their own learning. Summer staff opportunities include swimming instructors, outdoor educators, natural-craft teachers, song leaders, ropes-course facilitators, trip leaders, canoeists, hike masters, story tellers, riding instructors, potters, and weavers—and the list goes on! Training, certification, and staff development begin in mid-May or June (depending on program). A salary, room, and board are provided. Call for more information.

For More Information:
Don Webb, Director
Nature Camps, Inc.

17433 Big Falls Rd.
Box 240
Monkton, MD 21111-0240
(800) 606-3381 • (410) 343-0223 • (410) 378-5439 (fax)
naturecampsinc@aol.com

NORTH FORK GUEST RANCH

Guest Ranch • Colorado • Summer
www.northforkranch.com

NORTH FORK GUEST RANCH, a small, family-oriented ranch, lies on the gorgeous banks of the rushing North Fork of the South Platte River and adjoins a national wilderness area in the heart of the Rockies. The ranch offers everything an outdoor enthusiast could want, including great horseback riding, white-water rafting, overnight pack trips, hiking, trapshooting, terrific fishing, and the unique opportunity to meet and make friends from all over the world.

What You'll Be Doing: Because the ranch is a people-serving business, they do not hire people merely to get a job done. You will be expected to give totally of yourself, sharing with and caring for their guests. Positions include cooks, kids' counselor, office/kitchen, wrangler, maintenance, and housekeeper/wait staff.

Commitment: They are primarily interested in those who can arrive in May and stay through August.

Perks and Rewards: Staff members receive $650 per month, plus room and great home-style meals. (Yes, there will be many barbecues and steak cookouts!) On your day off and after daily duties, you can enjoy all ranch activities.

The Essentials: Simply stated: dedicated, dependable, and dynamic individuals.

Your First Move: Call for application materials. The ranch begins their review of applications starting in January and tries to have its entire staff hired by May 1.

For More Information:
Dean and Karen May, Owners
North Fork Guest Ranch
P.O. Box B
Shawnee, CO 80475
(800) 843-7895 • (303) 838-9873 • (303) 838-1549 (fax)
northforkranch@worldnet.att.net

*Do you love people?
Do you love to work? Are you willing
to learn and do new things?
Are you flexible and willing to help out anytime,
anywhere, and do anything? Are you
enthusiastic and excited about other people
enjoying their vacation? Would you involve
yourself in the basic ranch objective of making
the guests' stay at North Fork Ranch a
great experience? If you answered yes to
these questions, you are the type of person
we are looking for!*

OAKLAND HOUSE SEASIDE RESORT

Resort • Maine • 2–12 Weeks
www.oaklandhouse.com

LIFE AT OAKLAND House Seaside Resort is more "like it used to be," with creative use of time and leisure hours spent by their guests and staff. At the turn of the nineteenth century, the first guests were the "Rusticators," who arrived on steamships from Boston, New York, and places beyond. They were writers, artists, and educators seeking respite from city bustle. Today Oakland House offers a half-mile of prime oceanfront, ocean and lakeside beaches, hiking trails, a dock, rowboats, and, of course, relaxation.

Photo Credit: Sally Littlefield

The Oakland House culinary staff meet in the organic gardens to discuss what herbs and vegetables will be harvested for the evening's five-course meal.

What You'll Be Doing: No matter the position, Oakland House staff members are there to make guests feel welcome in a family-style atmosphere. Positions include waitstaff, grounds and gardens attendants, cabin stewards, housekeepers, first mate (for boat trips), and assistants for the office/reservation desk, kitchen, and maintenance. Culinary internships with a seasoned culinary staff are also available. Interns will learn how to create five-course dinners that emphasize the use of locally harvested seafood and meats along with vegetables and herbs from their organic garden. At season's peak, you'll find twenty-five to thirty staff members working together.

Commitment: Positions begin in mid-May, with staggered completion terms through the end of October. In addition, two- to eight-week culinary internships are available throughout the season. The normal workweek ranges from forty- to forty-eight hours per week, six days a week.

Perks and Rewards: The pay varies with each position. Staff members will live on the second and third floor of the two-hundred-year-old hotel with single beds (in rooms that sleep either one or two staff members) for a fee of $50 per week, which includes meals. Due to the general long-term nature of guest visits (one-week minimum in cottages), there are many opportunities for friendships and cordial staff relationships.

The Essentials: Applicants must be at least eighteen years of age, and staff members often return year after year as they work through college. Because of its rural location, it's helpful if employees bring a car. International applicants must have a J-1 visa.

Your First Move: Detailed information and applications can be obtained online.

For More Information:
Jim and Sally Littlefield, Innkeepers
Oakland House Seaside Resort
435 Herrick Rd., Herricks Landing
Brooksville, ME 04617
(207) 359-8521 • (207) 359-9865 (fax)
jim@oaklandhouse.com

PEACEFUL VALLEY RANCH

Guest Ranch • Colorado • Summer
www.peacefulvalley.com

As ONE OF Colorado's oldest and largest guest ranches, Peaceful Valley Ranch treats guests to the true meaning of Western fun. Along with riding horses, campfires, horse-drawn hayrides, barn dances, backcountry tours, fly-fishing, hiking, and recreational activities, participants also have the chance to participate in a "gymkhana," a cross between a horse show and rodeo. Dressed in denim shirts, wranglers, cowboy boots, and western hats, summer staff members are generally hired in administration, housekeeping, kitchen and waitstaff, or barn and maintenance; however, everyone will chip in where needed (which means getting involved in sing-a-longs, square dancing, talent shows, and campfire programs). Wages start at $1,200 per month and are based on a six-day, forty-eight hour workweek from May 1 through the end of September. Everyone receives housing and meals along with the benefits of working and playing at the ranch. Applicants must be at least eighteen, hardworking, flexible, and guest/team oriented. Applications can be filled out online.

For More Information:
Staffing Director
Peaceful Valley Ranch
475 Peaceful Valley Rd.
Lyons, CO 80540-8951
(800) 955-6343 • (303) 747-2881 • (303) 747-2167 (fax)
howdy@peacefulvalley.com

POINT REYES NATIONAL SEASHORE ASSOCIATION

Ocean-Based Camp • California • Summer
www.ptreyes.org

POINT REYES OFFERS a six-week residential Science Camp for kids aged seven to twelve, who explore the rich coastal environment and diverse habitats of the region, as well as a six-day Adventure Camp for teens, aged thirteen to sixteen, who are led on a four-day backpack trip focusing on self-esteem, teamwork, and backpacking skills.

What You'll Be Doing: Naturalist intern/counselors primarily assist with guided natural history and environmental education programs, mealtime supervision, free-time activities, and cabin supervision for children attending the Science Camp. Not only will interns work with experts in the field of environmental and outdoor education, they will also have the chance to obtain training in educational and behavior-management techniques, natural history interpretation, and recreational leadership skills. Other summer staff positions include six naturalists, a director, and three kitchen workers.

Commitment: Summer positions start in late June (with staff training) and end in late August.

Perks and Rewards: A $175 to $200 per week stipend is provided, along with room and board. This is a great way to experience the warmth and camaraderie of living and working with other staff members in a residential camp environment.

The Essentials: Applicants should enjoy working with children and the outdoors, have a knowledge of ecological concepts/communities, and be first-aid and CPR certified. Preference is given to those who are in college; who are willing to work and live with campers in a rustic setting; and who are creative, enthusiastic, flexible, self-motivated, and have a sense of humor. Experience in supervising or teaching students is a bonus.

Your First Move: Call for application materials. On-site interviews are preferred, but phone interviews are acceptable.

For More Information:
Scott Wolland, Education Programs Director
Point Reyes National Seashore Association
Point Reyes Station, CA 94956
(415) 663-1224 • (415) 663-8174 (fax)
summercamp@ptreyes.org

RAMAPO ANCHORAGE CAMP

Therapeutic Camp • New York • Summer
www.ramapoanchorage.org

RAMAPO ANCHORAGE CAMP fosters the development of positive social and learning skills for children who have a wide range of emotional, behavioral, and learning problems. Counselors work individually with children through educational and outdoor-adventure programming, helping them to develop their school readiness and the communication skills necessary for healthy growth. The staff consists mostly of college students and recent graduates who have strong leadership and caring qualities that enable them to motivate and relate to young people. A stipend, room, and board are provided. Application forms can be found online. Ramapo also conducts "Field Experience in Special Education," an on-site, year-round college course where participants can receive academic credit.

For More Information:
Tom Decker, Assistant Director
Ramapo Anchorage Camp
P.O. Box 266
Rhinebeck, NY 12572-0266

(845) 876-8403 • (845) 876-8414 (fax)
office@ramapoanchorage.org

REDFISH LAKE LODGE

Lodge • Idaho • Summer
www.redfishlake.com

ESTABLISHED IN 1929, Redfish Lake Lodge is a family-oriented rustic lodge located on the northern shore of Redfish Lake in the rugged Sawtooth Mountains. The area is known for its incredible backpacking, horseback riding, white-water rafting, rock climbing, mountain-bike riding, and fishing. From May through the end of September, a crew of fifty seasonal staff members join Redfish. Summer positions include food service staff, service station attendants, housekeepers, marina staff, store assistants, front-desk clerks, and maintenance people (with a six-day workweek). Wages range between $1,162 and $1,254 per month, with perks including a Redfish-sponsored employee activities program. Because of their remote location, Redfish offers room and board (which most employees take advantage of). Rustic, dormitory-style housing, within walking distance of the lodge, is provided for $180 per month; and wholesome, family-style meals are provided three times a day, seven days a week for $210 per month. First consideration is given to those who can work at least through Labor Day weekend (and preferably through the end of September). The minimum age is seventeen; and for waitstaff, store clerk, and bartender positions, the minimum is nineteen. Applications are available online, and are accepted beginning in February.

For More Information:
Human Resources
Redfish Lake Lodge
P.O. Box 43
Jerome, ID 83338
(208) 644-9096 • (208) 644-9616 (fax)
hr@redfishlake.com

RESORT AT SQUAW CREEK

Resort • California • Seasonal
www.squawcreek.com

IDEALLY SITUATED AT the base of Squaw Valley USA, the Resort at Squaw Creek offers more than four hundred rooms, five restaurants, a fitness center, a full-service spa, and unlimited recreation in the beautiful setting of the Sierra Nevada Mountains. Whether you're looking for a summer, winter, or year-round job, positions are available as food servers, conference service attendants, retail sales clerks, fitness attendants, drivers, and spa hosts. It's always best to look for housing early and keeping roommates in mind is a good idea. The average rent for a studio ranges from $550 to $700 a month while houses start at about $1,000 a month. Specific job openings can be found online, or call/email for more information.

For More Information:
Human Resources Department
Resort at Squaw Creek
400 Squaw Creek Rd.
Olympic Valley, CA 96146
(530) 581-6642 • (530) 581-6681 (job hotline)
info@squawcreek.com

RIVER WAY RANCH CAMP

Camp • California • Seasonal
www.riverwayranchcamp.com

LOCATED IN THE foothills of Sequoia/Kings Canyon National Parks, River Way Ranch Camp offers fun and excitement for children from all over the world, with over sixty different specialized activities (from photography and martial arts to a ropes course). Along with a variety of counselor and activity specialists, River Way also hires camp interns (who assist in marketing, evaluations, public relations, and behind the scenes) and resort interns (who program and lead activities for the public). Most counselor-type positions are offered during the summer months; however, intern opportunities are available year-round. Benefits include a $1,944 to $2,300 stipend for the season, plus room and board. Employment is open to all who would like to learn more about the resort and camp industry, have a love for children, and outgoing and creative. Applications can be filled out online.

For More Information:
Nancy Oken Nighbert, Director
River Way Ranch Camp
6450 Elwood Rd., "BD"
Sanger, CA 93657
(800) 821-2801 • (559) 787-2551 • (559) 787-3851 (fax)
rwrcamp@aol.com

ROCKY MOUNTAIN VILLAGE

Therapeutic Camp • Colorado • Summer
www.eastersealsco.org/rmvillage

ROCKY MOUNTAIN VILLAGE, owned and operated by Easter Seals Colorado, serves as a residential camp for children and adults with physical and/or cognitive disabilities. Seasonal positions include activity director, registered nurse, cabin counselors, kitchen/cooks, maintenance, and specialists in these areas: trips/travel, ropes course, outdoor education, arts and crafts, aquatics, horseback riding/animals, and media. Those who have a desire to work with children and adults with disabilities are preferred. A weekly stipend of $175 is provided (along with a $200 bonus if you work the entire season).

For More Information:
Roman Krafczyk, Director
Rocky Mountain Village
Easter Seals Colorado
P.O. Box 115
Empire, CO 80438
(800) 692-5520 • (303) 569-2333 • (303) 569-3857 (fax)
campinfo@cess.org

SEACAMP

Ocean-Based Camp • Florida • Summer
www.seacamp.org

ESTABLISHED IN 1966, Seacamp is dedicated to the study of marine communities and island habitats, with courses led by academically trained marine-science instructors. Over seventy-five hundred teenagers have attended one of Seacamp's eighteen-day programs, which focus on everything from sailing, scuba, and kayaking to photography and arts and crafts. Although their backgrounds vary, participants share at least one common interest: the importance of oceans and marine life to their world.

Your Surroundings: With its beautiful location at Newfound Harbor, Seacamp is minutes from the only living coral reef in North America. Opportunities abound to explore the exciting waters of the Florida Keys, both in the Atlantic Ocean and the Gulf of Mexico. Indians, pirates, and Flagler's Railroad all contribute to the heritage of this subtropical area.

What You'll Be Doing: A variety of instructor positions are available, including those in arts and crafts, board sailing, photography, sailing, science, and scuba, as well as other positions as counselors and kitchen and maintenance staff. Whatever the position, each staff member participates in all camp activities. The camp experience is a unique learning environment that combines the living and working aspects of the staff member's life, and many times it becomes hard to distinguish between learning and teaching experiences.

Commitment: The summer season runs from late May through late August. For those who would like to continue to teach young people about the sea, Newfound Harbor Marine Institute (a Seacamp program) provides workshops and residential programs from early September through late May. See their listing on page 207 for more information.

Perks and Rewards: Benefits include a weekly salary, lodging, meals, and health insurance. A four-week pre-camp training program provides American Red Cross lifeguarding, first-aid, and CPR certification, NAUI skin-diving instruction, a forty-hour workshop in seamanship and boat handling, and if scuba certified, rescue-diver training.

The Essentials: The minimum age for employment is nineteen years, and most candidates are either in college or have just graduated. With the heart of Seacamp's program focused on marine-science education, the best applicants possess an interest in working with teenagers in a water-oriented setting.

Your First Move: Call for application materials. Phone interviews begin in March and continue through April.

For More Information:
Grace Upshaw, Camp Director
Seacamp
1300 Big Pine Ave.
Big Pine Key, FL 33043-3306
(305) 872-2331 • (305) 872-2555 (fax)
seacamp98@aol.com

SKIING

Working at a Ski Resort

Photo Credit: David Nagel

If you have a love for children, there are plenty of ski instructor opportunities with kid friendly resorts.

The popular saying among employees at the Village at Breckenridge Resort is "you move here for the winters, but end up staying for the summers." This appears to be the common theme for thousands of snow enthusiasts who work seasonally at ski resorts all over the country. Beyond a work environment that provides breathtaking scenery, one of the biggest perks of becoming a "ski bum" for the winter is the coveted ski pass (along with free ski rentals and lessons, as well as discounts on just about everything offered at the resort).

Most ski resorts generally offer the same types of seasonal jobs, which fall under the categories of administration, food and beverage, hospitality services, mountain operations, and ski services. So whether you want to become a snowboard instructor, teach children how to ski, serve meals to guests, or assist with marketing efforts, opportunities abound. In general, people from all walks of life are hired—from those who recently finished their college studies to those looking for a lifestyle change.

SO YOU WANT TO BE A SKI INSTRUCTOR?

For those interested in ski and snowboard instructor positions, sometimes it's not enough to be an excellent skier. Certification in your specialty is often a requirement. Ski instructors should contact the Professional Ski Instructors of America (www.psia.org/education/certification.htm). For ski patrol positions, the National Ski Patrol (www.nsp.org) provides courses and certification. Similarly, the American Association of Snowboard Instructors (www.aasi.org) provides snowboarding certification. You'll also find that ski resorts look for those who are effective communicators and have a knowledge of teaching and learning theory, biomechanics and kinesiology, and human development.

The soul is healed by being with children. —FYODOR DOSTOYEVSKY

CALIFORNIA
ALPINE MEADOWS

LAKE TAHOE—site of the highest concentration of ski areas in the nation. Alpine Meadows is one of the "Big Six" among fourteen ski areas located in or near the Tahoe Basin with plenty of cross-country and backcountry skiing and snowboarding. It is also home to the Alpine Meadows Eco-Trail, providing kids and parents with information about the mountain's unique plant and animal life, and encouraging guests to learn about winter ecology, plants, and animals specific to the Sierra. With your typical ski-resort opportunities available, the winter staff at Alpine Meadows come to Lake Tahoe for the great lifestyle it affords, along with the great perks—including free skiing and snowboarding at Alpine Meadows, Boreal & Soda Springs, and Park City Mountain Resort in Utah (Alpine's corporate siblings) as well as at Sugar Bowl on Donner Summit. Housing will be a bit of a challenge in Tahoe unless you start your search early (it's best to do so by September). Applications can be obtained by calling or through email. Alpine Meadows also applies for six-month H-2B Visas for international applicants—call for more information if you fit under this category.

For More Information:
Human Resources Department
Alpine Meadows
P.O. Box 5279
Tahoe City, CA 96145
(800) 441-4423 • (530) 581-8302 • (530) 583-0963 (fax)
hr@skialpine.com • www.skialpine.com

BEAR VALLEY MOUNTAIN RESORT

LOCATED IN THE Stanislaus National Forest (between Lake Tahoe and Yosemite), Bear Valley boasts over thirty feet of snow each year with 1,280 acres of skiable terrain. In late November, hundreds of seasonal employees come to Bear Valley to work, learn, and play. Typical ski jobs can be found, ranging from lift operations and waitstaff to ski and snowboard instructors, with positions generally running through April 15. Along with an hourly wage, benefits include generous ski/snowboard privileges, family and friends passes, and ski/snowboard lessons. Limited employee housing is also available. Applicants are encouraged to attend the resort's annual job fair in late October. Applications are available online or call/write for more information.

For More Information:
Arrah Mann, Personnel Director
Bear Valley Mountain Resort
P.O. Box 5038
Bear Valley, CA 95223
(209) 753-2301, ext. 104 • (209) 753-6421 (fax)
work@bearvalley.com • www.bearvalley.com

BOREAL MOUNTAIN RESORT

BOREAL MOUNTAIN RESORT includes both Boreal and Soda Springs Ski Areas, which are located at the top of historic and scenic Donner Summit Pass in the Lake Tahoe region. Cleverly timed, Boreal opens on Halloween; Soda Springs on Thanksgiving. Boreal is best known for its night skiing and radical terrain-parks and half-pipes. Soda Springs was the first ski area in Tahoe to offer lift access tubing as an added snow sport. Typical seasonal jobs are offered, and employees can work one of two shifts, up to forty-eight hours per week, to accommodate day and night skiing. Along with a weekly wage, food is discounted at 50 percent, and merchandise from the sport shop is discounted at 25 percent. Along with complimentary ski rentals, employees can also ski free at Alpine Meadows, and Park City, Utah, which are owned by the same corporation. A pass-exchange program allows employees to check out Donner Ski Ranch, Royal Gorge, and Sugar Bowl midweek, and a new summer Sports Action Park makes it possible to work seasonally during the summer months.

For More Information:
Human Resources Dept.
Boreal Mountain Resort
P.O. Box 39
Truckee, CA 96160
(530) 426-3666, ext. 357 • (530) 426-3173 (fax)
hr@borealski.com • www.borealski.com

HEAVENLY SKI RESORT

SPREAD OVER FORTY-EIGHT hundred acres of Tahoe's majestic terrain with the highest skiable peak rising to over ten thousand feet, the mountain itself certainly draws many to Heavenly Ski Resort. However, those who join the Heavenly team also join a community of people who share a common bond: a love for mountain living, outdoor adventuring, and, well, living life to the fullest. In addition to great alpine skiing, Heavenly offers a snowboard park (with a snowboard-cross course and a half-pipe) and an adventure park (at 9,100 feet), that showcases a tubing run, wide-open terrain for snow play and sledding, cross-country skiing, and snowshoeing. Seasonal staff come from all over the world and work in every conceivable area on the mountain and at the resort. If working and playing at Heavenly isn't benefit enough, additional perks include a free ski pass (for Heavenly and eight other ski resorts), lessons, and discounts galore. For those who make at least a three-month commitment, limited employee housing is an option (units fit four to six people and are fully furnished). The majority of employees, however, live in the cities of South Lake Tahoe (California) and Stateline (Nevada). As a general rule, expect to pay $300 to $500 per month per person for rent. Current job openings are constantly updated online with an online application available.

For More Information:
Human Resources
Heavenly Ski Resort
P.O. Box 2180
Stateline, NV 89449
(775) 586-7000, ext. 6255 • (530) 541-2643 (fax)
personnel@skiheavenly.com • www.skiheavenly.com

HOMEWOOD MOUNTAIN RESORT

HOME-AWAY-FROM-home for many, Homewood Mountain Resort is a place you won't find lift lines, traffic hassles, and congestion—just wide open spaces for great skiing. During the winter months, seasonal staff have the opportunity to work in the ski school, the race team, lift operations, parking and transportation, food and beverage, building maintenance, ticketing, or children's services. Positions run from mid-December through mid-April, with most of the hiring done by the end of October. Generous benefits are provided as is limited employee housing. (However, if you'll be looking for your own digs, an early house-hunting trip is strongly recommended.) Call or email for the latest line on job opportunities.

For More Information:
Human Resources Director
Homewood Mountain Resort
P.O. Box 165
Homewood, CA 96141
(530) 525-2992, ext. 126 • (530) 525-0417 (fax)
smile@skihomewood.com • www.skihomewood.com

IVGID-DIAMOND PEAK SKI RESORT

LOCATED ON THE beautiful north shore of Lake Tahoe, Incline Village General Improvement District (IVGID) facilities include Diamond Peak Ski Resort, two eighteen-hole golf courses, a recreation center, beaches, and parks—with employment opportunities available in each! Seasonal positions range from day-camp leaders and recreation hosts to food and beverage and ski resort staff (during the winter months). In addition, recreation interns spend half their time in paid work assignments, while the other half is spent volunteering. Hourly wages vary and perks include free access to private beaches, food and beverage discounts, membership to the Incline Village Recreation Center, golfing privileges, and during the winter months—complimentary skiing/snowboarding, ski equipment rental, and lessons. Those who possess a good work ethic, enjoy the outdoors and beautiful mountain settings, have a flexible schedule, and are customer-service focused will thrive at IVGID. Call or email for specific job descriptions and an application.

For More Information:
Lisa Hoopes, Human Resources Analyst
IVGID/Diamond Peak Ski Resort
893 Southwood Blvd.
Incline Village, NV 89451
(775) 832-1205 • (775) 832-1359 (fax)
jobs@ivgid.org • www.ivgid.org

KIRKWOOD MOUNTAIN RESORT

OVER ONE HUNDRED years ago, Zachary Kirkwood found himself in awe of a landscape of vibrant meadows surrounded by towering peaks. This High Sierra valley now bears his name and your reaction to this protected enclave may well be the same—that is, if you decide to explore the opportunities at Kirkwood Mountain Resort. As with most ski resorts, you'll find the usual seasonal employment opportunities—from lodging and housekeeping staff to skier services and ski/snowboard instructors. The snow season is always contingent on snow conditions, but usually runs from Thanksgiving through the end of April. Along with an hourly wage, there are a plethora of perks, including a free season pass, group ski and snowboarding lessons, cross-country trail use and lessons, lift tickets for family and friends, and an employee shuttle from surrounding towns (South Lake Tahoe and Gardnerville, Nevada, are about forty miles from the resort). Onsite housing is available for about 20 percent of the employees, so apply early! The rent runs $200 to $320 per month, including utilities and a furnished apartment. Applications can be obtained online, although it's best to apply in person at the hiring fair held in October.

For More Information:
Human Resources Manager
Kirkwood Mountain Resort
P.O. Box 1
Kirkwood, CA 95646
(209) 258-7385 • (209) 258-7340 (job hotline)
(209) 258-7368 (fax)
scota@ski-kirkwood.com • www.kirkwood.com

MAMMOTH MOUNTAIN SKI AREA

DRIVING ALONG CALIFORNIA's Highway 395 on the eastern side of the Sierra Nevada mountain range, Mammoth Mountain is impossible to miss: its 11,053-foot summit dominates the skyline as the highway moves from desert to forest. One look at Mammoth any time between October and June will be explanation enough for Mammoth's claim to skiing fame: the mountain gets an average of 385 inches of snow per year! In addition to epic skiing at Mammoth Mountain, the resort also operates June Mountain, a smaller "boutique" resort, as well as a number of other recreational and lodging facilities.

Seasonal positions are offered in four areas—skier services, outside operations, food services, and hotel operations—with the bulk of positions available during the winter from late November through April. Along with a weekly wage (starting at $8 per hour), winter housing is provided for first-year seasonal employees who are part of the Mammoth entry-level staff or those participating in the Foreign Exchange Program. Housing varies from private rooms to bunk beds at a cost of $9 to $16 per night (over six hundred beds in the Mammoth Lakes area are committed to employees). Yes, there are plenty of perks as well, including complimentary skiing, snowboarding, and cross-country skiing privileges and lessons. International applicants need to apply for winter employment by September 1 in order to insure adequate time to process documentation and guarantee housing.

For More Information:
Jeff Byberg, Recruiting Manager
Mammoth Mountain Ski Area
Human Resources Department
P.O. Box 24
Mammoth Lakes, CA 93546
(800) 472-3160 • (760) 934-0654 • (760) 934-0608 (fax)
personnel@mammoth-mtn.com
www.mammothmountain.com

NORTHSTAR-AT-TAHOE

LOCATED AT LAKE TAHOE in the majestic northern Sierra Nevada (where the sun shines 80 percent of the time), Northstar offers winter, summer, and year-round seasonal positions. The majority of positions are during the winter months (mid-December through mid-April), with a focus on mountain operations, food and beverage, housekeeping, ski rental, retail, and lodging. Along with a weekly wage, benefits include a complimentary ski/snowboard pass and skiing privileges at all Booth Creek resorts as well as participation in employee events, such as parties, ski races, and golf tournaments throughout the year. Most of the hiring is done at job fairs at the end of October, which gives applicants the chance to meet managers in person. Interviews can be arranged after the job fairs depending on what positions are still available. Employment packets for the winter season are available at the beginning of September, and can be obtained by calling the job hotline.

For More Information:
Employee Services
Northstar-at-Tahoe
P.O. Box 129
Truckee, CA 96160
(530) 562-3510 • (530) 562-2217 (job hotline)
jobs@skinorthstar.com • www.skinorthstar.com

ROYAL GORGE CROSS-COUNTRY SKI RESORT

WITH OVER NINE thousand acres of private lands and a network of eighty-eight trails, Royal Gorge is the largest cross-country ski resort in North America. Guest services include two overnight lodges, a day lodge, and ten warming huts sprinkled throughout the track system on historic Donner Summit. From mid-November through mid-April, seasonal employees are hired in administration, mountain operations, resort services, the ski school,

Photo Credit: David Madison

Seasonal ski instructors at Royal Gorge Cross Country Ski Resort help novices fine-tune their cross-country skiing abilities.

and the wilderness lodge. As in any ski area, work hours are entirely dependent upon the weather. Along with a weekly wage, perks include a free season pass, use of rental equipment, and ski school lessons, as well as discounted meals. For those who need housing, Royal Gorge has several furnished houses that are usually within walking (or skiing) distance of the resort, with rents ranging from $80 to $270 per month plus utilities. Bunkhouse-style accommodations are also available for part-time employees. Send a resume and cover letter to begin the application process or attend the job fair in mid-October.

For More Information:
Director of Operations
Royal Gorge Cross-Country Ski Resort
P.O. Box 1100
Soda Springs, CA 95728
(800) 500-3871 • (530) 426-3871 • (530) 426-9221 (fax)
hr@royalgorge.com • www.royalgorge.com

SNOW SUMMIT MOUNTAIN RESORT

WITH AN AVERAGE snowfall of seventy-five inches, Snow Summit Mountain Resort is located in Southern California's pristine Big Bear Lake area. Over one thousand winter seasonal positions are available in all areas of operation, ranging from the ski school and rental shop to food and beverage and marketing. Wages range from $6.75 to $17 per hour (depending on position and experience),

and benefits include complimentary lift tickets and lessons as well as discounted ski and snowboard rental, meals, and retail purchases. Most of the seasonal staff is hired at the resort's October job fair, where managers and supervisors from every department will be on hand to conduct personal interviews and make job offers on the spot. Those who cannot make it to the job fair must submit their applications in person to the personnel department.

For More Information:
Personnel Director
Snow Summit Mountain Resort
880 Summit Blvd.
P.O. Box 77
Big Bear Lake, CA 92315-0077
(909) 866-5766, ext. 141 • (909) 866-6806 (fax)
employeeservices@snowsummit.com
www.snowsummit.com

SQUAW VALLEY USA

WHETHER WORKING AS a children's ski instructor or as one of their cable car operators, winter seasonal staff at Squaw Valley have high expectations of them, but are also offered fun and recreation, lifetime friendships, personal achievements, and a valuable work experience in return. Flexible hours, competitive wages, and the benefits alone (a free ski pass, lessons, and discounts galore) make this a great way to spend a season in Lake Tahoe. It's always best to visit the personnel office in person or attend the job

Life would be infinitely happier if we could only be born at the age of eighty and gradually approach eighteen. —MARK TWAIN

WORKING AT A SKI RESORT

WORKING AT A SKI RESORT

fair in October (where they'll be doing interviews and making job offers on the spot); however, if you won't be in the Tahoe area, either fill out the online application or call for an employment booklet.

For More Information:
Jim Brady, Personnel Department
Squaw Valley USA
P.O. Box 2007
Olympic Valley, CA 96146
(530) 581-7112 • (530) 581-7117 (job hotline)
(530) 581-7202 (fax)
personnel@squaw.com • www.squaw.com

SUGAR BOWL SKI RESORT

HOME TO THE first chairlift in California and first gondola in the country, Sugar Bowl is known for its rich history and deep powder—over 1,500 acres of challenging terrain, four picturesque mountain peaks, and three day lodges. Those who come to work for Sugar Bowl are lured by the mountains, an enjoyable working experience, and an enriching lifestyle. Benefits include a season pass and complimentary lift tickets for friends and family, discounts on just about everything, and flexible schedules. Limited housing is also available: dorm rooms have two or three people per room, community bathrooms down the hall, and are $225 to $250 per month, while semiprivate "hotel-style" rooms have two people per room, a private bath and TV, and run $275 to $300 per month. It's recommended that you attend the Sugar Bowl job fair, which is normally conducted the last two Saturdays of October. Applications are available online.

For More Information:
Personnel Department
Sugar Bowl Ski Resort
P.O. Box 5
Norden, CA 95724
(530) 426-6730 • (530) 426-6731 (job hotline)
(530) 426-3723 (fax)
personnel@sugarbowl.com • www.sugarbowl.com

COLORADO

ASPEN SKIING COMPANY

ASPEN SKIING COMPANY operates four ski resorts in Aspen, including Snowmass, Aspen Mountain, Aspen Highlands, and Buttermilk Mountain. Seasonal and year-round opportunities are available, with the bulk of positions offered in the winter months on and off the mountain. One of the biggest perks is a complimentary four-mountain ski pass (which is also good for summer gondola rides), along with skiing and snowboarding clinics, tickets to five neighboring ski resorts, and discounted health insurance. Housing is available, although limited and in high demand (translation: the early bird gets the worm). Their website provides extensive information on the best ways to find housing (along with application materials).

For More Information:
Jenny Lee, Recruiting Specialist
Aspen Skiing Company
Human Resources Department
P.O. Box 1248
Aspen, CO 81612-1248
(800) 525-6200 • (970) 920-0946
(970) 923-0499 (job hotline) • (970) 920-0771 (fax)
hr@aspensnowmass.com • www.jobswithaltitude.com

COPPER MOUNTAIN RESORT

BLESSED WITH A nearly perfect mountain (naturally divided into a variety of terrain features for expert, intermediate, and beginner skiers), Copper Mountain Resort is both a "local's choice" and a popular destination resort for people who love the mountains. Winter seasonal employees begin their adventures in early November and work in a variety of on- and off-the-mountain positions. The average entry-level wage is $8 per hour, along with a season pass and free lessons. However, to keep your season filled with glades, half-pipes, parks, bowls, and cruisers, you'll also have unlimited skiing access at an additional sixteen ski areas managed by Intrawest (see listing on page 144). Employee housing is limited and most find housing in the surrounding towns of Frisco, Dillon, Silverthorne, Breckenridge, or Leadville (with the average cost of housing ranging from $350 to $650 per month, per person.) For those interested in booking short-term temporary housing, one of these three hostels will get you started: Alpen Hutte (www.alpenhutte.com); Just Bunks (www.hostels.com/justbunks); and Leadville Hostel (www.leadvillehostel.com).

For More Information:
Employment Manager
Copper Mountain Resort
P.O. Box 3548
Copper Mountain, CO 80443
(800) 458-8386 • (970) 968-3060 • (970) 968-3165 (fax)
humanresources@coppercolorado.com
www.coppercolorado.com

Helpful application tips from Copper Mountain:

- List specific jobs that you are applying for on your application (which can be filled out online).
- Be specific about your employment-history details in your application/resume.
- If you intend to apply in person, bring your resume on disk so you can cut and paste it into the resort's application. On-the-spot interviews are arranged whenever possible.
- Don't be afraid to follow up on your application. If you don't hear from someone, give the resort a call. Since your application/resume is routed to the department to which you applied, you are free to contact that department directly.

CRESTED BUTTE MOUNTAIN RESORT

KNOWN FOR ITS extreme skiing and its funky Victorian architecture, Crested Butte remains one of the last undiscovered ski towns in the West and home to the U.S. Extreme Skiing and Snowboarding Championships. College students take note—in additional to seasonal employment opportunities, Crested Butte also has a winter and summer internship program, with positions in business, early childhood development, food and beverage, hospitality management, sales, and ski-area management. So while you're earning academic credit, you're also gaining experience in the field and making the same wages as other seasonal employees. Starting wages range from $6 to $7.25 per hour along with a "Real Deal" ski pass that not only gives you ski privileges at Crested Butte, but also at Aspen, Copper Mountain, Durango, Loveland, Steamboat, Sunlight, and Winter Park! Limited employee housing is available at the resort (from $370 to $415 per month) and in rustic cabins in Almont (about eighteen miles south of the ski area) for $200 to $450 per month (typical rent in the area runs $500 to $1,000). Check online for the latest openings and application details.

For More Information:
Elaine Crumpton, Human Resources Director
Crested Butte Mountain Resort
12 Snowmass Rd.
P.O. Box 5700
Mt. Crested Butte, CO 81225
(970) 349-4606 • (970) 349-4777 (job hotline)
(970) 349-2250 (fax)
jobs@cbmr.com • www.skicb.com

DURANGO MOUNTAIN RESORT

AS A SMALL and unique extension of the mountain community of Durango (on the southern rim of the Rockies), Durango Mountain Resort offers a variety of seasonal ski jobs during the winter months as well as year-round opportunities at the resort itself. Benefits include a free ski pass at Durango along with skiing privileges at other major ski resorts in Colorado, including Copper Mountain, Steamboat Springs, and Winter Park. The majority of winter staff is hired at the job fair held each October. Check out current openings on the Web.

For More Information:
Human Resources Department
Durango Mountain Resort
#1 Skier Place
Durango, CO 81301
(970) 385-2162, ext. 4 • (970) 247-9000 (job hotline)
hr@durangomountain.com
www.durangomountainresort.com

STEAMBOAT SKI AND RESORT CORPORATION

STEAMBOAT SPRINGS HAS the distinction of being the home of more winter Olympic athletes than any other town in North America (with forty-seven and still counting). Not only is this a great place to ski (averaging over 300 inches of snow and 2,900 acres of skiing terrain), the town is rich in Western heritage with a lifestyle that includes a true Ranching community, many cultural events, a great night life, and endless outdoor and sporting activities.

What You'll Be Doing: Staff positions are available either indoors or out, and your new mode of transportation to work just may be a high-speed gondola with your skis attached! Close to a thousand full-time staff members are hired on the mountain in these areas: accounting, competition services, courtesy patrol, mountain operations, food and beverage, kids' vacation center, lift ticket office, reservations, real estate and facilities, resort services, security, and ski and snowboard school, along with positions at the Steamboat Grand Resort Hotel.

Commitment: Winter staff are generally hired from Thanksgiving until mid-April . . . and don't forget about the summer months. Summer operations normally begin in early June through Labor Day (with positions that range from adventure-club counselors to mountain trail crew). A variety of administrative, management, and year-round positions are also available.

Perks and Rewards: Many jobs don't require that you know how to ski or snowboard, but if you'd like to learn, they'll be happy to teach you—just one of the many staff benefits. Others include competitive wages, a free ski pass (including dependents), access to a health insurance plan, and limited staff housing. Housing is maintained in two-bedroom, two-bath units located approximately one mile from the base area. These units are fully furnished (down to the pots and pans). Rent is based on two people per room (total of four occupants in one unit) at $300 per month plus utilities, and units are filled on a first-come, first-served basis.

Your First Move: Applications are available online and the resort's annual job fair is held in early November each year. Instructors and patrol candidates must attend a hiring clinic in late November or early December.

For More Information:
Karen Goedert, Human Resources Manager
Steamboat Ski and Resort Corporation
2305 Mt. Werner Circle
Steamboat Springs, CO 80487
(970) 871-5132 • (970) 871-5130 (fax)
personnel@steamboat.com • www.steamboat.com

TELLURIDE SKI AND GOLF COMPANY

IN ADDITION TO your typical ski-resort jobs that are available in the winter months and throughout the year, Telluride offers a twelve-week internship program that allows interns to work in different departments and perform varied tasks. For interns, a $1,000 stipend is provided, along with a free ski pass if working during the winter months. Employee housing is limited; however, they will assist you in finding suitable accommodations (the local paper, *The Daily Planet,* is a good source of available rentals). To begin the internship application process, send a resume, a letter of reference, a copy of your school's internship manual, and a letter detailing your skills and internship goals. For seasonal employment, applications are available online.

For More Information:
Heather Young, Human Resources Manager
Telluride Ski and Golf Company
565 Mountain Village Blvd.
Telluride, CO 81435

(888) 754-1010 • (970) 728-7331 • (970) 728-7443 (fax)
jobs@telluridecolorado.net •
www.tellurideskiresort.com

VAIL RESORTS

VAIL RESORTS (WWW.VAILRESORTS.COM) owns and operates four ski resorts—Vail, Beaver Creek, Breckenridge, and Keystone—which are all located within a forty-mile radius of each other. That's good news for seasonal and year-round employees coming to the Rocky Mountains of Colorado, as your ski and snowboard pass is good at each of them. And that's just the beginning. In addition to free ski/snowboard lessons, health benefits, and resortwide meal, lodging, and retail discounts, employee housing is available to thirty-five hundred employees. All housing is furnished and cable ready, with dormitory- or apartment-style options, and rents ranging from $200 to $490 per month.

Employment information can be found at www.skijob1.com (providing a searchable database of current employment opportunities), through the job hotline at (888) SKI-JOB1, or by contacting each resort individually:

▶ Breckenridge

OVER FIFTEEN HUNDRED employees come to Breckenridge to enjoy alpine and nordic skiing, snowboarding, and ice-skating during the winter months, while the summer is filled with white-water rafting, mountain biking, hiking, and a summer music festival on Maggie Pond. In addition to on-the-mountain ski positions, those who want to advance their careers in the resort and hospitality field will find plenty of opportunities at the Village at Breckenridge and the Great Divide Lodge.

Ski Positions:
Breckenridge Resort
Human Resources
P.O. Box 1058
Breckenridge, CO 80424
(970) 453-3238 • (970) 453-3260 (fax)
breckjobs@vailresorts.com • www.breckresort.com

Lodging and Hospitality Positions:
The Village at Breckenridge/Great Divide Lodge
Human Resources
P.O. Box 8329
Breckenridge, CO 80424
(970) 453-3120 • (970) 453-3127 (fax)
breckhr@vailresorts.com

▶ Keystone

WITH A NATURALLY spectacular setting in the Arapaho National Forest, Keystone Resort offers a variety of year-round employment opportunities in addition to those on the slope during the winter months. Keystone's best kept secret is its summer. More than eighteen hundred employees work year-round at the conference center, lodges, restaurants, or golf courses.

For More Information:
Keystone Resort
Human Resources
P.O. Box 38
Keystone, CO 80435
(970) 496-4157 • (970) 496-4310 (fax)
keyjobs@vailresorts.com • www.keystoneresort.com

▶ Vail/Beaver Creek Resorts

MOST EMPLOYEES COME to Vail for the skiing; however, the small-town atmosphere, active outdoor lifestyle, and the friendly people lure them for more than just a season. Vail Resort features the biggest network of high-speed quad lifts in North America, while Beaver Creek is home to the Birds of Prey Downhill Course, designed for the 1999 World Alpine Skiing Championships—and if you love skiing with sunny skies, the area averages over 275 days of sunshine per year.

Ski Positions:
Vail/Beaver Creek Resorts
Human Resources
P.O. Box 7
Vail, CO 81658
(970) 845-2460 • (970) 845-2465 (fax)
vbcjobs@vailresorts.com • www.vailresorts.com

Hospitality Positions:
The Lodge at Vail
Human Resources
174 E. Gore Creek Dr.
Vail, CO 81657
(970) 477-3751 • (970) 477-3746 (fax)
lavjobs@vailresorts.com • www.lodgeatvail.com

For Vail/Beaver Creek Ski School employment information, visit www.vailbcschools.com

Photo Credit: Helen Norman

Whether it's Glow Bug Skate Night or a pick-up hockey game after work, Keystone's ice-skating rink serves as a hub of winter activities for Keystone Village. The lake is the largest Zamboni-maintained outdoor rink in North America.

WINTER PARK RESORT

COME ENJOY THE year-round beauty of the Rockies—and don't forget to bring your adventurous spirit with you. Winter Park is the fifth-largest ski area in Colorado although it manages to avoid the mainstream crowds of the "rich and famous." Popular activities at Winter Park include skiing, snowboarding, snowshoeing, ice-skating, snowmobiling, tubing, mountain biking, rafting, hiking, camping, fishing, stargazing, hunting, and enjoying beautiful scenery. For applicants with a limited skiing or snowboarding background, positions are available in food service, facilities, grounds crew and parking, ticket and lesson sales, reservations, and children's center staff. For applicants with some basic skiing or snowboarding ability, there are numerous openings for lift attendants. Advanced skiers and snowboarders may apply for positions as race-crew members and ski and snowboard instructors. Wages start at $8.25 per hour for entry-level positions, with benefits including a free season pass, discounted lift passes for friends, free ski and snowboard lessons, group health insurance, and food and beverage

There's always something to suggest you'll never be who you want to be.
Your choice is to take it or keep on moving. —PHYLICIA RASHAD

WORKING AT A SKI RESORT

discounts. Employees can also use the Sports Science Fitness Center or the Early Education Center (day care for employees' children) for a nominal fee. Winter Park also offers a limited amount of subsidized employee housing in nearby condos. Applications are available online.

For More Information:
Recruiting Office
Winter Park Resort
P.O. Box 36
Winter Park, CO 80482
(888) 562-4525 • (970) 726-1536 • (303) 892-5823 (fax)
wpjobs@mail.skiwinterpark.com
www.winterparkresort.com

IDAHO

SUN VALLEY RESORT

NESTLED IN THE Idaho Rockies, Sun Valley Resort is home to Bald Mountain (also known as "Baldy"), which boasts great alpine and nordic skiing as well as snowboarding (with a perfect pitch and 3,400-foot vertical drop!) during the winter months and incredible hiking and mountain biking during the summer. In addition to Baldy, Dollar Mountain caters to beginners, and has been dubbed "the finest teaching mountain in the world." At this year-round destination resort, seasonal staff members are able to work in the summer, winter, or year-round. You'll find your typical resort positions available and most first-year employees work in food and beverage, mountain operations, or retail. Wages start above minimum wage, with a slew of benefits including access to the employee fitness center and pools, first-run movies at the Opera House, year-round ice-skating, bike rentals, discounts on just about everything, and low-cost meals at the employee cafeteria. Current job opportunities can be found online, or call/email for more information.

For More Information:
Human Resources Department
Sun Valley Resort
P.O. Box 10
Sun Valley, ID 83353
(800) 894-9946 • (208) 622-2078 • (208) 622-2082 (fax)
svpersonnel@sunvalley.com • www.sunvalley.com

MAINE

SUGARLOAF–USA

As YOU ROUND the "Oh My Gosh Corner" on Route 27 and are confronted with Sugarloaf Mountain for the very first time, this spectacular sight will surely take your breath away. Sitting at 3,000 feet above the leafy floor of the Maine woods and way above the tree line, Sugarloaf has 1,400 skiable acres and is home to the state's largest nordic trail network (not to mention a solar-heated lodge with magnificent views, trailside warming huts, and an Olympic-size skating rink). Whether working as a ski instructor or a food server during the winter months, seasonal employees come to Sugarloaf for the small-town mountain lifestyle that it promotes. A great community, sunrises, and snow are definitely not the only perks. Seasonal staff receive a season pass for alpine and cross-country skiing (and snowboarding), a membership to the sports and fitness club, group skiing and riding clinics, and ski/snowboard rentals. Current jobs are posted online, as is an application.

For More Information:
Human Resources Office
Sugarloaf/USA
R.R. 1, Box 5000
Carrabassett Valley, ME 04947
(800) 843-5623 • (207) 237-2000, ext. 6932
jobs@sugarloaf.com • www.sugarloaf.com

SUNDAY RIVER SKI RESORT

While Sunday River boasts great skiing and snowboarding with the "most dependable snow in New England," it offers a wide range of additional services including the innovative Perfect Turn Ski and Snowboard Program, six full-service restaurants, three pubs, two slopeside cafes, three food courts, and the mountaintop Peak Lodge.

What You'll Be Doing: Sunday River provides an exciting and diverse work environment for the more than thirteen hundred seasonal staff employed each winter season (including more than one hundred international staff each year). Positions include lift operators, housekeepers, snowmakers, food and beverage staff, ski/snowboard instructors, ticket sales, lodging, retail, and maintenance.

Commitment: Most positions are available from mid-December to mid-April, with varied start and finish

WORKING AT A SKI RESORT

dates. Typical workdays run from as early as 6:00 A.M. to after the lifts close; most positions require working weekends and some holidays.

Perks and Rewards: Wages vary between departments, but range from $6 to $7.50 per hour. Employee housing is limited and given out on a first-come, first-served basis. Housing is offered (by law) to all international staff. Benefits include a free season pass (including dependents), which is valid at all American Skiing Company Resorts (including Sunday River and Sugarloaf in Maine, Killington/Pico and Mount Snow/Haystack in Vermont, Attitash/Bear Peak in New Hampshire, The Canyons in Utah, Heavenly in California, and Steamboat Springs in Colorado).

The Essentials: Sunday River strives to hire energetic staff who are hardworking, dependable, flexible, and customer-service minded.

Your First Move: Hiring begins in September, with application materials available online. International staff who wish to be hired on an H-2B Visa must begin the application process in August; those on a J-1 visa may apply in September.

For More Information:
Callie Phillips, Human Resources Recruiter
Sunday River Ski Resort
P.O. Box 450
Bethel, ME 04217
(877) 476-6956 • (207) 824-3000 • (207) 824-5381 (fax)
jobs@sundayriver.com • www.sundayriver.com

MONTANA

BIG MOUNTAIN SKI AND SUMMER RESORT

LOCATED IN THE Rocky Mountains of northwest Montana (just thirty miles west of Glacier National Park), Big Mountain is one of the largest ski resorts in the U.S. and Canada, featuring three thousand acres of skiable terrain along with twenty miles of mountain-bike trails. Whether working seasonally during the winter or summer months (or both!), Big Mountain is a great place to begin your mountain lifestyle. Seasonal positions are generally found in lift operations, ticket and ski lesson sales, hotel operations, retail sales, and parking, although ski patrol and ski school instructor positions are also available. Since most are entry-level positions, no prior experience is required and training will be provided. The ski season typically opens on Thanksgiving Day and closes in mid-April,

while the summer season opens the first Saturday in June and closes in early October. There is also a need for additional short-term employees during the holiday period in late December and early January; this is a great opportunity for students who are on holiday break. Entry-level wages range from $6.60 to $7 per hour along with great benefits. Most employees live in the nearby towns of Whitefish (eight miles from Big Mountain), Columbia Falls (sixteen miles), or Kalispell (twenty-five miles). Applications can be found online.

For More Information:
Human Resources Department
Big Mountain Ski and Summer Resort
Attn: Winter Sports, Inc.
P.O. Box 1400
Whitefish, MT 59937
(800) 858-3930 • (406) 862-1937 • (406) 862-2995 (fax)
jobs@bigmtn.com • www.bigmtn.com

BIG SKY RESORT

HOME TO THE "huge, wonderful, uncrowded hill" in the winter, Big Sky Resort offers skiing and snowboarding on over thirty-six hundred acres across three mountains. Winter opportunities include ski patrol, snowboard, ski, and child instructors, guest services, lift operations, accounting staff, retail, food and beverage, hotel operations, and housekeeping. Look under "current openings" on the Web for a complete list of seasonal and potential full-time year-round positions (along with downloadable application forms). Most positions pay between $6 and $7 per hour along with a ski pass in the winter or a golf pass during the summer. Dorm-style housing is offered on a space-available basis either in the rustic Mountain Lodge ($200 per month) or in the dorms ($160 per month). In addition to the many outdoor activities in the area, Big Sky has an activities director who plans in-house activities for employees. Past activities have included dance parties, fly-fishing lessons, movie nights, golf tournaments, and group hikes. It's noted that the resort is looking for adventure-seeking outdoor enthusiasts who are not desiring much nightlife.

For More Information:
Velvet Williams, Human Resources Department
Big Sky Resort
1 Lone Mountain Trail
P.O. Box 160001
Big Sky, MT 59716
(406) 995-5812 • (406) 995-5001 (fax)
jobs@bigskyresort.com • www.bigskyresort.com

Photo Credit: David Nagel

WORKING AT A SKI RESORT

NEW HAMPSHIRE

LOON MOUNTAIN RESORT

WHY WOULD YOU name a ski resort after a powerful flying waterbird with red eyes and the ability to dive to depths of two hundred feet and fly up to eighty miles per hour? Well, legend has it that loons once nested (and mated for life) on the pond at the summit, and the loons' beauty, strength, and commitment to family were an inspiration to all humans at this special mountain. Maybe you, too, can find out what's special here. Just two hours from Boston, Loon Mountain offers forty-four trails that wind down 2,100 vertical feet spread over 275 acres. Those who love a resort atmosphere, enjoy helping people have fun on their vacations, and have a "can do" attitude are the optimum Loon seasonal staff members. Along with competitive wages and benefits, seasonal workers also have the opportunity to live in employee housing, which runs $60 per week for a double or triple room and $85 per week for a single room. Current job opportunities can be found online (or by calling).

For More Information:
Human Resources
Loon Mountain Resort
R.R. 1, Box 41
Kancamagus Highway
Lincoln, NH 03251-9711
(603) 745-6281, ext. 5581
gclark.lm@boothcreek.com • www.loonmtn.com

NEW MEXICO

ANGEL FIRE RESORT

CENTURIES AGO, NATIVE AMERICANS revered the Moreno Valley as the land of angel fire, a name they gave to the phenomenon which occurs when sunlight reflects off the morning frost on the branches of mountaintop trees. Today this valley and the Sangre de Cristo Mountains are home to Angel Fire Resort. Along with skiing, cross-country skiing, and snowboarding, thrill seekers will definitely appreciate Liberation Park, which includes a four-hundred-foot half-pipe at the summit (along with numerous moguls). With seasonal and year-round staff opportunities available, it's more than just skiing at Angel Fire—especially if you like golfing and fishing! One of the biggest perks is employee housing. While you will be sharing a condominium with three other employees, these large two-bedroom, three-bath units are available for only $175 a month per person. Applications are available online.

For More Information:
Human Resources Department
Angel Fire Resort
P.O. Drawer B
Angel Fire, NM 87710
(800) 633-7463 • (505) 377-4227 • (505) 377-4240 (fax)
hr@angelfireresort.com • www.angelfireresort.com

OREGON

MT. BACHELOR

MT. BACHELOR IS nestled in the heart of Central Oregon near Bend, where winter and summer collide in an explosion of exciting activities. From skiing, snowboarding, snowmobiling, and backwoods excursions to fishing, golfing, rafting, rock climbing, and mountain biking, there is always something to do. With a staff of over eight hundred team members (working in your typical ski resort jobs), Mt. Bachelor is looking for reliable team members who are enthusiastic and like to have fun while they work. Winter seasonal positions run from approximately mid-November through April, and team members are expected to commit to a full season. The hiring process starts in mid-September, with a variety of job fairs scheduled in early November. Housing isn't provided; however, there are ample options in Bend and the surrounding areas; for more information call *RENT Magazine* at (541) 617-1367. Applications can be found online; in-person interviews are required.

For More Information:
Human Resources Dept.
Mt. Bachelor
P.O. Box 1031
Bend, OR 97709-1031
(800) 829-2442 • (541) 382-2442 • (541) 382-6536 (fax)
jobs@mtbachelor.com • www.mtbachelor.com

MT. HOOD MEADOWS SKI RESORT

MT. HOOD MEADOWS features 2,150 acres of rugged terrain, complete with mogul-filled bowls, chutes, ridges, and outback skiing in Heather Canyon. Winter positions (from early November to late April) include lift operators, ski patrol, snow groomers, rental technicians, cashiers, ticket checkers, bus drivers, and food-service staff. Wages range from $6.50 to $10 per hour. Perks include a free season pass, lessons, and shuttle bus transportation. Discounts on food and ski shop purchases are also available. Applicants should be gregarious, neat, and have previous service-oriented experience and the tenacity to work in a mountain environment. It's highly recommended that applicants attend the job fair the first week of October. Applications are available online.

For More Information:
Human Resources Dept.
Mt. Hood Meadows Ski Resort
P.O. Box 470
Mt. Hood, OR 97041
(503) 337-2222, ext. 338 • (503) 337-2218 (fax)
hr@skihood.com • www.skihood.com

TIMBERLINE LODGE

YOU'LL RECOGNIZE A "sense of place" (and some of nature's most scenic country) at Timberline Lodge. Constructed of mammoth timbers and native stone, the lodge, registered as a National Historic Landmark, stands today as tribute to the rugged spirit of the Pacific Northwest. Seasonal positions are available in lift operations, skier services, front desk, rental shop, lodge services, and kitchen and banquets; however, if you love teaching, many opt for instructor positions at the ski school. Hourly wages range from $6.50 to $16 (plus tips), depending on position. Employee housing is available in Government Camp, with rents that range from $275 to $325 per month. All housing features private sleeping quarters, private or limited-share bathrooms, shared kitchen, common area, washers, dryers, telephone, and is cable-ready. Timberline has one of the most competitive benefit packages around. A free season pass, a uniform, and meal and retail purchase discounts are only the tip of the iceberg. Their winter season is also one of the longest in the world (they typically open in mid-September andrun straight through the summer). Call or email for more information.

For More Information:
Bruce Clifton, Human Resources Manager
Timberline Lodge
Timberline Ski Area
Timberline Lodge, OR 97028
(503) 622-0715 • (503) 622-0710 (fax)
jobs@timberlinelodge.com • www.timberlinelodge.com

UTAH

ALTA SKI LIFTS COMPANY

DEEP POWDER SNOW, rugged terrain, and spectacular scenery are characteristics synonymous with Alta. Seasonal staff opportunities run from mid-November through April on and off the slopes, including ski school and ticket sales, kitchen and restaurant help, lift operators, Snowcat mechanics and operators, parking attendants, and PSIA-certified ski instructors. Benefits include free skiing privileges (there's no snowboarding on the mountain), ski school lessons, a season-end bonus, and employee housing at the ski area. Applications are available online.

For More Information:
Staffing Director
Alta Ski Lifts Company
P.O. Box 8007
Alta, UT 84092-8007
(801) 359-1078
info@alta.com • www.alta.com

WORKING AT A SKI RESORT

PARK CITY MOUNTAIN RESORT

As one of the hosts for the 2002 Olympic Winter Games (with venues including the alpine giant slalom and snowboarding events, along with Picabo Street as the Director of Skiing), Park City Mountain Resort is home to some great skiing and snowboarding terrain, with over one hundred trails—the longest running three-and-a-half miles. Winter seasonal workers have the opportunity to work in food and beverage, mountain operations, and skier services (which has a great kids' school)—and if you are a certified ski or snowboard instructor, Park City is definitely interested. The resort doesn't provide housing, although it does offer great wages and benefits. No worry, because housing always can be found in the surrounding areas of Park City, Heber, Salt Lake City, and Provo (and those without cars can always hop on the free Park City shuttle). All positions require an in-person interview and favorable references. In some instances, phone interviews are conducted for people with prior experience and outstanding references. It's strongly recommended that you attend one of the job fairs in the fall if you are interested in multiple positions. Applications are available online.

For More Information:
Human Resources
Park City Mountain Resort
P.O. Box 39
Park City, UT 84060
(435) 647-5421
hr@pcski.com • www.parkcitymountain.com

SNOWBIRD SKI AND SUMMER RESORT

With a mid-mountain average annual snowfall of more than five hundred inches, Snowbird boasts more fresh powder snow than almost any other resort in the country. Snowbird's mountain trails cover more than two thousand skiable acres. Seasonal staff positions include food service personnel, front desk clerks, reservation clerks, sales clerks, security officers, switchboard operators, valets, tram operators, ski hosts/hostesses, housekeeping, parking attendants, warehouse laborers, ski school, and mountain operations. Wages start at $7.50 per hour, with perks featuring a generous ski privilege program that includes dependent passes, group health/hospitalization, life insurance, free transportation, and discounts on food, ski lessons, and lodging. Most Snowbird employees live in and commute from the Salt Lake City area. Snowbird not only hires seasonal employees for the winter and summer months, but has many year-round positions as well.

For More Information:
Recruiting
Snowbird Ski and Summer Resort
c/o Snowbird Canyon Racquet and Fitness Club
7350 S. Wasatch Blvd.
Salt Lake City, UT 84121
(801) 947-8240 • (801) 947-8244 (fax)
employment@snowbird.com • www.snowbird.com

VERMONT

KILLINGTON RESORT

With two hundred trails spread over seven mountains (with views of five states and Canada!), Killington is definitely a skier's paradise. For snowboarders, there's a superpipe right outside the base lodge, along with Snowshed Trail and the Beach Terrain Park. Each winter the resort hires over one thousand seasonal employees in positions on and off the mountains—from ski coaches and snowmakers to guest services and food and beverage staff. The ski season begins in mid-November and continues all the way through June, although most seasonal jobs come to an end on April 1. Along with competitive wages and skiing privileges, Killington offers limited employee dorm-style housing at Green Mountain College. Shared, semiprivate rooms run $107.50 per person, per week, which includes a kitchenette, private bath, microwave oven, refrigerator, heat, cable television, and a set of linens. Applications for winter employment are accepted beginning in August. One of the best times to apply is at one of the job fairs held throughout the fall.

For More Information:
Human Resources
Killington Resort
4763 Killington Rd.
Killington, VT 05751
(800) 300-9095 • (802) 422-6100 • (802) 422-6294 (fax)
humres@killington.com • www.killington.com

OKEMO MOUNTAIN RESORT

Aside from Okemo's incredible terrain, it's the family-friendly atmosphere that sets this resort apart from the rest. Families can ski and ride together from virtually any lift or participate in instructional programs at the Learning Center, which features a staff of 250 professional (and young-at-heart) ski and snowboard instructors as well as

"Snow Stars" who assist with trailing children's classes. In addition to instructor positions, seasonal opportunities exist in administration, culinary services, grounds maintenance, lift and mountain operations, rentals and repairs, traffic control, and retail services. A competitive salary and an extensive list of benefits are provided. Applications are available online.

For More Information:
Human Resources
Okemo Mountain Resort
77 Okemo Ridge Rd.
Ludlow, VT 05149
(802) 228-4041
jobs@okemo.com • www.okemo.com

SMUGGLERS' NOTCH

KNOWN FOR THEIR unique family-programming throughout the year, Smugglers' Notch offers incredible skiing and snowboarding in the winter months and literally hundreds of outdoor activities during the summer (boasting the single largest summer day camp operation in the U.S.). As a seasonal staff member, the opportunities are limitless: dress up as Mogul Mouse for the children; work as a ski/snowboard instructor at the adaptive ski school; provide massages or create meals for guests; host recreation games in the clubhouse; lead hikes in the great outdoors; teach swimming in the aquatics facility; or deliver educational programs at the summer camp. Competitive wages and great benefits are provided. Applications are available online.

For More Information:
Human Resources
Smugglers' Notch
4323 Vermont Route 108 South
Smugglers' Notch, VT 05464-9537
(888) 754-7684 • (802) 644-8585 • (802) 644-8580 (fax)
employment@smuggs.com • www.smuggs.com/jobs

STOWE MOUNTAIN RESORT

SINCE THE SKI area shares its name with the town, there's no confusion about where seasonal employees are headed when they come to Stowe Mountain. Beyond the great skiing and resort atmosphere, the unique thing about Stowe is their AAA philosophy: attitude, awareness, and accountability—that positive vibe and respect for others that they instill in their guests and employees alike (who all wear the AAA pendant as a simple reminder of these golden rules). Seasonal jobs abound—housekeepers,

repair and rental technicians, child-care workers, food and beverage staff, lift and parking attendants, custodians, ski patrol and ski instructors—as do the benefits! Full-time staff members receive free skiing and snowboarding privileges (as do spouses and children), lessons, rentals, and discounts on just about everything (including the fitness center). Although employee housing is not available, a two-bedroom apartment or condominium ranges from $400 to $700 per month. Send off a cover letter and resume to begin the application process.

For More Information:
Human Resources
Stowe Mountain Resort
5781 Mountain Rd.
Stowe, VT 05672-4890
(802) 253-3541 • (802) 253-3544 (fax)
info@stowe.com • www.stowe.com

SUGARBUSH RESORT

THERE ARE FEW places as beautiful and charming as Sugarbush and the Mad River Valley in the Northeast. This is quintessential Vermont at its best—from classic-style New England skiing and boarding to covered bridges and steepled churches. Each winter over seven hundred seasonal employees come to this quaint area and work in a variety of positions on and off the mountain and at the lodge. Along with a weekly wage, full-time staff receive a free ski pass (as do spouse and/or children), rental equipment use for $5 per day, 50 percent discounts at cafeterias and the repair shop, and complimentary golfing (well, when it's not snowing . . .). Applications are available online.

For More Information:
Human Resources Department
Sugarbush Resort
R.R. 1, Box 350
Warren, VT 05674
(802) 583-6400 • (802) 583-6495 (fax)
hr@sugarbush.com • www.sugarbush.com

WASHINGTON

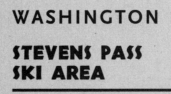

STEVENS PASS SKI AREA

TUCKED IN BETWEEN Mt. Baker–Snoqualmie and the Wenatchee National Forest, Stevens Pass is part of the scenic Cascade Loop, a unique location filled with snow—and lots of it—during the winter months. Covering 1,125 acres of skiable terrain, alpine and nordic skiers have their choice of numerous bowls, glades, faces, and pristine area, including the ominous Cowboy Mountain, which rises to 5,845 feet! Each winter, over eight hundred seasonal employees come to the mountain to work, play, and enjoy a plethora of benefits, with positions ranging from accounting and guest services to lift operators and snowboard instructors. Applications are available online.

For More Information:

Human Resources Department
Stevens Pass Ski Area
P.O. Box 98
Skykomish, WA 98288
(206) 812-4510 • (206) 812-4517 (fax)
humanresources@stevenspass.com
www.stevenspass.com

WYOMING

GRAND TARGHEE SKI AND SUMMER RESORT

GRAND TARGHEE IS a small, family-oriented resort nestled in the pines at eight thousand feet on the west side of the spectacular Teton Mountains. Over five hundred inches of annual snowfall provide some of the best skiing conditions during the winter, with miles of mountain-bike trails and terrain available during the summer. For music lovers, Targhee is known for their great summer music festivals. Targhee offers typical resort jobs in these departments: mountain, guest services, accounting/administrative, maintenance, lodging, food and beverage, retail, and rental. The summer season runs from June 15 to October 1; winter, November 15 to April 15. Seasonal employees receive an hourly wage, a free season pass with skiing privileges in Jackson Hole and Big Sky, and employee meal and retail discounts. Reasonable housing is available nearby, and the resort's free employee bus accommodates most work schedules. The resort begins hiring employees for the winter starting in August; for the summer, in March.

For More Information:

Joni Dronen, Human Resources Office
Grand Targhee Ski and Summer Resort
Ski Hill Rd.
Box Ski
Alta, WY 83422
(800) 827-4433 • (307) 353-2300, ext. 1310
(307) 353-8148 (fax)
info@grandtarghee.com • www.grandtarghee.com

USA/CANADA

INTRAWEST SKI RESORTS

INTRAWEST OFFERS SEASONAL employment opportunities at some of the most unique village-centered destination resorts in the U.S. and Canada. Be it high on a mountaintop, on a quiet, isolated beach, deep in a sand bunker, or in the hustle and high energy of an urban environment, they have jobs in locations across North America (and some as far away as Europe). Name a hospitality job and Intrawest has it—guest services, ski operations, golf course maintenance, marketing and sales, hotel and resort, retail, human resources, and accounting. The majority of jobs are seasonal in nature with most winter openings available the first week of December through mid-April. The summer season typically is busy from mid-June until Labor Day. Pay and benefits vary; however, you can be assured there is a whole list of perks for each resort. To view a complete list of opportunities, visit www.wework2play.com.

For More Information:

Chris Wrazej, Director of Recruitment
Intrawest Ski Resorts
Panorama, BC V0A 1T0
Canada
(800) 579-3777 • (250) 342-0639 • (250) 342-0659 (fax)
cwrazej@intrawest.com • www.wework2play.com

SOL DUC HOT SPRINGS

Hot Springs Resort • Washington • Summer
www.northolympic.com/solduc

THE QUILEUTE INDIANS called it Sol Duc—a land of sparkling water. The original resort was built in 1912 and was conceived as a health spa in the European tradition. Today the main attraction to the area is the three hot spring mineral pools. These soaking pools are man-made circular pools supplied with all natural, mineral rich, hot-spring water. Staff opportunities during the summer months include your typical resort-type positions (from food and beverage staff to lifeguards). They also have internship opportunities for those who want to be immersed in all aspects of resort management. Wages start at $6.50 per hour, with coed, dormitory-style housing and three meals provided at $8.50 per day. The rooms vary in size, with the largest housing up to six staff members at peak season. The employee lounge has games, books, a VCR, and over two hundred videos to choose from. Accommodation for married couples is limited. The biggest perk is a lively family atmosphere and work environment, not to mention free use of the hot spring mineral pools and swimming pool. Those who have previous hotel or restaurant experience are preferred; however, positive energy and attitude, with a willingness to learn and put forward your best effort is even better. Few on-site interviews are conducted due to their isolated location.

For More Information:
Human Resources Manager
Sol Duc Hot Springs
Olympic National Park
P.O. Box 2169
Port Angeles, WA 98362-0283
(360) 327-3583 • (360) 327-3593 (fax)
sdrjob@aol.com

SQUAM LAKES ASSOCIATION

Outdoor Conservation • New Hampshire • Summer
www.squamlakes.org

WORKING TO PRESERVE the character of the Squam Lakes since 1902, Squam Lakes Association offers a variety of unique programs and service for people of ages. Visitors can take advantage of twelve backcountry campsites (on Moon Island, Bowman Island, and the Chamberlain Reynolds Memorial Forest), boat along sixty-five miles of shoreline, or get involved in the community youth sailing or summer discovery-camp programs. Seasonal opportunities include an environmental coordinator, boat attendants, kayak instructor, camp counselors, and visitor assistants, with various start and finish dates that fall between Memorial Day and Labor Day. Weekly salaries range from $240 to $400. Call for more information.

For More Information:
Staffing Director
Squam Lakes Association
P.O. Box 204
Holderness, NH 03245
(603) 968-7336
info@squamlakes.org

STANFORD SIERRA CONFERENCE CENTER

Conference Center • California • 2–3 Months

STANFORD SIERRA CONFERENCE Center (SSCC) provides full-service lodging and meeting facilities for conferences, business retreats, weddings, and social events for groups ranging in size from twenty to two hundred people. Many of the conference guests return year after year for four-star meals, comfortable lodging, a beautiful location, and—above all—professional, efficient, and friendly service from the SSCC staff!

Your Surroundings: The center is located just five miles from South Lake Tahoe on the shores of Fallen Leaf Lake, a gorgeous Sierra lake with a breathtaking mountain backdrop. Behind the resort is Desolation Wilderness, a national wilderness area with some of the best hiking and scenery in the Sierras. The solitude of nature will certainly be right outside your back door.

What You'll Be Doing: Every spring and fall SSCC forms a tight-knit community in their beautiful mountain environment. First-year staff members generally work in the kitchen or as all-purpose staff (with a majority of the workload in housekeeping and in the dining room). In addition, time is spent shuttling guests to the airport, monitoring the boat dock, washing dishes, cleaning the main lodge, and working in the center's store. Specialized positions are also available as office assistants, host/hostess, housekeeping, evening manager, and night watchman.

Commitment: The spring conference season begins mid-April and ends mid-June; the fall conference season begins the first week in September and ends

When we do the best we can, we never know what miracle is wrought in our life, or in the life of another. —HELEN KELLER

mid-November. The workload varies widely according to conference size; however, plan on thirty to forty hours per week, with shifts spread throughout the day (and two days off per week). Opportunities for extended employment and increased responsibility may become available.

Perks and Rewards: Wages start at $6.75 per hour, plus room and board, gratuities, and an end-of-season bonus (at least $150). Staff are housed in lake-view rustic cabins (some have roommates and a communal bathroom/shower area). The food is delicious, healthful, and plentiful, with vegetarian and vegan options available. (You will eat what the guests do—everything from salmon and prime rib to burgers and the salad bar.) One of the biggest perks is use of the facilities, including boating, sailing, waterskiing, tennis, volleyball, basketball, and miles of hiking trails.

The Essentials: Self-motivated, hardworking, and reliable people who have an excellent sense of professionalism, a warm personality, and a high level of maturity will thrive at SSCC. Applicants also must be able to handle the responsibilities of living and working in a diverse community. The staff comes from all walks of life—college students, professionals between jobs, experienced workers in the service industry, travelers, or people taking time off. Two years of college or more is preferred, but not required.

Your First Move: Call or email for application materials. Phone interviews and hiring will occur during the week following the application deadline (mid-March for the spring; mid-August for the fall.) Face-to-face interviews, if possible, usually work to the applicant's advantage.

For More Information:
Maren Ewers, Conference Staff Director
Stanford Sierra Conference Center
P.O. Box 10618
South Lake Tahoe, CA 96158-3618
(530) 541-1244, ext. 106 • (530) 541-2212 (fax)
mwe@stanford.edu

SUNDANCE TRAIL GUEST RANCH

Guest Ranch • Colorado • Summer
www.sundancetrail.com

RIDE THE TRAILS and meadows of the Roosevelt National Forest by horse, explore the wild by jeep, try your hand at fishing or rock climbing, snooze in a hammock, enjoy hearty Western meals, evening campfires, a soak in the Jacuzzi, or a good book on the porch. This is the life for guests at Sundance Trail. Because the ranch is smaller (no more than seven guest families come at a time), the lifestyle at the ranch is a bit more flexible and carefree. Although carefree for guests, it's hard work with long hours for the summer staff. Having a "love for horses and the great outdoors" is not enough for Sundance—past experience with people, horses, kitchen, housekeeping, maintenance, child care, fishing, or whatever the position requires is a must. Although each staff member will have a specific responsibility, everybody helps in all areas of the ranch, including washing dishes, housekeeping, shoveling manure, clearing trail in the high country, assisting with ranch entertainment, and telling endless jokes and humorous stories. All staff live and eat at the ranch, and receive a weekly wage. Those who are mature, self-directed, well rounded, happy, people-friendly, and physically fit are desired. Current-first aid and CPR certification is required, and wrangler applicants must submit a videotape (details are online or call for more information). Applications are accepted beginning in the winter months with hiring decisions made as early as January.

For More Information:
Ellen and Dan Morin, Summer Staffing
Sundance Trail Guest Ranch
17931 Red Feather Lakes Rd.
Red Feather Lakes, CO 80545
(800) 357-4930 • (970) 224-1222
sundancetr@aol.com

SUNRIVER RESORT

Resort • Oregon • Seasonal
www.sunriver-resort.com

WITH OVER THIRTY-THREE hundred acres in and around the Cascade mountain range (and including Mt. Bachelor), Sunriver Resort offers numerous recreational opportunities, including white-water rafting, canoeing, fishing, and swimming. The resort is surrounded by golf courses, tennis courts, pools, thirty miles of bike paths, a marina (with canoe, kayak, raft, and fishing rentals), a bike shop with over 450 bikes, and a complete stable operation.

What You'll Be Doing: Resort internship positions focus on social activities, youth programs, the bike shop, and the marina. Each intern will gain exposure to various departments to complete a well-rounded internship (such as sales and marketing, special events, recreation department, management, and tours, just to name a few). Each intern will also be responsible for completing and presenting a special project beneficial to both the intern and Sunriver. In addition, over 250 seasonal positions are available, including youth program leaders, bike shop mechanics, marina program leaders, food and beverage, front desk, recreation, housekeeping, and golf staff.

Commitment: Most positions are twelve weeks, mid-June through Labor Day, with varying work schedules. Some year-round positions are available, and limited positions are available in May and June.

Perks and Rewards: Interns receive a stipend of $950 per month; seasonal employees receive $6.50 to $7 per hour. Housing is not provided; however, efforts are made to help employees find adequate housing. In addition to your wages, employees are welcome to take part in numerous free recreation amenities. Discounts in all the restaurants and resort shops are available along with a 50 percent discount on accommodations for your immediate family. Your summer work attire is provided—Sunriver shirts and shorts. Oh, and don't forget your bike. It's the best way to get around.

The Essentials: Applicants must be friendly and outgoing, enjoy working with people, and physically able to meet the demands of the job. Intern candidates must be juniors or seniors studying recreation, physical education, elementary education, sports management, or hotel management. First-aid and CPR certifications are required for all recreation employees. For those wanting a full-time job at Sunriver, get your foot in the door by working a summer seasonal job. The best employees receive offers to stay on through winter.

Your First Move: Call for application materials (or apply online). The best time to apply is generally in February or March, and a personal interview is a prerequisite to employment.

For More Information:
Joyce Luckman, Human Resources Director
Sunriver Resort
P.O. Box 3609
Sunriver, OR 97707
(503) 593-4600 • (503) 593-4411 (fax)
personnel@sunriver-resort.com

SUPERCAMP

Academic Camp • Worldwide • 3–6 Weeks
www.supercamp.com

SUPERCAMP IS AN academic and personal-growth camp for teenagers. Each program teaches academic skills that help campers succeed in any subject, at any level, and also addresses life skills—to help develop friendships, resolve conflicts, and communicate more clearly. Camps are held on academic campuses across the country, including the Claremont Colleges, Colorado College, Hampshire College, Stanford University, University of Wisconsin, U.S. International University, and Wake Forest. SuperCamp also has international programs in Australia, Hong Kong, Indonesia, Malaysia, Mexico, Singapore, Switzerland, and Thailand.

What You'll Be Doing: Team leaders head up SuperCamp activities, supervise students, facilitate team meetings, and create camp spirit, as well as serving as a role model for teens. A team usually consists of two or three team leaders, plus eleven to fourteen students. Facilitators set camp direction, inspiration, guidance, and tone, and are the most visible leaders at camp. The curriculum they present consists of personal growth (communication, team building, relationships, and motivation) and academic growth (memory, creativity, power writing, quantum reading, and academic strategies). Other staff personnel include medical personnel, counselors, and office managers.

Commitment: Staff usually work three to six weeks during the summer; dates vary with each position and camp location.

Perks and Rewards: An honorarium of $300 to $2,350 per camp session is provided, along with room and board. All staff members will attend a four- to five-day staff training session and learn accelerated-learning philosophies and techniques, communication and leadership skills, and gain experience working with teens.

The Essentials: Applicants must be at least eighteen years of age, physically fit and energetic, comfortable relating to teenagers, highly committed to others, self-motivated, full of playful energy, willing to work long hours, and do whatever it takes to get the job done!

For More Information:
Kevin T. Irvine, Director
SuperCamp
1725 South Coast Highway
Oceanside, CA 92054-5319
(800) 285-3276 • (760) 722-0072, ext. 180
(760) 722-3507 (fax)
staffing@supercamp.com

I started with SuperCamp on a whim, looking for something fun to do with my summer, and it was the most profound, life-changing experience ever. The benefits I've received from this experience are priceless. I've been working with SuperCamp for five years, and have had the opportunity to travel and work in places like Colorado, Texas, Illinois, Massachusetts, Singapore, and Hong Kong—yes, I worked at a summer camp in Southeast Asia! These experiences not only boosted my self-confidence and self-esteem, but also gave me the satisfaction that I truly had made an impact on young people's lives (along with helping me carve out my own career path).

If you care about making a difference for people by inspiring them to live up to their potential; if you want an experience that will have a lifelong impact on you; if you are interested in learning skills that will take your life to the next level, personally and academically, then grab on to this opportunity. You will come home not only with an incredible experience, but also with a fresh, new outlook on life.

—CONTRIBUTED BY TROY STENDE, who spends his summers with SuperCamp, and in the off-season, as a professional college speaker with the Good Thinking Company (www.goodthink.com/troy/troy.htm). Troy would love to hear from you at tstende@earthlink.net.

SYLVAN DALE GUEST RANCH

Guest Ranch • Colorado • Seasonal
www.sylvandale.com

SYLVAN DALE is nestled in a peaceful river valley at the mouth of Colorado's Big Thompson Canyon between Estes Park and Fort Collins, Colorado. As a working horse and cattle ranch since 1946, Sylvan Dale helps their guests discover their inner cowboy—and you can too! Seasonal opportunities throughout the year are available in administration, food service, housekeeping, grounds keeping, and as wranglers and youth counselors.

Along with competitive wages, housing is available for wranglers and cooks during the summer months. Applications are available online.

For More Information:
Rick Krause, Staffing Coordinator
Sylvan Dale Guest Ranch
2939 NCR 31D
Loveland, CO 80538
(877) 667-3999 • (970) 667-3915 • (970) 635-9336 (fax)
ranch@sylvandale.com

WAUNITA HOT SPRINGS RANCH

Guest Ranch • Colorado • Summer
www.waunita.com

ONCE A SUMMER gathering area for the Ute Indians and a noted health spa in the early 1900s, Waunita is now a family-style ranch owned by the Pringle family—with over three generations of family members working on the grounds. Whether enjoying the ninety-five-degree hot-spring fed pool, a cookout horseback ride, or the toe-tapping music show with the Pringle boys, there are always unexpected discoveries to be found for Waunita's guests. During May through September, the Pringles hire an entourage of seasonal staff members who guide horseback trail rides, housekeep, cook, wait tables, maintain the grounds, and entertain. Work at the ranch is often repetitious and sometimes downright hard (six days per week); however, if you enjoy meeting, living, and working with a tight group of people, this will be a summer you won't forget. The Pringles attempt to live their lives and run the affairs of the ranch with the highest standards of Christian conduct in mind, and hire staff based on that fact. Pay starts at $6 per hour along with meals and housing at the ranch. Call or email for an application packet.

For More Information:
Tammy Pringle, Owner/Manager
Waunita Hot Springs Ranch
8007 County Rd. 887
Gunnison, CO 81230
(888) 232-9337 • (970) 641-1266
rpringle@gunnison.com

WILDERNESS CANOE BASE

Wilderness Education/Ministry • Minnesota • Summer
www.wildernesscanoebase.org

As THE CAMPING ministry of Plymouth Christian Youth Center and the Lake Wapogasset Lutheran Bible Camp, Wilderness Canoe Base provides outdoor-challenge adventures and life experiences for youth from the upper Midwest. Set on two islands on Seagull Lake, the education base is in the very heart of the famed Boundary Waters Canoe Area Wilderness at the end of the historic Gunflint Trail.

What You'll Be Doing: As a summer staff member, you will live in a vital, diverse community, helping young people to better know themselves, to live creatively with others, and to experience "the greatness of God's love." Opportunities include guides and counselors, pontoonists, cooks, and Island Camp staff, as well as health and safety director, waterfront coordinator, environmental-education coordinator, rock-climbing technician, youth-hostel manager, pastor-in-residence, spotlessness coordinator, trail director, swamper coordinator, and many, many volunteers for all areas.

Commitment: Staff orientation and training begins in early June. Summer contracts end around the third week of August. Volunteers must make a commitment of at least two weeks.

Perks and Rewards: A salary of $1,400 along with room, homemade meals, and health and accident insurance are provided; however, the biggest perks may be the two-week staff training, the supportive staff community, the healthy outdoor environment, and the challenges for personal and interpersonal growth.

The Essentials: Applicants must have a basic commitment to the Christian faith and be willing to participate in the community process of work, worship, fellowship, affirmation, empowerment, and responsibility. All staff must have current certifications in CPR and first aid. Preference is given to those who have certification in First Responder, Wilderness First Responder, or Emergency Medical Training.

Your First Move: Call for application packet. All applications and in-person interviews must be completed by March 1.

For More Information:
Director
Wilderness Canoe Base
12477 Gunflint Trail
Grand Marais, MN 55604
(800) 454-2922 • (218) 388-2241
paddle@wildernesscanoebase.org

WILDERNESS TRAILS RANCH

Guest Ranch • Colorado • Summer
www.wildernesstrails.com/jobs

EXPERIENCE THE AMERICAN WEST where the lifestyle of the American cowboy still lingers. Don your hat, mount your trusty horse, and ride into Wilderness Trails Ranch, where guests experience everything from learning how to speak to horses in their own language to participating in Western dance and sing-alongs (combined with some great wilderness adventures). Seasonal staff are hired to emulate the dude ranch experience and are encouraged to participate fully in all that they have to offer. Whether you are working as a wrangler or as a cabin supervisor, the entire staff works as a team and plays an extremely important role in the operation of the ranch. Applicants must be available to work the entire season, which runs from mid-May to the end of August, and be at least eighteen years of age. In addition to a monthly salary ranging from $750 to $1,000, meals and dormitory-style accommodations are provided. Applications can be downloaded from the ranch's website.

For More Information:
Jan Roberts, Owner
Wilderness Trails Ranch
23486 CR 501
Bayfield, CO 81122
(800) 527-2624 • (970) 247-0722 • (970) 247-1006 (fax)
jobs@wildernesstrails.com

YMCA CAMP ERDMAN

Ocean-Based Camp • Hawaii • Seasonal
www.camperdman.net

KNOWN FOR BEING one of the oldest YMCA camps in the U.S., Camp Erdman is located on the north shore of Oahu (right on one of the most famous surf beaches in the world). During the fall, spring, and summer, the camp recruits counselors and instructors who teach physical science, nature studies, and a team-building program to kids and youth, from elementary to high school. Volunteers receive room and board, while instructors receive $175 per week, room and board, and health benefits. (Yes, you'll earn enough for a round-trip ticket to Hawaii!) Applicants can work one or all seasons. Call for application materials.

For More Information:
Stephanie MacDougall, Staffing Director
YMCA Camp Erdman
69-385 Farrington Highway
Waialua, HI 96791
(808) 637-4615 • (808) 637-8874 (fax)

YMCA CAMP SURF

Ocean-Based Camp • California • Seasonal
www.ymca.org/camp

SAN DIEGO, CALIFORNIA. A temperate climate year-round. Forty acres of beachfront property on the Pacific Ocean. The sound of rhythmic surf. Polynesian-theme cabins and bathhouses nestled in and around sand dunes. Young and old learning how to surf, body-board, kayak, or sculpt the sand. This is YMCA Camp Surf—outdoor and waterfront activities at their best.

What You'll Be Doing: Whether it be surfing or sailing, a science class on intertidal marine life, or leadership development using the low ropes course, program instructors during the spring and fall are trained to lead and teach a variety of recreational activities. In addition, lifeguards and program coordinators are hired during this time frame, and some staff also lead work projects as part of their Missions program in Tijuana, Mexico. During the summer months, cabin counselors, program-specialty counselors, and camp coordinators come to Camp Surf to teach and impact children's lives.

Commitment: The spring and summer are definitely their busiest and longest seasons. Spring instructors generally

begin in early February, with groups arriving mid-March through the first week of June; summer camp staff begin in early June and finish in late August; and instructors in the fall work from September through mid-November.

Perks and Rewards: Base wages range from $180 to $270 per week depending on position and qualifications. Spring and fall staff are assigned to either a private or shared room in the waterfront facility. (Yes, you'll sleep to the sounds of the pounding surf and start your day by stepping out the door into the sand!) Summer camp staff housing is in the cabins with campers. All staff receive meals (with a vegetarian option).

The Essentials: Strong water skills are needed for all program positions at YMCA Camp Surf. In addition, all staff must be certified in first aid and CPR prior to their arrival. Spring and fall staff should have a background in outdoor education, recreation, or leadership development, and a college degree is preferred.

Your First Move: Applications can be filled out online or submittd by mail. Their website also provides details on seasonal work opportunities at other YMCA camps in San Diego.

For More Information:
Zayanne Gardner Thompson, Camp Director
YMCA Camp Surf
106 Carnation Ave.
Imperial Beach, CA 91932
(619) 423-5850 • (619) 423-4141 (fax)
campsurf@ymca.org

> *Watching something grow is good for morale. It helps you believe in life.*
>
> —MYRON S. KAUFMANN

YMCA WILLSON OUTDOOR CENTER

Outdoor Education • Ohio • Seasonal
www.ymcawillson.org

WITH A FOCUS on outdoor-education activities, YMCA Willson Outdoor Center provides programs that include a summer camp, weekend retreats, outdoor education, conference/group camping, and horseback riding. The camp sits on 409 acres of land, with a 40-acre glacial kettlehole lake, a 1860s log cabin, and a 35-foot climbing wall. Year-round, outdoor education naturalists and interns are responsible for teaching classes in natural science and history, team building, and early American curriculum, as well as leading recreational activities. During the summer months, camp positions are available, including outpost counselors, waterfront director, sports coordinator, western horseback riding instructors/counselors, and leadership/trip directors. A wage of $155 to $240 per week is provided along with room and board. Send a cover letter and resume to begin the application process.

For More Information:
Kori Keck, Outdoor Education Director
YMCA Willson Outdoor Center
2732 County Rd. 11
Bellefontaine, OH 43311-9382
(800) 423-0427 • (937) 593-9001 • (937) 593-6194 (fax)
willson4@brightusa.net

RECOMMENDED RESOURCES...............

CAMPS

Each January, the **American Camping Association** (www.acacamps.org) publishes the *Summer Camp Employment Booklet,* a free guide highlighting hundreds of nationwide job listings for day and resident camps accredited by the ACA. Detailed descriptions, salary ranges, employment benefits, and contact information are provided for most camps. For a copy, give the ACA a call at (800) 428-2267 or download it from www.acacamps.org/jobs.htm. In addition, the latest line on job fairs, career information, education and training programs, as well as bimonthly email job listing subscriptions are featured at ACA's website.

The Learning Disabilities Association of America (www.ldanatl.org) publishes *The Summer Camp Directory,* a great resource for those who want to work with children with learning disabilities in a camp setting (plus it's only $4). Although it doesn't provide a listing of jobs, it does serve as a source of contacts for your own job development. The association also publishes many other booklets and pamphlets on various subjects for the learning disabled. Contact them to receive a free packet of information. For more information contact Learning

Disabilities Association of America, 4156 Library Rd., Pittsburgh, PA 15234-1349; (412) 341-1515, info@ldaamerica.org.

The Western Association of Independent Camps (www.waic.org) provides a directory of western U.S. camps, including those in Arizona, California, Colorado, Utah, Washington, and Wyoming. Although there aren't any job opportunities posted on their site, you will find a brief description of each camp, including contact/website information.

Kidscamps.com offers an extensive database of more than twelve thousand programs—from art camps to community service programs (just for starters!) in the U.S. and abroad. Most search results include direct links to the camp's website. For job opportunities, head on over to www.campjobs.com—their companion job site—listing hundreds of summer camp jobs.

For further exploration of summer camp job opportunities on the Web, be sure to check out these sites:
www.campchannel.com
www.campsearch.com
www.campstaff.com

LESSONS LEARNED AROUND THE CAMPFIRE

Simply consider the lessons I was taught by the campfire. Every time I was on fire detail, the situation and challenge was different. But, every time the rich reward was the same as we simply sat and enjoyed our consuming creation. And, there was one aspect in particular that never failed to intrigue me, and that was the process of seeing the single small flame of the match spread to the kindling and then the twigs and then the smaller branches and finally the larger logs. It didn't dawn on me until years later, but this was the perfect metaphor for the creative process. In much the same way, the fragile spark of an idea can spread to become a great work of art or a movie or a political movement or an automobile or a Space Shuttle or a new communications technology. But, these blazing achievements can only happen if the initial idea is cared for, protected, and nurtured until it is ready to spread. —MICHAEL EISNER (Disney's CEO)

If you want to be successful, know what you are doing, love what you are doing, and believe in what you are doing. —WILL ROGERS

RESOURCES

DUDE RANCHES

The Colorado Dude and Guest Ranch Association (www.coloradoranch.com) publishes a directory of approved ranches in Colorado. Although the directory really acts as a vacationer's guide, it lists thirty-six ranches (all of which hire seasonal employees), complete with contact information and phone numbers. Call or write for your complimentary copy or explore some of their job opportunities on the Web (www.coloradoranch.com/emplymnt.html). For more information contact the Colorado Dude and Guest Ranch Association, P.O. Box 2120, Granby, CO 80446; (970) 887-3128

To assist individuals seeking employment at a ranch, the **Dude Ranchers' Association** (www.duderanch.org) provides a couple of great services. First off, they publish *The Dude Rancher Directory,* listing contact information, amenities, and services for more than one hundred member dude ranches in twelve western states and two Canadian provinces. Dude ranches vary from working cattle ranches to more luxurious resort-type facilities. Although it doesn't list seasonal jobs at each ranch, it's a great resource for contact information—plus it's free. In addition, they publish a biweekly in-house newsletter that is sent directly to all member ranches. For a $5 fee, you can place an "employment wanted" ad in the newsletter. Simply send your name, address, phone number, dates of availability, type of positions preferred, and two to three sentences describing your experience or qualifications. Many ranchers do use these ads when hiring. Of course, there are no guarantees, but it is a good and inexpensive way to contact all the ranchers at one time. On the Web (www.duderanch.org/employment.html), you can view a listing of current ranch job opportunities. For more information contact the Dude Ranchers' Association, P.O. Box 2307, Cody, WY 82414; (307) 587-2339

> Dude and guest ranching is more than a vacation; it is a spirit, a tradition of Western hospitality, warmth, honesty, family, and natural beauty. It is, indeed, a ministry that touches lives and helps to make this a better world in which to live.
>
> —GENE KILGORE

Have you ever marveled at the geysers of Yellowstone, explored the verdant mountains of the Rockies, paddled a canoe in the Boundary Waters of Minnesota, or walked across a glacier in Alaska and wondered what it would be like to work in such magnificent places? These are the types of opportunities that thousands of seasonal workers enjoy with organizations such as the National Park Service, hospitality services within the parks, or those that maintain thousands of miles of hiking trails. From jobs as campground hosts and interpretative rangers to trail-maintenance laborers and guest-services staff, you'll explore every conceivable assignment while working in the wild.

Climb the mountains and get their good tidings. Nature's peace will flow into you as sunshine flows into trees. The winds will blow their own freshness into you, and the storms their energies, while cares will drop off like autumn leaves.

—JOHN MUIR

Unique Opportunities to Explore in This Section:

- Outdoor expert Bill Borrie believes that those who succeed in the future are those who learn how to make wonderful things happen with a can-do attitude, regardless of what the naysayers might suggest. Explore his get-up-and-go approach to kick-starting a federal agency career (page 154).

- From the architectural relics of the Anasazi in Mesa Verde to geysers bursting in Yellowstone, the National Park Service offers seasonal workers some of the most incredible places to work in the U.S. (page 172). Explore your working options at other public agencies, including the Bureau of Land Management (page 159), the U.S. Fish and Wildlife Service (page 179) and the U.S. Forest Service (page 180).

- Can you see yourself patrolling a remote island wilderness in Alaska by kayak, or playing the role of an 1800s resident of historic Ft. Laramie? These are just a few of the assignments participants enjoy with the Student Conservation Association (page 178).

Photo Credit: John Spring

A conservation intern with the Student Conservation Association (page 178) involved in a surveying assignment at Olympic National Park.

THE GREAT OUTDOORS:
WORK AT STATE AND NATIONAL PARKS

A GET-UP-AND-GO APPROACH TO KICK-STARTING A FEDERAL AGENCY CAREER

Dr. Borrie in the "outback" of the Upper Missouri River Breaks National Monument, Montana.

Are you considering a career in one of the four federal land management agencies (National Park Service, Forest Service, Bureau of Land Management, Fish and Wildlife Service)? Good for you! What a great opportunity to get involved and make a difference!

But it's going to take a little dogged determination and careful thinking to get where you want to go. Briefly put, I believe that the federal agencies will always find a way to hire good people. The leaders of these agencies know that long-term effectiveness depends on the creativity and enthusiasm of its personnel. True leadership requires constantly energizing and reinventing the agency. And this requires younger, competent people with the drive to provide true public service and stewardship of the national estate.

However, you will still have to work hard to blast off your career. You may also need to shift some of

your expectations and change your sights as to what you can achieve in the short term. For instance, you may have to reconsider the hope of immediately working in your favorite state. Instead, you may have to go somewhere new, such as Georgia, which does have some wonderful wilderness areas! Similarly, you might not get to live in the size of town that you prefer. Instead, you might have to consider living in Washington, D.C., or Sacramento, California, or Glendive, Montana. You might also have to work on projects that are not your obvious choice. But the more you learn about the agency and all of its missions, the more effective you become. You may even get to work for a different agency (for instance, the Bureau of Land Management). In each case, you should view each of these as stepping stones, learning opportunities, and necessary experiences. And, you never know, you might like what you see!

You guys and gals are training for careers that will require different skills than what many current employees have. You have new perspectives, new experiences, and new ideas. This can be threatening to older employees, and one of their strategies for coping with this is to discourage or disparage you. But you will be the ones guiding the agency in the future—with your abilities, knowledge, and get-up-and-go. Those who succeed in the future, I believe, will be those who learn how to make wonderful things happen, regardless of what the naysayers are suggesting. A can-do attitude will win in the long run.

Part of what I think older employees are communicating to you is that some of the old assumptions within the agencies no longer hold. For instance, it could be said that you no longer have a job for life. Others will tell you that it is no longer who you know that matters. And it is no longer reasonable to expect the government to look after your career. In short, *you* now have much more responsibility for your career. It's no longer an automatic rise through the levels. This is unsettling for people who still believe in the old ways, and one way of communicating that is to warn new people not to enter into the organization.

But, if you really, really want to work for a particular agency, then I say go out and work for them! Don't let anybody tell you that you can't! If you believe that what you should be doing is working for the government—and that is the best use of your skills and enthusiasm—then you are a

Photo Credit: Bob Cleaver

Do you have the determination of a wombat? This adolescent critter is cared for by wombat experts Jan and Bob Cleaver, who received an award for having achieved first recorded captive breeding of the southern hairy-nosed wombat in South Australia.

good prospect to hire. And managers worth their salary will go out of their way to find a way to help you. They will give you a chance to show your worth, and if they like what they see, they will want to keep you on. The decision they face is how many chips to spend on your behalf—how much are you worth? So, work hard, be reliable and energetic, and show how much the public lands and public service mean to you.

Maybe I should be recommending that you think like a wombat!? (Wombats are stocky Australian marsupials.) Once there was a young wombat that was being raised by a park ranger after its mom got hit by a car. Well, as it grew to be a solid adult wombat, the critter didn't quite understand the human concept of doors. As a result, the walls of the house it lived in (which were made of thin cement sheets) had little wombat-shaped holes in them! You just can't stop a determined wombat from getting where he or she wants to go!

So, set your sights high and work hard toward getting there. These are magnificent places to manage and important benefits to be providing to the American public. You should be honored to have the opportunity to serve but also congratulated on your decision to do so. Be proud of the small contributions you can make—those contributions will grow.

—CONTRIBUTED BY DR. BILL BORRIE, who recently received the Faculty Member of the Year Award in the School of Forestry at the University of Montana. Montana Public Radio also channels his voice across the airwaves of western and central Montana. To learn more about Dr. Borrie's work and passions, visit www.forestry.umt.edu/personnel/faculty/borrie.

ADIRONDACK MOUNTAIN CLUB

Conservation Education • New York • Seasonal
www.adk.org

KNOWN FOR ITS rugged mountains (with forty-six peaks over four thousand feet high), rivers, streams, lakes and bogs, and a profusion of wildlife, Adirondack Park covers over six million acres and is the largest U.S. park outside of Alaska. The Adirondack Mountain Club is responsible for the protection and responsible use of this extraordinary wilderness area. Educational workshops, wildflower and birding field trips, guided hikes, kayaking, and winter cross-country skiing are among the many programs of this venerable club for nature lovers. Seasonal opportunities may include assisting with the maintenance and reconstruction of backcountry hiking trails, working in a backcountry information center, interpreting Adirondack regional natural history, and/or operating two mountain lodges. Pay is based on position, and meals and housing in tents or rustic wilderness cabins may be provided. Applicants must have a strong outdoor orientation and public service skills, and positions are often filled by outgoing, highly motivated, and independent individuals. Call for application materials (or you can download them online). Applications are due by February 15 for the summer; other seasons have rolling deadlines.

For More Information:
Applications
Adirondack Mountain Club
P.O. Box 867
Lake Placid, NY 12946-0867
(518) 523-3441 • (518) 523-3518 (fax)
adkinfo@northnet.org

ALASKA STATE PARKS

State Park • Alaska • Seasonal
www.dnr.state.ak.us/parks

CREATED IN 1970, Alaska State Parks manages more than 130 state park units with more than six million visitors each year. These park units range in size and character from the half-acre Potter Section House State Historic Site to the 1.5-million-acre Wood-Tikchik State Park. In general, state parks are accessible by road and offer a host of visitor facilities including campgrounds, boat launches, hiking trails, and visitor centers.

What You'll Be Doing: The majority of volunteer positions are campground hosts, who assist rangers with campground maintenance and visitor contact. Other typical volunteer and internship assignments include archaeological assistant, backcountry-ranger assistant, natural-history interpreter, park caretaker, ranger assistant, and trail crew.

Commitment: Most positions are full-time during the summer; however, a few positions are part-time, and a handful of positions are offered during the winter. Time off is usually given during the middle of the week.

Perks and Rewards: Most positions offer an expense allowance of $100 to $300 per month, uniforms, rustic housing (RV/trailer hook-ups for campground hosts), and, of course, the state's beauty. Transportation to and from Alaska is the responsibility of the volunteer.

The Essentials: Applicants must be eighteen years or older and have U.S. citizenship.

Your First Move: Their website provides current volunteer opportunities and an application; however, you are welcome to call for the volunteer program catalog that becomes available each October. Applications are accepted between November 1 and April 1 (with some exceptions), and you may apply for as many positions as you like.

For More Information:
Lynn Blessington, Volunteer Coordinator
Alaska State Parks
550 W. 7th Ave., Suite 1380
Anchorage, AK 99501-3561
(907) 269-8708 • (907) 269-8907 (fax)
volunteer@dnr.state.ak.us

Many positions are filled before April 1, so it is best to send your application in as soon as possible. Some of our rangers work seasonally, so do not be concerned if you do not receive an immediate reply, particularly from November through January.

AMERICAN HIKING SOCIETY

Trail Maintenance • USA • 1–2 Weeks
www.americanhiking.org

THE AMERICAN HIKING Society (AHS) is a national non-profit organization dedicated to establishing, protecting, and maintaining foot trails in America. Serving as the voice of the American hiker in our nation's capital, American Hiking Society works to educate the public about the benefits of hiking and trails, to increase the following for trails, and to foster research on trail issues.

What You'll Be Doing: AHS Volunteer Vacations offers an inexpensive way to visit a new part of the U.S., work with your hands, and help conserve and revitalize America's trails. Vacationers rake, shovel, trim, lop, and chop hundreds of trail miles in America's national parks, forests, and rangelands. Volunteering affords you an opportunity to whip some trail miles—and your mind and body—into shape. You'll spend your days performing rewarding trail work. During late afternoon and evening hours, you'll explore the countryside, photograph wildlife, relax by a mountain stream, or simply enjoy the fellowship of people who share your passion for the outdoors. Most projects require a hike into a remote base camp; some offer bunkhouse or cabin accommodations. For each project, American Hiking Society chooses an experienced volunteer team-leader to serve as the liaison between your crew and the host agency. If you are interested in serving as a leader, just indicate that on your registration form.

Commitment: On a typical day, after a hearty breakfast, you will be on the trail at 9 A.M., work for six to eight hours, and return to base camp by 4 P.M., just in time to enjoy the long summer afternoons. On two-week vacations, you will get the weekend off.

Perks and Rewards: Host agencies provide tools, safety equipment, workers' compensation, and project leaders. Most agencies also provide food; however, for some projects, volunteers may be asked to donate an additional $40 per week. Registration requires a nonrefundable $100 registration fee, which includes a one-year membership to American Hiking Society. AHS members pay $80 for the first trip, and each additional trip costs $60.

The Essentials: Participants should possess a desire to improve America's trails, and be in good physical condition (able to hike five miles or more a day) and at least eighteen years of age. Volunteers supply their own camping equipment (tent, sleeping bag, personal items) and arrange their own transportation to and from the work site (although many agencies provide pickups at major airports near the work sites).

Your First Move: Call to receive a project schedule and registration form (or check out the Web for complete details).

For More Information:
Volunteer Vacations Coordinator
American Hiking Society
1422 Fenwick Ln.
Silver Spring, MD 20910
(800) 972-8608 • (301) 565-6704, ext. 206
volvac@americanhiking.org

Photo Credit: American Hiking Society

Participants on a volunteer vacation with the American Hiking Society help construct a footbridge.

I only went out for a walk, and finally concluded to stay out until sundown; for going out, I found, was really going in. —JOHN MUIR

APPALACHIAN MOUNTAIN CLUB

Conservation Education • East Coast • Seasonal
www.outdoors.org

APPALACHIAN MOUNTAIN CLUB (AMC), the nation's oldest and largest recreation and conservation organization, offers a smorgasbord of projects for volunteers, interns, and seasonal workers. Seasonal crews have the opportunity to work in the White Mountain National Forest in New Hampshire, Mount Desert Island in Maine, or in the hiking/canoeing center at the Delaware Mountain Gap in New Jersey—to name just a few! Crews generally work in base camps, shelters, huts, visitor centers, or youth hostels, with positions ranging from backcountry staff, trail crew, and educational instructors. The average weekly pay for seasonal workers ranges from $250 to $340 after deductions for room and board. Interns get more involved in the business end of operations—everything from working on their website to assisting with the *AMC Outdoors* magazine. Volunteers for AMC help maintain more than 1,300 miles of recreational trails, including 350 miles of the Appalachian Trail. Volunteers also lead nature hikes, fill in for hut crews, and give public information talks. Call for a copy of the annual *Trail Volunteer Opportunities* catalog, which lists more than seven hundred opportunities.

For More Information:
Pat McCabe, Human Resources/Seasonal Employment
Appalachian Mountain Club
Pinkham Notch Visitor Center
P.O. Box 298
Gorham, NH 03581
(603) 466-2721, ext. 145 • (603) 466-2822 (fax)
amcemployment@outdoors.org

APPALACHIAN TRAIL CONFERENCE

Trail Maintenance • East Coast • 1–6 Weeks
www.appalachiantrail.org

HELP BUILD A piece of the Appalachian National Scenic Trail, one of the most famous footpaths in the world. Winding along the peaks of the Appalachian chain from Georgia to Maine, this trail exists thanks to dedicated volunteers who planned, constructed, and now maintain and manage the trail by participating in ATC's Volunteer Trail Crew Program. In cooperation with the U.S. Forest Service, National Park Service, and trail-maintaining clubs, the crews design and build new trail segments, shelters, and bridges, rehabilitate damaged trails, improve wildlife habitat, and preserve open areas. Food, accommodation, equipment, and on-the-job training are provided, and participants must be at least eighteen years of age. No prior experience is necessary. Crews operate from May through October from base camps in Tennessee, southern Virginia, south-central Pennsylvania, Vermont, and Maine. Participants may volunteer for up to six weeks. Although coed crews are the norm, ATC also sponsors two-week all-women crews.

For More Information:
Jody Bickel, Associate Regional Representative
Appalachian Trail Conference
ATC Trail Crew Program
P.O. Box 10
Newport, VA 24128
(540) 544-7388 • (540) 544-6880 (fax)
crews@appalachiantrail.org

BADLANDS NATIONAL PARK

Natural Resources • South Dakota • Summer
www.nps.gov/badl/exp/volunteer.htm

BADLANDS NATIONAL PARK consists of 244,000 acres of fossil-rich eroded sedimentary formations and mixed-grass prairie. In the summer, the weather is hot and dry and always windy. To hint at the beauty of the park, it was recently voted as having the best sunrises and sunsets in the world by International Nature Photographers. Summer interns staff park visitor centers; provide interpretive walks, children's hikes, and slide-show presentations; patrol the backcountry; or engage in research and writing programs. Positions begin in mid-May and continue for twelve weeks. Applicants must be friendly and have strong public speaking skills and the ability to work in a high-stress environment and/or extremely remote setting. Housing is provided just a short walk from the visitor center, as is a reimbursement of expenses up to $1,000.

For More Information:
Marianne Mills, Resource Education Chief
Badlands National Park
P.O. Box 6
Highway 240
Interior, SD 57750
(605) 433-5245 • (605) 433-5248 (fax)
badl_internship@nps.gov

BUREAU OF LAND MANAGEMENT

I look forward to an America which will not be afraid of grace and beauty, an America which will protect the beauty of our natural environment....

—JOHN F. KENNEDY

The Bureau of Land Management (BLM) is responsible for managing about one-eighth of the land in the United States. Most of these public lands are located in the western U.S., including Alaska, and are dominated by extensive grasslands, forests, high mountains, arctic tundra, and deserts.

VOLUNTEERING AND CAREER OPPORTUNITIES

Volunteers help the BLM educate others and instill a pride in the public lands that is crucial if these lands are to be held in trust for future generations. Volunteers improve the health of the public lands by restoring riparian areas across the West, building and repairing fences to protect special areas, planting trees, pulling weeds, and helping in many other ways.

Many students—from high school through college—can participate in one of two paid seasonal programs offered by the BLM: the Student Career

Experience Program and the Student Temporary Employment Program. Positions include natural resources, wildlife, cultural resources, recreation, information resources, and administration.

Fire-fighting jobs are mostly seasonal positions during the months of May through September, depending upon the fire season in a particular area. Jobs include not only fire fighting (hand crews, engine crews, smoke jumpers) but also many fire support positions in dispatching, warehousing, and equipment operations. Once they have become experienced wildland firefighters, many opt for the coveted smoke jumper position (a wildland firefighter who parachutes into remote areas to provide initial attack on wildfires). Smoke jumpers usually travel for 100 days out of a 120-day fire season (and it's noted that candidates should keep up a year-round physical fitness program to complete four weeks of rookie training—one of the hardest training programs to go through to get a job).

Photo Credit: Bureau of Land Management

Maintenance crews repair a BLM cabin along the Iditarod National Historic Trail. Extending from Seward to Nome, Alaska, the trail is famous for the annual dogsled race.

Those who contemplate the beauty of the earth find reserves of strength that will endure as long as life lasts. —RACHEL CARSON

BUREAU OF LAND MANAGEMENT

Photo Credit: Bureau of Land Management

A BLM plant specialist gives a young student a hands-on lesson about one of Utah's many wild plant species.

FOR MORE INFORMATION:

HEADQUARTERS
Bureau of Land Management
Environmental Education and Volunteers Group
1849 C St., NW, Suite 406-LS
Washington, D.C. 20240

EMPLOYMENT OPPORTUNITIES
Call (202) 501-6723 or visit www.blm.gov/careers

(including student, seasonal, temporary, and welfare-to-work)

VOLUNTEER OPPORTUNITIES
Call (202) 452-5078 or
visit www.blm.gov/volunteer

BLM STATE OFFICES

ALASKA STATE OFFICE
222 W. 7th Ave., Suite 13
Anchorage, AK 99513-7599
(907) 271-5960
www.ak.blm.gov

ARIZONA STATE OFFICE
222 N. Central Ave.
Phoenix, AZ 85004-2203
(602) 417-9200
www.az.blm.gov

CALIFORNIA STATE OFFICE
2800 Cottage Way
Sacramento, CA 95825
(916) 978-4400
www.ca.blm.gov

COLORADO STATE OFFICE
2850 Youngfield St.
Lakewood, CO 80215-7076
(303) 239-3600
www.co.blm.gov

EASTERN STATES OFFICE
7450 Boston Blvd.
Springfield, VA 22153
(703) 440-1713
www.blm.gov/eso

(including Arkansas, Iowa, Louisiana, Minnesota, Missouri, and all states east of the Mississippi River)

IDAHO STATE OFFICE
1387 S. Vinnell Way
Boise, ID 83709-1657
(208) 373-4000
www.id.blm.gov

NEVADA STATE OFFICE
P.O. Box 12000
Reno, NV 89520-0006
(775) 861-6400
www.nv.blm.gov

NEW MEXICO STATE OFFICE

P.O. Box 27115
Santa Fe, NM 87502-0115
(505) 438-7471
www.nm.blm.gov

(including Kansas, Oklahoma, and Texas)

MONTANA STATE OFFICE

5001 Southgate Dr.
Billings, MT 59101
(406) 896-5000
www.mt.blm.gov

(including North Dakota and South Dakota)

OREGON STATE OFFICE

1515 S.W. 5th Ave.
P.O. Box 2965
Portland, OR 97208-2965
(503) 952-6287
www.or.blm.gov

(including Washington)

UTAH STATE OFFICE

324 S. State St., Suite 301
P.O. Box 45155
Salt Lake City, UT 84145-0155
(801) 539-4001
www.ut.blm.gov

WYOMING STATE OFFICE

5353 Yellowstone Rd.
P.O. Box 1828
Cheyenne, WY 82003
(307) 775-6314
www.wy.blm.gov

NATIONAL OFFICE OF FIRE AND AVIATION

3833 S. Development Ave., FA-106
Boise, ID 83705
(208) 387-5458
www.fire.blm.gov

NATIONAL TRAINING CENTER

9828 N. 31st Ave.
Phoenix, AZ 85051-2517
(602) 906-5500
www.ntc.blm.gov

Come spend eight weeks during the summer in beautiful southwestern Colorado working in a "hands-on" museum committed to the preservation and interpretation of the northern San Juan Anasazi. Interns in collections management and cultural-resources management are provided with a realistic and well-rounded experience in a federal museum setting. Interns are expected to be self-motivated and able to work with a minimum amount of supervision once the task is understood. Interns receive a $50 per week stipend, plus communal housing. Send a resume and cover letter before April 1.

FOR MORE INFORMATION

Curator
Anasazi Heritage Center
Bureau of Land Management
27501 Highway 184
Dolores, CO 81323
(970) 882-4811
www.co.blm.gov/ahc/hmepge.htm

BUREAU OF LAND MANAGEMENT

The world is a sacred vessel, which must not be tampered with or grabbed after. To tamper with it is to spoil it, and to grasp it is to lose it. —Lao-Tzu

CARLSBAD CAVERNS NATIONAL PARK

Caving • New Mexico • 10+ Weeks
www.nps.gov/cave

ESTABLISHED TO PRESERVE Carlsbad Cavern and numerous other caves within this Permian fossil reef, the park contains more than ninety caves. Carlsbad Cavern, with one of the world's largest underground chambers and countless formations, is also highly accessible, with a variety of tours offered year-round. Special opportunities are available for people interested in caves, natural resources, and working with the public. Volunteer positions include park interpretation, visitor services, maintenance, environmental education, history and curatorial, resource management, and cave restoration. A minimum commitment of thirty-two hours per week for at least ten weeks is needed. In return, the park provides dormitory-style housing or an RV site with full hook-ups.

For More Information:
Volunteer Coordinator
Carlsbad Caverns National Park
3225 National Parks Hwy.
Carlsbad, NM 88220
(505) 785-2232 • (505) 785-2302 (fax)
cave_volunteers@nps.gov

THE COLORADO TRAIL FOUNDATION

Trail Maintenance • Colorado • Summer
www.coloradotrail.org

THE COLORADO TRAIL Foundation recruits and trains over 350 volunteers to help maintain five hundred miles of trails stretching from Denver to Durango—and across eight mountain ranges and seven national forests! Volunteers can participate in weeklong trail crew work (that usually runs from mid-June through early August) with teams made up of twenty individuals. Trail crews are highly participatory, and all volunteers are encouraged to join in daily camp life. Volunteers bring their own tents, sleeping bags, and personal gear, but all meals, tools, and instruction are included for a nominal fee of $40 per week. Crews generally fill by April, so it's best to get on the mailing list by February 1. It's also noted that partici-

pants should establish an exercise program prior to their arrival on the crew to minimize sore muscles. Application materials and registration forms can be obtained online.

For More Information:
Suzanne Reed, Volunteer Coordinator
The Colorado Trail Foundation
710 10th St., Suite 210
Golden, CO 80401-5843
(303) 384-3729, ext. 113 • (303) 384-3743 (fax)
ctf@coloradotrail.org

CUSTER STATE PARK RESORT COMPANY

Guest Services • South Dakota • Seasonal
www.custerresorts.com

IN THE SUMMER of 1874, Major General George Custer led a scientific expedition through the Black Hills of Dakota Territory. When word spread that the expedition had discovered gold near the present-day city of Custer, prospectors and settlers soon followed. After the turn of the twentieth century, visionaries like South Dakota Governor Peter Norbeck realized that our environment was more precious than gold. In 1919, he urged the South Dakota State Legislature to preserve our natural resources and designate forty-eight thousand acres near Custer as a permanent state park. Today Custer State Park spreads across a total of seventy-three thousand acres. Seasonal employees have the opportunity to work in one of four resorts that are managed by Custer State Park Resort Company: the State Game Lodge and Resort, Blue Bell Lodge and Resort, Legion Lake Resort, or Sylvan Lake Resort. Typical seasonal positions are available; the more unique positions include entertainers, jeep drivers, interpretive guides, and wranglers. They also have a management-trainee internship program, with interns trained in all areas of resort operations. A monthly salary is provided, along with meals (and housing, if needed). An end-of-season bonus is also available to all who finish their agreements.

For More Information:
Human Resources Department
Custer State Park Resort Company
HC 83, Box 74
Custer, SD 57730
(800) 658-3530 •
(605) 255-4541 • (605) 255-4706 (fax)
e-mail@custerresorts.com

DENALI NATIONAL PARK AND PRESERVE

National Park • Alaska • Summer
www.nps.gov/dena

DENALI NATIONAL PARK and Preserve features North America's highest mountain, Mt. McKinley, and encompasses more than six million acres filled with spectacular scenery and large mammals. (Yes, you'll see grizzly bears and moose!) Summer volunteer positions include interpretative naturalists, campground hosts, backcountry patrol, resource management assistants, and visitor services. Housing is extremely limited and very rustic; campground hosts must provide their own RV or trailer. A small weekly stipend may be provided and some positions have a one- to two-week training period. In general, volunteers are needed between May and September. Applications are due by March 15 (and can be obtained at www.nps.gov/volunteer).

For More Information:
Theresa Philbick, VIP Program Coordinator
Denali National Park and Preserve
P.O. Box 9
Denali Park, AK 99755
(907) 683-2294 • (907) 683-9617 (fax)
Theresa_Philbick@nps.gov

DENALI PARK RESORTS

Guest Services • Alaska • Summer
www.denaliparkresorts.com

DENALI NATIONAL PARK has more than six million acres of pristine wilderness, including some of the most awe-inspiring scenery and wildlife in North America, including Mt. McKinley, which rises over twenty thousand feet into the Alaskan sky. Denali Park Resorts operates four lodges and resorts as well as Alaska Raft Adventures and Tundra Wildlife Tours.

What You'll Be Doing: Adventure awaits in the heart of the last frontier with Denali Park Resorts! Whether working as a hospitality staff member, a dinner theatre performer, or a tour or river guide, those who enjoy a busy work environment with extensive guest contact will thrive here. Each summer over 950 seasonal staff come to Denali to work, play, and explore.

Commitment: The season runs from May through mid-September, with preference given to those who can work the entire season.

Perks and Rewards: Most first-year employees earn $5.50 to $8.00 per hour and a bonus of approximately $300 for the season. Room and board are available for $12 per day, and all employees have free use of laundry facilities. A variety of rustic, dormitory-style company housing units (shared rooms with one or two others) with a central bathhouse are available. Perks include a hodgepodge of employee activities, free rafting, and discounted tours, flight-seeing, and retail purchases. And don't forget about your new playground—millions of acres of pristine Alaskan wilderness to hike, climb, bike, fish, kayak, and explore.

The Essentials: Applicants must be at least eighteen for housing, although many jobs require that you be at least twenty-one. Local services are limited in Denali, which is 120 miles from Fairbanks, the nearest city. Therefore applicants should have a strong desire to enjoy and discover the wilderness.

Your First Move: Applications are accepted from December through August.

For More Information:
John Tsoutsouvas, Human Resources Director
Denali Park Resorts
241 W. Ship Creek Ave.
Anchorage, AK 99501
(907) 264-4600 • (907) 264-4680 (fax)
denalijobs@lprm.aramark.com

FLAGG RANCH RESORT

Guest Services • Wyoming • Seasonal
www.flaggranch.com

CENTRALLY LOCATED BETWEEN Yellowstone and Grand Teton National Parks, Flagg Ranch is a privately owned company that operates visitor services for the National Park Service. Summer and winter seasonal positions are available in all areas of hospitality management (from lodging and food and beverage staff to river guides and naturalist/activities coordinators). An hourly wage is provided, along with room and board for a nominal cost deducted from your paycheck. The ranch also has a limited number of full hookup sites for employees with their own trailers or motor homes. Applicants must be at least eighteen years of age. Note that Flagg Ranch conducts its recruiting efforts from Tempe, Arizona.

Be glad of life, because it gives you the chance to love and to work and to play and to look at the stars. —HENRY VAN DYKE

For More Information:
Jennifer Anderson, Human Resources Coordinator
Flagg Ranch Resort
3207 S. Hardy Dr.
Tempe, AZ 85282
(800) 224-1384 • (480) 829-7600 • (480) 829-7460 (fax)
info@flaggranch.com

FLAMINGO LODGE AND MARINA

Guest Services • Florida • Seasonal
www.flamingolodge.com

SEASONAL POSITIONS AT Flamingo Lodge (in the heart of Everglades National Park) range from food and beverage and hotel services to marina staff and accountants. The summer season runs from May 1 through the end of October, with the winter season spanning from November 1 through the beginning of May. Generally, the earlier you can start and the later you can stay, the better your chances will be of receiving an offer of employment. Wages for most positions start at $5.50 per hour and include low-cost dormitory-style housing or full RV hookup. Other benefits include complimentary Florida Bay and Back Country Boat Cruises, and rental of canoes, kayaks, and skiffs. Applicants must be at least eighteen years of age.

For More Information:
Human Resources Department
Flamingo Lodge, Marina, and Outpost Resort
Everglades National Park, Xanterra Parks and Resorts
#1 Flamingo Lodge Highway
Flamingo, FL 33034-6798
(239) 695-3101, ext. 285 • (239) 695-3921 (fax)
jos-flamingo@xanterra.com

FLORISSANT FOSSIL BEDS NATIONAL MONUMENT

National Monument • Colorado • Summer
www.nps.gov/flfo

FLORISSANT FOSSIL BEDS National Monument sits at an elevation of 8,400 feet and preserves fossil remains and geologic evidence of a far different world, from thirty-five million years ago. The fossil beds are named after a nearby small town, Florissant, which takes its name from the French word for flowering or blooming.

What You'll Be Doing: Interpretative interns provide information on natural and cultural resources, explain area significance, and communicate National Park Service philosophy to the visiting public. Paleontology interns are involved with projects relating to the geological or paleontological resources of the park, including resource management, museum collection curation, and technical assistance with excavating and monitoring of paleontological sites. All interns participate in a one-week orientation training session, including standard first aid and CPR. Training in other park operations, basic wildland fire fighting, and natural and paleontological resources monitoring is scheduled throughout the twelve weeks (beginning in late May).

Perks and Rewards: A $12-per-day stipend is provided, along with housing and uniforms.

The Essentials: Interpretive applicants must have effective communication skills, the ability to work comfortably with a variety of people of all ages, the ability to work independently and as part of a team, and an interest and ability to work outdoors. Paleontology applicants must have completed basic undergraduate course work in geology or biology. Since there is no public transportation in the area, and housing may be several miles from the park, a personal vehicle is highly recommended.

Your First Move: Send a cover letter, stating your interest in the position, and a resume with two references (with contact information) by mid-March.

For More Information:
Volunteer/Intern Coordinator
Florissant Fossil Beds National Monument
Field Internship Program
P.O. Box 185
Florissant, CO 80816-0815
(719) 748-3253 • (719) 748-3164 (fax)

FREDERICKSBURG AND SPOTSYLVANIA NATIONAL MILITARY PARK

Military Park • Virginia • Seasonal
www.nps.gov/frsp/vc.htm

FREDERICKSBURG WAS THE scene of four major Civil War battles, resulting in more than one hundred thousand casualties. No other area of similar size witnessed such heavy losses. The boundaries encompass more than eight thousand acres, making the park the largest military preserve in the world.

What You'll Be Doing: Various seasonal, volunteer, and internship positions are available: historical interpreters provide information and conduct walking tours for park visitors; historical researchers complete projects to help the staff access specific information easily; education-coordinator assistants develop lesson plans and visuals for the park staff or teachers to use for student programs; curatorial assistants help with cataloging museum artifacts; cultural-resource management assistants help to identify and preserve military and civilian landmarks of the Civil War era; restoration assistants properly protect and repair monuments, historic buildings, and other cultural resources; and administrative assistants may learn various federal personnel, budgeting, or purchasing practices.

Commitment: Most volunteers must make a commitment of at least 100 hours and internships range from 120 to 480 hours for the term. Schedules vary with each position.

Perks and Rewards: Housing is provided when available. Seasonal wages vary.

Your First Move: Request application materials and specific descriptions of volunteer work or internships. It's best to apply at least three months before your desired start date. As a reminder, paid seasonal employment applicants must go through the National Park Service website, www.sep.nps.gov.

For More Information:
Gregory Mertz, Supervisory Historian
Fredericksburg and Spotsylvania National Military Park
120 Chatham Ln.
Fredericksburg, VA 22405
(540) 373-6124 • (540) 371-1907 (fax)
greg_mertz@nps.gov

FURNACE CREEK INN AND RANCH RESORT

Guest Services • California • Seasonal
www.furnacecreekresort.com

IMAGINE WORKING AT 200 feet below sea level while being surrounded by a vast and arid desert region with mountains that rise to 11,500 feet. Yes, this is the desolate landscape of Death Valley National Park, where the contrasting lush oasis of Furnace Creek Inn & Ranch Resort emerges for guests and staff alike. Seasonal guest-service and hospitality opportunities abound at Furnace Creek throughout the year—from guest-room attendants and

groundskeepers to front-desk clerks and accountants. Staff will work at one of four properties, including Furnace Creek Inn, a 68-room historic inn; Furnace Creek Ranch, a 224-room resort; Stove Pipe Wells Village, an 82-room motel; and Scotty's Castle. All staff receive an hourly wage along with housing and meals available for a nominal fee. Rustic double-occupancy cabin or dorm-style housing is provided at $25 per week, which includes bedding, towels, utilities, and cable TV hook-ups (don't forget your TV!). Breakfast and lunch are provided at no cost (dinner is $2.50 per day). RV spaces are also available at $30 per week. For those who love the outdoors, the biggest perk may well be exploring the three million square miles of Death Valley. Staff also have free rein on ranch activities, including tennis, volleyball, and basketball courts, the golf course, spring-fed swimming pools, a new employee fitness/weight room, and horseback riding October through May. Applicants must be at least eighteen years old and willing to work any day of the week (shifts may include weekends and holidays). Applications can be obtained online.

For More Information:
Cyndi MacDougall, Human Resources Director
Furnace Creek Inn and Ranch Resort
P.O. Box 187
Death Valley, CA 92328
(760) 786-2311 • (760) 786-2396 (fax)
hr@furnacecreekresort.com

THE GLACIER INSTITUTE

Outdoor Education • Montana • 2–7 Months
www.glacierinstitute.org

THE GLACIER INSTITUTE is based at two facilities in and adjacent to Glacier National Park in northwest Montana and is governed by a working board of directors who aren't afraid to get dirty. Outdoor enthusiasts will enjoy that most of their work is conducted outside in this rugged and beautiful mountainous region. The institute courses often bring in local natural-resource specialists and employees from Montana Fish, Wildlife and Parks; Flathead National Forest; Flathead Valley Community College; Glacier Natural History Association; and Glacier National Park.

Your Surroundings: Both their facilities are rustic, historic sites in spectacular settings. Opportunities for river floating, hiking, wildlife viewing, and backcountry camping abound. During time off, the towns of Columbia Falls, Kalispell, and Whitefish are close enough for movies, restaurants, and shopping.

What You'll Be Doing: As an intern at The Glacier Institute, you become a full-fledged staff member and are responsible for all facets of running a residential outdoor-education center, both as a teacher of youth programs and an assistant during adult classes. At the Big Creek facility, you will help with all organizational, programmatic, and facility aspects concerning on-site operations of the program. This includes cooking with students, teaching evening programs, creating and implementing curriculum, and helping with facility upkeep. At the field camp, you will fill a similar role. Responsibilities include staffing the office, accompanying instructors on field trips, trail and first-aid support, and developing and teaching youth programs. As a teacher/naturalist at Big Creek, your responsibilities increase as you serve as a mentor to interns.

Commitment: Programs run from the mid-March until the end of October (interns can work two to seven months). The work schedule is very irregular and busy. There may be times with no programs and times when programs run nonstop.

Perks and Rewards: Interns receive $200 to $300 per month; teachers/naturalists earn $550 to $600 per month. Housing as well as food or a food stipend is also provided. Because they are a small organization, they rely heavily on staff creativity and input, so there are many opportunities to become involved in program enhancement and development.

The Essentials: Applicants should be at least nineteen years old and have two years of college or more, and some prior experience teaching or working with youth. All staff must have CPR and first-aid certification.

Your First Move: Call for job descriptions and application. Most interviews are done over the phone, but they prefer personal interviews if at all possible. It's best to apply by the end of January.

For More Information:
RJ Devitt, Program Director
The Glacier Institute
P.O. Box 7457
Kalispell, MT 59904
(406) 755-1211 • (406) 755-7154 (fax)
glacinst@digisys.net

Staff members really enjoy working and living with people of all ages, are enthusiastic and energetic, love learning and being outside, and are creative and flexible. We need people who can be happy working and living in a residential, remote setting with rustic accommodations. Self-directed people who can work without much supervision and are willing to do anything will do very well in our program.

GLACIER PARK

Guest Services • Montana • Seasonal
www.gpihr.com

Rising from the plains of northwest Montana and southern Alberta, the jagged peaks of the Rocky Mountains make up the heart of Waterton-Glacier International Peace Park. This serves as the backdrop for seasonal employees at Glacier Park, which operates seven historic hotels, nine restaurants, five retail gift shops, a pro golf shop, four camp stores, and thirty-three famous (and recently restored) 1930s red tour buses. Whether working as a baker, waitstaff, bellhop, accounting clerk, guest service agent, or a tour driver, Glacier Park is a great place to begin your budding hospitality career.

Perks and Rewards: Wages range from $5.15 to $7.25 per hour, depending on the position and whether you work in the U.S. or Canada. Housing in Glacier is *extremely* rustic. The "structures" are located in remote Rocky Mountain settings, weathering extreme winter elements and hundreds of new tenants each season. All housing is dormitory-style, with triple or quad accommodations. There is also limited trailer/RV space. Housing is charged at $2.50 per day, and meals are $6.50 per day.

The Essentials: The minimum working age is eighteen years old (although waitstaff, bartenders, and drivers must be at least twenty-one). Applicants will be considered based on their work availability dates (a full season is preferred), qualifications, and experience in the respective position.

Your First Move: Call for application materials (which can also be filled out online). Most positions are filled by May 1, although midsummer opportunities, which begin as early as June 1 or as late as August 15, are available.

For More Information:
D. Leon Stiffarm, Human Resources Director
Glacier Park
106 Cooperative Way, Suite 104
Kalispell, MT 59901
(406) 755-3325 • (406) 755-3394 (fax)
May through September: P.O. Box 147,
East Glacier, MT, 59434; (406) 226-5600
jobs@gpihr.com

GLACIER PARK BOAT COMPANY

Tour Boat Outfitter • Montana • Summer
www.digisys.net/gpboats

A BANK TELLER turned boat builder started a family legacy in Glacier National Park. In the summer of 1937, Glacier Park Boat Company launched its first boat tours in the park with two classic-style wooden boats. Four generations later, this family-run operation has five locations throughout the park and boats that now carry from forty-five to eighty passengers. Seasonal staff captain the tour boats from June 1 through September 15, while giving commentaries on the historic and natural aspects of "America's little Switzerland." Extensive preseason training in tour-boat operation and history of the region is provided (which also prepares each staff member for boat certification exams). Applicants must be at least eighteen years of age, possess current CPR and first-aid certificates, pass a physical exam and drug test, enjoy working with the public, and have good communication skills—especially public speaking. Benefits include minimum wage pay, along with family-style housing and meals (for $8 per day). It's suggested you apply by January or February.

For More Information:
Susan Burch, Director
Glacier Park Boat Company
P.O. Box 5262
Kalispell, MT 59903-5262
(406) 257-2426 • (406) 756-1437 (fax)
gpboats@digisys.net

GRAND CANYON NATIONAL PARK LODGES, SOUTH RIM

Guest Services • Arizona • Seasonal
www.grandcanyonlodges.com

GRAND CANYON NATIONAL Park Lodges, located on the South Rim of Grand Canyon, is the authorized concessionaire providing hospitality services for the park. There are no easy jobs at Grand Canyon—the staff are known to work hard and play ferociously. Positions include food and beverage, retail sales, housekeeping, front desk, and accounting. Many employees start in entry-level positions and advance during the season. Positions are offered year-round or on a seasonal basis, beginning as early as March and ending as late as mid-October. Preference is given to those who can work at least a three- or four-month period. Wages start at $6 per hour for non-tipped positions. Dormitory-style housing (two to a room) is provided for $16 per week, and RV spots are available for $90 per month. A low-cost employee meal plan is also offered. Applicants must be eighteen years of age to live in company-provided housing. Deadlines are rolling; however, it's best to apply in early January.

For More Information:
Employment Office
Grand Canyon National Park Lodges, South Rim
P.O. Box 699
Grand Canyon, AZ 86023
(888) 224-0330 • (928) 638-2343 • (928) 638-9247 (fax)
jobs@grandcanyonlodges.com

GRAND TETON LODGE COMPANY

Guest Services • Wyoming • Seasonal
www.gtlc.com

GRAND TETON LODGE Company manages four unique resorts in the heart of Grand Teton National Park. Jackson Lake Lodge is their largest hotel resort, situated on a bluff overlooking Jackson Lake and the skyline of the Tetons; Colter Bay Village, on the shores of Jackson Lake, is a family resort offering cabins, tent cabins, and RV park accommodations; Jenny Lake Lodge is a small, elegant resort located in the shadow of the towering Tetons; and Snake River Lodge & Spa is located in Teton Village near Jackson Hole.

Now I know the secret of making the best persons; it is to grow in the open air and to eat and sleep with the earth. —WALT WHITMAN

167

What You'll Be Doing: Whether for a summer or many seasons, employment with Grand Teton provides a unique experience in one of the most beautiful and rugged areas in the world. (The first time you get a glimpse of the Tetons, you'll truly be amazed.) While the work is demanding and the summer cannot be considered a vacation, Grand Teton Lodge Company offers employees an opportunity to live in an area that annually attracts well over three million visitors. Hospitality-type jobs run the gamut here and include accounting, employee services (including recreation staff and personnel clerks), food and beverage, guest activities (wranglers, river guides, and van/bus drivers), hotel services, maintenance, and retail.

Commitment: The Grand Teton season runs from May through October. Depending on the position, various starting and ending dates can be accommodated. Preference will be given to applicants who can work through Labor Day (or the end of the season), and positions beginning in July and August are also available. Work schedules vary but in most cases are six days, forty-eight hours per week.

Perks and Rewards: Entry-level salaries begin at $7 per hour, and dormitory-style housing is provided at no charge (RV sites are $4.35 per day). There is a $47.25 per week fee for employee services, which include cafeteria meals, laundry facilities, and laundered linens. Employee recreational activities, such as dances and sporting events, are scheduled throughout the summer.

The Essentials: A minimum age of eighteen is required for all employees housed in company-maintained facilities.

Your First Move: Applications can be filled out online.

For More Information:
Personnel Manager
Grand Teton Lodge Company
P.O. Box 250
Moran, WY 83013
(800) 350-2068 • (307) 543-3068 • (307) 543-3139 (fax)
personnel@gtlc.com

GREAT SMOKY MOUNTAINS INSTITUTE AT TREMONT

Environmental Education • Tennessee • 3–12 Months
www.gsmit.org

LOCATED DEEP IN the heart of the largest mountain wilderness in the eastern U.S., the Great Smoky Mountains Institute (GSMI) offers residential, hands-on environmental education programs for children, adults, teachers, and people of all ages and walks of life. Using its classroom of 522,000 acres of forest, field, and stream in the Great Smoky Mountains National Park, GSMI is dedicated to creating "environmentally literate" students who want to help preserve and protect places like the Smokies for the future. Year-round offerings include Elderhostel programs, teacher-training weeks, backpacking courses, summer youth camps, and weekend to weeklong adult workshops on topics from wildflowers to local culture and history.

What You'll Be Doing: For those who are excited about environmental education and want to gain practical experience in the field, GSMI offers a variety of summer and year-round opportunities. Summer teacher/naturalists work in all aspects of the GSMI youth camps, including developing and teaching daily natural history activities, coleading backpacking trips, conducting evening programs, supervising campers in the dormitory, and a variety of other summer camp–related activities. A number of internships are also available for the summer season and those from abroad can participate in the International Volunteer Work Study program (six-month to one-year positions beginning in January and June).

Perks and Rewards: A $75 to $250 per week stipend (depending on position and experience) is provided, along with housing and meals.

The Essentials: Naturalists must have experience and training in environmental education and natural history, and experience working with children and adults in outdoor educational settings. A minimum of two years of college in a related field/summer camp experience, and first-aid and CPR certification is required.

Your First Move: Call for application materials. Naturalists and interns must apply by February 1. International applicants must apply through the National Park Service's Office of International Affairs at (202) 565-1293.

For More Information:
Staffing Director
Great Smoky Mountains Institute at Tremont
9275 Tremont Rd.
Townsend, TN 37882
(865) 448-6709 • (865) 448-9250 (fax)
mail@gsmit.org

THE GREEN MOUNTAIN CLUB

Trail Maintenance • Vermont • Seasonal
www.greenmountainclub.org

MIDWAY BETWEEN WATERBURY and Stowe, Vermont, you'll find the headquarters for the Green Mountain Club along with its thousands of members and volunteers who preserve, protect, and maintain Long Trail, Vermont's "footpath in the wilderness" and the oldest long-distance hiking trail in America. Seasonal opportunities on the trail include maintenance activities, working with the Long Trail Patrol trail crew, volunteering as a caretaker, or leading interpretive hikes. Off-the-trail volunteers can get involved in everything from publications and grant writing to membership development. Stipends range from $50 to $300 per week, and some positions include meals and/or rustic housing.

For More Information:
Jane Coffey, Volunteer Coordinator
The Green Mountain Club
4711 Waterbury-Stowe Rd.
Waterbury Center, VT 05677
(802) 244-7037, ext. 24 • (802) 244-5867 (fax)
gmc@greenmountainclub.org

HOPEWELL FURNACE NATIONAL HISTORIC SITE

Historic Site • Pennsylvania • 3–4 Months
www.nps.gov/hofu

HOPEWELL FURNACE IS one of the finest examples of a restored charcoal-burning iron furnace, which once dominated life in southeastern Pennsylvania and provided the foundations for the industrial development of this country. Hopewell Furnace operated from 1771 until 1883, spanning several generations of our industrial history, from its infancy in the colonial period to the giant steel and railroad industries at the turn of the twentieth century. As an active living history site, Hopewell features first-person interpretation of colliers, blacksmiths, farmers, housewives, servants, cooks, and members of the ironmaster's family. The interpretive program also includes an active farm with horses, sheep, and cows. In addition, Hopewell conducts its own charcoal burn twice a year in an effort to preserve the otherwise lost skill of producing charcoal from cord wood. The charcoal pro-

duced in these burns is used as fuel in molding, casting, and blacksmithing demonstrations.

What You'll Be Doing: Seasonal staff positions may include museums and cultural-resource preservation, historical interpretation, living history, and visitor-center operations. Duties are determined by the needs of the site and interests of the intern.

Commitment: Internship dates are variable, full- or part-time. In general, positions last three to four months at a minimum of twenty hours per week.

Perks and Rewards: Although no stipend is available, shared housing and reimbursement for miscellaneous expenses are provided.

The Essentials: Applicants must show a willingness to work with and get along with a wide variety of coworkers and visitors. A genuine desire to ensure that each visitor has an enjoyable experience at Hopewell is essential.

Your First Move: A National Park Service volunteer application may be obtained through the Volunteers in Parks website at www.nps.gov/volunteer. Completed applications should be sent by email to Hopewell. Those who do not have Web access should send a cover letter and resume.

For More Information:
Frank Hebblethwaite, Volunteer Coordinator
Hopewell Furnace National Historic Site
National Park Service
2 Mark Bird Ln.
Elverson, PA 19520-9505
(610) 582-8773, ext. 229 • (610) 582-2768 (fax)
hofu_superintendent@nps.gov

ISLE ROYALE NATIONAL PARK

National Park • Michigan • Summer
www.nps.gov/isro

In LAKE SUPERIOR's northwest corner sits a wilderness archipelago, a roadless land of wild creatures, unsoiled forests, refreshing lakes, and rugged, scenic shores accessible only by boat or floatplane. Volunteer positions are available in the park library, photo darkroom, resource management, backcountry campground, interpretation, and assistance with monitoring projects on park wildlife and vegetation. A stipend of $60 to $70 per week is provided as well as meals and comfortable dormitory-style housing on Mott Island, the park's summer headquarters.

A great flame follows a little spark. —RALPH WALDO EMERSON   169

For More Information:
Volunteer Coordinator
Isle Royale National Park
800 E. Lakeshore Dr.
Houghton, MI 49931
(906) 487-7153 • (906) 487-7170 (fax)

LAKE POWELL RESORTS AND MARINAS

Guest Services • Arizona • Summer
www.visitlakepowell.com

LAKE POWELL RESORTS and Marinas, managed by
Aramark Corporation, operates five marinas and resort
properties as well as Wilderness River Adventures, a river
guide company. The vermilion ridges, towering mesas,
long and twisting canyons, deep and clear mirrors of
water, arching rainbows, and play of light and shadow in
Glen Canyon that inspired Zane Grey in 1915 will instill
similar feelings of supernatural awe in you. Positions are
available in the marina (marina utility, fuel attendant, boat
rental attendant, boat instructor, marine mechanic, truck
driver, maintenance, and rental clerk), food and beverage
(food and cocktail servers, bus people, bartender, cook,
cashier, dishwasher, and food and beverage utility), hotel
(front desk clerk, night auditor, housekeeper, bellhop,
maintenance, utility, laundry, van driver, and bus driver),
and retail (sales clerk). Seasonal wages start at $5.70 per
hour and dormitory-style housing (single and double
occupancy options) is offered for a monthly fee.

For More Information:
Carol Mehler, HR Director
Lake Powell Resorts and Marinas
Glen Canyon National Recreation Area
P.O. Box 1597
Page, AZ 86040
(928) 645-1081 • (928) 645-1016 (fax)
mehler-carol@aramark.com

LAKE TAHOE BASIN MANAGEMENT UNIT

Natural Resources • California • Seasonal
www.r5.fs.fed.us/ltbmu

COORDINATED BY THE U.S. Forest Service at Lake Tahoe,
the interpretive services program provides informational

and interpretive materials through a visitor center, stream
profile chamber, self-guided trails, brochures, displays,
and guided activities. Year-round opportunities abound
for seasonal interpretive naturalists. Summer naturalists
assist with campfire programs, environmental education
activities, living-history programs, exhibits for display,
natural history information, recreational activities, and
various special projects; fall naturalists teach third
and fourth graders about the life cycle of the Kokanee
salmon, which spawn in a creek near the visitor center;
and winter naturalists serve fifth and sixth graders, interpreting Lake Tahoe's winter environment in a classroom
setting and outdoors on snowshoes. A subsistence
allowance, training, and complimentary government
housing (on the shores of Lake Tahoe in a historic estate)
are provided.

For More Information:
Michael St. Michel, Visitor Center Director
Lake Tahoe Basin Management Unit
U.S. Forest Service
870 Emerald Bay Rd., Suite #1
South Lake Tahoe, CA 96150
(530) 573-2600 • (530) 573-2693 (fax)
mstmichel@fs.fed.us

Photo Credit: Michael St. Michel

A summer naturalist with the Lake Tahoe Basin Management
Unit helps children collect aquatic insects on a creek walk.

LAND BETWEEN THE LAKES

Natural Resources • Kentucky • 3–12 Months
www.lbl.org/internships.html

LOCATED IN WESTERN Kentucky and Tennessee, Land Between the Lakes (LBL) offers 170,000 acres of wildlife, history, and outdoor-recreation opportunities, wrapped by three hundred miles of undeveloped shoreline. Interns and apprentices work closely with professionals and receive firsthand experiences in everything from recreation and environmental education to history and photography. Work locations might be in a family campground, a resident group camp, a living-history farm, a nature center, or the LBL administrative office. Internships last from twelve to sixteen weeks, while apprenticeships are available for up to one year. A weekly stipend of $150 to $200 is provided along with housing in a fully-furnished home or house trailer. Prospective interns must have completed at least two years of college course work, while apprentice applicants must have at least a bachelor's degree. Someone with the ability and enthusiasm for working with a variety of people in the outdoors has as good a chance as someone with all the experience in the world. Call for application materials.

For More Information:
Tamara Neukam, Intern/Apprentice Coordinator
Land Between the Lakes, U.S. Forest Service
100 Van Morgan Dr.
Golden Pond, KY 42211
(270) 924-2006 • (270) 924-2060 (fax)
tneukam@fs.fed.us

MAINE APPALACHIAN TRAIL CLUB

Trail Maintenance • Maine • Seasonal
www.matc.org

VOLUNTEER OPPORTUNITIES ABOUND in the Maine Appalachian Trail Club. More than five hundred members and volunteers help maintain 261 miles of the Appalachian Trail in Maine, from Mt. Katahdin to Route 26 in Grafton Notch, including thirty-seven lean-tos and tent sites. Trail-crew leaders, assistants, and interns provide everything from logistical support to path reconstruction. Positions begin as early as May and include a travel grant, stipend (up to $400), lodging, and meals.

Caretaker positions are available at various campsites throughout Maine from mid-May to late October. Duties include greeting and registering hikers, performing maintenance tasks, and providing overnight backpacking hikes. A stipend of $270 to $310 per week is provided along with housing, cook stove, work tools, and gear. Applications are accepted in late fall for the following season. View the club's website for a listing of positions and where to send your application materials.

For More Information:
Tom Lohnes, Corresponding Secretary
Maine Appalachian Trail Club
P.O. Box 283
Augusta, ME 04332-0283
tlohnes@pivot.net

MINNESOTA CONSERVATION CORPS

Conservation Education • Minnesota • Summer
www.dnr.state.mn.us/mcc

THE MINNESOTA CONSERVATION Corps summer program provides the chance for Minnesota youth, ages fifteen to eighteen, to work on various natural resource projects while learning basic work skills. The summer staff, ranging from site directors, work-project coordinators, crew leaders, and education coordinators, supervise and work with the youth corps members, along with instructing them in environmental awareness, life skills, and career development. Past projects have included erosion control, building and maintaining hiking trails, historical restoration, tree planting, and building bridges. Depending on the position, a weekly stipend of $290 to $440 is provided, along with room, board, and transportation while on the job. Applicants who thrive in these positions aren't afraid of mosquitoes, rain, heat, and other challenges that the outdoors presents. Individuals who are sign language interpreters and/or skilled in American Sign Language are also encouraged to apply. In addition, those who are deaf or hard-of-hearing are needed for leadership roles. Application materials must be received by mid-March.

For More Information:
Greg Hall, Summer Program Coordinator
Minnesota Conservation Corps
500 Lafayette Rd.
St. Paul, MN 55155-4029
(651) 296-9165 • (651) 297-5818 (fax)
greg.hall@dnr.state.mn.us

We sleep, but the loom of life never stops and the pattern which was weaving when the sun went down is weaving when it comes up tomorrow. —HENRY WARD BEECHER

WORKING FOR THE NATIONAL PARK SERVICE

Many Americans have had love affairs with the national parks since Yellowstone, the first national park, was created in 1872. Today the National Park Service preserves and manages more than 370 national sites across the U.S. (including Guam, Puerto Rico, and the Virgin Islands). From the architectural relics of the Anasazi in Mesa Verde, the historical treasures of Gettysburg Battlefield, the fossil reefs of Carlsbad Cavern, the geysers bursting in Yellowstone, or, say, the awesome coastal redwood forest in Redwood National Park, the National Park Service personnel are there to protect these awe-inspiring places and to teach and educate the millions of people who visit. All national park employment opportunities can be found online at www.nps.gov/personnel.

SEASONAL JOBS

Seasonal workers are hired every year to help permanent staff, especially during peak visitation seasons. Jobs range from carpenters, campground hosts, fee collectors, firefighters, historians, laborers, landscape architects, naturalists, law-enforcement rangers, lifeguards, park rangers, tour guides, visitor-use assistants, to so much more. Seasonal jobs are very competitive, although competition is usually less keen at smaller, lesser-known parks and for seasonal jobs in the winter season. Application forms, including a list of parks hiring for a particular season, are available from any regional office or the Seasonal Employment Program, Human Resources Office, National Park Service, P.O. Box 37127, Mail Stop 2225, Washington, D.C. 20013-7127; (202) 208-5074. The filing period for winter employment is June 1 through July 15 (postmarked); the summer employment filing period is November 15 through January 15 (postmarked). Applicants are encouraged to use the seasonal employment website at www.sep.nps.gov (questions can be directed to nps_sep@nps.gov).

VOLUNTEERS IN PARKS (VIP) PROGRAM

VIPs work in almost every park in the National Park System and perform varied duties that might include working at information desks, presenting living history demonstrations in period costume, serving as campground hosts, leading guided nature walks and evening campfire programs, or maintaining and patrolling trails. All VIPs are given special training, and some parks reimburse volunteers for some out-of-pocket expenses, such as local travel costs, meals, and uniforms. Visit www.nps.gov/volunteer on the Web (which includes an extensive list of volunteer and artist-in-residence program opportunities), or call the VIP coordinator at the national park where you would like to volunteer. Be sure to ask for the Volunteers in Parks brochure, which provides a nifty map of all the national parks (with contact information) and application materials.

The NPS manages more than just our national parks—the National Park system (encompassing more that 83.6 million acres!) is broken down by a variety of unique designations, including monuments, preserves, historic sites, memorials, battlefields, cemeteries, recreation areas, seashores, lakeshores, rivers, parkways, and trails—more than 370 national sites in all! To find out more information on a specific park (including job/volunteer opportunities), use the NPS Park Guide at www.nps.gov/parks.html.

INTERNSHIP OPPORTUNITIES

Whether you are a college student or a retiree, the Student Conservation Association (SCA) is one of the best ways to land a paid seasonal internship with the National Park Service (as well as other federal agencies, like the Bureau of Land Management and U.S. Forest Service). Throughout the year, SCA publishes a catalog of opportunities that range from educating people to save the Florida manatee to providing guided nature and historic talks at a national monument. More information on SCA can be found on page 178, or visit them on the Web at www.sca-inc.org.

A variety of current opportunities can also be viewed in the volunteer section of the NPS employment website at www.nps.gov/volunteer; however, it's best to contact the SCA or each park for specific information.

PARK CONCESSIONAIRES

Hotels, lodges, restaurants, stores, transportation services, marinas, and many other visitor facilities in the National Park System areas are operated by private companies that hire their own employees. This section of your guide features the details for many—from Denali Park Resorts (page 163) to Furnace Creek Inn and Ranch Resort (page 165)—or contact one of the regional offices found below.

NATIONAL PARK SERVICE REGIONAL CONTACTS

Below you'll find contact information for the seven field offices in the U.S. with national parks noted in parenthesis (where most seasonal and volunteer job opportunities can be found). Contacting a regional office—or the park itself—is a great starting point for current job opportunities. A directory of all 370 parks can be found on the Web at www.nps.gov/parks.html.

ALASKA REGIONAL OFFICE
National Park Service
2525 Gambell St., Room 107
Anchorage, AK 99503-2892
(907) 257-2574

Includes Denali, Gates of the Arctic, Glacier Bay, Katmai, Kenai Fjords, Kobuk Valley, Lake Clark, and Wrangell–St. Elias.

INTER-MOUNTAIN REGIONAL OFFICE
National Park Service
12795 W. Alameda Parkway
Denver, CO 80225-0287
(303) 969-2020

Includes Arizona (Grand Canyon and Petrified Forest), Colorado (Mesa Verde and Rocky Mountain), Montana (Glacier), New Mexico (Carlsbad Caverns), Oklahoma, Texas (Big Bend and Guadalupe Mountains), Utah (Arches, Bryce Canyon, Canyonlands, Capitol Reef, and Zion), and Wyoming (Grand Teton and Yellowstone).

MIDWEST REGIONAL OFFICE
National Park Service
1709 Jackson St.
Omaha, NE 68102-2571
(402) 221-3456

Includes Arkansas (Hot Springs), Illinois, Indiana, Iowa, Kansas, Michigan (Isle Royale), Minnesota (Voyageurs), Mississippi, Missouri, Nebraska, North Dakota (Theodore Roosevelt), Ohio, South Dakota (Badlands and Wind Cave), and Wisconsin.

NATIONAL CAPITAL REGIONAL OFFICE
National Park Service
1100 Ohio Dr., SW
Washington, D.C. 20242
(202) 619-7256

Includes Washington, D.C., and nearby areas in Maryland, Virginia, and West Virginia.

NATIONAL PARK SERVICE

NORTHEAST REGIONAL OFFICE

National Park Service
U.S. Custom House
200 Chestnut St., Room 322
Philadelphia, PA 19106
(215) 597-4971

Includes Connecticut, Delaware, Maine (Acadia), Massachusetts, New Hampshire, New Jersey, New York, Pennsylvania, Rhode Island, Vermont, and most areas of Maryland, Virginia (Shenandoah), and West Virginia.

PACIFIC WEST REGIONAL OFFICE

National Park Service
One Jackson Center
1111 Jackson St., Suite 700
Oakland, CA 94607
(510) 817-1300

Includes California (Channel Islands, Kings Canyon, Lassen Volcanic, Redwood, Sequoia, and Yosemite), Guam (National Park of American Samoa), Hawaii (Haleakala and Hawaii Volcanoes), Idaho, Nevada (Great Basin), Oregon (Crater Lake), and Washington (Mount Rainier, North Cascades, and Olympic).

SOUTHEAST REGIONAL OFFICE

National Park Service
Richard B. Russell Federal Building
75 Spring St., SW, Suite 1130
Atlanta, GA 30303
(404) 331-5711

Includes Alabama, Florida (Biscayne and Everglades), Georgia, Kentucky (Mammoth Cave), Louisiana, North Carolina, Puerto Rico, South Carolina, Tennessee (Great Smoky Mountains), and the Virgin Islands (Virgin Islands National Park).

NORTHWEST YOUTH CORPS

Conservation Education • Pacific Northwest •
2–4 Months
www.nwyouthcorps.org

THE NORTHWEST YOUTH Corps (NYC) is a summer education and job-training program for high school youth. Youth crews work on projects for government agencies and private landowners in a format stressing environmental education and development of basic job skills. Crews typically live and work in remote locations throughout Oregon and in parts of Washington and Idaho. During the week, crews set up primitive camps near their job sites, live in tents, and cook their own meals over a campfire or Coleman stove. On weekends, three to four crews rendezvous for recreational outings and educational activities. NYC is the only fully mobile conservation corps in the country.

What You'll Be Doing: More than seven hundred youth crew members maintain wilderness trails, build fences, pull debris from creeks, restore wildlife habitat, plant trees, enhance fisheries, or work to save endangered species. Crew leaders and assistants work shoulder to shoulder with their crew while supervising the successful completion of a wide variety of manual labor projects and providing environmental education programs.

Commitment: Positions, with various start/finish dates, begin in mid-April and continue throughout the summer months into October. The program requires long days, high energy, and a love for challenge. Time off is limited.

Perks and Rewards: Crew leaders average $4,700 to $5,300 per summer (about $70 to $80 per day), plus meals and rustic housing.

The Essentials: The ideal candidate has a youth leadership background, experience in professional positions, a solid environmental ethic, and a diverse set of conservation skills. Current first-aid and CPR certifications are required, and lifesaving certification is desirable.

Your First Move: Applications can be filled out online.

For More Information:
Ethan Nelson, Program Director
Northwest Youth Corps
2621 Augusta St.
Eugene, OR 97403
(541) 349-5055 • (541) 349-5060 (fax)
work@nwyouthcorps.org

OLYMPIC NATIONAL PARK

National Park • Washington • 2–6 Months
www.nps.gov/olym

OLYMPIC NATIONAL PARK occupies nearly one million acres in Washington State, established to preserve primeval forests and the largest natural herd of Roosevelt elk. In 1976, it was designated a Biosphere Reserve, and soon thereafter, it was designated a World Heritage Site. The park consists of a rugged and spectacular glacier-capped mountainous core penetrated by deep valleys, some with lush temperate rainforests, a separate fifty-seven-mile-long coastal strip, and some one hundred offshore islands.

What You'll Be Doing: In addition to a variety of volunteer opportunities (ranging from campground hosts to back-country rangers), Olympic National Park has an extensive internship program for the budding outdoor enthusiast. Whether working as an interpretive ranger on Hurricane Ridge, at the visitor center at Lake Crescent, or at the Port Angeles wilderness information center, interns have the chance to work behind the scenes and develop the necessary skills to further their career with the National Park Service. A two-week training program is provided for most positions.

Commitment: Positions are generally available throughout the year, including the summer months. Visitor center internship positions vary seasonally, although plan on two or three months or longer. A minimum commitment of two-and-a-half months is generally needed.

Perks and Rewards: Interns receive a stipend of $50 to $100 per month, along with shared bunkhouse or dorm-style housing. Housing or RV/trailer hookups (electrical, water, and sewer) are provided for volunteers.

The Essentials: Applicants should have a strong background in natural science, park management, or interpretation. Some knowledge of ecological processes and natural history is desirable as is the ability to work independently and with people.

Your First Move: Call for application materials and details of all their internship and volunteer opportunities. (It's extensive!) Phone calls are welcomed, and it is suggested you send your application one to three months before the season begins.

For More Information:
Maurie Sprague, Information Specialist
Olympic National Park

600 East Park Ave.
Port Angeles, WA 98362-6798
(360) 565-3000 • (360) 565-3015 (fax)
maurie_sprague@nps.gov

POTOMAC APPALACHIAN TRAIL CLUB

Trail Maintenance • Virginia • Summer
www.patc.net

THE POTOMAC APPALACHIAN Trail Club is a volunteer trails organization that provides upkeep and improvement of 970 miles of hiking trails, thirty shelters, and twenty-eight cabins in Virginia, Maryland, West Virginia, Pennsylvania, and the District of Columbia. Work on trails, shelters, and cabins is performed solely by volunteer overseers, interns, trail crews, and ridge runners. Volunteers generally sign up for a one-week block in the months of May through September. Accommodations are in either tents or cabins, and longer-term volunteers may receive a weekly stipend of $220. This is a great way to meet new people with outdoor interests and an outstanding way to make a real contribution to the hiking public.

For More Information:
Volunteer Coordinator
Potomac Appalachian Trail Club
118 Park St., SE
Vienna, VA 22180-4609
(703) 242-0693, ext. 12 • (703) 242-0968 (fax)
info@patc.net

PRIEST LAKE STATE PARK

State Park • Idaho • Summer
www.idahoparks.org

AT AN ELEVATION of about 2,400 feet, Priest Lake offers an abundance of beautiful scenery and recreational opportunities. Visitors enjoy the dense cedar-hemlock forests and have ample opportunity to observe nature's inhabitants such as whitetail deer, black bear, moose, and bald eagles. Noted for its clear water, Priest Lake extends nineteen miles and is connected to the smaller Upper Priest Lake by a placid two-mile-long thoroughfare. Priest Lake offers park visitors a diversity of outdoor enjoyment, ranging from boating and fishing to snowmobiling and cross-country skiing.

However much you knock at nature's door, she will never answer you in comprehensible words. —IVAN TURGENEV

What You'll Be Doing: Located either in the Indian Creek or Lionhead Unit, interns work as crew leaders, interpretaters, maintenance crew, registration aides, and store clerk and manager. Interns will have the opportunity to observe and learn about park operational and administrative methods, and acquire skills and experience necessary to pursue a career in parks and recreation.

Commitment: The internship begins one week prior to Memorial Day weekend and runs through Labor Day.

Perks and Rewards: Maintenance, clerical, and interpretive positions are paid up to $7.50 per hour; others are nonpaid. Housing is available for a nominal fee and all interns are required to purchase and wear a park-approved uniform.

The Essentials: CPR and first-aid training is required prior to starting employment.

Your First Move: Applications are accepted from January 1 through March 15, and can be found online. A personal interview with qualified applicants is generally required at the park.

For More Information:
Park Manager
Priest Lake State Park
314 Indian Creek Park Rd.
Coolin, ID 83821-9706
(208) 443-2200 • (208) 443-3893 (fax)
pri@idpr.state.id.us

THE RESORT AT GLACIER, ST. MARY LODGE

Guest Services • Montana • Seasonal
www.glacierparkjobs.com

GLACIER NATIONAL PARK is a two-million-acre masterpiece of unsurpassed beauty. Conquer the challenge of biking the famous Going-to-the-Sun Highway, adventuring on a fifty-mile hike along the Continental Divide, or touring through this pristine wilderness. To guests visiting Glacier, the family-owned St. Mary Lodge offers the park's most complete guest facilities (and one of the most magnificent views in the world).

What You'll Be Doing: Positions include food and beverage staff, housekeeping, sales and administration, front desk clerks, gas station attendants and mechanics, maintenance and grounds personnel, night security, and resident assistants, as well as internships in accounting, hospitality, retail management, and recreation. The work

required is challenging both mentally and physically; however, the atmosphere of the Rocky Mountains and the companionship of fellow employees make it seem less strenuous than it would elsewhere.

Commitment: The lodge is open from May 15 to October 1, although staff members can begin their summer employment as early as May 1 and end it as late as October 15.

Perks and Rewards: Most positions pay between $5.15 and $5.75 per hour. Food servers can gross about $4,400 for the summer. All employees receive room and board (three meals a day) for $8.95 per day. Employees are housed in new dormitories by seniority and age.

The Essentials: St. Mary Lodge attracts people who have high energy and are looking for the experience of a lifetime.

Your First Move: Online applications are available for download or call for more information. Late-season help is always needed (from mid-August through October 15). Between mid-April and mid-October, contact St. Mary Lodge in Montana at (406) 732-4431.

For More Information:
Dustin Wyant, Assistant General Manager
The Resort at Glacier, St. Mary Lodge
P.O. Box 1808
Sun Valley, ID 83353
(800) 368-3689 • (208) 726-6279 • (208) 726-6282 (fax)
jobs@glcpark.com

SAGAMORE INSTITUTE

Historic Site • New York • 4–5 Months
www.sagamore.org

BUILT IN 1897 as the wilderness retreat of the Vanderbilt family, Sagamore's twenty-seven rustic buildings include the architectural prototype for many National Park Service designs. Mostly a U.N.–designated Biosphere Reserve, the park is a historic laboratory for evolving land-use policy. Offered to the public during the summer and fall seasons, a two-hour guided tour engages guests in a twenty-five-minute slide presentation followed by a walking narrative of the grounds and many of the buildings.

What You'll Be Doing: After intensive training, historic preservation interns conduct tours that interpret the institute's socioeconomic and architectural history in light of American cultural and land-use history, as well as the history and uncertain future of the Adirondack park. Outdoor/environmental education interns deliver programs involving canoeing, hiking, swimming, and nature interpretation to residential guests. Other opportunities include actors and a technician as well as a museum/café intern. A weekly seminar with common readings and guest speakers is also provided.

Commitment: Summer interns are in residence between mid-May and mid-June and continue through Labor Day; fall residencies run September through October. Sagamore welcomes those who can work the entire season.

Perks and Rewards: A weekly stipend of $150, along with room and board, is provided. Interns also have the opportunity to participate in residential programs, which might include workshops on Adirondack ecology, history, arts and crafts, or education and professional development, as well as engage in outdoor programs ranging from backpacking to llama trekking.

The Essentials: Interns often come fresh out of college or on summer break, in the period of career change, on sabbatical, or are retired professionals who often have taken an Elderhostel course at Sagamore.

Your First Move: Their website outlines detailed application materials that are required. During June through August, address correspondence to: P.O. Box 146, Raquette Lake, NY 13436; (315) 354-5311, sagamore@telenet.net.

For More Information:
Michael Wilson, Internship Director
Sagamore Institute
9 Kiwassa Dr.
Saranac Lake, NY 12983
(518) 891-1718 • (518) 891-2561 (fax)
mwilson@northnet.org

SHENANDOAH NATIONAL PARK

Guest Services • Virginia • Seasonal
www.visitshenandoah.com

KNOWN AS VIRGINIA's mountain playground, Shenandoah National Park is situated close to Washington, D.C., and is encompassed by the Blue Ridge Mountains and the historic Appalachian Trail. From April through November, seasonal staff converge on the park and work in the lodges, dining facilities, camp stores, craft and gift shops, and stables. Competitive wages are offered (based on your experience), along with health-insurance benefits. Dormitory-style housing with a shared bath or individual

rooms with bath are limited (so be sure to apply early!) and cost $20 per week. Meals are $2 to $6 per day. All applicants must be at least eighteen years of age.

For More Information:
Debbie Zinn, Human Resources Dept.
Shenandoah National Park
ARAMARK
P. O. Box 727
Luray, VA 22835
(540) 743-5108 • (540) 743-7883 (fax)
zinn-debbie@aramark.com

SIGNAL MOUNTAIN LODGE

Guest Services • Wyoming • Seasonal
www.signalmtnlodge.com

SIGNAL MOUNTAIN LODGE is a privately owned company that operates visitor services in the spectacular Grand Teton National Park, with over two hundred miles of hiking trails and some of the best rock climbing in North America. Signal Mountain is located directly on Jackson Lake, just thirty miles from the town of Jackson Hole and twenty-five miles from the south entrance of Yellowstone National Park. Their operation includes seventy-nine guest units, two restaurants, two gift shops, a bar, a grocery/gas station, and a marina, along with Leek's Pizzeria and Marina, just ten miles north of the lodge. From early May through mid-October, over 150 seasonal workers come to Signal Mountain and work in a variety of hospitality-related positions. Hourly wages vary, and all employees live and eat on the property (which runs $250 per month). Benefits include free Internet access, a variety of sporting events, and outdoor recreation at its best! Applicants with retail, food-service, or hotel experience, and a genuine, enthusiastic desire to work with the public are most likely to get hired. Those with the longest dates of availability will be given first consideration. Hiring begins in January.

For More Information:
Megan Dorr, Personnel Manager
Signal Mountain Lodge
Grand Teton National Park
P.O. Box 50
Moran, WY 83013
(800) 672-6012
(307) 543-2831 • (307) 543-2569 (fax)
personnel@signalmtnlodge.com

Forget not that the earth delights to feel your bare feet and the winds long to play with your hair. —KAHLIL GIBRAN

STUDENT CONSERVATION ASSOCIATION

Conservation Education • USA • 3–12 Months
www.sca-inc.org

CENTRAL TO THE Student Conservation Association's (SCA) mission is the goal of educating students and professionals of all ages about the need for active stewardship of the environment, and encouraging them to pursue life-long careers focused on conservation and care of the earth's natural resources.

What You'll Be Doing: Can you see yourself . . . patrolling a remote island wilderness in Alaska by kayak? Assisting with desert tortoise research in Southern California? Leading canoe trips and giving talks in northern Minnesota? Playing the role of an 1800s resident of historic Ft. Laramie? These are just a few of the assignments participants in the resource-assistant or conservation-associate programs enjoy. Participants will also have the chance to live and work in America's spectacular national parks, wildlands, and historic sites, ranging from California's Joshua Tree to the Great Smoky Mountains. For those aged twenty-one and over, SCA also offers paid leadership positions, working with fifteen- to nineteen-year-old volunteers through their summer conservation work-crew program.

Commitment: Depending on your availability and background, opportunities range from twelve weeks to twelve months.

Perks and Rewards: Benefits include a food allowance (which is generally $50 to $200 per week), free housing, travel to and from position site, free or low-cost health insurance, and valuable training packages. Conservation interns are also eligible for education awards of $1,180 to $4,725 from the Corporation for National Service.

The Essentials: A majority of participants are college students or recent graduates; however, teachers, career changers, and retirees join SCA each year. (There's a minimum applicant age of eighteen.) In general, applicants are seeking real-life experiences in the conservation field to further academic, career, or personal goals.

Your First Move: SCA publishes *Make Contact,* a catalog of opportunities (including application materials) printed on a monthly basis. This information is also available online and updated weekly. The extensive application (along with a $20 fee) is forwarded to various agencies (who do the hiring) based on your choices. There are no program deadlines; however, to enhance your chances of being selected, you should apply by these dates: spring—January 15; summer—March 1; fall—June 1; early winter—September 15; and late winter—November 15.

For More Information:
Student Conservation Association
689 River Rd.
P.O. Box 550
Charlestown, NH 03603-0550
(603) 543-1700 • (603) 543-1828 (fax)
internships@sca-inc.org

U.S. ARMY CORPS OF ENGINEERS VOLUNTEER CLEARINGHOUSE

Conservation Education • USA • Seasonal
www.orn.usace.army.mil/volunteer

THE U.S. ARMY CORPS of Engineers, the steward of almost twelve million acres of land and water, offers many volunteer opportunities in recreation and natural resources management. These include trail building and maintenance, park attendant, campground hosting, wildlife habitat construction, educational interpretation, visitor center staffing, photography, and dozens of other unique and challenging opportunities. Benefits vary with the position and may include reimbursement for out-of-pocket expenses and free camping. To learn of these opportunities, call the Corps nationwide, toll-free hotline number. Before you call, you should be ready to provide information about your interests, talents, and the locations where you may want to volunteer. The clearinghouse, in turn, will provide you with contact information for the area you have requested, as well as written information about volunteer opportunities there. An application and details of opportunities are also available on the Web.

For More Information:
Volunteer Coordinator
U.S. Army Corps of Engineers Volunteer Clearinghouse
P.O. Box 1070
Nashville, TN 37202-1070
(800) 865-8337
gayla.mitchell@usace.army.mil

U.S. FISH AND WILDLIFE SERVICE

Imagine banding birds at a national wildlife refuge, raising fish at a national fish hatchery, conducting wildlife surveys, leading a tour, or assisting in laboratory research. You can engage in these exciting opportunities by volunteering at national wildlife refuges, fish hatcheries, research stations, and administrative offices. The work may be hard, the conditions harsh, and living quarters primitive, but it is well worth the experience—a commitment made by more than thirty-six thousand volunteers each year.

The U.S. Fish and Wildlife Service manages more than five hundred wildlife refuges and nearly eighty national fish hatcheries that raise more than two hundred million fish each year, from the arctic north coast of Alaska to tropical Caribbean islands. These sites cover over ninety million acres and include virtually every kind of habitat necessary for survival of America's wildlife. As our world forges into the twenty-first century, U.S. Fish and Wildlife personnel are challenged by pollution, deforestation, and the continued loss of wetlands and other vital wildlife habitat.

For information on specific volunteer positions in certain geographic locations or for general information on employment, contact the volunteer coordinator at the nearest regional personnel office listed below. You can also visit their website at http://volunteers.fws.gov, which has a searchable database of current opportunities (or you can email the volunteer coordinator at volunteers@fws.gov). Most volunteers receive room and board, and sometimes travel expenses. Summer employment applications generally need to be submitted sometime between January and April.

U.S. FISH AND WILDLIFE SERVICE FIELD OFFICES

SERVICE HEADQUARTERS
U.S. Fish and Wildlife Service
4040 N. Fairfax Dr.
Room 300, Webb Building
Arlington, VA 22203
(703) 358-1724 • www.fws.gov

ALASKA REGION
U.S. Fish and Wildlife Service
1011 E. Tudor Rd.
Anchorage, AK 99503-6199
(907) 786-3328 • http://alaska.fws.gov

GREAT LAKES/BIG RIVERS REGION
U.S. Fish and Wildlife Service
BHW Federal Building, 1 Federal Dr.
Fort Snelling, MN 55111-4056
(612) 713-5316 • http://midwest.fws.gov

(Illinois, Iowa, Indiana, Michigan, Minnesota, Missouri, Ohio, and Wisconsin)

MOUNTAIN PRAIRIE REGION
U.S. Fish and Wildlife Service
134 Union Blvd.
Lakewood, Colorado 80228
(303) 236-7919 • (303) 236-4733
(Job Information Line)
http://mountain-prairie.fws.gov

(Colorado, Kansas, Montana, Nebraska, North Dakota, South Dakota, Utah, and Wyoming)

A pond-frog cannot imagine the ocean, nor can a summer insect conceive of ice. Remember, you are restricted by your own learning. —CHUANG-TSU

NORTHEAST REGION

U.S. Fish and Wildlife Service
300 Westgate Center Dr.
Hadley, MA 01035-9589
(413) 253-8315
http://northeast.fws.gov

(Connecticut, Delaware, Maine, Maryland, Massachussetts, New Hampshire, New Jersey, New York, Pennsylvania, Rhode Island, Vermont, Virginia, and West Virginia)

PACIFIC REGION

U.S. Fish and Wildlife Service
Eastside Federal Complex
911 N.E. 11th Ave., 6th Floor West
Portland, OR 97232-4181
(503) 231-2260
(503) 231-2018 (Job Information Line)
http://pacific.fws.gov

(California, Hawaii, Idaho, Nevada, Oregon, Washington, and the Pacific Islands)

SOUTHEAST REGION

U.S. Fish and Wildlife Service
1875 Century Center Blvd., Suite 400
Atlanta, GA 30345
(404) 679-7077 • http://southeast.fws.gov

(Alabama, Arkansas, Florida, Georgia, Kentucky, Louisiana, Mississippi, North Carolina, South Carolina, Tennessee, Puerto Rico, and the Virgin Islands)

SOUTHWEST REGION

U.S. Fish and Wildlife Service
500 Gold Avenue, SW
Albuquerque, NM 87102
(505) 248-7838 • http://southwest.fws.gov

(Arizona, New Mexico, Oklahoma, and Texas)

U.S. FOREST SERVICE

If you've heard of Smokey Bear or Woodsy Owl, you're familiar with the U.S. Forest Service. With twenty-nine thousand permanent employees and a temporary workforce that typically exceeds fifteen thousand workers in the summer, the Forest Service is one of the government's major conservation organizations. The agency manages 191 million acres of federal lands, assists state and private landowners, conducts research, and works with international organizations and other countries to build a better world. Employees are stationed at more than nine hundred separate work locations—most of which are in national forests; however, many work on college campuses, at research laboratories, or in office buildings in cities or towns.

Although the largest number of jobs are in forestry, there's something for everybody. Here's a snapshot of some of the most sought-after seasonal and volunteer positions:

• Archaeologists help inventory national forest lands for prehistoric and historic sites (Indian burial grounds hunting sites, old mining camps, or homesteads). Fieldwork varies but may involve inventory surveys, photography, mapping, and test excavation.

• Backcountry rangers are jacks-of-all-trades. They educate the public to practice sound land ethics, as well as practice fire prevention, camping ethics, assist in clearing and maintaining trails, maintain fire lookouts, inventory campsites, and record wildlife observations.

• Campground hosts serve as picnic ground or campground resource people—greeting visitors, providing information, and maintaining the camp.

• Wilderness rangers meet wilderness visitors and provide information on proper wilderness use and ethics. These rangers are usually in the field for one-week to ten-day periods.

• Other seasonal and volunteer opportunities include positions in administration, cartography, education, fire fighting, guard stations, historical research, human resources, hydrology, interpretation, range management, recreation, research, visitor centers, and wildlife and fish management.

As many Forest Service employees reach retirement age, employment opportunities will increase over the next couple years, especially in the fields of conservation, wildlife, and communications.

TIPS ON GETTING IN WITH THE FOREST SERVICE:

Contact local Forest Service offices to learn what types of seasonal positions are available, how best to find out about them, and what skills and abilities you need to develop. Although the regional offices are the forest hubs, there are more than nine hundred separate work locations across the U.S. Most regional offices publish volunteer opportunity directories that you can obtain for free.

Summer job opportunities begin approximately mid-May and end September 30. Applications are typically accepted from December through April 15. Applicants must be at least sixteen years of age and qualify for a position based on work experience and/or education. Beyond the summer, positions can last a couple months or as long as four years.

Job Connections with the U.S. Forest Service: An overview of employment opportunities can be found on the Web at www.fs.fed.us/fsjobs/ forestservice

All temporary employment opportunities (including fire, nonfire support, resource technicians, internships, and student programs) can be found through their Automated Staffing Application Program at www.fs.fed.us/people/ employ/asap.

For information on the Student Career Experience Program (SCEP) or the Student Temporary Employment Program (STEP), applicants can also write:
USDA Office of Human Resources Management
Department of Student Programs Manager
1400 Independence Ave., SW
Room 309-W, Jamie L. Whitten Federal Building
Washington, D.C. 20250-9600

U.S. FOREST SERVICE REGIONAL OFFICES

REGION 1—NORTHERN REGION
U.S. Forest Service
Federal Building
200 E. Broadway
P.O. Box 7669
Missoula, MT 59807
(406) 329-3511
www.fs.fed.us/r1

(northern Idaho, Montana, North Dakota, northwestern South Dakota)

REGION 2—ROCKY MOUNTAIN REGION
U.S. Forest Service
740 Simms St.
P.O. Box 25127
Lakewood, CO 80225-0127
(303) 275-5350
www.fs.fed.us/r2

(Colorado, Kansas, Nebraska, South Dakota, and eastern Wyoming)

REGION 3—SOUTHWESTERN REGION
U.S. Forest Service
Federal Building
517 Gold Avenue, SW
Albuquerque, NM 87102
(505) 842-3292
www.fs.fed.us/r3

(Arizona and New Mexico)

REGION 4—INTERMOUNTAIN REGION
U.S. Forest Service
324 25th St.
Ogden, UT 84401
(801) 625-5297
www.fs.fed.us/r4

(southern Idaho, Nevada, Utah, and western Wyoming)

FOREST SERVICE

FOREST SERVICE

REGION 5—PACIFIC SOUTHWEST REGION

U.S. Forest Service
1323 Club Dr.
Vallejo, CA 94592
(707).562-8737
www.r5.fs.fed.us

(California, Hawaii, Guam, and Trust Territories of the Pacific Islands)

REGION 6—PACIFIC NORTHWEST REGION

U.S. Forest Service
333 S.W. 1st Ave.
P.O. Box 3623
Portland, OR 97208-3623
(503) 808-2971
www.fs.fed.us/r6

(Oregon and Washington)

REGION 8—SOUTHERN REGION

U.S. Forest Service
1720 Peachtree Rd., NW
Atlanta, GA 30309
(404) 347-4177
www.southernregion.fs.fed.us

(Alabama, Arkansas, Florida, Georgia, Kentucky, Louisiana, Mississippi, North Carolina, Oklahoma, Puerto Rico, South Carolina, Tennessee, Texas, Virgin Islands, and Virginia)

REGION 9—EASTERN REGION

U.S. Forest Service
310 W. Wisconsin Ave., Suite 500
Milwaukee, WI 53203
(414) 297-3601
www.fs.fed.us/r9

(Connecticut, Delaware, Illinois, Indiana, Iowa, Maine, Maryland, Massachusetts, Michigan, Minnesota, Missouri, New Hampshire, New Jersey, New York, Ohio, Pennsylvania, Rhode Island, Vermont, West Virginia, and Wisconsin)

REGION 10—ALASKA REGION

U.S. Forest Service
Federal Office Building
709 W. 9th St.
P.O. Box 21628
Juneau, AK 99802-1628
(907) 586-8863
www.fs.fed.us/r10

This is sand dune country! Oregon Dunes National Recreation Area is unique in that it is one of only a few areas where windswept open dunes, some towering over four hundred feet, are bordered by the beach to the west and the coastal forest to the east. Volunteer and intern positions include overlook hosts, headquarters hosts, guided field-trip and nature-walk interpreters, campground hosts, recreation (including off-road vehicle) assistants, fish and wildlife assistants, writers, illustrators, photographers, graphic designers, and office help. If you have a special skill or talent you think is valuable in managing the Oregon Dunes, let them know. Work one month or six, a few hours a week or full-time! Help is generally needed most from May through September. A small stipend and uniforms are provided, and housing is available to volunteers who work at least twenty-four hours per week. Housing, complete with kitchen, bathroom, and laundry facilities, is located two miles north of where you will be working. Campground hosts receive a campsite with hookups.

For More Information:

Volunteer Coordinator
Oregon Dunes National Recreation Area, Siuslaw National Forest
855 Highway 101, Reedsport, OR 97467
(541) 271-3611
www.fs.fed.us/r6/siuslaw/oregondunes

VEGA STATE PARK

State Park • Colorado • Seasonal
www.coloradoparks.org/vega

VEGA STATE PARK, located at an elevation of eight thousand feet on the eastern edge of the spectacular Grand Mesa, is one of forty state parks in Colorado. Vega Reservoir and the meadows that surround it are rich in history and natural beauty; the area was once a mountain meadow where cattle ranchers grazed their herds from the late 1800s until 1962. *Vega* is the Spanish word for "meadow."

What You'll Be Doing: Year-round seasonal positions include rangers, maintenance workers, and gate attendants, along with volunteer campground hosts. With a relatively small staff, all workers, regardless of the position, help each other in completing tasks. As a result, job duties can be highly variable, and employees find it nearly impossible to be bored.

Perks and Rewards: Seasonal workers receive a wage of $6.28 to $11.83 per hour, along with low-cost housing and training. Volunteers receive free housing (or RV site) and an annual pass to forty Colorado state parks after volunteering forty-eight hours. This is an excellent opportunity to learn about park management, meet wonderful people, and make lifelong friendships.

The Essentials: Applicants must be highly energetic, friendly, outgoing, and motivated, and able to work independently with little supervision. Good public relations skills are a must.

Your First Move: Applications are accepted year-round; however, summer applications must be received by March 31. Top applicants will be interviewed by phone.

For More Information:
Chris Childs, Park Manager
Vega State Park
P.O. Box 186
Collbran, CO 81624
(970) 487-3407 • (970) 487-3404 (fax)
vega.park@state.co.us

Crew leaders with the Vermont Youth Conservation Corps learn the ropes of trail maintenance before leading their team.

Photo Credit: Vermont Youth Conservation Corps

VERMONT YOUTH CONSERVATION CORPS

Conservation Education • Vermont • Seasonal
www.vycc.org

THE VERMONT YOUTH Conservation Corps (VYCC) is a nonprofit service, conservation, and education organization that strives to instill the values of personal responsibility, hard work, education, and respect for the environment in young adults. Corps members, who are between the ages of sixteen and twenty-four, work, live, and study together in small groups, completing priority conservation and park management projects throughout Vermont under the guidance of highly trained leaders. Projects focus on a daily integrated cycle of reading, discussion, writing, and team-building activities, with assignments that may include trail construction and maintenance, watershed restoration, bridge construction, park management, and facility improvement. A diverse team is a key component to the VYCC experience. Corps members may be economically disadvantaged, college-bound, high school dropouts, or learning disabled youth. This extraordinary diversity helps break down traditional social and economic barriers and provides a rich and challenging environment for participants to learn from one another.

What You'll Be Doing: With a variety of field staff opportunities available, each staff member will colead groups of four to ten corps members in completion of their work project. In addition, each staff member will train, motivate, supervise, and support corps members, facilitate VYCC's daily education program, and create a sense of community within a diverse crew of young people. Park managers (and assistants) will manage all aspects of a Vermont State Park and campground and perform park-ranger duties, such as leading nature and recreation programs, enforcing park regulations, and managing facilities and park finances. Crew leaders will complete high priority conservation projects throughout Vermont, including stream bank stabilization, trail maintenance, bridge construction, and carpentry projects.

Commitment: Park-manager positions run from late April to mid-September or mid-October; assistant positions run from early May to late August/early September; and crew-leader positions run from mid-May to late August.

Perks and Rewards: Park-manager and crew-leader positions wages range from $360 to 480 per week; assistant wages range from $320 to $340 per week. Most positions include room and board, and all staff receive nationally recognized training and are eligible for an AmeriCorps education award.

The Essentials: Candidates must have a strong desire to change young people's lives, a high level of maturity, a strong work-ethic and self-confidence, and the ability to actively motivate young adults. Outdoor leadership experience, knowledge of trail work or natural resource management and experience with group facilitation techniques is very helpful. The minimum age for park managers and crew leaders is twenty-two and for assistants is twenty.

Your First Move: Applications are available online, or request a complete job description and application by phone or email.

For More Information:
Recruitment Coordinator
Vermont Youth Conservation Corps
92 S. Main St.
Waterbury, VT 05676
(800) 639-8922 • (802) 241-3699 • (802) 241-3909 (fax)
ycorps@together.net

WILDERNESS VOLUNTEERS

Wilderness Service • USA • 1 Week
www.wildernessvolunteers.org

FROM THE TRINITY ALPS Wilderness to Hawaii Volcanoes National Park, Wilderness Volunteers organizes over forty one-week volunteer service adventures with public land agencies across the U.S. Following a "leave no trace" (www.lnt.org) philosophy of outdoor-living skills and ethics, trips (with active, strenuous, and challenging options) are limited to twelve or fewer participants and led by volunteer leaders (in cooperation with land-agency representatives). Tools for the work project are provided and each adventure gives ample time to explore and enjoy the surrounding region. Participants must be at least sixteen years of age (the average age is forty-five) and all trips require regular conditioning for at least two months prior to the trip. Program fees for mainland trips run $198, for Hawaii, $220. Food is provided for all trips along with cooking gear, and participants are responsible for any travel costs. Specifics on all trips can be found online, or call for further information.

For More Information:
Volunteer Coordinator
Wilderness Volunteers
P.O. Box 22292
Flagstaff, AZ 86002-2292
(928) 556-0038 • (928) 779-6339 (fax)
info@wildernessvolunteers.org

WIND CAVE NATIONAL PARK

National Park • South Dakota • 3–4 Months
www.nps.gov/wica

LOCATED IN THE southern Black Hills (also known as Custer Country), Wind Cave National Park features some of the most pristine mixed-grass prairies found in the U.S., including a world-renowned cave with over one hundred miles of passages. Large herds of free-roaming bison, elk, pronghorn, and deer inhabit the grasslands and forest. Three- or four-month seasonal positions are available year-round in interpretation/visitor services, resource management, and as campground hosts. In addition, students (with at least two years of college) have the opportunity to participate in the park's summer park ranger/interpretation internship program (with an application deadline of March 1). Experience in interpretation, public speaking, environmental education, or caves would be helpful, but is not required. Benefits for all opportunities include training, rent-free shared housing, and a weekly stipend. Interns also receive up to $150 for round-trip travel to the park. Call for application materials.

For More Information:
Phyllis Cremonini, Assistant Chief of Interpretation
Wind Cave National Park
Rt. 1, Box 190
Hot Springs, SD 57747-9430
(605) 745-4600 • (605) 745-4207 (fax)
phyllis_cremonini@nps.gov

YELLOWSTONE NATIONAL PARK LODGES

Guest Services • Wyoming • Seasonal
www.yellowstonejobs.com

IMAGINE WATCHING BEEHIVE geyser shoot its hot water and steam hundreds of feet into the air . . . fly-fishing for acrobatic rainbow trout on the Fire River . . . hiking on Hayden Pass Trail and spotting a herd of buffalo . . . or trekking to the top of Mt. Washburn (from which on clear days you can see the Grand Teton). Well, these are just some of the things you can do in your new backyard—that is, you can if you join the thirty-five hundred other adventurous workers in Yellowstone National Park this summer. Of course it's not all play; however, time will be well spent working for Xanterra Parks and Resorts (www.xanterra.com), who operates the major visitor-services concession facilities in Yellowstone, including lodging, restaurants, shops, boat and horse activities, campgrounds, and transportation services.

What You'll Be Doing: Yellowstone must be approached with a "work hard, play hard" mentality. You'll definitely work hard in the position you take on; however, you'll also have the opportunity to play hard in time off. Seasonal staff come from all over the world and are hired in practically every conceivable resort-related field, ranging from lodging services to employee recreation. A majority of the staff works at one of six major locations around the park—Mammoth Hot Springs, Roosevelt Lodge (the dude ranch of Yellowstone), Canyon Village, The Lake Area, Grant Village, and Old Faithful—each with its own unique charm and features. For many, a summer in Yellowstone is an unforgettable and once-in-a-lifetime experience.

Commitment: Applicants who can work from mid-April or early May to October are preferred; however, shorter terms are available. Yellowstone also offers positions during the winter months (with many filled by summer employees).

Perks and Rewards: The pay for entry-level positions begins at $6 per hour and many positions are salaried. Cafeteria-style meals, shared lodging, and laundry facilities are provided at a cost of $68.25 per week. Employee residence facilities range from rustic cabins to a typical dorm complex. (Note that you can request to live with a friend or, perhaps, someone that you meet in your orientation seminar.) Summer employees who choose to return for a winter season can become eligible for health insurance, paid vacation and holidays, and other benefits. The biggest perk, however, is the employee recreation program, with activities that include outdoor adventure programs (from white-water rafting trips to fly-fishing trips), outdoor equipment rental, slide shows and seminars, live bands, sports leagues, video rental, a photography and T-shirt design contest, and a year-end talent show.

The Essentials: People who are willing to work hard, who enjoy working with and for others, and who take pride in a job well done make the best employees.

Your First Move: Applications are available online; however, you can also call to request one. Positions fill very quickly, so it is best to apply by early February. Note that applications are accepted into the summer, especially for those who can arrive in August (when many students go back to college) and work through September/October.

For More Information:
Melissa Sutherland, Employment
Opportunities Manager
Yellowstone National Park Lodges
P.O. Box 165
Yellowstone, WY 82190
(307) 344-5324 • (307) 344-5627 (application request)
(307) 344-5441 (fax)
info@yellowstonejobs.com

After spending twenty years working in corporate America, I realized that my most rewarding experiences inside work were guiding, educating, and mentoring others. Those outside of work were my artistic pursuits, travel, health and fitness, and environmental projects. Changes in my personal life have made it possible for me to change direction now and integrate my career with the real passions in my life. My resume outlines specific skills, but cannot possibly convey the positive energy, enthusiasm, and creativity I bring to my work.

Coming to Yellowstone was just a step in breaking away from the mind-set that money and possessions are the measure of a person and his or her success in life. Being here has shown me that some people value other things and live a totally different way. Now I seek people who are doing what they really love, filled with creative force, shaping their own lives, and having a positive influence on the lives of others.

—SANDRA ALDRICH,
seasonal worker at Old Faithful

YELLOWSTONE PARK SERVICE STATIONS

Gas Station • Wyoming • Summer
www.ypss.com

WHATEVER HAPPENED TO full-service gas stations? You know, when the service attendant comes out of the office in overalls and a blue baseball cap, stops by your car to greet you, then fills your tank, washes the windows, and checks under the hood? Nowadays it's "pay at the pump" and you are off (with gas-covered hands)—that is, unless you are cruising through Yellowstone National Park and need a fill-up. Yellowstone Park Service Stations still rely on traditions of years past where service attendants take first-rate care of you. Summer seasonal employees (over seventy of them!), from service station attendants to automotive technicians, earn $6.10 per hour (and a

season-end bonus). A payroll deduction of $9.75 per day is made for dormitory-style housing, with meals served in employee dining rooms.

For More Information:
Hal Broadhead, General Manager
Yellowstone Park Service Stations
P.O. Box 11
Gardiner, MT 59030-0011
(406) 848-7333 • (406) 848-7731 (fax)
jobs@ypss.com

YOSEMITE CONCESSION SERVICES CORPORATION

Guest Services • California • Seasonal
www.yosemitepark.com

EL CAPITAN, ONE of the largest exposed monoliths in the world. The awe-inspiring Half Dome. Beautiful hikes to Mirror Lake or Yosemite Falls. Nordic skiing at Badger Pass. This is Yosemite National Park—a place that John Muir spoke about with passion: "a landscape that after all my wanderings still appears as the most beautiful I have ever beheld." As the host for the park, Yosemite Concession Services Corporation provides all the guest services to the park's nearly four million annual visitors—ranging from the impressive National Historic Landmark Ahwahnee Hotel to guided tram and horseback tours, rafting along the Merced River, or the renowned Yosemite Mountaineering School (which offers rock-climbing lessons, guided climbs, and backpacking trips in both Yosemite Valley and the High Sierra of Tuolumne Meadows).

What You'll Be Doing: First-season staff members are generally given an "unassigned" hire, which means they're given a current job opening that's available upon their arrival to Yosemite. Entry-level positions include housekeeping, guest services, food and beverage staff, security officers, retail, and bus drivers. Management and professional positions are also offered to those with more experience.

Commitment: Seasonal and year-round schedules are available, with most positions available during the week before Easter through mid-September (over eight hundred positions are filled in this time frame). A minimum two-month commitment is needed; however, longer terms are preferred.

Perks and Rewards: Wages begin at $6.75 per hour. Employee housing consists of shared rustic tents or wooden cabins and a limited number of dormitory rooms for $15 to $20 per week. A 50 percent discount is provided at most eating establishments and all housing areas have a community kitchen where employees may prepare their meals. One of the biggest perks during time off is participation in Yosemite's employee recreation program. A variety of activities and facilities are available to staff, including a fitness and wellness center, organized sports and hikes, craft classes, rafting trips, dances, movies, and barbecues. Yosemite also supports and encourages employee involvement in GreenPath, an internationally certified environmental management program.

The Essentials: Employees must be at least eighteen years of age to room in employer-provided housing, and foreign applicants must possess the right to work in the U.S. prior to applying.

Your First Move: Applications are available online or call/email for more information.

For More Information:
Lisa Abbott, Human Resources Director
Yosemite Concession Services Corporation
P.O. Box 578
Yosemite, CA 95389
(209) 372-1236 • (209) 372-1050 (fax)
ycshr@dncinc.com

YOSEMITE NATIONAL PARK

National Park • California • Summer
www.nps.gov/yose/learn/intern.htm

YOSEMITE'S INTERNSHIP PROGRAM is sponsored by the Yosemite Association, a nonprofit organization that raises money to be used for special projects in the park. Interpretation interns will work in visitor centers and provide walks, talks, and campfire programs, as well as rove specific areas discussing upcoming activities, park policies, and natural and cultural history with visitors. Wilderness interns will spend time in a wilderness permit office, issuing backcountry permits and discussing weather, equipment, and trail conditions with day hikers and overnight backpackers. A variety of other internships are available, including resource management/archaeology, natural history, search and rescue, and deaf services. In general, there are twenty-five openings each summer.

Commitment: The summer kicks off with a week-long orientation session held in mid-June. Interns then work full-time for twelve weeks through Labor Day.

Perks and Rewards: Interns receive a $10-per-day stipend to defray the cost of food during the working day, along with a $1,000 scholarship upon successful completion of the twelve-week commitment. Shared housing, ranging from canvas-covered tent cabins to large houses, is also provided. Perks include one Yosemite Association seminar during the summer, a packet of books, maps, and other materials about Yosemite, a privilege card for discounts with the park concessionaire, and up to $300 for round-trip travel to the park.

The Essentials: The program is limited to undergraduate students with above-average scholastic records. Applicants should have a strong interest in resource preservation and management, and have an ability to communicate ideas effectively, a genuine liking for people, and enthusiasm for sharing knowledge with others. Maturity, a sense of responsibility, creativity, and a willingness to work hard are essential.

Your First Move: Visit their website for more information and application materials. All applications must be postmarked by February 1.

For More Information:
Kathy Dimont, Student Intern Coordinator
Yosemite National Park
Wawona Ranger Station
P.O. Box 2027
Wawona, CA 95389
(209) 375-9505 • (209) 375-9525 (fax)
yose_education@nps.gov

RECOMMENDED RESOURCES. . . . .

The National Association for Interpretation
(www.interpnet.com) publishes the biweekly *Jobs in Interpretation* newsletter, which provides listings of internships, seasonal jobs, and career opportunities in the natural and cultural interpretation field (about eighty listings per issue). Members of the association ($15 for students, $45 for professionals) receive five issues for free; thereafter it's $5 per issue through regular mail or $2 per issue through email. Subscriptions are also available for nonmembers, and a small listing of job opportunities can be viewed online. To connect more with others in the interpretation field, don't miss the National Interpreters Workshop, their annual conference held each November. For more information contact the National Association for Interpretation, P.O. Box 2246, Fort Collins, CO 80522; (888) 900-8283, membership@interpnet.com.

To explore a variety of job opportunities and essential resources for working at state or national parks, check out **About.com's Guide to U.S./Canadian Parks** (www.usparks.about.com/cs/jobs), hosted by park expert Darren Smith.

Passport in Time Clearinghouse
(www.passportintime.com), commonly known as PIT, invites you to share in the thrill of discovery through archaeological and historical research on national forests and grasslands throughout the U.S. Forest service archaeologists and historians guide volunteers in activities ranging from excavating sites to historic-building restoration. Many projects involve backcountry camping in which volunteers supply their own gear and food. Some projects offer meals for a small fee; others might provide hookups for your RV. Project length ranges from a weekend up to a month, and there is no registration fee or cost for participating. *The PIT Traveler,* a free newsletter/directory, announces current projects every March and September (however, see their website for late-breaking project opportunities). For more information contact Passport in Time Clearinghouse, P.O. Box 31315, Tucson, AZ 85751-1315; (800) 281-9176, pit@sricrm.com.

Have you ever wanted to explore Colorado's mountains, parks, trails, and open spaces? With **Volunteers for Outdoor Colorado's** (VOC) network of volunteer opportunities, you can spend some quality time getting dirty, working your muscles and mind, meeting people, and giving something back to Colorado. Each April VOC publishes a catalog profiling more than eight hundred volunteer opportunities around Colorado with agencies including the U.S. Forest Service, the Bureau of Land Management, Colorado state parks, and various other state programs. From building rock walls to developing new trails, projects focus on backcountry monitoring, conservation action, environmental education and interpretation, fieldwork, forestry, gardening, recreation, trail construction and maintenance, visitor information, wildlife studies, and Youth Corps opportunities. Projects can range from a few hours per month up to full-time for one year. For some projects, training, housing, and a stipend are provided. Listings of current opportunities can be found by clicking on the "VOC Network" section of their website (www.voc.org), and their catalog can be downloaded as a PDF file (or call for your complimentary copy). For more information contact Volunteers for Outdoor Colorado, 600 S. Marion Parkway, Denver, CO 80209-2597; (800) 925-2220, voc@voc.org.

Those who have a deep care for the earth and have a love for nature will find endless opportunities in this section. Whether you'll be leading educational canoe trips in a swamp forest, teaching children about native wildlife of the area, or developing programs that help to protect the integrity of the earth's natural systems, your adventures will help to promote a personal responsibility for our natural world.

As long as I live, I'll hear waterfalls and birds and winds sing. I'll interpret the rocks, learn the language of floods, storms, and avalanche. I'll acquaint myself with the glaciers and the wild gardens, and get as near the heart of the world as I can.

—JOHN MUIR

Unique Opportunities to Explore in This Section:

- Does studying insects, learning where food comes from, turning lunch scraps into compost, or exploring Native American history and culture get you excited? Find out what's so special about Foothill Horizons and what Jacob Sackin has to say about his internship experience (page 198).

- Each year, hundreds of men and women from across the country spend months at a time aboard commercial fishing vessels operating off the Alaskan coast as fisheries observers, all made possible by the North Pacific Fisheries Observer Training Center (page 209).

- Interns with the School for Field Studies head off to exotic places such as Australia, the British West Indies, and Costa Rica, while teaching and engaging others in environmental problem solving (page 213).

- Raise the sails on a fifty-foot schooner. Track and research some of the world's rarest marine animals. Hold living sea cucumbers in your hands. Kayak along cliffs where peregrine falcons nest. Photograph puffins at close range. As a seasonal staff member with the Whale Camp, you'll help participants discover, enjoy, understand, and preserve the incredible natural world found in Canada's Grand Manan Island (page 220).

Photo Credit: Dennis Bowen

Summer staff members at the Whale Camp (page 220) set sail aboard the fifty-foot Schooner *d'Sonoqua*.

- How often do you find yourself taking extravagant pleasure in being alive? Learn about the Alaskan Inuit expression of *Nuanaarpuq* (page 226).

NATURE LOVER JOBS

AMERICAN HORTICULTURAL SOCIETY-RIVER FARM

Agriculture • Virginia • 4–6 Months
www.ahs.org/riverfarm/river.htm

RIVER FARM SERVES as the headquarters of the American Horticultural Society (AHS), and is situated on a historic twenty-five-acre property along the Potomac River. Throughout the farm, visitors will find several home demonstration gardens, plant collections, perennial gardens, a wildlife habitat garden, boxwood hedges, theme gardens, fruit orchards, and shade gardens. Interns assist with renovation, restoration, and maintenance of the gardens and grounds, and help with the children's gardening program and other special projects. Six distinct opportunities are available, including Seed Exchange, Propagation, Living Lab, Gardeners Information Service, Integrated Pest Management, and Plant Records/Signage. Interns also participate in society programs and projects, such as their annual seed program, open house events, lectures, and seminars, as well as guided field trips to sites such as the U.S. National Arboretum, Dumbarton Oaks, and Mt. Vernon. Internships of four to six months are available, with various start dates throughout the year. An $8-per-hour wage is provided and AHS will recommend housing in a local neighborhood. Applications are available online.

For More Information:
Janet Walker, Director of Horticulture
American Horticultural Society—River Farm
7931 E. Boulevard Dr.
Alexandria, VA 22308
(800) 777-7931 • (703) 768-5700, ext. 112
(703) 765-8700 (fax)
jwalker@ahs.org

ANITA PURVES NATURE CENTER

Nature Center • Illinois • 3–12 Months
www.prairienet.org/upd/
anitapurvesnaturecenter.html

DEDICATED IN 1979, the nature center is named in honor of Anita Parker Purves, a concerned citizen who initiated interest in environmental awareness in Urbana. The center provides environmental recreation programming for all segments of the community, promoting appreciation, understanding, and responsible use of the earth.

What You'll Be Doing: The assistantship and internship program is designed to provide an opportunity to develop programming and leadership skills in environmental education activities by working with students, park district staff, and cooperating organizations. Duties include developing curricula for environmental programs; providing leadership for programs; recruiting and training volunteers; participating in the planning, implementation, and evaluation of workshops and special events; assisting with development of displays and exhibits; and preparation and administration of program budgets.

Commitment: Programs run for a minimum of three months and a maximum of twelve months.

Perks and Rewards: Assistants receive a stipend of $350 per month, while interns receive $150 per month.

The Essentials: Assistantship candidates must have either a bachelor's or master's degree in environmental education/science, while internship applicants must have at least junior status. Each applicant must have a genuine interest in working with people of all ages and intend to pursue a career in environmental education.

Your First Move: Call for application materials. Interviews include a panel interview, tour of the facilities and programs, and a written exercise.

For More Information:
Judy Miller, Environmental Program Manager
Anita Purves Nature Center
Urbana Park District
1505 N. Broadway Ave.
Urbana, IL 61801
(217) 384-4062 • (217) 384-1052 (fax)

ASPEN CENTER FOR ENVIRONMENTAL STUDIES

Nature Center • Colorado • Summer
www.aspennature.org

SINCE ITS FOUNDING in 1968 by Aspen resident Elizabeth Paepcke, the nonprofit Aspen Center for Environmental Studies has been educating people to be environmentally responsible. Managing the 25-acre Hallam Lake sanctuary and another 175-acre natural area, the center offers hikes and nature classes to children and adults. It also runs the Environmental Learning Center, which houses the Scott

Field Laboratory, Pinewood Natural History Library, Gates Visitor Center, and a bookstore informally known as "the Den."

What You'll Be Doing: Summer naturalist interns get involved in just about everything that has to do with maintaining the center—landscaping, giving talks on the birds-of-prey program, providing wildlife information, teaching natural history classes to children and adults, and leading nature walks. Interns teach all the summer programs, from leading a troop of adults on a sunset walk by the lake to teaching children about the rich diversity of insects in the area. After spending a summer leading interpretive walks, learning to handle birds of prey for educational programs, and teaching children about the environment, interns are sure to leave with a newfound appreciation of nature.

Commitment: Mandatory staff training begins in early June with the season continuing through Labor Day.

Perks and Rewards: A weekly stipend of $125 and housing are provided. Interns often cook and eat dinners together, forming friendships that the center's communal atmosphere encourages. Interns are also allowed to take at least one class for free from the center's naturalist field school. Following the internship, summer naturalists have the opportunity to apply for winter-naturalist and academic-year educator positions.

The Essentials: College juniors, seniors, graduate students, and recent graduates are eligible, although the bulk of interns have received college degrees by the start of the internship. The center strongly prefers students who have studied the natural sciences or environmental studies and have experience working at other nature centers. First-aid certification is required.

Your First Move: Submit a completed application (which can be found on their website), a resume, and three letters of recommendation (the letters are suggested, but not required) by March 1. Top candidates are interviewed over the phone.

For More Information:
Jim Kravitz, Interpretation Director
Aspen Center for Environmental Studies
Summer Naturalist Internship
100 Puppy Smith St.
Aspen, CO 81612
(970) 925-5756 • (970) 925-4819 (fax)
jkravitz@aspennature.org

AUDUBON NATURALIST SOCIETY

Natural History • Maryland • Seasonal
www.audubonnaturalist.org

FOUNDED IN 1897, the Audubon Naturalist Society (not to be confused with the National Audubon Society) pioneered the linking of natural history studies with conservation activities. Interns serve as coteachers of children's classes (ages four to ten) for twelve weeks during the summer. In seasons other than the summer, part-time positions are available. Full-time interns receive a $200-per-week stipend along with room and kitchen privileges. Perks include a 20 percent discount at the bookshop and free (or at-cost) participation in most programs. First-aid and CPR certification are required, as is a car or bike. Send off a cover letter, resume, and two letters of recommendation three months prior to your start date.

For More Information:
Andrew Vernor, Education Program Coordinator
Audubon Naturalist Society
8940 Jones Mill Rd.
Chevy Chase, MD 20815
(301) 652-9188 • (301) 951-7179 (fax)
hq@audubonnaturalist.org

AUDUBON SHARON

Nature Center • Connecticut • 2–4 Months
www.audubon.org/local/sanctuary/sharon

SPREAD OVER ONE thousand acres with protected ponds, streams, forests, fields, and wildlife, Audubon Sharon offers hands-on education experiences for people of all ages, wildlife rehabilitation, live animal exhibits, a children's adventure center, a nature store, and a natural history library.

What You'll Be Doing: During the spring and fall, environmental education interns get involved in all aspects of the center's operation, with a primary focus of developing educational materials and teaching a wide variety of topics—discovery walks, pond exploration, birds of prey, insect investigation, and maple sugaring—to audiences of all ages. Summer naturalist interns primarily oversee the weeklong Summer Explorers and Eye on Nature programs for children ages ten to fourteen. In addition, a bird-banding internship (with two weeks of intensive training) and a research apprenticeship are offered from May through August.

Perks and Rewards: A salary of $100 to $200 per week is provided. In addition, each intern receives a furnished suite in the main building, with a private bedroom and shared kitchen, bath, and living area.

The Essentials: Some teaching experience or curriculum development is necessary; however, the most important assets include a strong natural history background, enthusiasm, commitment, a desire to learn, flexibility, and the ability to work well with others (especially children). Completion of at least two years of college course work in environmental studies is required.

Your First Move: Send a cover letter, resume, and three references with contact information. For bird-banding internships, contact Scott Heth (sheth@audubon.org); research apprenticeships, Mike Dudek (mdudek@ audubon.org).

For More Information:
Joseph Markow, Environmental Education Specialist
Audubon Sharon
325 Cornwall Bridge Rd.
Sharon, CT 06069
(860) 364-0520 • (860) 364-5792 (fax)
jmarkow@audubon.org

AULLWOOD AUDUBON CENTER AND FARM

Environmental Education/Farming • Ohio • 10–20 Weeks
http://aullwood.center.audubon.org

AULLWOOD AUDUBON CENTER and Farm is one of the five original environmental education centers in the U.S. owned and operated by the National Audubon Society. With over seventy-five thousand visitors per year, they reach far with their message about "promoting awareness of the relationships within natural and agricultural systems, with humans as an integral element."
Environmental education and organic agriculture interns are involved in an extensive orientation and then gradually assume the same kinds of responsibilities as full-time staff, with a concentration on education and farming activities. All facets of an environmental education center and organic farm are explored, including work with the public in program presentation, animal care at the nature

center and farm, store operations, and maintenance. Positions are offered in January for twenty weeks; June for ten weeks; and August for eighteen weeks. A $110-per-week stipend and furnished housing (and utilities) on the Aullwood property are provided, along with field study and visits to similar organizations. All interns must be high school graduates; however, having finished at least the sophomore year of college works out to the applicant's advantage. Call or email for further information and application materials.

For More Information:
Alison Verey, Intern Coordinator
Aullwood Audubon Center and Farm
1000 Aullwood Rd.
Dayton, OH 45414-1129
(937) 890-7360 • (937) 890-2382 (fax)
averey@audubon.org

BRUKNER NATURE CENTER

Wildlife • Ohio • 3–9 Months

SURROUNDED BY 165 acres of rolling hills accessed through six miles of hiking trails, Brukner Nature Center endeavors to provide meaningful experiences that emphasize natural history and the environment. Over sixty permanently injured native Ohio animals and birds are housed on the property and used for educational programming.

What You'll Be Doing: Interns assist in planning, preparing, and conducting natural history, historical, and native wildlife programs for school-age children and the public. Extensive work is also done with the wildlife, including daily husbandry and care of the animals and birds as well as work with injured and orphaned native wildlife in the wildlife rehabilitation unit. This is a great program for those who want an in-depth experience at a nature center.

Commitment: A commitment of three months is required; however, longer terms, from six to nine months, are preferred.

Perks and Rewards: Housing and a $75-per-week food stipend are provided.

The Essentials: A background in natural history or animal husbandry and previous experience working with wildlife, planning educational programs, and guiding interpretive hikes are preferred.

Your First Move: Send cover letter and resume. Opportunities are offered year-round; however, there is less competition for openings in the school year.

For More Information:
Debbie Brill, Administrative Director
Brukner Nature Center
5995 Horseshoe Bend Rd.
Troy, OH 45373
(937) 698-6493 • (937) 698-4619 (fax)
brukner@juno.com

CAMP HIGH TRAILS OUTDOOR SCIENCE SCHOOL

Outdoor Education • California • 4 Months
www.camphightrails.com

IF YOU HAVE a college degree, a healthy amount of experience both with kids and the outdoors (or a strong and eager desire to learn), and the willingness to work and live in a small, close-knit staff community, Camp High Trails Outdoor Science School is a perfect place to begin new adventures. Located in the mountains of Southern California, this residential center gets sixth graders connected to nature. As an outdoor-education instructor, you'll have the opportunity to create fun, educational, and meaningful experiences with classes and activities such as: climbing, low ropes, archery, forest ecology, water study, outdoor-living skills, astronomy, and nighttime wildlife. The benefits are also great—room, board, health insurance, and a nice paycheck! Seasonal contracts begin either in September or January for four months. Check out their website first to explore all the opportunities, then send your resume, cover letter, and three references.

For More Information:
Chris Hoyt, Program Director
Camp High Trails Outdoor Science School
4650 Jenks Lake Road East
Angelus Oaks, CA 92305
(909) 228-4199 • (909) 752-5301 (fax)
work@camphightrails.com

CAMP MCDOWELL ENVIRONMENTAL CENTER

Outdoor Education • Alabama • 4 Months
www.campmcdowell.com/cmec

SHARE CAMP MCDOWELL's eight hundred acres of secluded forests, streams, waterfalls, and canyons in northwest Alabama with groups of up to twelve students

(ranging from grades four through eight). Environmental education instructors teach hands-on classes with subjects and activities including forest ecology, earth and water science, insects and wildlife, canoeing, map and compass, low and high ropes, Native American history, arts and crafts, astronomy, fishing, and field games. Programs run from February through May and late August through November. Staff receive a $200-per-week stipend, meals, and private rooms in a newly renovated house, complete with kitchen, living room, laundry, and screened porch with rocking chairs! To apply, send a cover letter, resume, and references.

For More Information:
Jennifer Arnold, Staffing Director
Camp McDowell Environmental Center
105 DeLong Rd.
Nauvoo, AL 35578
(205) 387-1806 • (205) 221-3454 (fax)
cmec@campmcdowell.com

> *We're seeking applicants who have maturity, enthusiasm, initiative, a sense of humor, flexibility, and team spirit. In addition, applicants must have a demonstrated respect and affinity for children and a desire to help them learn and grow, as well as a desire to work outside and to be a member of a friendly and supportive team.*

CENTRAL WISCONSIN ENVIRONMENTAL STATION

Environmental Education • Wisconsin • 9–12 Months/Summer
www.uwsp.edu/cnr/cwes/

AS A FIELD STATION of the University of Wisconsin Stevens Point's College of Natural Resources, the Central Wisconsin Environmental Station is a three-hundred-acre teaching and environmental learning center for K–12 students. Through hands-on environmental education activities, the station provides a foundation for the study of ecological principles and concepts as they relate to people and their environment.

What You'll Be Doing: Throughout the year (for nine to twelve months), environmental education/interpretation interns serve as regular staff members and provide

I frequently tramped eight or ten miles through the deepest snow to keep an appointment with a beech tree, or a yellow birch, or an old acquaintance among the pines. —HENRY DAVID THOREAU

193

instruction in environmental studies for groups of students. During the summer months, staff counselors and specialists are responsible for carrying out overall camp operation, with an emphasis on environmental and outdoor education. Staff will participate in one of three residential camps, including the Sunset Lake adventure camp (for ages seven to fourteen), the adventure expeditions camp (for ages eleven to seventeen), or the high school workshops (which focus on outdoor leadership or natural resources careers).

Perks and Rewards: A $1,800 stipend, plus a $300 living allowance, is provided for interns. On-site housing may be available, and some meals are provided. Summer staff pay ranges from $155 to $175 per week along with room and board.

The Essentials: Intern applicants must have reached at least their junior year in college and have completed course work in methods of environmental education or interpretation. Previous practical experience in environmental education, outdoor education, or natural history interpretation is desirable. Summer staff applicants should have training or experience in one or more of the following areas: recreation, environmental education, water or field sports, backpacking, canoeing, or arts and crafts. Preference will be given to applicants with a college background.

Your First Move: Call or email for additional information.

For More Information:
Rebecca Clarke, Program Manager
Central Wisconsin Environmental Station
10186 County MM
Amherst Junction, WI 54407
(715) 824-2428 • (715) 824-3201 (fax)
cwes@uwsp.edu

CHICAGO BOTANIC GARDEN

Gardens • Illinois • 3–12 Months
www.chicagobotanic.org

RECOGNIZED FOR THE most diverse botanic garden internship in North America, the Chicago Botanic Garden strives to stimulate and develop an appreciation and understanding for gardening, horticulture, botany, and conservation. Just a half-hour drive from downtown Chicago, its unique design of islands, water, and twenty-three specialty-display gardens attracts almost three-quarters of a million visitors annually and provides a dramatic setting for the interaction of plants and people.

College interns have the chance to experience a wide variety of horticulture activities at Chicago Botanic Garden, one of the world's premier horticultural institutions.

What You'll Be Doing: Interns work in a one-on-one setting with professionals who share their experience and expertise in every conceivable area of operation—from conservation ecology and environmental education to community gardening and visitor/school programs.

Commitment: Internships vary in length from three to twelve months, with varying start and finish dates.

Perks and Rewards: A $7.50-per-hour wage is provided, and the garden will assist in finding affordable housing in the area. Interns have the use of library and research facilities and may attend seminars, classes, and field trips. A car or bicycle is recommended.

The Essentials: Applicants should be enthusiastic, energetic, positive thinking, and willing to "grow" with the gardens. Preference is given to those with some experience and a background in horticulture, botany, ecology, or conservation.

Your First Move: Review the application process through their website or call for an application packet. The priority deadline is March 1, or until all twenty-one positions are filled.

For More Information:
Aviva Levavi, Intern Coordinator
Chicago Botanic Garden
1000 Lake Cook Rd.
Glencoe, IL 60022-8264
(847) 835-8263 • (847) 835-1635 (fax)
alevavi@chicagobotanic.org

THE CONSERVANCY OF SOUTHWEST FLORIDA

Conservation • Florida • 3–9 Months
www.conservancy.org

SINCE 1964, THE Conservancy has served as the region's environmental leader, spearheading the conservation of more than 300,000 acres of environmentally sensitive land. In addition to an environmental protection and research division, this progressive organization includes two nature centers, a wildlife rehabilitation center, and an environmental education department.

Your Surroundings: The climate of this region is sub-tropical, with a strong marine influence from the Gulf of Mexico. The average annual temperature is approximately seventy-five degrees and rainfall averages about fifty-four inches annually, with most precipitation occurring during the summer.

What You'll Be Doing: Whether leading interpretive canoe, boat, and beach programs for children and adults (at the Briggs Nature Center), implementing weeklong specialty day camps for students on marine ecology (at Naples Nature Center), teaching ecology of south Florida to school children, or working with the environmental protection staff monitoring sea turtles, this is an ideal place for interns to gain knowledge and experience in the field. Approximately thirty interns are hired throughout the organization each year.

Commitment: Positions are available year-round, although a three- to nine-month commitment is necessary.

Perks and Rewards: Interns receive a weekly cost-of-living assistance of $125 and optional free housing. Perks include uniform shirts, free accident insurance, and Conservancy membership.

The Essentials: Applicants must have at least junior status in college (or be recent graduates) with a background in biology, ecology, conservation, wildlife, research, teaching, elementary education, environmental education/science, or marine science. Those who are quick and eager learners and enjoy being outdoors are preferred.

Your First Move: Details on each internship and applications are available online or email/call for more information.

For More Information:
Sharon Truluck, Human Resources Director
The Conservancy of Southwest Florida
1450 Merrihue Dr.
Naples, FL 34102
(941) 262-0304 • (941) 262-0672 (fax)
humanresources@conservancy.org

DAHLEM ENVIRONMENTAL EDUCATION CENTER

Nature Center • Michigan • 3 Months
www.dahlemcenter.org

KNOWN FOR ITS award-winning elementary education curriculum, the Dahlem Environmental Education Center strives to bridge the gap between humans and the natural environment. Operating on Jackson Community College property as a nonprofit organization, the center generates its own revenue via memberships, user fees, gifts, grants, fund-raising projects, and special events. A professional staff, supplemented with seasonal interns and trained community volunteers, provides educational services for more than twenty-six thousand visitors annually, including more than four hundred school and youth groups.

What You'll Be Doing: Naturalist interpretive interns primarily teach in the center's school program. Along with exposure to all aspects of nature center operations, interns will have the opportunity to engage in exhibit design, assist in program development, write for nature center publications, provide animal care, participate in special events, and work with volunteers. Summer ecology camp counselors develop and implement their own activity plans for ten to twelve elementary school campers each week, and summer wildlife-biologist interns coordinate research and work with staff in the center's countywide bluebird recovery project.

Perks and Rewards: On-site housing, staff training, and a weekly stipend of $231 are provided.

The Essentials: Applicants should have college-level training in an environmental field and previous teaching/programming experience, especially with children in an outdoor educational setting. The ideal applicant is responsible, flexible, creative, and enthusiastic, with a "do and discover," rather than a "show and tell," teaching style.

Your First Move: Call or write for application materials and deadlines. Telephone interviews are provided for qualified applicants.

Adopt the pace of nature, her secret is patience. —RALPH WALDO EMERSON

For More Information:
Susan Larson, Youth Services Coordinator/Naturalist
Dahlem Environmental Education Center
7117 S. Jackson Rd.
Jackson, MI 49201
(517) 782-3453 • (517) 782-3441 (fax)
susan_larson@jackson.cc.mi.us

DEEP PORTAGE CONSERVATION RESERVE

**Environmental Education • Minnesota •
3–9 Months**
www.deep-portage.org/jobs.html

EACH YEAR THOUSANDS of students from Midwest schools explore conservation and environmental education activities at Deep Portage Conservation Reserve. In addition, Deep Portage serves area residents and visitors with weekly classes, interpretive programs, wildflower garden displays, land-use demonstrations, and recreational opportunities for birding, hiking, hunting, and skiing.

What You'll Be Doing: Seasonal staff and intern duties include preparing and presenting interpretive and environmental education programs for school groups and the general public, hosting visitors in the interpretive center, assisting professional staff in curriculum development and assessment, and special-project work. The recreation program teaches every kind of outdoor recreation skill for appreciating lake and forest country. Participating in this program will help each staff member to become a forester, wildlife manager, recreation leader, or a K–12 formal-education teacher.

Commitment: Positions are offered year-round (beginning in January, June, or September) and last from three to nine months.

Perks and Rewards: A weekly stipend of $150 to $250 is provided, along room and board.

The Essentials: Along with enthusiasm, applicants should have a variety of skills and, whenever possible, certifications in these skills.

Your First Move: Submit cover letter, resume, and three letters of reference at least twelve weeks before your requested start date.

For More Information:
Molly Malecek, Program Director
Deep Portage Conservation Reserve
2197 Nature Center Dr., NW
Hackensack, MN 56452-9720
(218) 682-2325 • (218) 682-3121 (fax)
portage@uslink.net

DELAWARE NATURE SOCIETY

Nature Center • Delaware • Seasonal
www.delawarenaturesociety.org

CREATED BY A handful of concerned people in 1964, the Delaware Nature Society fosters understanding, appreciation, and enjoyment of our natural world. Interns at the Ashland Nature Center teach and coteach children's classes, and have the opportunity to work with people of all ages and interests, design curriculum, work with farm and wild animals, and develop their own special skills and interests. A stipend of $2,000 helps to alleviate the costs of housing, food, and transportation. Applicants must have completed their junior or senior year in college and be pursuing a career in environmental education or natural sciences. Send a cover letter, resume, and two letters of recommendation by March 15 for summer positions. For other times during the year, applications are accepted on a rolling basis.

For More Information:
Karen Travers, Member Programs Coordinator
Delaware Nature Society
Ashland Nature Center
P.O. Box 700
Hockessin, DE 19707
(302) 239-2334, ext. 15 • (302) 239-2473 (fax)
karen@dnsashland.org

EAGLE BLUFF ENVIRONMENTAL LEARNING CENTER

Environmental Education • Minnesota • 9 Months
www.eagle-bluff.org

EAGLE BLUFF ENVIRONMENTAL Learning Center is a nonprofit environmental school dedicated to developing and fostering educational opportunities that will create universal awareness, enhance respect, and promote personal responsibility for the natural world. Twelve participants in the naturalist fellowship program spend nine months (beginning in late August) developing teaching, public relations, and many other skills related to residential environmental education. Fellows kick off the program with a two-week training period, then coordinate, teach, and lead residential and day-use naturalist programs for visiting groups. Fellows live in private rooms with a communal living area, dining room, and kitchen (the center's website has some great photos). In addition to room and board, a monthly stipend of $600 is provided. Applicants must have a bachelor's degree, experience working with children, and CPR and first-aid certification. Applications are accepted year-round with hiring beginning on March 1.

For More Information:
Fellowship Coordinator
Eagle Bluff Environmental Learning Center
1991 Brightsdale Rd.
Route 2, Box 156A
Lanesboro, MN 55949
(507) 467-2437 • (507) 467-3583 (fax)
fellowship@eagle-bluff.org

FERNWOOD BOTANICAL GARDEN AND NATURE CENTER

Nature Center • Michigan • 8 Months
www.fernwoodbotanical.org

FERNWOOD IS A combined one-hundred-acre nature center, botanic garden, and arts-and-crafts center that provides a sense of environmental awareness, cultural appreciation, and education for the community. Seasonal naturalists (from late March through mid-November) develop and conduct natural history programs for school groups and weekend visitors, maintain and design educational displays, supervise care of animals, supervise and assist in the daily operations of the nature center, and provide grounds maintenance. A $6-per-hour wage is provided along with housing, workshops, classroom training, and discounts in gift shops and the cafeteria. Applicants should have an interest and training in natural history, ecology, or biology. Previous experience (paid or

volunteer) in environmental education or work with children improves your chances tremendously. Also, a good knowledge of plant and animal identification is very helpful. Send a cover letter, resume, and references to begin the application process.

For More Information:
Wendy Jones, Head Naturalist
Fernwood Botanical Garden and Nature Center
13988 Range Line Rd.
Niles, MI 49120-9042
(616) 695-6491 • (616) 695-6688 (fax)

FIVE RIVERS METROPARKS

**Natural History/Farm Education • Ohio •
3–12 Months**
www.metroparks.org

INTERNSHIPS AND APPRENTICESHIPS at Five Rivers Metro Parks provide practical on-the-job experience in outdoor/farm education, natural history, and park management. Positions are available in the following areas: Possum Creek Farm (lead school tours or youth groups through the barn and trails and care for farm animals), Carriage Hill (historical farm restoration and agriculture/farm maintenance), Cox Arboretum (horticultural education); Germantown MetroPark (natural history), North Metro-Parks (natural history); Wesleyan MetroPark (natural history and youth programming); and Wegerzyn Horticultural Center (horticulture and education). Programs are offered during the summer and for nine or twelve months beginning each fall, with an average thirty-two-hour work week. A $7-per-hour wage is provided along with housing at several work sites. It's noted that with the summer positions being so highly sought, it's recommended that you apply for a nine- or twelve-month apprenticeship.

For More Information:
Lyn Modic, Chief of Education and Programming
Five Rivers MetroParks
1375 E. Siebenthaler Ave.
Dayton, OH 45414
(937) 275-7275 • (937) 278-8849 (fax)
email@metroparks.org

The old Lakota was wise. He knew that man's heart, away from nature, becomes hard; he knew that lack of respect for growing, living things soon led to lack of respect for humans too. —LUTHER STANDING BEAR

197

FOOTHILL HORIZONS OUTDOOR SCHOOL

Outdoor Education • California • Academic Year
www.stan-co.k12.ca.us/scoe/outdoor-ed/foothill

DURING THE SCHOOL year, sixth-grade students spend an entire week at Foothill Horizons Outdoor School. During this time, the students participate in a variety of activities to increase their knowledge and awareness of nature, and take part in nature classes, campfires, dancing, free play, night hikes, and field trips. A school garden and cob/straw-bale greenhouse gives students the opportunity to see where food comes from, to study insects in the butterfly garden, and to learn how their lunch scraps are turned into soil in the compost and worm bins.

What You'll Be Doing: Interns begin the first three weeks of their ten-month internship (beginning in early August) training, observing naturalists, and team teaching. From the fourth week on, interns lead groups of students on hikes, teaching them about ecology, conservation, Native American history and culture, and sensory awareness. After several weeks of teaching, interns rotate through other support positions. The head naturalist will observe each intern twice each semester to help refine the intern's teaching technique. Interns are encouraged to use any and all resources available to improve their teaching, including Project Learning Tree and Project Wild workshops, regularly scheduled in-services, conferences, curriculum guides in the library, and, of course, the knowledge of the naturalists.

Commitment: Foothill honors a forty-hour work week; however, the nature of an internship requires study and preparation beyond scheduled work hours. A commitment for the full school year (ten months) is essential.

Perks and Rewards: A daily stipend of $40 is provided, along with room, board, and health fund. Lucrative weekend and overtime work as a site host and counselor trainer is also available on an optional basis. Beyond the extensive training interns receive, the biggest perks are paid site visits to other outdoor schools, paid admission to professional conferences and fairs, and career support and guidance during and after the internship.

The Essentials: Applicants must be college graduates who have concentrated in the areas of natural and environmental sciences, resource management, parks and recreation, child development, or education. Beyond that, Foothill is looking for people who are passionate about making a positive impact on kids' lives.

Your First Move: The application process requires either an on-site visit and mini-teaching demo by the applicant, or a phone interview and a videotaped lesson presented by the applicant to a group. Positions are filled between the months of January and May.

For More Information:
Dan Webster, Head Naturalist
Foothill Horizons Outdoor School
Stanislaus County Office of Education
21925 Lyons Bald Mountain Rd.
Sonora, CA 95370
(209) 532-6673 • (209) 533-1390 (fax)
foothill@sonnet.com

> As a young teacher who wasn't sure of the exact path I wanted to take, working at Foothill Horizons has given me the opportunity to teach outdoor education and help me with the decision of where I belong in the world. I learned about science, nature, Miwuk Indians, and classroom-management skills from experienced naturalists. I have never worked in an environment where I have received so much support and enthusiasm from coworkers who love their jobs. I can already feel that my experience has helped me to stay on a path with heart, guiding me to whatever comes next—whether it be teaching or doing something completely different. I consider it a great gift to have spent a year of my life at Foothill Horizons. I am already a better person because of the time I have spent here.
>
> —JACOB SACKIN, intern

4-H ENVIRONMENTAL EDUCATION PROGRAM

Environmental Education • Georgia • 3–4 Months
www.georgia4h.org

THE 4-H ENVIRONMENTAL Education Program, the largest residential environmental education program in the nation, is part of Georgia's 4-H and Youth Program (first implemented at Rock Eagle 4-H Center in 1979). More than four hundred thousand students from five hundred different schools have participated in the program.

What You'll Be Doing: Do you enjoy working outside and have an interest in teaching children? The 4-H Environmental Education Program hires forty to forty-five enthusiastic, creative, and motivated seasonal instructors and interns to join their staff in teaching science and outdoor education to grades three through eight. If selected, you will work at one of four 4-H state facilities, Rock Eagle (central Georgia piedmont), Jekyll Island (coastal barrier island), Wahsega (north Georgia mountains), or Tybee Island (coastal barrier island).

Commitment: The spring season runs from mid-February to late May, with the fall season running from early September to late November.

Perks and Rewards: Seasonal staff will receive a stipend of up to $240 per week, housing, meals, a limited health-insurance policy, and extensive training in environmental education.

The Essentials: Applicants should have a genuine interest in children, a dynamic personality, well-developed communication skills, creativity, and leadership abilities. A bachelor's degree in education, natural science, environmental education, or outdoor recreation is preferred.

Your First Move: Details on specific positions for each facility can be found on their website or by calling. To begin the application process, submit a resume with references and a cover letter.

For More Information:
Diane Davies, State 4-H Specialist
4-H Environmental Education Program
Rock Eagle 4-H Center
350 Rock Eagle Rd., NW
Eatonton, GA 31024-6104
(706) 484-2872 • (706) 484-2888 (fax)
ddavies@uga.edu

Jekyll Island: Donna Stewart, Jekyll Island,
201 S. Beachview Dr., Jekyll Island, GA 31527,
(912) 635-4117, donnast@uga.edu

Rock Eagle: Steve Dorsch, Rock Eagle
350 Rock Eagle Rd., NW, Eatonton, GA 31024-6104;
(706) 484-2862, sdorsch@uga.edu

Tybee Island: Katie MacNichols, Tybee Island,
P.O. Box 1477, Tybee Island, GA 31328
(912) 786-5534, tybee4h@uga.edu

Wahsega: Paul Coote, Wahsega, 77 Cloverleaf Trail,
Dahlonega, GA 30533; (706) 864-2050, paulc@uga.edu

GARDEN IN THE WOODS

Gardens • Massachusetts • 3–6 Months
www.newfs.org/volunteers.html

ON A FORTY-FIVE-ACRE landscape of rolling hills, ponds, and streams, emerges Garden in the Woods, with over sixteen hundred kinds of plants grown in a naturalistic fashion. As the headquarters for the New England Wild Flower Society, Garden in the Woods offers educational programming and garden walks and operates a native plant nursery that produces over thirty-five thousand plants for garden displays and sale to the public.

What You'll Be Doing: Since 1979, the New England Wild Flower Society has offered an internship/fellowship program to train interns in the practical aspects of native plant cultivation and propagation. Interns can focus on either propagation and nursery management or native plant horticulture. For horticulture interns, regular on-site activities are supplemented by field trips to nearby gardens, arboretums, nurseries, and natural areas. In addition, interns are assigned a small special project based on their area of interest, which might include nursery sales, interpretation, design, or writing. Just recently the society introduced a unique conservatory fellows program that begins each March for six months. Fellows will administer all conservation programs. Contact Chris Mattrick (cmattrick@newfs.org; (503) 877-7630, ext. 3203) for more information.

Commitment: Programs run for six months beginning in March; there is also a three-month opportunity for the native plant horticulture internship, which begins in mid-May.

Perks and Rewards: A weekly stipend of $230 and off-site/shared housing within walking distance provided. Perks include participation in selected field trips and a wide range of optional natural history classes provided by the education department, including a native-plant certificate program.

The Essentials: Preference is given to applicants who have career aspirations and at least two years of educational course work in plant-related fields, previous work experience, and the ability to engage in rigorous outdoor work.

Your First Move: Call or download application materials from their website. Applications are due the first week of February for the six-month internship and mid-March for the three-month program. Depending on distance, applicants may be interviewed in person or over the phone.

For More Information:
Tom Smarr, Horticulture Internships/Fellowships
Garden in the Woods
New England Wild Flower Society
180 Hemenway Rd.
Framingham, MA 01701-2699
(508) 877-7630, ext. 3404 • (508) 877-3658 (fax)
tsmarr@newfs.org

GLEN HELEN OUTDOOR EDUCATION CENTER

Environmental Education • Ohio • 4–5 Months
www.glenhelen.org

THE GLEN HELEN Outdoor Education Center is a residential outdoor-education program serving more than three thousand elementary school students annually. Six biotic communities and a raptor center comprise this thousand-acre nature preserve owned and operated by Antioch College. Naturalist interns plan and lead small groups of residential environmental education programs, care for hawks or owls in the raptor center, and actively participate in a comprehensive training program. Interns also portray a living history character from the late 1700s during the fall and winter terms. Positions are offered from early January to early June or from mid-August to mid-December, with a possibility of summer work. A stipend of $250 per month, along with room and board, is provided. In addition, interns have access to all the facilities at Antioch College and are able to receive twelve undergraduate or ten graduate credits (with tuition waived). Applicants must have completed at least two years of college (though a degree is preferred), enjoy working with a close-knit staff, and have an interest in working with children in a residential outdoor-education setting.

For More Information:
Sue Feller, Assistant Director
Glen Helen Outdoor Education Center
1075 SR 343
Yellow Springs, OH 45387
(937) 767-7648 • (937) 767-6655 (fax)
ghelen@antioch-college.edu

HAWK MOUNTAIN SANCTUARY ASSOCIATION

Wildlife • Pennsylvania • Seasonal
www.hawkmountain.org

HAWK MOUNTAIN SANCTUARY Association is a private, nonprofit organization with programs in education, research, and conservation policy that are national and international in scope. Hawk Mountain, established in 1934, is the world's first sanctuary for hawks, eagles, and other birds of prey. Science-education interns learn how to guide field trips and present on-site and off-grounds interpretive programs to schoolchildren and the general public; ecological-research interns learn how the sanctuary studies raptors and Appalachian mountain fauna and flora; and biological interns assist with censuses of songbirds, raptors, and other flora and fauna, and maintain databases. Along with a monthly stipend of $500, interns receive free housing on the sanctuary grounds.

For More Information:
Dr. Keith Bildstein, Director of Research and Education
Hawk Mountain Sanctuary Association
1700 Hawk Mountain Rd.
Kempton, PA 19529-9449
(610) 756-6961 • (610) 756-4468 (fax)
bildstein@hawkmountain.org

HEADLANDS INSTITUTE

Environmental Education • California • Seasonal
www.yni.org/hi

HEADLANDS INSTITUTE, OPERATING out of historic Fort Cronkhite in the Marin Headlands (north of San Francisco), is an educational nonprofit organization that provides field-based science programs in nature's classroom to inspire a personal connection to the natural world and responsible actions to sustain it. Educational adventures engage students in interactive learning through outdoor activities, learning games, team-building exercises, and classroom instruction.

What You'll Be Doing: Field instructors develop a set of activities and hikes for ten to fifteen students (a majority are in the fourth through sixth grade) that meld the clients' needs with the instructor's unique strengths and the institute's core themes. The three broad core themes are "sense of place," interconnections, and stewardship.

In addition, each instructor is expected to attend weekly staff meetings and present a one-hour evening program once or twice a week for groups of up to eighty students. Education interns will have a rotating schedule that includes observing instructors in the field, working on administrative projects in the office, delivering promotional slide presentations, and developing an educational project.

Commitment: Field teaching positions begin in late August, early January, and mid-June. Internships begin in January and June for a duration of six months.

Perks and Rewards: Instructor positions start at $66 per day and include housing, partial board, medical/dental plan, retirement plan, paid training, and vacation benefits. Part-time and substitute instructor positions are also available. Education interns receive room, partial board, and a small stipend of $150 per week.

The Essentials: Candidates for either position must have at least a four-year degree in a related field and current first-aid/CPR certification. Successful candidates for field-instructor positions generally have a minimum of two years' experience teaching in the outdoors. Intern applicants must have demonstrated interest (education or experience) in natural science and experience working with children. Although not required, applicants are encouraged to complete a Wilderness First Responder, EMT, or other advanced first-aid training.

Your First Move: Applications are accepted on a rolling basis, but priority is given to those received by October 15 (for positions starting in January) and March 15 (for summer and fall positions). Top candidates are invited to Headlands for an interview and an opportunity to observe a field program.

For More Information:
Duffy Ross, Education Director
Headlands Institute
GGNRA, Building 1033
Sausalito, CA 94965
(415) 332-5771 • (415) 332-5784 (fax)
hi@yni.org

THE HOLDEN ARBORETUM

Gardens • Ohio • 3–12 Months
www.holdenarb.org

As a NONPROFIT museum with over thirty-five hundred acres of horticultural collections and natural areas, the Holden Arboretum connects people with nature for inspiration and enjoyment, fosters learning, and promotes conservation.

What You'll Be Doing: The internship program is designed to give a balance of hands-on experience and educational programming. The educational aspect of the program has four parts: an arboretum orientation that combines lectures and tours; educational sessions; field trips to other horticultural institutions in northeast Ohio and Canada; and demonstrations, which give interns an opportunity to learn additional skills on equipment they might not otherwise use during the summer. Internships are available in horticulture, horticulture maintenance, landscape gardening, conservation, horticulture therapy, and education.

Commitment: The internship is a full-time position offered during the summer with terms up to one year. Interns spend between five and ten hours each week in educational programs—most of them taking place during work hours.

Perks and Rewards: Along with housing, interns recieve wages starting at $7 per hour. The intern campus promotes bonding on a social level through activities including picnics, ball games, and nights out.

The Essentials: Applicants must be studying horticulture, natural history, or related fields. Current students and recent grads receive first consideration.

Your First Move: Submit cover letter, resume, and names of three references by February 1.

For More Information:
Greg Wright, Intern Coordinator
The Holden Arboretum
9500 Sperry Rd.
Kirtland, OH 44094-5172
(440) 946-4400 • (440) 602-3857 (fax)
gwright@holdenarb.org

HORIZONS FOR YOUTH

Environmental Education • Massachusetts • Seasonal
www.hfy.org

HORIZONS FOR YOUTH offers outdoor environmental education programs in the fall through spring and a camp during the summer months. Field-teacher instructors and interns develop and teach lessons and activities in the outdoors, focusing on ecology, environmental science, conservation, and group dynamics. Adventure

A field instructor at Horizons for Youth teaches children about the buzzing world of bees.

leaders plan and implement twenty-three-day wilderness trips, and environmental camp leaders plan and implement a five-day environmental camp experience. Most staff receive $250 per week, plus room and board. For more information on becoming a summer camp counselor, contact Ally McDonagh (camp@hfy.org).

For More Information:
James Barnett, School Program Director
Horizons for Youth
121 Lakeview St.
Sharon, MA 02067
(781) 828-7550 • (781) 784-1287 (fax)
outdoors@hfy.org

INTERNATIONAL CRANE FOUNDATION

Birding • Wisconsin • 6 Months
www.savingcranes.org

THE INTERNATIONAL CRANE Foundation is a nonprofit organization dedicated to conservation and preservation of the world's cranes and the natural wetland and grass-

land communities in which they live. Aviculture interns receive hands-on training in the care, breeding, and management of endangered cranes. Caring for the adult cranes and chicks comprises half of the job; other tasks include annual facilities maintenance, video-monitoring of crane behavior, and speaking to the public. Internships are available each season for a six-month period. A stipend of $350 to $600 per month is provided along with housing. Senior undergraduates through recent college graduates may apply, and individuals seeking graduate training are especially encouraged. Send cover letter, resume, and three letters of recommendation.

For More Information:
Mike Putnam, Curator of Birds
International Crane Foundation
Aviculture Internships
P.O. Box 447
Baraboo, WI 53913-0447
(608) 356-9462 • (608) 356-9465 (fax)

KALAMAZOO NATURE CENTER

Environmental Education • Michigan • Summer
www.naturecenter.org

NATIONALLY RECOGNIZED FOR their outreach, education, and avian-research programs, the Kalamazoo Nature Center, partnering with Michigan state parks, coordinates the Michigan State Parks Adventure Program. Within the system's 260,000 acres there are over 140 miles of Great Lakes frontage; 460 miles of lakes, rivers, and streams; virgin timber stands; waterfalls; and plenty of recreational opportunities. Summer staff, known as Adventure Rangers, develop and implement naturalist programs for adults and youth within thirty-eight of the ninety-six Michigan state parks, as well as schedule and promote all programs. A salary of $290 to $310 per week and assistance in securing housing are provided. Candidates must have degree work in environmental education, parks, or biology. Send a resume and cover letter (including three references with contact information).

For More Information:
Sarah Reding, Adventure Program Director
Kalamazoo Nature Center
7000 N. Westnedge Ave.
Kalamazoo, MI 49009-6309
(616) 381-1574 • (616) 381-2557 (fax)
sreding@naturecenter.org

KEEWAYDIN ENVIRONMENTAL EDUCATION CENTER

Environmental Education • Vermont • 8–12 Weeks
www.keewaydincamps.org

KEEWAYDIN ENVIRONMENTAL EDUCATION Center is a nonprofit organization that provides short-term residential environmental education programs for public school groups. Many students and their teachers raise the necessary funds to pay for their trip to Keewaydin, which not only allows the whole class to participate but also gives the kids a sense of ownership. The role of environmental education instructors at Keewaydin is challenging, fun, demanding, and rewarding. For eight weeks during the spring, instructors lead field investigations and teach students about natural science, local history, human impact, communities, and land issues. During the summer months, camp counselors, lifeguards, water-safety instructors, and trip leaders are hired for Songadeewin of Keewaydin (a girls' camp) and Keewaydin Camp for Boys. A $275-per-week salary is provided for instructors, while summer staff receive $1,600 to $2,600 for the season, plus a bonus. All staff receive housing (in wooden cabins or platform tents close to the lake) and family-style meals. Enthusiasm for learning, living, and working with children, as well as caring deeply for the earth and all its inhabitants, are qualities found in the Keewaydin staff. Send a resume and cover letter to begin the application process. It's best to apply at least two to three months ahead of time. For summer camp positions, check out their website for the most current contacts. Telephone interviews are common for all positions.

For More Information:
Dave Konopke, Director
Keewaydin Environmental Education Center
10 Keewaydin Rd.
Salisbury, VT 05769
(802) 352-4247 • (802) 352-4772 (fax)
dave@keewaydincamps.org

KEWALO BASIN MARINE MAMMAL LABORATORY

Marine Science • Hawaii • 3–4 Months
www.dolphin-institute.org

THROUGH A CAREFULLY designed full-time apprentice-ship-training program, interns work directly with the dolphins and researchers to learn effective dolphin and whale behavior teaching techniques and research skills. Projects include exploring dolphin perception, intelligence, and communication; assisting with dolphin husbandry and care; assisting the staff in the research laboratory; and orientating Dolphin Institute volunteers. Interns must provide their own transportation, living accommodations (the institute will assist in arranging group housing), and daily expenses. Applicants must have at least two years of college experience. If you are no longer a student, they also have short-term projects and a volunteer program. Internship application deadlines: spring—September 15; summer—January 15; and fall—April 1.

For More Information:
Internship Coordinator
Kewalo Basin Marine Mammal Laboratory
The Dolphin Institute
1129 Ala Moana Blvd.
Honolulu, HI 96814
(808) 593-2211 • (808) 597-8572 (fax)
participate@dolphin-institute.org

LONG LAKE CONSERVATION CENTER

Experiential Education • Minnesota • 3–9 Months
www.llcc.org

ESTABLISHED IN 1963, Long Lake Conservation Center (LLCC) is Minnesota's original environmental learning center. Each year thousands of students and adults explore LLCC's 760-acre outdoor classroom and learn about the environment and conservation of natural resources through school-year programs, a summer camp, and public programs.

What You'll Be Doing: In a spirit of symbiosis, Long Lake views each fieldwork experience as an opportunity for the intern and the center to benefit equally. You'll be at

Some trees grow very tall and straight and large in the forest close to each other, but some must stand by themselves or they won't grow at all. —OLIVER WENDELL HOLMES

the heart of the environmental education world, through both learning and teaching. You'll learn through observation of and interaction with the center's creative and dynamic year-round staff. You'll teach by sharing knowledge with students, bringing fresh insights, and lending individual expertise to the community. You'll become proficient at teaching a number of topics, which vary with the season, including aquatic biology, archery, canoeing, cross-country skiing, predator/prey relationships, fire building and wilderness ethics, human ecology, orienteering, and many games and activities. Summer counselors will supervise, organize, and assist campers during Junior Naturalist, Advanced Ecology, and River Trip sessions.

Commitment: Many interns opt for an entire academic year, beginning in September; however, opportunities are available throughout the year for a minimum commitment of ten weeks.

Perks and Rewards: Interns receive at least a $100-per-week stipend (summer counselors receive $175 per week), along with room and board, liability coverage, and limited attendance at professional workshops and meetings. Each staff member has private sleeping quarters in the North Star Lodge, with shared kitchen, lounge, and two complete bathrooms.

The Essentials: Intern candidates seeking experience in teaching and developing communications skills are ideally suited to this program. Applicants must be working toward a degree in a related field, or have already graduated and be seeking to gain experience. Nontraditional students (i.e., older adults seeking a career change or reentry into the workforce) are also welcome to apply. Counselor applicants must be at least high school seniors and enjoy working with adolescents and the outdoors. Swimming and/or lifesaving is highly desirable.

Your First Move: Request an application packet. Applications are considered on a first-come, first-served basis, and many candidates apply nine to twelve months in advance.

For More Information:
Bob "Schwampy" Schwaderer, Executive Director
Long Lake Conservation Center
28952 - 438th Lane
Palisade, MN 56469
(800) 450-5522 • (218) 768-4653 • (218) 768-2309 (fax)
llcc@mlecmn.net

LONGWOOD GARDENS

Gardens • Pennsylvania • 3–24 Months
www.longwoodgardens.org

LOCATED IN THE culturally rich and historic Brandywine Valley, Longwood Gardens is one of the world's premier display gardens, with nearly four acres of greenhouses and conservatories, flower gardens, fountain gardens, century-old trees, and natural areas encompassing one thousand acres. Longwood offers six training programs geared for high school and college students as well as professional gardeners. In general, interns and trainees specialize in one work area, such as curatorial, arboriculture, greenhouse display, greenhouse production, research, education, or performing arts, supplemented by seminars, workshops, continuing education courses, and field trips over a three- to twenty-four-month period. All participants receive a stipend and are able to live rent-free on the grounds of the former estate of industrialist Pierre S. du Pont. The student houses are furnished and include kitchen utensils and dishes, laundry facilities, study areas, and nearby garden space. Their website provides all the details, including job openings and an application form.

For More Information:
Bill Simeral, Student Programs Coordinator
Longwood Gardens
Route 1, P.O. Box 501
Kennett Square, PA 19348-0501
(610) 388-1000 • (610) 388-2908 (fax)
studentprograms@longwoodgardens.org

Photo Credit: L. Albee

The philosophy of "learning by doing" is the best teacher for interns at Longwood Gardens.

MISSION SPRINGS CONFERENCE CENTER

Outdoor Education/Ministry • California • Academic Year/Summer
www.missionsprings.com

MISSION SPRINGS CONFERENCE Center hosts an outdoor-education program in the redwoods for students in grades five to eight from both Christian and public schools. The program is affiliated with the Pacific Southwest Conference of the Evangelical Covenant Church and serves sixty schools with about three thousand students annually. The proximity to Santa Cruz, the beach, and many other natural attractions makes this a great place to work, live, and learn.

What You'll Be Doing: Over ten naturalists lead natural science classes, Bible studies, field trips, and other activities throughout the school year. Naturalists have the opportunity to gain work experience in outdoor education, Christian camping, and youth ministry; obtain training in natural history interpretation and recreational leadership skills; and enjoy living in a tight-knit Christian community. Check out their website for other employment opportunities, including summer-camp counselors and guest-service positions.

Commitment: Naturalists work full-time weekly from September to June, with a two-month winter break. In general, summer opportunities begin in early June and continue through Labor Day.

Perks and Rewards: A stipend of $250 per week is provided, along with room, meals (when groups are being served), and limited health insurance. Lodging is also provided during the winter break.

The Essentials: Individuals with emotional maturity, excellent physical health, enthusiasm, teaching experience, enjoyment of the outdoors, ability to teach Bible classes, concern about environmental issues, a bachelor's degree, and current first-aid certification are desired.

Your First Move: Submit cover letter and resume, then follow up with a phone call or email.

For More Information:
Scott Smithson, Outdoor Education Director
Mission Springs Conference Center
1050 Lockhart Gulch Rd.
Scotts Valley, CA 95066
(800) 683-9133 • (831) 335-3205 • (831) 335-7726 (fax)
outdooreducation@missionsprings.com

> *I'm looking for solid Christians interested in teaching environmental education. Previous youth ministry and teaching experience are desirable. Guitar players and bilingual applicants are strongly encouraged.*

MONTSHIRE MUSEUM OF SCIENCE

Science Museum • Vermont • 15 Weeks
www.montshire.org

LOCATED A STONE's throw from Dartmouth College, Montshire Museum of Science serves as a hands-on education center that creates its own natural history, physical science, and technology exhibits. The museum conducts a variety of programs, trips, and other activities for children and families, as well as courses, workshops, and forums for community groups.

What You'll Be Doing: Throughout the year, fifteen-week internships are available with options including science education programming, exhibit design and fabrication, membership and development, public relations, Internet and education, land management, and exhibit maintenance and reconstruction. During the summer months, Montshire offers extensive summer environmental and science programming for children of preschool, elementary, and middle-school age with most programs taking place entirely outdoors. Summer staff positions (which range from environmental educators to museum exhibit hosts) begin with a week of training that includes a variety of sessions ranging from leadership skills to ecology to group management.

Perks and Rewards: For interns, a $600 stipend is provided, and, if desired, Montshire will provide free housing hosted by local families. Summer staff wages range from $280 to $370 per week.

The Essentials: Prerequisites include an interest in science and a desire to work with people. Familiarity with natural and physical science, communications, and education is useful.

Your First Move: Call for application materials. Upon receiving your application, a staff member will call or send a letter to arrange an interview. In-person interviews

---

The moment one gives close attention to anything, even a blade of grass, it becomes a mysterious, awesome, indescribably magnificent world in itself. —HENRY MILLER

are held with applicants who live nearby and telephone interviews with more distant applicants.

For More Information:
Lou-Anne Conroy, Intern Coordinator
Montshire Museum of Science
One Montshire Rd.
Norwich, VT 05055
(802) 649-2200 • (802) 649-3637 (fax)
mms-education@montshire.org

MOTE MARINE LABORATORY

Marine Science • Florida • 2–4 Months
www.mote.org

MOTE MARINE LABORATORY is a nonprofit organization dedicated to research in marine and environmental sciences, with a focus on the southwest Florida coastal region. College interns have the opportunity to participate in scientific literature review, project development, data processing and analysis, and report writing. Internships are available in all research areas of the laboratory as well as such support areas as the aquarium, communications, and education. Although a volunteer position, interns receive all the benefits of membership, including free aquarium admission, gift shop and cafe discounts, special event discounts, and lecture and seminar admission. Housing is also available at $75 per week. Positions are available from two to four months throughout the year (note that it's best to apply during the fall for summer internships).

For More Information:
Andrea Davis, Volunteer/Intern Coordinator
Mote Marine Laboratory
1600 Ken Thompson Parkway
Sarasota, FL 34236
(800) 691-6683 • (941) 388-4441 • (941) 388-4312 (fax)
adavis@mote.org

THE NATURE CONSERVANCY

Conservation • Virginia • Summer
www.nature.org/volunteer

THE NATURE CONSERVANCY, founded in 1951, is an international conservation organization committed to preserving natural diversity by finding and protecting lands and waters supporting the best examples of all elements of the natural world. Hands-on conservation internships at nationwide field offices and preserves include administrative, naturalist, preserve, and stewardship positions. Call for the latest line on opportunities and application materials. Each office conducts its own recruiting, so it's best to apply to the state office that interests you. (Their website provides contact information.)

For More Information:
HR Coordinator
The Nature Conservancy
Worldwide Office Divisions
4245 N. Fairfax Dr., Suite 100
Arlington, VA 22203-1606
(800) 628-6860 • (703) 841-5379
(703) 247-3721 (job hotline)

NATURE'S CLASSROOM ATOP LOOKOUT MOUNTAIN

Experiential Education • Alabama • 3 Months
www.naturesclassroom.com

STARTED AS AN experiential education program with an environmental foundation, Nature's Classroom is designed to support traditional classroom learning by teaching creative and practical applications of subjects taught in school. Students enjoy the informal, outdoor atmosphere, opening themselves to new growth experiences.

Your Surroundings: The facility is located on the picturesque and rural Lookout Mountain, on the Little River (one of only two rivers that begin and end on a mountain), bordering Tennessee and Georgia.

What You'll Be Doing: Teachers work with public- and private-school children from the third to eighth grade, teaching hands-on classes in all curriculum areas as well as leading field groups in the outdoors. Small-group activities are designed to foster group cooperation, communication, and team-building concepts using group initiatives and a low-ropes challenge course. A large-group activity may include a simulation of the Underground Railroad, an environmental hearing, or a night hike.

Commitment: Contracts are available from mid-February through end of May and/or mid-September through mid-December. Most staff work up to thirteen hours a day, three to four days a week.

Perks and Rewards: Along with a private cabin or room, meals, training, access to canoes and climbing gear, and the chance to work with a diverse staff, teachers receive a weekly stipend of $190 (and up). Health insurance, up to $150 per year for incidental medical expenses, and use of a washer and dryer are also provided.

The Essentials: Teachers must have a four-year degree and be at least twenty-one, while interns must be at least eighteen and working on a college degree. A sense of humor is very helpful and appreciated, and being able to put the needs of the program and children first is a must. Although individuality and diversity are celebrated, a professional appearance (woodsy professional, that is) is just as important. Emotional maturity is needed to be a success and have fun.

Your First Move: Call for application materials. Candidates are welcome to stay for a few days during their on-site interview.

For More Information:
Krista Coffey, Program Director
Nature's Classroom atop Lookout Mountain
P.O. Box 400
Mentone, AL 35984-0400
(800) 995-4769 • (256) 634-4443 • (256) 634-3601 (fax)
natures@hiwaay.net

NEW CANAAN NATURE CENTER

Nature Center • Connecticut • Academic Year/Summer
www.newcanaannature.org

ESTABLISHED IN 1960, New Canaan Nature Center is a nonprofit nature center serving a wide range of students and visitors, with a focus mainly on the education of students in grades K–8. During the academic year, teacher/naturalists present and help develop school and public programs for all ages, on local wildlife, ecology, environmental issues, and natural history. Summer camp naturalists plan and team-teach diverse programs in sensory awareness, natural science, and general environmental education. Applicants must have a heartfelt desire to teach, an interest in experiencing a nature center setting, and a fairly strong background working with kids. Academic-year staff must have a bachelor's degree and summer staff must be at least eighteen years of age. A weekly stipend of $250 is provided along with possible free housing.

For More Information:
Ann Kozlowicz, Director of School Programs
New Canaan Nature Center
144 Oenoke Ridge
New Canaan, CT 06840
(203) 966-9577, ext. 38 • (203) 966-6536 (fax)
akozlowicz@newcanaannature.org

NEWFOUND HARBOR MARINE INSTITUTE

Marine Science • Florida • Academic Year
www.nhmi.org

NEWFOUND HARBOR MARINE Institute, sponsored by the Seacamp Association, offers programs in marine science and environmental education to school groups (from elementary to high school). Designed to awaken the senses and gain a better understanding of the natural features of the ocean and its ecosystems, the institute allows participants to explore the dynamics of natural communities in a variety of habitats including the opportunity to snorkel and wade with instructors as they experience the wonders of the Florida Keys. More than eight thousand students participate in the program annually.

Your Surroundings: The institute is located 120 miles southwest of Miami—an ideal site for exploring the subtropical marine and terrestrial habitats of the Lower Keys—and is within the boundaries of the Florida Keys National Marine Sanctuary (where the year-round temperature averages seventy-nine degrees).

What You'll Be Doing: Instructor positions and internships are designed to provide college students and preprofessionals with a variety of experiences—from developing their ability to lead interpretive programs to snorkeling among coral reefs with visiting school groups. Over six to eight weeks of intensive training are provided; staff learn boat-handling skills and U.S. Coast Guard boating rules to captain their twenty-six-foot oceanic research vessels. Seminars and hands-on training workshops are conducted on topics including mangrove ecology, reef fish ecology, coastal ecology, shark biology, coral reef ecology, and field techniques. Staff also participate in teaching techniques seminars, program observations, and teamteaching sessions. Other seasonal opportunities exist in photography, marketing, maintenance, food service, and support staff.

If you give a person a fish, you feed him for a day. If you train a person to fish, you feed him for a lifetime. —CHINESE PROVERB

Photo Credit: Seacamp

Newfound Harbor Marine Institute instructors help participants gain an understanding of the natural features of the Florida Keys and its ecosystems.

Commitment: Interns and instructors work eight to ten hours per day, five or six days per week throughout the academic year. For those who would like just a summer experience teaching youth about the sea, the Seacamp Association offers a residential program from late May through late August. See their listing on page 128 for more information.

Perks and Rewards: A monthly stipend (interns start at $50 per week), room and board, a travel bonus, and access to staff boats are provided. American Red Cross certification in advanced first aid, CPR, and lifeguarding is also provided.

The Essentials: Applicants should have an interest in children and marine environment, boating and waterfront experience, and a college degree (or current study) in biology or environmental science.

Your First Move: Send cover letter, resume, transcripts, and three letters of recommendation to receive an application. Deadlines: fall—July 1; spring—October 15.

For More Information:
Judy Gregoire, Intern Coordinator
Newfound Harbor Marine Institute
1300 Big Pine Ave.
Big Pine Key, FL 33043-3336
(305) 872-2331 • (305) 872-2555 (fax)
info@nhmi.org

NEW YORK STATE DEPARTMENT OF ENVIRONMENTAL CONSERVATION

Environmental Education • New York • 10–12 Weeks
www.dec.state.ny.us/website/education/5river.html

THE NEW YORK State Department of Environmental Conservation operates three centers: Five Rivers Environmental Education Center (Delmar), Rogers Environmental Education Center (Sherburne), and Stony Kill Farm Environmental Center (Wappingers Falls). With programming for teachers, school groups, youth groups, conservation organizations, and the public, the three state-run centers promote an understanding of natural history, ecology, environmental science, and natural resources.

What You'll Be Doing: Working at one of the three centers, intern naturalists receive training in a wide variety of education-center programs, the operations and activities of a nature center, and principles of environmental interpretation. Duties range from leading environmental activities to designing educational exhibits.

Commitment: Positions are available for ten to twelve weeks with sessions beginning in January, April, June, and September.

Perks and Rewards: Each center provides a $200-per-week stipend, along with a private bedroom, furnished living room, and fully-equipped kitchen.

The Essentials: Applicants must be eighteen and older, with at least two years of college study in environmental education, science education, or natural resources. Enthusiasm, love of the outdoors, and a desire to work with people are required.

Your First Move: Send your completed application three months before your desired start date. It's noted that summer is ten times as popular as other seasons and the spring session (April through June) is actually the most interesting.

For More Information:
Anita Sanchez, Naturalist Intern
    Program Coordinator
NYS Department of Environmental Conservation
Five Rivers Environmental Education Center
56 Game Farm Rd.
Delmar, NY 12054
(518) 475-0291 • (518) 475-0293 (fax)
amsanche@gw.dec.state.ny.us

NORTH CASCADES INSTITUTE

Environmental Education • Washington • 4 Months
www.ncascades.org

NORTH CASCADES INSTITUTE (NCI) is a nonprofit organization dedicated to increasing understanding and appreciation of the natural, historical, and cultural landscapes of the Pacific Northwest. Each spring and fall, NCI conducts Mountain School, a field program for upper-elementary-school classes who camp in North Cascades National Park. Intern instructors serve as their core teaching staff in this innovative outdoor experience for students, teachers, and parent chaperones. At minimum, applicants should love the outdoors and have a desire to teach children and an ability to live and work with eight other educators in an intensive outdoor environment that is often wet and challenging. Although a volunteer position, perks include room and board, extensive training, teaching materials, and participation in field seminars.

For More Information:
Internship Coordinator
North Cascades Institute
810 Route 20
Sedro-Woolley, WA 98284-9394
(360) 856-5700, ext. 209 • (360) 856-1934 (fax)
nci@ncascades.org

An observer measures the width of a crab onboard a commercial crabbing vessel in Alaska with the North Pacific Fisheries Observer Training Center.

NORTH PACIFIC FISHERIES OBSERVER TRAINING CENTER

Fishery Observer • Alaska • Seasonal
www.uaf.edu/otc

EACH YEAR HUNDREDS of men and women from across the country spend months at a time aboard commercial fishing vessels operating off the Alaskan coast as fisheries observers. Working independently alongside the fishermen, observers collect data on species and quantities of fish caught, fish lengths, weights, and sex, and sightings of marine mammals and seabirds for federal and state agencies that manage Alaska's fisheries. Observers are hired by one of five private contractors. Once accepted by a contractor, a potential observer must successfully complete a two- to three-week training course that covers sampling responsibilities, fish identification, and safety at sea. Observers generally work under a ninety-day contract, although their actual time at sea can vary from three weeks to three months. It's noted that there is a very high demand for observers (about 375 people per year) and most observers can find work year-round if they want.

To the attentive eye, each moment of the year has its own beauty, and in the same field, it beholds, every hour, a picture which was never seen before, and which shall never be seen again. —RALPH WALDO EMERSON

Photo Credit: North Pacific Fisheries Observer Training Center

Wages between $120 and $170 per day are provided, along with transportation expenses and insurance. A bachelor's degree in biology, natural science, or environmental science is required.

For More Information:
Peter Risse, Director
North Pacific Fisheries Observer Training Center
University of Alaska, Anchorage
707 A St., Suite 207
Anchorage, AK 99501-3600
(907) 257-2770 • (907) 257-2774 (fax)
otc@uaa.alaska.edu

PEACE VALLEY NATURE CENTER

Nature Center • Pennsylvania • 10–12 Weeks

PEACE VALLEY NATURE Center began in 1975 with a mission to educate schoolchildren and the general public about the natural world. The nature center features nine miles of trail winding through five hundred acres of diverse natural communities, including fields, deciduous forests, thickets, streams, ponds, coniferous forests, and a portion of Lake Galena. The center is home to a solar building that houses displays, a shop, and a Clivus Multrum composting toilet.

What You'll Be Doing: Each season, interns are required to observe and teach programs, complete and present a project, write a natural history article, attend a board meeting, participate in bird walks, keep a daily diary, and attend staff meetings.

Commitment: Positions run ten weeks during the summer and twelve weeks during the spring and fall. Interns must work every other weekend; Mondays are days off.

Perks and Rewards: A $5.15-per-hour wage is provided, along with housing and the opportunity to gain experience teaching and observe various teaching styles and methods.

The Essentials: Preference is given to applicants with two years of study in environmental education, biology, or environmental studies. Applicants must be interested in teaching children of all ages about the natural world.

Your First Move: Send a resume, references, and cover letter requesting an application. Candidates within a two-hour drive are interviewed on-site; others are interviewed by phone. Applying for the spring or fall internships increases the candidate's chances of employment.

For More Information:
Craig Olsen, Assistant Naturalist
Peace Valley Nature Center
170 Chapman Rd.
Doylestown, PA 18901
(215) 345-7860 • (215) 345-4529 (fax)

POCONO ENVIRONMENTAL EDUCATION CENTER

Environmental Education • Pennsylvania • 6–10 Months
www.peec.org

LOCATED IN THE Delaware Water Gap National Recreation Area, Pocono Environmental Education Center's (PEEC) outdoor classroom consists of a thirty-eight-acre campus with access to over two hundred thousand acres of public land—fields, forests, ponds, waterfalls, and scenic hemlock gorges. Throughout the year, PEEC hosts school groups, religious organizations, universities, professional conferences, and workshops. PEEC also sponsors Elderhostel programs, family nature-study vacations, and professional-development workshops on topics ranging from ornithology and wildflowers to photography and Native American studies.

What You'll Be Doing: Environmental education instructors provide programming, development, and service programs; program-planning interns assist in scheduling, implementing, and coordinating educational programs; and public-relations interns focus on the publications and marketing of PEEC.

Commitment: Six- to ten-month staffing assignments begin in February, June, or September.

Perks and Rewards: A $500 to $800 per month stipend is provided, along with lodging in heated cabins with a private bath (usually shared with one roommate), a shared staff lounge, and meals served in the dining hall.

The Essentials: Enrollment in or completion of a degree program in English, communications, environmental/outdoor education, natural sciences, or related fields is required. Applicants must demonstrate experience working with people and interest in working in a residential setting. Certification in lifeguarding, first aid, or CPR is preferred.

Your First Move: Submit resume, cover letter, and two references. Selected candidates will have on-site interviews to observe the typical operation of the center.

For More Information:
Flo Mauro, Director
Pocono Environmental Education Center
R.R. 2, Box 1010
Dingmans Ferry, PA 18328
(570) 828-2319 • (570) 828-9695 (fax)
peec@ptd.net

RAINFOREST ACTION NETWORK

Environmental Advocacy • California • Seasonal
www.ran.org/vip

RAINFOREST ACTION NETWORK (RAN) works to protect the earth's rain forests and support the rights of their inhabitants through dynamic, hard-hitting campaigns that work to bring corporate and governmental policies into alignment with popular support for rain-forest conservation. Intern opportunities at their headquarters in San Francisco include media operations, database coordination, campaign administration and coordination, executive administration, development assistance, and writing, layout, and research. Interns work on a volunteer basis; however, local commuting costs up to $7 per day are reimbursed. A minimum commitment of three months is required. A letter of reference, a complimentary year's membership to RAN, and a T-shirt are provided after completion of the internship.

For More Information:
Adrienne Blum, Volunteer and Intern
    Program Director
Rainforest Action Network
221 Pine St., Suite 500
San Francisco, CA 94104
(415) 398-4404 • (415) 398-2732 (fax)
helpran@ran.org

RICHARDSON BAY AUDUBON CENTER AND SANCTUARY

Natural Science • California • Summer
www.bayaudubon.org

SURROUNDED BY ELEVEN acres of land and nine hundred acres of tidal wetlands (preserved for wintering water-birds) on San Francisco Bay, Richardson Bay is composed of a wildlife preserve and nature education center.

Summer environmental education interns primarily assist with teaching in the center's nature day-camp program (for children ages three to ten), which includes six to eight weeklong programs with a variety of different natural history and environmental science themes. A $75 per week food stipend is provided, and housing is sometimes available. Candidates should deal effectively with people, be well organized, and have an interest in natural history. Experience working with children or teaching is helpful. To begin the application process, send a cover letter and resume.

For More Information:
Meryl Sundove, Education Coordinator
Richardson Bay Audubon Center and Sanctuary
National Audubon Society
376 Greenwood Beach Rd.
Tiburon, CA 94920
(415) 388-2525 • (415) 388-0717 (fax)
msundove@audubon.org

RIVER BEND NATURE CENTER

**Environmental Education • Minnesota •
3 or 9 Months**
www.rbnc.org

HOME TO ACTIVE wetlands, maple and basswood forests, and restored prairies, River Bend helps people "discover, enjoy, understand, and preserve the incredible natural world that surrounds us." Intern naturalists develop and teach programs, providing hands-on teaching experiences for children from preschool through age twelve in environmental day camps during the summer and for school groups throughout the academic year. In addition, interns design and teach public weekend programs for all ages, including youth, families, seniors, and special-needs groups. Academic-year interns receive a $150 weekly stipend, two weeks paid vacation, seasonal bonus, and housing; summer interns receive a $175 weekly stipend plus housing. A minimum of three years of college study is required. Send off a cover letter, resume, and list of three references.

For More Information:
John Blackmer, Chief Naturalist
River Bend Nature Center
100 Rustad Rd.
P.O. Box 186
Faribault, MN 55021-0186
(507) 332-7151 • (507) 332-0656 (fax)
blackmer@rbnc.org

RIVERBEND ENVIRONMENTAL EDUCATION CENTER

Environmental Education • Pennsylvania • Summer
www.riverbendeec.org

HOUSED IN A 1923 converted barn and surrounded by thirty-one acres of forest, fields, and streams, Riverbend provides a unique setting for educational activities designed to establish an awareness and understanding of the principles upon which our natural world is based. Spend time at Riverbend using your creative abilities and love of natural history while sharing the joy of discovery with children. Environmental education interns prepare and teach classes to schools, organized groups, and the public while gaining an orientation to environmental education, a working knowledge of ecological and environmental concepts, and experience developing and implementing educational goals and lesson plans. Environmental educator/camp staff work at the Exploration Camp and are directly responsible for the creation and implementation of hands-on, exploration-based activities. Benefits include $150 to $275 per week and housing if needed.

For More Information:
Timshel Purdum, Education Director
Riverbend Environmental Education Center
1950 Spring Mill Rd.
Gladwyne, PA 19035-1000
(610) 527-5234 • (610) 527-1161 (fax)
tpurdum@riverbendeec.org

RYERSON WOODS

Environmental Education • Illinois • 10–48 Weeks
www.ryersonwoods.org

AS THE HEADQUARTERS of the Lake County Forest Preserve, Ryerson Woods is home to several rare species, including the blue-spotted salamander, wood frog, eastern Massasauga rattlesnake, red-shouldered hawk, and purple-fringed orchids. The visitors center houses an extensive natural science library and is punctuated with changing art exhibits depicting the beauty and wonder of nature. As paraprofessional naturalists, environmental education instructors are exposed to all operations of the center. A large portion of time is spent developing, preparing, and presenting programs to youth and adults throughout the year and for the nature and adventure camps during the summer months. Other responsibilities may include participation in volunteer- and teacher-training programs or special events. Positions run from ten to forty-eight weeks with start dates in February, March, May, June, and September. Stipends range from $2,700 for summer nature-camp instructors on up to $15,862 for forty-eight-week instructors. Furnished housing can be arranged for a fee of $100 per month. Ideally, applicants should have at least two years of course work in biology or education along with an enthusiasm and respect for both people and the environment. Call or email for application materials.

For More Information:
Mark Hurley, Education Instructor Coordinator
Ryerson Woods
Lake County Forest Preserve
21950 Riverwoods Rd.
Deerfield, IL 60015
(847) 968-3324
mhurley@co.lake.il.us

SALISH SEA EXPEDITIONS

Marine Science • Washington • 4 Months
www.salish.org

SALISH SEA EXPEDITIONS provides boat-based research expeditions to groups of students ranging from fifth to twelfth grade. Aboard the research ship, a sixty-one-foot yawl, students rotate through tasks such as helping handle sail, cooking meals, launching and recovering scientific gear, evaluating data, plotting a course, or standing a watch. In the classroom, marine-science educators help students develop their itinerary and research plan; then, while aboard the ship, they double as watch leaders and scientific-study teachers. On board, logistics coordinators assist students with food preparation, and also the educators and sail crew as needed. Prior to working with students (either during the spring or fall term), all staff members participate in a one-week training period that focuses on Puget Sound ecology, program methodology, safety procedures, and ship operations. Along with room and board, base salaries range from $1,000 to $1,600 per month. All marine science positions require a college degree and a demonstrated ability to teach and design/implement scientific research projects. Basic first-aid and CPR certificates are required; however, advanced certificates in EMT or WFR are highly encouraged. Hiring begins in May for the fall, and in October for the spring.

For More Information:
Lori Midthun Mitchell, Program Director
Salish Sea Expeditions
647 Horizon View Place
Bainbridge Island, WA 98110
(206) 780-7848
lori@salish.org

For More Information:
Dianne Braybrook, Internship Coordinator
Sarett Nature Center
2300 Benton Center Rd.
Benton Harbor, MI 49022
(616) 927-4832 • (616) 927-2742 (fax)
dianne@sarett.com

SARETT NATURE CENTER

Nature Center • Michigan • 3–4 Months
www.sarett.com

MORE THAN TWENTY-FIVE thousand students from pre-school through college follow the Sarett Nature Center staff naturalists down the pathway to environmental education each year. The center owns eight hundred acres along the Paw Paw River, manages another twelve hundred acres of wooded dunes for the Nature Conservancy, and provides nature interpretation at Grand Mere State Park, a wilderness area along Lake Michigan.

What You'll Be Doing: Intern naturalists teach a variety of natural history programs to school groups, primarily preschool through sixth grade. During these programs, interns lead interpretive nature walks, teach cross-country skiing (winter), lead sixth-grade students on an overnight wilderness camping experience (spring/summer), aid in developing educational programs and weekend activities for the public, and care for resident educational animals. Interns also complete a special project ranging from an interpretive program or display to writing a natural history article for publication to engaging in field research.

Perks and Rewards: Interns receive $5.15 per hour, plus housing.

The Essentials: Biology or environmental science college graduates interested in sharing their knowledge of the natural world with children of all ages are ideal. Useful skills include bird, tree, insect, animal track, and woodland/wetland wildflower identification for the northeastern U.S.; cross-country skiing and snowshoeing; canoeing and lifesaving; and low-impact wilderness camping.

Your First Move: Submit cover letter (including the season you wish to work), resume, and three or four references. Deadlines: winter/spring—October 1; summer—March 1; and fall—June 1.

THE SCHOOL FOR FIELD STUDIES

Environmental Studies • Worldwide • 1 Year
www.fieldstudies.org

THE SCHOOL FOR Field Studies (SFS) is the country's oldest and largest educational institution exclusively dedicated to teaching and engaging undergraduates in environmental problem solving. Students will learn about environmental issues and work to solve them by actually living within the ecosystems and communities where they take place. In one of their more recent projects, students at their Center for Rainforest Studies in Australia are engaged in rain-forest restoration and have assisted the communities there in replanting more than twenty thousand trees.

What You'll Be Doing: Participating in a practical education in environmental studies, interns will assist staff members with organizational and academic tasks, group dynamics, administrative support and logistics, site management, and the academic and research programs. Placements are offered in Australia, the British West Indies, Canada, Costa Rica, Kenya, and Mexico.

Commitment: Interns must make a commitment of one year. Start dates begin in late January, June 1, and September 1.

Perks and Rewards: Benefits include a stipend of $750 for each semester and $500 for both summer sessions ($2,000 total), along with on-site room and board, evacuation/repatriation insurance coverage, and reimbursement for any required visas and/or work permits. Half of the direct round-trip airfare is also reimbursed at the conclusion of service. Interns must have adequate, internationally valid, health insurance for the entire internship period.

The Essentials: Applicants must be college graduates (twenty-one years or older) and have valid certification in first aid and CPR (lifeguard certification preferred), as well as experience in group dynamics, leading groups, or teaching. Ideal candidates are energetic, motivated individuals who seek out new challenges and enjoy a group living

Photo Credit: Schuylkill Center for Environmental Education

Participants learn more about the streams and ponds at the Schuylkill Center for Environmental Education.

environment. Some programs also require a specific language proficiency, and those who have been through an SFS summer or semester program are given preference.

Your First Move: Their website outlines specific application materials (or call for a packet). Deadlines: summer/fall—February 1; spring—September 1.

For More Information:
Mary Shattuck, Staff Recruitment Coordinator
The School for Field Studies
16 Broadway
Beverly, MA 01915-4499
(800) 989-4435 • (978) 927-7200, ext. 304
(978) 927-5127 (fax)
jobs@fieldstudies.org

SCHUYLKILL CENTER FOR ENVIRONMENTAL EDUCATION

Environmental Education • Pennsylvania • 10 Weeks
www.schuylkillcenter.org

As PHILADELPHIA'S OLDEST and largest environmental education facility, the Schuylkill Center offers five hundred acres of varied habitats and resources and a multitude of opportunities for teaching and learning.

What You'll Be Doing: Interns become environmental educators-in-training, working closely with the professional teaching staff, then practicing newly acquired skills firsthand with the children and adults who visit the center. Duties include teaching daily environmental education programs for preschool level through twelfth grade; assisting with the center's daily operations; conducting weekend natural history programs; surveying environmental education curriculum materials; designing and constructing displays and exhibits for the discovery museum; and observing and assisting with adult workshops, teacher in-services, and college credit courses.

Commitment: The program is offered each spring and fall for ten weeks.

Perks and Rewards: A small stipend is provided along with an invaluable experience. Periodic teacher workshops in national environmental education curriculum and materials are also available.

The Essentials: Applicants must have a minimum of two years of college in the field of environmental education, biology, natural sciences, or elementary education, with an interest in the environment and desire to work with people. Those with a combined background of natural sciences and teaching experience are preferred.

Your First Move: Call/email for more information and application materials.

For More Information:
Kathy Bright, Director of Education
Schuylkill Center for Environmental Education
8480 Hagy's Mill Rd.
Philadelphia, PA 19128-1998
(215) 482-7300, ext. 124 • (215) 482-8158 (fax)
kbright@schuylkillcenter.org

SCICON

Outdoor Education • California • 10 Months
www.tcoe.org/scicon

EXPERIENCING NATURE AND science firsthand, more than eleven thousand students each year participate at the Clemmie Gill School of Science and Conservation (SCICON), a residential outdoor-education school operated by the Tulare County Office of Education. With community involvement as its backbone, every acre has been acquired through donations, and every building and facility built through volunteers and contributions. A museum of natural history, planetarium, observatory, raptor rehabilitation center, and over seventeen miles of trails are just some of the highlights of this beautiful eleven-hundred-acre campus.

What You'll Be Doing: The internship program kicks off with an in-depth orientation program, which includes guest speakers, field trips, and an intensive training workshop. Interns then gain experience in every facet of outdoor-school operation, and learn to teach basic concepts of outdoor education in all areas of natural history. In addition, interns gain skills in large-group management, program scheduling, and administration. There is also a California teaching credential program in which you can enroll concurrently with the internship.

Commitment: Internships begin in mid-August with three weeks of staff training and continue with program operation through the end of June (a ten-month commitment). Interns can expect long days with irregular hours, Monday through Friday.

Perks and Rewards: A stipend of $54 per day is provided, along with room, board, and health insurance.

The Essentials: Applicants with a bachelor's degree in science, education, or recreation are preferred (although upper-division students will also be considered). Applicants must have a high energy level, professional appearance, and a real love for children and the outdoors. The program is ideal for those considering careers and leadership roles in outdoor education.

Your First Move: Send off your resume and cover letter before March 1; an application packet will be sent to you upon receipt.

For More Information:
Rick Mitchell, Administrator/Director
SCICON
P.O. Box 339
Springville, CA 93265
(559) 539-2642 • (559) 539-2643 (fax)
rickmit@tcoe.org

THE SCOTT ARBORETUM OF SWARTHMORE COLLEGE

Gardens • Pennsylvania • 3–12 Months
www.scottarboretum.org

THE SCOTT ARBORETUM, which is uniquely situated on the campus of Swarthmore College (a small, outstanding, coeducational liberal arts college with a student population of 1,375), was established in 1929 for the purpose of cultivating and displaying trees, shrubs, and herbaceous plants suited to the climate of eastern Pennsylvania and which are suitable for planting by home gardeners.

What You'll Be Doing: Summer internships offer a broad range of practical work experience to those interested in the ornamental horticulture field. Interns work with the staff and volunteers in gardening, plant propagation, plant records, educational programs, and special events.

A curatorial intern leads a tour at the Scott Arboretum on Arbor Day.

Photo Credit: Harry Kalish

How wonderful it is that nobody need wait a single moment before starting to improve the world. —ANNE FRANK

In addition, a yearlong curatorial internship is offered, with duties including supervision of volunteers and summer interns along with assisting in educational events.

Commitment: Summer internships are available for a minimum of ten weeks, April through September; the yearlong position begins in June.

Perks and Rewards: Summer interns receive $8.50 per hour, while the yearlong intern receives $1,500 per month plus full benefits. Assistance with locating housing will be provided, though it will be your responsibility. Swarthmore is a college community, so you shouldn't have a problem here. Other perks include free admission to college events such as concerts and plays, as well as free use of the college's sports facilities.

The Essentials: Applicants must have a keen interest in horticulture and enjoy working with people and plants.

Your First Move: Submit cover letter, resume, and three references (with contact information) by March 1.

For More Information:
Claire Sawyers, Director
The Scott Arboretum of Swarthmore College
Swarthmore College
500 College Ave.
Swarthmore, PA 19081-1397
(610) 328-8025 • (610) 328-7755 (fax)
csawyer1@swarthmore.edu

SEA TURTLE RESTORATION PROJECT

Ecotourism • Costa Rica • 2 Weeks–2 Months
www.seaturtles.org

VOLUNTEERS ARE NEEDED for beach patrols and sea-turtle hatchery work from mid-July to mid-January at Punto Banco, on the Pacific coast of Costa Rica (a place surrounded by black sand, warm ocean waters, and a tropical rain forest). Volunteers work with a Costa Rican biologist and community members, with activities that include walking the beaches at night searching for nesting turtles, moving turtle nests to the hatchery, and participating in environmental education programs in the community. Adult turtles will be tagged and measured, and data on hatching success will be recorded. It's definitely not all work while volunteering; leisure activities include jungle hikes and snorkeling. Volunteers stay in rustic cabins operated by Tiskita Jungle Lodge (www.tiskita-lodge.co.cr) along with enjoying local (and delicious) cuisine. One to

four volunteers participate at a time, and a two-week commitment is required. Volunteers with some knowledge of Spanish and who are willing to participate in environmental education programs with local children are highly desirable. There is a program fee of $500 for two weeks, $700 for one month, $1,200 for two months, and discounts for those receiving academic credit. (Transportation is additional.) Call or email for application materials or visit www.tortugamarina.org.

For More Information:
Randall Arauz, Central American Director
Sea Turtle Restoration Project
Costa Rica Volunteer Project
P.O. Box 400
Forest Knolls, CA 94933
(800) 859-7283 • (415) 488-0370 • (415) 488-0372 (fax)
rarauz@tortugamarina.org

SHAVER'S CREEK ENVIRONMENTAL CENTER

Environmental Education • Pennsylvania • 3–6 Months
www.shaverscreek.org

SHAVER'S CREEK, ADMINISTERED by Penn State's Continuing Education program, is an environmental education laboratory seeking to enhance the quality of life by providing exemplary outdoor learning opportunities. This multifaceted center offers environmental education programs for group visits, natural/cultural history exhibits, live amphibians and reptiles, hiking trails, herb gardens, and more. The raptor center, providing perpetual care and housing for eagles, falcons, hawks, and owls, is one

of the few federally and state-licensed raptor facilities in Pennsylvania.

What You'll Be Doing: Environmental education interns become an integral part of the staff and are encouraged to participate in all aspects of the center's operation. A two-week orientation and training period is followed by seasonal program opportunities in both day and residential settings. Interns work with all ages, preschool to adult, as they lead natural and cultural history programs for school and community groups, families, and the general public. Interns also have the opportunity to contribute articles to the members' newsletter, lead adventure and team-building programs, participate in the care and handling of the live animal collection, and assist in the general operation of the center. Observations, recordings, and videotaping are used in evaluation, and interns are encouraged to keep a journal.

Commitment: Positions are available year-round, from three to six months, with the opportunity to work multiple seasons.

Perks and Rewards: A weekly stipend of $150 and on-site housing (nestled in the woods away from park visitors, with a private sleeping room) are provided. Interns are encouraged to participate in professional development workshops and regional conferences, and each season includes a three-day staff trip to another environmental center or a facility of interest. Macintosh computers are used on-site, and access to the Internet is available. Career counseling, job-listing resources, and assistance with resume writing are also provided.

The Essentials: Successful candidates have a strong desire to teach and share their knowledge and enthusiasm for the natural world. A background in education or the natural sciences is helpful but not necessary. International students are encouraged to apply (as the center can assist with the J-1 Visa application process).

Your First Move: Interested candidates can call, fax, or write for an application. Deadlines: winter/spring—November 1; summer—March 1; and fall—July 1. Interviews with top candidates are conducted in person or by phone.

For More Information:
Doug Wentzel, Internship Coordinator
Shaver's Creek Environmental Center
The Pennsylvania State University
RR1, Box 325, Discovery Road
Petersburg, PA 16669-9317
(814) 863-2000 • (814) 865-2706 (fax)
shaverscreek@outreach.psu.edu

The most successful candidates have some experience in working with children. A site visit and meeting with the intern coordinator is beneficial but not necessary. Many first-time undergraduate candidates who are not accepted mistakenly fail to reapply for an upcoming season.

SQUAM LAKES NATURAL SCIENCE CENTER

Environmental Education • New Hampshire • Summer
www.nhnature.org

LOCATED IN A beautiful countryside in central New Hampshire, the Squam Lakes Natural Science Center is a unique outdoor classroom offering people of all ages the opportunity to discover and explore New Hampshire's natural world. Through the classroom and using the center's two-hundred-acre site, summer interns lead programs on natural history and environmental awareness. Interns are also involved in exhibit design and construction as well as care of the center's native wildlife collection. A $100-per-week stipend is provided along with on-site housing, including a private bedroom, shared bath, and kitchen use. College undergraduates with at least junior status or graduate students studying the natural sciences, education, or environmental education are most desirable. Enthusiasm, motivation, and a desire to work with people and animals are a must. Send resume and a cover letter (with three professional references). Applications must be received by February 1.

For More Information:
Amy Yeakel, Director of Education
Squam Lakes Natural Science Center
P.O. Box 173
Holderness, NH 03245-0173
(603) 968-7194 • (603) 968-2229 (fax)
info@nhnature.org

Each year Squam Lakes also hires an assistant naturalist who is responsible for teaching school and natural adventure programming. The position begins in mid-March for one year; a weekly stipend of $175, housing, benefits and health insurance are provided. Applicants must be college grads.

STARR RANCH SANCTUARY

Ecology • California • 3 Months
www.starrranch.org

LOCATED IN THE foothills of the Santa Ana Mountains in a mild and semiarid Mediterranean climate, Starr Ranch Sanctuary is a four-thousand-acre preserve owned and operated by the National Audubon Society. Interns participate in an independent research project while assisting researchers and leading nature walks during public events. Positions run for three months each season except the winter. Applicants must be undergraduate or graduate students with some ecological, biological, or conservation background. A $150-per-week stipend is provided along with housing. Send cover letter stating career goals, resume, and two letters of recommendation.

For More Information:
Dr. Sandy DeSimone, Research Director
Starr Ranch Sanctuary
Audubon California
100 Bell Canyon Rd.
Trabuco Canyon, CA 92679-3511
(949) 858-0309 • (949) 858-1013 (fax)
sdesimone@audubon.org

TREES FOR TOMORROW

Natural Resources • Wisconsin • Academic Year
www.treesfortomorrow.com

TREES FOR TOMORROW is one of the Midwest's oldest conservation education centers, with a "classroom" that includes miles of surrounding state and national forests, lakes and streams, and abundant wildlife. From their thirty-acre campus in Eagle River, participants travel to nearby demonstration areas to learn firsthand about forest management, wildlife habitat, water systems, and conservation practices. Whether bouncing on a bog, collecting critters from a stream, or learning how to weave a snowshoe, a "learn by doing" approach resonates throughout their entire programming.

What You'll Be Doing: After an extensive training period, naturalist interns will give evening naturalist programs, teach a variety of indoor and outdoor classes, and develop an interpretive display or environmental education curriculum. The changing seasons offer additional duties ranging from teaching cross-country ski techniques to leading bog studies and orienteering classes.

Commitment: Four naturalists are hired from early September to early June.

Perks and Rewards: A stipend of $700 to $750 per month is provided, along with full room and board. Perks include catastrophic health insurance, paid holiday and vacation days, a staff jacket and curriculum guides, and the chance to tour other nature centers and network with professionals in the field.

The Essentials: A willingness to learn, coupled with good people skills and the ability to teach others about natural resources, are the key ingredients for the ideal intern. Recent graduates in biology, forestry, environmental education, or natural resource management are preferred, although students at the junior or senior level are also welcome.

Your First Move: Send cover letter, resume, and a list of three references by May 15. Telephone interviews are given to the most promising applicants.

For More Information:
Sandy Lotto, Intern Coordinator
Trees For Tomorrow
Natural Resources Education Center
P.O. Box 609
Eagle River, WI 54521-0609
(800) 838-9472 • (715) 479-6456 • (715) 479-2318 (fax)
trees@nnex.net

A UGA Marine Education Center intern introduces some muddy students to a salt marsh snail.

UNIVERSITY OF GEORGIA MARINE EDUCATION CENTER AND AQUARIUM

Marine Science • Georgia • 1 Year
www.uga.edu/aquarium

LOCATED ON SCENIC Skidaway Island, the University of Georgia's Marine Education Center and Aquarium (MECA) includes a 19,000-square-foot education center with a teaching aquarium, classrooms and exhibit space, a sixty-bed dormitory, a cafeteria, and three research vessels. Each year, over thirteen thousand students from Georgia and adjacent states receive formal education from programs here.

What You'll Be Doing: Over the course of a one- to two-month intensive training period, interns will learn how to teach and convey marine-related content to children of all ages and adults, through lectures, labs, coastal field studies, and distance learning. Interns are also in charge of maintaining touch-tank animals and assisting staff in other specialty areas. Each intern will also complete an education project for the MECA facility.

Commitment: This is a full-time, fifty-week program that begins in early September. In the months of June and July, interns work with several weeklong science-camp programs for children.

Perks and Rewards: A $249-per-week stipend is provided along with single occupancy, studio apartments in the dormitory and free meals (whenever groups are scheduled to eat in the cafeteria). Perks include access to the on-site research library, the nearby Skidaway Institute of Oceanography, and the opportunity to attend local workshops and educational meetings.

The Essentials: Internships are geared for recent graduates who would like some teaching experience in the marine realm and have not yet decided whether to go to graduate school or take a full-time permanent position. A degree in science or science education is required; however, university seniors may apply before graduation if their degree will be awarded before the internship begins. Marine-science experience is not necessary and applicants must be physically fit and able to do fieldwork. Cheerfulness and flexibility are very important!

Your First Move: Consult their website for detailed application instructions and qualifications. All application materials must be received by April 30 for internships beginning the following September.

For More Information:
Dr. Maryellen Timmons, Internship Coordinator
UGA Marine Education Center and Aquarium
30 Ocean Science Circle
Savannah, GA 31411
(912) 598-2496 • (912) 598-2302 (fax)
mare@uga.edu

UP YONDA FARM

Environmental Education • New York • Summer
www.upyondafarm.com

WITH A SPECTACULAR view of Lake George, Up Yonda Farm sits upon a seventy-two-acre property surrounded by beauty (and lots of butterflies during the summer months). The environmental education center features wildlife exhibits and nature trails and offers a variety of interpretive programs to schools and the general public. During the summer months, naturalists are the backbone of the programming to visitors. Typical activities include providing information to visitors; conducting interpretive walks, developing presentations; designing and creating exhibits and displays; preparing and distributing promotional materials; and providing routine grounds and trail maintenance. Candidates must have great communication skills, the ability to work with the public, and degree studies in interpretation or environmental science. Housing is available along with an $8.38-per-hour wage ($1 more if you have your own housing). To apply, send resume, references, and a college transcript. A personal interview is required for placement.

In hot pursuit of Monarch butterflies for a tagging and identification research project at Up Yonda Farm, a summer naturalist explains catching techniques to two energized workshop participants.

For More Information:
Matt Sprow, Internship Coordinator
Up Yonda Farm
P.O. Box 1453
Bolton Landing, NY 12814
(518) 644-9767 • (518) 644-3824 (fax)
upyonda@capital.net

UPHAM WOODS 4-H EE CENTER

Environmental Education • Wisconsin • Seasonal
www.uwex.edu/ces/4h/uphamwoods

PART OF THE University of Wisconsin system since 1950, Upham Woods provides environmental education programs for more than nine thousand adult and youth clients each year. Residential programs focus on animals, plants, water, and the unique geological formations of the region.

What You'll Be Doing: Seasonal naturalists teach natural science and lead activities primarily for middle-school clientele. Other responsibilities include developing and leading challenge activities on-site, as well as planning, designing, and developing educational displays, activities, or curriculum.

Commitment: Positions are offered year-round, with a five-day, irregular workweek scheduled between the hours of 7 A.M. and 11 P.M.

Perks and Rewards: A $250-per-week stipend is provided, along with on-site staff-only housing and meals.

The Essentials: Applicants must have completed introductory courses in natural resources, recreation, or education (at least junior status for college students). Demonstrated success in working effectively with individuals and groups is preferred. Lifesaving, advanced first aid, and current CPR are required for summer positions.

Your First Move: Call for application materials. Personal interviews are preferred, although phone interviews are acceptable.

For More Information:
Bob Nichols, Director
Upham Woods 4-H EE Center
N194, County Highway N
Wisconsin Dells, WI 53965
(608) 254-6461 • (608) 253-7140 (fax)
bob.nichols@ces.uwex.edu

WHALE CAMP

Marine Science • Canada • Summer
www.whalecamp.com

LOCATED ON CANADA's Grand Manan Island in the mouth of the Bay of Fundy between Maine and Nova Scotia, the Whale Camp provides fun and adventuresome marine learning experiences for youth and adults throughout the summer months. Its unique location lures some of the world's rarest marine mammals each summer, providing direct observation of species ranging from right whales, humpback whales, and white-sided dolphins to colonies of puffins and peregrine falcons. Along with three boats used for ocean exploration (including a fifty-foot traditionally rigged schooner), the tools of scientific inquiry help residential camp participants (ages ten to seventeen) learn about the geology of the region, the marine life in the bay, and the land-based life of Grand Manan. Beyond the residential camp, Whale Camp also offers specialty courses for educators and birders, including the Authors of the Sea session. In this program, students work alongside a published author and professional artist to create a high-quality, professionally published book documenting their experiences on Grand Manan.

What You'll Be Doing: With each youth session combining the elements of field experiences; hands-on marine science, coastal ecology, and oceanography activities; sailing and kayaking adventures; and classroom activities, seasonal staff members joining the Whale Camp will have their hands full. Exercises in the development of self-esteem, trust, and cooperation are woven throughout the program, allowing students to develop a deeper understanding of themselves, others, and the world around them. Whether working as an environmental science instructor, outdoor recreation and dormitory instructor, logistic coordinator, or program director, staff members are the heart and soul of Whale Camp—providing participants with continual guidance and support along with educating and fostering an awareness and respect for the entire environment.

Commitment: Positions begin in late May or early June and continue through early September (with varied start and finish dates). Those arriving at the beginning of the season will participate in an eleven-day training period. Although the positions are seasonal, there is opportunity in the off-season to do some recruiting and curriculum projects.

Perks and Rewards: All staff receive a salary along with room and board. With the exception of the outdoor recreation and dormitory instructors (who live in the dorms with students), staff members live in a cottage that overlooks the Bay of Fundy. The cottage has a wood-burning stove, full kitchen, washing machine/dryer, two private bedrooms (the rest are doubles), and phone lines. Internet access is available on the island at the local school. Perks include the opportunity to go on kayak excursions, trips to Machias Seal Island (to view Atlantic puffins), whale/sail trips on the camp's schooner, and other boat trips throughout the summer.

The Essentials: Ideally, applicants should have at least one to two seasons of outdoor education experience, a marine/coastal-ecology background, enthusiasm working with youth in the outdoors, and demonstrated leadership skills (along with a strong work ethic and an innovative and patient attitude!). Since there is creativity and flexibility in the Whale Camp curriculum, candidates who can walk into the job with a solid set of teaching skills and have the motivation to take the program to new levels will thrive here. All applicants must be at least twenty-one and have CPR and first-aid certification (advanced medical certification is encouraged). Both Canadian and U.S. citizens are eligible; others must have a current work visa.

Your First Move: It's preferred that you download an application online. In addition to a completed application, a resume, list of references, and copies of your certification cards are needed. Hiring begins in January.

For More Information:
Dennis Bowen, Director
Whale Camp
P.O. Box 63
Cheyney, PA 19319
(888) 549-4253 • (610) 399-1463 • (610) 399-4482 (fax)
employment@whalecamp.com

WHITE MOUNTAIN RESEARCH STATION

Natural Resources • California • Summer
www.wmrs.edu

THE WHITE MOUNTAIN Research Station (WMRS), a multicampus research unit of the University of California, was established over fifty years ago to provide laboratory, teaching, and housing facilities for researchers doing fieldwork in the eastern Sierra Nevada. WMRS has four laboratory facilities spanning a 10,000-foot elevation range, including the highest laboratory in North America at 14,246 feet on White Mountain peak. Each summer, researchers from around the world (representing over one hundred institutions) and interns come together to work on current issues in resource management, conservation biology, and physical change of the environment.

What You'll Be Doing: Internships with the Interagency Resource Team are ideal for undergraduate students with limited experience in resource management and field research, while advanced internships are geared for upper-division undergraduates with academic experience in the field. Interns kick off their summer in mid-June with an orientation week, which focuses on training in first aid, orienteering (map and compass use), global positioning system use, 4WD truck driving, and backpacking skills. While out in the field, interns will conduct monitoring and research (under the guidance of experienced field supervisors) and are responsible for communal camping and cooking activities.

Perks and Rewards: There is a participation fee of $2,100 (for room and board) for Interagency Resource Team internships; however scholarships are available. Advanced interns receive room and board, along with a stipend up to $2,500 depending on the project. All interns live in dormitory-style housing with research assistants of their own age and gender.

The Essentials: Applicants must be undergraduates or recent college grads with an ecology, biology, or conservation background. No field experience is necessary; however, an interest in backpacking in rugged, alpine environments is a must. Those who are preparing for graduate studies or professional careers in natural resource fields will thrive in this learning experience.

For More Information:
Susan May Szewczak, Ph.D., Academic Coordinator
White Mountain Research Station
3000 E. Line St.
Bishop, CA 93514
(760) 872-4214 • (760) 873-7830 (fax)
susan@wmrs.edu

WILDLANDS STUDIES

Endangered Species • Worldwide • Seasonal
www.wildlandsstudies.com/ws

SPONSORED BY San Francisco State University's College of Extended Learning, Wildlands Studies participants work with field teams searching for answers to important environmental problems affecting endangered wildlife and threatened wildland ecosystems in areas of the mainland U.S., Alaska, Hawaii, New Zealand, Fiji, Canada, Belize, Thailand, or Nepal. Research projects occur entirely in the field and involve extensive on-site experiences in wildlife preservation, resource management, conservation ecology, and cultural sustainability. Prior fieldwork experience is not necessary and academic credit can be arranged. There is a program fee that ranges from $425 to $1,900.

For More Information:
Crandall Bay, Program Director
Wildlands Studies
3 Mosswood Circle
Cazadero, CA 95421
(707) 632-5665 • (707) 632-5665 (fax)
wildlnds@sonic.net

WILDLIFE PRAIRIE STATE PARK

Wildlife • Illinois • 12 Weeks

WILDLIFE PRAIRIE STATE Park covers two thousand acres of grazing land, lakes, and forests, and presents wild animals native to Illinois in their natural habitats. It con-

trasts the rugged heritage and simple lifestyles of Illinois's past with the complex, energy-demanding society of the future, and provides a better understanding of our environment through education, conservation, and recreation.

What You'll Be Doing: Student naturalist interns work under the direction of the park's education department, with duties that include special interpretive projects, trail monitoring and development, and presenting public educational programs. These varied duties will entail both indoor and outdoor tasks, require physical and mental skills, and provide working experience with park staff, volunteers, and the general public.

Commitment: Internships are offered year-round for a minimum of twelve weeks.

Perks and Rewards: Spring, summer, and fall interns are provided with a minimum-wage salary, uniform shirts, and possible on-site lodging. Interns for the winter semester are on a voluntary basis.

The Essentials: Candidates must be recent graduates or those pursuing a degree in outdoor/environmental education, interpretation, parks and recreation, or biology.

Your First Move: Send a cover letter and resume.

For More Information:
Rebecca Rees, Intern Coordinator
Wildlife Prairie State Park
3826 N. Taylor Rd., R.R.2, Box 50
Hanna City, IL 61615-9617
(309) 676-0998 • (309) 676-7783 (fax)
wppnat@aol.com

WOLF RIDGE ENVIRONMENTAL LEARNING CENTER

Environmental Education • Minnesota • 3–9 Months
www.wolf-ridge.org

WOLF RIDGE ENVIRONMENTAL Learning Center is an accredited residential school that provides people of all ages (from school groups to Elderhostel participants!) with the opportunity to develop their understanding and appreciation of the environment and their responsibility for stewardship of the earth. Seasonal employment opportunities abound at Wolf Ridge. During the summer months, naturalists and instructors teach ten to fourteen classes per week, with topics that cover ecology, cultural history, and adventure education. Benefits include a stipend of $250 per week, meals, and staff lodging with a private bedroom. Applicants must be at least twenty-one and have certificates in first aid, CPR, and lifeguarding. Get your applications in early as the deadline generally falls toward the end of January.

Beyond the summer months, Wolf Ridge offers a post-baccalaureate certificate in environmental education (teaming up with the University of Minnesota in Duluth). This is an intense training program combined with an academic year of graduate study, designed for people interested in entering the naturalist field. Learning comes through direct experience, ongoing evaluations, seminars, workshops and field trips, and university classes. Participants receive a private room, partial board, a tuition scholarship paid directly to the University of Minnesota, a certificate in environmental education, special consultant weekends at cost, and occasional pro deals on equipment. (Note that this program is highly competitive, so communicate well about yourself and your experiences through the application.) This position demands a person who truly enjoys being with people, especially children, and is a hard worker with community focus. Applications are accepted through March 31, and more information on all the opportunities can be found online.

For More Information:
Naturalist Training and Summer Programs
Wolf Ridge Environmental Learning Center
6282 Cranberry Rd.
Finland, MN 55603-9700
(800) 523-2733 • (218) 353-7414 • (218) 353-7762 (fax)
mail@wolf-ridge.org

WOODS HOLE SEA SEMESTER

Marine Science • Worldwide • 8–12 Weeks
www.sea.edu

THE WORLD'S OCEANS cover upwards of 70 percent of the planet, but our understanding of the ocean as a physical system and as a vital element in human culture and history is still in its infancy. The mission of Sea Education Association is to give students the practical and theoretical experience necessary to contribute to our understanding of the ocean environment.

What You'll Be Doing: This is a uniquely challenging program. SEA Semester students spend six weeks at the Woods Hole campus (the world capital of ocean science) receiving intensive classroom instruction in oceanography, nautical science, and maritime studies. Each student works closely with the oceanography faculty to design a research project, using the resources of the nearby Marine Biological Laboratory. Upon successful completion of course work on shore, each student takes a berth as a crew member on one of SEA's two research vessels—120-foot blue-water "tall ships." Each vessel will then undertake its unique scientific mission during the second six weeks, to places as far as the shores of Venezuela. On board, students become active members of the ship's crew and conduct oceanographic research and gather data for research projects.

Commitment: The semester program runs twelve weeks, five times per year. An eight-week summer class begins in early June.

Perks and Rewards: The cost of SEA Semester is about the same as a semester at a private university—approximately $17,000 ($12,000 for the summer course). Financial aid is available. Housing is provided on shore; room and board are provided at sea. Students typically earn seventeen academic credits from Boston University, as well as 102 "sea days" toward the 180 days required to sit for a U.S. Coast Guard Able-Bodied Seaman's license.

The Essentials: Previous sailing or marine science experience is not required. SEA Semester stresses problem solving, critical thinking, and teamwork. College-bound students seeking a rigorous academic experience prior to starting college, and college graduates seeking some practical experience before grad school or job hunting are welcome.

Your First Move: Call or email for materials and program video. Application materials are also available through their website. Enrollment is limited to forty-nine spaces in each class. It's best to apply early.

For More Information:
Brian Hopewell, Dean of Enrollment
Woods Hole SEA Semester
Sea Education Association
171 Woods Hole Rd., P.O. Box 6
Woods Hole, MA 02543
(800) 552-3633 • (508) 540-3954 • (508) 457-4673 (fax)
admission@sea.edu

When you work, you fulfill a part of earth's fondest dream assigned to you when that dream is born. —KAHLIL GIBRAN

YMCA CAMP WIDJIWAGAN

Adventure Education • Minnesota • 3–9 Months
www.widji.org

LOCATED AT THE edge of the Boundary Waters Canoe Area Wilderness, Widgiwagan is a place of beauty, solitude, and peace. Instructors use the boreal forest as their classroom to engage students in hands-on learning about the environment, outdoor skills, and teamwork. Residential programs are offered throughout the year, and focus on wilderness adventure trips for twelve- to eighteen-year-olds and hands-on environmental education experiences for school groups.

What You'll Be Doing: Each year Widjiwagan hires over eighty summer trail staff and up to fifteen environmental education instructors during the school year. Summer wilderness trail counselors primarily lead canoe and backpack trips ranging in length from five to twelve nights, while support staff (including trail-building coordinators, office staff, cooks, and maintenance assistants) are the "grease" of the in-camp programs. Instructor naturalists have the opportunity to work with small groups and exercise their own creative style in developing a range of lesson plans. Responsibilities might include leading a variety of instructional hikes, leading team building exercises, or chaperoning a student cabin at night. Finally, interns in the wilderness or environmental education program receive extensive training in all aspects of the program while developing their abilities in natural history programming, wilderness skills, and youth leadership.

Perks and Rewards: Wilderness trail staff wages range from $1,500 to $1,900 per summer; instructors, $650 to $700 per month; and interns receive a stipend. All staff receive room and board as well as expert staff training in leadership, teaching and outdoor skills, and wilderness medicine.

The Essentials: Applicants must have experience teaching in an outdoor setting, skills in wilderness canoeing and/or backpacking, or training in the natural sciences. Interns must have a desire to develop youth leadership skills, have confidence working in an outdoor setting, and be pursuing (or have) a degree in an environmental field. Current certification in CPR and first aid is required (lifeguarding and Widerness First Responder may also be needed).

Your First Move: Application requests should be done through the mail. For specific questions on the summer program, contact Tracy Whitcher at (651) 645-6605; for the environmental education program, contact Karen Pick at (218) 365-2117. Inquire early as staff are hired on a rolling application basis.

For More Information:
Environmental Education Program Director
YMCA Camp Widjiwagan
2233 Energy Park Dr.
St. Paul, MN 55108-1533
(651) 645-6605 • (612) 646-5521 (fax)
widji@spacestar.net

RECOMMENDED RESOURCES. . . . .

Do you have a green thumb? Membership in the **American Association of Botanical Gardens and Arboreta** (www.aabga.org) is one way to further your career goals and keep you in touch with what's happening at public gardens throughout the U.S. and Canada. Their annual internship directory, available for $10, lists more than one hundred summer jobs and internships in fields including horticulture, conservation, education, collections, children's programs, historic garden restoration, horticultural therapy, and zoo horticulture programs. For more information contact the American Association of Botanical Gardens and Arboreta, 351 Longwood Rd., Kennett Square, PA 19348; (610) 925-2500, resources@aabga.org.

If you are a birding enthusiast looking for an interesting life experience or a new way to spend your vacation, explore the possibilities with the **American Birding Association**. Each January, they publish *Opportunities for Birders,* listing more than 650 volunteer projects for birders in the U.S., Canada, and an ever increasing list in other countries. Short- and long-term opportunities are available, and some offer a stipend. A copy of the directory is sent to each ABA member in February (membership is $20 for students; $40 for individuals); listings can also be viewed through www.americanbirding. org/opps/voldintr.htm, which is updated regularly. For more information contact Dr. Paul Green, Executive Director, American Birding Association, P.O. Box 6599, Colorado Springs, CO 80934-6599; (800) 850-2473, paulgrn@aba.org.

Whether you want to intern at a drive-through safari zoo, a freshwater aquarium, or a three-thousand-acre wildlife center, the **American Zoo and Aquarium Association** has hundreds of opportunities to explore at www.aza.org/joblistings.

The Massachusetts Audubon Society
(www.massaudubon.org) provides an online directory of seasonal employment, internship, and volunteer opportunities at Audubon sanctuaries throughout the state—from Cape Cod to the Berkshires. Typical assignments range from environmental education and naturalist internships to camp counselors and shorebird nesting monitors. More information can also be found through their job hotline at (781) 259-9506.

Do you need to make vital contacts with influential nature lovers? **The National Wildlife Federation (NWF),** the nation's largest member-supported conservation education and advocacy organization, offers an internship program for college graduates with an interest and knowledge in environmental issues. Each intern is given a responsible role and becomes an essential part of NWF's conservation and education efforts. Typical assignments are programs with animal tracks, backyard wildlife habitats, conservation summits, campus ecology, population and environment, and schoolyard habitats, as well as in the communications, legal, outdoor education, publications, or public lands divisions. The internship length varies from a summer on up to a year, with stipends ranging from $300 to $350 per week. Opportunities are available at their national headquarters in Virginia and at offices all over the U.S., with destinations as far as Anchorage, Alaska! Internships are posted online and removed once filled—thus, it's to your advantage to keep an eye on their website. Applications are available as a PDF download and resumes are accepted only for posted positions. Due to the large size of the organization, don't expect any correspondence from the NWF unless they're interested in you. For more information contact the National Wildlife Federation, 11100 Wildlife Center Dr., Reston, VA 20190-5362; (703) 790-4545, internopp@nwf.org, www.nwf.org/careergateway.

Whether you want to work in the U.S. or abroad, **Environmental Career Opportunities** (www.ecojobs.com) lists current jobs in conservation, environmental policy, science and engineering, and education. A sampler of current listings is provided online; however, ECO's biweekly newsletter provides over five hundred job opportunities for a fee. A four-month subscription (with an online or newspaper format option) runs $49. (Shorter and longer subscriptions are available.) For more information contact Betty Brubach, Publisher, Environmental Career Opportunities, P.O. Box 678, Stanardsville, VA 22973; (800) 315-9777, betty@ecojobs.com.

The Job Seeker is a biweekly newsletter that provides extensive listings of environmental and natural resource work opportunities—from internships to career-track jobs—throughout the U.S. The newsletter is a perfect complement to your job search, and can be received

RESOURCES

TREES

I think that I shall never see
A poem lovely as a tree.

A tree whose hungry mouth
    is pressed
Against the Earth's sweet
    flowing breast;

A tree that looks at God all day,
And lifts her leafy arms to pray.

A tree that may in Summer wear
A nest of robins in her hair;

Upon whose bosom snow has lain;
Who intimately lives with rain.

Poems are made by fools like me,
But only God can make a tree.

—JOYCE KILMER

either through regular mail or email. Email subscriptions are available for three months ($19.50), six months ($36), or one year ($60), or you may want to invest in the *Summer Jobs Special,* which costs $10 for nine issues during the months of December through April (subscriptions through the regular mail are a little higher in price). For more information contact the Job Seeker, 24313 Destiny Ave., Tomah, WI 54660; (608) 378-4450, www.thejobseeker.net.

NUANAARPUQ

How often do you find yourself taking extravagant pleasure in being alive? As we hike over the crest of a snowy ridge in the heart of the vast wilderness, the world seemingly unfolds in front of us. At once, we can embrace endless miles of ridges, peaks, and valleys. An inner joy bubbles up within each of us. Overtaken with the beauty of the moment, one of us spontaneously shouts out, "Nuanaarpuq!"

Is it possible to express the feelings of such special moments in words? We used to be skeptical, feeling that the joy of the moment alone would suffice. That was until we learned the Alaskan Inuit expression "Nuanaarpuq." Those who live by this expression live with a deep respect for the natural world and have learned to appreciate and celebrate all the wonders of nature. It is expressed with both reverence and pleasure.

Are you aware of such moments of extravagant pleasure? Do you share this with others?

Nuanaarpuq is about awareness, about finding and celebrating beauty in the simple things in life. It is the key word for opening up eyes and creating an excitement for life. It is a way to express our celebration of the present moment and for expressing deep joy. Begin making this newfound awareness a daily part of your life and extend your joy to others. After all, excitement for life is contagious.

—CONTRIBUTED BY CHRISTIAN BISSON AND JULIE GABERT, who work as outdoor educators at Hollins College in Virginia during the academic year and teach seasonally for the National Outdoor Leadership School in Wyoming. Through these experiences, they find many moments of Nuanaarpuq!

In a world focused on technology and getting ahead at all costs, it might be time to look at life in a different way and focus on what's really important. This section is about the simple life and living more sustainably. It's for those who want to transform their world into something completely different—learning to become more self-reliant, connecting with the earth, integrating skills from the "good old days" that many of us take for granted, and leading a more balanced and harmonious lifestyle. It is the same spirit referred to by the poet Gary Snyder when he advised, "Find your place on the planet and dig in." This section will give you the tools to do just that.

It is thus with farming; if you do one thing late, you will be late in all your work.

—CATO THE ELDER

Unique Opportunities to Explore in This Section:

- As you dig into the organic farming opportunities in this section, the overviews of Community Supported Agriculture (page 229) and Rudolph Steiner's biodynamic method of farming (page 232) will be helpful in your new journey.

- Are you in search for some food for the soul? The importance of the whole—the balance of the mind, body, and spirit—is essential for anyone who wants to make a personal commitment to self-exploration, growth, and sustainable living. Come indulge in a variety of retreat centers with a holistic twist (page 235) as well as Catharine Sutherland's captivating story of her Hawaiian experience at Kalani Oceanside Retreat, which offers the promise of a new direction, a new adventure, and a new way of life (page 239).

- Is it true that we can live out our dreams by creating our own realities? Find out how Cori Stennett's internship at Hidden Villa unlocked her door of opportunity (page 252).

- Working in exchange for your keep is the basis of Willing Workers on Organic Farms. As a short-term volunteer, you'll help with organic farming, gardening, homesteading, or other environmentally conscious projects, in exchange for room and three wholesome meals. Check out this special section to job-hop all over the world (page 266).

Michaela Farms (page 259) provides interns with the opportunity to experience all aspects of farm life, including a lifestyle that fosters simple and holistic living.

SUSTAINABLE
LIVING AND FARMING

ANANDA MARGA LAKE HUGHES PEACH FARM

Yoga Farm • California • Seasonal
www.amps.org/us/ca/peachfarm

♥ 🏠 🌐

Situated within the Angeles National Forest at an elevation of 3,250 feet, Ananda Marga Lake Hughes Peach Farm is a nonprofit yoga/meditation, ecological, and social-service organization. More than twenty-five hundred peach trees and one hundred cherry trees are intercropped with twenty thousand Japanese and globe eggplants and melons. Interns are welcome year-round and participate in all activities of the farm, which may include transplanting, mulching, weeding, harvesting, packing, marketing, and transport. The hours are flexible, but usually six to eight hours per day, and conditions range from intense to laid-back depending on the time of the year or day of the week. Benefits include a shared room in a large house, vegetarian meals, and a yoga/meditation lifestyle (including free instruction). They also have a good supply of spiritual and farming/gardening reading material. Send a resume and letter including such things as educational background, work experience, farming experience, hobbies and interests, and background in meditation, yoga, or other spiritual disciplines.

For More Information:
Allen Thurm, Director
Ananda Marga Lake Hughes Peach Farm
42310 Lake Hughes Rd.
Lake Hughes, CA 93532
(323) 225-3290 • (661) 724-1161 (farm)
amurtla@igc.org

ANGELIC ORGANICS

Organic Farming • Illinois • 3–7 Months
www.angelicorganics.com

💰 🏠 🌐

For those who haven't worked on a farm before, Angelic Organics describes it this way: "It's chaotic, messy, unpredictable, tiring, low-paying, uncomfortable, and unforgiving in ways that probably go beyond your normal understanding of these words (we love what we do, but we want people to know that farm life is not a

Farmer John Peterson of Angelic Organics talks to interns about greenhouse operations during a Collaborative Regional Alliance for Farmer Training field day, a program that brings all farming interns from northern Illinois and southern Wisconsin together for a day of learning and camaraderie.

Photo Credit: Tony Ends

pastoral paradise)." At Angelic Organics, interns will practice the hands-on work of organic and biodynamic farming for their Community Supported Agriculture (CSA) program: everything from planting and harvesting to packing and creating a beautiful presentation for CSA shareholders. The experience begins with a four-day training beginning mid-April, and includes informal discussions, seminars, conferences, and visits to other farms throughout the course of the internship. Benefits include a $300 monthly stipend ($500 for those with at least one year of experience), shared furnished housing and meals, and staples and produce from the garden. Call for their internship booklet, which contains application materials and articles on farming practices. The best time to apply is late fall/early winter and it's highly suggested that you visit the farm for a couple days to a week on a trial basis. International applicants are accepted on a three-month or less basis.

For More Information:
John Peterson, General Manager
Angelic Organics
1547 Rockton Rd.
Caledonia, IL 61011-9572
(815) 389-2746 • (815) 389-3106 (fax)
csa@angelicorganics.com

APROVECHO RESEARCH CENTER

Sustainable Living • Oregon • 10 Weeks
www.efn.org/~apro

APROVECHO, WHICH MEANS "make best use of" in Spanish, is the central theme of the center—to learn how to live together sustainably and ecologically and to help others around the world to do the same. The center is located in the abundant ecosystem of Oregon's Willamette Valley. Culturally rich Eugene is just thirty minutes away.

What You'll Be Doing: Groups of up to fourteen interns join ten resident staff members for an intensive ten-week learning experience. Daily classes and activities teach interns basic principles of sustainable forestry, organic gardening, indigenous skills, and appropriate technology. Classes combine a holistic approach of lecture and discussion formats with practical, hands-on activities. Readings, independent projects, and field trips supplement other course work. Applying newly learned skills, interns will cook with food from the garden, heat and build with wood from the forest, make use of native

WHAT IS COMMUNITY SUPPORTED AGRICULTURE?

Community Supported Agriculture, commonly known as CSA, is an innovative program connecting local consumers with a local farmer for fresh and sustainably produced food. With its roots reaching back some forty years ago in Japan, the CSA concept soon traveled throughout Europe and was formally introduced in the U.S. in 1985 at a farm in Massachusetts.

One has to wonder why the CSA movement didn't start sooner than it did. Just turn to your parents or grandparents to uncover these answers. You'll find that most families lived more sustainably in years past—growing their own vegetables or raising chickens as a way of putting food on the table. But as supermarkets emerged as an easy way of getting these staples, the small family gardens of the U.S. soon diminished. Today you only have to bite into a tasteless tomato purchased from a supermarket to understand why there's nothing like indulging in the sweet taste of a locally grown one.

With over one thousand CSA farms in the U.S. alone, CSA shareholders make a commitment to support the farm throughout the season, while also assuming the costs, risks, and bounty of the harvest along with the farmer. In this way, farmers and members become partners in the production, distribution, and consumption of locally grown food.
A season's share generally amounts to about $50 per month, and in return, a weekly bag of fresh vegetables, herbs, fruits, milk, eggs, meat, flowers, and/or crafts is provided, depending on the season. Many farms also include newsletters filled with recipes and unique activities and events at the farm. *This community-spirited CSA concept forms the framework for most internships and apprenticeships at farms in this section.*

plant species for food, medicine, and crafts, and utilize resource-conserving technologies to build a solar oven.

Commitment: Internships span ten weeks, beginning in early March, June, and September. Classes typically run from 8 A.M. to 5 P.M., Monday through Friday. Weekends are open so interns can take advantage of Oregon's beautiful coastline, mountain ranges, and lakes and rivers.

Perks and Rewards: The sliding scale tuition of $1,800 to $2,500 covers room, board, and instruction for the term. Interns generally need only a small amount of spending money, as most necessities are provided on-site. All interns live in an eco-friendly, straw-bale dormitory.

The Essentials: Acceptance into the program is based on enthusiasm, a sincere interest in the subjects of study, and a willingness to join in a cooperative learning experience. Participants come from varied backgrounds and have ranged in age from seventeen to sixty-four. Interns who want to learn how to live in ways that are more ecologically and socially sustainable and to acquire specific practical and intellectual skills that will aid them on this path will thrive in this program.

Your First Move: Call for a brochure and application. Internships are offered on a space-available basis to qualified applicants.

For More Information:
Internship Coordinator
Aprovecho Research Center
80574 Hazelton Rd.
Cottage Grove, OR 97424
(541) 942-8198
apro@efn.org

ARCOSANTI

Sustainable Living • Arizona • 5 Weeks+
www.arcosanti.org

BACK IN THE early 1970s, an experimental town called Arcosanti emerged in the high desert of Arizona. Built as a model for how the world might build its cities in an energy-efficient way, Arcosanti intends to house seven thousand people living and working together. Designed with the concept of arcology (the synthesis of architecture and ecology), Arcosanti hopes to demonstrate ways to improve urban conditions, prevent the spread of suburban sprawl, and lessen our destructive impact on the earth while simultaneously allowing interactions with the surrounding natural environment.

What You'll Be Doing: Arcosanti's five-week workshop introduces participants to building techniques and an intensive look at Paolo Soleri's concept of arcology by incorporating independent, creative thinking and a "learn by doing" approach. The first week is dedicated to seminar topics ranging from exposure to drawings and plans and a surveying class to site tours and discussions with Paolo Soleri. The rest of the time is spent working on projects, participating in cultural events, and taking a field trip to Phoenix to see sites of architectural interest. Completion of the Arcosanti workshop qualifies individuals to be considered for a three-month internship. Positions are available in permaculture/organic gardening, ceramics (creating windbells and planters that fund the Arcosanti project), construction, landscaping, planning and drafting, and woodworking.

Perks and Rewards: The five-week program fee is $950. (The first-week seminar runs $450.) The fee covers tuition, room and board, and use of the site facilities. Workshop participants generally stay in a camp that is equipped with electricity, toilets, showers, and simple living shelters. Interns only pay for meals and a weekly co-use fee.

The Essentials: Although there is a need for skilled workers, most participants are novices. Individuals must be at least eighteen years of age (or be accompanied by a parent).

Your First Move: Call for application materials. A nonrefundable registration fee of $50 is required with the application, which is applied to the workshop fee total.

While driving through Arizona, plan on a side trip to Arcosanti, an experimental town in the high desert, just seventy miles north of Phoenix. Learn about Paolo Soleri's concept of arcology (the synthesis of architecture and ecology), tour the grounds, or purchase one of the world-famous Soleri Bells. Concerts and other events in the Colly Soleri Music Center also allow visitors to experience Arcosanti. Shows include dinner and are often followed by a light show on the opposite mesa. Limited overnight guest accommodations are available by reservation. The simple guest rooms, beginning at $20 a night, provide "no frills" accommodations. The Sky Suite, at $75 a night, includes a kitchenette and a panoramic view of this beautiful valley.

For More Information:
Wes Ozier, Workshop Coordinator
Arcosanti
HC 74, Box 4136
Mayer, AZ 86333
(520) 632-7135 • (520) 632-6229 (fax)
workshop@arcosanti.org

ARCTIC ORGANICS

Organic Farming • Alaska • 6 Months
www.arcticorganics.com

ARCTIC ORGANICS, A twenty-acre farm set at the base of the Chugach Mountains in Alaska, focuses on intensive organic-vegetable production. Interns interested in small-scale organic farming are needed from mid-January through mid-September, with benefits including a stipend of $200 per month, along with bunkhouse living and kitchen privileges. (Meals are not included.)

For More Information:
River and Sarah Bean, Owners
Arctic Organics
HC04, Box 9043
Palmer, AK 99645
(907) 746-1087
beans@alaska.com

ATLANTIS YOUTH EXCHANGE

Farming/Au Pair • Norway • 2 Months–2 Years
www.atlantis-u.no

ENJOY A FEW months living with a Norwegian host family on a farm or up to two years as an au pair, in the beautiful countryside of high mountains, deep fjords, and the midnight sun. Sponsored by Atlantis Youth Exchange, the working guest and au pair programs are a great way to get to know the Norwegian people, culture, customs, and lifestyle from the inside, rather than as an ordinary tourist.

What You'll Be Doing: Working guests take part in the daily life on the farm, both in work and in leisure, as a member of the host family and the local community. During working hours participants are expected to help in the agricultural work on the farm, which might include haymaking, weeding, milking, picking berries and vegetables, painting, or light housework. As an au pair, participants will live as a member of the family, look after the children, and help with household duties, along with attending Norwegian classes for free.

Commitment: Most families invite working guests for two- or three-month stays (which are offered throughout the year) for up to thirty-five hours per week. The minimum stay as an au pair is six months (thirty hours per week), with a maximum stay of two years. The majority of families prefer to have an au pair for nine to twelve months.

Perks and Rewards: A minimum wage of 800 Norwegian kroner (NOK) per week (which equals about $90 in U.S. dollars) is provided, along with a private room and meals with the family. Au pair participants receive a minimum of 2,800NOK per month, plus a travel card, and are entitled to one week of vacation after six months of work. Each applicant is responsible for obtaining a work permit and travel arrangements to Oslo.

The Essentials: Applicants must be between eighteen and thirty years old and have the ability to communicate in English. Successful applicants are open-minded and able to adapt to the host family's way of life. Life will often be quite different from what most participants are accustomed to at home.

Your First Move: Applications, along with a fee of 2,500NOK (about $280US), are due at least three to four months ahead of your preferred arrival date (which is generally plenty of time to obtain a visa). Applicants should provide a positive, honest, and smiling impression in their application.

For More Information:
Inbound Manager
Atlantis Youth Exchange
Kirkegata 32
N-0655 Oslo, Norway
(011) 47 2247 7170 • (011) 47 2247 7179 (fax)
post@atlantis-u.no

BENEFICIAL FARM

Biodynamic Farming • New Mexico •
1 Week–9 Months

AS AN OFF-THE-GRID homestead in the piñon-juniper wilderness at seven thousand feet (near Santa Fe), Beneficial Farm uses biodynamic preparations and the Stella Natura calendar for growing vegetables, herbs, and flowers as well as raising seven hundred hens. A variety of short-term employment opportunities are available: apprentices work anywhere from three to nine months; working visitors have three-week to three-month stays;

BIODYNAMIC FARMING AND RUDOLPH STEINER

When you begin your journey with biodynamic farming, you don't get very far into it before you are confronted with the philosophies from the forefather of the movement—Rudolf Steiner. Based on a series of lectures given by Dr. Steiner, the biodynamic concept centers around an organic method of agriculture that actively works with the health-giving forces of nature and the cosmic rhythms of the Stella Natura calendar. In essence, this means growing food with a strong connection to a healthy, living soil, and recognizing the basic principles at work in nature as well as those "from above."

Obviously the biodynamic concept has a jargon of its own, and, perhaps, is best learned experientially from a farmer practicing these methods. (You'll find plenty of opportunities in this section!) A good introduction to these philosophies can also be found in the book, *Gardening for Health and Nutrition: An Introduction to the Method of Biodynamic Gardening* by John and Helen Philbrick (Anthroposophic Press, $9.95).

In the seed we have an image of the whole universe. Each single time a seed is formed, the earthly organizing process is led to its end, to the point of chaos. And each time, within the seed-chaos, a new organism is built up out of the whole universe.

—RUDOLF STEINER

and working guests can come to the farm for five days to three weeks. Rustic housing, common meals, and weekly classes and activities are provided. Apprentices also receive a modest stipend, while working guests are encouraged to make a donation for their farm experience. Santa Fe has a Waldorf School, an anthroposophical members group, and an active farmers' market. Call for more information.

For More Information:
Steve Warshawer, Working Visitor Program
Beneficial Farm
286 Arroyo Salado
Santa Fe, NM 87505
(505) 422-2238

BROOKFIELD FARM

Biodynamic Farming • Massachusetts • 8 Months
www.brookfieldfarm.org

As a LIVING-LEARNING center dedicated to promoting the development of healthy agriculture, Brookfield Farm is a 120-acre biodynamic farm which raises produce and meat for over four hundred CSA subscribers. Seasonal festivals, social events, and educational opportunities for children and adults provide a unique opportunity to create a community of people connected to each other through their connection to the earth. In 1986, Brookfield Farm was one of only three CSA farms in the U.S. Now there are over one thousand CSAs breathing new life into American farming.

What You'll Be Doing: If you are looking for an apprentice program that will teach you how to manage a mixed organic/biodynamic farm, not just how to "go out and hoe," Brookfield is the place for you. During the course of the full season, apprentices work in all aspects of the farm's production, from soil preparation to harvest, tractors to hand hoes, and administration to marketing farm products. In addition, all apprentices may take part in the Collaborative Regional Alliance for Farmer Training (CRAFT) program, which offers visits to a wide variety of organic and biodynamic farms in the Northeast for in-depth tours.

Commitment: The program begins April 1 and concludes the day before Thanksgiving (no partial-season apprenticeships are possible). The work schedule is Monday through Friday, 6 A.M. to 5 P.M. (with one-hour breaks for breakfast and lunch) and Saturdays until noon.

Perks and Rewards: A stipend of $500 per month, housing with a private room (with shared kitchen, living room, and bathroom), farm produce (vegetables, fruits, flowers, and herbs), weekday lunches at the farmhouse, and full health insurance are provided. Apprentices can also purchase Brookfield Farm meat for half price and take up to fifty pounds of produce per year as gifts for family and friends.

The Essentials: Anyone with a serious interest in agriculture and the physical ability to work the long hours of a farming schedule will be considered—from inexperienced city folks looking to explore agriculture as a career option to experienced farmers looking for a new approach to agriculture.

Your First Move: To start the application process, send a letter of intent and resume. All interested applicants are encouraged to set up a time to visit and work on the farm. All hiring decisions will be made on a first-come, first-served basis.

For More Information:
Dan Kaplan, Apprenticeship Program
Brookfield Farm
24 Hulst Rd.
Amherst, MA 01002
(413) 253-7991
info@brookfieldfarm.org

COLD POND COMMUNITY FARM

Horse-Powered Farm • New Hampshire • 1 Year

COLD POND COMMUNITY FARM, a biodynamic, horse-powered farm in the hills of New Hampshire, offers a yearlong apprenticeship for singles or couples. A small rustic cabin, a share of all produce, and a stipend are provided in exchange for labor in the fields and woodlot four days a week . Activities include working with a CSA and market garden, maple syrup, honey bees, food preservation, orchard and berries, dairy cows, poultry, logging, woodshop, and pottery. Apprentices are involved in the year-round cycle of activities that the farm community depends on for their own food and the income to meet expenses, with work that is highly dependent on the seasons and the weather. The emphasis is on producing high-quality food and crafts for themselves and for their shareholders, and on developing an ecologically sustain-able small farm that will continue to be productive in years to come. The farm is specifically looking for motivated and energetic individuals interested in learning the skills needed to work on sustainable farms and in farming in the future.

For More Information:
Steve Davis, Owner
Cold Pond Community Farm
Apprentice Program
P.O. Box 95, Cold Pond Rd.
Acworth, NH 03601
(603) 835-2403
cpclt1@email.com

COMMON GROUND ORGANIC FARM

Farming • Pennsylvania • Seasonal
www.commongroundfarm.com

COMMON GROUND IS a sixty-acre diversified organic farm in the Appalachian Mountains of central Pennsylvania. Along with vegetable production, the farm raises lamb, chicken, and eggs for a fifty-member CSA and two local farmers' markets. Each year three to six apprentices have the opportunity to gain experience on what it takes to create a successful organic-farming system. Interns work with the farmer and farm manager, performing a variety of tasks that are always determined by the season and weather (from livestock care and vegetable harvesting to selling produce and farm tours). Along with a $100-per-month stipend, housing (in a cabin, camper, or farmhouse) and meals are provided. Educational activities include field trips to other farms, conferences, seminars, and workshops (whenever possible). Send a resume and letter of intent by mail or email anytime during the year.

For More Information:
Leslie Zuck, Apprenticeship Program
Common Ground Organic Farm
176 Zuck Rd.
Spring Mills, PA 16875
(814) 364-9171 • (814) 364-2330 (fax)
commongro@aol.com

The reason a lot of people do not recognize opportunity is because it usually goes around wearing overalls looking like hard work. —THOMAS EDISON

EAST WIND COMMUNITY

Community Living • Missouri • 3 Weeks+
www.eastwind.org

You'll FIND A unique group of people in the beautiful Ozarks of southern Missouri. It's called East Wind—a community of seventy-five members (as of printing) that have left mainstream America to form a place where all can live together in a diverse, nonexploitive, nonviolent, democratic, and ecologically responsible way. Utopia it is not, but those that come to stay will find that the diversity here is the greatest attribute as is the community itself—the "glue" of East Wind. Along with three acres of organic vegetables, herbs, berries, and orchards (as well as a dairy, beef cattle, pigs, and chickens on the ranch), East Wind has three very successful businesses, including East Wind Nutbutters, Twin Oaks Hammocks, and Utopian Rope Sandals.

What You'll Be Doing: Work—and there's plenty of it. The members work hard, but they keep the work week short by working smart and sharing resources. In addition to work in one of the many agriculture areas, one may also work in forestry, carpentry, cooking, child care, cleaning, auto maintenance, accounting, or in one of the community's three businesses (which is preferred by many). Everyone chips in with various chores—from cooking to child care—throughout the week.

Perks and Rewards: Membership includes a private room, meals (as a community of vegans, vegetarians, mellow omnivores, and avid meat-eaters, food for all types is provided at meals), co-op membership, a stipend of $90 per month (with the option of earning more by working extra hours in the businesses), and medical benefits after six months. One of the biggest perks is the region and community itself. Whatever your tastes, they're bound to have it—canoeing and camping supplies, a swimming hole and sweat lodge, an extensive library (touted the largest in the Ozarks), a pottery studio, a metal shop, a music practice space, and a lifestyle that promotes being very social if you choose.

The Essentials: The reasons that people have come to East Wind are vastly different—some for security, some for adventure, some for idealism, some for escapism, some for the simple lifestyle, some for the complex human interactions, some to build and join an extended family. Whatever your reason, living in community—in the purest sense of the term—is reason enough.

Your First Move: To be considered for membership, a three-week stay during a visitor period is necessary (so you'll get a good feel for East Wind). There's a visitor fee of $5 per day, but this can be waived for folks for whom this is a hardship. Short-term visits are fine, but they need to be arranged at least a few days in advance. Call, write, or email (the easiest) to obtain more information, including the dates for the next visitor period.

For More Information:
Visitor Manager
East Wind Community
HC-3 Box 3370
Tecumseh, MO 65760
(417) 679-4682 • (417) 679-4684 (fax)
visit@eastwind.org

FOOD FOR THE SOUL:
Retreat Centers with a Holistic Twist

The journey to wholeness requires that you look honestly, openly, and with courage into yourself, into the dynamics that lie behind what you feel, what you perceive, what you value, and how you act. It is a journey through your defenses and beyond, so that you can experience consciously the nature of your personality, face what it has produced in your life, and choose to change that. Words lead to deeds. They prepare the soul, make it ready, and move it to tenderness.

—GARY ZUKOV

Photo Credit: Aaron Mitchell

Meditation—aerobic conditioning for the mind

In the silence of meditation, the soulful songs of Sufi dance, the vitality and healthful benefits of yoga, the study of ancient disciplines of the East, or the healing techniques of Gestalt therapy, holistic retreat centers are providing something that's missing in so many people's lives—food for the soul. From eco-villages and monasteries to yoga institutes and Zen centers, this special section offers unique opportunities for hard work, personal growth, reflection and rejuvenation, spiritual exploration, and community building. The work component at each center is generally basic and rudimentary (from working in the gardens to housekeeping); however, the real draw is participation in a collection of stimulating classes and workshops, connecting with inspiring and supportive people, and indulging in fresh, organic meals. With a one-month commitment for most programs, this may be the hiatus you need to reawaken your soul.

The whole soul is composed into a kind of real harmony the instant one sets oneself to work. —THOMAS CARLYLE

FOOD FOR THE SOUL

MEDITATION BASICS

1. Pick a focus word or short phrase that's firmly rooted in your belief system.

2. Sit quietly in a comfortable position.

3. Close your eyes.

4. Relax your muscles.

5. Breathe slowly and naturally, and as you do, repeat your focus word, phrase, or prayer silently to yourself as you exhale.

6. Assume a passive attitude. Don't worry about how well you're doing. When other thoughts come to mind, simply say to yourself, "Oh, well," and gently return to the repetition.

7. Continue for ten to twenty minutes.

8. Do not stand immediately. Continue sitting quietly for a minute or so, allowing other thoughts to return. Then open your eyes and sit for another minute before rising.

9. Practice this technique once or twice daily.

—From the book *Timeless Healing: The Power and Biology of Belief,* by Herbert Benson, M.D., with Marg Stark (Fireside, $14)

ESALEN INSTITUTE

Holistic Education • California • 1–2 Months
www.esalen.org

FOUNDED IN THE early 1960s, the world's first alternative education/holistic center has flourished, continually pushing the envelope of human potential. Once home to a Native American tribe known as the Esselen, Esalen is situated on twenty-seven acres along the spectacular Big Sur coastline. Many first-timers to the center opt for the "Experiencing Esalen" workshops, which provide an introduction to holistic practices, such as Gestalt therapy, massage, sensory awareness, creative arts, and meditation. For those interested in a more intense and complete involvement in the center, Esalen offers a twenty-eight-day work-study program. Participants work thirty-two hours per week in one of Esalen's departments—kitchen, housekeeping, garden/farm, maintenance, or grounds—along with staff and long-term students. During most

evenings and one weekend intensive, students are together in one of two groups exploring different practices and approaches available at the center, with assigned leaders who are with the group throughout the month. The fee of $795 also covers shared housing and healthful food. In addition, a more rigorous two-month work-study program is offered twice a year for a fee of $1,740. Applications and specific details about each session can be found online.

For More Information:
Patrice Hamilton, Work Study Coordinator
Esalen Institute
Highway 1
Big Sur, CA 93920-9616
(831) 667-3010 • (831) 667-2724 (fax)
workstudy@esalen.org

HOLLYHOCK

Holistic Education • Canada • 4–6 Weeks
www.hollyhock.ca

LOCATED ON AN island north of Vancouver, British Columbia, Hollyhock offers a hodgepodge of workshops, one-month intensive programs, meditation retreats, and kayak and wilderness adventures—ranging from a writer's retreat and Esalen massage training to the alchemy of relationships and yoga teacher training. Those who wish to receive discounted room and board can participate in their work/study program, which combines a structured learning component with service over a four-to six-week period. Each weekday, participants spend half the day on study, instruction, and practice; the other half of the day is then focused on service work, mostly on outdoor projects. Programs begin in early May, June, and September, with fees that range from $1,238 to $1,795. Application deadlines generally fall one month prior to the start date; however, an early application is advised. Call or email for application materials.

For More Information:
Work-Study Program Coordinator
Hollyhock
Box 127, Manson's Landing
Cortes Island, BC V0P 1K0
Canada
(800) 933-6339 • (250) 935-6576 • (250) 935-6424 (fax)
registration@hollyhock.ca

THE PROMISE OF A NEW DIRECTION, A NEW ADVENTURE, AND A NEW WAY OF LIFE

When I arrived at Kalani Oceanside Retreat on the Big Island of Hawaii one warm, rainy November afternoon, I thought my story would be startlingly unique. I mean, how many people in the world quit their jobs, pack their lives into storage units, and fly to Hawaii to spend their days peeling carrots at a tiny resort tucked into a tropical jungle—with no idea of what they'll do next, or even where they'll live when three months are up? At age twenty-five, I'd recently quit my job as an assistant editor at a successful publishing house to test the waters of freelance writing. After six months, I was ready to kiss my keyboard good-bye, leave the mountains for the sea, and get my fingernails dirty. "Why was I working? What, other than paying the light bill, was I accomplishing?" I thought, frustrated. I sought a life with meaning and direction, and I had no qualms about leaving job and home security to find it.

Much to my surprise, neither did anyone else at Kalani! My first evening dining on the lanai, or outdoor patio, I quickly discovered that I was surrounded by fellow work-scholars who had come to Kalani for exactly the same reasons I had: to escape the push-button, digitized, ATM-everything, mile-a-minute lifestyle that has become so rampant in the world and the computer-keyboard-phone-desk-chair routine of daily office existence; to find a place where nature's sweet and soothing song could be savored one fragrant pau-kini-kini blossom at a time; and, most of all, to become quiet enough to hear our inner voices speak, and to slow down enough to listen to them. For many of us, Kalani held the promise of a new direction, a new adventure, and a new way of life.

Kalani's work-scholar volunteer program, as it turned out, was a magnet for individuals in life transition—as well as those who simply desired a sabbatical from fulfilling careers or a three-month vacation in the sun. From burnt-out New York City "dot-commers" to carefree Kansas retirees, the staff I grew to know and love was home to all kinds. We'd found our way there through friends who had visited, Internet searches, and, in my case, this guidebook! I worked in the kitchen, putting my interest in culinary school to the test. Slicing pineapples and bananas as the sun rose over coconut palms and doing dishes by candlelight when the generator shut down was unlike any other restaurant experience I'd had. I also helped on the waitstaff, coaxing tiny geckos away from the sugar bowl and serving bountiful plates of whole-food meals to delighted guests hungry after a day of yoga or snorkeling. Other volunteers toted their weight in sheets and towels on the housekeeping crew or built new A-frame huts as grounds maintenance staff.

When I wasn't working, I walked or rode a staff bike a mile and a half down the Red Road (a two-lane road that retains its familiar name, despite a recent coat of black asphalt) to Kehena Beach, a secluded strip of black sand accessible only by descending a winding, stairstep path along the black lava cliffs. Clothing on the beach was optional and the water sparkled, brilliantly blue and clear. I swam with dolphins in the small bay twice during the winter months, and once, pedaling home, a friend and I stopped and stared, awestruck, at a humpback whale a short distance offshore. She was slapping her huge tail against the water over and over, as if in a greeting to us. We hardly breathed until she disappeared beneath the blue water, and even then we looked at each other so full of joy and amazement

FOOD FOR THE SOUL

we couldn't speak; instead, we whooped and sang all the way home.

I spent early mornings, late afternoons, and moonlit nights on the point, a grassy knoll perched above thrashing white foam where the sea crashed into black cliffs. It was the perfect spot to watch the sun rise out of the ocean or to gather for a drum circle after dark. Riding bikes to the tidal pools and thermal baths, we often stopped to pick fresh guava from the lush green foliage on the roadside. The fruits were bright yellow like lemons, with a pink, succulent flesh full of seeds. I trekked across a lava field to see hot, flowing, orange lava, and placed a red leaf in its path—an offering to Pelé, revered goddess of the volcano, who hungrily engulfed and accepted it. Lying in bed in my open-air A-frame hut after such full days, I could hear the waves of the ocean and see banana trees silhouetted in the moonlight.

In the midst of captivating beauty and activity, I learned many new things: the basics of Zen Buddhist meditation, Reiki healing techniques, the songs of Sufi dancing. Yet the most important thing I brought home from Kalani was a strong certainty about something I already suspected: that the universe operates perfectly, and that by trusting my inner guidance and a higher universal power, I will be guided along the path I am to walk in this lifetime. There is no need to worry. I am a wonderfully powerful being, capable of creating my own reality with my thoughts and actions—for better or for worse. The most magical part of my Hawaiian experience was being surrounded by people who embraced this view of the world in everyday life.

I left Kalani in May, two months later than planned, but at exactly the right time. My homeward

Catharine Sutherland outside her open-air A-frame hut at Kalani, just a short walk to the black sands of Kehena Beach.

journey was a complete test of the faith I'd strengthened during my sun- (and rain-) drenched days on the Big Island. I had to have faith; I had no job, no money, and nowhere to call home! I was not disappointed. Thanks to my family, my college degree, and the infallibility of the universe, I followed my path to a job in college public relations and a perfect apartment just blocks from my childhood home in a city I never dreamed I'd return to. It all fell so beautifully into place that I now feel sure of a truth I didn't even realize I was seeking: I'm in the writing business for a reason greater than paying the light bill. And, my curiosity piqued, I plan to stick around and see what it is.

—CONTRIBUTED BY CATHARINE SUTHERLAND, who is enjoying a return to professional life that involves shoes, earrings, and deodorant! In addition to her work as a public information specialist at Greensboro College in North Carolina, Catharine practices yoga daily (and hopes to create a yoga class for children), cohosts a kids' poetry club, happily creates art, and treads softly upon the earth. You can reach Catharine at yippeecat_2000@yahoo.com.

KALANI OCEANSIDE RETREAT

Retreat Center • Hawaii • 1–3 Months
www.kalani.com/volunteer.htm

SURROUNDED BY THERMAL springs, orchid farms, tidal pools, waterfalls, botanical gardens, historic villages, and spectacular Volcanoes National Park, Kalani treats guests to Hawaii's aloha comfort—offering personal retreats that encompass adventure, wellness, natural steam baths, yoga, Hawaiian dance, music, art, and food for the soul.

What You'll Be Doing: Throughout the year, volunteers at Kalani support the day-to-day activities of the center, and provide assistance in maintenance, food service, housekeeping, and gardening. Resident volunteers must commit to a three-month period, volunteering thirty hours per week in an assigned department, while volunteer scholars commit to a one-month period and assist twenty hours per week.

Perks and Rewards: A participation fee of $900 includes organic and locally grown vegetarian meals (with a fish and poultry option at dinner), community living in A-frame structures, a week of free time (for personal relaxation, explorations, or intensive study), and the option of instruction in a Level I Kalani Wellness Practitioner certification. Ongoing activities and instruction include volcano and native plant treks, dolphin swims, snorkeling, hula, Lauhala weaving, massage, Hawaiian mythology and language classes, ecstatic dance; shiatsu, and yoga. Upon arrival at the center, each volunteer is provided with a journal to capture his or her own growth and lessons learned, through writing and artwork—a necessary tool to prepare for life's next adventure.

The Essentials: Strong and self-motivated individuals will thrive at Kalani. Volunteers must provide their own medical insurance to cover their entire stay and proof of a return airline ticket.

Your First Move: Applications can be found online, or call/email for more information.

For More Information:
Resident Volunteer Coordinator
Kalani Oceanside Retreat
R.R. 2, Box 4500, Pahoa–Beach Rd.
Kehena Beach, HI 96778-9724
(800) 800-6886 • (808) 965-7828 • (808) 965-0527 (fax)
volunteer@kalani.com

> If I could have my way about it, I would go back there and remain the rest of my days. It is paradise! If a man is rich, he can live expensively and his grandeur will be respected as in other parts of the earth. If he is poor, he can herd with the natives and live on next to nothing; he can sun himself all day long under the palm trees, and be no more troubled by his conscience than a butterfly would. When you are in that blessed retreat, you are safe from the turmoil of life. The past is a forgotten thing, the present is forever, the future you leave to take care of itself.
>
> —MARK TWAIN, on Hawaii

FOOD FOR THE SOUL

Meditate. Live purely. Be quiet. Do your work with mastery. Like the moon, come out from behind the clouds. Shine! —BUDDHA

FOOD FOR THE SOUL

KRIPALU CENTER FOR YOGA AND HEALTH

Yoga Center • Massachusetts • 1–12 Weeks
www.kripalu.org

LOCATED IN A former Jesuit seminary in the Berkshires of Massachusetts, Kripalu guest programs serve up every possible permutation of yoga—ranging from yoga camp for grown-ups and Thai yoga massage to exploring your life's mission and meditation retreats. A day at Kripalu is filled with workshops, daily yoga, meditation, Dans-Kinetics® classes, relaxing in whirlpools and saunas, and healthful vegetarian food choices—a sanctuary for your body and soul.

What You'll Be Doing: Based on the yogic principle of "seva," or selfless service, Kripalu volunteers serve in "off the mat" karma-yoga programs by sharing their time and energy—a lifestyle that supports the discovery of new ways to express each participant's energy and reveal his or her highest potential. With programs available throughout the year, the most popular is the one- to four-week Seva Program where participants live a balanced spiritual lifestyle while serving forty hours per week alongside the staff. Be prepared to engage in an active vigorous work-

week that may involve chopping vegetables, cleaning bathrooms, or performing basic clerical tasks. Those who desire a more in-depth transformation at all levels (physical, emotional, mental, and spiritual) opt for the intensive, three-month Spiritual Lifestyle Program.

Perks and Rewards: Volunteers receive dorm-style housing (with plenty of private space) and three healthy vegetarian meals per day (with a fresh salad bar and homemade breads). When not serving, volunteers can attend daily classes on yoga and meditation, workshops, evening concerts, and satsangas (spiritual gatherings), and have access to the sauna, whirlpool, and weight room. Some yoga and evening workshops are required.

The Essentials: Although practically every age and professional background is represented in Kripalu programs, volunteers all have a strong personal intention to learn and practice the techniques that bring transformation and inner harmony. Participants must be at least eighteen; a willingness to serve others is essential.

Your First Move: It's strongly recommend that you attend a guest program or two days of rest and renewal before volunteering. The Seva Program runs weekly from Sunday to Sunday; the three-month Spiritual Lifestyle Program is offered each month. It's suggested that you apply at least two to three months prior to your anticipated start date (and at least six months in advance for the Spiritual Lifestyle Program).

For More Information:
Karma Yoga Dept. (Volunteer Programs)
Kripalu Center for Yoga and Health
P.O. Box 793
Lenox, MA 01240-0793
(800) 546-1556 (job hotline) • (413) 448-3123
(413) 448-3384 (fax)
longterm@kripalu.org

Photo Credit: Kripalu Center for Yoga and Health

Along with a day filled with daily yoga, meditation, and healthful vegetarian meals, a volunteer with Kripalu shares her time and energy in an "off the mat" work assignment.

LOSANG DRAGPA BUDDHIST CENTRE

Buddhist Center • United Kingdom • Seasonal
www.losangdragpa.com

LOSANG DRAGPA BUDDHIST CENTRE, located in an unusual and picturesque Victorian castle surrounded by twenty-four acres, is a college and retreat center that is home to thirty-five (and growing) lay and ordained Buddhists of all ages and backgrounds. The center provides a place where people can learn about the Buddhist

Photo Credit: K. Tsewang

Work-exchange participants at Losang Dragpa Buddhist Centre learn about the Buddhist way of life at this unusual and picturesque Victorian castle.

way of life through meditation classes, study programs, and retreats. The activities of the community reflect the Buddhist principle of leading a pure and simple way of life. In exchange for thirty-five hours a week on projects including gardening, decorating, and building, participants receive food, warm and cozy dormitory-style accommodations, and meditation sessions and evening classes.

For More Information:
Working Holiday Program
Losang Dragpa Buddhist Centre
Dobroyd Castle, Pexwood Rd.
Todmorden, West Yorkshire OL14 7JJ
United Kingdom
(011) 44-1706-812247 • (011) 44-1706-818901 (fax)
info@losangdragpa.com

MAHO BAY CAMPS

Sustainable Resort • The Virgin Islands • 1–6 Months
www.maho.org

♥ 🏠 🌍

MAHO BAY RESORTS combine an environmental consciousness and green philosophy—pioneering the latest techniques in sustainable resort development, conservation, recycling, and site restoration, along with close-to-nature experiences and economy. Tent-cottages

and architecture, which are surrounded by Virgin Islands National Park and the turquoise waters and white sandy beaches of the Caribbean, provide plenty of creature comforts without disturbing the creatures that were there before we were. Activities on the premises range from sailing and snorkeling to educational programs and yoga. For those who wish to blend a vacation adventure along with some work, Maho provides a work exchange program. Volunteers contribute four hours per day of work to the Maho community, and in return, receive a low-cost Caribbean vacation, with free lodging and a nonoptional meal plan at $55 per week. No experience is necessary; however, volunteers must be at least eighteen years of age, and stay a minimum of one month during the time frame of May 1 to October 15. Work assignments might include housekeeping, maintenance, food services, store assistance, or guest registration.

For More Information:
Personnel Recruiter
Maho Bay Camps
4-Hour Worker Program
Box 310
Cruz Bay, VI 00831-0310
(800) 392-9004 • (340) 776-6226 • (340) 776-6504 (fax)
mahobay@maho.org

FOOD FOR THE SOUL

OMEGA INSTITUTE FOR HOLISTIC STUDIES

Holistic Learning • New York • 2–7 Months
www.eomega.org

OMEGA INSTITUTE BEGAN in the mid-1970s when holistic health, psychological inquiry, and new forms of spiritual practice were just budding in American culture. Since then, they have become one of the country's largest alternative education and retreat centers, focusing on every imaginable aspect of mind, body, and spirit. More than twelve thousand guests come to Omega each year to participate in workshops and professional-training seminars in diverse areas such as psychology, health, spiritual studies, communication, sports, the arts, the environment, and social action. The Rhinebeck campus is spread over 150 acres of rolling hills, an inviting waterfront, and garden areas in the Hudson Valley (just two hours north of New York City).

What You'll Be Doing: A season at the institute offers a unique opportunity for hard work, personal growth, spiritual exploration, and community building. Each year four hundred staff members (from all ages and backgrounds) join together to work and grow alongside like-minded people. The work itself is basic and rudimentary, with a majority of jobs that focus on maintenance, housekeeping, food service, and luggage handling. There are also a number of jobs in administration, as well as lifeguard and first-aid staff (along with a limited number of supervisory positions). The real draw, however, is participation in a stimulating collection of staff classes taught by respected faculty, with a curriculum designed to support the process of self-discovery within the context of community life. Topics include bodywork, yoga, tai chi, alternative health, psychological studies, performing and visual arts, sports and play, and esoteric studies.

Commitment: Participants must commit to at least one work period (approximately seven weeks) or stay for the entire seven-month season, which begins in April/May and continues through September.

Perks and Rewards: Benefits include a stipend of $50 per week (for full-time work), housing in the dorms or camp, wholesome meals, and use of the facilities.

The Essentials: Whether you are a college student looking to gain work and life skills over the summer, in career transition, or an active retiree who wants to participate in community living and could offer mentoring to younger staff, anyone over the age of eighteen is considered for seasonal opportunities.

Your First Move: Applications are available online (or by fax, phone, or email). It's important that you read the Myths and Realities form (which is online) prior to submitting your application. Hiring starts in early February.

For More Information:
Toni Sinopoli, Staff Recruitment Manager
Omega Institute for Holistic Studies
150 Lake Dr.
Rhinebeck, NY 12572-3212
(845) 266-4444, ext. 304 • (845) 266-8691 (fax)
sdd@eomega.org

THE OPTION INSTITUTE

Happiness Center • Massachusetts • 2 Months
www.option.org

IMAGINE MAKING A conscious commitment to help yourself and others live happier, more successful, and more peaceful lives! The Option Institute offers a two-month residential volunteer program six times each year, where you'll work on various community service projects and at the same time experience a lifestyle that fosters personal happiness. The service component entails support staff work in the areas of food service, housecleaning, office support, and grounds maintenance. You'll also be serving people—oftentimes people who are having incredible difficulties and have come to the institute to reconstruct their lives. In weekly classes, you'll learn tools and ideas that participants have used to profoundly improve the quality of their lives, with the challenge of choosing how you want to be in this world. Volunteers also support the work of the Son-Rise Program, a unique method of working with children with special needs and their families. Room, vegetarian meals, weekly classes, "Option Process" dialogues, and a personal "happiness coach" are the biggest perks, not to mention being located in one of the most beautiful regions of New England—the Berkshires in western Massachusetts.

For More Information:
Christopher Treciokas, Volunteer Program Manager
The Option Institute
2080 S. Undermountain Rd.
Sheffield, MA 01257-9643
(800) 714-2779 • (413) 229-2100 • (413) 229-8931 (fax)
volunteer@option.org

FOOD FOR THE SOUL

We seek enthusiastic, energetic individuals who want to wholeheartedly serve others, and who want to explore the idea of learning through service.

ROCKY MOUNTAIN SHAMBHALA CENTER

Meditation Center • Colorado • 2 Days–6+ Months
www.rmsc.shambhala.org

LOCATED ON SIX hundred acres in northern Colorado, Rocky Mountain Shambhala Center (RMSC) offers hundreds of programs on Buddhist meditation, yoga, and other contemplative disciplines. Tamed by thirty years of use as a contemplative retreat center, RMSC is a place where one of the basic truths of Buddhism—that people can be profoundly open to the wisdom of the present moment—is always readily available. Throughout the year there are many opportunities to join the community as a volunteer or work/study-intensive participant for a weekend, a week, several weeks, or for the entire program. Positions range from helping with setting-up the tent village in the spring to work in the botanic gardens. The schedule follows six hours of work each day (six days a week), daily group meditation, weekly meditation instruction/discussion, and activities ranging from volleyball to movie nights. Room and hearty meals are provided, along with ongoing classes in Buddhism and Shambhala training. Those willing to make a longer-term commitment will receive a stipend. Call or email for more information.

For More Information:
Ann Bodnar, Director of Human Resources
Rocky Mountain Shambhala Center
4921 County Rd. 68C
Red Feather Lakes, CO 80545
(970) 881-2184, ext. 308 • (970) 881-2909 (fax)
hr@rmsc.shambhala.org

TASSAJARA ZEN MIND TEMPLE

Monastery • California • Summer
www.sfzc.com/zmcindex.htm

SET IN THE wilderness of California's Santa Lucia Mountains behind Big Sur, Tassajara Zen Mind Temple is a working Zen Buddhist monastery that invites guests who wish to participate in some Zen practice along with the students and monks who live there. You'll rise with the residents and the sun (around 5:30 A.M.), then join them for a period of zazen meditation, morning service, temple cleaning, and breakfast, followed by three and a half hours of community work then lunch. Afternoons and evenings are free to enjoy hiking, swimming, relaxing at the baths, and simple vegetarian cuisine for dinner. The program also includes an invitation to attend classes, lectures, and community discussions. There is a fee of $50 per person per day (with a minimum stay of three days). From April through September, Tassajara offers a work-practice program, where volunteers get the chance to assist with the maintenance of the facilities and follow the daily resident schedule of meditation and work. A minimum commitment of five days is required and applicants must be at least eighteen years of age. A $70 fee covers room and board, as well as lectures and classes on Buddhism. For those planning on staying at least five months, a small stipend is available.

For More Information:
Guest Practice Program Coordinator
Tassajara Zen Mind Temple
39171 Tassajara Rd.
Carmel Valley, CA 93924
(415) 865-1899
tassrez@sfzc.org

TREE OF LIFE REJUVENATION CENTER

Retreat Center • Arizona • Seasonal
www.treeoflife.nu

USING THE METAPHOR of the "Tree of Life"—working with all the forces in our lives such as air, earth, sun, water, love, wisdom, joy, peace, right livelihood, and the Divine Presence—is at the heart of this eco-retreat center. Employment with the Tree of Life Rejuvenation Center

FOOD FOR THE SOUL

offers the opportunity to live in a spiritually based community, serve others who are on the path of awakening, and join in spiritual practices and celebrations. Positions are available in the kitchen, maintenance, housekeeping, and organic/biodynamic gardening (with projects that include work in the center's circle garden, solar greenhouse, the children's educational garden and park, two orchards, and vineyards). The seven-hour workday is shared with other interns and includes classes in yoga and meditation, with ample time available for quiet reflection and development of a healthy, holistic, and sustainable lifestyle. Interns start out in a three-month trial period, with one-year terms available after that point. A small stipend, rustic lodging, and "live-food" vegan meals are provided. Applications are available online and in-person interviews are required.

For More Information:
Doug Busch, Apprenticeship Coordinator
Tree of Life Rejuvenation Center
P.O. Box 1080
Patagonia, AZ 85624
(520) 394-2520, ext. 206 • (520) 394-2099 (fax)
doug@treeoflife.nu

TRILLIUM COMMUNITY LAND TRUST

Intentional Community • Oregon • 3+ Months
www.deepwild.org

As a WILDERNESS sanctuary and eco-village in the Siskiyou Mountains of southern Oregon, the Trillium Community is a unique place to spend a season or two as an intern in their rustic wilderness homestead and college campus immersed in intentional community. Areas of service include event coordination (such as the Spring Ecostery event, an intensive eight-week residential academic program focusing on environmental studies), organic gardening and permaculture, environmental activism and education, grounds and maintenance, construction, and office work—there is definitely something of interest for everybody. Time at Trillium should be looked at holistically, understanding that there is a blend between work, play, service, and creativity. Internships are available for three months at the start of the changing seasons, with each offering a variety of projects, programs, celebrations, and special events on the equinoxes and solstices. A fee of $375 is charged for each three-month session, which includes shared living space in a rustic cabin and use of the facilities. All residents also share in community food staples, to which all contribute about $25 to $50 per month. There are also opportunities to earn academic credit through self-directed, experiential courses offered by Dakubetede Environmental Education Programs (Antioch University) for an extra fee of $375 for a three-credit course. Those who are highly motivated vegetarian folks, who love the natural world and approach life with an attitude of integrity and optimism, and who are willing to learn new ways of living, working, and serving are desired. Call or email for more information.

For More Information:
Internship Program Coordinator
Trillium Community Land Trust
Dakubetede Environmental Education Programs
P.O. Box 1330
Jacksonville, OR 97530
(541) 899-1712
trillium@deepwild.org

RECOMMENDED READING . . . .

Looking to rejuvenate the spirit and soul or for an unconventional lodging arrangement on your next journey? *Sanctuaries—The Complete United States* by Marcia and Jack Kelly (Bell Tower, $18) features over twelve hundred monasteries, abbeys, and retreat centers. Although the guide focuses mainly on Catholic and Episcopalian havens, it's also filled with Buddhist, Hindu, Sufi, and other places to find quiet and seclusion.

For those who want to challenge the mind, body, and spirit, *Vacations That Can Change Your Life* by Ellen Lederman (Sourcebooks, $16.95) provides listings of more than two hundred soul-enriching vacations, including meditation and spiritual retreats, empowerment weekends, wilderness survival excursions, and weeks spent swimming with dolphins.

EDUCATIONAL CONCERNS FOR HUNGER ORGANIZATION

**Farming/Ministry/Hunger Awareness •
Florida/Haiti • 15 Months**
www.echonet.org

EDUCATIONAL CONCERNS FOR Hunger Organization (ECHO) cultivates one of the largest collections of tropical food plants in the U.S. The twenty-one-acre farm serves as a training tool for interns, as an educational tool for public tours, and as a production farm for seeds and nursery plants.

What You'll Be Doing: Interns spend twelve months in Florida engaging in hands-on, experiential learning activities related to sustainable agriculture in the tropics. Common activities include growing tropical foods (including underexploited plants and fruit and multi-purpose trees), caring for animals, and maintaining the various demonstrations. All interns help harvest, process seed orders, supervise the work of local volunteers, and lead educational tours for visiting individuals and groups. The climax of the internship is a three-month, cross-cultural experience in Haiti, which gives interns an opportunity to live and work in an actual third-world setting while working with farmers or urban gardeners.

Perks and Rewards: Benefits include apartment-style dorms, a $350 to $450 monthly stipend, health insurance, and travel expenses to Florida. Interns must raise their own support for the three months in Haiti, which is usually done through churches, friends, and relatives. ECHO often has matching funds available for up to 50 percent of the expenses and stipend for each intern.

The Essentials: A degree in agriculture or previous farm or gardening experience in not required, although it is helpful. A sincere Christian commitment and a strong body able to do manual work are essential. Most interns come to ECHO right after getting their bachelor's degree.

Your First Move: Application materials can be found online, or call/email for more information. Completed applications must be received by September 15 for positions opening January through May, and by February 1 for positions opening June to December.

For More Information:
David Balsbaugh, Educational Programs Director
Educational Concerns for Hunger Organization
17391 Durrance Rd.
North Ft. Myers, FL 33917
(941) 543-3246 • echo@echonet.org

EMANDAL-A FARM ON A RIVER

Sustainable Farm/Camp • California • 1–9 Months
www.emandal.com

EMANDAL—A FARM on a River serves as an environmental education facility for school groups. It also offers a small children's group during June and July, a family vacation farm during August, a pseudo-working cattle and pig ranch, and it produces fine jams, jellies, pickles, and salsas. The philosophy is one of self-sufficiency, both mental and physical, as an individual and as part of a community, to ensure viability in our changing world.

Your Surroundings: Emandal is located in the heart of Mendocino County, on the main fork of the Eel River. This is a land where biomes of the arid Southwest and rainy Northwest overlap and interact, creating an incredible diversity of plants and wildlife. Set into this wilderness is the farm, with acres of fruits and vegetables that feed all who experience life on the farm.

What You'll Be Doing: Emandal provides a learning environment and a chance to do something constructive while pondering life's choices. Explore the cycle of employment opportunities throughout the year: February—gardeners/apprentices and farm workers; March/April—naturalists, cooks, and assistant gardeners; June—children's camp counselors, camp cooks, backpack counselor, program director, and teen programs director; July—family camp workers, pickle packers, and scrapbook editor; September through November—farm workers/gardeners; November through December—mail-order

An organic-farm instructor teaches participants about the wonders of growing vegetables at Emandal—A Farm on a River.

I often hesitate to say we own this land. How can a person own what he has not created? The earth is the Lord's and the fullness thereof. We are only its custodians. —JOSEPHINE DUVENECK

workers. Typical job assignments include trail building, firewood gathering, painting cabins, fixing fences, planting seeds, washing clothes, making jam, labeling brochures, feeding animals, butchering chickens, building compost, teaching soap making, building rock walls, gardening, or creating meals.

Commitment: Positions are full- or part-time or any other times that can be negotiated (with the exception of December and January, which are the farm's down time). The days in summer are long—working up to twelve hours per day. A farmworker follows the sun. Days off and time off change dramatically with the seasons.

Perks and Rewards: Most stipends range from $100 to $250 per week, plus room and board. Emandal is known for its incredible family-style meals. The living space is in bunkhouses, cabins, the schoolhouse, tents, or the carriage house, depending on the season.

The Essentials: The farm is ideal for transitioning from one experience to another—whether the end of school, between jobs, before a trip around the world, or while making a decision about a career change. Those who want to make a difference in children's lives and connect with the earth will thrive.

Your First Move: To begin the application, email or fax a letter of interest and resume.

For More Information:
Clive and Tamara Adams, Owners
Emandal—A Farm on a River
16500 Hearst Post Office Rd., Willits, CA 95490
(707) 459-5439 • (707) 459-1808 (fax)
emandalkidscamp@pacific.net

We're always looking for good people, eager to learn and work, who are interested in others. We especially need grandparents for the summer camp!

FEATHERSTONE FRUITS AND VEGETABLES

Organic Farming • Minnesota • 4–7 Months
www.featherstonefarm.com

FEATHERSTONE IS A thirty-acre certified organic farm which grows a large variety of fruits and vegetables (from asparagus to zucchini) and is part of the five-hundred-

acre Zephyr Valley Community Cooperative, a seven-family community that "lives lightly on this rich fertile valley." The farm serves a ninety-member CSA along with selling to grocery stores, restaurants, and local farmers' markets. The internship program is a great hands-on opportunity to learn all aspects of organic vegetable production. Interns will participate in planting, harvesting, and marketing of produce as well as learn greenhouse management, organic pest and disease control, crop rotation, and cover cropping. Interns also choose one area of the farm to learn, manage, and develop with the help of experienced growers, including greenhouse tomato and pepper production, harvest management, CSA newsletter writing/editing, and tractor tool operation. Applicants should be hardworking, open-minded, willing to learn, and passionate about organic farming. Their growing season is from April through October, and applications are considered for anyone able to work four of these months or more. Monthly stipends start at $500, along with a food stipend of $100 per month, farm produce, and housing in a trailer (near a tree-lined creek) or furnished cabin. Kitchen, employee lounge areas, and rustic bathing facilities are also provided.

For More Information:
Rhys Williams, Partner
Featherstone Fruits and Vegetables
Apprenticeship Program
R.R. 1, Box 121F
Rushford, MN 55971
(507) 453-9621 • jack@featherstonefarm.com

FOOD BANK FARM

Organic Farming • Massachusetts • 1–8 Months
www.foodbankwma.org/farm.htm

LOCATED IN THE "five college area" of western Massachusetts (also known as the "happy valley"), Food Bank Farm grows and harvests organic vegetables, flowers, and small fruits for over six hundred CSA shareholders. But they don't stop there—the farm also donates almost half of its production to the nonprofit Western Massachusetts Food Bank. The farm is a constant bustle of community activity. From sunup to sundown, shareholders can be found picking up veggies, using the farm as a personal retreat, or participating in the full-moon potlucks at a bonfire under the stars. Meanwhile apprentices are hard at work learning about all aspects of the farm's operation—from planning and land preparation to harvesting and planting of cover crops. Apprentices have the option of a full-season apprenticeship (from April or May to December 15) or a summer-season "planting" apprenticeship (from mid-May to mid-June). A stipend of $550 to $750 is provided, along with housing in a renovated eighteenth-century farmhouse, all the organic produce you can eat, and weekly yoga classes. Those who have an interest in both agriculture and feeding those in need, plenty of stamina and spirit, and who enjoy working with others will thrive at Food Bank. Send off a cover letter, resume, and three references, or call/email for more information. It's best to apply between the months of December and March.

For More Information:
Michael Doctor, Apprenticeship Coordinator
Food Bank Farm
121 Bay Rd.
Hadley, MA 01035
(413) 582-0013
foodbankfarm@yahoo.com

GARDEN HARVEST

Farming/Hunger Awareness • Maryland • 10+ Weeks
www.gardenharvest.org

GARDEN HARVEST IS a one-hundred-acre organic farm, which also doubles as an educational center that works to alleviate hunger and improve nutrition of the disadvantaged. One hundred percent of the organic fruit and vegetables grown are distributed fresh to soup kitchens and emergency food pantries in the area. Apprentices will receive extensive training and education in organic farming and sustainable agriculture, develop leadership and supervisory skills, gain experience in the operation of a nonprofit, and have exposure to issues of hunger and homelessness. Duties range from planting, growing, harvesting, and composting, to bee-keeping, delivery of produce, and supervision of volunteers. Positions are available from April through November (forty hours spread over five days), with a ten-week minimum commitment. No previous farming experience is necessary; however, applicants must be at least eighteen years of age, have a sincere interest in organic farming and/or helping humanity, and be capable of strenuous physical work outside in various weather conditions. Room, meals, and a stipend are provided. If housing becomes unavailable, Garden Harvest will assist with nearby housing, and pay a wage to help cover this cost.

For More Information:
Jim Dasher, Executive Director
Garden Harvest
14045 Mantua Mill Rd.
Glyndon, MD 21071
(410) 526-0698 • (410) 429-3946 (fax)
garharvest@aol.com

GEORGE WASHINGTON'S MOUNT VERNON

Living History • Virginia • Summer
www.mountvernon.org/pioneer

MOUNT VERNON IS a nonprofit organization created to preserve George Washington's home. Located just outside Washington, D.C., the estate welcomes more than one million visitors each year.

What You'll Be Doing: After completion of a short training program, which includes several field trips to related historic sites, interns act as living history guides, teaching visitors about Washington's innovative approach to farming and his stature as a progressive leader in early American agriculture. Interns also demonstrate Washington's farming practices, working with livestock (horses, mules, and sheep), using period-style farm tools, and discussing such things as Washington's crop rotation schemes, his use of fertilizers, and the diet of the field workers.

Commitment: Internships run ten weeks during the summer months beginning in June.

Perks and Rewards: Interns are provided round-trip travel to Mount Vernon, a weekly stipend of $200, housing on the Mount Vernon estate, and period attire (eighteenth-century field-hand clothing).

The Essentials: Mount Vernon recruits as many as six graduating high school seniors and undergraduate students (aged eighteen to twenty-two) who have a strong background in agriculture and history as well as good public speaking skills.

Your First Move: Applications are available online or contact Jinny through e-mail or regular mail.

For More Information:
Jinny Fox, Supervisor of Interpretation
George Washington's Mount Vernon
Pioneer Farmer Internships
P.O. Box 110, Mount Vernon, VA 22121
(703) 799-8611 • (703) 799-8609 (fax)
jfox@mountvernon.org

A talent is something given, that opens like a flower, but without exceptional energy, discipline, and persistence will never bear fruit. —MAY SARTON

A pioneer-farming intern at George Washington's Mount Vernon demonstrates hoeing practices of years past for a group while teaching them about the historical relationship between farmers and slaves.

Mount Vernon also offers four-week, unpaid internships for retired agricultural teachers, who receive compensation for round-trip travel to Mount Vernon, as well as free housing on the estate. (Spouses are welcome!)

GREEN GULCH FARM AND ZEN CENTER

Organic Farming/Zen Center • California • 6 Months
www.sfzc.com/ggfindex.htm

GREEN GULCH FARM and Zen Center, nestled in a valley bordered by the Pacific Ocean, Golden Gate National Recreation Area, and Mount Tamalpais, offers a residential apprenticeship in organic gardening and farming from mid-April through mid-October each year. Along with hands-on experience and instruction in organic-gardening/farming methods, the apprenticeship also emphasizes Zen meditation practice and study/instruction in Buddhist teachings. Daily work includes harvesting, sowing, transplanting, compost making, tractor cultivation, raised-bed flower and vegetable

gardening, fruit cultivation, craft production, and opportunities to market the produce at the farm and regional farmers' markets. Room, board, a small stipend, and weekly classes and seminars with resident and visiting teachers are provided. Prior to applying, a two-week stay as a guest student is required (at a cost of $15 to $20 per day). Call or write for further information or to inquire about a guest student visit.

The application deadline is March 1.

For More Information:
Liz Milazzo, Farm Manager
Green Gulch Farm and Zen Center
1601 Shoreline Hwy.
Sausalito, CA 94965
(415) 381-0253 • (415) 383-3134 (Main Office)
(415) 383-3128 (fax)

GUIDESTONE CSA FARM

Organic Farming • Colorado • 3–12 Months
www.stewardshipcommunity.org

LOCATED ONE HOUR north of Boulder, one and a half hour south of Ft. Collins, Guidestone CSA Farm includes a 150-acre organic farm, a diversified livestock program (that includes raising sheep, pigs, laying hens, turkeys, and working with three draft horses), a four-acre vegetable garden, and a small cow dairy that provides milk for its shareholders. The farm also sponsors a summer farm camp for children, educational programs, and adult workshops relating to alternative energy and natural home building.

What You'll Be Doing: Interns have the opportunity to focus on organic gardening, animal husbandry, creating a farm business, or farming. Although a specific area is chosen, everyone has an opportunity to learn and experience organic vegetable production, work with the animals, baking on a wood-fired brick oven, running a CSA farm, teaching educational programs to children, learning various skills (such as tree grafting and permaculture), and natural home building and alternative-energy technologies.

Commitment: The length of internships can range from three months to a year. The growing season is from April to November, while animal care and milking are year-round activities.

Perks and Rewards: A stipend of $150 per month is provided, along with housing and food from the farm. Accommodations are simple and range from a three-person cabin to yurts overlooking the pond. Kitchen and bathroom facilities are also available, and include solar showers, an innovative solar moldering outhouse, and a semi-outdoor kitchen. All facilities were built using alternative building methods such as straw-clay construction and cob construction.

Your First Move: Call for a detailed internship packet. If possible, prospective interns should visit Guidestone prior to committing to a position in order to make sure that the program and living situation is right for them.

For More Information:
David Lynch, Internship Program
Guidestone CSA Farm
Center for Sustainable Living
5943 N. County Road 29
Loveland, CO 80538
(970) 461-0271 • info@stewardshipcommunity.org

HARTFORD FOOD SYSTEM

Organic Farming • Connecticut • 2 Months–1 Year
www.hartfordfood.org

THE HARTFORD FOOD SYSTEM is a nonprofit organization that strives to increase the access to high-quality, affordable food for lower-income and elderly Hartford residents. In addition to its development and management of community food programs, such as a farmers'

markets, Holcomb Farm CSA, and grocery delivery service, the Food System develops policy initiatives designed to influence the response of the local, state, and federal governments to food-system issues. Food-policy and CSA-farm interns with a strong commitment to social justice and hunger issues, as well as an interest in sustainable agriculture, are needed throughout the year. CSA interns are primarily involved in the planting, cultivating, harvesting, and distribution of vegetables and fruit using organic growing principles. All interns will receive a stipend of $600 per month, fresh vegetables from the farm, participation in the farm and food-system education program, plus assistance with housing. A two- to three-month commitment is required; however, a six-month to one-year commitment is preferred. To apply, send a resume and letter stating educational goals, reasons for seeking the internship, and three references. Applicants are strongly encouraged to visit the farm before making a commitment to the position. Positions are filled on a first-come, first-served basis.

For More Information:
Liz Wheeler, Program Director
Hartford Food System
Holcomb Farm CSA
509 Wethersfield Ave.
Hartford, CT 06114
(860) 296-9325 • (860) 296-8326 (fax)
lwheeler@hartfordfood.org

HAWTHORNE VALLEY FARM

Biodynamic Farming/Education • New York • 3–12 Months
www.hawthornevalleyfarm.org

HAWTHORNE VALLEY FARM was founded in 1972 by a group of experienced educators and farmers who recognized a growing need to create a place where children and young people might experience life in its wholeness and gain the inner strength and the practical abilities that they would need as adults. At Hawthorne Valley, farmers, artists, and teachers working out the insights of Rudolf Steiner have joined together to create such a place. The four-hundred-acre biodynamic farm is home to a K–12 Waldorf day school, a children's residential school and summer camp program, a cheese and yogurt production dairy (with a sixty-head dairy herd), a full bakery, a ten-acre market garden which supplies a 225-member CSA program, a Green Market stand in New York City, and a retail natural foods and grocery store on the premises.

The harvest is plenty, laborers are few. Come with me into the fields. —MATTHEW 9:37–38

What You'll Be Doing: Whether as a Visiting Students Program intern, a summer camp counselor, or a farm apprentice, the farm provides ample opportunities to learn in new and exciting ways. As the Waldorf educational arm of the farm, the Visiting Students Program brings students and teachers from public and private schools to spend a week on the farm. Interns and staff host the classes and conduct activities such as animal feeding, gardening, barn cleaning, sourdough bread baking, butter making, and seasonal projects including apple cider pressing and maple syrup making. During the summer months, camp counselors teach either in the House Camp for nine- to eleven-year-olds or the Field Camp for teens aged twelve to fifteen. These programs seek to build reverence for life and community awareness through living, playing, and working together on an active farm. Camp assistant cooks are also needed during this time frame. Farm apprentices do whatever needs to be done during their on-the-job training. You'll find them milking the cows, haying, caring for the livestock, cleaning the dairy barn, repairing machinery, planting or tending the garden crops, harvesting vegetables, or driving to the Green Market in New York City.

Commitment: Internships begin with a two-week training period and are available during the school year, either for a semester or on a yearlong basis. Camp counselors kick off the summer in mid-June with a one-week training and work through mid-August. The apprentice program runs from February through November with the option to stay through the winter. Interactive sessions on biodynamic farming practices, informative talks with local geology and nature experts, and field trips to other farms round out apprentice training.

Perks and Rewards: Camp counselor stipends range from $1,500 to $1,700; camp cooks receive $2,250; and apprentices receive $400 per month. While on the farm, all staff members live as a community and eat family-style meals (consisting of whole foods, grains, and fresh vegetables). Home is a comfortable nineteenth-century farmhouse (counselors have private tents).

Your First Move: Call or email for an information packet. Additional information on the camp can be found at www.camppage.com/hawthorne; and for more information on the apprentice program, contact Rachel Schneider at (518) 672-4465, ext. 105.

For More Information:
Ruth Bruns, Program Director
Hawthorne Valley Farm
327 Route 21C
Ghent, NY 12075
(518) 672-4790 • (518) 672-4887 (fax)
vsp@taconic.net

Hawthorne Valley Farm summer campers and staff make their way to the biodynamic gardens to help out the farm team with the day's harvest.

Photo Credit: Hawthorne Valley Farm

NOWHERE ELSE I'D RATHER BE

When I was first considering a farm apprenticeship at Hawthorne Valley, I was still teaching in Brooklyn. I had spent four months at a farm in Kentucky before moving to New York City to study and teach in the inner city, and by my third year there, the concrete hurt. It was difficult to find a common language with children who were taught from the beginning to be removed from the sources of their sustenance. And I, too, was growing disconnected: if I wanted to eat mindfully, my choices seemed limited to organic foods grown by California migrant workers and trucked thousands of miles. I began to research CSA. I realized that my work with children needed to happen within the context of farming, not only so that I could be sustained, but also so that I could contribute to the making of a sustainable world.

As a farm apprentice for the past two seasons, I've had my share of long, hot, hard days. (Also long, cold, hard days!) I have grown strong and have felt a certainty deep in my bones that I have found a calling. I love hearing the cows coming in early in the morning and knowing that it's about time for me to rise too. I love harvesting out in the garden as the sun rises and knowing that, if the cows are going back out to pasture, it must be 7:15.

This year I have learned more about tractor operation, and recently, I spent the day raking hay on a big Belarus. I have witnessed the birth of three calves and saw one stillborn. The cycles of life and death are immediate, tangible, and an intimate part of what we do every day. Grass and hay become manure which becomes compost, which is added to the soil to nourish more pasture or vegetables, which are, in turn consumed or (through the process of feeding hay to the cows) used to create milk, and on and on.

This morning I transplanted our fall beets. Now, this afternoon, I am about to go milk the cows. Children from the summer camp will probably be in and out of the barn as they do afternoon chores and help us bring in the heifers. We'll all fan ourselves and comment on the weather and pray for rain, and I will feel grateful, for this will be a time when there is nowhere else I would rather be.

—CONTRIBUTED BY REBECCA NELLENBACK, former Hawthorne Valley Farm Apprentice

HEARTWOOD SCHOOL

House Building • Massachusetts • 1–10 Weeks
www.heartwoodschool.com

HEARTWOOD TEACHES THE skills and knowledge it takes to build an energy-efficient house as well as offering workshops on all aspects of the home-building crafts, including timber framing, cabinetmaking, and finish carpentry. Those who come to Heartwood range from students to retirees, and most have little or no previous construction experience; however, they all share a "clear determination to empower their hands, to train their eyes for quality and beauty in the design of things, and to question and explore the ways we might live in a more honest relation with our planet."

What You'll Be Doing: In addition to attending a workshop as a participant, Heartwood invites four apprentices-in-residence who help with workshops and maintain tools and facilities in exchange for reduced rates in tuition. Apprentices will not only gain a comprehensive knowledge of house building and timber framing, but also a clear, concise methodology of problem solving and training of the eyes and hands for quality and beauty— yes, true craftsmanship! Note that the main purpose of the apprenticeship program is to train individuals who are interested in timber framing as a career. Upon conclusion of the program, apprentices must agree to continue working with a member timber company (Heartwood arranges this) for a minimum of eight months (which includes a stipend).

Commitment: One-week workshops are offered from early May through mid-October (enrollment averages ten students); the three-week home-building course begins in early July. Apprentices must commit to seven weeks of residency (from mid-June through early August). This time period coincides with their core timber framing curriculum and also includes the three-week house-building workshop.

Perks and Rewards: Those participating in one-week workshops pay a tuition fee of $500 ($900 per couple); the three-week house-building course runs $1,350 ($2,400 per couple). The fee include materials and hearty lunches. Special weekly rates at nearby hotels, bed-and-breakfasts, and campgrounds are offered. Apprentices pay a fee of $1,750, which includes housing, lunch, and a one-year membership in the Timber Framers Guild (www.tfguild.org). Housing consists of use of a kitchen and bath and one of four sleeping areas: two lofts in the schoolhouse and two cabins behind it.

Your First Move: Call for application materials. The apprentice application deadline is March 15 (with notification by April 15).

For More Information:
Will and Michele Beemer,
Workshop/Apprentice Coordinators
Heartwood School
Johnson Hill Rd.
Washington, MA 01223
(413) 623-6677 • (413) 623-0277 (fax)
info@heartwoodschool.com

HEIFER INTERNATIONAL RANCH

**Hunger Awareness • Arkansas/California/
Massachusetts • Seasonal**
www.heifer.org

HEIFER INTERNATIONAL IS a Christian nonprofit development organization working in forty-eight countries (including the U.S.) to help alleviate world hunger. Their three learning centers (in California, Arkansas, and Massachusetts) are hands-on campuses that teach the public about the root causes of hunger and poverty and the way animals and people can make a difference. Volunteers are needed to work in the organic gardens and with the livestock, as well as to assist with the education program (including field trips for children, alternative spring break, and tours), office work, and maintenance. Volunteers receive a monthly stipend of $200 and on-site housing. Applicants must be at least eighteen, and applications are accepted year-round.

For More Information:
Volunteer Coordinator
Heifer International Ranch
55 Heifer Rd.

Perryville, AR 72126
(800) 422-0474 • (501) 889-5124 • (501) 889-1574 (fax)
ranchvol@heifer.org

HIDDEN VILLA

**Farm Education • California •
12–15 Months/Summer**
www.hiddenvilla.org

CONNECTING CHILDREN TO the earth and instilling a sense of responsibility for their environment, Hidden Villa engages participants in hands-on innovative programs promoting environmental awareness, multicultural understanding, and humanitarian values. Located in the foothills of the Santa Cruz Mountains on a sixteen-hundred-acre wilderness preserve and organic farm, Hidden Villa features a multicultural summer camp (for ages six to eighteen), a school-year environmental education program for elementary school children, a youth hostel, a CSA program, and a variety of community programs. For many visitors, Hidden Villa provides an opportunity to walk in the woods, come face to face with a large, friendly farm animal, and see where milk and eggs come from.

An environmental education intern inspires children through Hidden Villa's science-based teaching curriculum.

THE REALITY OF DREAMS

Upon discovering a special place called Hidden Villa, I became enthralled by the opportunity to live on a farm and help children connect with nature. I realized this was the job I had been preparing myself for without even knowing it:

an internship experience representing a unique integration of the mind, body, and soul through work and recreation.

Imagine a long, narrow valley surrounded by lush tree-covered mountains glowing under a cloud-studded sky. Lichen and mosses ensure the air is crisp and pristine, as fragrant smells swim through the atmosphere, invigorating the lungs and spirit. Waterfalls gliding down the mountains soothe the mind under a canopy of green hues. Birds are chirping, frogs croaking, and in the distance the sounds of sheep ring through the valley.

As an intern at Hidden Villa, days are spent outside in the foothills of the Santa Cruz Mountains guiding children around the farm and wilderness preserve, fostering their connection to the natural world. For many children, Hidden Villa becomes their first exposure to a farm: eating food grown directly from the gardens, appreciating worms for their wonderful work of making dirt, or, perhaps, seeing and touching a pig, chicken, sheep, cow or goat—something only previously seen in storybooks or on television, yet such an integral part of our lives. We hike the trails of a mossy enchanted forest, exploring and sharing its awe and wonder.

Experiencing nature with children as they foster connections with their roots is an amazing journey. Today, many children are being raised with no concept of the interconnectedness and balance of all living things. Our intricate relationship and reliance on the earth's energies for survival and happiness has become something we buy in a box on a shelf in a building. We cannot endure this disconnection and expect our children to clean up the environmental and social destruction that has been created. Healing begins now—by the way we live each day and by

Photo Credit: Justin Halgren

Using Hidden Villa's hands-on approach to learning, Cori Stennett and her team of children pause and reflect upon our links to the Earth.

the way we teach our children that we are interconnected with all life that surrounds us.

Working at Hidden Villa has been far more than a job—it has been a remarkable adventure of life. Challenges, truths, and realizations have been crucial contributors along this pathway for me. Existing in a new environment, developing new relationships with people and animals, and opening up to the myriad of possibilities has invigorated my soul. Living a lifestyle that offers a connection to the earth while devoting energy to an enjoyable job and meaningful purpose have helped me evolve toward the person I want to be. And the journey has just begun!

This experience has unlocked many doors of opportunity and many more positive situations to discover, learn, share, play, live, and evolve; much like *The Back Door Guide* unlocked the door to Hidden Villa for me. Beyond each description Michael Landes has given each of us in this book lies a world of pure imagination, as the Great Willy Wonka would say:

If you want to view paradise,
Simply look around and view it.
Anything you want, you do it.
Want to change the world?
There's nothing to it.

Fortunately, we have the ability to make conscious decisions influencing our growth, discovery, and purpose. Where we position ourselves on this earth and the energies with which we come into contact create the scenes of our lives. Choosing a pathway that positively impacts the environment and human conscience is a dream of interdependence. Each of us can live our dreams by creating our own realities. What are yours?

—Contributed by Cori Stennett,
Hidden Villa Intern

What You'll Be Doing: Environmental education interns spend one day each week working on the farm and studying agriculture and animal care with the ranch staff. The other four weekdays are dedicated to teaching. Duties include giving short tours of the farm for preschoolers, educating and working with elementary schoolchildren on the farm, or giving presentations to classrooms at surrounding schools. With an emphasis on fun and interactive education, interns will learn leadership skills as well as hands-on and creative teaching techniques (through the use of slides, puppets, music, role playing, and storytelling). Practical living skills, organic gardening, and the realities of life on a small farm round out the learning experience. Note that opportunities also exist at Hidden Villa during the summer months, with positions ranging from residential counselors and trip leaders to ropes-course and rock-climbing coordinators to garden/farm staff—and much more!

Commitment: Internships begin either in September for fifteen months or January for twelve months. Camp positions are offered during the summer months.

Perks and Rewards: Interns receive a monthly stipend of $500, shared housing, seasonal food from the farm, and full medical benefits. Summer wages start at $235 per week plus rustic housing and meals. One of the biggest perks is the chance to live in a beautiful place, meet inspiring people, and receive lots of experience with children, teaching, and farms.

The Essentials: Those who have an interest in organic farming, the outdoors, and children, and can show how an internship might benefit their career path are preferred. It's also helpful to have experience in teaching, counseling, or working with children in other ways. Traits found in their interns include a fun-loving spirit, maturity, and energy over the long haul.

Your First Move: Call, email, or write for application materials. Internship deadlines: mid-April for positions starting in September; mid-September for positions starting in January. All applicants are interviewed by telephone.

For More Information:
Internship Coordinator
Hidden Villa
26870 Moody Rd.
Los Altos Hills, CA 94022-4209
Environmental Education: (650) 949-8643
hveep@hiddenvilla.org
Summer Camp: (650) 949-8641
camp@hiddenvilla.org

HOWELL LIVING HISTORY FARM

Sustainable Farm • New Jersey • 3–12 Months
www.howellfarm.com

Howell Living History Farm is a 130-acre farm where the techniques that farm families used to feed and clothe themselves at the turn of the twentieth century are practiced and demonstrated to thousands of visitors each year. Hand, horse, ox, and steam- and gas-engine power are used to operate field, barn, and other equipment. As a working farm, Howell Farm offers recreational and educational opportunities to its visitors, involving them in the work and play of a traditional family farm.

What You'll Be Doing: The internship program at Howell Farm is designed to teach participants skills for their interpretation of turn-of-the-century farm life. These skills may be useful to those working with small farmers in developing countries, working at other living history farms or agricultural museums, or to the twenty-first-century homesteader. The internship program is integrated with the overall needs of a historical farm, which include cropping, equipment restoration and repair, site maintenance, an introduction to woodworking and metalworking, and educational programs for schools and the general public. The program is designed to involve participants in as many of the seasonal activities as possible.

Commitment: Program dates vary from year to year, but generally the twelve-week sessions start in March, June, and September. The yearlong program is designed as an advanced-level program, so a college degree related to agriculture and/or farming experience is necessary.

Perks and Rewards: A stipend, living quarters, hands-on training, and farm products are provided. Living accommodations are modest, with each intern having a private room and access to a shared kitchen, living room, and bathroom.

The Essentials: Past interns have been returned Peace Corps volunteers looking to continue in the field of international agriculture, college students exploring careers related to agriculture, and people of all ages interested in sustainable agriculture.

For More Information:
Rob Flory, Intern Coordinator
Howell Living History Farm
101 Hunter Rd.
Titusville, NJ 08560
(609) 737-3299 • (609) 737-6524 (fax)
thefarm@bellatlantic.net

INTERNATIONAL AGRICULTURAL EXCHANGE ASSOCIATION

Agriculture • Worldwide • 4–12 Months
www.agriventure.com

Do you have an agricultural or horticultural background? Have you always dreamed of working abroad? The International Agricultural Exchange Association (IAEA), along with a strong international network of past trainees and host families, connects participants to farming and agriculture jobs in the U.S., Canada, Australia, New Zealand, Japan, Western Europe, and the United Kingdom. There is more to life than what you can see out your back door!

What You'll Be Doing: Experience the thrill of herding cattle in the outback of Australia, milking two hundred cows in less than two hours in New Zealand, or working in the flower market in Amsterdam—not to mention the adventures you can experience on your days off. IAEA is

a great way to meet people from all over the world, to experience a different culture, and to live as a member of a host family.

Commitment: Departure dates are in March, April, July, August, September, October, and November, and programs range in duration from four to twelve months. "Flex" programs can be arranged to accommodate most schedules; and longer programs can combine work and travel in two countries.

Perks and Rewards: Host families generally pay trainee allowances once per month, along with room and board. Program fees range from $2,595 to $5,895 and cover work visas, medical and travel insurance, a round-trip airline ticket, an orientation seminar in the host country, supervision, and a two-year membership with IAEA.

The Essentials: Candidates must be citizens of one of the member countries (the U.S. is one of them!); have the desire to work overseas; be eighteen to thirty years old; have practical experience in agriculture, horticulture, or home management; have a valid driver's license; have no criminal record; have no children; be in good mental and physical health; and have a basic understanding of the English language.

Your First Move: Call or write for more information, application, and current program fees.

For More Information:
Program Coordinator
International Agricultural Exchange Association
Agriventure
1000 1st Ave. South
Great Falls, MT 59401
(800) 272-4996 • (406) 727-1999 • (406) 727-1997 (fax)
usa@agriventure.com

LOST VALLEY EDUCATIONAL CENTER

Intentional Community • Oregon • 1–8 Months
www.lostvalley.org

Structured as an intentional community, Lost Valley is a nonprofit educational center that organizes and hosts conferences, workshops, and retreats that focus on personal growth and sustainable living. Committed to the pursuit of a more sustainable lifestyle, twenty-two adults and seven children live year-round on the grounds (located on eighty-seven acres in the foothills of western Oregon's Cascade Range and eighteen miles from Eugene).

The future must be seen in terms of what a person can do to contribute something, to make something better, to make it go where he believes with all his being it ought to go. —Frederick Kappel

What You'll Be Doing: The apprenticeship program is an opportunity to immerse yourself in the seasonal cycles of organic gardening and working on the land, while experiencing the ebb and flow a cooperative living lifestyle. Apprentices will explore the interrelationship of food, medicine, the growing cycle, the land, emotional and spiritual life, and connections with other people. Activities vary depending on time of year, but may include mulching, soil preparation, sowing and seed saving, transplanting and fertilizing, composting, weeding, harvesting and food preservation, growing medicinal herbs and mushrooms, greenhouse management, and fence making. Weekly classes and field trips to other farms and organic innovators round out the experience. Other opportunities include an eight-month "work/trade" internship program beginning in mid-February (for those with experience), Community Experience Week workshops held three times per year, and a two- to three-month vegetarian cooking or service and sacred-space internship/apprentice program.

Commitment: A three- to six-month commitment is suggested; however, apprentices must commit to at least one month. The program generally begins the first weekday of each month throughout the year. All participants work forty hours per week, which includes participation in community cooking shifts, chores, and weekly "well-being" meetings.

Perks and Rewards: There is a one-time $100 registration fee/deposit, plus a $400 monthly food and lodging fee (which includes organic vegetarian meals and lodging or campsite accommodations in the summer). A swimming hole and a sweat lodge are available to rejuvenate the mind and body.

The Essentials: Apprentices are selected based on their excitement about working, learning, and confronting challenges with a positive attitude. No previous gardening experience is necessary, only a willingness to work hard, to abide by apprentice commitments, and to be open to the multifaceted learning that occurs in the community.

Your First Move: Call or write for application materials. Qualified applicants are accepted on a first-come, first-served basis.

For More Information:
Tammy Davis, Apprenticeship Coordinator
Lost Valley Educational Center
81868 Lost Valley Ln.
Dexter, OR 97431
(541) 937-3351 • (541) 937-2243 (fax)
garden@lostvalley.org

A *"journal of our evolving ecological culture,"* Talking Leaves *is filled with feature articles, essays, and other writings contributed by people working to restore healthy human relationships with the natural world, with one another, and with self. Each issue also includes an extensive book and music review section, announcements, poetry, and art. Published by Lost Valley Educational Center four times per year, subscriptions run $20. Visit* Talking Leaves *on the web at www.talkingleaves.org or contact Chris Roth at editor@talkingleaves.org.*

MAST INTERNATIONAL

Agriculture • Worldwide • 3–12 Months
http://mast.coafes.umn.edu

MAST International offers those between the ages of eighteen and thirty the opportunity to participate in three- to twelve-month training assignments in agriculture, horticulture, or forestry around the globe. Applicants must have a minimum of six months practical or work experience, and knowledge of the host country's language is preferred, but only required in France. Participants generally receive an allowance plus room and meals with a host family. There is a program fee of $400 (airfare, insurance, visa, personal expenses, and in-country program fees are additional). Apply a minimum of three months prior to your preferred start date; four months for Germany and Denmark.

For More Information:
Susan Von Bank, Program Coordinator
MAST International
R395 VoTech Building
1954 Buford Ave.
St. Paul, MN 55108-6197
(800) 346-6278 • (612) 624-3740 • (612) 625-7031 (fax)
mast@umn.edu

MAYSIE'S FARM CONSERVATION CENTER

Farming • Pennsylvania • Seasonal
www.maysiesfarm.org

·····································

PURE AND SIMPLE, Maysie's Farm is dedicated to increasing the public's understanding of ecological living and the importance of communities based on local, sustainably produced food supplies. Along with their sixty-five-acre farm, the farm's unique educational activities include a certified organic CSA farm (with 150 subscribers), school and youth programs, a community learning series, and sustainable-agriculture internships.

What You'll Be Doing: Since the farm is based on education rather than solely dedicated to production, interns have the opportunity to really learn and understand soil fertility practices, crop rotation principles, organic pest control, and other aspects of the art and science of growing great vegetables. Additionally, interns will participate in the development of a community focused on a local food supply and are able to observe firsthand the benefits of its community spirit. Maysie's also founded the Agriculture Internship Training Alliance of Southeastern Pennsylvania (SAITA), which brings interns, farmers, and volunteers together for a Saturday workshop and farm tour at one of ten farms each month.

Commitment: Typically interns work at least forty hours per week, with longer hours in the spring and summer months. The internship term varies to meet personal or academic needs, with four to six interns at the farm at any given time.

Perks and Rewards: Housing is provided in a renovated farmhouse near the farm. A local university professor (who is also on the board of directors) lives in the house to ensure a healthfully functioning communal home and a model of ecologically responsible living. Interns also receive a moderate stipend and food from the garden.

The Essentials: Individuals who have an interest in sustainable agriculture, are in good health, and have the ability to work independently and in groups will thrive at Maysie's.

Your First Move: Call or email for more information.

For More Information:
Sam Cantrell, Internship Director
Maysie's Farm Conservation Center
15 St. Andrew's Ln.

Glenmoore, PA 19343
(610) 458-8129 • (610) 469-9662 (fax)
sam@maysiesfarm.org

MERCK FOREST AND FARMLAND CENTER

Sustainable Farm • Vermont • Seasonal
www.merckforest.org

·····································

AS A 3,150-ACRE preserve located in the Taconic Mountains of southwestern Vermont, Merck Forest and Farmland Center is a nonprofit conservation and education organization. Facilities include a small-diversified organic farm, working forest, maple sugar operation, rustic cabins and shelters, group camping area, solar-powered visitor center, and twenty-eight miles of trails for hiking and skiing.

What You'll Be Doing: During the summer months, outdoor-camp leaders teach environmental education programs that emphasize sustainable land use, ecology, community living and low-impact camping skills as well as lead backpacking, site-based camping, and other outdoor-activity experiences for children of all ages. Throughout the year, internships in sustainable farm and forest resources are also offered. Depending on seasonal needs and intern interests, responsibilities may include animal care, organic farming (everything from planting to harvesting), use of power tools and tractors, firewood and Christmas tree harvest and production, sugaring, and marketing.

Perks and Rewards: Interns receive a stipend of $65 per week (camp leaders start at $260 per week), housing, and complimentary farm produce, maple syrup, and meats as available. Training will also be offered in SOLO wilderness first-aid for camp leaders. (SOLO, which stands for Stonehearth Open Learning Opportunities, is one of the leading organizations in the field of wilderness emergency medicine.) During the summer, housing is provided at the upper and lower barn cabins, each which have wooden bunks and a woodstove (and just outside, a cook-house with a stove, refrigerator, and gravity-fed water). During the winter and fall, housing is provided at the lodge, which has running water, shower, gas lights, stove, and refrigerator.

The Essentials: Interns must have an interest in sustainable forestry and farming, a willingness to work hard and a positive attitude. Experience in backcountry leadership, teaching, backcountry medicine, water safety, and work with children is desired for camp leaders.

Your First Move: Submit cover letter, resume, and three letters of reference to begin the application process.

For More Information:
Staffing Coordinator
Merck Forest and Farmland Center
Route 315, Rupert Mountain Rd.
P.O. Box 86
Rupert, VT 05768
(802) 394-7836 • (802) 394-2519 (fax)
merck@vermontel.com

MICHAEL FIELDS AGRICULTURAL INSTITUTE

Farming • Wisconsin • 7 Months
www.mfai.org

Photo Credit: Tony Ends

A pair of interns pause to display freshly harvested onions as they make their way to the washing and packing station at Michael Fields

UP AT DAWN for orders of the day at 6 A.M. Muscle-straining, perspiration-dripping, back-aching work—all day long. Knock off when the mosquitoes or darkness drive you inside. And follow this routine for seven months. It's a training ground in organic garden and field. It's a hands-on program of instruction in lessons ranging from hand-to-hand combat with weeds to planting and cultivation by tractor. "It" is Michael Fields's Garden Training Program, which teaches a broad range of fundamental skills in a working CSA and market garden.

What You'll Be Doing: Ten students are selected each year to participate in this self-imposed boot camp for the mind, body, and soul. Along with learning the fundamentals of organic gardening (on twenty acres of French-intensive raised garden beds and field sites) and building relationships with communities and markets, students will also learn about traditional farm-life skills—yogurt and cheese making, food preservation, butchering, and knitting. Students also take part in the Collaborative Regional Alliance for Farmer Training (CRAFT), visiting other market-garden and subscription-farming operations in southern Wisconsin and northern Illinois periodically during the summer.

Commitment: Students work very long days, six days per week. Vegetable production is labor intensive, and the program strives to give a realistic introduction to the rigors that go along with farming without chemical shortcuts or large-scale mechanization. Training begins in mid-April with an intensive four-day CRAFT orientation workshop hosted at Michael Fields. Internship training runs well into October.

Perks and Rewards: Students are housed primarily in a historic dairy barn that has been renovated into an energy-efficient, comfortable dormitory and study space. Meals are cooked largely with produce that the students grow, with shared cooking responsibilities (which expand the students' sales knowledge of advantages, recipes, and best uses of specific vegetable varieties). A small, weekly stipend is also provided.

The Essentials: Those who love the outdoors, revere nature, and appreciate both the spiritual and physical qualities of intensive organic vegetable production will thrive at Michael Fields. Stamina and strength to keep up with production, cultivation, and harvest—in rain or shine, cool season or hot—are absolutely essential. Applicants must also be willing to take on individual responsibility for completing scores of specific garden tasks as well as working well in a team on group tasks. At minimum, students must be college graduate–age or older.

Your First Move: An application can be downloaded through their website, or you can request a student handbook, brochures, and application by mail, phone, or email.

For More Information:
Therese Philipp, Training Program Registrar
Michael Fields Agricultural Institute
Garden Training Program

W2493 County Road ES
East Troy, WI 53120
(262) 642-3303 • (262) 642-4028 (fax)
mfai@mfai.org

MICHAELA FARM

Organic Farming • Indiana • 7–8 Months
www.oldenburgfranciscans.org

BEGUN BY THE Sisters of St. Francis in 1854, Michaela Farm provides a center for organic food production, ecological education, and spiritual renewal. Farm resources and facilities include vegetable and flower gardens, a greenhouse, a pumphouse (which has been renovated into a hermitage), a retreat cottage, and a herd of beefalo that helps create a more "whole" farm system. Community Supported Agriculture (CSA) members subscribe to a weekly box of produce from June through October and a farm store supplies fresh produce and merchandise.

What You'll Be Doing: If you're looking for a supportive environment to gain hands-on skills in organic gardening and marketing, Michaela Farm is a wonderful place to be. The CSA program forms the framework for this intensive seven- to eight-month intern program. This time frame affords interns the opportunity to experience all aspects of farm life, including planning, greenhouse operation, field planting, harvesting, and packing produce for the CSA program (along with other chores including fence work, livestock care, or tree work).

Commitment: Interns begin either in March or April and continue through mid-November.

Perks and Rewards: Along with formal (and informal) instruction, a monthly stipend, meals (usually vegetarian), and housing are provided. Interns all live in one of two farmhouses in private rooms with a shared common space. Interns also get the chance to share in seasonal celebrations, biweekly community gatherings, and other events that contribute to community development.

The Essentials: Focused individuals with an exuberant love of the land and a willingness to work hard and learn will thrive at Michaela.

Your First Move: To begin the application process, call or email Michaela with the details of your interest and availability. A cover letter, resume, and references are required. Selected candidates are asked to come to the farm for a work experience and interview.

For More Information:
Ann Marie Quinn, Intern Director
Michaela Farm
P.O. Box 100
Oldenburg, IN 47036
(812) 933-0661 • (812) 933-6403 (fax)
michaelafarm@seidata.com

NEW MORNING FARM

Farming • Pennsylvania • 9 Months

NEW MORNING FARM is a family organic farm located in the rural ridges and valleys of south-central Pennsylvania. Over forty crops are grown, including berries and herbs, spread over twenty-five acres. They have also founded and actively participate in a successful wholesale marketing cooperative, representing a community of twenty farms. Six apprentices are hired each year for a full-season stay (usually beginning sometime in April and finishing in late November), with a primary role of assisting in management of crops, equipment, and marketing. A $600 monthly stipend is provided, along with training, all-inclusive board, and private rooms in one-person cabins with shared cooking and washing facilities. Besides on-the-job training, New Morning Farm always takes time for orderly discussions and seminars on topics of interest to apprentices.

For More Information:
Jim Crawford, Apprenticeship Program
New Morning Farm
HCR 71, Box 168
Hustontown, PA 17229
(814) 448-3904

NORTH COUNTRY FARMS

Organic Farming • Hawaii • 6 Months
www.skyfamily.com/northcountryfarms

LOCATED ON A "four-acre piece of heaven," North Country Farms serves a seventy-five-member CSA, runs a co-op, and operates a bed-and-breakfast on the grounds of the organic farm. Each year a hard-working couple interested in an apprentice lifestyle is needed to help in a variety of tasks in exchange for a redwood studio cottage. A six-month commitment is necessary.

Remember that your work comes only moment by moment, and as surely as God calls you to work, he gives the strength to do it. —PRISCILLA MAURICE

For More Information:
Lee Roversi, Owner
North Country Farms
P.O. Box 723
Kilauea, Kauai, HI 96754
(808) 828-1513 • (808) 828-0805 (fax)
ncfarms@aloha.net

QUAIL HILL COMMUNITY FARM

Organic Farm • New York • 3–8 Months
www.peconiclandtrust.org/preserve.htm

As A STEWARDSHIP project of the Peconic Land Trust, Quail Hill Farm is a certified organic farm located on the Long Island Sound (and ninety miles north of the Big Apple). The crop list features 225 varieties of vegetables, herbs, and flowers, along with a mature apple orchard, young peach trees, several varieties of raspberries, a few hives of bees, and a small flock of hens. In addition to educational programs and the sale of produce to local restaurants, over 160 CSA families visit the farm twice a week to harvest their own share of vegetables. From March 15 through November 15 (with various start dates), three to four apprentices learn the ropes of organic farming and work with CSA members. Housing and a $175 weekly stipend is provided. Call for more information.

For More Information:
Scott Chaskey, Apprenticeship Program
Quail Hill Community Farm
P.O. Box 1268
Amagansett, NY 11930
(631) 267-8492
schaskey@peconiclandtrust.org

RAPHAEL GARDEN

Biodynamic Farming • California • 1 Year
www.steinercollege.edu/biodynamics.html

As ONE OF America's leading Waldorf teacher-education colleges, Rudolf Steiner College offers a variety of teacher and training programs based on the innovative ideas and discoveries of Rudolph Steiner as well as an anthroposophical training center. Raphael Garden serves as the training ground for many activities at this thirteen-acre campus, including a one-year apprenticeship for those looking for a vocation in small-scale farming, gardening, or teaching. A combination of practical and theoretical skills in biodynamic and CSA farm production comprise this unique program. There is no fee for the training; however, it does involve hard work (from seven to ten hours per day, with occasional weekend chores). Housing in a new dormitory, vegetables, four weeks of vacation, and a $100-per-month stipend is provided. An application consists of a biography that answers why you'd like to become an apprentice and your future aspirations, two references, and when you are able to start the program. Further details can be found online or by calling.

For More Information:
Harald Hoven, Farmer
Raphael Garden
Apprenticeship Training Program
3937 Bannister Rd.
Fair Oaks, CA 95628
(916) 965-0389

INSPIRATIONS FROM RUDOLPH STEINER

Born in Austria in 1861, Dr. Steiner studied modern science and philosophy, edited Goethe's scientific works, and developed anthroposophy—the science of the spirit. Echoing the ancient Greek axiom, "Man, know thyself," Dr. Steiner described anthroposophy as an "awareness of one's humanity." Humanity (anthropos) has the inherent wisdom (sophia) to transform both itself and the world. Anthroposophy is a path in which the human heart, hand, and especially one's capacity for thinking are essential—and at the heart of Rudolph Steiner College and the apprenticeship experience.

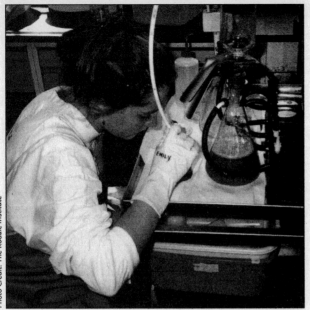

An intern at the Rodale Institute analyzes organic matter from the soil.

THE RODALE INSTITUTE EXPERIMENTAL FARM

Experimental Farm • Pennsylvania • 2–9 Months
www.rodaleinstitute.org

RODALE-STYLE FARMING has changed over the years—from organic and low-input to sustainable and regenerative—but the intent is unchanged: to provide more healthful food by creating and maintaining healthy soil. Each year more than twenty-five thousand visitors see the results of health-based growing techniques first-hand in both the field crops and the demonstration garden; it is hoped that each visitor will rediscover that the food they eat is a primary tool in achieving optimum health and avoidance of illness and disease. At the experimental farm, interns assist the staff in a variety of projects while gaining hands-on study and educational experience. Internships are generally available in the following departments (but may change due to funding): creative-education team, farm operations (a complete view of what it takes to run and profit from an organic farm), international programs (developing self-sustaining organic models within other countries), and soil health. Interns receive an hourly wage and generally work between the months of March and November for two to nine months. Priority will be given to applications received prior to February 15. Unpaid internships are available year-round and can be arranged in cooperation with a college or university for credit or with funding from a scholarship or other grant.

For More Information:
Sandra Strausser, Human Resources
The Rodale Institute Experimental Farm
Internship Program
611 Siegfriedale Rd.
Kutztown, PA 19530-9749
(610) 683-1428 • (610) 683-1431 (fax)
sandra.strausser@rodaleinst.org

ROXBURY FARM

Farming • New York • 1–9 Months
www.roxburyfarm.com

ROXBURY FARM, A 650-member CSA farm in upstate New York, is located on 150 acres in the Hudson Valley and serves CSA members locally, in the Capital District (Albany), and New York City. Members pay for twenty-seven weeks of fresh, in-season, organic vegetables before the season begins. This provides the farm with committed support to pay for the actual cost of the farm operation.

What You'll Be Doing: Each season the farm looks for four to five apprentices to learn about farming while they take part in all aspects of the operation—from field preparation and greenhouse work to harvesting and distribution. Apprentices will also take part in the Collaborative Regional Alliance for Farmer Training (CRAFT) program, with a chance to visit twelve to fifteen farms, attend workshops, and meet other farmers and apprentices. The CRAFT training program was founded at Roxbury Farm and is a great opportunity to create a network of farming resources.

Commitment: The season runs from April until December; however, apprenticeships can be arranged for all or part of the season. During the peak of the season, apprentices can figure on ten hours per day and during the spring and late fall the workload falls to eight to nine hours a day. Every other Saturday apprentices travel to a CRAFT farm visit.

Perks and Rewards: A stipend reflecting experience and responsibility is paid monthly. On-farm housing with full facilities, along with vegetables and fruit produced on the farm are also provided. Many agricultural resources such as harvest manuals, seeding schedules, and biodynamic farming resource books are available for use.

A man's accomplishments in life are the cumulative effect of his attention to detail. —JOHN FOSTER DULLES

The Essentials: Candidates should have some farming experience as well as the desire to learn how to farm efficiently in order to produce affordable food. Those who are self-motivated, have a love for hard work, and who have good organizational skills do best. Many of Roxbury's past apprentices have gone on to have their own successful farm operations.

Your First Move: Send a letter of interest, including a short description of future goals and why this apprenticeship interests you, along with a resume and two references, either by email or mail. Candidates are also asked to visit the farm before a final commitment is made (so you'll get a good feeling for the farm and the work).

For More Information:
Jody Bolluyt, Intern Coordinator
Roxbury Farm
2501 State Route 9H
P.O. Box 338
Kinderhook, NY 12106
(518) 758-8558
info@roxburyfarm.com

SHELBURNE FARMS

Farm Education • Vermont • 3–6 Months
www.shelburnefarms.org

LOCATED IN VERMONT's Champlain Valley, Shelburne Farms is a fourteen-hundred-acre working farm and dairy (known for their incredible farmhouse cheddar cheese) and offers year-round conservation education programs and events for students, teachers, and people of all ages. Organic Gardening apprentices work alongside a master gardener in the two-acre market garden, with organic vegetables, herbs, and fruits that are grown for the Inn (the farm's historic guesthouse). Positions begin in April for six months, with job responsibilities ranging from planting and cultivating to assisting with animal care and educational garden programs. Education apprentices instruct and assist with the development of agricultural and natural resource education programs for preschool children through adults throughout the year (usually one or two seasons). Individuals holding a degree in environmental studies, education, or agriculture are preferred. All apprentices receive a stipend of $180 per week, along with participation in orientation and training events, on-site housing, and access to in-season garden produce and inn meals (and an abundance of free-range,

organic chicken eggs!). Send a cover letter and resume to begin the application process.

For More Information:
Amy Powers, Work and Learn Coordinator
Shelburne Farms
1611 Harbor Rd.
Shelburne, VT 05482
(802) 985-8686 • (802) 985-8123 (fax)
apowers@shelburnefarms.org

SISTERS HILL FARM

Organic Farming • New York • 3–7 Months

WITH A MISSION to "grow healthy food which nurtures bodies, spirits, communities, and the earth," Sisters Hill Farm is guided by a heartfelt reverence for creation. Owned by the Sisters of Charity (advocates of the poor for over two hundred years), four acres of the 150 are dedicated to high-quality organic produce and flowers that support a 170-member CSA (with over ten thousand pounds donated to local charities).

What You'll Be Doing: The farm is committed to creating the best learning environment possible for their apprentices. Each apprentice will be exposed to and expected to competently perform all farm operations—from greenhouse management to driving a tractor. The work will definitely be physically demanding; however, many hands make for light work. Since it is a small, innovative farm, interns will also have ample hands-on learning opportunities, with projects in the past that have included a custom greenhouse, a walk-in cooler, and a root-washing machine.

Commitment: Two apprentices are needed each year—one for the full season (from mid-April to the end of November) and one for the summer months. The normal workweek consists of five- to eight-hour weekdays and five hours on Saturday.

Perks and Rewards: A stipend of $800 per month is provided along with farm produce and housing. A one-bedroom apartment with a screened-in porch (complete with swing!) is available for the full-season intern. The summer apprentice will have a small, private room with bath inside the barn. There is also an in-ground pool on the property (there's nothing more refreshing than a cool dip after a long sweaty workday). It's noted that the farmer is an avid cyclist, runner, canoe enthusiast, and rower and is always looking for partners in these activities!

The Essentials: Those who have a passion for agriculture, a love for physical labor and the outdoors, an openness to learning, curiosity, and who enjoy a good laugh will thrive here.

Your First Move: Call for an application packet.

For More Information:
David Hambleton, Farmer
Sisters Hill Farm
Apprenticeship Program
P.O. Box 22
Stanfordville, NY 12581
(845) 868-7048
shfarm@earthlink.net

SLIDE RANCH

Sustainable Education • California • 11 Months
www.slideranch.org

As a NONPROFIT education center, the 134-acre Slide Ranch teaches respect for the human role in the web of life by hands-on experience. Educational programs encourage participants to touch, taste, smell, hear, and observe plants, sea life, and the earth. Whether milking a goat, observing bees make honey, searching for worms, turning compost, making solar ovens, or exploring the tidepools, visitors will gain an understanding of organic-food production, animal husbandry, recycling, open-space conservation, and the responsibility each of us has for sustaining a healthy environment.

Your Surroundings: As a park partner with the Golden Gate National Recreation Area, Slide Ranch is nestled in the rugged coast on the ocean side of Highway One (just north of San Francisco). A short hike from the farm and residential areas of Slide Ranch bring visitors to the shore itself, where an abundance of coastal marine life thrives in the inter-tidal zone tide pools. Most people who come here feel they've discovered something very special.

What You'll Be Doing: Upon arrival, teachers-in-residence participate in a three-week intensive training program, and throughout the program, they receive ongoing support, supervision, staff development, and enrichment. Under the guidance of a head teacher and program director, teachers gain valuable outdoor-education teaching experiences by teaching groups of all ages. Beyond your responsibilities in the teaching programs, teachers-in-residence are also responsible for a chore area, which includes caring for the garden and compost or one of the many animals on the ranch.

Commitment: Positions begin in early February and end in mid-December. Living at the ranch is more than a nine-to-five job; it's a full-time commitment. Operating as a small community that works, lives, and plays together, all residents are expected to take part in the shared decision making and domestic responsibilities that go along with being part of a community.

Perks and Rewards: A monthly stipend is provided. While each teacher is provided with an individual room and full board, cooking and dining space is shared, and all residents help in the preparation of food and the maintenance of the facilities. There is a five-day community trip scheduled, and each teacher is given several flexible vacation days to schedule during their tenure. Many former Slide Ranch teachers now teach professionally, while others work in the social services, community-development organizations, sustainable agriculture, and environmental organizations.

The Essentials: Candidates must have a keen interest in environmental education and community spirit.

Your First Move: Call for a brochure and application guidelines. Speaking other languages or having experience working with low-income or special populations is pertinent information that should be included in your application.

For More Information:
Program Director
Slide Ranch
2025 Shoreline Highway
Muir Beach, CA 94965
(415) 381-6155 • (415) 381-5762 (fax)
slideranch@igc.org

STILL POINT COMMUNITY FARM

Biodynamic Farming • New York • 1 Week–1 Year
www.bestweb.net/~stillpt

SPREAD OVER EIGHTY acres (including woodlands, a large creek, open fields, and twenty acres of cropland), Still Point Community Farm is a biodynamic vegetable farm, with produce marketed through both local and New York City CSAs and farmers' markets. What's unique about Still Point is the philosophy behind the farm: how to lead a meaningful, satisfying existence while meeting the demands of life in the modern world. This revolves around physical work, close contact with like-minded people, and "real" food.

Do not wish to be anything but what you are, and try to be that perfectly. —ST. FRANCIS DE SALES

What You'll Be Doing: Six apprentices join the farm each year (two for a year and up to four in the summer). Each apprentice will take responsibility for a specific aspect of farm life and work, depending on individual interests and abilities. Most of the work on the farm is group oriented; however, through specialization, each person gains an intimate knowledge of some aspect of farming.

Commitment: Full-year apprentices begin in January, while summer apprentices begin in May.

Perks and Rewards: Apprentices receive full room and board and a modest stipend.

The Essentials: Farming experience is welcomed but not necessary. The people who tend to thrive at Still Point come with a curiosity and openness that allows them to accept what is without trying to change it. Short-term visitors are also welcome, particularly foreign travelers looking for the farm's unique way of life. Visitors participate in all aspects of farm life and may stay from one week to three months or longer. In return, room and board is provided.

Your First Move: Call or email for more information or to schedule a farm visit.

For More Information:
Nathaniel Thompson, Apprenticeship Director
Still Point Community Farm
103 Amenia Union Rd.
Amenia, NY 12501
(845) 373-7189
stillpt@bestweb.net

TILLERS INTERNATIONAL

Traditional Farming • Michigan • 3–9 Months
www.wmich.edu/tillers

TILLERS TRAINING CENTER offers learning opportunities in traditional farming and crafting techniques, including classes in alternative energy, animal power, blacksmithing, farming, rope and broom making, and woodworking, as well as old-time barn raising. Classes and activities are available year-round with fees ranging from free to $310. In addition to classes, Tillers offers internships in farming and woodworking. Two to four interns help with the farm, shop, and organizational work over a three- to nine-month period. While the pay is modest, most of the compensation comes from the opportunity to learn rare skills. On the farm, interns learn to drive oxen and horses in an array of tasks from manure spreading to haymak-

ing. In the wood shop, interns learn to shape ox yokes, bend bows, and construct joinery for timber frames. An old abbey farmhouse serves as a guest house for students and interns working at Tillers. (Breakfast and lunches are provided; there is a kitchen to prepare evening meals.) Contact Tillers for their most recent catalog and application materials.

For More Information:
Dick Roosenberg, Program Organizer
Tillers International
5239 S. 24th St.
Kalamazoo, MI 49002
(800) 498-2700 • (616) 344-3233 • (616) 344-3238 (fax)
tillersox@aol.com

WOLLAM GARDENS

Flower Farm • Virginia • 10 Weeks
www.wollamgardens.com

AT WOLLAM GARDENS, three apprentices have the opportunity to learn all aspects of a cut-flower growing operation—from seeding, planting, and weeding to cutting and bouquet making. Most of the flowers are propagated in a small greenhouse and grown outdoors on almost five acres. Flowers are sold to florists and at three large farmers' markets in the Washington, D.C., area. A $150-per-week stipend is provided, along with a private room in a historic colonial farmhouse, meals, laundry, and an Internet connection. Note that life on the farm is a shared-living experience—all share in the chores of cooking, shopping, and cleaning. Positions are available beginning mid-March through October, and most apprentices make a commitment of ten weeks (although

shorter/longer time frames are possible). To begin the application process, contact them by phone or email.

For More Information:
Bob Wollam, Owner
Wollam Gardens
5167 Jeffersonton Rd.
Jeffersonton, VA 22724
(540) 937-3222 • (540) 937-8290 (fax)
wollam@summit.net

WORLD HUNGER RELIEF

Farming/Ministry/Hunger Awareness • Texas/Haiti/Mexico • 15 Months
www.worldhungerrelief.org

AT THE HEART of World Hunger Relief Inc. (WHRI) is the philosophy to live simply, helping those who struggle to meet their basic needs by sharing and investing what God has given us into others. Their program roots encompass three key elements: training in intensive, natural, sustainable farming techniques for those who are hungry and whose work does not provide sustenance; education in methods of conserving and sharing resources for those with an abundance; and on-site training and assistance in sustainable development in specific locations around the world. At their demonstration farm and training center in Texas (which includes a new straw-bale visitor/education center), WHRI runs a CSA and farm market, offers seminars on intensive organic gardening and hunger awareness, and works with low-income, elderly, and disabled individuals on community garden projects. WHRI also supports a twenty-two-acre training center in northeastern Haiti.

What You'll Be Doing: Each year, WHRI selects ten interns to participate in a twelve-month sustainable farming and development program, followed by a three-month field experience in Ferrier, Haiti. From day one, interns become a major part of the farm. Along with the daily (and intensive) labors of running a vegetable farm and goat dairy, interns are also involved in leading tours, teaching classes, giving devotions, and running a small-business (using farm produce). The facilities are to be used as a training tool for the interns to practice all aspects of development work for developing countries.

Perks and Rewards: Dormitory-style housing and fresh organic produce are provided. Outside financial support is needed for an intern to work on the farm; however,

Photo Credit: Matthew Lester

A World Hunger Relief intern prepares for his three-month field experience in Haiti.

these financial needs can be fairly minimal. In addition, WHRI supports interns in traveling to Educational Concerns for Hunger Organization (see page 245 for more information) for their annual conference in Fort Myers, Florida. This conference is an excellent opportunity for interns to talk with fellow workers in developing countries and participate in workshops.

The Essentials: Candidates must be eager, creative, industrious, committed, willing to be taught, and able to work independently when needed.

Your First Move: Call or email for more information. A visit to the farm for an interview is welcomed.

For More Information:
Dale Barron, Development Director
World Hunger Relief
P.O. Box 639
Elm Mott, TX 76640
(254) 799-5611
whri@hot.rr.com

Real development is not leaving things behind, as on a road, but drawing life from them, as from a root. —G.K. CHESTERTON

265

WILLING WORKERS ON ORGANIC FARMS

WWOOF (wuf), v. [O.E. woef, to travel in search of organic farms; to pull weeds in exchange for alms.]—From *The Shorter Oxford Dictionary*

Established in the United Kingdom in the seventies, Willing Workers on Organic Farms (commonly known as WWOOF) was initially designed to allow people from the city to experience rural areas of the U.K. Today its purpose is to promote the organic agricultural movement in the global village in which we live. Working in exchange for your keep is the basis of WWOOFing. As a short-term volunteer, you'll help with organic farming, gardening, home-steading (animal care, weeding, harvesting, and construction projects), or other environmentally con-scious projects in exchange for room and board (usually three wholesome meals). A half-day's work for a full-day's keep seems to be a good rule of thumb, with the length of stay varying from a few days to several months (and sometimes longer). Of course, this varies with each country and farm.

This type of lifestyle affords the opportunity to obtain firsthand experience in organic/biodynamic growing methods by working with experts in the field; a chance to meet, talk, learn, and exchange views with others in the organic movement; the abil-ity to learn about life in the host country by living and working as a family; and the opportunity to travel in areas of a country that might have been overlooked.

GETTING INVOLVED

Details of farms registered with WWOOF in each country are available through the various programs listed on the following pages. Each organization pub-lishes a directory of opportunities that you can obtain for a fee that generally ranges from $20 to $40 (cash), plus one or two International Reply Coupons (IRC) for programs outside the U.S. Fees for each program are listed in U.S. currency unless otherwise noted.

Once you have received the WWOOF listings, it's then your responsibility to contact the farm directly and arrange a mutually convenient time and period of work. Telephoning or emailing the host seems to be the most convenient method. For those with families, some farms are prepared to take chil-dren, with meal and supervision arrangements agreed upon between the WWOOF member and host beforehand.

If you'll be working in a country other than your own, be sure to read through the visa requirements. According to most immigration departments, WWOOFing is seen as voluntary work and therefore can be done by holders of a regular or tourist visa, provided that it is not the main reason for coming to a country.

WHAT IS AN IRC?
This acronym stands for International Reply Coupon, which serves as a form of payment for sending a twenty-gram letter anywhere in the world. IRCs are available at most post offices and cost slightly more than the cost of an international stamp (generally $1).

WWOOF CONNECTIONS AROUND THE WORLD

▶ North America

HAWAII

Ever heard of "lilikoi" or "awapuhi?" As an apprentice on a Hawaii Organic Farmers Association (HOFA)-sponsored farm on the Hawaiian Islands, apprentices will plant, harvest (and taste) these and hundreds of other tropical fruits and vegetables. And what's unique about the Hawaiian Islands is that they contain eleven of the thirteen microclimates found throughout the world. Thus, apprentices have the opportunity to work in dry, wet, coastal, or mountainous regions. HOFA provides all the details of farm opportunities—including contacts and a short description of each farm—for a fee of $20. Most farms offer room and board, a stipend, or both. Positions are available year-round; however, if you're interested in a particular crop, be sure to do some research. Some crops, like pineapples, are generally harvested in July and August, while bananas and papayas can be harvested year-round. Call or email for more information or fill out the questionnaire that's found online. By the way, lilikoi is a wild passion fruit and awapuhi is edible-root ginger.

For More Information:
Farm Apprentice Program Director
Hawaii Organic Farmers Association
P.O. Box 6863
Hilo, HI 96720
(877) 674-4632 • (808) 969-7789
(808) 969-7759 (fax)
hofa@nethawaii.net
www.hawaiiorganicfarmers.org

MAINE

The Maine Organic Farmers apprenticeship program places individuals in one of forty working sustainable farms in Maine. Participants learn rural skills and gain firsthand experiences in market growing, livestock management, marketing techniques, food preservation, homesteading, and dairy farming. Opportunities are available year-round; however, most farmers look for apprentices from March through October. Room, board, instruction, practice, and a stipend are provided in exchange for your labor. There is a $20 application fee.

For More Information:
Farm Apprentice Placement Program
Maine Organic Farmers and Gardeners Association
P.O. Box 170
Unity, ME 04988-0170
(207) 568-4142 • (207) 568-4141 (fax)
mofga@mofga.org
www.mofga.org

VERMONT

Certified Organic. This is at the heart of the Northeast Organic Farming Association of Vermont (NOFA-VT). Along with summer workshops, a winter conference, and certifying over 225 organic farms each year, NOFA-VT programs include getting organic produce into elementary school lunch programs (and agriculture education into the curriculum!), making organic food more accessible to limited-income individuals, and apprenticeship and WWOOF opportunities. Each year Vermont farmers provide exciting opportunities for young farmers interested in learning about mixed vegetable production, greenhouse tomato operations, maple syruping, haying, growing berries or apples, raising poultry or beef, or producing cheese. For a fee of $25, NOFA-VT will send you a directory (published each year in February) of over sixty-five farmers looking for apprentices and willing workers, as well as information that will help you locate the appropriate apprenticeship. In addition, discounts on books and free admission to all NOFA-VT training sessions and workshops are provided. Applications for apprenticeships are accepted year-round, although most placements are made March through October.

For More Information:
Apprenticeship Program Coordinator
Northeast Organic Farming Association
   of Vermont
P.O. Box 697
Richmond, VT 05477
(802) 434-4122 • (802) 434-5154 (fax)
info@nofavt.org
www.nofavt.org

WWOOF

WWOOF

▸ Canada / USA / Hawaii

John Vanden Heuvel states that WWOOF Canada continues to grow (organically and sustainably) and now has over four hundred hosts all across Canada with two hundred of these in British Columbia. Just recently they have introduced WWOOF opportunities in the U.S. and Hawaii (over 120 farms and other hosts). Most opportunities are offered spring through fall; however, volunteers are needed year-round. Send a letter outlining when you'd like to come and where you're thinking of going to. With your request include two International Reply Coupons (IRCs) if you are in the U.S., three IRCs if you are outside of North America, along with a membership contribution of $30 (cash only). As soon as WWOOF Canada receives your materials, they will immediately send a booklet listing farms, descriptions, and contact information.

For More Information:
John Vanden Heuvel, Director
WWOOF Canada
4429 Carlson Rd.
Nelson, BC V1L 6X3
Canada
(250) 354-4417 • (250) 354-4417 (fax)
wwoofcan@uniserve.com
www.wwoofusa.com/canada

CityFarmer.org promotes the new and growing field of urban agriculture, which encompasses a wide variety of interests and concerns ranging from rooftop gardens and composting toilets to air pollution and mental/physical health. Information can be found on short- and long-term job openings (www.cityfarmer.org/jobs.html) and WWOOF-related opportunities (www.cityfarmer.org/wwoof.html) situated mostly in North America.

▸ Asia

JAPAN

For $40, you can obtain the WWOOF Japan host list (with text in both English and Japanese), which consists of contact information for twenty farms (and growing).

For More Information:
Glenn Burns
WWOOF Japan
Kita 7-Jo, Nishi 1-Chome, 1-11-601
Kita-Ku, Sapporo 060-0807
Japan
wwoofjapan@thejapangroup.com
www.thejapangroup.com/wwoofjapan

KOREA

WWOOF Korea (www.wwoofkorea.com/english.html) provides a free listing of thirty-six farms in South Korea through their website, or you can order the book for 15,000WON (about $12). Opportunities include everything from growing grapes and working on a potter's wheel at a Buddhist farm to growing herbs and vegetables on Cheju Island, touted in travel magazines as Korea's Hawaii.

▸ Australia / New Zealand

WWOOF Australia publishes a handful of organic farming books that include their network of hosts in Australia and throughout the world. Their flagship list, *The Australian WWOOF Book* (commonly known as the AUSlist), includes more than fifteen hundred participating hosts who are mainly pursuing a simple, sustainable lifestyle. Also included are nurseries, schools, and people running home businesses such as guest houses, publishers, and writers, who have a willingness to host visitors for a cultural exchange experience. The list runs $50AUS (which includes shipping) and is updated every six months. Other publications include the *WWOOF Independent Host List* (which includes more than six hundred hosts in forty-eight countries, for $27AUS), the *WWOOF Organic Bed & Breakfast List* for $11 AUS, and the *Organic Travelers Spiritual Retreat and Communities List* for $11 AUS. See their website for details and payment options in other currencies (offering secure, credit card payments).

For More Information:
Garry Ainsworth
WWOOF Australia (WWOOF Pty Ltd)
Mt. Murrindal Co-op
Buchan, Victoria 3885
Australia
(011) 61 03 5155-0218
wwoof@wwoof.com.au
www.wwoof.com.au

The Australian WWOOF Training Centre is mostly for students and travelers from non-English-speaking countries who need preparation for working and living on an organic farm in Australia (with training ranging from horse riding to sheep shearing). One- and four-week training courses are offered for a tuition fee of $270AUS to $1,000AUS. Housing is provided on the G'day Farmstay with the college principal and his family.

For More Information:
Australian WWOOF Training Centre
P.O. Box 60
Gulargambone NSW 2828
Australia
(011) 61 02 6825-1076
info@wwoof-australia.com.au
www.wwoof-australia.com.au

For $20, WWOOF New Zealand provides a listing of more than six hundred properties, including farms, permaculture properties, market gardens, communities, and ventures in self-sufficiency in which organic growing plays some part. Take a tour of some of the farms on their website.

For More Information:
Andrew and Jane Strange
WWOOF New Zealand
P.O. Box 1172
Nelson
New Zealand
(011) 64 3 544-9890
support@wwoof.co.nz
www.wwoof.co.nz

It's the good, the bad, and the ugly: accommodations can range from a bike shop to a retreat center to a biodynamic farm in the hills.

—ALONA JASIK (a *Back Door* reader) on her experience at organic farms in New Zealand

► Europe / United Kingdom
AUSTRIA

Looking to get into the Austrian countryside? A one-year membership with WWOOF Austria provides a detailed listing of over one hundred farms along with four newsletters throughout the year. The fee runs $20 plus two IRCs. Check out a sample of farm descriptions online.

For More Information:
Hildegard Gottleib
WWOOF Austria
Langegg 155, A 8511
St. Stefan ob Stainz
Austria
(011) 43 3463-82270
wwoof.welcome@telering.at
http://members.telering.at/wwoof.welcome/
    english.htm

WWOOF

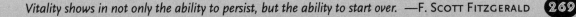

BULGARIA

Upon becoming a member of New Century, you'll receive a WWOOF book outlining all the farms in Bulgaria as well as gain access to the hosts online. Current membership pricing is available online.

For More Information:
Youth Exchange Centre—New Century
P.O. Box 169
Plovdiv 4023
Bulgaria
(011) 359 88 1235
wwoof@abv.bg
www.newcentury.hit.bg/wwoof.html

DENMARK

Getting involved with WWOOF Denmark is ideal for those who want to spend an active and inspiring "time off" experience getting to know aspects of organic farming and environmentally friendly living, along with learning more about the Danish culture. In Denmark, WWOOF is called Vi Hjaelper Hinaden (VHH for short), which means "we help each other." Programs range from a few days to a few months, with most hosts using biodynamic and organic farm methods. In addition, activities such as sustainable house building, renewable energy, and permaculture-style farming are also common. The directory can be ordered for $50DKK (about $6).

For More Information:
Inga Nielsen
VHH/WWOOF Denmark
Asenvej 35
9881 Bindslev
Denmark
(011) 45 9893 8607
info@wwoof.dk
www.wwoof.dk

GERMANY

Each March, WWOOF Germany publishes a booklet (available in English) containing contact information for over 150 farms for $18EUR (cash only).

For More Information:
WWOOF Deutschland
Freiwillige Helfer auf ökologischen Höfen E.V.
Postfach 210259
01263 Dresden
Germany
info@wwoof.de
www.wwoof.de

ITALY

The WWOOF Italia list includes biodynamic and organic farms throughout the entire country. Some hosts are farmers that sell their products for a living, while others just want to be self-sufficient, or simply grow their own organic vegetables. Membership runs 45,000LIRE (around $20), which includes an official membership card, insurance coverage in Italy for a twelve-month period, and the most current listings (which you can receive through either email or regular mail). Their website has a nifty currency converter so you'll know exactly how much to pay.

For More Information:
Bridget Matthews
WWOOF Italia
Via Casavecchia 109
57022 Castagneto Carducci, Livorno
Italy
(011) 39 0565-765001
info@wwoof.it
www.wwoof.it

WWOOF

INSIDER TIPS FROM WWOOF ITALIA

- Always telephone or write before visiting a farm (if you expect a reply, always enclose an IRC or stamp). Try to plan your movements well in advance and keep hosts informed of changes in your plans. Never turn up unexpectedly on a host's doorstep expecting to be made welcome.
- Make sure that you have a clear agreement with your host as to the basis of your stay (e.g. working hours, food, accommodation, facilities, arrangements if you take children with you, and so forth) before you arrive.
- Always take working clothes (i.e. gloves and good shoes or boots). Sometimes it may be necessary to take a sleeping bag.
- It would be a good idea to make sure you and your host have a language in common!

SWITZERLAND

Details of organic farms (from big to small and rural to urban) that are registered with WWOOF Switzerland can be obtained by sending $2 or two IRCs (for postage) and $15 (no checks).

For More Information:
WWOOF Switzerland
Postfach 59
CH-8124 Maur
Switzerland
wwoof@dataway.ch
www.dataway.ch/~reini/wwoof

UNITED KINGDOM

(including England, Scotland, Wales, and North Ireland)

WWOOF UK publishes a newsletter every month, which contains details of longer stays, events, developments, training and opportunities in the organic movement and includes members' contributions and advertisements. For an annual membership fee of $20 you will receive six issues. Details can be found through their website.

For More Information:
Fran Whittle
WWOOF United Kingdom
P.O. Box 2675
Lewes, East Sussex BN7 1RB
England
United Kingdom
www.wwoof.org/wuk2.html

Check out the
International WWOOF Association
at www.wwoof.org to see what's new
in the WWOOF movement.

WWOOF

Individuality is the salt of common life. You may have to live in a crowd but you do not have to like it, nor subsist on its food. You may have your own orchard. You may drink at a hidden spring. Be yourself if you would serve others. —HENRY VAN DYKE

RECOMMENDED RESOURCES. . . . .

Every December the **Alternative Farming Systems Information Center** publishes *Educational and Training Opportunities in Sustainable Agriculture,* a sixty-page resource listing hundreds of opportunities in organic, alternative, or sustainable agriculture work, education, and training. The majority of listings are in the U.S. and Canada, although a handful are overseas. Call for your free copy—(301) 504-6422—or view the listings at www.nal.usda.gov/afsic (click on the publications link or type in www.nal.usda.gov/afsic/afsic_pubs/edtr.htm). Each listing is verified with the organization every year, with changes and additions incorporated throughout the year on their web version.

Appropriate Technology Transfer for Rural Areas, commonly known as ATTRA, publishes a 120-page listing of programs offering internships and apprenticeships on farms, sustainable living centers, and the like. Updated each January, the listing is a gold mine of opportunities for the budding farmer, with extensive program details broken down by four regions in the USA and Canada. The complete listing is accessible through www.attra.org (click on "Resources"), with the option of a PDF download. For those without web access, call for your complimentary copy at (800) 346-9140.

From mango and wine-grape picking to orange and peach harvests, there is a way to continually be employed in Australia. Sponsored by **Australian JobSearch** (www.jobsearch.gov.au/harvesttrail.asp), visitors can choose various harvest trail options to explore the opportunities, complete with contact information and dates of harvest.

The Biodynamic Farming and Gardening Association provides an abundance of information on the biodynamic movement as well as a bimonthly magazine of opportunities for biodynamic apprenticeships. Single copies cost $6, or an annual subscription runs $45 (which includes a one-year membership). You can also explore current and ongoing internships and apprenticeships through www.biodynamics.com. For more information contact the Biodynamic Farming and Gardening Association, Building 1002B, Thoreau Center, The Presidio, P.O. Box 29135, San Francisco, CA 94129-0135; (888) 516-7797, biodynamic@aol.com.

For a fee of $20, the **Ohio Ecological Food and Farm Association** (www.oeffa.com) links prospective apprentices and farmers seeking apprentices through a special matching service. After submitting application materials (by January 15), applicants will receive mailings of potential hosts. Farmer and apprentice applicants contact each other for mutual "sizing up," farm visitations, and making arrangements. Apprentices must be eighteen or older and no previous farm experience is necessary. For more information contact Sean McGovern, Apprenticeship Program Coordinator, Ohio Ecological Food and Farm Association, P.O. Box 82234, Columbus, OH 43202; (614) 421-2022, seanmcgovern@oeffa.com.

As a match-making service for those looking for an apprenticeship, internship, or employment in the organic farming movement in the U.S., **OrganicVolunteers.com** offers hundreds of opportunities that cover everything from programs in ecotourism and education to gardening and construction.

The Robyn Van En Center for CSA Resources (www.csacenter.org) provides a searchable directory (by zip or state) of CSA farms throughout the U.S., as well as an extensive list of organizations involved in the CSA movement.

The **Rural Heritage Good Farming Apprenticeship Network** (www.ruralheritage.com/apprenticeship) is designed to link future farmers with experienced handlers of working draft horses, mules, and oxen to ensure that animal-powered farming and logging practices are passed down through the generations. The participating farmers—ranging from British Columbia to Tennessee and from California to Nova Scotia—offer a broad range of learn-by-working experiences. Participating farms can be viewed on the Web, or for $10 you can obtain a printout (or email list). For more information contact the Rural Heritage Good Farming Apprenticeship Network, 281 Dean Ridge Ln., Gainesboro, TN 38562-5039; (931) 268-0655, editor@ruralheritage.com.

The **Seattle Tilth Association** (www.seattletilth.org) promotes the art of organic gardening in an urban setting and maintains gardens at the Good Shepherd Center in Seattle's Wallingford district. Volunteers are an integral part of Tilth operations and a great way to learn organic gardening through hands-on experiences. A listing of Washington organic farms looking for seasonal workers is available through the association for $3 (to cover copying and postage costs). Explore the possibilities on the Web. For more information contact Lisa Taylor and Olga Schifani, Garden Coordinators, Seattle Tilth Association, 4649 Sunnyside Ave. N., Room 1, Seattle, WA 98103; (206) 633-0451, tilth@speakeasy.org.

FURTHER READING.....................

We're living in a society where more and more people take things for granted and do not learn important skills for leading a self-reliant and simple lifestyle. *Back to Basics* (Reader's Digest, $30) provides practical and useful information that brings you back to the "old-fashioned" way of doing things—such as from converting trees to lumber and building a home from them, growing and harvesting your own vegetable garden, learning traditional crafts and homesteading skills, or enjoyable activities that don't hurt your pocketbook. The pages are filled with building a new way of life.

Nothing could be more fundamental to the needs of an increasingly crowded world than food. Based on biointensive gardening techniques, *How to Grow More Vegetables* (Ten Speed Press, $17.95) will show you how to raise enough fresh, healthy, organic vegetables for a family of four on a parcel of land as small as eight hundred square feet. John Jeavons provides the ultimate how-to manual for sustainable gardening, with results that are more bountiful.

Work is not always required . . . there is such a thing as sacred idleness, the cultivation of which is now fearfully neglected —GEORGE MACDONALD

A FARMER'S CREED

I believe a man's greatest possession is his dignity and that no calling bestows this more abundantly than farming.

I believe hard work and honest sweat are the building blocks of a person's character.

I believe that farming, despite its hardships and disappointments, is the most honest and honorable way a man can spend his days on this earth.

I believe my children are learning values that will last a lifetime and can be learned in no other way.

I believe farming provides education for life and that no other occupation teaches so much about birth, growth, and maturity in such a variety of ways.

I believe many of the best things in life are indeed free: the splendor of a sunrise, the rapture of wide open spaces, the exhilarating sight of your land greening each spring.

I believe true happiness comes from watching your crops ripen in the field, your children grow tall in the sun, your whole family feel the pride that springs from their shared experience.

I believe that by my toil I am giving more to the world than I am taking from it, an honor that does not come to all men.

I believe my life will be measured ultimately by what I have done for my fellow men, and by this standard I fear no judgement.

I believe when a man grows old and sums up his days, he should be able to stand tall and feel pride in the life he's lived.

I believe in farming because it makes all this possible.

—Written for the New Holland America,
originally published in 1975

o one can tell you how to live your life. You are the artist and must shape your experiences with your own hand. Whether working as an accomplished artist or just starting out in the field, creative-minded painters, writers, photographers, actors, musicians, dancers, crafters, filmmakers, architects, exhibit designers, museum enthusiasts, living-history performers, archaeologists, historians, and researchers will find a supportive arts environment to learn and grow from in this section. Come take your career to new heights, explore your options, and learn what it takes to do what you love and make enough money to support your creative passions.

A musician must make his music, an artist must paint, a poet must write if he is to ultimately be at peace with himself.

—ABRAHAM MASLOW

Unique Opportunities to Explore in This Section:

- Recognizing the need for artists and writers to set aside periods of time to work intensively on projects away from the distractions of everyday life but still have a social connection, artist communities and resident programs offer a unique way to foster your creative pursuits virtually expense-free (page 280).

- Whether you'd like to gain more experience in stage management, artistic design, or any other facet of professional theatre, the Seattle Repertory Theatre's training program has something for each budding artist (page 304)—as do plenty of other theatres, play houses, and music and dance festivals profiled in this section.

- The Smithsonian Institution is the world's largest museum and, quite possibly, has the world's largest museum internship program. The Center for Education and Museum Studies coordinates the central referral service for all internship programs, including sixteen museums and galleries, and the National Zoo (page 305).

Photo Credit: Phil Grant

The chamber music class with Eagle's Nest Foundation (page 112) performs barefoot as their music lifts through the trees.

- At some point in our life, we all come to a place where we long to uncover our mission—a lifelong "assignment" that evolves from deep within our soul. Join David Lyman, the founder of the Workshops, in his journey of uncovering a deeper "calling" and building his place in the world (page 310).

ARTISTIC PURSUITS

ACADEMY OF TELEVISION ARTS AND SCIENCES FOUNDATION

Television • California • Summer
www.emmys.org

THE ACADEMY OF Television Arts and Sciences (ATAS) is a nonprofit awards organization, with a professional membership of nearly ten thousand. In addition to sponsoring the Emmy Awards, ATAS runs the College Television Awards, faculty seminar and visiting artists programs, publishes *Emmy* magazine, and offers an eight-week summer college internship program. Each internship is hosted by an organization—children's shows, prime-time sitcoms, talent agencies, studios, and production companies—with opportunities available in all areas of professional television production (from animation and casting to news and scriptwriting). Interns receive in-depth exposure to facilities, techniques, and practices and are paired with past interns through the academy's mentor program. Each intern receives a stipend of $2,500 (and those residing outside Los Angeles County receive an additional $500 to offset travel expenses). Any full-time college student can apply, although junior, senior, or graduate students are preferred. Applications are available online, with an entry period from January 1 through mid-March (finalists will be notified by April 15). All finalists will then have to submit a videotaped interview for their final screening.

For More Information:

Education Director
Academy of Television Arts and Sciences Foundation
Internship Program
5220 Lankershim Blvd.
North Hollywood, CA 91601-3109
(818) 754-2830 • (818) 761-2827 (fax)
internships@emmys.org

AMERICAN CONSERVATORY THEATER

Theatre • California • 2–10 Months
www.act-sfbay.org

SAN FRANCISCO'S TONY Award–winning American Conservatory Theater (ACT) is one of the largest and most active of the nation's resident professional theaters. In their magnificently restored Geary Theater, ACT presents a season of the classics of dramatic literature and outstanding works of Modern theatre. In addition to housing a prestigious actor-training program, ACT employs more than eight hundred people annually, including actors, directors, teachers, designers, administrators, technicians, and craftspersons.

What You'll Be Doing: Since 1976, ACT has provided in-depth training for individuals seeking a career in theatre arts by offering internships in theatre production and administration. These programs provide students and other interested people the opportunity to work closely with top professionals in the field. The Production Department includes positions in stage management, production management, properties, technical design, sound design, lighting design, costume rentals, costume shop and wig construction/makeup. The Artistic and Administrative Departments offer positions as assistant directors, artistic staff, marketing/public relations, literary/publications, arts management, and development.

Commitment: Production Department internships are full-time positions that parallel the Geary season, approximately August to June. Due to the program's variable hours of the program and the intense nature of the work, it is impossible to hold an outside job during the internship period. Artistic and Administrative internships are generally flexible, lasting from two to six months throughout the year, and work schedules that accommodate outside employment may be arranged.

Perks and Rewards: A small hourly wage is available to all interns. ACT will provide housing assistance, but securing housing is the responsibility of each intern. Perks include complimentary tickets to ACT productions (and other local theater productions), monthly intern roundtables with guest speakers, and a resume/portfolio workshop.

The Essentials: Most departments require previous experience in their area of production, but a sincere and enthusiastic personality may compensate for a lack of experience in some cases. Due to the high costs of living in the Bay Area, all applicants must have additional independent funding for living expenses while in residence.

Your First Move: Visit ACT's website for complete details and an application, or call for a brochure. Production Department internship applications are due April 15. Notification of acceptance will be made by June 1, after an in-person or telephone interview. Artistic and Administrative internship applications are accepted anytime.

For More Information:
Jennifer Caleshu, Internship Coordinator
American Conservatory Theater
30 Grant Ave.
San Francisco, CA 94108-5800
(415) 834-3200 • (415) 439-2447 (internship hotline)
(415) 834-3326 (fax)
jacaleshu@act-sfbay.org

AMERICAN DANCE FESTIVAL

Dance Festival • North Carolina • Summer
www.americandancefestival.org

HERE'S A CHANCE to become part of an exciting community of dancers, students, choreographers, teachers, performers, critics, body therapists, dance medical specialists, scholars, and arts managers from all over the U.S. and around the world. Held for six weeks each summer at Duke University, the American Dance Festival offers internships in the box office, facilities services, food and housing, merchandising, performances, press, schools and workshops, and production. In addition to a $950 to $1,100 stipend, interns will receive one complimentary ticket to one night of each performance. Interns may also take one dance class per day and can observe panel discussions, seminars, and lectures by distinguished visitors as the work schedule permits. Apartments and shared housing are conveniently located near the festival site. Those needing housing assistance are encouraged to seek the festival's assistance. Interns also have full use of Duke facilities, including swimming pools, tennis courts, bookstores, and libraries. Applications must be received by February 15.

For More Information:
Kimberly Quick, Intern Coordinator
American Dance Festival
Box 90772
Durham, NC 27708-0772
(919) 684-6402 • (919) 684-5459 (fax)
internships@americandancefestival.org

AMERICAN THEATRE WORKS

Theatre Festival • Vermont • Summer
www.theatredirectories.com

AMERICAN THEATRE WORKS presents the Dorset Theatre Festival each summer at the Dorset Playhouse, built from two prerevolutionary barns in the historic village of Dorset. The festival's apprenticeship program adheres to the traditional sense of the word "conservatory": learning a craft by working closely with professionals for an intense and extended period of time. The program focuses on performance, production, a series of seminars, and contact with professionals. For those with more experience, internships are available in arts management, technical theatre, and the acting apprentice company. Housing is provided; interns also receive a $125-per-week stipend.

For More Information:
John Nassivera, Artistic Director
American Theatre Works
Dorset Theatre Festival Conservatory Program
P.O. Box 510
Dorset, VT 05251-0510
(802) 867-2223 • (802) 867-0144 (fax)
theatre@sover.net

APERTURE FOUNDATION

Photography • New York • 6 Months
www.aperture.org

DEVOTED TO PHOTOGRAPHY and the visual arts, the Aperture Foundation promotes the development of photography as one of the most powerful forms of human expression, helping to illuminate important social, environmental and cultural issues. While working with a small, committed staff and some of the greatest living photographers and photography writers, work-scholar program participants engage in all facets of Aperture activities—from writing and design to production and traveling exhibitions. A monthly stipend of $250 is provided along with discounts on books, magazines, and prints. Work-scholars also receive a limited edition print upon completion of their internship as well as a letter of recommendation. Applicants are selected on the basis of their interest and motivation in working for Aperture, the ability to contribute significantly to the program, and an

You've got to dance like there's nobody watching; you've got to love like you've never been hurt;
you've got to sing like there's nobody listening; you've got to live like it's heaven on earth.

277

openness in gaining a meaningful work experience. Send a resume, two short writing samples, and a cover letter describing your background, special skills, and personal objectives.

For More Information:
Maria Décsey, Work-Scholar Coordinator
Aperture Foundation
20 East 23rd St.
New York, NY 10010-4463
(212) 505-5555, ext. 336 • (212) 475-8790 (fax)
mdecsey@aperture.org

> *Be concise in your letter; please let us know what positions you are most interested in and exactly when you can start. Enthusiasm and interest are the most important tips on getting accepted into the program. Staff members want to know that you are interested and that you will work hard once you arrive.*

APPEL FARM ARTS AND MUSIC CENTER

Performing Arts • New Jersey • 3–9 Months
www.appelfarm.org

APPEL FARM IS renowned for its evening concerts and family matinee series, annual Arts and Music Festival and country music events, summer camp, and community arts outreach program—programs that provide people of all ages a supportive environment to study, appreciate, and present work in the creative and performing arts.

What You'll Be Doing: Interns work side by side with Appel Farm staff either in marketing/box office or outreach/event coordination. Summer-camp staff positions are available in theatre, music, fine arts, media, dance, and sports/swimming. Along with specific projects, interns will be expected, as is everyone at Appel Farm, to pitch in where help is needed. Everyone will do his or her share of envelope stuffing, data entry, filing, and other office work.

Commitment: Interns should plan to make at least a three-month commitment, although positions may be extended up to six to nine months and are available

September through June. Summer camp positions span from late June through late August.

Perks and Rewards: Interns receive a $300-per-month stipend along with meals and on-site housing in Appel's original farmhouse. Summer staff wages vary based on experience, with meals and on-site housing in bunkhouses provided. Since the farm is located in a quiet country setting, most staff bring along a car to explore the surrounding region. (Philadelphia is just a half-hour away.)

The Essentials: If you want to gain administrative experience in the arts while being in a supportive atmosphere, contribute to a growing arts center, and thrive on being given responsibility and hard work, then Appel is an ideal place to work and learn. Camp staff must be at least twenty-one years of age, available for the entire camp season, and nonsmokers.

Your First Move: Applications and detailed staff descriptions can be found online. An application, resume, and three references are required.

For More Information:
Matina Lagakos, Office Manager
Appel Farm Arts and Music Center
457 Shirley Rd.
P.O. Box 888
Elmer, NJ 08318-0888
(800) 394-8478 • (856) 358-2472, ext. 100
(856) 358-6513 (fax)
appelarts@aol.com

ARENA STAGE

Theatre • Washington, D.C. • 6–40 Weeks
www.arenastage.org

FOUNDED IN 1950, Arena Stage was an early pioneer in the resident theatre movement, which sought to establish living theatre in communities outside of New York. Today they present an expansive spectrum of dramatic literature that encompasses both classic and new American plays and musicals.

What You'll Be Doing: Arena Stage offers practically every conceivable type of internship related to the theatre field. Interns will work with seasoned professionals in the areas of artistic and technical production, in arts administration, or at Living Stage (their social outreach theatre). The work experience is supplemented with seminars provided by Arena's directors, designers, and administrators.

Commitment: Administrative internships are available throughout the year. Directing, stage management, and technical production internships are available during the season (August through June) only. The duration of internships may vary from six to eight weeks (a production schedule) to forty weeks (a full season).

Perks and Rewards: A $120-per-week stipend is provided, along with complimentary tickets to Arena performances and regular informational seminars with Arena's staff of professionals and guest artists.

The Essentials: The program is designed for people interested in pursuing a career in the professional theatre. Applicants should be serious-minded, highly motivated individuals who have basic training and experience in theatre and are willing to engage in the creative process and to test the limits of their own ingenuity.

Your First Move: Call for their internship program brochure, which provides details on each position and application information. Deadlines: winter/spring—October 1; summer—March 1; and fall—May 1. An interview is mandatory and can be handled in person or by telephone.

For More Information:
Intern Program Coordinator
Arena Stage
1101 6th St., SW
Washington, D.C. 20024
(202) 554-9066 • (202) 488-4056 (fax)
interns@arenastage.org

> Don't wait until the last minute to apply. Keep the coordinator abreast of the progress of your application if you are having trouble getting all of the materials in on time.

ARROWMONT SCHOOL OF ARTS AND CRAFTS

**Traditional Crafting • Tennessee •
2–5 Weeks/11 Months**
www.arrowmont.org

ARROWMONT SCHOOL OF Arts and Crafts, located adjacent to the Great Smoky Mountain National Park, serves as a cultural and educational center for visitors and

students. Workshops lure those who wish to learn traditional and contemporary crafts, with classes in weaving, fabric design, quilting, jewelry making, wood turning, clay and metal working, enameling, photography, papermaking, drawing, and painting.

What You'll Be Doing: Each spring and summer, Arrowmont sponsors a two- to five-week work-study and studio assistantship program. Work-study individuals assist the full-time support staff in the kitchen, housekeeping, maintenance, gardening, or office, while studio assistants (who must have four years of completed course work in a specific media) work alongside the support staff assisting with the studios, gallery installations, book and supply store, and clerical functions. In addition, Arrowmont selects five artists each year to participate in their eleven-month artist-in-residence program (beginning mid-June), where artists work both in their private studios and in workshops, special media conferences, seminars, retreats, Elderhostel classes, and eight hours for Arrowmont.

Perks and Rewards: Room, board, and tuition for classes (and, if needed, course credit for classes is available through the art department at the University of Tennessee, Knoxville) are provided for work-study/studio assistants. Resident artists receive a private room with bath, meals, and private studios in the spacious resident-artist studio complex. A modest monthly fee is charged per resident for housing, studio, and utilities. Several paid teaching opportunities are also available.

Your First Move: Work-study/studio assistant applicants must apply by January 15 for the spring and March 15 for the summer; artist-in-residence program applicants must apply by February 1. Applications are available online.

For More Information:
Work Study Program Coordinator
Arrowmont School of Arts and Crafts
P.O. Box 567
Gatlinburg, TN 37738-0567
(423) 436-5860 • (423) 430-4101 (fax)
info@arrowmont.org

Love is the spirit that motivates the artist's journey. The love may be sublime, raw, obsessive, passionate, awful, or thrilling, but whatever its quality, it's a powerful motive in the artist's life. —ERIC MAISEL

ARTIST COMMUNITIES AND RESIDENT PROGRAMS:

Special Places to Create

If you are looking for an inspiring setting that's rich in stimulation and fellowship to encourage and nurture your creative pursuits, this section will provide you with a variety of creativity-stirring colonies, communities, and resident programs. Geared to both the emerging and the established artist, residence programs generally run from one week on up to nine months throughout the year. Undoubtedly, the biggest lure for many artisans is the ability to create without interruption in beautiful and unique surroundings. Most programs also take care of all your daily needs—including housing, meals, studio space, equipment, and even supplies—while providing common areas to socialize and collaborate with other talented people.

> *Creation is a peculiar process. It is something that happens between the earth, sun, and the human mind. . . . In creation we must have both leisure to think and dream and means to execute.*
>
> —MARY CROVATT HAMBIDGE

DJERASSI RESIDENT ARTISTS PROGRAM

Artist Retreat • California • 4–5 Weeks
www.djerassi.org

FOR EMERGING AND mid-career artists in the disciplines of choreography, literature, music composition, visual arts, and media arts/new genres, Djerassi might have a place for you. Located in a spectacular rural setting in the Santa Cruz Mountains overlooking the Pacific Ocean,

Djerassi's residency experience centers around its genuine retreat atmosphere over a four- to five-week term during late March through late November. Residents work and are housed in two buildings on the ranch according to artistic discipline and creative project. The Artists' Barn contains three visual art studios, a large dance studio, a darkroom, a music composition studio with a baby grand and an electric piano, and a multimedia lab (equipped with Windows and Mac platforms, Internet access, and all the software you'll need). Living quarters and studio space consist of a four-bedroom house and a unique, remodeled twelve-sided barn (complete with wood-burning stove and modest sleeping lofts). A chef prepares communal dinners Monday through Friday, and stocks the kitchen for resident meals at other times. Applications must be received by February 15 for a residency in the following year.

For More Information:
Djerassi Resident Artists Program
2325 Bear Gulch Rd.
Woodside, CA 94062-4405
(650) 747-1250 • (650) 747-0105 (fax)
drap@djerassi.org

DORLAND MOUNTAIN ARTS COLONY

Artist Retreat • California • 1–2 Months
www.ez2.net/dorland

AS A PRIMITIVE retreat for creative people (just an hour north of San Diego), Dorland Mountain Arts Colony offers a natural setting without distractions or interruptions. What's unique about Dorland is the total absence of electricity, which enables residents to detach from the outside world and tap further into their inner resources. The colony encourages visual artists, poets, writers, playwrights, composers, photographers, and other artists to apply for one- to two-month residencies. Each artist is provided with an individual cottage containing a simple kitchen, bathroom, and living and working areas (cooking and refrigeration is powered by propane, a woodstove keeps the cottage warm, and lamps come to life with kerosene). Accommodations run $300 per month, and each artist provides his or her own food (Temecula is about eight miles away) and artist materials. For relaxation, Dorland offers miles of natural trails, a spring-fed pond, scenic overlooks, and an eclectic library. Applications are reviewed twice a year, with deadlines on March 1 and September 1.

For More Information:
Admissions Committee
Dorland Mountain Arts Colony
P.O. Box 6
Temecula, CA 92593
(909) 302-3837
dorland@ez2.net

DORSET COLONY FOR WRITERS

Artist Retreat • Vermont • Seasonal
www.theatredirectories.com/colony.html

RECOGNIZING THE NEED for writers to set aside periods of time to work intensively on projects away from the distractions of everyday life but still have a social connection, Dorset Colony for Writers provides a quiet working retreat for writers and other artists. September through November and April through May, eight private rooms, along with public areas where conversation and fellowship are encouraged, are available for a fee of $120 per week. Residency lengths vary and rooms are filled as requests come in. To apply, submit a letter with requested dates of residency, description of the project to be worked on while in residence, and a resume of publications.

For More Information:
John Nassivera, Executive Director
Dorset Colony for Writers
P.O. Box 510
Dorset, VT 05251
(802) 867-2223 • theatre@sover.net

THE HAMBIDGE CENTER FOR CREATIVE ARTS AND SCIENCES

Artist Retreat • Georgia • 2–6 Weeks
www.hambidge.org

NESTLED WITHIN THE lush forests of northeast Georgia's Blue Ridge Mountains and covering six hundred acres, The Hambidge Center's natural environment provides the atmosphere and connections that encourage human creativity—and the foundation for their resident artist program. Writers, poets, visual and environmental artists, photographers, composers, performers, and dancers are housed in eight individual cottages (which double as studios), complete with bath and kitchen facilities. The Rock House serves as a communal place for residents and houses a laundry area, phones, and dining room where dinner is served May through October. The center offers a warm weather clay studio (with electric and kick wheels and two electric kilns), a performance studio with Steinway grand, an artists' gallery, and a working grist mill. Various nature trails on the property lead to streams, waterfalls, and wildflower coves. Residents can stay from two to six weeks for a fee of $125 per week. An application (with a $20 processing fee), samples of work, and letters of recommendation are due by May 1 (for September through February residencies) or November 1 (for March through August residencies). The review process usually takes from six to eight weeks.

For More Information:
The Hambidge Center for Creative Arts and Sciences
P.O. Box 339
Rabun Gap, GA 30568
(706) 746-5718 • (706) 746-9933 (fax)
center@hambidge.org

KALANI OCEANSIDE RETREAT

Artist Retreat • Hawaii • Seasonal
www.kalani.com/artist.htm

LOCATED ON OVER one hundred acres on Hawaii's Big Island, Kalani Oceanside Retreat provides resident artists with the impetus to complete works in progress, strike out in new directions, or simply exchange ideas with other resident artists from varied disciplines, backgrounds, and cultures. Living accommodations and working/performance space are provided for visual,

It is the function of art to renew our perception. What we are familiar with we cease to see. The writer shakes up the familiar scene, and as if by magic, we see new meaning in it. —ANAÏS NIN

literary, folk, and performing arts. Kalani's Monkeypod tree houses, wooden lodges, and private cottages provide simple but comfortable accommodations. Lodging runs $105 to $210 per night; however, half-off lodging cost stipends are available during the less busy periods (May to July and September to December). Healthful and delicious meal options are also available for a fee. More information about Kalani can be found on page 239.

THE MACDOWELL COLONY

Artist Retreat • New Hampshire • 4–8 Weeks
www.macdowellcolony.org

FOUNDED IN 1907, The MacDowell Colony offers a place where emerging and well-established creative artists can find freedom to concentrate on their work. Architects, composers, filmmakers, photographers, printmakers, visual artists, and writers come to the colony each year for a four- to eight-week period (with twenty to thirty artists in residence at any given time). Most artists come to the colony to take advantage of uninterrupted time and seclusion in which to work as well as the experience of living in a community of gifted artists. Undoubtedly friendships established among artists in residence often lead to collaborations and connections beyond the colony. There are no residency fees, and each participant is provided with a private room and studio as well as three meals per day. Grants for travel to and from the colony are available based on need. Financial aid for writers is available through a special grant from an anonymous foundation. It's necessary to apply at least five to eight months before an anticipated residency. A two-page application form, a work sample, project description, two references and an application fee of $20 are required. Residence notification is given eight weeks after the application (call for upcoming deadlines).

For More Information:
Admissions Coordinator
The MacDowell Colony
100 High St.
Peterborough, NH 03458
(603) 924-3886 • (603) 924-9142 (fax)
info@macdowellcolony.org

MILLAY COLONY FOR THE ARTS, INC.

Artist Retreat • New York • 1 Month
www.millaycolony.org

THE MILLAY COLONY offers one-month residencies to talented writers, painters, sculptors, photographers, novelists, poets, playwrights, screenwriters, and performance artists in a setting that is designed to foster creativity. Whether you are just starting out in your career or need a place to be refreshed, the colony accepts six artists each month. A private studio and separate living quarters are provided in the renovated Millay Barn, which includes a kitchen, dining room, living room, library, and a sitting darkroom. Call for information and an application.

For More Information:
Ann-Ellen Lesser, Executive Director
Millay Colony for the Arts, Inc.
P.O. Box 3
Austerlitz, NY 12017-0003
(518) 392-3103
application@millaycolony.org

RAGDALE FOUNDATION

Artist Retreat • Illinois • 2–8 Weeks
www.ragdale.org

SITUATED ON FIFTY acres of prairie (and just thirty miles from Chicago), Ragdale is a unique place where writers, composers, and visual artists of all disciplines can find uninterrupted time to work in a beautiful setting. Two hundred residents come to Ragdale each year for a two- to eight-week period. Living (housing and meals) and working space is provided for a fee of $15 per day. (The majority of the actual cost is subsidized by the foundation.) A Creative Sabbatical Program is also available for career-changers wanting to focus on their creative work. Fees run $950 for one week, $1,750 for two. Applications (which require a $20 fee) must be received by January 15 for residencies from June through December, and June 1 for those between January and April. Decisions are made three months after the deadline and are based primarily on the panel's evaluation of your work sample and quality of proposal.

For More Information:
Susan Page Tillett, Executive Director
Ragdale Foundation
1260 N. Green Bay Rd.
Lake Forest, IL 60045
(847) 234-1063, ext. 202 • (847) 234-1075 (fax)
sptil@aol.com

VIRGINIA CENTER FOR THE CREATIVE ARTS

Artist Retreat • Virginia • 2–8 Weeks
www.vcca.com

LOCATED AT MT. SAN ANGELO, a 450-acre estate, the
Virginia Center for the Creative Arts offers residential
fellowships for writers, visual artists, and composers for
a two- to eight-week period. Every fellow has a private
studio in a renovated Normandy-style barn built in the
1930s (twenty-two studios in all) as well as a private
room in a separate residence (which offers a laundry
facility, satellite television, a collection of art books, and a
Steinway grand piano). Prepared breakfasts and dinners
are served in the residence, while lunches are brought to
the studio complex in lunchboxes. Art supplies are available at Sweet Briar College on a limited basis and a daily
fee of $30 is suggested. Admission is based on pro-
fessional achievement or the promise of achievement.
Applications revolve around three deadlines throughout
the year (January 15, May 15, and September 15) for residencies that begin approximately five to eight months
after the deadline. Notification is generally given two
months after the filing deadline. Applications are available online.

For More Information:
Admissions Committee
Virginia Center for the Creative Arts
Mt. San Angelo
Box VCCA
Sweet Briar, VA 24595
(434) 946-7236 • (434) 946-7239 (fax)
vcca@vcca.com

WATERSHED CENTER FOR THE CERAMIC ARTS

Artist Retreat • Maine • 2 Weeks–9 Months
www.watershedcenterceramicarts.org

IF YOU ARE a serious artist and need the time and space
to create in clay, Watershed offers an intimate communal
approach and peaceful environment for experimentation,
exploration, collaboration, and growth. The studio is
housed in a spacious old brickworks barn that provides
ample, flexible studio space. Equipment includes propane
car kilns, a wood and soda kiln, various electric kilns,
potter's wheels, clay mixers, slab rollers, extruders, and a
put mill. While a hillside of local earthenware brick clay is
free and abundant, standard clay and glaze materials are
available for a fee. A separate residence building provides
dorm housing for residents, including a central living area
for conversation and a dining room where healthy meals
are prepared by staff artists. Fully funded and partially
funded residencies run from two weeks on up to nine
months. Call for application materials and deadlines.

For More Information:
Lynn Thompson, Executive Director
Watershed Center for the Ceramic Arts
19 Brick Hill Rd.
Newcastle, ME 04553
(207) 882-6075 • (207) 882-6045 (fax)
h2oshed@midcoast.com

ARTIST PROGRAMS

RECOMMENDED RESOURCES..............

Whether located in a pastoral setting or in the middle of an urban warehouse district, the artist communities listed with **The Alliance of Artists' Communities** (www.artistcommunities.org) are a great starting point for your research. Over one hundred member programs are profiled on the Web, with the ability to search for programs by architecture and design, film/video and media, interdisciplinary, music/dance/performance, scholarship, visual arts, and writing. The Alliance also has a handful of great publications, including *Artist's Communities* (Allworth Press, $18.95), which is a must for those needing a creativity-stirring change of pace. The guide details seventy-nine residencies and retreats in the U.S. with descriptions of facilities, history, stipends and fees, selection processes, odds of acceptance, special programs,

admission deadlines, and contact information. In addition, contact information for over 150 residency programs in the U.S. and abroad is provided.

For more information contact the Alliance of Artists' Communities, 255 S. Main St., Providence, RI 02903; (401) 351-4320, aac@artistcommunities.org

If you have a creative project to work on and need a unique place to pursue your ambitions, *Artists & Writers Colonies* (Blue Heron Publishing, $19.95) explores over two hundred opportunities—including residencies and retreats, fellowships and grants, and colonies and creative spaces. Listings include facility descriptions, historical information, application requirements, and contact information.

ART WORKSHOPS IN GUATEMALA

Art Workshop • Guatemala • 10 Days
www.artguat.org

Art Workshops in Guatemala offers a wide variety of ten-day workshops for those who want to add an educational component to their travel experience. Known as "The Land of Eternal Spring" (because of its year-round seventy-degree weather), Guatemala is the kind of place travelers fall in love with and never want to leave. The pace is slower, less hectic. Cobblestone streets and colorful bougainvillea spilling over rocks of century-old ruins provide daily inspiration. The range of workshops is perfect for those who want to expand their creative horizons, with classes that extend from creative writing and photography to backstrap weaving. The price for each educational travel package is approximately $1,850 and includes airfare from most major U.S. cities, lodging in a beautiful old colonial home, hearty breakfasts, ground transportation, and some pretty interesting field trips.

For More Information:
Liza Fourre, Director
Art Workshops in Guatemala
4758 Lyndale Ave., South
Minneapolis, MN 55409-2304
(612) 825-0747 • (612) 825-6637 (fax)
info@artguat.org

ASTORS' BEECHWOOD MANSION

Theatre/Living History • Rhode Island • 7 Months
www.astors-beechwood.com

A visit to the Astor summer cottage is a bit different than your ordinary mansion tour. Guests are transported back in time through interaction with members of the Beechwood Theatre Company, who portray the Astor family, society friends, and servants, re-creating the lifestyle of Newport's vivid Victorian past.

What You'll Be Doing: As a living history museum, the Beechwood Theatre Company is not your traditional theatrical experience. Company staff members portray characters from the Victorian age (late 1800s), and take part in Victorian balls, teas, and murder mysteries. Five production team members perform in the Living History Museum as well as direct, teach, accompany, choreograph, and design costumes for the museum. All company members will be taught vintage dance, movement techniques, and Victorian etiquette as well as participate in classes that focus on improvisation.

Commitment: Company members must make a seven-month commitment, which runs from mid-May through mid-December.

Perks and Rewards: Stipends start at $115 per week (production staff make $200 or more per week), along with housing. There are also opportunities to make extra income by performing in murder mysteries as well as working weddings and corporate events (generally $10 per hour).

The Essentials: Applicants are expected to sing "like angels" and have strong improvisational skills. Beechwood is an opportunity for the young actor to gain confidence in self and skills. Living in a mansion is also a lifetime highlight for many.

Your First Move: Submit cover letter, resume, and photo, or send an e-mail for more information. Auditions usually include two contrasting monologues and a song (videos are accepted).

For More Information:
Charlotte Lee, Executive Director of Living History
Astors' Beechwood Mansion
580 Bellevue Ave.
Newport, RI 02840
(401) 846-3772 • (401) 849-6998 (fax)
casting@astors-beechwood.com

Photo Credit: Astors' Beechwood Mansion

Interns with Astors' Beechwood Mansion portray Victorian characters while entertaining guests.

AUGUSTA HERITAGE CENTER

Traditional Crafting • West Virginia • Seasonal
www.augustaheritage.com

THE HEART OF Augusta emanates the passing on of West Virginia's traditional folk arts and the documentation of regional folkways. A five-week summer workshop program covers a broad spectrum of traditional arts and folklore, with more than two hundred classes and seminars as well as studio work. To encourage and sustain the practice of this tradition through one-on-one teaching from master artists, the West Virginia Folk Art Apprenticeship Program was created. Serving as mentors, master artists guide apprentices through hands-on instruction in a variety of folk and traditional arts at their studios. Instruction might include traditional music and song, woodworking and carving, fiber arts, basket making, blacksmithing, or musical instrument construction. Becoming personally involved with the master artist gives the apprentice not only a good grasp of the technical aspects of their art but also a feeling for the context in which the tradition has survived. The apprenticeship program is available only to West Virginia residents, with applications due on either April 1 or October 1. The workshop program is open to all.

For More Information:
Gerry Milnes, Apprentice Coordinator
Augusta Heritage Center
West Virginia Folk Art Apprenticeship Program
Davis & Elkins College
Elkins, WV 26241
(304) 637-1334 • (304) 637-1317 (fax)
gcm@augustaheritage.com

BERKELEY REPERTORY THEATRE

Theatre • California • 11 Months
www.berkeleyrep.org

SINCE ITS FOUNDING in 1968, Berkeley Rep has focused on the development of a resident company of theatre artists, including actors, playwrights, directors, designers, and artisans. The sense of community and shared growth and knowledge that now exists within the Rep is one of its real strengths. The company mounts eight challenging productions each season, including three innovative Parallel Season productions and one fully produced school-touring production.

What You'll Be Doing: With positions available in every conceivable area of the theatre, interns have the opportunity to work closely with an accomplished company of artists, administrators, guest directors, and designers. The program includes regularly scheduled informal seminars every month throughout the season as the production schedule allows. The partnership between the theatre and the intern is intended to fulfill as many career-building goals and objectives as possible and to provide the intern with a variety of professional contacts and craft-building experiences.

Commitment: Internships usually begin in August or September and span full-time over an eleven-month period.

Perks and Rewards: A $400 stipend per month is provided, plus local housing for most positions.

The Essentials: Applicants should have already acquired basic training and experience in the theatre and be ready for the next step toward a career in professional theatre. Candidates should be willing to engage in the creative process and to test the limits of their own ingenuity. Serious-minded and highly motivated applicants are most often hired.

Your First Move: Send an email to obtain application materials (which are due by April 15). The Rep notes that if you have some solid experience, even if it's only in college, and you proofread your application, you'll definitely get an interview.

For More Information:
Intern Coordinator
Berkeley Repertory Theatre
2025 Addison St.
Berkeley, CA 94704
(510) 647-2900 • (510) 647-2929 (fax)
internship@berkeleyrep.org

CAREER DISCOVERY PROGRAM

Design • Massachusetts • 6 Weeks
www.gsd.harvard.edu/professional/career_discovery

WHETHER YOU ARE considering a career in architecture, landscape architecture, or urban planning and design, the summer Career Discovery Program at Harvard University can help you experience what it's like to be in these professions. Students participate in a core program of morning lectures and panel discussions, with most of the time devoted to studio work. Short, intensive projects simulate typical first-year experiences in a professional design program. Drawing and computer workshops, one-on-one instruction, career advising, and field trips and tours throughout the Boston area round out this six-week intensive program. Along with a $30 application fee, the tuition of $2,150 also includes a kit of basic studio supplies. On-campus housing is available for a fee starting at $875, although you might look for shared living possibilities that might be less expensive. The Harvard Square

subway stop makes it easy to live just about anywhere in the Boston area. The program is open to anyone that is seriously considering a career in the design professions. (At a minimum, applicants must be high school graduates.) Application materials are due in early May.

For More Information:
Program Coordinator
Career Discovery Program
Harvard University
Graduate School of Design
48 Quincy St.
Cambridge, MA 02138
(617) 495-5453 • (617) 496-8306
discovery@gsd.harvard.edu

CARIBBEAN VOLUNTEER EXPEDITIONS

Preservation • The Caribbean • 1–2 Weeks
www.cvexp.org

"PRESERVATION IN PARADISE" is the theme for volunteers who venture off to the islands with Caribbean Volunteer Expeditions (CVE). Having skills in preservation, architecture, history, carpentry, photography, or teaching, volunteers are typically those who are not satisfied by merely visiting an island, but are driven to record its architecture, document its heritage, and preserve its history. Working with local Caribbean preservation leaders, volunteers generally measure and document historical plantations, windmills, and other structures to help local Caribbean agencies keep a record of their architectural heritage. Typical expeditions last one to two weeks and volunteers should be prepared for thorns, mosquitoes, and other Caribbean conditions. But don't worry, the beach is never far away. CVE charges a fee to cover room, board, tours, and local transportation; airfare is the responsibility of each volunteer.

For More Information:
Anne Hersh, Program Director
Caribbean Volunteer Expeditions
P.O. Box 388
Corning, NY 14830
(607) 962-7846 • (607) 936-1153 (fax)
ahershcve@aol.com

Photo Credit: Caribbean Volunteer Expeditions

A National Park Service archaeologist discusses the day's game plan with his Caribbean Volunteer Expeditions team in the Virgin Islands.

CENTER FOR AMERICAN ARCHEOLOGY

Archaeology • Illinois • Summer
www.caa-archeology.org/intern.htm

NEAR THE CONFLUENCE of the Mississippi and Illinois rivers, the Center for American Archeology helps to unfold the unbroken record of nearly ten thousand years of human habitation in an area that has been called "The Nile of North America."

Each summer the center offers budding female archaeologists the chance to participate in their Women in Archeology Internship program. Interns will teach various interactive museum education curricula for students of all ages, provide residential and tour-group learning experiences, and engage in research. Yes, this means the opportunity is only open to college women (and advanced high school students) who have either course work or field experience in archaeology. But, don't panic males, because they also offer summer field assistant/chaperone positions for all. Applicants need to be at least twenty-one years of age and have completed an archaeological field school as well as have archaeological excavation experience. All summer staff receive a salary, living accommodations, and some meals.

For More Information:
Mary Pirkl, Director of Education
Center for American Archeology
P.O. Box 366

Kampsville, IL 62053
(618) 653-4316 • (618) 653-4232 (fax)
caa@caa-archeology.org

CENTER FOR INVESTIGATIVE REPORTING

Journalism • California • 5 Months
www.muckraker.org

THE CENTER FOR Investigative Reporting serves as a base for journalists in pursuit of hidden stories about the individuals and institutions that shape our lives. Since the center's founding in 1977, the staff and associates have completed hundreds of major investigations that have resulted in stories for major newspapers, national magazines, radio, and television. Their stories have spurred interest and action in Congress, the courts, and the United Nations, and have forced changes in multinational corporations, government agencies, and other organizations. Media outlets such as *60 Minutes,* the *CBS Evening News with Dan Rather,* National Public Radio, and the *Los Angeles Times* have relied on the center to produce similar types of stories for them.

What You'll Be Doing: One of the center's most important functions is to teach investigative reporting skills to novice reporters. After a half-day orientation, six to eight interns are paired with senior reporters. Under the guidance of these senior journalists, interns follow the full cycle of a major project from concept to publication or broadcast. Interns will conduct interviews, gather information and search through public records, and often contribute to final stories with sidebars or other reporting. Research projects generally include investigations into the environment, public health, constitutional government, national security, the economy, and social justice. In addition, interns participate in a series of seminars on investigative techniques, searching for public records, media ethics and law, and other issues.

Commitment: The duration is approximately five months, with a minimum commitment of fifteen to twenty hours per week. Start dates begin around February 1 for winter/spring and July 1 for summer/fall.

Perks and Rewards: A $500-per-month stipend is provided. Interns also interact with prominent local and national producers, reporters, and journalism instructors.

The Essentials: Students and career changers with writing and research skills, as well as an interest in investigative reporting and a self-directed work style, are encouraged to apply.

Your First Move: Submit resume, cover letter (describing interests and background), and a few clips or writing samples. (If you haven't been published, make sure you send in vivid writing samples.) Deadlines: winter/spring—December 1; summer/fall—May 1.

For More Information:
Internship Coordinator
Center for Investigative Reporting
131 Steuart St., Suite 600
San Francisco, CA 94105
(415) 543-1200 • (415) 543-8311 (fax)
center@cironline.org

CENTER FOR PHOTOGRAPHY AT WOODSTOCK

Photography • New York • 3–6 Months
www.cpw.org

SINCE 1979, THE center has presented the Woodstock Photography Workshops, an education series where national and international photographers serve as teachers. Workshop students come from all over the U.S. as well as from other countries to study with working photographers who have the skills and desire to share their experiences with a peer group.

What You'll Be Doing: The intern experience is unlike traditional classroom education. In a matter of months, interns have the opportunity to meet an average of fifteen different guest teachers and hundreds of students. An entire range of topics—from teaching strategies to professional image-making—is presented in a relatively short span. Fridays through Sundays are reserved for providing general hospitality and support for guest artists. In addition to the four workshop internships that are available, Woodstock also offers an arts administration internship with training opportunities ranging from exhibition design to fund-raising strategies.

Commitment: Workshop internships are available full-time from June through October; arts administration positions are available year-round (one to three days for three to six months).

Perks and Rewards: Workshop interns have the opportunity to participate in workshops and the photography lecture series tuition-free (a $5,000 value); arts administration interns are on a volunteer basis. A fully equipped

professional darkroom and use of the library are also available free of charge.

The Essentials: Individuals who are curious, highly motivated, technically skilled, and able to handle a diverse audience and a fast-paced work environment are encouraged to apply.

Your First Move: Workshop-intern applicants are required to schedule a personal interview on Fridays at 2 P.M. during the last two weeks of March or in the month of April. A personal portfolio (ten prints), resume, and three references (with phone numbers) are required for the interview. Deadlines for arts-administration interns are rolling.

For More Information:
Kate Menconeri, Program Director
Center for Photography at Woodstock
59 Tinker St.
Woodstock, NY 12498
(845) 679-9957 • (845) 679-6337 (fax)
info@cpw.org

CENTER STAGE

Theatre • Maryland • 9–10 Months
www.centerstage.org

CENTER STAGE STRIVES to explore a wide range of dramatic literature and production approaches, from fresh visions of the classics to active support of contemporary writing. Production internships are available in stage management, scenic shop, painting, properties, costumes, electrics, and sound. Administrative interns work in development/fund-raising, public relations, marketing, dramaturgy, education, volunteer service, or company management. Positions begin in late August for a nine- to ten-month period. A stipend of $85 per week is provided along with a fully-furnished efficiency apartment in one of three newly renovated row houses close to the theatre. Perks include tickets to all productions at Center Stage (and often to other local theatres and concerts) as well as participation in biweekly seminars. Applicants should have a proven ability in their area of specialization and a willingness to work hard. It's best to apply by March for the following season. It's noted that applications or resumes should not be sent by email.

For More Information:
Katharyn Davies, Internship Coordinator
Center Stage

Photo Credit: Kate Gust

Working from a sketch-board, a production intern at Center Stage adds her artistic touches to a background scene for an upcoming show.

700 N. Calvert St.
Baltimore, MD 21202-3686
(410) 685-3200, ext. 330 • (410) 539-3912 (fax)
kdavies@centerstage.org

CENTRAL CITY OPERA HOUSE ASSOCIATION

Opera Festival • Colorado • Summer
www.centralcityopera.org

BUILT IN 1878 by Cornish and Welsh miners, Central City Opera House hosts one of the oldest opera festivals in the U.S. The 552-seat theatre, a historic landmark in an old mining town, affords an intimate experience with opera. Summer festival staff positions include assistants in public relations, house management, production, and stage management/props, as well as positions in the music library, costume shop/wardrobe, gardening, gift shop, facility maintenance, and office administration. A $225-per-week salary is provided, along with housing (with kitchen and laundry facilities) and a travel stipend for those residing outside of Colorado. It's best to request an application by January as materials are due by the end of

February (although applications will be taken until positions are filled). Applicants must be at least eighteen years of age and exude a positive attitude. An interest in opera is helpful, but not required.

For More Information:
Rebecca Graham Forbis, Festival Manager
Central City Opera House Association
11825 W. 66th Pl., Unit A
Arvada, CO 80004-2497
(800) 851-8175 • (303) 421-3977 • (303) 421-4313 (fax)
info@centralcityopera.org

CHESAPEAKE BAY MARITIME MUSEUM

Museum • Maryland • 10–13 Weeks
www.cbmm.org

ENTER A FULLY restored 1879 Hooper Strait lighthouse and feel what it must have been like to guide ships to safety. Or climb aboard the skipjack *Rosie Parks* and experience the daily drudgery of sailing a large wooden boat while hauling up heavy oysters in freezing temperatures and wind. With engaging exhibitions, boat-building classes, and outdoor summer concerts, the Chesapeake Bay Maritime Museum explores how the bay shaped the lives of everyone who has lived around it.

What You'll Be Doing: The museum's internship program is an integral part of its educational activities. Interns will have the opportunity to develop and support family and on-site interpretive programs, assist in the documentation of folklife and folk arts, work with museum collections, or assist in public relations. Internships are available in the research/curatorial, education, exhibits, boatyard, marketing and public relations, membership, and museum advancement departments.

Commitment: Internships span thirteen weeks during the summer months (with the exception of curatorial and education positions, which are also available in the winter and spring for ten to thirteen weeks).

Perks and Rewards: A weekly stipend of $125 plus housing is provided. Interns will also have exposure to the entire museum through attendance at staff meetings, rotation through the institution, opportunities to shadow key staff, and field trips or independent visits to other museums.

The Essentials: Individuals working toward undergraduate or graduate degrees in museum studies or history are encouraged to apply.

Your First Move: Application information can be found through their website, or call for more information. Applications must be in by March 15 for summer positions.

For More Information:
Leigh Ann Gay, Internship Program Coordinator
Chesapeake Bay Maritime Museum
P.O. Box 636
St. Michaels, MD 21663-0636
(410) 745-2916, ext. 122 • (410) 745-6088 (fax)
lgay@cbmm.org

CHILDREN'S MUSEUM OF INDIANAPOLIS

Children's Museum • Indiana • 10 Weeks
www.childrensmuseum.org

THE CHILDREN'S MUSEUM of Indianapolis is the largest and fourth-oldest children's museum in the world. This five-story brick museum (356,000 square feet) houses ten major galleries exploring the sciences, history, foreign cultures, and the arts. In addition, it regularly offers thousands of nontraditional programs for children and their families, hosting over 1.3 million visitors each year. The museum itself includes a sweeping atrium entrance (complete with a unique water clock) an education center, a world-class planetarium, and an IWERKS CineDome Theater. The museum also operates Ritchey Woods, a 180-acre environmental learning center for children and their families.

What You'll Be Doing: With the goal of providing opportunities to form a well-rounded, professional experience, the museum provides enthusiastic staff members as mentors and a customized experience for each intern. Interns will have the opportunity to work with the public, design and implement activities, discover the inner workings of a major museum, experience the day-to-day business of meetings and brainstorming, and, of course, have a lot of fun! Placements are generally in education, programs and events, collections, exhibit production, marketing, communication services, finance, and multimedia technology; however, new ideas are encouraged and new opportunities for internships are continually being developed.

Commitment: A minimum commitment of ten weeks is required; however, the best experiences usually come from a full-time internship for a three- to four-month period. The longer your commitment, the more substantive the assignments.

Perks and Rewards: Although the positions are on a volunteer basis, the museum offers behind-the-scenes field trips to area and regional arts institutions, professional development workshops, restaurant and store discounts, comprehensive orientation programs, reciprocal admission to area arts organizations, discounts on health club memberships, and free parking.

The Essentials: Applicants must be college students, recent graduates, or graduate students. The most successful interns are interested in working with and for children, have good interpersonal skills, and can articulate their goals. It's noted that the program is highly competitive, with enthusiasm invariably being more important than your academic background.

Your First Move: Applications should be sent at least six to eight weeks prior to your anticipated start date. After an interview with a staff member, the museum will provide a more specific job description proposal and try to accommodate any other needs.

For More Information:
Internship Coordinator
Children's Museum of Indianapolis
P.O. Box 3000

Indianapolis, IN 46206-3000
(800) 826-5431 • (317) 334-3322 • (317) 920-2047 (fax)
internresume@childrensmuseum.org

Museums are an increasingly tough field to break into, so previous experience is more important than ever. We are dedicated to providing professional, positive experiences for interns interested in working with children.

THE CLEARING

Art Discovery • Wisconsin • Seasonal
www.theclearing.org

As an "adult school of discovery in the arts, nature, and humanities," an experience at the Clearing is a unique combination of simplicity, small classes, and artistic surroundings, all taking place in a family-like atmosphere of living and learning together. Founded and designed by the renowned Danish landscape architect Jens Jensen, all buildings are log or native stone, blending with the rustic natural setting—a setting meant to provide a clearing of the mind. Offered as a summer residential program or autumn and winter day programs, courses range from "Career Development for the Best Work of Your Life" and "Recreating Body As Home" to watercolor, Navajo rug-weaving, and writing classes.

For More Information:
Program Coordinator
The Clearing
12171 Garrett Bay Rd.
P.O. Box 65
Ellison Bay, WI 54210
(877) 854-3225 • (920) 854-4088 • (920) 854-9751 (fax)
clearing@theclearing.org

CREEDE REPERTORY THEATRE

Theatre • Colorado • 4 Months
www.creederep.com

Began as a silver-mining town over one hundred years ago, the town of Creede is situated at 9,000 feet near the headwaters of the Rio Grande. This incredible backdrop along with dramatic weather conditions make for a

unique living experience for interns and staff at Creede Repertory Theatre. Four-month internships are available in business, costume design, light and sound, shop set, and stage management. A $175 weekly stipend is provided as well as double-occupancy housing in the newly refurbished historical Rio Grande Hotel (where all staff live), which overlooks the amphitheater. Opportunities are available during the summer and fall months.

For More Information:
Maurice LaMée, Artistic Diretor
Creede Repertory Theatre
124 N. Main St.
P.O. Box 269
Creede, CO 81130
(866) 658-2540 • (719) 658-2541 • (719) 658-2343 (fax)
crt@creederep.com

Theatre interns at Creede Repertory Theatre will enjoy the pedestrian-friendly downtown that's been transformed from a roaring mining town of yesteryear to a place that's now rich in the arts and outdoor activities.

CROW CANYON ARCHAEOLOGICAL CENTER

Archaeology • Colorado • Seasonal
www.crowcanyon.org

Crow Canyon archaeologists have been carefully piecing together information that will help them understand the prehistoric people who once flourished in this majestic land of mesas, mountains, and canyons. Participants join archaeologists in their effort and learn the process of excavation, artifact identification, and interpretation by working on a dig site. The center's goal is to reconstruct the prehistoric cultural and natural environment in order to understand how the relationship between the two brought about a change in ancestral Pueblo Indian life. With that knowledge, they may also recognize those dynamics in modern cultures and environments, including our own! The Crow Canyon campus covers 170 acres, with hiking trails snaking through the juniper-covered terrain.

What You'll Be Doing: Field, laboratory, and environmental archaeology research interns work closely with experienced professionals to assist them in excavating and recording archaeological contexts, in site surveying and mapping, in laboratory processing and analysis, or in studies of present and past environments. In addition, interns will be responsible for helping supervise small groups of program participants who are engaged in field or lab work. Interns may also be asked to give lectures or demonstrations to help participants prepare for fieldwork. Education interns work closely with experienced educators to assist them in preparation and teaching, including the development of a research project that assesses how and what students are learning.

Commitment: Positions are offered year-round; call for specific time frames. Interns will work a five-day week, normally Monday through Friday.

Perks and Rewards: There is a modest stipend of $50 to $100 per week, plus meals at the center's dining hall and lodging in rustic cabins. Interns scheduled in the cold season will be provided with indoor housing. Everyone eats well at Crow Canyon; the resident chef serves up three delicious meals every day, including homemade salsas, luscious guacamole, gourmet tacos, and blue-corn chicken enchiladas! Interns will also attend research staff meetings where they may participate in discussions of research strategies, organization, and scheduling of work. Interns are welcome to attend evening educational programs and have the option of giving an evening lecture.

The Essentials: Advanced undergraduate or graduate course work in archaeology, anthropology, or related fields, along with the ability to work as an effective member of a small research team with lay participants, and a strong interest in improving field, lab, and teaching skills is required. Experience in either archaeological field work or lab/museum work is a must to be accepted for a research internship.

Your First Move: It's recommended that you call for application materials by December for internships the following year. Deadlines vary and phone interviews may be conducted.

For More Information:
Education/Research Intern Program
Crow Canyon Archaeological Center
23390 County Rd. K
Cortez, CO 81321
(800) 422-8975 • (970) 565-8975 • (970) 565-4859 (fax)
Education: edu_interns@crowcanyon.org
Research: research_interns@crowcanyon.org

We do call references, so it's advisable to list people who have actually worked with you and are accessible by phone. Research internships are highly competitive; list any and all experiences that are applicable. Education internships are not as competitive, but a demonstrated interest in teaching is necessary.

DIRECTORS GUILD-PRODUCER TRAINING PLAN

Television • California • 400 Days
www.dgptp.org

ESTABLISHED IN 1965 and sponsored by the Directors Guild of America and the Alliance of Motion Picture and Television Producers, the Assistant Directors Training Program trains second assistant directors for the motion picture and television industry. Since its inception, more than 450 participants have graduated from the program and gone on to successful careers in the business.

What You'll Be Doing: The program is designed to provide a basic knowledge of the organization and logistics of motion picture and television production, including set operations, paperwork, and the working conditions and collective bargaining agreements of more than twenty guilds and unions. Trainees are assigned to work projects on episodic television, television movies, pilots, miniseries, and feature films with various studios and production companies, and learn to deal with all types of cast and crew members while solving problems in highly varied and sometimes difficult situations. The trainee work is physically demanding and is characterized by long hours.

Commitment: If accepted into the program, trainees will be required to complete four hundred days of on-the-job training and attend regular seminars. During this time you must live in the Los Angeles area, have a car, and be licensed to drive it.

Perks and Rewards: A salary of $521 to $640 per week is provided, plus medical benefits. Upon satisfactory completion of the program, trainees will be placed on the Southern California Area Qualification List, providing eligibility for employment as a second assistant director.

The Essentials: Applicant must be at least twenty-one years old and have either an associate's or bachelor's degree, or two years of paid work in any industry.

Your First Move: Applicants who meet the basic eligibility requirements must first take a written test ($75 fee). The test assesses job-related skills, including verbal, reasoning, and mathematical abilities, as well as organizational and interpersonal skills. The test is given once per year, usually in January, and is administered in Los Angeles and Chicago. The final selection of trainees is based on test scores and group and individual interviews. Deadline: mid-November for the following year.

For More Information:
John Slosser, Administrator
Directors Guild—Producer Training Plan
14724 Ventura Blvd., Suite 775
Sherman Oaks, CA 91403
(818) 386-2545
trainingprogram@dgptp.org

FLAT ROCK PLAYHOUSE

Theatre • North Carolina • Summer
www.flatrockplayhouse.org

FROM BUILDING AND running shows to attending classes, assisting patrons, or performing at the Sandburg Home (a National Historic Site across the street) and on the main stage, apprentices are constantly on the move. Flat Rock Playhouse believes that hands-on professional training is essential to any drama student's education. That's why they expose over twelve apprentices each year to as many facets of theatre as possible. Daily "master classes" range from acting and improvisation to costume design and professional preparation. Other opportunities exist in weekly technical-crew assignments and performing in as many as five venues. The room and board fee of $300 (for a ten-week period starting in early June) includes three meals a day and on-site dormitory-style housing. Some scholarship and work-study money is available and is based on talent and financial need. Apprentices must be at least high school graduates with prior theatrical experi-

ence and committed to the development of the art form. Applications (which can be printed from the Web) are due by March 15.

For More Information:
Apprentice Program Director
Flat Rock Playhouse
P.O. Box 310
Flat Rock, NC 28731-0310
(828) 693-0403, ext. 18 • (828) 693-6795 (fax)
design-education@flatrockplayhouse.org

GEVA THEATRE

Theatre • New York • 1 Year
www.gevatheatre.org

OCCUPYING A BUILDING that is on the National Registry of Historic Places, Geva Theatre offers a distinctive season that includes a wide variety of classics, revivals, musicals, and contemporary drama representing the whole body of American and international dramatic literature. Yearlong apprenticeships starting in August are available in administration, stage management, scenery/prop construction, electrics, and education. A stipend of $250 per week is provided. Send resume, cover letter, and three references.

For More Information:
Skip Greer, Director of Education
Geva Theatre
75 Woodbury Blvd.
Rochester, NY 14607
(716) 232-1366 • (716) 232-4031 (fax)
sgreer@gevatheatre.org

GREEK DANCES-THEATRE DORA STRATOU

Performing Arts • Greece • Seasonal
http://users.hol.gr/~grdance

EACH EVENING, IN the open-air theatre of Dora Stratou, a living reminder of the continuity and vitality of Greece's ancient heritage comes alive. Seventy dancers and folk musicians in authentic costumes present a unique spectacle with songs and dances from all over Greece. Positions in dance, theatre management, ethnographic field research, and costume maintenance are available. This is an unpaid position, so interns must have their own financial resources.

The world is moving so fast these days that the man who says it can't be done is generally interrupted by someone doing it. —HARRY EMERSON FOSDICK

For More Information:
Alkis Raftis, President
Greek Dances—Theatre Dora Stratou
8 Sholiou Str., Plaka
Athens 105 58
Greece
(011) 30 1 3244395
grdance@hol.gr

HENRY FORD MUSEUM AND GREENFIELD VILLAGE

Museum • Michigan • Seasonal
www.hfmgv.org/employment

HENRY FORD MUSEUM and Greenfield Village is the nation's largest indoor/outdoor museum complex and has the goal of "inspiring people to learn from America's traditions of ingenuity, resourcefulness, and innovation to help shape a better future." Part-time employment opportunities are available in virtually every facet of village operation, including historical presenter, glassblower, carriage driver, conservation technician, food service, visitor services, retail, and grounds maintenance. Along with a weekly wage, benefits include discounts on food and retail items, and the ability to admit up to four people into the village or museum. The ideal candidate possesses outstanding hospitality and communication skills, enjoys dealing with the public, is flexible regarding scheduling, and exhibits pride and enjoyment in working for the village.

For More Information:
Workforce Development
Henry Ford Museum and Greenfield Village
20900 Oakwood Blvd., Lovett Hall
P.O. Box 1970
Dearborn, MI 48121-1970
(313) 982-6090 • (313) 982-6226 (fax)
employment@hfmgv.org

THE HERMITAGE

Archaeology/History • Tennessee • 5 Weeks
www.thehermitage.com

SINCE 1987 ARCHAEOLOGICAL fieldwork has been performed on the grounds of the Hermitage. By exploring the foundations and other subsurface artifacts adjacent to President Andrew Jackson's family mansion, archaeologists and interns reconstruct what plantation life was like at the Hermitage of Jackson's time.

What You'll Be Doing: After a brief orientation meeting and a welcoming barbecue, interns begin their five-week adventure in historical archaeology during the summer months (with two terms available). With trowel in hand and sweat on brow, interns are fully immersed in archaeological excavation. The internship experience provides a full range of activities, including testing and model building as well as excavation and lab work. Interns will have the chance to unearth all sorts of artifacts, including pieces of pottery and glass, animal bones, rusty nails, glass beads, and coins from the 1850s. An integral part of life as a Hermitage intern is interaction with the public. Hundreds of tourists visit the grounds every day, and inevitably they encounter interns hard at work excavating. Although a sign explains the basics of the project, it's up to interns to answer any questions visitors have about the excavation. The Hermitage's current fieldwork focus is on investigations of slave dwelling sites in two different areas of Hermitage property.

Perks and Rewards: Housing and a stipend of $1,000 are provided. Interns live in one of two 1930s-era farmhouses located on the Hermitage property, about a half-mile from the mansion. Each has a bathroom, a few pieces of furniture, and a fully equipped kitchen. Six people live in each house, with two or three to a bedroom.

The Essentials: The program is intended for advanced undergraduates and early phase graduate students who have had some field training in archaeology and who are looking for more experience in a research-oriented setting.

Your First Move: The application deadline is mid-April, with selections made by May 1.

For More Information:
Elizabeth Kellar, Director of Archaeology
The Hermitage
4580 Rachel's Ln.
Hermitage, TN 37076-1331
(615) 889-2941 • (615) 889-9909 (fax)
hermitage@mindspring.com

HISTORIC DEERFIELD

Museum • Massachusetts • Summer
www.historic-deerfield.org

ART AND HISTORY. This is at the heart of Historic Deerfield. Carefully preserved eighteenth- and nineteenth-century houses, the Flynt Center of Early New England Life, and the decorative art pieces within them allow visitors to see what life once was like in this unspoiled village.

What You'll Be Doing: Attention college students: every year since 1956, Historic Deerfield has offered summer internships and fellowships for those who desire a rare behind-the-scenes view of the workings of a museum, and a thorough investigation of early American history and material life. The unique "learning and living" fellows program provides hands-on research of daily life and cultural history of New England, the ability to interpret the American past through objects, and to meet visitors from throughout the U.S. and around the world. Along with seminar sessions in a classroom setting, on walking tours, and in the museum houses, fellows also go on weekly field trips to other museums in New England, including Old Sturbridge Village and Plimoth Plantation. At the end of the summer the fellows take a weeklong trip to the South, visiting the Winterthur Museum in Delaware, the city of Annapolis, and Colonial Williamsburg in Virginia. Interns have the opportunity to work with museum staff in every department at the museum—from curatorial, archives, and collections management, to architectural conservation, development, and research.

Perks and Rewards: The $7,500 fellowship covers tuition, books, field-trip expenses, housing, and meals for nine weeks. In addition, a limited number of awards of $1,000 to $1,500 will be given to offset lost summer income to students of exceptional promise and with demonstrated financial need. Interns receive a $3,000 stipend (for a nine- to twelve-week summer experience) and housing may be available. Historic Deerfield can also arrange academic credit through the history department at the University of Massachusetts at Amherst.

The Essentials: Fellows must have completed two years of college and still be in school. Interns must be undergraduate or graduate students with a background in history, art, American studies, museums, or public history.

Your First Move: Call for application materials, which are due by March 1 and include a $15 nonrefundable application fee. Decisions will be announced in early April.

For More Information:
Jessica Neuwirth, Director of Academic Programs
Historic Deerfield
P.O. Box 321
Deerfield, MA 01342-0321
(413) 775-7207 • (413) 775-7224 (fax)
jneuwirth@historic-deerfield.org

JACOB'S PILLOW DANCE FESTIVAL

Dance Festival • Massachusetts • Summer
www.jacobspillow.org

"How FITTING THAT many in the dance world refer to Jacob's Pillow as the Dance Farm, for it is indeed a place that nurtures." Jacob's Pillow is America's oldest dance festival, presenting ten weeks of dance performances (modern, ballet, jazz, and cultural dance), and conducting a professional dance school each summer. Professional-track dancers, choreographers, and students from all over the world come together to create a unique and exciting environment.

Your Surroundings: Located in the Berkshire Hills of western Massachusetts, the campus includes 150 acres of woodlands, two theaters, four studios, and an outdoor stage.

What You'll Be Doing: Working closely with staff members in all aspects of festival operation, interns receive extensive on-the-job training and experience. Visiting artists and professionals offer additional insights and the oppor-

People are like stained-glass windows. They sparkle and shine when the sun is out; but when the darkness sets in, their true beauty is revealed only if there is a light from within. —ELIZABETH KÜBLER-ROSS

Photo Credit: Mike Van Sleen

A documentation intern with Jacob's Pillow videotapes a summer outdoor performance.

tunity to make valuable contacts. Positions are available in archives/preservation, the business office, development, education, marketing/public relations, operations, programming, technical theatre, ticket services, and video/photography.

Commitment: All positions begin in late May and finish at the end of August. A limited number of fall and spring internships are also available.

Perks and Rewards: A stipend of $500 is provided, along with housing at the Pillow's cottages and meals served in the Pillow's resident cafeteria. Beyond living and working with a diverse community of artists, faculty, students, and staff, interns may also attend performances, community and master classes, and festival events.

Your First Move: Before submitting application materials (two copies of your resume, two work-related references, two letters of recommendation, and a cover letter), be sure to check out the specifics of the position you are applying for on the Web, or call for more information. Although summer applications are accepted through March 1, it's best to apply before February 15 for priority consideration.

For More Information:
Internship Program
Jacob's Pillow Dance Festival
P.O. Box 287
Lee, MA 01238
(413) 637-1322 • (413) 243-4744 (fax)
info@jacobspillow.org

THE JOHN F. KENNEDY CENTER FOR THE PERFORMING ARTS

Performing Arts • Washington, D.C. • 3–4 Months
www.kennedy-center.org

THE KENNEDY CENTER is one of the country's foremost performing arts institutions. Founded in 1971 as a memorial to JFK, the center not only was a sorely needed addition to Washington's cultural scene but also quickly became an arts center of national and international importance. Today the center attracts the country's finest music, dance, and theatre companies, while also providing a home to the National Symphony Orchestra, the American Film Institute, and the Washington Opera. It also runs an admirable array of educational programs and competitions for students of all ages. The center's grand marble exterior is matched by a foyer, regal red carpet, and an eighteen-foot bust of JFK.

What You'll Be Doing: Up to twenty students are selected each semester to participate in the Kennedy Center's Vilar Institute for Arts Management internship program. Positions may be available in advertising, development, education (local and national programs), press, the National Symphony Orchestra, special events, production, programming, and volunteer management. In addition to creating a list of learning objectives and goals with their supervisor, interns will develop a special project that they will complete during their time at Kennedy. Interns also submit a weekly journal, maintain a working portfolio, attend required intern events, and participate in midsemester and final evaluations. In addition, interns will attend a weekly Executive Seminar Series, which involves presentations by executives of the center and other major arts institutions in Washington, D.C.

Commitment: Internship assignments are full-time and available during the fall (September to December), winter/spring (January to May), and summer (June to August).

Perks and Rewards: A stipend of $800 per month is provided to help defray housing and transportation costs. Interns also have the chance to attend performances, workshops, classes, and courses presented by the center free of charge.

The Essentials: Internships are designed to offer meaningful learning experiences for those interested in careers in performing arts management and/or arts education. Upper-level undergraduate students (juniors and seniors), graduate students, and students who have graduated but have not been out of school for more than two years are eligible.

Your First Move: Applications are available for download on the Web, or call/email for more information. Phone interviews may be conducted.

For More Information:
Jennifer Schmidt, Internship Program Coordinator
The John F. Kennedy Center for the Performing Arts
Education Department
2700 F St., NW
Washington, D.C. 20566
(202) 416-8821 • (202) 416-8853 (fax)
jlschmidt@kennedy-center.org

JUILLIARD SCHOOL

Theatre • New York • Academic Year
www.juilliard.edu

THE JUILLIARD SCHOOL has various facilities that serve various types of theatre productions. The Juilliard Theatre, seating more than nine hundred people, and with a sixty-foot proscenium stage, houses Juilliard's opera and dance productions, concerts, recitals, and special events. The Drama Theatre contains a large thrust stage that supports drama productions ranging from classical Greek to modern avant-garde plays, as well as lectures, workshops, and spring repertory. Juilliard also has black box studios for performance, drama, and opera.

What You'll Be Doing: Technical theatre internships are available in costumes, electrics, production, props, scene painting, stage carpentry, stage management, and wigs and makeup. The arts administration internship covers a variety of areas and departments including concert office, dance division, drama division, facilities management, orchestra library and management, and vocal arts. Many former interns now work at Juilliard as administrators or as theatre technicians.

Commitment: Full-time internships begin in September and end in May. Although reasonable working hours are generally maintained, the interns' weekly schedules will vary with their duties and the requirements of the overall production schedule.

Perks and Rewards: A stipend of $241 per week is provided in addition to basic student medical coverage. Keep in mind that you will be living in New York and may need more income in order to cover living expenses. Housing in New York is expensive and requires careful consideration.

Your First Move: Call for application materials (which are due by June 1).

For More Information:
Helen Taynton, Professional Intern Program Director
Juilliard School
60 Lincoln Center Plaza
New York, NY 10023-6588
(212) 799-5000, ext. 7102 • (212) 724-0263 (fax)
htaynton@juilliard.edu

KENTUCKY SHAKESPEARE FESTIVAL

Theatre • Kentucky • Summer
www.kyshakes.org

As THE OLDEST independently operated professional Shakespeare company in North America, the Kentucky Shakespeare Festival produces a variety of plays in Central Park (in a thousand-seat outdoor amphitheatre) that are free of charge to the public. In addition, the festival offers "Will on Wheels," an educational outreach program, and Camp Shakespeare during the summer months. The festival's professional internship program offers participants the opportunity to make the transition from their training program to the professional theatre world. Positions are available in acting, stage and production management, costuming, promotion/marketing, and education. A stipend of $100 per week and housing in shared dormitory-style housing are provided. Company members can also opt for a single room for $35 per week. Acting interns also participate in free workshops led by members of the resident acting company and other theatre professionals from the Louisville arts community. Send a current head shot and resume to begin the application process; all internships require an audition and/or

No one can whistle a symphony. It takes an orchestra to play it. —HALFORD LUCCOK

interview. For technical or administrative positions, contact Celeste Santamassino (celeste@kyshakes.org); and for education internships, contact Doug Sumey (doug@kyshakes.org).

For More Information:
Celeste Santamassino, Associate Producing Director
Kentucky Shakespeare Festival
1114 S. Third St.
Louisville, KY 40203
(502) 583-8738 • (502) 583-8751 (fax)
info@kyshakes.org

THE KITCHEN

Performing Arts • New York • 2–3 Months
www.thekitchen.org

THE KITCHEN IS a small nonprofit organization dedicated to the presentation and promotion of emerging artists and experimental art forms. Located in the Chelsea neighborhood of New York City, the Kitchen originally began in an unused kitchen of the Mercer Arts Center in the early seventies. Today it houses two of the largest black box theatres in the country. Its performance season (from September through May) features more than two hundred evenings of dance, music, performance, literature, and new media. The internship program is loosely structured around the interest, background, and schedule of each applicant, with positions available in technical, marketing, fund-raising, administrative, and media services. Although financial remuneration is not offered, interns do receive free access to all Kitchen performances, an invaluable work experience, and contact with world-class artists. A two- to three-month commitment is necessary.

For More Information:
Intern Coordinator
The Kitchen
512 W. 19th St.
New York, NY 10011
(212) 255-5793 • (212) 645-4258 (fax)
info@thekitchen.org

LA SABRANENQUE

Restoration • France/Italy • 1 Week–3 Months
www.sabranenque.com

LA SABRANENQUE PROGRAMS offer the chance to discover French village life "from the inside" through dynamic and genuine immersion in regional life and historic preservation. As a grassroots, nonprofit organization created in 1969, La Sabranenque has won several national awards for its restoration work and its international cultural activities.

Your Surroundings: Most activities are based in the restored old quarter (with full modern comfort) in the village of Saint Victor la Coste (near Avignon, southern France), listed as one of the "most beautiful villages in France." Projects are also conducted in various hamlets in Italy.

What You'll Be Doing: Volunteers have the opportunity to become actively and directly involved in preservation and reconstruction work on sites and monuments often dating back to the Middle Ages. Volunteers learn the traditional construction techniques on the job from experienced technicians and, in a short period, experience the satisfaction of making a lasting contribution to the preservation of the villages of southern France. Work is shared with a diverse multinational team and can include stone masonry or cutting, tile floor or roof restoration, dry-stone walling, or vault construction. This is a different and unique way to see the beautiful villages of southern France and, at the same time, participate in a creative experience.

Commitment: Projects range from a minimum of one week to three months in the months of April through October.

Perks and Rewards: Participants pay a $550 program fee (for a two-week session) which includes room and board.

The Essentials: Applicants must be at least eighteen years of age.

For More Information:
Jacqueline Simon, Restoration Projects Coordinator
La Sabranenque
124 Bondcroft Dr.
Buffalo, NY 14226-3427
(716) 836-8698
info@sabranenque.com

In France:
Marc Simon
La Sabranenque
rue de la Tour de l'Oume
30290 Saint Victor la Coste
France
(011) 33 (0) 466 500 505

LATIN AMERICAN ART RESOURCE PROJECT

Art Education • Maryland/Honduras • 1–3+ Months
www.hood.edu/academic/art/laarp

. . . .

WILLIAM AND SARA Swetcharnik, painter and sculptor, have supported themselves as professional artists for over twenty-five years, producing figurative artwork using traditional media from different cultures. William also supports and directs the Latin American Art Resource Project (LAARP), a development program that teaches Central American artists, artisans, and art educators how to work with low-cost, sustainable resources.

Your Surroundings: After seven years based in Honduras, the artists have moved their home base back to their converted barn in the Maryland countryside, near Washington, D.C. Interns may focus on studio arts or preparation for art resource projects in Honduras. Periodic field projects in Honduras are located in the Miskito and Tawahka communities along the Patuca River rainforest corridor and in Garífuna (African-Caribbean) communities in the Cayos Cochinos coral reef islands.

What You'll Be Doing: The LAARP internship program is an excellent opportunity for anyone interested in a first-hand experience of what it takes to run a development project in a poor country. A great deal of this experience consists of learning to navigate within a culture that operates very differently from, and not nearly as efficiently as, those of Europe and North America. Patience, love, and creativity are required to make things work. Some aspects of the work fit the training profile for any arts administrator: maintaining lines of communication and coordination of activities with collaborating institutions, presentations, and exhibitions. The fieldwork includes setting up regional workshops, researching local materials and methods at each site, and, of course, helping with the workshops themselves. To help effectively with the workshops, interns need firsthand experience with materials and methods, which entails a fair amount of studio work, particularly in the production of demonstration pieces for art and artisanry.

Perks and Rewards: The fee for field internships in Honduras ranges from $2,200 for three weeks to $4,800 for nine weeks. Internships in the U.S. range from $1,100 for three weeks to $2,400 for nine weeks. If the intern applicant is highly qualified, part or all of that fee may be waived. Please note that the internship fee helps support ongoing art resource projects and defrays long-term operating costs of the art resource program. The fee does not cover food, lodging, transportation or any other of the intern's personal expenses.

The Essentials: No special skills are required, only emotional maturity and an eagerness to learn, attested through good school records, work history, and letters of reference. A good working knowledge of Spanish is helpful but not necessary.

Your First Move: To receive more information, send a letter or email to the Swetcharniks. After the initial exchange of information, there is a $100 application fee.

For More Information:
William and Sara Swetcharnik, Artists
Latin American Art Resource Project
7044 Woodville Rd.
Mt. Airy, MD 21771
(301) 831-7286 • (301) 694-7653 (fax)
swetcharnik@hood.edu

MAINE STATE MUSIC THEATRE

Theatre • Maine • Summer
www.msmt.org

. . . .

MAINE STATE MUSIC Theatre is Maine's only professional resident music theatre where interns are put in the midst of some of the best professionals from around the country. Internships are available in performance and production (administration, box office, carpentry, costumes, house management, lighting, marketing, music direction, painting, props, stage management, and sound). All interns attend classes given by various members of the professional company and are overseen by an academic supervisor. Because team playing is essential for the summer, interns will also be required to work outside their particular concentration. A weekly stipend of $60 is provided along with room and a food stipend.

For More Information:
Kathi Kacinski, Company Manager
Maine State Music Theatre
14 Maine St., Suite 109

Let your dreams bind your work to your play. —BOB FRANKE

Brunswick, ME 04011
(207) 725-8769 • (207) 725-1199 (fax)
msmtjobs@blazenetme.net

THE METROPOLITAN MUSEUM OF ART

Art Museum • New York • Summer
www.metmuseum.org

THE METROPOLITAN MUSEUM of Art (the Met) is the largest and most diverse museum in the Western Hemisphere, containing two million pieces that cover nearly five thousand years of history. Summer interns are placed in a variety of areas, including conservation, library, education, administration, or one of their nineteen curatorial departments. The program begins with a two-week whirlwind orientation, where interns visit each curatorial department. This prepares college students to give gallery talks and work at the visitor information center. Graduate students begin work on projects related to the museum's collections or to a specific exhibition. The Met also sponsors other programs, including a six- or nine-month internship program, fellowships, and a nine-week summer internship program at the Cloisters (a branch of the Met that resembles a twelfth-century monastery and is devoted to the art of medieval Europe). Both paid and volunteer positions exist, and applicants must be college or graduate students. Specific details on all the opportunities can best be viewed on the Web. (Just type "internship" into the search box.) Electronic applications are encouraged.

For More Information:
Internship Program Coordinator
The Metropolitan Museum of Art
Education Department
1000 Fifth Ave.
New York, NY 10028-0198
(212) 570-3710 • (212) 570-3872 (fax)
mmainterns@metmuseum.org

NAVAL HISTORICAL CENTER

History • Washington, D.C. • Seasonal
www.history.navy.mil

TIRED OF CONDESCENDING internships? The Naval Historical Center treats its interns well. (Admittedly, they must perform herculean amounts of work, but isn't that the nature of the position?) Internships here excite people about history. With a staff of less than one hundred, the center produces books, exhibits, and brochures. The museum and art gallery have less than a tenth of the National Air and Space Museum's annual visitors, but they provide their interns with greater insight into museum operations. The center serves a large branch of the federal government; it is the only organization dedicated to the history of all aspects of the U.S. Navy. Internships here consistently garner good reviews, and many former interns return as volunteers. It is no platitude to say that an internship at the center enhances one's academic and employment prospects.

What You'll Be Doing: Each intern works on a personal project, with possibilities in archives, editing, design, historical research and writing, collections management, curation, education, publicity, documentary editing, and library science. Archival and collections management interns catalog new material and assist with accounting for items already in the collection. Editing interns help with the publication program. In design, interns work on invitation and exhibit layouts and silk-screening. Research and writing form the backbone of work in the branches dealing with post-1945 history, ships, and naval aviation, but interns also learn about museum curation. Library interns work in one of the oldest federal libraries. Everyone, just like the paid staff, turns to the more mundane pursuits: answering inquiries, addressing mass mailings, short bursts of office work, assisting with public programs, and organizing educational tour materials.

Commitment: Have your weekends free. Interning hours are Monday through Friday, excluding federal holidays. You won't make a fortune at the Naval Historical Center, but you will be able to arrange a schedule convenient for your academic or employment needs.

Perks and Rewards: A small stipend is offered, and you will receive sound information on housing options. When intern numbers warrant (generally in the summer), the coordinator arranges field trips; and on the same note, intern T-shirts are designed and produced in-house. Interns have the social cachet of inviting their friends to public programs and private exhibit openings. In addition, each branch sends off its interns with a farewell lunch, and each intern will receive the services of excellent reference writers.

The Essentials: The Naval Historical Center wants everybody to have the opportunity to work in naval history. Past interns have included history majors (naturally) but also those in museum studies, studio art, anthropology, English, French, political science, computer science, international relations, and geography.

Your First Move: Call for application materials (or download them from the Web). Send a completed application along with a writing sample, unofficial transcripts, and an academic letter of reference. Design interns must submit a portfolio (call for specifics). Interviews by telephone or in person form part of the application process.

For More Information:
Edward Furgol, Curator
Naval Historical Center
The Navy Museum
Washington Navy Yard
805 Kidder Breese St., SE
Washington, D.C. 20374-5060
(202) 433-6901 • (202) 433-8200 (fax)
furgol.edward@nhc.navy.mil

> *Be enthusiastic and open to new experiences. It's hard sometimes, but try to submit a complete application packet. We love organizational skills.*

NEW STAGE THEATRE

Theatre • Mississippi • 9 Months
www.newstagetheatre.com

FOUNDED IN 1965, New Stage Theatre is the only fully professional theatre in the state of Mississippi. Under the leadership of its staff, the theatre operates year-round, offering an ambitious season that includes six main-stage productions, two second-stage shows, the premiere of a new play, and a main-stage production for young audiences.

What You'll Be Doing: Acting-intern company members tour the state of Mississippi with three arts-in-education productions for a variety of audiences. Interns also teach creative dramatics for children, conduct theatre workshops in area schools, assist with teacher workshops, and help coordinate equity auditions. When not performing or rehearsing, acting interns assist in the daily operation of the theatre, including technical and administrative duties as well as the strike of all productions. Technical interns participate in the building of all New Stage productions by assisting in the areas of design, carpentry, scenic painting, props, lighting, sound, and costuming.

Commitment: Internships run nine months, starting in September. Interns usually work an average of forty hours per week with one day off.

Perks and Rewards: Stipends range from $6,000 to $7,000, with limited housing available within walking distance of the theatre. Acting interns are given an opportunity to earn equity points toward their Actor's Equity Association card by being cast in understudy roles in equity productions.

The Essentials: New Stage prefers recent college graduates with theatre experience, although others may apply. Applicants must have a good attitude, dedication to the theatre, as well as the ability to adapt and get along with others.

Your First Move: Call for application materials (which are due in mid-April).

For More Information:
Patrick Benton, Education Director
New Stage Theatre
1100 Carlisle St.
Jackson, MS 39202-2127
(601) 948-3533 • (601) 948-3538 (fax)
newstage@netdoor.com

Rain puts a hole in stone because of its constancy, not its force. I just kept knocking on doors until the right one opened. —H. JOSEPH GERBER

NORFOLK CHAMBER MUSIC FESTIVAL

Music Festival • Connecticut • Summer
www.yale.edu/norfolk

How WOULD YOU like the opportunity to work with world-renowned musicians, help produce a concert three to five times per week, and play softball with the Tokyo String Quartet on your day off? The Norfolk Chamber Music Festival, tucked away in Connecticut's Litchfield Hills, is definitely a foot in the door for those exploring the performing arts field—that is, if you can handle the insane pace of work at a summer festival! From mid-June to late August more than thirty concerts are presented with the help of seasonal staff and interns. Positions include associate administrator, facilities manager/artist liaison, box office manager, concert hall manager, music librarian, and recording engineer. Internships are available in administration and recording/production. A stipend of $1,000 to $1,500 is provided for seasonal staff; interns are unpaid. However, everybody receives room, board, and training. The ideal candidate loves the arts and the fast pace that goes hand-in-hand with this exceptional summer event. Send resume, cover letter, and references. Phone interviews are acceptable for those residing out of town.

For More Information:
Festival Manager
Norfolk Chamber Music Festival
Yale Summer School of Music
P.O. Box 208246
New Haven, CT 06520-8246
(203) 432-1966 • (203) 432-2136 (fax)
norfolk@yale.edu

NORLANDS LIVING HISTORY CENTER

Living History • Maine • 2+ Months
www.norlands.org

EMPHASIZING THE FRUGAL lifestyle of the northern New England farm family as expressed in a "use it up, wear it out, make it do, or do without" philosophy, Norlands Living History Center offers the visitor an in-depth experience of nineteenth-century rural life. The programs are unique and innovative, encouraging visitors to participate in history with the hope of developing an appreciation of the present! Thus, visitors might bake cornbread on a woodstove, drive a team of oxen in the fields, or worship in church while learning from "local characters."

What You'll Be Doing: With the goal of making the sights, sounds, smells, and citizens of the nineteenth-century come to life, interns will portray a local character while educating guests. Prior to choosing a character, a thorough training period on local history and everyday lifestyles of the area is provided. In addition, interns will assist with and/or participate in the interpretation of daily scheduled programs, living-history techniques, historic agriculture, archives and research, outreach programs, public festivals and meals, hayrides, site maintenance, and special projects (not to mention learning about business aspects of running a nonprofit museum).

Commitment: The program is offered year-round with flexible start dates; however, due to the training required to fully participate in an internship, a two-month minimum requirement is necessary.

Perks and Rewards: A $200 monthly stipend is provided, along with on-site staff housing in a Cape Cod–style house. Each intern has a private sleeping room and shares a kitchen, living room, and bath. Meals are not provided except when interns are participating in a program. In addition, interns attend one of Norlands' seventy-two-hour Adult Live-In programs (a three-day/three-night experience of nineteenth-century rural New England life) free of charge.

The Essentials: As interpreters of a rural lifestyle, interns should be comfortable with barns and livestock, dirt paths, outhouses, kerosene lamps, and cooking and heating with woodstoves. Those with a high energy level, initiative, enthusiasm, and the willingness to communicate the heritage of rural Maine to people of all ages and backgrounds will thrive here.

Your First Move: Applications are available online, or call/email for further information.

For More Information:
Judy Bielecki, Executive Director
Norlands Living History Center
209 Norlands Rd.
Livermore, ME 04253
(207) 897-4366 • (207) 897-4963 (fax)
norlands@norlands.org

ORLANDO–UCF SHAKESPEARE FESTIVAL

Theatre • Florida • 6 Weeks–10 Months
www.shakespearefest.org

WITH A BRAND new three-hundred-seat Elizabethan-inspired thrust theatre and newly renovated 120-seat theatre, the Orlando–UCF Shakespeare Festival, in partnership with the University of Central Florida, produces six main-stage productions and a staged workshop/reading series from September through May. As the festival's training wing, the education department teaches Shakespeare in over ninety central Florida classrooms each year as well as offers a summer camp for middle school students, a training program for high school students, and an internship and apprenticeship program. Over a nine-month period (forty to sixty-five hours per week), interns work in performance, education, stage management, and/or administration/box office. Interns are usually offered main-stage roles and participate in a variety of classes and workshops. Apprentices work more in a specific capacity for a shorter-term contract (six weeks to ten months). A stipend of $125 per week along with housing is provided (add $50 per week if you have your own housing)—not to mention Disney, Universal, Sea World, and the beach in your own backyard. Auditions and interviews are held locally and at the Southeastern Theatre Conference (www.setc.org).

For More Information:
Sarah Hankins, Intern Coordinator
Orlando–UCF Shakespeare Festival
812 E. Rollins St., Suite 100
Orlando, FL 32803
(407) 447-1700, ext. 214 • (407) 447-1701 (fax)
sarahh@shakespearefest.org

We are looking for hard-working, creative, and dedicated individuals who can work well with a variety of supervisors in a fast-paced environment. We especially appreciate challenge-seeking self-starters with positive attitudes and time-management skills. Our internships are adjustable to all levels of training: from beginners to recent undergraduate students to MFA graduates.

THE PEARL THEATRE COMPANY

Theatre • New York • 6 Months
www.pearltheatre.org

THE PEARL IS a resident acting company that produces five classical plays in its 160-seat theatre in Manhattan's East Village. Emphasis is put on the actor's craft. Audiences are transported to the world of the play rather than adapt the play to conform to modern idiom. Administrative, stage management, and costume internships are available over a six-month period. Hours vary; however, most full-time interns can expect to work at least fifty hours per week and may work as many as seventy hours during load-in and tech week. A weekly stipend of $175 is provided ($200 for costume positions). Those receiving academic credit are unpaid. The Pearl is one of the few theatres in New York authorized to grant Equity membership candidacy points to stage management interns.

For More Information:
Meghan Beals, Programs Manager
The Pearl Theatre Company
80 St. Mark's Pl.
New York, NY 10003
(212) 505-3401 • (212) 505-3404 (fax)
mbeals@pearltheatre.org

REPORTERS COMMITTEE FOR FREEDOM OF THE PRESS

Journalism • Washington, D.C. • 12–14 Weeks
www.rcfp.org

LOCATED ONE METRO stop from Washington, D.C., the Reporters Committee for Freedom of the Press is a voluntary association of reporters and editors dedicated to protecting the First Amendment interests of the news media by providing cost-free legal defense and research services to journalists throughout the U.S.

What You'll Be Doing: Journalism interns have the opportunity to report, write, and edit the committee's publications. These stories cover a broad range of issues, from the arrests of journalists to military press-pool restrictions and access to executions. Interns also attend weekly seminars by prominent media and legal experts in the field, along with attending congressional hearings and media conferences relevant to the committee's work.

Commitment: Internships are offered three times a year for twelve to fourteen weeks.

Perks and Rewards: Full-time interns receive a stipend of $650 to $1,000 per semester; part-time interns receive proportional shares, based on hours worked.

The Essentials: Juniors, seniors, or graduate students are encouraged to apply. A strong background in journalism or political science is required.

Your First Move: Submit resume, short writing sample (clips and/or a short research paper), and a cover letter describing interest.

For More Information:

Rebecca Daugherty, Internship Coordinator
Reporters Committee for Freedom of the Press
1815 N. Fort Myer Dr., Suite 900
Arlington, VA 22209
(703) 807-2100 • (703) 807-2109 (fax)
rcfp@rcfp.org

Our interns go immediately to work here. They are very much a part of the committee's work in this small-staffed office. We generally consider those who are the best writers and are clearly professional in attitude and demeanor.

SEATTLE REPERTORY THEATRE

Theatre • Washington • 9 Months
www.seattlerep.org

Producing plays that excite the imagination and nourish a lifelong passion for the theatre, the Seattle Repertory Theatre is America's largest professional, nonprofit theatre. Receiving international renown for its consistently high production and literary standards, the Rep is in a unique position to offer aspiring theatre professionals top-notch training through its Professional Arts Training Program.

What You'll Be Doing: Interns participating in the Professional Arts Training Program will undertake responsibilities as members of the staff, contribute ideas, participate in department and staff meetings, and complete projects under the guidance of their supervisors. Staff members

guide the work of each intern to help prepare them for a career in professional theatre. Internships are available in the artistic department, arts management, communications, costume shop, education, production management, properties, scenic art (paints), stage management, technical production, and scenic and lighting design. The Seattle Rep also provides a unique learning opportunity to all interns through a series of professional workshops. These workshops provide a chance for interns to learn more about the many different departments at the Rep and connect with theatre staff, guest artists, and members of the Seattle arts community—along with enjoying a late morning snack!

Commitment: Internships begin in September 2002 and continue through the following May on a full-time basis. Please note that you must be available for the complete duration of the internship. (However, on rare occasions, there may be some flexibility on your time commitment.)

Perks and Rewards: Interns will receive at least a weekly stipend of $145, and college students may also arrange academic credit through their internship department. Although housing is not provided, the Rep is happy to provide information regarding housing options and other resources. Check out their "Living in Seattle" link on the Web for more housing information and other resources.

The Essentials: The Rep seeks bright, creative, reliable and self-motivated individuals with basic training and experience in theatre, who are committed to strengthening their skills and talents.

Your First Move: The application process for the September season-opener begins on January 1 and concludes on March 15. To apply, send off the following in one packet: a resume of theatre and related experience; a letter of intent listing internship desired (you may choose up to three areas) and how you heard about the program; and two letters of recommendation from people who know your work. A photo is optional.

For More Information:

Internship Coordinator
Seattle Repertory Theatre
155 Mercer St.
Seattle, WA 98109
(206) 443-2210 • (206) 443-2379 (fax)
interns@seattlerep.org

*The Rep's tech people don't seem
to have a limit to what they can do.
When you have ideas at other theatres
you get excuses why they can't be done.
But when you have an idea at the Rep,
the tech people think about it for awhile
and then say "yes we can do that."*

—ACTOR, DIRECTOR,
AND INSPIRED CLOWN,
BILL IRWIN

SMITHSONIAN CENTER FOR EDUCATION AND MUSEUM STUDIES

Museum • Washington, D.C. • 2–12 Months
http://museumstudies.si.edu

THE SMITHSONIAN CENTER for Education and Museum Studies (SCEMS) coordinates a central referral service for all internship programs at the Smithsonian Institution. Incorporating sixteen museums and galleries plus the National Zoo, the Smithsonian is the world's largest museum complex and offers, quite possibly, the world's largest museum internship program.

What You'll Be Doing: Interns at the Smithsonian develop job skills, expand expertise in academic disciplines, learn about museum careers, and see the workings of a major institution from the inside out. Smithsonian interns learn by doing, working closely with an internship supervisor in a tutorial setting. Interns are placed in one of forty museums, administrative offices, and research programs—there is truly something for everyone. Remember that the Smithsonian Institution is more than just the science, art, and history museums. The great size of this cultural institution means that there are many interns here doing a wide variety of work, from exhibit design to research to conservation to public programs and education. There are also internships in areas not normally associated with a museum, such as photography, computer science, public affairs, administration, product development, and library science. Most museums also have enrichment programs for interns, which include career seminars, behind-the-scenes tours, and such.

Commitment: Most interns work at the Smithsonian for a period of two months to one year, for a minimum of twenty hours per week.

Perks and Rewards: Unless otherwise noted, internships at the Smithsonian do not carry a stipend. Perks include enrichment events and a 20 percent discount at museum gift shops.

Your First Move: Visit SCEMS online for many links to institution-wide programs, or email for information and an application. Applicants can apply directly to each museum/office or through the Central Referral Service. For the latter, you must submit five sets of application materials for each museum/office where you wish to be considered for an internship. This includes a completed application form, a two- to three-page essay, two letters of reference, and transcripts. Deadlines: spring—October 15; summer—February 15; and fall—June 15. No interviews are conducted.

For More Information:
Tracie Spinale, Internship Coordinator
Smithsonian Center for Education and
    Museum Studies
Arts & Industries Bldg., Room 2235
P.O. Box 37012
Washington, D.C. 20013-7012
(202) 357-3102 • (202) 357-3346 (fax)
interninfo@scems.si.edu

Make sure you find out about the internship program you are applying for. A good way to get information is to contact the intern coordinator for each specific program; and it is better to ask any questions you might have about the process before you apply. Don't ever think a question is stupid or irrelevant. Some of us were interns before and probably had the very same question. The most important thing to remember when applying is being yourself and letting you and your interests be apparent in your application. This way the project you may be selected for will truly match your interests and help you to fulfill your goals. The application essay gives you the opportunity to do this.

SPOLETO FESTIVAL USA

Music Festival • South Carolina • 3–6 Weeks
www.spoletousa.org

THE SPOLETO FESTIVAL produces and presents world-class opera, dance, theatre, chamber music, symphonic and choral music, jazz, and literary and visual arts—more than 120 events in seventeen days, playing to an international audience of more than seventy-five thousand in a variety of theaters and other performance sites throughout historic Charleston.

What You'll Be Doing: In what is called "a short-term, intensive, and exciting opportunity to learn about the world of the performing arts," apprentices work with arts professionals to produce and operate this extravagant event (from May to mid-June, full-time). Administrative apprenticeships are available in media relations, development, finance, box office, housing, general administration, merchandising, orchestra management, chamber music, and rehearsal. Production apprenticeships include stage carpenters, stage electricians, sound, properties, wardrobe, wigs and makeup, and administration.

Perks and Rewards: A $250 per week stipend is provided along with housing at the College of Charleston. Out-of-town apprentices also receive $50 toward travel expenses. Other perks include a welcoming party, a participant badge (open access to all events), and excellent career training in the arts.

The Essentials: Applicants should have excellent organization, communication, and administrative skills. Familiarity with the arts is also a plus.

Your First Move: Applications are available online, and are due by February 1. Secondary material or an interview may be required.

For More Information:
Apprentice Program Coordinator
Spoleto Festival USA
P.O. Box 157
Charleston, SC 29402-0157
(843) 722-2764 • (843) 723-6383 (fax)
apprentice@spoletousa.org

STAGEDOOR MANOR

Performing Arts • New York • Summer
www.stagedoormanor.com

EVERY SUMMER MORE than 245 talented kids and 100 staff members from all over the world travel to Stagedoor (in the Catskills Mountains) to produce thirty-three full-scale productions in five on-site theaters. In addition to these productions, Stagedoor offers a full program of classes in dance, TV, video production, directing, vocal training, acting technique, stage combat, technical skills—every facet of theatre and performance is covered. Staff and participants alike come to Stagedoor for experience and to fulfill professional and personal goals. They also come for fun, laughter, and friendships that last a lifetime. Their classrooms, video labs, dance studios, and costume and scenic shops are alive with the energy and enthusiasm of theatre.

What You'll Be Doing: Positions at Stagedoor require great flexibility. The staff must have a commitment to teamwork and a true enjoyment of the energy and honesty of children. The days are long and the daily schedule of each staff member includes a variety of responsibilities and functions. Camp counselors double as stage managers, production assistants, dance captains, or sports personnel. Directors, musical directors, and choreographers teach classes in their craft and must hold professional credits. Technicians and designers have little interaction with campers, and focus most of their time with work behind the scenes. Stagedoor also hires office, housekeeping, and kitchen personnel, registered nurses, American Red Cross lifeguards, and swim and tennis instructors.

Commitment: The program runs ten weeks, from mid-June to late August.

Perks and Rewards: Salaries vary according to age and experience and range from $900 to $2,500 for the season, along with dormitory-style housing and meals. Perks include working for an internationally famous training center with staff and children from all over the world.

The Essentials: Staff members must be twenty-one or older, with previous experience working with children and the theatre. Most staff members are between the ages of twenty-three and thirty.

Your First Move: Call to request an application and brochure. Application materials are due by April 15, although it is best to apply by February because a high percentage of staff return each season!

For More Information:
Carl Samuelson, Co-Director
Stagedoor Manor
150 Karmel Rd.
Loch Sheldrake, NY 12759-5308
(888) 782-4388 • (845) 434-4290 • (845) 434-1466 (fax)
info@stagedoormanor.com

WESTPORT COUNTRY PLAYHOUSE

Theatre • Connecticut • Summer
www.westportplayhouse.com

EACH SUMMER SINCE 1931, a series of comedies, dramas, and musicals has been presented in the Westport Country Playhouse. One feels the history and charm of the playhouse just by walking through the lobby, with walls covered with posters advertising shows dating from the beginning of the theatre's history.

What You'll Be Doing: Each intern will work directly under a department head, with positions including, administration, company management, directing, electrics, playhouse operations, properties, scenic construction, scenic painting, stage management, and wardrobe. To supplement the internship experience, interns will partake in a series of seminars and workshops designed to provide a look into the inner workings and operations of a regional summer theatre as well as connect with playhouse staff, guest artists, and members of the local arts community. For those who are in high school and between the ages of sixteen and nineteen, the playhouse also offers an eight-week volunteer apprenticeship program. The program is designed to provide an in-depth exposure to the theatre with a chance to rotate through various work assignments and performance responsibilities.

Commitment: Internships begin in early June and continue through mid-September. A minimum commitment of twelve weeks is required.

Perks and Rewards: Interns receive a $100-per-week stipend, along with housing.

The Essentials: The internship is best suited for those who have already acquired basic training and experience in the theatre, and are ready for the next step toward a career in professional theatre. Applicants must be serious-minded, highly motivated, and at least nineteen.

Your First Move: Application materials are available online, or call for more information. Applications are due by the end of March.

For More Information:
Hyla Crane, Education Coordinator
Westport Country Playhouse
P.O. Box 629
Westport, CT 06881
(203) 227-5137, ext. 16 • (203) 221-7482 (fax)
hcrane@westportplayhouse.com

Interns must be willing to engage in the creative process, test the limits of their own ingenuity, and have a willingness to work hard. In return, interns are treated as members of the professional staff and receive intensive hands on experience crucial to a professional resume and professional contacts that will help the interns get that "foot in the door."

WILLIAMSTOWN THEATRE FESTIVAL

Theatre Festival • Massachusetts • Summer
www.wtfestival.org

ONCE A SMALL summer company, the Williamstown Theatre Festival (in northwest Massachusetts) has grown into a major theatrical event and has acquired a national reputation for the artists it attracts and the gifted young actors, designers, and directors it sends out into the world. Interns concentrate in one of the following areas: box office, design (sets, costumes, lights, and sound), directing, general/company management, literary management, photography, producing, publicity, production management, publications management, stage management, or technical production. Interns work from early June through the end of August and are responsible for their own daily living expenses, including $500 for Williams College housing. An acting-apprentice program is offered as well as a few fellowships and paid staff positions.

For More Information:
Anne Lowrie, Company Manager
Williamstown Theatre Festival
229 West 42nd St., Suite 801
New York, NY 10036-7201
(212) 395-9090 • (212) 395-9099 (fax)
alowrie@wtfestival.org

The notes I handle no better than many pianists. But the pause between the notes—ah, that is where the art resides. —ARTUR SCHNABEL

Operated in partnership with the National Park Service, Wolf Trap's Filene Center offers a magical outdoor venue for world-class performances of every genre.

WOLF TRAP FOUNDATION FOR THE PERFORMING ARTS

Performing Arts • Virginia • Summer
www.wolftrap.org

KNOWN AS AMERICA's national park for the performing arts, Wolf Trap's mission since its inception in 1971 has been to "enrich, educate, and provide enjoyment to the widest possible audiences through a broad range of accessible, high-quality activities in the performing arts." To reach the community, the country, and the world, Wolf Trap not only presents outstanding performances, including world premieres, national radio and television broadcasts, and events that preserve culturally diverse art forms, but provides educational opportunities in the arts to people of all ages and backgrounds.

Your Surroundings: Wolf Trap is situated on an expanse of Virginia farmland a half hour from Washington, D.C., and has an open-air amphitheater with thousands of lawn seats.

What You'll Be Doing: Wolf Trap's Internship Program provides meaningful hands-on training and experience in the areas of arts administration, education, and technical theatre. These internships offer a practical opportunity to become an integral member of the staff and work side-by-side with professionals producing, promoting, and administering the full spectrum of the performing arts.

Positions are available in every conceivable area of the theatre—from stage management, directing, and costuming to graphic design, Internet programs, and catering. A complete list can be found on the Web.

Commitment: Internships are available for twelve weeks, full-time (forty hours per week) during the summer, and part-time (twenty-four hours per week) in the fall and spring.

Perks and Rewards: Summer interns receive a stipend of $210 per week, while fall and spring interns receive up to $126 per week. Housing is the responsibility of each intern, although guidance is available. Perks include the opportunity to attend a variety of performances and events (two complimentary tickets for each), field trips and facility tours, and educational seminars on topics relating to careers in arts management, as well as participation in "brown bag lunch" presentations by department heads and guest speakers.

The Essentials: Internships are designed for students who have completed a minimum of one year of undergraduate study, as well as graduate students and recent graduates. Wolf Trap is not accessible by public transit, thus interns must have a reliable mode of transportation.

Your First Move: Specific application materials can be found on the Web, or call for a brochure. The majority of interviews take place over the phone, but in-person meetings can be arranged. Deadlines: spring—November 1; summer—March 1; and fall—July 1. An early application is advised.

For More Information:
Mia DeMezza, Assistant Director, Education Outreach
Wolf Trap Foundation for the Performing Arts
1624 Trap Rd.
Vienna, VA 22182
(800) 404-8461 • (703) 255-1933 • (703) 255-1924 (fax)
internships@wolftrap.org

WOMEN'S STUDIO WORKSHOP

Art Studio • New York • 4–8 Months
www.wsworkshop.org

FOUNDED IN 1974, the Women's Studio Workshop (WSW) is a nonprofit artists' space founded and run by women to serve as a supportive working environment for all people interested in the visual arts. WSW staff artists coordinate grants, fellowships, internships, exhibition opportunities, and the Summer Arts Institute—WSW's primary education program for visual artists.

Your Surroundings: Located in the beautiful Hudson Valley, in the foothills of the Shawangunk and Catskill Mountains, WSW is surrounded by acres of marsh and woodlands. It is housed in the Binnewater Arts Center, a hundred-year-old mercantile building that has been completely renovated to accommodate specialized studios in printmaking, papermaking, photography, and book arts. The five thousand square feet of studio space have been carefully designed, localizing work and printing areas, all with plenty of natural light and direct access to the outdoors.

What You'll Be Doing: Interns work alongside the artist staff on projects in papermaking, printmaking, book arts, and arts administration, as well as assist in the Artists-in-Residence program, work with artists and educators in the Art in Education program, and participate in the Summer Arts Institute classes as studio assistants. Tasks

vary throughout the internship, but may include preparing studios, designing brochures and posters, assisting in all aspects of the exhibition program, preparing the apartment for visiting instructors, setting up for evening programs, managing the setup and breakdown of lunch each day, staffing the annual fund-raising auction, and assisting in the day-to-day running of the organization.

Commitment: Interns have the option of working from January through mid-August (Session I) or mid-August to mid-December (Session II).

Perks and Rewards: A monthly stipend of $100 is provided along with housing, a communal staff potluck lunch each workday, and unlimited access to studios after hours.

The Essentials: Ideal applicants must have an undergraduate degree, experience in studio arts, an ability and willingness to work in a close-knit community, and enjoy working at a variety of tasks. Applicants must understand that their internship experience does not serve as an artist's residency program.

Your First Move: Send a cover letter, resume, ten to twenty slides of your work, and three letters of reference. Postmark deadlines: Session I—October 15; Session II—April 1.

For More Information:
Internship Coordinator
Women's Studio Workshop
P.O. Box 489
Rosendale, NY 12472
(845) 658-9133 • (845) 658-9031 (fax)
wsw@ulster.net

Do not send old recommendation letters. We would rather hear from a friend who knows you well than a professor who does not. In your cover letter, address why you want to come here, specifically how we will benefit from having you here, as well as how a WSW internship can help further your professional ambitions. A strong body of work is essential, as shown through good-quality slides.

IN SEARCH OF A MISSION—
A DEEPER CALLING

Photo Credit: The Workshops

David Lyman teaches creative people to become better at what they do at a total-immersion workshop.

At some point in our lifetime, we come to a place where we long to uncover our mission—a lifelong "assignment" that evolves from deep within our soul. Here's the story, as told by David Lyman, about his journey of uncovering a deeper calling and building his place in the world:

My father, the son of a New England minister, described one's mission in life as a "calling." However, a calling is not exactly a job. That was something you did to support your lifestyle. Nor was a calling exactly a profession, which is earning a living by doing something you like to do. A calling was more. It was something you had to do, loved doing, and loved doing for others.

For me, it began as photography. After a year covering the war in Vietnam as a Navy journalist, I went to work for a variety of adventure and sports magazines. By the age of thirty-two, I was feeling pretty good about my achievements, but I'd become bored. I longed to make photographs and tell stories that made a difference. When I learned that Robert Gilka, then Director of Photography at *National Geographic* magazine, was to teach a workshop at The Center of the Eye in Aspen, I signed up, was accepted, and arrived at the workshop with portfolio in hand. To work for *National Geographic* and to travel the world making photographs of my adventures were lifelong dreams.

It was the summer of 1972, and I was thrilled to be among twenty other would-be photojournalists, all hoping to be discovered. Appearing before Gilka at the workshop, I presented my portfolio. He opened my book, turned a few pages, closed it, and pushed it back across the table. Then, in his famous drill sergeant's voice he said, "You earn a living with this stuff?"

I left the room in disillusionment and spent the remainder of the day in shock. I finished the workshop with thoughts racing through my mind about my future. However, I realized that if I were to make a statement with my photography, I would need to learn from the best. All fall I thought about what to do. The Center of the Eye went out of business. My research turned up only a few other workshops and none that fit my requirements. Jokingly I said to myself, "Why don't I start my own workshop right here on the coast of Maine?"

Soon thereafter, with the help of a photographer and designer, the Workshops became a reality. One hundred and fifty students attended twelve workshops that first summer. It all started with $1,000 in my pocket and a $3,000 loan. I lost money the first summer, and again after the second, but the realization of what was happening drove me on. During the winters I recouped my losses by photographing ski races, sports personalities, and resorts. Sooner than I could imagine, I was surrounded by the greatest minds in photography.

Twenty-five years later, we have a new campus with eight buildings, a summer enrollment of twenty-seven hundred, and have become a well-established international center. As I look back over the years, I see that Gilka had given me just the right assignment after all—not the glamorous one I sought but an assignment that answered a deeper calling. It has been a gift to be able to build not only a place where creative people can come and learn but also a place that provides support and encouragement for those developing their own "calling." That is what I intended to do all along.

—CONTRIBUTED BY DAVID LYMAN,
director and founder of the Workshops

Work-study students learn new processes, tools, and techniques for mastering the craft of black-and-white photography.

THE WORKSHOPS

Photography • Maine • 7 Weeks+
www.theworkshops.com/jobs

THE PICTURE-PERFECT Maine coast village of Rockport serves as a backdrop for inspiration and subject matter for one of the nation's leading educational centers for photography, film and video, and creative writing. Referred to by students as the "Outward Bound School of Photography," more than 250 one-week workshops, master classes, and expeditions are conducted by some of the most successful visual minds in the field. The curriculum is designed for budding enthusiasts to professional actors, filmmakers, photographers, storytellers, and writers.

What You'll Be Doing: The Workshops hires nearly one hundred energetic people each summer to help run their "creative community of visual artists." Interns and staff members work as teachers and teaching assistants, technical and lab assistants, office and kitchen help, studio and darkroom assistants, video and computer technicians, gardeners, store clerks, drivers, administrative assistants, and publicity people. Another option you might consider is the highly praised seven-week work-study program (offered twice during the summer), which includes a comprehensive course in black-and-white photographic craft and vision, along with practical assignments, critiques, classes, field trips, lectures, slide presentations, and a term-end group exhibition in the Workshops' gallery. Students attend this course in exchange for twenty hours per week of work in a variety of roles.

Perks and Rewards: Interns receive room and board, and paid staff start at $6 per hour. There is a fee of $2,195 for the work-study program, which covers tuition, lab fee,

and shared room and board for seven weeks. All participants have access to darkrooms, editing suites, studios, and the library and gallery.

The Essentials: In addition to practical skills of darkroom work, film and video training, and experience, characteristics of the summer staff include high energy, enthusiasm, responsibility, and punctuality; they are people who want to make a contribution as well as improve their career options.

Your First Move: Write or call for a listing of openings and positions. A majority of the positions are filled at the three-day summer job fair, held the first weekend of April (provided it's not Easter).

For More Information:
David Lyman, Founder and Director
The Workshops
2 Central St.
P.O. Box 200
Rockport, ME 04856
(877) 577-7700 • (207) 236-8581 • (207) 236-2558 (fax)
info@theworkshops.com

In addition to their summer staff opportunities, you may want to participate in one of the one- to three-week learning vacations, photographic expeditions, or workshops that can take you to all corners of the world! These unique programs focus on travel photography, documentary photography, documentary film, documentary video, and photojournalism.

RECOMMENDED RESOURCES. . . . .

"An organization of people who bring history to life," the **Association for Living History, Farm, and Agricultural Museums (ALHFAM)** has more than nine hundred members who work in living history sites as volunteers or paid staff. Their website provides a listing of more than eighty international programs with living history programming. For more information contact ALHFAM, Brownwood Farm, 8774 Route 45 NW, North Bloomfield, OH 44450-9701; (440) 685-4410, www.alhfam.org.

The **American Association of Museums (AAM)** represents the entire scope of museums, including art, history, science, military and maritime, and youth museums, as well as aquariums, zoos, botanical gardens, arboretums, historic sites, and science and technology centers. *Aviso,* AAM's monthly newsletter, provides listings for museum positions and internships as well as information on upcoming seminars, workshops, and other museum activities. AAM members receive it as part of their membership ($50 per year for students), or it can be purchased as a yearly subscription for $40. The online version can be found at http://aviso.aam-us.org (which has a searchable database of current opportunities). AAM also sponsors a job placement center, resume review, and mentoring opportunities forum at its annual meeting held in mid-May each year. For more information contact the American Association of Museums, 1575 Eye St., NW, Suite 400, Washington, D.C. 20005; (202) 289-9122, www.aam-us.org.

Have you always wanted to participate in an archaeological dig? With the *Archaeological Fieldwork Opportunities Bulletin,* you just might find the perfect project. Researched and edited by the Archaeological Institute of America (and updated for release each year in January), this comprehensive guide lists over two hundred excavations, field schools, and special programs with openings for volunteers, students, and staff throughout the world. The majority of the opportunities listed take place over the summer (and generally have late spring/early summer application deadlines). The guide can be purchased directly through the David Brown Book Company for $15.95 (www.oxbowbooks.com; 800-791-9354) or visit the AIA website at www.archaeological.org.

The *New England Conservatory (NEC) Job Bulletin* is one of the most comprehensive resources for music-related jobs around. Listings include teaching positions in higher education and K–12, orchestral, choral, and church, as well as military jobs, and arts administration opportunities. The newsletter also includes interesting information on grants, festivals, and competitions as well as helpful career information. Once every two weeks you can have the newsletter delivered to your email box for a subscription fee of $35 (twenty-four issues total). To take a peek at a newsletter sampler along with other features of the NEC Career Services Center, visit their website at www.newenglandconservatory.edu/career.

If you are a storyteller, musician, magician, puppeteer, speaker, or theatre artist, you might consider taking to the road and performing at school assemblies across the nation. To get the inside scoop on developing a program, marketing yourself, and presenting at schools, check out *How to Make Money Performing in Schools* (Silcox Productions, $18.95) or just start doing it: contact schools locally and see what opportunities come forth. **Schoolgigs.com** and **Schoolshows.com** offer more information and links.

Need to feel empowered about your career as an artist? *How to Survive and Prosper As an Artist* (Owl Books, $17) will provide you with optimistic and helpful information to assist you in taking control of your career while creating a successful livelihood as an artist. As an author, sculptor, and veteran arts career counselor, Caroll Michels (www.carollmichels.com) provides advice and information on selling from a studio, working with galleries, generating exhibition opportunities, and understanding grants. She also offers thousands of resources—from art colonies and internships to online galleries and studios. If you're looking for further information, contacts, links, guidance, and advice on artist resources, stop by the author's latest creation, the Artist Help Network (www.artisthelpnetwork.com).

ShawGuides.com provides continually updated information on educational travel and creative career programs throughout the world (and access to all the content is free). Their online database contains more than thirty-five hundred programs ranging from cooking schools and writer retreats to art and craft workshops and language vacations.

Determine that the thing can and shall be done, and then we shall find the way. —ABRAHAM LINCOLN

If you're thinking of becoming an artist or craftsman (or wish to turn your hobby into a career), ***Opportunities in Arts and Crafts Careers*** (McGraw Hill, $11.95) will guide you in the right direction. Each artistic career path that Elizabeth Gardner profiles includes a brief history, a description of what's involved in the work, and discusses training options and job potential in the field. Another similar book—***Career Opportunities in Art*** (Facts on File, $10.95)—provides profiles for eighty arts careers, including a career ladder and skills necessary to break into the field.

As an introduction to careers in the artistic field, ***100 Best Careers for Writers and Artists*** (Arco, $15.95) by Shelly Field features a variety of opportunities to assist the budding artist to prepare now for an exciting job. Providing descriptive information, job tips, and additional resources, the guide covers everything from writing careers in television and book publishing to artistic pursuits in the theatre and fine arts.

Theatre Directories, the publishing wing of American Theatre Works (see page 277 or visit www.theatredirectories.com), provides some great directories that include information on apprenticeship, internship, and short-term employment opportunities throughout the U.S. The *Summer Theatre Directory* is filled with summer employment and training opportunities in summer stock theatres, Shakespeare festivals, theme parks, outdoor dramas, performing-arts camps, and cruise ships. Or to find a job or an internship as an actor, designer, technician, or staff in a professional regional or dinner theatre across the U.S., the *Regional Theatre Directory* provides endless leads ($19.95 for either book).

What Do Museum Professionals Do?

Not only are museums a powerful source of knowledge, they are also exciting places to work. People who work in this environment find that many of the rewards come from disseminating their knowledge to others. The museum field encompasses a variety of opportunities that include interpretive specialists and docents, collections managers and exhibition researchers, writers and designers, along with administrative positions ranging from membership coordinators to public-relations specialists. Potential employers are especially attracted to applicants who possess solid practical museum experience and can demonstrate a strong academic background. Many people secure practical, on-the-job training through internships or working as a museum volunteer.

For a listing of museum-related website links, visit www.aam-us.org.

The pay is modest. The work is important. The satisfaction is incredible. Whether working in soup kitchens or family shelters, teaching and inspiring at-risk youth, ministering to the abused or mentally ill, building houses for the poor, empowering people through ministry work, assisting the elderly, helping the fight against hunger or AIDS, or working to keep the world's population in check, this section has plenty of options to choose from. Your efforts may not immediately change the world or solve deep-rooted problems, but will serve as an ongoing commitment to helping others in need while promoting the integrity of creation. If you have a passion for service and are willing to go the extra mile to help a good cause, it's time to start making a difference—the world needs you!

Remember that when you leave this earth, you can take with you nothing that you have received—only what you have given: a full heart, enriched by honest service, love, sacrifice, and courage.

—SAINT FRANCIS OF ASSISI

Unique Opportunities to Explore in This Section:

- We all know the heartfelt work Habitat for Humanity provides—bringing people from all walks of life together to make affordable housing and better communities a reality for everyone. But did you know you can experience the work of Habitat around the globe? From joining an RV Care-A-Vanner program to volunteering at their national headquarters, this special section explores all your working options (page 328).

- All of us experience brief periods of confusion, anxiety, or sadness as a normal part of our everyday lives. However, there are many who are unable to cope with the daily struggles—not because of choice but because of mental illness. Programs such as Gould Farm (page 327), Innisfree Village (page 331), or Spring Lake Ranch (page 340) offer hope and a place for volunteers to help those in need.

- Just because you've reached your golden years doesn't mean there isn't a world of opportunities to explore. It's only too late if you don't begin your journey now. Those who are beyond the age of fifty will uncover some unique opportunities and resources in this special section (page 344).

Photo Credit: University for Human Goodness

Small class sizes and dynamic hands-on service learning experiences enrich University for Human Goodness (page 342) students of all ages and backgrounds.

HEART WORK

AMERICORPS

Service Learning • USA • 10–12 Months
www.americorps.org

AMERICORPS IS A national service movement that engages thousands of Americans of all ages and backgrounds in a domestic Peace Corps—that is, getting things done across America by meeting our education, public safety, environmental, and human needs. The work will be tough and AmeriCorps members won't solve all of America's problems, but those who join this effort will definitely make a difference.

What You'll Be Doing: AmeriCorps*VISTA has been helping to meet the needs of low-income communities since 1965, when it was first established as Volunteers in Service to America (VISTA). Members make a full-time, full-year commitment and are assigned to local public and private nonprofit organizations to work toward meeting the community needs determined by the community itself. VISTA members might mentor teens, teach elementary schoolchildren, walk the beat with community police officers, renovate low-income housing, help the homebound and disabled achieve self-sufficiency, or tackle one of the thousands of projects other VISTA members are conducting right now to help their communities. AmeriCorps*NCCC, the National Civilian Community Corps, is a ten-month residential national service program for those between the ages of eighteen and twenty-four. The program takes its inspiration from the Depression-era Civilian Conservation Corps (CCC), which put thousands of young people to work restoring our natural environment. Today corps members in NCCC work on environmental projects but also in disaster relief, education, and public safety; they also help address other unmet human needs.

Commitment: VISTA members serve one year, with opportunities available year-round. NCCC members begin with a three-week training class starting in October and continue with a ten-month commitment.

Perks and Rewards: All AmeriCorps members receive a modest living allowance, health coverage, travel expenses, and after completing one year of full-time service (from ten to twelve months), an education award of $4,725 ($2,362 for part-time service). NCCC members live on one of five campuses that serve five separate regions of the U.S., ranging from a closed military base in San Diego to the Veterans Administration Medical Center in Maryland.

The Essentials: Along with having a deep desire to make a difference, VISTA applicants must be at least seventeen years of age and U.S. citizens or permanent residents; NCCC members must be between eighteen and twenty-four.

Your First Move: Call for an information kit (plenty of info is also available online, including a searchable database of projects). Joining AmeriCorps is a highly competitive process. Members are selected through a review process involving an initial screening of the application, an interview, and a review of references. Once an applicant qualifies for service, a placement officer attempts to locate a suitable assignment, taking skills and preferences into account. This process may take a few months, so an early application is advised. The deadline for NCCC is March 15 for positions beginning in October.

For More Information:
Recruitment Administrator
AmeriCorps
Corporation for National and Community Service
1201 New York Ave., NW
Washington, D.C. 20525
(800) 942-2677 • (202) 606-5000 • (202) 565-2789 (fax)
questions@americorps.org

I will get things done for America—to make our people safer, smarter, and healthier.
I will bring Americans together to strengthen our communities.
Faced with apathy, I will take action.
Faced with conflict, I will seek common ground.
I will carry this commitment with me this year and beyond.
I am an AmeriCorps member, and I will get things done.

—AMERICORPS PLEDGE

BRETHREN VOLUNTEER SERVICE

Service Learning/Ministry • USA/Worldwide • 1–2 Years
www.brethrenvolunteerservice.org

SPONSORED BY THE Church of the Brethren, Brethren Volunteer Service (BVS) volunteers give their time and skills to help a world in need. It is a way for people to work at issues greater than themselves, recognizing that their efforts may not immediately solve deep-rooted problems but can be a part of ongoing work for justice, peace, and the integrity of creation.

What You'll Be Doing: Volunteers choose from a variety of projects (more than 150 are available in twenty-four states in the U.S. and in seventeen nations abroad) including those involving children, young adults, senior citizens, farmworkers, disabled persons, general community services, agriculture, hunger/homelessness, prisoners and the prison systems, refugees, domestic violence, housing, health care, camping ministries, community organizing and development, education and teaching, the environment, and congregational placements. A booklet describes the specifics of each position. Volunteers begin their term of service with ten to thirty other volunteers in a BVS three-week orientation (scheduled four times per year), which examines a wide range of topics, including peace and justice issues, hunger, cross-cultural understanding, and poverty.

Commitment: Positions in the U.S. require a one-year commitment; overseas positions require two years.

Perks and Rewards: Volunteers receive room, board, medical coverage, life insurance, transportation to and from the project, a monthly allowance of $60 to $80, and an annual retreat for those in the U.S. and Europe. Possible living environments include community-style with other volunteers, in an apartment (sometimes shared), with a family, or on the project site. The financial costs include transportation to orientation and an overseas travel fee of $400 for those going abroad. Some projects qualify for an AmeriCorps education award of $4,725.

The Essentials: BVS seeks those who are willing to act on their commitment and values. BVS challenges individuals to offer themselves, their time, and their talents to work that is both difficult and demanding, yet rewarding and joyful. The minimum requirements: eighteen years of age, sound physical and mental health, willingness to examine and study the Christian faith, and commitment to the goals of BVS. A college degree or equivalent life experience is required for overseas assignment.

Your First Move: Call for application materials. Applications are accepted year-round, although applicants are encouraged to apply four to six months prior to their availability.

For More Information:
Recruitment
Brethren Volunteer Service
1451 Dundee Ave.
Elgin, IL 60120-1694
(800) 323-8039 • (847) 742-5100 • (847) 742-0278 (fax)
bvs_gb@brethren.org

> *It is essential that each volunteer bring a willingness to grow and a desire to serve. Important work toward peace, justice, and meeting the needs of humanity and the environment calls out for persons willing to serve.*

CAMP WOODSON

Therapeutic Camp • North Carolina • 17 Weeks

CAMP WOODSON IS a year-round therapeutic, adventure-based wilderness program operated by the North Carolina Department of Juvenile Justice. Activities such as hiking, rock climbing, canoeing, urban exploring, and horseback riding are used to address issues of troubled youth (who are all involved in the court system). The camp's approach is to challenge individuals and provide opportunities for success.

What You'll Be Doing: Interns will conduct and process initiatives and perform both individual and group counseling for students, aged thirteen to seventeen, who have come from unstable family situations and have failed in the traditional school system. (Their range of offenses might include breaking and entering, assault, substance abuse and drug violations, auto theft, or sexual offenses, and their attendance at the camp is voluntary.) Interns become role models and friends, with their goal to capture the lesson from difficult and challenging situations and make that lesson real for the students.

Commitment: Three five-week sessions and a training week between each session are recommended.

Perks and Rewards: Although no compensation is provided, housing and food may be available. Perks include living in the beautiful western North Carolina mountains, where there are many opportunities for climbing, hiking, canoeing, and mountain biking. Interns should have their own transportation.

The Essentials: Interns typically have backgrounds in human-service fields and have experience in leading and facilitating outdoor-adventure activities.

Your First Move: Submit cover letter and resume, then call to arrange an interview.

For More Information:
Internship Director
Camp Woodson
741 Old U.S. Highway 70
Swannanoa, NC 28778
(828) 686-5411 • (828) 686-7671 (fax)

CAMPHILL ASSOCIATION

Community Building • USA • 3–12+ Months
www.camphill.org

AFTER FLEEING THE Nazi invasion of his own country, Dr. Karl Koenig (an Austrian pediatrician and educator) settled in Aberdeen, Scotland, to develop a community that focused on the abilities, talents, and gifts of each person—not their limitations. Inspired by Rudolf Steiner's philosophy of "anthroposophy" (see page 260 for details), Camphill attempts to foster and support lively, viable communities that celebrate the individual while making educational, social, cultural, and environmental contributions to society. Today the international Camphill movement consists of more than ninety communities in nineteen countries. In the U.S. alone, there are ten independent communities that are home to over eight hundred people.

What You'll Be Doing: Camphill is a way of life. It is not a job. There are no shifts, no salaries, no relative values placed on people according to the nature of the work they do. But it is certainly a life full of jobs to be done. There are meals to cook, floors to sweep, fields to mow, cows to milk. There are children in need of special care. Tasks are undertaken for the good of the whole, out of a sense of commitment and responsibility. To be able to do real, meaningful work gives purpose and dignity to life. The arts are also an important aspect of life in Camphill, with each center hosting concerts and other cultural activities. Thus, there are many participatory artistic activities, such as orchestra, choir, drama groups, community newspapers, folk dancing, music appreciation, and study groups.

Commitment: Whether you are looking for an internship opportunity, a formal training program, a short-term volunteer experience, or a new, fully committed lifestyle, Camphill offers a variety of time frames and commitments for its coworkers.

Perks and Rewards: There is no salary in the usual sense. Coworkers receive room, board, and a small stipend for personal expenses. Most of the Camphill centers offer formal courses on social therapy, and there are opportunities to learn many transferable and practical skills, including a variety of crafts, biodynamic gardening, farming, pruning fruit trees, baking, cooking, care giving, and homemaking. Those that provide a year of service are eligible for an AmeriCorps educational award of $4,725.

The Essentials: Camphill coworkers come from different countries, professional and educational backgrounds, age groups, and interests. Prospective coworkers with a genuine interest in others, a willingness to do what is needed, flexibility, tolerance, and cheerfulness are eagerly sought by each community. Coworkers are expected to share their lives with others, especially those with developmental disabilities.

Your First Move: Call or email for more information. Opportunities outside the U.S. can be found at www.camphill.org.uk.

For More Information:
Co-Worker Development
Camphill Association
20 Triform Rd.
Hudson, NY 12534
(518) 851-3260 • (518) 851-9257 (fax)
coworker@camphill.org

When I come here, I see the coworkers and the villagers in this kind of mutual "us" which, I have to say, is a quite unusual thing in the world. I come here not only to play concerts for people, but to feel a sort of spiritual refreshment that being here makes me feel. It's not very often that you feel this kind of harmoniousness in the world. It's a wonderful experience.

—RICHARD GOODE, pianist

THE CARTER CENTER

Think Tank • Georgia • 15 Weeks
www.cartercenter.org

GUIDED BY JIMMY CARTER and staffed with distinguished professionals, the Carter Center works with world leaders and dignitaries to promote democracy, resolve conflicts, protect human rights, eradicate disease, improve agriculture in developing countries, and tackle social problems in urban areas.

What You'll Be Doing: Supervisors in each program (ranging from global development to human rights) work with interns to establish weekly projects and long-term assignments. Interns are typically given a broad range of duties focusing on issues addressed by their program, but also dapple in office administration and issues cutting across other programs. To augment the intern's experience, a number of other educational and social opportunities are provided.

Commitment: Interns are required to commit a minimum of twenty hours per week for at least fifteen weeks.

Perks and Rewards: Graduate/professional students may be eligible for a $3,000 stipend during the summer session (for a fifteen-week, forty-hour-per-week term); otherwise positions are unpaid.

The Essentials: The program is open to undergraduate juniors and seniors, recent graduates, and graduate/professional students who are interested in contemporary international and domestic issues. Foreign language ability and travel abroad are very helpful.

Your First Move: Call or visit the Web for an application packet. Deadlines: spring—October 15; summer—March 15; and fall—June 15. Recognizing the need of some applicants to apply for funding or to make alternative plans, program staff strive to complete the process within a month.

For More Information:
Educational Programs Director
The Carter Center
453 Freedom Parkway
One Copenhill
Atlanta, GA 30307
(404) 420-5151 • (404) 420-5196 (fax)
carterweb@emory.edu

CATHOLIC NETWORK OF VOLUNTEER SERVICE

**Social Justice/Ministry • Worldwide •
2 Weeks–2 Years**
www.cnvs.org

THE CATHOLIC NETWORK of Volunteer Service (CNVS) publishes *Response,* an annual directory of volunteer opportunities that includes over two hundred faith-based, full-time volunteer programs in the U.S. and in more than one hundred countries worldwide. Volunteers of all ages, committed to social justice, spirituality, and a simple lifestyle, work in soup kitchens or family shelters, direct programs for at-risk youth, teach in schools, minister to the abused, provide health care, build houses, or offer service to refugees—to name just some of the many opportunities. Programs vary in length from a few weeks to a few years, although the average length of a domestic placement is one year and an international program, two years. Each program has its own combination of benefits and compensation; most include a stipend, room and board, and health insurance. All provide orientation and training, and some may offer retreats or language training. Call for your free copy of the directory, or view the most current listings (including urgent opportunities) on the Web. Long-term, full-time administrative volunteers are also needed at the CNVS office in Washington, D.C. Benefits include a stipend, health insurance, and housing in a Christian community setting.

For More Information:
Matthew Koerner, Membership and
    Recruitment Coordinator
Catholic Network of Volunteer Service
1410 Q St., NW
Washington, D.C. 20009-3808
(800) 543-5046 • (202) 332-6000, ext. 12
(202) 332-1611 (fax)
volunteer@cnvs.org

The healthy social life is only found when in the mirror of each human soul the whole community finds its reflection and when in the community the virtue of each one is living. —RUDOLF STEINER

319

The Catholic Network is a wonderful resource for finding a well-rounded, faith-based volunteer program. Each program in the network has something different to offer and each is run by an incredible staff that carries such a passion for the work that they do. I have never worked in an environment where the people I corresponded with every day (the program directors) were so understanding, loving, and full of energy for their daily work. If you are looking to begin or enhance your spiritual journey while participating in a wonderful, year-long volunteer experience, the Catholic Network is an ideal program.

—THERESE STRASSER, participant

CENTER FOR STUDENT MISSIONS

Ministry • USA/Canada • 3–8 Months
www.csm.org

IF YOU ARE interested in youth ministry and want to participate in an urban short-term mission experience, the Center for Student Mission can provide you with an extraordinary opportunity. As a city host, you'll be responsible for "bridging the gap" between suburban/rural people and city people. Duties include facilitating groups of youth and adults (from junior high school to college), while making a profound impact on their relationship with God. With various start dates throughout the year, over seventy positions are available from three to eight months in eight major cities throughout the U.S. and in Toronto, Canada. A stipend of $350 per month, along with housing, food while hosting, training, and supervision is provided. Applicants must be from either the U.S. or Canada and at least eighteen years old, have excellent people and leadership skills, and have the desire to be a servant and leader. Applications can be downloaded online.

For More Information:
Kyle Becchetti, Director
Center for Student Missions
P.O. Box 900
Dana Point, CA 92629-0900
(949) 248-8200 • (949) 248-7753 (fax)
kyle@csm.org

CHILDREN'S DEFENSE FUND

Child Advocacy • Washington, D.C. • 10–12 Weeks
www.childrensdefense.org

THE MISSION OF the Children's Defense Fund (CDF) is to "leave no child behind" and to ensure every child a "healthy start, a head start, a fair start, a safe start, and a moral start" in life and successful passage to adulthood with the help of caring families and communities. CDF provides a strong, effective voice for all the children of the U.S. who cannot vote, lobby, or speak for themselves. They pay particular attention to the needs of poor and minority children and those with disabilities. CDF educates the nation about the needs of children and encourages preventive investments before they get sick, into trouble, drop out of school, or suffer family breakdown.

What You'll Be Doing: Interns are assigned to one of CDF's several divisions, providing administrative and program support to their professional staff of researchers, lobbyists, public interest lawyers, trainers, community organizers, media and communications specialists, fund-raising officers, event planners, administrative managers, and computer technology experts. Interns also have the chance to attend weekly brown-bag discussions on substantive issues, engage in hands-on advocacy skills training, and participate in national grassroots and mobilization efforts.

Commitment: Preference is given to those who can commit to a minimum of three days per week for ten to twelve weeks.

Perks and Rewards: Commuter reimbursement costs are provided (and paid at the end of service).

The Essentials: Candidates must be undergraduate or graduate students who have a passion for progressive social change, an interest in working on children's issues, and a track record of activism or community involvement.

Your First Move: Applications are available online. The review process generally takes four to six weeks and includes a telephone interview for finalists. While there are no application deadlines for the quarterly internship periods, candidates are encouraged to apply early due to the limited number of highly competitive positions in each division.

For More Information:
Herman Piper, Internship Coordinator
Children's Defense Fund
25 E St., NW
Washington, D.C. 20001
(202) 662-3797 • (202) 662-3680 (job hotline)
(202) 662-3570 (fax)
cdfinfo@childrensdefense.org

CHOATE ROSEMARY HALL

Teaching • Connecticut • Summer
www.choate.edu/summer

CHOATE ROSEMARY HALL, a secondary school spread over four hundred acres, offers one of the oldest summer enrichment programs in the country. Each summer thirty to thirty-five teaching interns are hired as members of the faculty, with senior teachers serving as mentors. Whether in the classroom, on field trips, or in the dorms, interns become engaged, stimulated, and supported in every facet of resident school life. Applicants must have completed three years of college and have a strong interest in exploring teaching as a potential career. A salary of $2,300 ($2,400 for graduates) is provided, along with room and board. It is advised that you submit application materials by the end of January; selected candidates will be invited to Choate Rosemary Hall for a campus tour and interviews.

For More Information:
Jim Irzyk, Director of Summer Programs
Choate Rosemary Hall
333 Christian St.
Wallingford, CT 06492-3800
(203) 697-2365 • (203) 697-2519 (fax)
jirzyk@choate.edu

CHRISTIAN APPALACHIAN PROJECT

Social Service/Ministry • Kentucky •
3 Weeks–1 Year
www.chrisapp.org

THE CHRISTIAN APPALACHIAN PROJECT serves economically, socially, and/or physically challenged people in eastern Kentucky through programs ranging from adult education and teaching independent-living skills, to garden programs and home repair. Volunteers live together and share household duties, meals, and prayer as they support each other through their strong motivation to serve people. One-year volunteers receive room and board, a monthly stipend, health insurance, loan deferment information, and a potential AmeriCorps educational award. Summer-camp counselors, who must be over eighteen, are needed to staff four summer camps in eastern Kentucky (room, board, orientation and training, and daily prayer are provided). A limited number of short-term opportunities are available for three weeks to eight months. Call for specific details and an application.

For More Information:
Elizabeth Fritz, Coordinator of Volunteer Recruitment
Christian Appalachian Project
322 Crab Orchard St.
Lancaster, KY 40446
(800) 755-5322 • (859) 792-3051
volunteer@chrisapp.org

A CHRISTIAN MINISTRY IN THE NATIONAL PARKS

National Parks/Ministry • USA • 3–15 Months
www.acmnp.com

A CHRISTIAN MINISTRY in the National Parks is an interdenominational movement recognized by over forty Christian denominations. It extends the ministry of Christ to the millions of people who live, work, and vacation in our national park. This ministry serves government personnel and their families who live in these areas, students and professional resort workers who are employed to operate the resort facilities during the summer and winter vacation seasons, and the millions of tourists visiting the parks. This ministry cooperates with support committees in each area to provide regular inter-

Photo Credit: Richard P. Camp, Jr.

From Rocky National Park (shown here!) to Acadia in Maine, participants with A Christian Ministry in the National Parks lead interdenominational services of worship during the summer months.

denominational services, religious education, and Christian fellowship.

What You'll Be Doing: Worship, work, and wilderness! This theme pervades the whole meaning of the ministry as it provides opportunities for Christian witness and service. Each member of the staff has a full-time job with either a park company or the National Park Service. Participants work as desk clerks, housekeepers, bellhops, store clerks, trail crew, rangers, tour guides, or food and beverage staff. Participants also plan and lead interdenominational services of worship on Sundays and Bible studies throughout the week. An important aspect of the program is being a positive Christian witness in the workplace. All staff leaders are encouraged to attend one of ten regional spring orientation conferences throughout the U.S.

Commitment: A three-month commitment is necessary. Most participants arrive at the parks between late May and mid-June and stay through Labor Day, although some parks are open from May 1 through November 1. Year-round and winter placements are available for those who are able to commit to periods of six to fifteen months, depending on the area assigned.

Perks and Rewards: Participants are paid for their work by the park companies, with most earning between $1,800 and $2,400 (after room, board, and taxes) for a three-month period. Of course, having a national park as your back yard is the biggest perk to many.

The Essentials: The program seeks individuals who are least eighteen years of age, imaginative, dedicated, and open to creative service. The ministry demands maturity of thought and conduct, and applicants must have the ability to understand and live amiably with other people and other faiths.

Your First Move: Applications are accepted year-round, although early applications are given first preference. Offers for summer positions are sent to qualified applicants starting in December, and applicants who wish to qualify for government jobs must apply by January 15.

For More Information:
Rev. Richard Camp, Jr., Director
A Christian Ministry in the National Parks
10 Justin's Way
Freeport, ME 04032
(207) 865-6436 • (207) 865-6852 (fax)
acmnp@juno.com

CITY YEAR

Service Learning • USA • 10 Months
www.cityyear.org

EVER SINCE THEIR beginning in Boston in 1988, the vision of City Year has remained the same: the hope that one day the most commonly asked question of an eighteen-year-old will be, "Where are you going to do your service?" Each year, beginning in September, City Year unites diverse groups of young people, ages seventeen to twenty-four, for a full year of rigorous community service, leadership development, and civic engagement in communities from coast to coast. Teams of corps members work in a variety of service opportunities, from teaching social issues on topics such as HIV/AIDS and domestic violence prevention to running after-school programs and organizing and leading out-of-school programs such as Camp City Year and Young Heroes (a service-learning corps for middle school students). Corps members receive a weekly stipend, health insurance coverage, and, upon graduation, are eligible for a postservice AmeriCorps education award up to $4,725, job training, and other life-changing opportunities.

Application materials, which are available online, must be sent in by April 30.

For More Information:
Jean Seigle, National Director of Recruitment
City Year
285 Columbus Ave., 5th Floor
Boston, MA 02116
(888) 424-8993 • (617) 927-2500 • (617) 927-2510 (fax)
info@cityyear.org

While browsing the City Year website, be sure to take a look at the history of their logo, which will provide you with interesting information for your interview. For instance, did you know the seven triangles in each segment of the log represent the days of the week and the American Indian belief that in every major decision we should consider the impact of any decision we make on the next seven generations?

CONFRONTATION POINT MINISTRIES

Youth Development/Ministry • Tennessee • Summer
www.confrontationpoint.org

CONFRONTATION POINT MINISTRIES offers opportunities to lead weeklong mission trips with youth groups doing home repairs (on the homes of poverty-stricken people) or outdoor-adventure trips (which are designed to teach leadership development). The programs run from late May to early August, with training provided for the adventure staff. Besides having a solid Christian faith, applicants must have group-leadership skills, maturity (not necessarily age, but twenty or over is better), a valid driver's license, and be hardworking, fun loving, and adventurous. Leaders receive a salary of $1,500, plus half of all partnerships that they raise (they provide a partnership-raising packet that will help you raise partners effectively), plus room and board. Over forty positions are offered each summer; applications can be found on the Web.

For More Information:
Randy Velker, Summer Staff Coordinator
Confrontation Point Ministries
P.O. Box 572
Crossville, TN 38557
(800) 884-8483 • (931) 484-7819 (fax)
randy@confrontationpoint.org

CONGRESSIONAL HUNGER CENTER

Hunger Awareness • USA/Washington, D.C. • 1 Year
www.hungercenter.org

DID YOU KNOW that more than one billion people throughout the world are denied the most basic of human rights—access to food? In the U.S. (the richest country in the world), one in ten people suffer from hunger and malnutrition. The Mickey Leland–Bill Emerson Hunger Fellows Program, a program of the Congressional Hunger Center, helps to make an impact by developing leaders in the fight against hunger.

What You'll Be Doing: Each year a select group of twenty-two participants are chosen to be fellows in this twelve-month program (beginning in late August). After an intensive ten-day orientation and training period in Washington, D.C., fellows are placed for six months, in teams of two, in grassroots organizations at sites throughout the U.S. to learn about hunger and poverty through hands-on experiences. The following six months are spent in Washington, D.C., at national nonprofit organizations working on hunger and poverty policy. During this time, fellows attend professional development seminars. Also inquire about their two-year international fellows program, with placements in South Asia, sub-Saharan Africa, and Latin America/Caribbean. (There's an April 30 application deadline for this program.)

Perks and Rewards: Designed to experience living at the poverty level, fellows receive a modest living allowance that averages $10,000 for the year. Benefits include health insurance, relocation stipends, and an end-of-service cash award of $3,500. Housing is provided in the host community during the six-month field placement and assistance in locating housing in Washington, D.C., is offered for the policy-placement segment of the program. Travel to and from training sessions and placements is also provided.

The Essentials: Applicants are chosen on the basis of their commitment to social change, diversity of experience and perspective, vision for the future, demonstrated leadership potential, and willingness to learn and have their lives changed by this experience. All applicants over the age of eighteen will be considered.

Your First Move: Call, email, or visit the Web for application materials, which are due by the end of January. Openings may occur late in the hiring process, so qualified candidates are encouraged to contact the center after the priority deadline.

For More Information:
John Kelly and Kristin Anderson, Codirectors
Congressional Hunger Center
Mickey Leland–Bill Emerson Hunger Fellows Program
229½ Pennsylvania Ave., SE
Washington, D.C. 20003
(202) 547-7022 • (202) 547-7575 (fax)
fellows@hungercenter.org

CONGRESSIONAL YOUTH LEADERSHIP COUNCIL

Education • Washington, D.C. • 4 Months
www.cylc.org

AS A NONPROFIT organization, the Congressional Youth Leadership Council focuses on leadership development for more than eight thousand outstanding high school juniors and seniors each year. Students from the U.S. and abroad come to Washington, D.C. and New York City to participate in educational programs, which inspire them to assume greater leadership roles locally, nationally, and internationally. In addition to inspiring young people to achieve their full leadership potential, the council provides internships for college students in education (conference planning and coordination), enrollment (admissions and alumni/teacher relationships), and public relations (congressional outreach and public affairs). Full- and part-time positions span four months with start dates available in January, May, and September. A $9-per-hour stipend is provided; applications are available online.

For More Information:
Dr. Marguerite Regan, Director of Curriculum
Congressional Youth Leadership Council
1110 Vermont Ave., NW, Suite 320
Washington, D.C. 20005
(202) 777-4050 • (202) 777-4050 (fax)
mregan@cylc.org

CO-OP AMERICA

Social Justice • Washington, D.C. • Seasonal
www.coopamerica.org/internships

CO-OP AMERICA IS a nonprofit membership association of individuals and organizations working to build a more cooperative and socially responsible economy. They strive to educate their members to use their buying power more effectively to create change. Co-op America serves as a link between socially conscious consumers and responsible businesses by providing a variety of benefits, including a quarterly publication and the *National Green Pages* to their members.

What You'll Be Doing: While at Co-op America, interns are exposed to the world of marketing and development in the nonprofit, social-change sector. Internships are available in these departments: corporate accountability, executive, foundation fund-raising, Internet marketing, magazine and publications, marketing analysis, media, *National Green Pages* advertising, research, and socially responsible business research. All positions involve work in developing programs, research and writing, and general organizational strategy. Co-op America has a progressive office, treats interns as part of the team, and encourages interns to participate in all staff activities.

Commitment: Internships are offered year-round, although they prefer those who can work a minimum of two months. Schedules and length of internships vary depending on the project and intern's availability.

Perks and Rewards: A stipend of $150 per month is provided, except for summer interns sponsored by the Everett Public Service Internship Program, which carries a stipend of $230 per week. All interns receive a two-year membership to Co-op America, a number of "intern appreciation lunches" (free food!), and every so often they close the office to do something fun together (such as tubing or bowling).

The Essentials: Those who are interested in the environmental- and social-change movement, hardworking, able to work independently and as part of a team, and willing to work in a cooperative environment make ideal candidates.

Your First Move: Detailed position descriptions can be viewed on the Web (or call for more information). Send your resume and cover letter stating why you want to work for Co-op America and which position you are interested in and why.

For More Information:
Internship Coordinator
Co-op America
1612 K Street, NW, Suite 600
Washington, D.C. 20006
(800) 584-7336 • (202) 872-5307 • (202) 331-8166 (fax)
internships@coopamerica.org

Let us know which internship you would like. Don't make us guess. Make sure there are no typos in your letter and resume. Be clear and concise about what you are looking for and what your skills are. Know something about the organization you are writing to. Let us know why you want to work at Co-op America rather than some other organization.

FARM SANCTUARY

Animal Rights • New York/California • 1–3 Months
www.farmsanctuary.org

DEDICATED TO ENDING the exploitation of animals used for food production, Farm Sanctuary (located both in the heart of upstate New York and in a small farming community in Northern California) serves as a refuge for hundreds of abused or badly injured farm animals—a haven where "food animals" come to live, not die. More than three hundred animals reside in twelve shelter barns at the farms. A "People Barn" functions as a learning center where visitors can find out more about factory farming and the harsh realities of the "food animal" industry.

What You'll Be Doing: The sanctuaries' well-established internship program allows volunteers to learn firsthand about the day-to-day responsibilities of farm work, farm-animal care, educational programming (from staffing and maintaining the visitor center to conducting tours), and the practical applications of grassroots participation.

Commitment: Full-time positions are available year-round, so volunteers can join the sanctuary any time. It's preferred that volunteers make a commitment of at least one month, and two- or three-month internships are encouraged.

Perks and Rewards: Volunteers receive shared housing, with access to kitchen facilities.

The Essentials: Anyone who has a strong commitment to animals and wants to experience the joy of doing outdoor work is welcome.

Your First Move: Fill out an application on the Web (click on the Volunteer/Jobs link), or call/write for more information.

For More Information:
Michelle Waffner, Education Coordinator
Farm Sanctuary
P.O. Box 150
Watkins Glen, NY 14891-0150
(607) 583-2225 • (607) 583-2041 (fax)
education@farmsanctuary.org

FRONTIERS FOUNDATION

Community Service • Canada • 3–6 Months
www.frontiersfoundation.org

FRONTIERS FOUNDATION IS a voluntary service program for people from Canada and around the world who are interested in volunteering their time to help others help themselves. The foundation works in partnership with communities in low-income, rural areas across northern Canada (and other areas of the world) with the hope of making a distinct impact on human poverty. Volunteers, working on projects that are locally initiated, might build or renovate homes, conduct training programs, or organize recreational activities in developing regions. Projects run year-round for three to six months. Accommodations, food, and travel at the project site are provided. Volunteers must be at least eighteen and in good physical condition. Application forms can be downloaded from the Web.

For More Information:
Marco Guzman, Executive Director
Frontiers Foundation
2615 Danforth Ave., Suite 203
Toronto, ON M4C 1L6
Canada
(800) 668-4130 • (416) 690-3930 • (416) 690-3934 (fax)
frontiersfoundation@on.aibn.com

The greatest challenge of the day is how to bring about a revolution of the heart, a revolution which has to start with each one of us. —DOROTHY DAY

GLOBAL CHILDREN'S ORGANIZATION

Community Service • California/Croatia • 2 Weeks
www.globalchild.org

THROUGH COMMUNITY SUMMER camps, Global Children's Organization helps "restore children to childhood"—that is, children who live in deprived, disrupted, and stressful circumstances resulting from armed conflict, war, inner-city violence, political and economic upheaval, or hatred and intolerance. Volunteers have the opportunity to participate in a two-week camp at a former monastery on a small island off the Adriatic coast or at the peace-building program in the mountains of Southern California during the summer months. (Other camp sites are in the works.)

What You'll Be Doing: Prior to the two-week experience, volunteers are trained in skilled peer counseling, working with traumatized children, conflict resolution/mediation, peace-building skills, and community-building exercises. Then the work begins—the beginnings of personal healing and play through games, sports, music, dance, and drama. Counselors also encourage children to express their painful experiences through art and dialogue—and to appreciate and celebrate their differences and find nonviolent solutions to conflict.

Perks and Rewards: Volunteers pay their own way to either Croatia ($1,280) or Southern California ($600), which includes participation for one child, along with housing and meals. Travel to the site and any other related expenses are the responsibility of each volunteer.

The Essentials: Volunteers come from the U.S. and all over the world. There are also volunteers from local areas who have, themselves, been victimized by the violence in their own communities. Applicants for the Croatia camp must be at least seventeen; for the Southern California camp, sixteen.

Your First Move: Call for application materials, which are due by the end of February. Applicants will be interviewed in person or via phone during the month of March. There is a nonrefundable $35 application fee.

For More Information:
Judith Jenya, Volunteer Coordinator
Global Children's Organization
10524 W. Pico Blvd., Suite 216
Los Angeles, CA 90064
(310) 842-9235 • (310) 842-9236 (fax)
gco@globalchild.org

GOOD SHEPHERD VOLUNTEERS

Community Service/Ministry • USA/Paraguay • 1–2 Years
www.goodshepherdvolunteers.com

FOUNDED BY THE SISTERS of the Good Shepherd (www.goodshepherdsistersna.com), Good Shepherd Volunteers is a faith-based volunteer program that places Christian men and women in jobs working with children, teens, and women in social service agencies.

What You'll Be Doing: Volunteers live together in communities that focus on simplicity, spirituality, and social justice, with typical service placements that include teaching (and range from an inner-city junior high to a domestic violence center), child care, outreach coordination, youth development, activities coordination, and counseling. Programs are offered in the U.S. in Los Angeles, New Jersey, New York, Philadelphia, and Washington, D.C., and abroad in Paraguay and other nations in South America (depending on need).

Commitment: Placements begin in late August with an initial weeklong orientation and continue for one to two years. Throughout the year, there are four weekend retreats as well as opportunities for work-related training and workshops.

Perks and Rewards: Benefits include professional support and supervision, a $100 monthly stipend, assistance with travel costs, full medical coverage, deferred student loans, and an AmeriCorps education award. A private room in community-style housing is also provided along with an $80-per-month food stipend.

The Essentials: Most volunteers are between the ages of twenty-two and twenty-five and have either just graduated from college or graduate school or have graduated in the past couple of years; others have taken a break from school to volunteer or were working and decided that they really wanted to try something else with their lives. At minimum, applicants must be twenty-one years of age and a high school graduate as well as have two years of work experience or some college education.

Your First Move: Applications are available online and are accepted on a rolling basis; however, many people submit their application materials starting in January.

For More Information:
Maureen McGowan, Director
Good Shepherd Volunteers
333 E. 17th St.

New York, NY 10003
(888) 668-6478, ext. 780 • (212) 979-8604 (fax)
goodshpvol@aol.com

GOULD FARM

**Therapeutic Community/Social Service •
Massachusetts • 1 Year**
www.gouldfarm.org

GOULD FARM IS a compassionate, respectful family environment where people with mental illness learn to build more meaningful lives for themselves. The services at the farm remain rooted in the belief that every person has something valuable to contribute to the community despite mental or emotional limitations. Central to the farm model is a structured, supportive work program with all community members helping to run the six-hundred-acre farm, whether tending to the gardens or the roadside store, pasteurizing milk, or preparing the meals. Volunteers generally work in one specific area of the farm, which might include gardening, farming, forestry, dairy management, livestock, cooking, child care, administration, or clinical work. Serving as informal counselors, work team leaders, and role models, most volunteers lead a small group of people through work tasks that are required to run the farm and maintain the community. A total of twelve positions (which require a one-year commitment) are usually filled throughout the year, along with occasional summer opportunities (from two weeks to four months) based on housing availability. Benefits for those who commit for one year include a monthly stipend of $250, a private bedroom in shared staff housing on the grounds, farm-fresh meals, full medical coverage, and the possibility of an AmeriCorps Education award. One of the biggest perks may be the spirit that resides in this rural, community lifestyle, which is filled with lots of work along with singing, crafts, music, art, weaving, and the celebration of nature and life!

For More Information:
Cynthia Meyer, Human Resources Director
Gould Farm
Box 157, 100 Gould Farm Rd.
Monterey, MA 01245-0157
(413) 528-1804, ext. 17 • (413) 528-5051 (fax)
humanresources@gouldfarm.org

GREEN CHIMNEYS CHILDREN'S SERVICES

**Farming/Therapeutic Community • New York •
3–5 Months**
www.greenchimneys.org

GREEN CHIMNEYS IS dedicated to the development of basic education and daily-living skills for children and adults to restore and strengthen their emotional health and well-being. The main campus is situated on a 150-acre farm where injured animals also have the chance for rehabilitation through the help from participants. The lessons learned from the animals become the stepping stone for a human connection and healing.

What You'll Be Doing: A typical day at Green Chimneys includes special education classes, vocational education, life skills, therapy, therapeutic activities, and recreation. Internships are available in the farm program, as well as the special education, recreation, and child-care departments. Farm interns work with children who are participating in daily barn chores and special projects (such as grooming animals, painting signs, or creating educational displays). Interns are offered the chance to participate in a variety of activities, including public programs and tours, teacher workshops, and weekend events.

Commitment: Programs vary in length from three to five months, with start dates beginning in January, June, and September.

Perks and Rewards: A small stipend is provided, along with room and board. Interns are housed in shared rooms in a residence located across the street from the campus.

The Essentials: Applicants must have a keen interest or background in children, animals, farms, and outdoor education, and must be at least twenty years of age (at least a junior in college or equivalent).

Your First Move: To hear a recorded message on current employment opportunities, dial extension 501 when calling.

For More Information:
Jackie Ryan, Internship Coordinator
Green Chimneys Children's Services
400 Doansburg Rd., Caller Box 719
Brewster, NY 10509-0719
(845) 279-2995, ext. 158 • (845) 279-2714 (fax)
info@greenchimneys.org

*The best and most beautiful things in the world cannot be seen or even touched.
They must be felt with the heart.* —HELEN KELLER

WORKING OPTIONS WITH HABITAT FOR HUMANITY INTERNATIONAL

Volunteers with Habitat's RV Care-A-Vanners program "take five" from their "Building on Faith" housing project in Seattle.

It's not what's out there in the world that you have to worry about.
It's what's in your heart and your head.

—JOSEPH M. McINTYRE

Putting faith into action, Habitat for Humanity brings people from all walks of life together to make affordable housing and better communities a reality for everyone. Habitat volunteers provide their construction and administrative skills for the vision of eliminating poverty housing from the face of the earth.

OPPORTUNITIES IN GEORGIA

Something new to Habitat's campus in Americus is the creation of the Global Village and Discovery Center—and they need plenty of volunteers to help out! Phase one of the village began in 2002 and calls for fifteen replica homes to be built, representing fifteen of eight-three countries in which Habitat works. The village will be built in five phases over the course of five years; and once completed, the village will be an interactive museum where visitors can wind their

way through multimedia displays on world housing, and then wander through a village to see replicas of houses from places such as such as Tanzania, Kenya, and Sri Lanka.

Teams of volunteers work to build the homes, with the first step of making each brick by hand (with the aid of a manual machine). The experience is unique in that you'll learn just how difficult it is for people in other countries to have a home of their own (who do most of the labor themselves). A three-week, full-time commitment is necessary, although volunteers can stay on up to three months. Construction skills are not a prerequisite as Habitat will teach you—if you have the will to learn! For further information about this new program, contact Volunteer Support Services (see page 330).

Other volunteer opportunities in Americus

include positions in administration, child care, fund-raising, graphic arts, information systems, language translation, photography, or public relations. Internships are also available for college students. Furnished housing and a food stipend are provided for all volunteer programs (and some positions include health insurance). Check out www.habitat.org/hr for more information.

ATTENTION RVers—ROAD TRIP USA?

Do you want to blend the fun of RV travel with a fulfilling Habitat for Humanity experience? Habitat's RV Care-A-Vanners organize caravans of six to ten RVs whose owners have a commitment to eliminate substandard housing and a willingness to learn from and partner with local affiliates and homeowner families. In general, these nationwide projects run two weeks, with a typical workday beginning with devotions and lasting about seven hours. Each volunteer must own a recreational vehicle (motor home, trailer, or van), along with a few basic tools, and have energy and a spirit of enthusiasm and flexibility. A caravan is time for growth and fellowship, as well as for service and hands-on experience. Activities may include work at any stage of new house construction, occasionally the renovation of an older home, or building awareness of Habitat's mission at churches, civic groups, or the local media. Participants must be financially able to travel to the project site and cover personal expenses while there; host affiliates provide a safe place to park your RV (water and electrical hookups and waste disposal). To get the

wheels of your RV turning, call for a packet or visit www.habitat.org/gv/

GLOBAL VILLAGE PROGRA

The Global Village Program (www. provides participants with a uniqu become active partners with people of another culture. Team members work alongside people of the host community, raising awareness of the burden of poverty housing and building decent, affordable housing worldwide. As partners, team members help build a true "global village" of love, homes, communities, and hope! Unlike tour groups, Global Village hosts offer team members a "back-door" welcome to their community and encourage teams to visit some of their cultural and national treasures available locally. One- to three-week itineraries are balanced with plenty of work, recreational activities, and free time. In addition to short-term missions here in the U.S., Mexico, and Canada, over sixty international destinations include Africa (Ethiopia, Ghana, and Tanzania), Asia/Pacific Rim (Fiji, India, Nepal, New Zealand, and Sri Lanka), Central America/Caribbean (Honduras and Nicaragua), and South America (Bolivia, Brazil, Ecuador, and Guyana). Program fees vary depending on the country and length; however, in general they range from $1,200 to $4,000. The fees cover international airfare, room and board, travel insurance, plus a donation toward the construction cost of houses built in the host country. Habitat provides simple, respectful ideas for fundraising efforts. Applicants include individuals, couples, groups, and families.

HABITAT FOR HUMANITY

To the full-time RVer, home is where you park it. In years past, RVers were synonymous with retired folks, but there is a growing trend of people of all ages who have taken to the road seeking recreation, friendships, new opportunities, and exciting jobs, while traveling around in motor homes and travel trailers. *Workamper News,* published bimonthly, provides information on short-term jobs and opportunities in places all around the country, specifically for those who travel RV-style. Yearly subscriptions run $23, and a sampler of listings is provided on their website (which includes a bookshop on other pertinent RV resources and guides).

GREG AND DEBBIE ROBUS, Workamper News, 201 Hiram Rd., Heber Springs, AR 72543-8747; (800) 446-5627, info@workamper.com, www.workamper.com

When our eyes see our hands doing the work of our hearts, the circle of Creation is completed inside us, the doors of our souls fly open and love steps forth to heal everything in sight. —MICHAEL BRIDGE

DON'T SKIP THE TRIP

I am still surprised from time to time when I hear from people who are not aware that Habitat for Humanity is an international ministry. They ask, "Do you mean that Habitat builds houses in Nepal too?" I am even more surprised when I think that people might not realize that Habitat *started* as an international ministry. Yes, houses were built on a no-profit, no-interest basis by Millard and Linda Fuller in Africa before the program ever began in the United States.

Photo Credit: Chris McGranahan

Global Village volunteers from the U.S. work alongside local volunteers to gather raw material for soil brick making in Urubamba, Peru.

My own personal experience with Habitat has had an international focus for over fifteen years, so my first thoughts always run to the international work. I often have to pause to think that hundreds of thousands of people may only be aware of Habitat's work in their own hometown. Perhaps that's what makes this Global Village work so much fun. Every single day we invite people to experience Habitat in another part of the world. We encourage them to go to Mongolia, to Tanzania, to El Salvador. We encourage them to taste and feel and smell the work of Habitat around the globe.

We also encourage them to help raise money to build more houses internationally. Some folks take the fund-raising challenge very seriously. The unstoppable Cynthia Kersey—a nationally-acclaimed writer and speaker—recently used a team experience to raise funds for one hundred homes in Nepal! Amazing! And she committed to a similar effort in Guatemala shortly thereafter. Yet I know that if I asked any of Cynthia's team members what was most important about their experience, they would say the trip itself.

Global Village brings people together in a spirit of partnership and camaraderie. We connect people who would never otherwise meet. We expose people to God's work with God's people in a powerful and meaningful way. No matter what your experience with Habitat is to date, I encourage you to get out and experience Habitat anew. Experience Habitat in another land. Don't skip the trip!

—CONTRIBUTED BY DAVID MINICH, director of the Global Village Program and together with his family served as an international partner in Papua New Guinea.

For More Information:
Habitat for Humanity International
121 Habitat St.
Americus, GA 31709
(800) 422-4828
www.habitat.org

- Human Resources
  Extension 2377
  hrstaffing@hfhi.org • www.habitat.org/hr

- Discovery Center Volunteering
  Volunteer Support Services
  Extension 2156
  vsd@hfhi.org

- RV Care-A-Vanners
  Extension 2466
  rvinfodesk@hfhi.org • www.habitat.org/gv/rv.html

- Global Village Program
  David Minich, Director
  Extension 2549
  gv@hfhi.org • www.habitat.org/gv

THE HOLE IN THE WALL GANG CAMP

Camp • Connecticut • Summer
www.holeinthewallgang.org

TUCKED AWAY FROM the outer roads in rural northeastern Connecticut's rising-and-falling hills and dense woods, you'll find a unique place called the Hole in the Wall Gang Camp. The tree-lined dirt road winds its way around paths into the woods until the main complex is revealed: log cabins, craft-making areas disguised as Western-style shops, a dining hall modeled from a Shaker barn, a theater, an Olympic-size swimming pool, and a recreation center. It is here that children with cancer, HIV/AIDS, or serious blood diseases find camaraderie and a renewed sense of being a kid. All of this is made possible because of the dream of and generosity of Paul Newman (and the hard work of hundreds of volunteers, staff, and donors). If you would like to help children do things that no one knew they were capable of doing, Hole in the Wall definitely needs you this summer. Cabin counselors serve as leaders and mentors for campers, while program specialists focus on activities ranging from adventure and sports programs to woodworking and writing. A salary, along with room and board, is provided. Applicants must be at least nineteen years of age and CPR certified. The website also highlights associated camps abroad (Ireland and France) and in the U.S. (California, Florida, New York, and North Carolina) that share in the same mission as Hole in the Wall.

For More Information:
Matthew Cook, Camp Director
The Hole in the Wall Gang Camp
565 Ashford Center Rd.
Ashford, CT 06278
(860) 429-3444 • (860) 429-7295 (fax)
ashford@holeinthewallgang.org

INNISFREE VILLAGE

Service Community • Virginia • 1 Year
http://monticello.avenue.org/innisfree

SET IN THE foothills of the Blue Ridge Mountains (and only seventeen miles from Charlottesville, Virginia), Innisfree Village is a life-sharing community for adults with mental disabilities. Sixty-five people live and

In the community of Innisfree Village, staff members and those with mental disabilities share in meaningful life and work experiences.

work together on a six-hundred-acre farm in a model therapeutic environment, emphasizing empowerment, interdependence, and mutual respect of all community members.

What You'll Be Doing: Volunteers and coworkers live together in family-style homes throughout the village. Generally two to four volunteers are assigned to each house and serve as "houseparents." Responsibilities include cleaning, cooking, laundry, shopping, and finances of the house as well as caring for the personal needs of each coworker. Volunteers are also engaged in therapeutic and meaningful work in the bakery, gardens, weavery, woodshop, and kitchens.

Commitment: One year minimum.

Perks and Rewards: One-year volunteers receive a private room, board, a monthly stipend of $215, fifteen paid vacation days, medical insurance, and two consecutive days off per week.

The Essentials: Fifteen to twenty people between the ages of twenty-one and sixty, all with various backgrounds and nationalities, are needed each year. Volunteers must be at least twenty-one years of age and able to commit for one year (although shorter-term positions are offered each year). The desire to live with adults with disabilities

We are here not to get all we can out of life for ourselves, but to try to make the lives of others happier. —WILLIAM OSLER

in a rural community is a must, as is a sense of humor, patience, flexibility, and common sense.

Your First Move: Call for application materials (which are accepted year-round). There is a one-month orientation period.

For More Information:
Recruitment Director
Innisfree Village
5505 Walnut Level Rd.
Crozet, VA 22932
(434) 823-5400 • (434) 823-5027 (fax)
innisfreevillage@prodigy.net

JESUIT VOLUNTEER CORPS

Service Learning/Ministry • USA/Worldwide • 1–2 Years
www.jesuitvolunteers.org

IN THE MID-1950s the first team of volunteers began their service to native people of Alaska with Jesuit Volunteer Corps (JVC). Since that time, over seven thousand volunteers have committed themselves to working with the poor, and hundreds of grassroots organizations across the country now count on JVC volunteers to provide social justice work to those who have few options. Volunteers also work in developing countries, often alongside Jesuits, in places as diverse as the coastal desert of Peru; the Pacific Islands of Micronesia; Tanzania, East Africa; and throughout Belize.

What You'll Be Doing: Jesuit Volunteers serve the homeless, the unemployed, refugees, people with AIDS, the elderly, street youth, abused women and children, the mentally ill, and the developmentally disabled. However, JVC is more than just a job. At the cornerstone of the volunteer experience are the four values of community, simple living, social justice, and spirituality. In addition to integrating these values, a series of retreats and workshops are offered throughout the year. These events include presentations by Jesuits and other resource people, discussion and reflection, personal and communal prayer, and time for rest and renewal.

Commitment: Domestic volunteers must make a one-year commitment, beginning in August with a one-week orientation; while international placements require a two-year commitment starting in July, with a two-week orientation.

Perks and Rewards: Housing, utilities, a food stipend, transportation to and from work (such as a bus pass or a

bicycle), medical insurance, and a small personal stipend of $75 per month are provided. JVC also provides travel from the orientation site to placement site (in the U.S. or abroad), transportation to and from retreats during the year, and transportation home upon conclusion of the program. Housing is community-style with three to nine other volunteers—a place to share in meals, conversation, and prayer, while encouraging each others' ministry.

The Essentials: JVC welcomes those who are at least twenty-one years old, have a college degree (or applicable work experience), and are self-motivated, mature, and stable. Some job placements require specific credentials or licenses; however, most can be done by people who have a general educational background and a willingness to learn new skills.

Your First Move: With six regional offices throughout the U.S. (Baltimore, Detroit, Houston, Portland, and San Francisco for U.S. programs; Washington, D.C., for international programs), applicants are encouraged to contact the JVC office nearest to their home. Contact information and application materials are available online or call for a brochure.

For More Information:
International Volunteer Coordinator
Jesuit Volunteer Corps
P.O. Box 3756
Washington, D.C. 20007-0256
(202) 687-1132
jvi@jesuitvolunteers.org

If you're looking for a volunteer experience abroad, be sure to explore more options found in the next section!

KITEZH CHILDREN'S COMMUNITY

Community Development • Russia • 1 Week–1 Year
www.ecologia.org.uk

AS A "REVOLUTIONARY" eco-village community, Kitezh offers a unique form of family-based care for homeless and orphaned children in Russia. Children find a positive experience of family life which enables them to recover from the trauma of earlier years to become open, loving, valuable, and contributing members of society. On 225 acres of land sit ten houses, a school, a church, and an organic farm, along with twenty permanent resident adults, who care for the children as foster parents and teachers. As an inspiring alternative model to the present state-run child-care institutions, the long-term intent is to create fifty villages elsewhere in Russia. Working visitors are welcome at any time to add their energy to building Kitezh. There is plenty of work to be done—from building and gardening to cooking and teaching English. There is also plenty of time to play with the children, participate fully in community life, and to practice your Russian language skills. First-time visitors are met in Moscow, which is 186 miles north of Kitezh (although a full-day's trip). Simple food (mostly home-grown) and housing with one of the families is provided (although some choose to live in the tents during the summer months). Applications must be received six weeks prior to arrival date. Call or email for further information.

For More Information:
Liza Hollingshead, Director
Kitezh Children's Community
Ecologia Trust
66 The Park, Forres
Morayshire IV36 3TZ
Scotland
(011) 44 1309 690995
all@ecologia.org.uk

LANDMARK VOLUNTEERS

Volunteer Service • USA • 2 Weeks
www.volunteers.com

LANDMARK VOLUNTEERS is a nonprofit summer service organization for high school students who are looking for an opportunity to do something for others through community service. Under the supervision of an adult leader, volunteers are placed in teams of thirteen at host organizations ranging from Colonial Williamsburg in Virginia to the Grand Teton Music Festival in Wyoming. In return for lending a hand (primarily manual labor) over a two-week period, participants receive an exceptional learning opportunity and a chance to understand how voluntary service functions as an essential element of the American experience. Volunteers are admitted on a competitive basis with purpose, diligence, and responsibility as determining factors. Applicants must be at least fourteen and a half by June and be entering at least the tenth grade (sorry, no graduates). A program fee of $735 covers the cost of placement as well as food and housing.

For More Information:
Ann Barrett, Executive Director
Landmark Volunteers
P.O. Box 455
Sheffield, MA 01257
(413) 229-0225 • (413) 229-2050 (fax)
landmark@volunteers.com

LITTLE BROTHERS-FRIENDS OF THE ELDERLY

Aging • Illinois/Ireland/France • 3–12 Months
www.littlebrothers.org/chicago

No ONE PLANS to grow old alone, but it happens. Little Brothers—Friends of the Elderly serves lonely and isolated elderly over the age of seventy who live within the city of Chicago. These people most often lack a social network of family and friends, or have few social skills to build friendships, and identify themselves as lonely. Little Brothers' motto of "flowers before bread" points to their belief that hearts starve as well as bodies. Chicago is the original home of Little Brothers in the U.S., but programs also exist in six other U.S. cities and in Canada, France, Germany, Ireland, Mexico, Morocco, and Spain.

What You'll Be Doing: Summer interns will be part of a team of helpers who, together with the elderly, organize and go to their vacation home, a fifteen-room house set on seven acres just two hours outside of Chicago. Interns will have constant interaction with the elderly, prepare and assist with various group activities, help with personal hygiene, assist with meal preparation, and drive passenger vans. Although challenging, vacations are often the most rewarding intern experience at Little Brothers. Program assistants in Chicago make a one-year commitment and assist the program coordinators to ensure that every elderly "friend in the family" has a relationship with Little Brothers. This may include personal visits to nursing homes, assistance in helping the elderly meet their daily needs to live independently, or working with program coordinators to plan and carry out celebrations of life. Finally, there are also three- to twelve-month internships available in France (activities assistant) and six- to twelve-month internships in Ireland (program coordination).

Commitment: Positions are offered during the summer or for one year, full-time, with a flexible schedule, including some evening and weekend work.

Perks and Rewards: Program assistants receive $600 per month, plus lodging and health insurance; summer interns in Chicago receive $200 for a seven-week period along with room and board; and interns abroad receive approximately $100 per month, with room, board, and health insurance (for at least a six-month commitment in France). All interns will receive excellent training and experience in the field of aging, while working under the guidance of experienced volunteers and staff.

The Essentials: Applicants must have a sensitivity to the needs of elderly people who are growing old alone, a personal value system that emphasizes respect for the individual, a belief that friendship is essential in the lives of elderly people, and strong communication/inter-personal skills. Bilingual English/Spanish skills are welcomed for Chicago positions; applicants for positions in France must be fluent in French.

Your First Move: Applications and additional details can be found on the Web.

For More Information:
Christine Bertrand, Internship Coordinator
Little Brothers—Friends of the Elderly
355 N. Ashland Ave.
Chicago, IL 60607-1019
(312) 455-1000 • (312) 455-9674 (fax)
cbertrand.chi@littlebrothers.org

> *Before I started volunteering with Little Brothers, I believed the world would be a better place if we focused on friendship and celebrating life, but now I am convinced. I realized that friendship takes time to develop but that everyone needs it. I learned that through celebrating life, chronic pain can disappear, at least for a second, and that even death loses its sting.*
>
> —DAVID SCOTT, volunteer

A volunteer with Little Children of the World assists in the construction of a new house in this poverty-stricken community of the Philippines.

LITTLE CHILDREN OF THE WORLD

Volunteer Service/Ministry • Philippines • 1–3 Months
www.littlechildren.org

♥ 🏡

LITTLE CHILDREN OF the World is a nonprofit Christian service agency dedicated to helping create caring communities for children who are victims of poverty or abuse. Work is also done with other service agencies, including the Consuelo Foundation, Habitat for Humanity, and Teen Missions International.

Your Surroundings: Most of Little Children's work is concentrated in the central Philippines. Volunteers will work in Negros, a beautiful tropical island with sandy beaches and mountains climbing to 7,000 feet.

What You'll Be Doing: Health workers assist in a special community-based health program; housing helpers assist in the construction of new houses and the repair of old ones; education helpers teach in one of the preschools or the School on Wheels; livelihood workers help with organic farming and biointensive gardening to promote self-reliance among indigent families; and peace workers help with the Sunday school, weekly Bible study groups, daily staff devotions, and training in the theory and practice of peaceful conflict resolution.

Commitment: Most volunteers stay for three months or more for a full experience, but shorter terms of at least one month are also welcome.

Perks and Rewards: Housing is available, but volunteers are asked for a weekly contribution of $10 to help defray expenses for utilities and the use of facilities. Food expenses will be minimal; cooked meals generally cost about $5 per day.

The Essentials: Candidates must have at least a high school diploma, but most are college students or recent graduates. Adaptability, flexibility, and ability to work with people of a different race and culture, as well as a love of children and a willingness to work with poor families, are trademarks of the best candidates.

Your First Move: Call or email for an informational packet, which includes brochures, a newsletter, and an application form. It's best to apply a minimum of three months prior to your departure date.

For More Information:
Dr. Doug Elwood, Volunteer Service Coordinator
Little Children of the World
361 County Road 475
Etowah, TN 37331
(423) 263-2303 • (423) 263-2303 (fax)
lcotw@conc.tds.net

LOCH ARTHUR COMMUNITY

Therapeutic Community • Scotland • 1 Year

LOCH ARTHUR IS a working community of seventy people in the southwest of Scotland, where volunteers live with, support, and work with adults who have learning disabilities. The five hundred acres include an organic farm (using biodynamic-agriculture practices), market gardens, a large creamery (for cheese making), a bakery, weaving workshop, and seven large households. A sense of home, community, spirituality, cooperation, emotional support, relationship building, and encouragement are the key ingredients of this shared lifestyle. The work component is about cooperation rather than competition, and provides a sense of responsibility and satisfaction. Most volunteers make a one-year commitment (although shorter stays are possible), with flexible schedules and time off for "holidays." Applicants must be at least eighteen, physically and mentally healthy, and open to new challenges. Pocket money, lodging, and board are provided.

For More Information:
Lana Chanarin, Volunteer Coordinator
Loch Arthur Community
Stable Cottage
Loch Arthur
Beeswing, Dumfries DG2 8JQ
Scotland
(011) 44 1387 760687
D.channerin@talk21.com

LUTHERAN VOLUNTEER CORPS

Service Learning • USA • 1 Year
www.lvchome.org

THE LUTHERAN VOLUNTEER CORPS provides the opportunity for participants to work full-time in nonprofit agencies over the course of a year. Volunteers commit to exploring their spirituality while working for social justice, living in an intentional community, and simplifying their lifestyles. More than one hundred opportunities in a variety of organizations are available, including working with children and youth, counseling rape survivors and AIDS patients, organizing for better health care, advocating on behalf of refugees, staffing shelters for the homeless, tutoring adults, or working to preserve the environment. Life together with other volunteers includes sharing meals, chores, faith nights, and weekly community time. In addition, LVC schedules four regional retreats each year that provide time for personal reflection, recreation, and worship.

Commitment: The program year begins with a five-day orientation at the end of August, followed by the work placement that continues through late August of the following year. Positions are available in the inner cities of Baltimore, Chicago, Milwaukee, Minneapolis/St. Paul, Seattle, Tacoma (Washington), Washington, D.C., and Wilmington (Delaware).

Perks and Rewards: The biggest perks include a great work experience, new friends, urban living, and the opportunity to make a difference! Volunteers also receive a monthly stipend, room and board, medical insurance, transportation money, and two weeks of vacation. In addition, volunteers may be eligible for forbearance on student loans and an AmeriCorps education award of up to $4,725.

The Essentials: Applicants must be at least twenty-one years of age (with no upper age limit) and willing to commit to exploring their spirituality while working for social

justice, living in an intentional community, and simplifying their lifestyles. Married couples and committed
partners are also welcome to apply. Volunteers often find
themselves in new and unexpected situations, so flexibility, openness, and a sense of humor are essential. Most
volunteer placements can be done by people who have a
general educational background and a willingness to
learn new skills.

Your First Move: Program information and applications
are available upon request or on the Web. Applications
are accepted from February 1 through mid-May for positions beginning in the fall. Get your application in by
February 1 for the best selection of cities and agencies.

For More Information:
Joanne Roepke Bode, Recruitment Coordinator
Lutheran Volunteer Corps
1226 Vermont Ave., NW
Washington, D.C. 20005
(202) 387-3222 • (202) 667-0037 (fax)
staff@lvchome.org

MAKE-A-WISH FOUNDATION OF AMERICA

Social Service • USA • Seasonal
www.wish.org

MAKE-A-WISH FOUNDATION fulfills the wishes of
children between the ages of two-and-a-half and eleven
who have life-threatening illnesses. Only through the
hard work and commitment of more than thirteen thousand volunteers in eighty-one chapters across the country
is Make-A-Wish able to continue its work. Local chapters
are always looking for volunteers to help in several areas,
including wish granting, development and fund-raising,
special events, marketing, medical outreach, website
design, and administration. It's best to contact the local
chapter for opportunities; their website provides all of
this information.

For More Information:
Volunteer Director
Make-A-Wish Foundation of America
3550 North Central Ave., Suite 300
Phoenix, AZ 85012-2127
(800) 722-9474 • (602) 279-9474 • (602) 279-0855 (fax)
mawfa@wish.org

MERCY SHIPS

Sailing/Ministry • Worldwide • 2 Weeks–2 Years
www.mercyships.org

MERCY SHIPS is a nonprofit Christian humanitarian
organization committed to a threefold purpose of mercy
and relief, training, and ministry. Mercy Ships has served
the poor in over seventy-five port cities by providing
medical care (surgeries along with medical, dental, and
optical clinics and health-care teaching), assisting through
development projects, and fulfilling basic daily needs in
order to demonstrate the message of hope through Jesus
Christ. Whatever your interest or background, there
could be a place for you in Mercy Ships—at sea or on
land. Join Mercy Ships for as little as two weeks and up to
two years (although many make a lifetime commitment).
As a volunteer short-term crew member, you will have the
opportunity to take a look at missions as well as at Mercy
Ships. Openings are available in a variety of positions—
from bakers and carpenters to translators and deckhands.
Applicants must be at least eighteen.

For More Information:
Human Resources Director
Mercy Ships
P.O. Box 2020
Garden Valley, TX 75771-2020
(800) 637-2974 • (903) 882-0887 • (903) 882-0336 (fax)
info@mercyships.org

MOBILITY INTERNATIONAL USA

Disability Awareness/International Exchange • Oregon/Worldwide • 3–6 Months
www.miusa.org

MOBILITY INTERNATIONAL USA (MIUSA) is an innovative nonprofit organization that empowers people with
disabilities around the world through international
exchange, information, technical assistance, and training.
MIUSA also serves as the National Clearinghouse on
Disability and Exchange, which provides personalized
information, referrals, and support for those who are
disabled and interested in international exchange. Short-
term exchange programs specialize in leadership training,
community service, cross-cultural experiential learning,
adaptive recreational activities, and volunteer service

Are you about to go on your adventure with a disability? With adequate preparation, much of the world is accessible to a disabled traveler—especially with help from Mobility International. From spending a study abroad year in Spain to working in Australia, *A World of Options* explores travel options for people with disabilities. Six hundred pages of opportunities range from community service and travel to international educational exchange and personal accounts. The book runs $30 (plus $5 shipping) and can only be purchased through MIUSA. In addition, MIUSA also publishes *A World Awaits You,* an annual journal of success stories about people with disabilities who have participated in international exchange. Call for your complimentary copy.

projects for youth, adults, and professionals. In the past, exchanges have taken place in Azerbaijan, Bulgaria, China, Costa Rica, East Asia, the United Kingdom, Germany, Italy, Japan, Mexico, and Russia. (For more information on these programs, send an email to exchange@miusa.org or fill out the online application.)

What You'll Be Doing: Interns will work directly with staff volunteers and have the opportunity to develop skills and gain direct work experience in disability rights, international educational exchange, leadership, travel and recreational opportunities, research, article and grant writing, program development, public relations, computer graphics and layout, and the day-to-day operation of a nonprofit organization. Interns are encouraged to work independently on their own projects as well as assigned and supervised projects.

Commitment: Internship programs usually last between three and six months.

Perks and Rewards: For interns committed to six months or longer, a stipend of $125 per month is provided to help with living expenses.

The Essentials: Interest in people with disabilities and promoting cross-cultural understanding is necessary. Preference will be given to applicants with international exchange or travel experience or who have career or master's-project goals that mesh with the goals of MIUSA. Persons with disabilities are especially encouraged to apply.

Your First Move: Along with a resume, cover letter, and two letters of recommendation, applicants will need to complete an application.

For More Information:
Susie Grimes, Intern Coordinator
Mobility International USA
P.O. Box 10767
Eugene, OR 97440
(541) 343-1284 • (541) 343-6812 (fax)
admin@miusa.org

NANNIES PLUS

Child Care • USA • 1 Year
www.nanniesplus.com

NANNIES PLUS PLACES U.S. citizens into nanny positions throughout the U.S. Over a one-year period, nannies are responsible for the care and development of the children of busy professional parents. Salaries for novice nannies range from $300 to $800 per week (more for those with experience), and include private room, board, and car use; some families contribute toward medical insurance. Nannies generally work ten to twelve hours per day (five days per week), with some variation depending on the family needs. There is no program fee for participants.

For More Information:
Lynn Socci, Director
Nannies Plus
520 Speedwell Ave., Suite 114
Morris Plains, NJ 07950
(800) 752-0078
(973) 285-5100 • (973) 285-5055 (fax)
nannies@nanniesplus.com

NATIONAL 4-H COUNCIL

Youth Development • Maryland • 3–5 Months
www.n4h.org

RESEARCH CONFIRMS THAT our young people—the future citizens, workers, parents, and leaders of our society—face unprecedented challenges, making the business of growing up more complex than ever before. Obscured at times by statistics of youth violence, crime, substance abuse, and suicide is the equally tragic waste of our youths' creative talents and unique skills by the neglect or ineffective interventions of public and private institutions.

I just carry hope in my heart. Hope is not a feeling of certainty, that everything ends well. Hope is just a feeling that life and work have meaning. —VACLEV HAVEL

The National 4-H Council embraces these challenges by offering community youth development, youth leadership, and experiential educational programs for the young citizens of our world.

What You'll Be Doing: Program assistants (PAs) become licensed tour guides and facilitate the National 4-H Council's educational programs by leading groups of all ages through Washington, D.C., and at the National 4-H Center. Using the city and its sites as a classroom for learning, PAs provide commentary and site interpretation, and also serve as role models for school groups and 4-H members. The Wonders of Washington (WOW) program gives groups the ultimate Washington experience, and includes study-track options such as black heritage and science and technology. The Citizenship Washington Focus (CWF) helps teach youth how to become "better citizens today, better leaders tomorrow." When not escorting groups, PAs work with various center teams in sales, planning, billing, guest services, and education.

Commitment: The program lasts from three to five months during the spring (February to June), summer (mid-May to July), and fall (September to December). The workload averages between fifty to sixty hours per week (it's a long workday!), and may include evenings, weekends, and holidays.

Perks and Rewards: A weekly stipend of $250, on-campus dormitory-style living quarters, and cafeteria meals are provided. Interns will reside in Warren Hall, a large coed house with all the amenities of home. Warren Hall has nine bedrooms spread across three floors. Some bedrooms have private bathrooms, while others have community bathrooms on the floor.

The Essentials: Applicants must be at least eighteen years of age and a citizen of the U.S., and successfully complete a tour-guide exam and three-week training period. Experience, interest, and the ability to work with youth is essential. College students are encouraged to apply.

Your First Move: To download application materials, visit the internship portion of www.cwf.n4h.org, or call for more information.

For More Information:
Stephanie Misar, Youth Development Coordinator
National 4-H Council
7100 Connecticut Ave.
Chevy Chase, MD 20815
(800) 368-7432 • (301) 961-2801 • (301) 961-2922 (fax)
smisar@fourhcouncil.edu

My summer was about growing as a person. I moved out of Wisconsin to a place I knew nothing about to live with people I had never met. It was in this setting that I learned who I am and who I want to become. I know that when I return home I will never be the same, because I have worked and lived with twenty-four other people who have impacted my life in a way that cannot be described. It can only be experienced.

—MONICA MONFRE, participant

NETWORK, A NATIONAL CATHOLIC SOCIAL JUSTICE LOBBY

Social Justice/Ministry • Washington, D.C. • 11 Months
www.networklobby.org

THROUGH EDUCATION AND lobbying, NETWORK envisions a social, economic, and political order that ensures human dignity and ecological justice while promoting the common good and celebrating diversity. Current issues include welfare and health-care reform, affordable housing, and globalization of the economy. Eleven-month education and service associates provide continuing education in political ministry (faith-based advocacy) through the legislative process and assist in the ongoing mission and work of the organization. Associates are compensated with an in-depth learning experience, a stipend of $7,700, and a contribution to health benefits. Applicants must have excellent written and oral communication skills, and a willingness to do everything from analyzing legislation to stuffing envelopes. The program begins each September with applications due by February 1.

For More Information:
Linda Rich, Intern Coordinator
NETWORK, A National Catholic Social Justice Lobby
801 Pennsylvania Ave., SE, Suite 460
Washington, D.C. 20003-2167
(202) 547-5556, ext. 12 • (202) 547-5510 (fax)
lrich@networklobby.org

POPULATION CONNECTION FELLOWSHIP PROGRAM

Population Activism • Washington, D.C. • 5¹/₂ Months
www.populationconnection.org

AT LAST COUNT there were 6,274,192,739 people on this earth. That's a lot of people. This, of course, is creating a certain havoc in our circle of life: population growth disrupts a sustainable balance of the earth's people, environment, and resources. And this is the very premise of Population Connection, the committed folks who hand out condoms with the wrappers embossed, "Save the world: Use a condom." Well, there's a lot more to it than getting people to use condoms to keep the world's population in check. Population Connection deals with both the causes and the effects of overpopulation, from supporting international family planning, to suburban sprawl, to contraceptive coverage by insurance policies. Let's hope their message of action and hope won't come too late.

What You'll Be Doing: Grassroots organizing, attending hearings and coalition meetings, contacting the media, developing teaching materials—these are just some of the activities that fellows engage in while participating in a broad range of activities for the organization.

Commitment: Fellowships are full-time and offered in two, five-and-a-half month sessions: from January to mid-June and July to mid-December. Full- and part-time unpaid internships may occasionally be available for periods less than six months, and you can always lend a helping hand on Volunteer Night, held every Tuesday.

Perks and Rewards: Fellows earn $600 every two weeks along with full medical and dental insurance coverage, but the real benefits come from the connections you'll be making in the nation's capital.

The Essentials: Whether you are still in college or recently graduated, fellows must have an academic background and experience relevant to their work at Population Connection. You must also have excellent writing and communication skills, the ability to work independently, and be prepared to advocate the positions of Population Connection. Candidates with Spanish/English bilingual skills are encouraged to apply.

Your First Move: Explore the Web for details on each fellow position and application materials needed. Deadlines: January session—end of October; July session—April 15.

For More Information:
Jay Keller, Fellowship Director
Population Connection Fellowship Program
1400 16th St., NW, Suite 320
Washington, D.C. 20036
(800) 767-1956 • (202) 332-2200 • (202) 332-2302 (fax)
activist@populationconnection.org

THE POPULATION INSTITUTE

Population Awareness • Washington, D.C. • 1 Year
www.populationinstitute.org

THE POPULATION INSTITUTE is a small nonprofit organization working to increase public awareness of the world's constantly increasing population and to foster leadership that works on solutions to the overpopulation problem. Its headquarters are on Capitol Hill, with affiliates in Brussels, Belgium; Colombo, Sri Lanka; and Bogota, Colombia.

What You'll Be Doing: Many of the institute's accomplishments can be attributed to the hard work of the fellows participating in the Institute's Future Leaders of the World (FLW) program. The FLW program allows recent college graduates from around the world to develop interpersonal, organizational, public relations, and writing skills while learning about current problems faced by nations around the world, including the U.S., as a result of overpopulation. Besides their daily interactions with the institute's staff, the fellows also have ample opportunities to meet with staff members from other organizations working on population, environment, and women's issues.

Commitment: Fellows kick off the program in July with intensive training and commit to one year, full-time.

Perks and Rewards: Participants receive a $2,000 per month stipend, along with medical benefits and paid vacation time.

The Essentials: Applicants must have completed at least two years of college, be between twenty-one and twenty-five years of age, and able to demonstrate leadership qualities, international experiences and perspectives, a good academic record, and strong writing and oral skills. Knowledge of a foreign language is essential.

Your First Move: Send resume, cover letter, an official transcript, and three letters of recommendation (two from academic sources) by April 15. A personal interview in their D.C. office is required.

Both tears and sweat are salty, but they render a different result. Tears will get you sympathy; sweat will get you change. —JESSE JACKSON

For More Information:
Devinka Peiris, Education Coordinator
The Population Institute
107 2nd St., NE
Washington, D.C. 20002-7396
(800) 787-0038 • (202) 544-3300, ext. 121
dpeiris@populationinstitute.org

ROSE RESNICK LIGHTHOUSE FOR THE BLIND

Visually Impaired Services • California • Summer
www.lighthouse-sf.org

♥ ⌂ 🌐

ROSE RESNICK LIGHTHOUSE for the Blind serves blind, visually impaired, and deaf/blind persons of all ages by providing rehabilitation, social services, and recreational opportunities. During the summer, volunteers provide practical support services at Enchanted Hills Camp, located in the wine country of Northern California. Volunteers assist with arts and crafts, hiking, swimming, horseback riding, and a variety of special activities. Fun is the common theme for the camp experience; however, the most important goal is for campers to achieve independence and develop confidence in their abilities. Sessions run from mid-June through the end of August for four to twelve days. Volunteers receive room and board, training in sensitivity to blindness, and the ability to test their own boundaries of giving and caring.

For More Information:
Donna Amburn, Volunteer Coordinator
Rose Resnick Lighthouse for the Blind
214 Van Ness Ave.
San Francisco, CA 94102-4508
(415) 431-1481, ext. 237 • (415) 863-7568 (fax)
volunteers@lighthouse-sf.org

SPRING LAKE RANCH

Therapeutic Community • Vermont • 6 Months–2 Years
www.spring-lake-ranch.org

💰 ⌂

SPRING LAKE RANCH is a small, therapeutic-work community founded in 1932. Residents decide to come to the ranch because stress, breakdown, or illness has interrupted the normal progress of their lives. All share a need for time to identify and work on problems and to assess and develop abilities that can be a foundation for future life. It is much easier to make friends and focus on what one can do rather than what one can't when working together on a common task.

Your Surroundings: The ranch is situated in a small, rural New England town located in the Green Mountains of Vermont. The ranch covers six hundred acres, most of which is either farmland or forest, with the Appalachian Trail crossing the property and major ski areas nearby.

What You'll Be Doing: House advisor/work crew leaders are responsible for the residents with whom they share living space. They also lead or participate in a wide variety of manual tasks appropriate to the rural environment and dramatically changing seasons. These might include cutting wood, caring for animals, growing vegetables in the gardens for sale at the farmers' market in town, shoveling snow, maple sugaring, haying in meadows, and helping with ongoing chores of cooking, cleaning, sewing, and construction. The majority of people who have worked in the ranch community have found the experience both physically and emotionally demanding but intensely rewarding as well. Unlike many institutions for the chronically ill, the ranch program has little structure or job description and demands flexibility and emotional spontaneity from its staff.

Commitment: There is a minimum six-month commitment. The time spent at Spring Lake Ranch is an extremely demanding life experience, requiring balance, stability, and an ability to set limits on one's involvement and the use of one's energy to achieve a positive end.

Perks and Rewards: Interns receive a $193-per-week stipend, plus room and board. Acting as a house advisor, interns will live in one of nine cottages, supervising from two to nine residents. Perks include two weeks of vacation during the first year, comprehensive health insurance, and personal use of the auto and woodworking shop, computers, and laundry facilities. Interns also have the opportunity to attend seminars/workshops and other benefits that only come from working and living in a small community.

The Essentials: Applicants must be twenty years of age or older, and show a willingness to share life with a community of diverse people. A basic knowledge of and experience in farming, gardening, carpentry, cooking, sewing, auto mechanics, landscaping, and recreational skills are not necessary but can be very helpful.

Your First Move: Send resume and cover letter. A twenty-four-hour visit is strongly recommended as part of the interview process.

For More Information:
Lynn McDermott, Personnel Director
Spring Lake Ranch
Spring Lake Rd.
Box 310
Cuttingsville, VT 05738
(802) 492-3322 • (802) 492-3331 (fax)
lynnslr@mindspring.com

ST. ELIZABETH SHELTER

Homeless Shelter • New Mexico • 3–12 Months
www.saintelizabethshelter.org

THE ST. ELIZABETH SHELTER is a homeless shelter providing services to more than one thousand homeless individuals and families each year. Six live-in interns are responsible for most of the hands-on operation of the shelter, ranging from assisting homeless guests, organizing meals, processing donations, and maintaining the facilities. Past interns have noted that time spent with the guests is both the most rewarding and the most challenging aspect of the job. A modest stipend of $60 to $85 per week and a fully furnished, private suite above the shelter (with shared kitchen privileges) is provided, along with hands-on experience in crisis resolution, mediation, and nonprofit management. Positions are available from three months to one year, forty hours per week. Those willing to make a commitment of one year are eligible for health insurance and an exit stipend upon completion of the program. Spanish language ability and intercultural experience are a plus. Applications are available online.

For More Information:
Del Bomberger, Executive Director
St. Elizabeth Shelter
804 Alarid St.
Santa Fe, NM 87505-3040
(505) 982-6611 • (505) 982-5347 (fax)
director@saintelizabethshelter.org

TEACH FOR AMERICA

Teaching • USA • 2 Years
www.teachforamerica.org

AS A SENIOR at Princeton University in 1989, Wendy Kopp was troubled by the educational inequities facing children in low-income communities. She was also convinced that many of her classmates were searching for a way to assume a significant responsibility that would make a real difference in the world. Working on her senior undergraduate thesis, she developed a dream to create a national teacher corps that would recruit talented, driven graduating seniors to commit two years to teach in urban and rural public schools. The reality? The creation of Teach for America, a national corps that calls upon outstanding recent college graduates to teach in urban and rural public schools, ensuring that all our nation's children have an equal chance in life.

What You'll Be Doing: Today close to two thousand Teach for America corps members (with over six thousand alumni) are impacting student achievement in full-time teaching positions in seventeen sites throughout the U.S. Corps members kick off their two-year program with a rigorous preservice summer training program for five weeks in Houston or New York City. Here you'll learn basic teaching skills, receive feedback from experienced teachers, and teach in a summer school program. Once placed in your teaching assignment, you'll use leadership skills to have an immediate impact on the lives of children, while also gaining the insight, network, and credibility you need to affect long-term change.

Perks and Rewards: Corps members are paid full-time teaching salaries ranging from $22,000 to $40,347 per year. In addition, an AmeriCorps education award of $4,725 per year is provided along with student loan forbearance eligibility.

Your First Move: Applications can be found on the Web, with deadlines at the end of February and October. Five hundred teachers are generally hired annually.

For More Information:
Sarah Leonard, Applicant Communications Associate
Teach for America
315 W. 36th St., Sixth Floor
New York, NY 10018
(800) 832-1230 • (212) 279-2080, ext. 225
(212) 279-2081 (fax)
admissions@teachforamerica.org

*The more you learn what to do with yourself, and the more you do for others,
the more you will enjoy the abundant life.* —WILLIAM J.H. BOETCKER

THIRD WORLD OPPORTUNITIES

Community Service • Mexico • 1 Week

As A "DEVELOPMENTAL RESPONSE" to poverty (rather than through charity), volunteers with Third World Opportunities become involved in work projects at Ranch San Juan Home for Boys in Tecate, Mexico. About thirty-six boys, aged six to nineteen, live at the ranch, most of whom have been abandoned by parents and later picked up off the streets. Although there are many construction and maintenance tasks to perform, the most important part of volunteering is building relationships with the boys and community. For a fee of $225, participants are fed and housed at the project site. One of the highlights of the experience is the integration of work and worship, language development and play, and growth and fellowship with one another. The minimum age requirement is fifteen, and knowledge of Spanish and building experience are helpful but not necessary. Prospective candidates must have a keen interest in the third world and a desire to learn about the root causes of hunger and poverty. Projects are generally for one week during spring break and summer.

For More Information:
Rev. M. Laurel Gray, Program Director
Third World Opportunities
1363 Somermont Dr.
El Cajon, CA 92021
(619) 449-9381 • (619) 449-9381 (fax)
pgray@ucsd.edu

UCSF AIDS HEALTH PROJECT

AIDS Education • California • 1 Year
www.ucsf-ahp.org

THE UNIVERSITY OF CALIFORNIA at San Francisco (UCSF) AIDS Health Project (AHP) seeks to help people reduce the risk of HIV transmission, cope with the emotional challenges of HIV infection, and support friends and family who face the challenges of this epidemic. Since 1987, AHP has provided direct service to more than twenty thousand individuals and more than one thousand care providers annually.

What You'll Be Doing: Interns become an integral part of the Health Project and are expected to take on many

of the professional responsibilities of permanent staff. Encouragement and assistance whenever possible will be given for the individual intern's pursuit of academic and professional goals. Internships include training, client support services, development, research, and HIV counseling/testing services.

Commitment: Interns must make a one-year commitment (thirty-two hours per week) beginning in July.

Perks and Rewards: Interns will receive a monthly housing stipend of $800 (which is paid directly to a landlord) along with a wealth of learning experience. Perks include student/staff privileges at UCSF, including reduced rate membership in the Milberry Union health and fitness program, use of the UCSF library, and other educational programs. Many interns get part-time paid work to support their internship experience financially.

The Essentials: Applicants must have excellent interpersonal skills, including the ability and sensitivity to work with clinical and nonclinical staff; sensitivity to HIV-related needs and concerns; and the ability and sensitivity to work in a culturally diverse work environment. A bachelor's degree and strong computer skills (including MS Word) are mandatory.

Your First Move: Call for application materials (which are due by March 31), or you can fill out an application on the Web. Acceptance into the program is provided no later than May 31.

For More Information:
Carol Music, Staffing Coordinator
UCSF AIDS Health Project
P.O. Box 0884
San Francisco, CA 94143-0884
(415) 476-3890 • (415) 476-3613 (fax)
cmusic@itsa.ucsf.edu

UNIVERSITY FOR HUMAN GOODNESS

Service Learning • North Carolina • 1 Year
www.ufhg.org

WITH THEIR BEGINNINGS as an all-volunteer organization providing free care for the terminally ill, respite care for children with disabilities, and health and wellness programs for hundreds of individuals, Human Service Alliance has evolved into something very special. Now called the University for Human Goodness (UfHG), people of all ages have the opportunity to participate in the year-long Soul-Centered Education for a Lifetime program. What's really unique to the program is that there are no fees for tuition, room, and board, and all faculty are volunteers who do regular service tasks alongside the students.

What You'll Be Doing: Self-discovery. A sense of purpose. Roadblocks removed. The joys of group work and living. Lessons learned—some unexpected and some from surprising sources. These are just some of the experiences students at UfHG can expect. Each day students participate in various combinations of learning experiences: class work, group development, cooperative living, project creation, reflection and journalizing, recreation, and hands-on service in several laboratory settings, including the popular restaurant, California Fresh Buffet (where guests will find fresh food and inspiration on the menu, with all profits going to charities), as well as through the video, audio, and graphics production studio. The program combines the three elements of service, study, and reflection, and centers around four tracks: the Totally Responsible Person, Science of the Soul, Service Entrepreneurship, and Synthesis (which brings all the learning together).

Commitment: Students may enter the program in January or mid-July. The schedule runs forty-five hours per week over six days in classes and applied service learning. Sunday is a free day.

The Essentials: People of all faiths, backgrounds, and ages (ranging in age from twelve to eighty-two) come to UfHG to discover a common ground through their spiritual connection with the goodness or soul within. If you are ready for the challenge of a lifetime—ready to do what it takes to hone, refine, and polish yourself to be more of what you can really be, this just might be the place for you.

Your First Move: To get a real sense of the program, prospective students are invited to a "Come and See" weekend preview. An application (available online), three letters of reference, a full-length photo, and a personal interview are required. "Come and See" dates can be found online.

For More Information:
Joanna White, Coordinator of Admissions
University for Human Goodness
3983 Old Greensboro Rd.
Winston-Salem, NC 27101
(336) 761-8745 • (336) 722-7882 (fax)
inquiry@ufhg.org

In the midst of gathering doubt, there is a light for all to see.

It's the light of loving service given selflessly.

Let our hands be joined in joy, let our actions speak of love, guided by the greater wisdom from above.

From every corner of the earth, the light of loving service blazes forth and warms the chill inside those who need a hand.

Groups working in joyful harmony to build a planet united in love, so all may know the feel of the "fire of life."

Serving joyously is the goal. Open your heart to the light of your soul.

—These words are part of the University for Human Goodness's "Song of Service," written in 1991.

It's easy to make a buck. It's a lot tougher to make a difference. —TOM BROKAW

THE GOLDEN YEARS:
It's Only Too Late If You Don't Start Now

I think the most important thing is when we reach the point of acknowledging that we are aging, whether it's at retirement or after, that we pause for maybe a week or two and consult with people in whom we have confidence, to inventory every possible element of life that we in the past have enjoyed but had to put aside because we didn't have time to pursue it. We need to determine what things are interesting to us, and then constantly explore new ideas and be willing to take a chance.

—JIMMY CARTER

Just because you're getting older doesn't mean that you have reached the end of the road. This life transition can serve as a challenging and exciting beginning—the chance to take advantage of opportunities that you never had time to explore. Obviously there are some restraints (Maslow's Hierarchy of Needs on page 10 comes to mind), but beyond these things, you have to determine if you'd like to look at the world through curious eyes or not. Realize that you have a lifetime of experiences and abilities that will assist you in a new career, volunteer work, learning a new trade, or making a difference in the world. It's only too late if you don't begin your journey now. It's your choice.

Throughout your guide you'll find plenty of opportunities for active retirees. Each summer hundreds of retirees work and live in Yellowstone National Park (page 185); the average age of a Global Volunteers' (page 369) participant is fifty; and Emandal—A Farm on a River (page 245) looks for grandparents to work at their summer camp—and that's just for starters. Beyond the opportunities presented throughout your guide, here are some special programs and resources specifically for those in their golden years:

Elderhostel (www.elderhostel.org) offers those age fifty-five and over inexpensive, short-term academic and volunteer opportunities around the world. Participants, known as "Elderhostelers," participate in "lively and

social" one- to four-week adventures ranging from a jazz course in New Orleans to experiencing the works of Michelangelo in Florence. Those that shy away from an academically stimulating experience might choose to participate in one of their many service projects, affording the opportunity to contribute energy and experience to important causes throughout the world. These short-term volunteer projects range from conservation work at national parks to building affordable housing with Habitat for Humanity. The all-inclusive program fee averages around $105 per night; overseas programs average $190 per night and include round-trip airfare in most cases. Hotels and motels, inns, college dormitories, rustic lodges, tents, and shipboard cabins serve as a home base and meals sample the local flavor. Add yourself to their mailing list, and you will receive their 175-page newspaper-sized catalog jam-packed with more than two thousand opportunities. You can also receive catalog announcements online with their monthly *ENews Bulletin*.

For more information contact the Elderhostel, 11 Avenue de Lafayette, Boston, MA 02111-1746; (877) 426-8056, registration@elderhostel.org.

The **National Senior Service Corps** (www.seniorcorps.org) helps people aged fifty-five and older engage in community-based service opportunities right in their own backyard. Foster Grandparents offer

Photo Credit: Elder-Treks

The trails aren't always dry when adventuring in the wild, but the destination is definitely worth it.

emotional support to child victims of abuse and neglect, tutor children who lag behind in reading, or, perhaps, assist children with physical disabilities and severe illnesses. Senior Companions reach out to adults who need extra assistance to live independently in their own homes or communities. They provide companionship and friendship to isolated frail seniors, assist with chores, provide transportation, and add richness to their clients' lives. Both these programs offer modest stipends and other benefits to help offset the cost of volunteering. Retired and Senior Volunteer Program volunteers choose how and where they want to serve—from a few hours to over forty hours per week. They might tutor children in reading and math, help to build houses, plan community gardens, or offer disaster relief to victims of natural disasters. Together these programs involve over a half-million seniors serving in tens of thousands of sites across the country. For the Web-savvy, all the opportunities can be viewed online.

For more information contact the Senior Corps, Corporation for National Service, 1201 New York Ave., NW, 9th Floor, Washington, D.C. 20525; (800) 424-8867, nsscjoin@cns.gov.

Working Options (www.aarp.org/working_options/home.html), provided by the American Association of Retired Persons (AARP), serves as a resource center for midlife and older workers. The online guide explores information on everything from job searching to staying employable to overcoming barriers to employment. You might also consider a membership with AARP, which is open to anyone age fifty or older (whether you are working or retired). Membership runs $12.50 per year.

For more information contact the American Association of Retired Persons, 601 E. St., NW, Washington, D.C. 20049; (800) 424-3410, member@aarp.org.

Upon leaving the White House as president at age fifty-six, Jimmy Carter and his wife, Rosalynn, had to face the same questions many elder Americans encounter when retirement approaches: what are we going to do with the rest of our lives? In *The Virtues of Aging* (Ballantine Books, $11), Jimmy Carter urges you to take charge of your life and explore the endless opportunities that this time affords.

Imagine what a harmonious world it could be if every single person, both young and old, shared a little of what he is good at doing. —QUINCY JONES

RECOMMENDED RESOURCES.................................

Every day the **American Red Cross** (www.redcross.org) helps people in emergencies—whether it's a thousand disaster victims or one sick child who needs blood. Ninety-seven percent of the Red Cross workforce is made up of volunteers—people of all ages carrying out vital humanitarian work. Current volunteer opportunities, including thousands of one-time and ongoing positions, can be found through the searchable online database (by zip code, category, and date). More information on volunteering can also be obtained by calling (800) 797-8022, or get in touch with your local chapter.

What's your cause? With **DoSomething.org,** young people can make a difference and take action to change the world around them. You and your classmates identify the issues you care about and Do Something provides the resources and support to help you make your community projects happen.

Idealist.org, a project of Action Without Borders, is a nonprofit organization that promotes the sharing of ideas, information, and resources to help build a world where all people can live free, dignified, and productive lives. At one of the richest communities of nonprofit and volunteering resources on the Web, visitors can quickly find the information they need through a searchable database of current job, volunteer, and internship opportunities in the nonprofit/social-service field. Over twenty-five thousand organizations in some one hundred and fifty countries are tucked away inside. If you're leaning toward the nonprofit field, you're bound to find something with Idealist. In addition, daily job/internship alerts and a monthly newsletter will definitely keep you in the know.

Everyone is disabled and everyone is employable. These encouraging words are at the heart of *Job Hunting for the So-Called Handicapped* (Ten Speed Press, $12.95)—and the very philosophy that will encourage anybody with a disability to find a job and meaning in his or her work. Career guru Richard Bolles and disability expert Dale Brown have teamed up to provide a new way to look at the world of work. In addition to explaining the ins and outs of the Americans with Disabilities Act (ADA), the guide provides fresh perspectives, helpful job-hunting ideas, and plenty of resources to get on the right path. Connect with Dale at www.ldonline.com, where she hosts "Dialogue with Dale."

Known as the "Christian career specialists," **Intercristo** is a nonprofit ministry service dedicated to assisting Christians with their careers through career-building resources and a job-referral program. After filling out an extensive application through their website, you are provided with customized and up-to-date listings of short-term and career openings with nonprofit Christian organizations all over the U.S. and overseas. Most of the domestic job openings are salaried positions, and the majority of overseas positions require you to raise your own support. The fee of $29.95 is good for a three-month period. Check on the Web at www.jobsinaflash.org, or call (800) 426-1342.

The National Assembly (www.nassembly.org), an association of national nonprofit health and human-service organization, offers a searchable database of more than two thousand paid and unpaid internships in the youth development field. In addition, an updated list of job opportunities with member organizations is available.

> It is not by accident that the happiest people are those who make a conscious
> effort to live useful lives. Their happiness, of course, is not a shallow
> exhilaration where life is one continuous intoxicating party.
> Rather, their happiness is a deep sense of inner peace that comes when
> they believe their lives have meaning and that they are
> making a difference of good in the world.
>
> —ERNEST FITZGERALD

The **Quaker Information Center** provides a smorgasbord of Quaker and non-Quaker opportunities ranging from weekend work camps, volunteer service, internships, and alternatives to the Peace Corps, both in the U.S. and around the world. Detailed information and links to hundreds of listings (for people of all ages) are available for free on the Web or can be sent through the mail for a donation of $12. For more information contact Peggy Morscheck, Director, Quaker Information Center, 1501 Cherry St., Philadelphia, PA 19102-1479; (215) 241-7024, quakerinfo@afsc.org, www.afsc.org/qic.htm.

A program of Youth Service America (www.ysa.org) **SERVEnet.org** specializes in volunteer opportunit high school and college students. Along with an extensive database of opportunities (searchable by zip, city, state, skills, interests, and availability), SERVEnet also highlights volunteer calendar events, recommended reading, and inspirational quotes.

Get out. Do good. This is at the heart of **Volunteer Match.org**—a site where prospective volunteers can search for nonprofit and community service organizations according to interest, location, and age group. And if you don't want to leave the comforts of your home, be sure to check out the "virtual" volunteer opportunities.

> Our deepest fear is not that we are inadequate.
> Our deepest fear is that we are powerful beyond measure.
> It is our light, not our darkness, that most frightens us.
> We ask ourselves, Who am I to be brilliant, gorgeous, talented, and fabulous?
> Actually, who are you not to be?
> You are a child of God.
> Your playing small doesn't serve the world.
> There's nothing enlightened about shrinking so that other people won't feel insecure around you.
> We were born to make manifest the glory of God that is within us.
> It's not just in some of us; it's in everyone.
> And as we let our own light shine, we unconsciously give other people permission to do the same.
> As we are liberated from our own fear, our presence automatically liberates others.
>
> —FROM NELSON MANDELA'S INAGURAL SPEECH IN 1994, ORIGINALLY WRITTEN BY MARIANNE WILLIAMSON

RESOURCES

The ultimate measure of a man is not where he stands in moments of comfort and convenience, but where he stands at times of challenge and controversy. —MARTIN LUTHER KING, JR.

For many, working, learning, living, and traveling abroad for extended periods of time becomes the adventure of a lifetime. Many venture to unknown lands to fill a gap of time in their lives, improve their fluency in a foreign language, meet new and interesting people, and/or build self-reliance. Whatever your case, by traveling and working in a new land, you'll have the chance to immerse yourself in the culture and meet people on their own terms rather than experiencing it as a tourist would. This section will provide you with hundreds of working options to choose from along with the tools to shape your journey of self-discovery abroad.

The world only exists in your eyes. You can make it as big or as small as you want.

—F. Scott Fitzgerald

348

Unique Opportunities to Explore in This Section:

- Whether you are just exploring your options abroad or are ready to pack your bags and go for it, global expert Elizabeth Kruempelmann provides an introduction and essential tips for adventuring overseas (page 349).

- Did you know each section in your guide has a handful of programs that offer opportunities abroad? So you don't miss a beat, a special page-by-page directory provides all the details! (page 352)

- Do you need the security of a prearranged job and living situation prior to going overseas? There are plenty of programs that will help you with your efforts. Alliances Abroad (page 353) or InterExchange (page 372) will take care of all your overseas arrangements, while BUNAC USA (page 357) or Council Exchanges (page 360) will provide you with the coveted work permit to legally work in another country.

- Helping people help themselves is the heart behind volunteering abroad. This special section provides an overview of international volunteering, selecting the right program, ways to fund your life-changing pursuits, and essential resources (page 362).

- Is it possible that a honeymoon adventure can bring out one's calling in life? Find out how the founders of Global Volunteers turned a two-week vacation into their life's work (page 368).

Photo Credit: Cross-Cultural Solutions

A Cross-Cultural Solutions (page 361) volunteer makes a difference in India.

OPPORTUNITIES ABROAD

THE THRILL OF EXPERIENCING THE WORLD

If you are like most people, you want to make the most of your life. You crave exciting adventures in intriguing places that get your heart pumping and mind racing. You long for life experiences that make you feel alive! For many people, the thrill of experiencing the world is what life is all about.

Since you have found your way to this section, I assume you are ready for your life journey to take you somewhere abroad—be it Brazil, China, or southern France—or on an adventure, like helping indigenous tribes of the rain forest, restoring a historic piece of the past, or working on a community development project. You probably don't know the specifics of "where in the world am I going" and "how in the world am I getting there," but you can rest assured that your life will be unique, out of the ordinary, and a very rewarding adventure. How do I know? Because I've been traveling, studying, and working abroad in various countries for ten years and know there is no life more fulfilling than an adventurous life of a global citizen. How do you know if you're ready for an adventure abroad and ultimately destined to lead a longer-term life living, studying, working, and traveling overseas? Just answer these questions:

- Are you amazed at students and professionals who seem to casually decide to put aside their studies and work for a while in favor of throwing on a backpack to spend six months working and traveling around the world?

- Do you feel great respect and admiration for the dedicated volunteers who make a real difference to folks in other parts of the world by building schools, roads, and houses, or teaching them essential skills like farming, math, and English?

- Are you in awe of linguistically talented folks who speak Italian, German, and French fluently without even pausing to think about what they're saying?

- When someone's academic qualifications include studying abroad or a degree from a foreign university (in a foreign language), are you impressed and maybe even a slight bit envious?

- Do you want the life of the gal or guy whose international firm just sent her or him to live and work in Rome for a year with future opportunities to work in one of their other twenty offices in places like Tokyo, Mexico City, Melbourne, or Cape Town?

If you've said "yep" to at least one of these questions, or even if you have a slightly different vision of your life abroad, you're already thinking about how to build a global life for yourself. Just imagining what you would love to be doing overseas is the first step to making your dream come true. Here are two tips to think about:

Define your passion: What is it that pulls you out into the world? Foreign languages, international business, global issues, the love of discovering new people and places, or something completely different? Defining your real passion will help determine the steps you need to take to develop those interests abroad.

Find a program (or another way) to fulfill your global dreams: It all starts with your first experience overseas. If you want a personally rewarding and professionally fulfilling adventure in a foreign country, the options are endless: intern, work on a farm, volunteer on a community development project, teach, take a language course, build bridges, get an international MBA, be a nanny, join the Peace

EXPERIENCING THE WORLD

Corps . . . and the list goes on and on. In this section you'll find a ton of unique, short-term adventures that serve as a starting part for nearly every global citizen's life journey.

PACK YOUR BAGS AND GO!

Ready to go for it now? If you're already living your dream life abroad mentally and just need to know how to get your physical body there ASAP, here's a quick rundown of what to do:

- **Applications and Essential Documents**
  Applications can take a few weeks or up to a year to process, depending on the program, so get them in early. Once you are accepted into a program, gather the documents you'll need for work permits, residency visas, scholarships, directions for lodging and accommodations, addresses of important contacts, and any other documentation that you'll need. If you'll be going abroad on your own to travel or look for a job, be aware of how long you are allowed to travel within that country. Also be sure to learn about the work permit regulations of that particular country.

- **Passport**
  Apply for your passport now as it could take up to six weeks to be delivered. Depending on your nationality and where you are headed, you may also need a visa to travel to that destination. Check with an embassy or consulate for further information.

- **Travel Arrangements**
  Buy your plane ticket and make other travel arrangements. Don't forget to sign up for frequent-flier miles and pay with a credit card that also adds miles to your account. Take advantage of discounted travel offers you might find by booking online or that you are eligible for because of your age. (Students and seniors often get a travel discount.)

- **Money**
  Arrange to bring traveler's checks, a bank card that can be used at ATMs worldwide, and a bit of cash. Many ATMs overseas accept only four-digit pin numbers, so check with your bank to ensure your card will work in ATMs everywhere.

- **Connections**
  Gather the names of the contacts you have in the country you'll be visiting. Even if you don't know a soul, you can easily make contact with foreigners living in your destination through "expat" communities online, such as ExpatForum.com. If you're going abroad on your own, it is good idea to have at least your first few days of lodging reserved.

Other than a few details that will naturally fall into place—like packing your bags and saying your last good-byes—you can be on the way to your next overseas adventure in no time. Bon Voyage!

—CONTRIBUTED BY ELIZABETH KRUEMPELMANN, who currently lives with her German husband and two children in Portugal. Her international experience includes studying international business for a year in Denmark, interning and teaching English in Germany, working as a partner and marketing manager in a small advertising company in Poland, and selling cross-cultural training programs in Portugal. She has traveled to over thirty countries in Europe, Asia, and Africa, and speaks English, German, and Portuguese. You can reach her at ekruempe@hotmail.com or through the Global Citizen website at www.the-global-citizen.com.

Elizabeth Kruempelmann creates an international way of life in Portugal.

EXPERIENCING THE WORLD

If you decide that traveling, studying, volunteering, working, and living abroad are going to be a way of life for you, then Elizabeth Kreumpelmann's book, *The Global Citizen: A Guide to Creating an International Life and Career* (Ten Speed Press, $16.95), will lead you every step of the way. You'll find tips and resources for uncovering your global passion, take a mini-cross-cultural course to polish your cultural skills, and complete a self-survey to plan your international life and career. After this little bit of prep work, you'll be on your way to choosing from over two hundred ways to travel, learn, volunteer, and work abroad—the fabric of your global future. And once you know the next stepping stone in your journey, Elizabeth will help you out with the practical to-do's of making it happen, funding your sojourns, and optimizing your time overseas. Finally, you'll discover how other global citizens got started on their worldly paths and how you too can transform your international experience into a truly rewarding way of life.

The wonder of the world, the beauty and the power, the shapes of things, their colors, lights, and shades.
These I saw. Look ye also while life lasts. —FROM AN OLD GRAVESTONE IN ENGLAND

SECTIONAL DIRECTORY OF OPPORTUNITIES ABROAD

In addition to the unique opportunities abroad found in this section, your guide is filled with plenty of other overseas short-term job adventures. This page-by-page directory provides all the specifics.

ALLIANCES ABROAD

Work/Travel • Worldwide • 2 Weeks–1 Year
www.alliancesabroad.com

ALLIANCES ABROAD DESIGNS and delivers customized programs for individuals and groups around the globe who want to learn about other cultures by studying or working abroad. Programs focus on these areas: Teach (Mexico, China, Korea, Taiwan, and Costa Rica); Work (England, Ireland, Australia, and the U.S.); Internship (Spain, Ireland, Germany, England, and the U.S.), Volunteer (South Africa, Ghana, Australia, Costa Rica, Nepal, and Mexico); Specialty (culinary courses in Spain and Italy and art courses and photography in Italy); Youth (France, Spain, Germany, and the U.S.); and Language (France, Spain, Germany, Mexico, Costa Rica, and Italy). No matter which program you choose, how long you stay, or what language you speak, the goal of Alliances Abroad is to help you fully immerse yourself in another culture. Each program is structured to help you learn about the language, customs, and lifestyles of the local people. Program fees vary depending on program and location (ranging from $1,200 for a one-year internship in Ireland to $1,300 for a four-month paid work experience in Australia). Housing is always available for a fee and round-trip airfare is the responsibility of each participant. Call for more information or explore the opportunities on the Web.

For More Information:
Kathryn Rogers, Program Director
Alliances Abroad
2423 Pennsylvania Ave., NW
Washington, D.C. 20037
(888) 622-7623 • (202) 467-9467 • (202) 467-9460 (fax)
outbound@alliancesabroad.com

AMERICAN FIELD SERVICE INTERCULTURAL PROGRAMS USA

Volunteer Abroad • Worldwide • 1–12 Months
www.usa.afs.org

BUILDING A GLOBAL community through student exchange for more than fifty years, American Field Service (AFS) Intercultural Programs sends students and volunteers (over ten thousand each year!) to forty-five countries for a semester, a summer, or the year. Those who are at least eighteen years of age and have graduated high school can participate in the 18+ Community Service program. Participants volunteer in nongovernmental organizations in Belgium, Bolivia, Brazil, Costa Rica, Egypt, France, Ghana, Panama, Paraguay, Russia, South Africa, and Thailand, with work that includes everything from education and the environment to childhood development and cultural preservation. Volunteers work with AFS staff and in-country volunteers to design a work experience that best meets all needs. Programs are also available for high school students (volunteering done as a group) and current/future educators (through a one-month intensive teaching program). Program fees vary, and cover transportation from the U.S. departure city to the host community, meals, lodging, and several orientations throughout the program. 18+ Community Service program fees range from $5,000 for semester opportunities and $6,000 to $7,000 for year volunteer opportunities. Scholarships and financial assistance are available. Call or visit AFS online for all the details.

For More Information:
Program Director
American Field Service Intercultural Programs USA
198 Madison Ave., 8th Floor
New York, NY 10016
(800) 237-4636 • (212) 299-9000 • (212) 299-9090 (fax)
afsinfo@afs.org

AMERICAN FRIENDS SERVICE COMMITTEE

Community Service • Mexico • 7 Weeks
www.afsc.org

THE AMERICAN FRIENDS Service Committee (AFSC) is a Quaker organization supported by individuals who care about peace, social justice, and humanitarian service. Its work is based on the profound Quaker belief in the dignity and worth of every person and faith in the power of love and nonviolence to bring about change. Many divisions separate the people of North America, Latin America, and the Caribbean—divisions of history, economics, culture, and language. The understanding that enables people to overcome these divisions is best established by personal encounter, reflection, and action. To help in this process, the AFSC has supported short-term community service projects in Latin America since 1939.

More than four thousand volunteers have participated since that time.

What You'll Be Doing: Ten to twelve participants from different backgrounds are assigned to a particular community (some located in indigenous regions), where they work side-by-side with residents. This is not a program of adventure and travel, but rather an opportunity to experience a single community in some depth. The daily experience of participants follows the patterns of rural life, and volunteers must fit into and respect local social customs. The nature of the projects depends on the needs and interests of the local people; recent work projects have included construction and repair of schools, clinics, roads, small stores, irrigation, and water supply systems. Participants also help in the organization of recreation, education, agriculture, or health activities.

Commitment: The program begins in July and spans seven weeks.

Perks and Rewards: The participant's contribution of $1,250 ($150 of that amount is a nonrefundable registration fee) covers orientation, food, lodging, transportation during the project, and health and accident insurance. Volunteers are responsible for their own transportation to Mexico, a required health examination and inoculations, and personal spending money. Some scholarships are available for low-income participants.

The Essentials: Spanish is the only language used in the program; thus, every participant must be able to communicate effectively in Spanish. All applicants should be eighteen to twenty-six years old, healthy, hardworking, flexible, willing to adapt to group living, and familiar with issues in the developing world. Construction, gardening, crafts, and recreation skills are helpful. Note that participants need not be Quaker, but should support the principles of nonviolence and justice.

Your First Move: Participant applications must be received by March 1, with notice given by April 1.

For More Information:
Linda Oh, Recruitment Coordinator
American Friends Service Committee
Mexico Summer Programs
1501 Cherry St.
Philadelphia, PA 19102-1479
(215) 241-7295 • (215) 241-7247 (fax)
mexsummer@afsc.org

THE AMERICAN-SCANDINAVIAN FOUNDATION

Teaching • Finland • 2–10 Months
www.amscan.org/training.html

THE AMERICAN-SCANDINAVIAN Foundation, which promotes educational and cultural exchange between the U.S. and Nordic countries, offers a Teaching English as a Foreign Language (TEFL) program in Finland. English teachers work from three months up to an academic year (between the months of August and May) in Finnish public schools, institutes, or private firms, and earn approximately $800 to $900 per month. Participants are responsible for housing (which is approximately $200 per month) and travel costs, including round-trip airfare. The program is geared to students or recent graduates who are U.S. citizens (or permanent residents) between the ages of twenty-one and thirty. There is a fee of $50, with applications due by March 1. The Web provides specific information and a downloadable application form. ASF can also assist with work permits for those who have a job offer in Scandinavia.

For More Information:
Exchange Division Coordinator
The American-Scandinavian Foundation
Scandinavia House, 58 Park Ave.
New York, NY 10016
(212) 879-9779 • (212) 686-2115 (fax)
training@amscan.org

AMERISPAN UNLIMITED

Service Learning • Latin America • 2–6+ Months
www.amerispan.com

AMERISPAN'S VOLUNTEER/INTERNSHIP program offers a wide variety of work opportunities for adults in Mexico and various locales in Central and South America. Two to six-month placements are generally offered in social work, education and ESL teaching, health care, environmental programs, and student services, although customized placements are available for a variety of fields. Prior to the work assignment, volunteers participate in a mandatory four-week language/cultural component. A homestay experience along with meals is offered for most placements, which runs from $77 to $150 per week (with longer term commitments, this may be provided). Fees start at $350, plus the costs for language classes, housing, and airfare. Predeparture information, an in-country orientation, and travel insurance are provided. Applicants must at least have a college degree (or be currently enrolled), and some positions have special requirements. The Web provides a search engine that allows you to view placements by country or by type of work. A minimum two-month window is needed prior to your requested start date.

For More Information:
Elizabeth Gregory, Volunteer/
    Internship Program Director
AmeriSpan Unlimited
P.O. Box 40007
Philadelphia, PA 19106-0007
(800) 879-6640 • (215) 751-1100 • (215) 751-1986 (fax)
info@amerispan.com

AMIGOS DE LAS AMÉRICAS

Service Learning • Latin America • 6–8 Months
www.amigoslink.org

THROUGH THE UNPARALLELED "Amigos experience" more than nineteen thousand young volunteers have completed extensive leadership and community-service training programs that prepare them to spend a summer as volunteers in ongoing community health and environmental development projects throughout Latin America (including Bolivia, Brazil, Costa Rica, the Dominican Republic, Honduras, Nicaragua, Mexico, and Paraguay).

What You'll Be Doing: The program begins with an extensive six-month experience-based training program both in the U.S. and in Latin America. Once trained, volunteers are assigned to ongoing health, community-development, and environmental programs partnered with sponsoring agencies in the host countries, ranging from community sanitation and nutrition education to home improvement and family garden projects (generally from four to eight weeks during the summer months). Participants typically live with families in small communities in rural and semi-urban areas and are supervised by more experienced volunteers and officials of the host agency. Amigos volunteers who have participated actively in training programs and who excel in the Latin America program are always encouraged to apply for project staff positions.

Perks and Rewards: The program fee of $3,500 includes round-trip international airfare, training materials, orientation, weekly training sessions (for chapter volun-

teers), project supplies, professional staff support, and host-country room, board, and transportation. Many participants are able to cover program fees through fund-raising efforts. Amigos has put together a fund-raising booklet that contains suggestions that have been proven successful by veteran volunteers. Participation-fee scholarships up to $800 are available to applicants with proven financial need.

The Essentials: Volunteers must be at least sixteen years of age, have at least two years of Spanish or Portuguese study, and successfully complete the training requirements.

Your First Move: Visit the Web for more specifics, or call/email for an information packet.

For More Information:
Glenn Bayron, Director of Domestic Programs
Amigos de las Américas
International Office
5618 Star Ln.
Houston, TX 77057
(800) 231-7796 • (713) 782-5290, ext. 119
(713) 782-9267 (fax)
info@amigoslink.org

> *Amigos volunteers are flexible, motivated, able to live and work independently and as team members, energetic, adventuresome, enthusiastic, and interested in public health, quality of life, and community service.*

AMITY INSTITUTE

Teaching • Africa/China/Europe/Latin America • 4–12 Months
www.amity.org

VOLUNTEERS WITH AMITY have the opportunity to teach English language classes at schools in Africa (Ghana and Senegal), Asia (China and Taiwan), Europe (Germany and Spain), and Latin America (Argentina, the Dominican Republic, Mexico, Peru, and Venezuela). Although the majority of participants will teach in English-learning classrooms, in some cases volunteers will teach or assist in a mathematics, science, social studies, or history class. One semester, full-year, and short-term assignments are available, and participants generally teach twenty to twenty-five hours per week. Applicants must be native English speakers and have an undergraduate degree,

The world we have created is a product of our thinking. It cannot be changed without changing our thinking. —ALBERT EINSTEIN

previous experience working or traveling abroad, and a personal commitment to international education and teaching. The host school provides participants with room and meals in the home of a family and a weekly stipend of $15 to $25. Each candidate is responsible for round-trip transportation between his or her home country and the host school, international health insurance (about $50 per month), $150 per month for personal spending money, and an administration fee of $500 for most assignments (Africa is double).

For More Information:
Karen Sullivan, Volunteer Teacher Coordinator
Amity Institute
10671 Roselle St., Suite 100
San Diego, CA 92121-1525
(858) 455-6364 • (858) 455-6597 (fax)
avta@amity.org

> I was lucky to find home life so rich and open, ameliorating my fears of being so far from my real family. I quickly became fast friends with my large family, especially with my Argentinean "sister" who was studying to be an English professor. We are already devising plans for her visit to my home and miss being roommates, chatting to each other in Spanglish every night.
>
> —ELIZABETH TENNEY, participant

AMIZADE

Community Service • Australia/Bolivia/Brazil/ Nepal/USA • 1 Week–2 Months+
www.amizade.org

AMIZADE, THE WORD for "friendship" in Portuguese, is a nonprofit organization dedicated to promoting volunteerism, providing community service, encouraging collaboration, and improving cultural awareness in locations around the world. Short- and long-term volunteer programs offer a unique cross-cultural experience woven into community service and personal exploration. Amizade program sites abroad include the Brazilian Amazon, Bolivian Andes, Australia's Hervey Bay, and the Khumbu Region of Nepal; in the U.S., programs are offered in the Navajo Nation of Arizona, the greater Yellowstone region, and West Virginia. Volunteers work with members of the local community to complete a community-identified project that addresses needs in education, environment, or health and well-being. Short-term programs run one to three weeks, while long-term volunteers must commit to at least two months. The program fee (ranging from $475 for one week in Yellowstone National Park on up to $1,899 for two weeks in Nepal) includes meals, housing (dorms, tents, or rustic cabins), travel at the project site, project materials, and cultural/ recreational activities. Airfare, visas, and immunizations are additional. Volunteers from all backgrounds and nationalities are welcome to participate, and no special skills are needed—just a willingness to help. Individuals twelve to seventeen years of age must be accompanied by a chaperone. Program details and an application are available online or by calling.

For More Information:
Michael Sandy, Executive Director
Amizade
367 S. Graham St.
Pittsburgh, PA 15232
(888) 973-4443 • (412) 648-1492 (fax)
volunteer@amizade.org

AU PAIR IN EUROPE

Child Care • Europe • 3–12 Months
www.aupairineurope.com

SINCE 1969, AU PAIR in Europe has been offering au pair positions—today in more than twenty countries around the world—for those aged eighteen to thirty. Contracts range from three months (usually in the summer) to one year. Along with room and board, au pairs generally receive between $75 to $120 per week (for thirty hours work per week). In most countries, the English language is quite acceptable with the exception of Germany, which requires that you have a good command of the German language. Programs in France and Italy require au pairs to attend a language course (usually one to three classes per week) in order to obtain a working visa. There is a program fee of $425, which does not include airfare.

For More Information:
Corinne and John Prince, Program Directors
Au Pair in Europe
P.O. Box 68056
Blakely Postal Outlet
Hamilton, ON L8M 3M7
Canada
(905) 545-6305 • (905) 544-4121 (fax)
aupair@princeent.com

BUNAC USA

**Work/Travel • UK/Australia/New Zealand •
1–12 Months**
www.bunac.org

The British Universities North America Club—
commonly known as BUNAC—provides U.S. full-time
students aged eighteen and upward with the coveted Blue
Card, allowing participants to obtain paid work experiences for a maximum of six months in England, Scotland,
Wales, and Northern Ireland. An orientation is provided
in BUNAC's London and Edinburgh offices, where you'll
receive vital information on jobs and accommodations,
maps and student guides, advice and counseling, and
government paperwork. After filling out an application,
you'll receive a program handbook outlining general living and accommodation information, general advice, and
employer listings ranging from pubtenders to "career-
type" positions. There is a $250 application fee. Beyond
the U.K., programs are also offered in Auckland, New
Zealand, for up to one year ($450 fee) and Sydney, Aus-
tralia, for up to four months ($475 fee). For these
programs, applicants must be between the ages of eighteen and thirty. It's suggested participants bring along at
least $1,000 to cover personal and living expenses prior to
receiving a first paycheck. Applications and detailed
information is available online.

For More Information:
Program Director
BUNAC USA
P.O. Box 430
Southbury, CT 06488
(800) 462-8622 • (203) 264-0901 • (203) 264-0251 (fax)
info@bunacusa.org

CASA XELAJÚ

**Language/Community Service • Guatemala •
2–6 Months**
www.casaxelaju.com

Casa Xelajú (pronounced "shay-la-hoo") provides
Spanish and Mayan language study, internships and volunteer work experience, homestays, and tour and travel
programs in Guatemala. Internships might include work
in human rights, the medical field, education, social
work, or vocational education. The internship and volunteer program fee of $45 per week includes supervision,
homestay experience, and three meals per day; the language program tuition of $165 to $190 per week includes
five hours of instruction five days per week, daily social
and cultural activities, a homestay, and three meals per
day. Participants must make a minimum commitment of
two months. Visit their website, or call/email for more
information.

For More Information:
Julio Batres, General Manager
Casa Xelajú
3034 47th Ave. South
Minneapolis, MN 55406
(888) 796-2272 • (612) 729-9253 • (612) 729-9264 (fax)
info@casaxelaju.com

CATHOLIC MEDICAL MISSION BOARD

Medical • Worldwide • 2 Weeks–2 Years
www.cmmb.org

If you're a physician, nurse, or physical therapist with
a strong desire to serve overseas, the Catholic Medical
Mission Board's volunteer program will match you with
a challenging mission setting where you can fulfill your
personal goals and use your professional skills to make a
meaningful difference. Depending on skill and location,
the mission term may vary from two weeks on up to two
years. Room and board is provided; and those who make
a commitment of at least one year will receive travel costs,
health and medical evacuation insurance, and a stipend.

For More Information:
Rosemary DeCostanzo, Volunteer Program Director
Catholic Medical Mission Board
10 West 17th St.

*Each friend represents a world in us, a world possibly not born until they arrive,
and it is only by this meeting that a new world is born.* —Anaïs Nin

New York, NY 10011-5765
(800) 678-5659 • (212) 242-7757 • (212) 242-0930 (fax)
rdecostanzo@cmmb.org

CDS INTERNATIONAL

**International Education • Worldwide •
3–18 Months**
www.cdsintl.org

CDS (CARL DUISBERG SOCIETY) International is a
nonprofit organization dedicated to developing and
enhancing opportunities for Americans to participate in
meaningful, practical training opportunities in Germany,
Argentina, Singapore, Switzerland, and Turkey. While all
programs contain an internship component, some have
academic or language training elements as well.

What You'll Be Doing: CDS offers three unique programs
for those who want to broaden their professional and life
experience while living, working, and learning overseas.
The Work Authorization Program provides participants
with the necessary documents for employment in Germany, Switzerland, and Singapore once they have secured
an internship position on their own. The Placement
Program, for participants up to age thirty, provides
internship placements in Germany, Argentina, Turkey,
and Switzerland in the fields of business/finance, marketing, communications, engineering, information
technology, and hotel management/tourism. Finally the
Scholarship/Fellowship Program consists of three programs: the Congress-Bundestag Youth Exchange for
Young Professionals (a one-year work/study program),
the Robert Bosch Foundation Fellowship Program (for
those ages twenty-three to thirty-four with graduate
training), and the Work Immersion Study Program
(a three-month summer language/internship program
for students at U.S. community colleges).

Commitment: Programs offered through CDS vary in
duration, but are typically three to twelve months,
although some eighteen-month placements may be
available.

Perks and Rewards: Most internships are paid. Compensation varies depending on previous experience and
training, but generally covers basic living expenses.
Round-trip transportation, related travel to seminars in
Europe, and health insurance are provided for fellowship
programs; internship placement participants must cover

*Participating in CDS International's work exchange
program in Germany proved to be a turning point for
my personal and professional growth. CDS provided me
with the proper work and residency permits, a one-
month language course, and a homestay experience
with a family. Finding an internship and a permanent
place to live was my own problem. It was far from easy
trying to secure a job with hardly any work experience;
my rudimentary knowledge of the German
language and a high unemployment rate in
Germany made this difficult.*

*After several months of plugging away at the job search,
I was happy to land an internship at a management
consulting firm where I assisted with project presentations and proposal translations. As my internship came
to an end and my German gradually improved,
I decided to prolong my work and residency permits to
get more out of my stay in Germany.*

*I had made it over the hardest part of adapting to the
German culture and was finally starting to enjoy the
language and social life. By securing a flexible and well-
paying job teaching English at the local language
institute, I was not only able to extend my stay but also
had more time and money to travel and make friends
with other foreigners and Germans alike. Together we
enjoyed bike tours around the countryside, German
festivals, boat cruises on the Rhine, and weekends in
Paris and Amsterdam, among many other
unforgettable travel adventures.*

*At the time, CDS provided me with a window of oppor-
tunity to learn a language, get international work
experience, and travel relatively cheaply around Europe.
However, as I reflect now on my total experiences of
studying and working in four foreign countries, learning
two foreign languages, and traveling to thirty lands,
CDS was truly the catalyst for living out my dream of
an international way of life.*

—CONTRIBUTED BY ELIZABETH KRUEMPELMANN, who has
a lot more to say about the international experience in the
introduction to this section (page 349).

these costs. There is a participation fee of $300 to $700 for all programs.

The Essentials: Most programs require language proficiency. A high level of interest in working in and acclimating to a foreign culture is necessary.

Your First Move: Application deadlines vary with each program; however, most are generally five months prior to the departure date. Please contact CDS for specific application deadlines.

For More Information:
Program Officer
CDS International
871 United Nations Plaza, 15th Floor
New York, NY 10017-1814
(212) 497-3500 • (212) 497-3535 (fax)
info@cdsintl.org

CENTER FOR GLOBAL EDUCATION

Educational Travel • Worldwide • 1–3 Weeks
www.augsburg.edu/global

THE CENTER FOR Global Education takes participants around the world on short-term travel seminars, encountering the peoples and situations of Mexico, Central America, the Caribbean, and the southern Africa region. These one- to three-week educational trips will bring participants face to face with people of other cultures—people struggling for justice and human dignity. Each day consists of two to four meetings with community representatives, ranging from grassroots organizers to business leaders and representatives of the ruling and opposition political parties, as well as visits to key historical or archaeological sites. The program attracts a broad range of participants, from ages sixteen to eighty, from all ethnic backgrounds and from all professional areas. All have an interest in listening to and learning from people in the community. Seminar fees start at $1,600, and include meetings with community representatives, lodging, all meals, translation, local travel, and usually round-trip airfare. Participants must be at least eighteen. The center looks for a broad variety of ages, backgrounds, and occupations.

For More Information:
Travel Seminar Coordinator
Center for Global Education
Augsburg College

2211 Riverside Ave., Box 307
Minneapolis, MN 55454
(800) 299-8889 • (612) 330-1159 • (612) 330-1695 (fax)
globaled@augsburg.edu

CHÂTEAU DE JEAN D'HEURS

Castle • France • 1–8 Months

LIVE AND WORK in a French castle! Château de Jean d'Heurs is a superb example of eighteenth-century French château architecture. Officially classified as a national historic monument, it is noted for its majestic staircases and monumental ironwork. The castle is about a two-hour train ride from Paris (which will cost you about $30). Housekeeper/gardener and assistant art restoration painter/plasterer positions are available, each with a flexible twenty-hour-per-week work schedule that gives you plenty of time to explore this beautiful region. In exchange for work, housing is provided in the castle (with complete use of the castle's kitchen and laundry). Program dates are flexible, however, the château is open April 1 through November 30.

For More Information:
Fadel Mezian, Program Manager
Château de Jean d'Heurs
55000, Lisle en Rigault
France
(011) 33 3 29 71 31 77

CHINA TEACHING PROGRAM

Teaching • China • Academic Year
www.wwu.edu/~ctp

FOR A TUITION fee of $1,250 (lower for Washington State residents), the China Teaching Program provides a five-week training session at Western Washington University (WWU) followed by a teaching placement at a Chinese institution for an academic year. The training, which begins in mid-July of each year, focuses on the Chinese language, an overview of Chinese culture, practical preparation for living overseas, and teaching English as a Foreign Language. A TESOL (Teacher of English to Speakers of Other Languages) certification option is also available through WWU's TESOL program. Approximately $85 is needed beyond the program tuition for books and class materials, and participants must make arrangements for their own housing while attending the session in Bellingham. (Most live on campus in WWU apartments at a cost of $250 for a double room or $500 for a single.) In early September, participants begin their assignment in China, teaching English speaking, listening, writing, and reading as well as contemporary American culture. The salary of $200 to $450 per month is adequate for buying food and other necessities in China. Housing and basic medical care are provided by the host institution. Health examinations, passport and visa fees, travel, and vaccinations are additional costs to be considered. Applications are available online (in Word or PDF format), and must be sent in by early February.

For More Information:
Catherine Pease Barnhart, Program Director
China Teaching Program
Western Washington University
Old Main 530F, MS-9047, 516 High St.
Bellingham, WA 98225-9047
(360) 650-3753 • (360) 650-2847 (fax)
ctp@wwu.edu

CONCERN AMERICA

Community Development/Refugee Aid • Latin America/Africa • 2–3 Years
www.concernamerica.org

CONCERN AMERICA is an international development and refugee aid organization that has staffed development projects in more than a dozen countries since 1972. Healthy children, appropriate sanitation systems, potable water, public health systems, and lasting employment opportunities are a few of the results from the work of Concern America.

What You'll Be Doing: Through the work of volunteers, who are professionals in the fields of health, public health, nutrition, health education, adult literacy, sanitation, agroforestry, appropriate technology, and community organizing, Concern America assists impoverished communities and refugees in developing countries in their efforts to improve their living conditions. The program emphasizes empowering and training of community members in order to impart skills and knowledge that remain with the community long after the volunteer is gone. Volunteers currently serve in development projects in El Salvador, Guatemala, Honduras, Mexico, and Mozambique.

Commitment: There is a minimum two-year commitment.

Perks and Rewards: Concern America provides room and board, round-trip transportation, health insurance, a small monthly stipend of $250 per month, a repatriation allowance (first year—$50 per month, second year—$100 per month, third year—$150 per month), and support services from the home office.

The Essentials: Applicants must have a degree/experience in public health, medicine, nutrition, nursing, agriculture, community development, education, or appropriate technology. Fluency in Spanish (except for the project in Mozambique, where Portuguese is required) or ability to learn Spanish at one's own expense is also required. All candidates must be at least twenty-one years of age.

Your First Move: Send a cover letter and resume to begin the application process.

For More Information:
Janine Mills, Recruitment Coordinator
Concern America
2020 N. Broadway, Third Floor
P.O. Box 1790
Santa Ana, CA 92702
(800) 266-2376 • (714) 953-8575 • (714) 953-1242 (fax)
concamerinc@earthlink.net

COUNCIL EXCHANGES

Work/Volunteer/Teach Abroad • Worldwide • 1–10 Months
www.councilexchanges.org

SINCE ITS FOUNDING in 1947, Council Exchanges has been active in the development and administration of study, work, travel, and volunteer programs worldwide. Let's take a bird's-eye view of each program:

If you're a college student (at least eighteen years of age) or recent graduate who has three to six months to enjoy an unforgettable travel experience, you can take advantage of Council's Work Abroad Program in Australia, Canada, France, Germany, Ireland, and New Zealand. Most participants find short-term or seasonal service-industry positions, such as waiting tables, bartending, office temping, and retail sales. An orientation, employment information, counseling services, and the use of a council office from which to job-hunt is provided upon arrival. There is a program fee of $300 to $400 (depending on country), which includes the highly coveted work permit to legally work in another country. While working, most participants earn enough money to cover day-to-day expenses.

A program with less restrictions is Council's International Volunteer Projects, a two- to four-week work-camp experience in Europe, Africa, Asia, and the Americas—from national parks and forests to inner-city neighborhoods and small towns. Volunteers may choose to build a playground, plant trees, restore a castle, organize a festival, or implement a recreation program for at-risk children. There is a $300 placement fee, which includes room and board. To learn more about these opportunities, a project directory is available in late March (for a fee of $20). Placements begin in April and continue on a first-come, first-served basis until July, by which time most summer projects have been filled. The average age of participants is twenty to twenty-five (although you must be at least eighteen and some countries have upper age limits).

Finally, for those with a bachelor's degree (and under sixty-five years of age), you might consider Council's Teach in China or Thailand programs. You don't need teaching experience or a TEFL (Teaching English as a Foreign Language) qualification to apply—just a genuine interest in Asia and teaching along with an appetite for adventure. You'll have the option of a full-year (ten months) or semester (five months) teaching contract (Thailand departures—May and October; China—February and August). A salary of about $225 to $275 per month (depending on exchange rates), furnished accommodations, work visa, a week-long training and orientation program, and a *Lonely Planet Guidebook* are provided. Fees range from $1,300 to $1,500 plus international airfare.

After participating in one of the council's programs, you might even consider working for them—internship and seasonal employment opportunities are available at field offices in the U.S. and abroad. Detailed information can be found on the Web or by calling.

For More Information:
Outbound Exchange Coordinator
Council Exchanges
633 Third Ave., New York, NY 10017-5706
(888) 268-6245 • (212) 822-2649 (fax)
info@councilexchanges.org

CROSS-CULTURAL SOLUTIONS

Service Learning • Africa/Asia/Eastern Europe/Latin America • 2–24 Weeks
www.crossculturalsolutions.org

THESE UNIQUE SHORT- and long-term programs give volunteers from all over the world the opportunity to come face to face with global issues and become part of productive solutions. Cross-Cultural Solutions' programs promise to be one of the most exciting, thought-provoking, and enriching experiences of your life.

What You'll Be Doing: Volunteers engage in vital humanitarian work in Latin America, Asia, Africa, and Eastern Europe. You might teach English to adults and school-children, stimulate small business activities, initiate programming with women's-empowerment groups, observe and assist local doctors, improve the quality of life for senior citizens, or act as a mentor to orphans. Yes, the type of work is limitless! While in the host country, volunteers are divided into small groups of two or three, which provides a more productive, meaningful experience.

Commitment: Programs are offered year-round, begin on specified start dates, and last from two to twenty-four weeks.

Perks and Rewards: The program is entirely driven by each volunteer's contribution, which ranges from $1,855 (for a two-week program in Russia) to $6,123 (for a twenty-four-week experience in Peru). Your contribution pays for all country-based expenses, including three meals per day, modest accommodations with shared-occupancy rooms, airport transfers and daily transportation, professional-staff guidance and supervision, orientation, and program materials. Beyond the set program fee, you will also be responsible for your visa, shots, and international airfare. Those who need help with the program fee can access the Cross-Cultural Solutions Fundraising Kit on the Web.

Your First Move: All nationalities and backgrounds are welcome, and nearly every candidate is accepted into the program. Volunteers are encouraged to apply at least two months prior to the projected start date.

For More Information:
Steve Rosenthal, Executive Director
Cross-Cultural Solutions
47 Potter Ave.
New Rochelle, NY 10801
(800) 380-4777 • (914) 632-0022 • (914) 632-8494 (fax)
info@crossculturalsolutions.org

Three fundamental goals of international volunteerism shape Cross-Cultural Solutions' programs: providing service, learning about development work and the local culture, and educating volunteers' own communities upon their return home.

Once in a while it really hits people that they don't have to experience the world in the way they have been told to. —ALAN KEIGHTLEY

INTERNATIONAL VOLUNTEERING AND FUND-RAISING IDEAS

Everybody can be great because anybody can serve.
You don't have to have a college degree to serve.
You don't have to make your subject and your verb agree to serve. . . .
You only need a heart full of grace. A soul generated by love.

—MARTIN LUTHER KING, JR.

Traveling as a volunteer departs from conventional adventure-travel and cultural-immersion experiences in one very important way: the wondrous experience of giving. Volunteers live and work with local people who need assistance in fulfilling life's basic needs—food, shelter, clothing, education—development projects that help people to help themselves. Each volunteer's energy, creativity, and labor are put to use as he or she gains a genuine, firsthand understanding of other people.

First off, you must realize that for most programs, volunteering costs money. Many volunteer organizations are underfunded and understaffed (and their staffs are often overworked). They keep their efforts alive by the contributions volunteers provide for the experience. Program expenses, transportation costs, meals, rent, health insurance, and the cost of developing and maintaining volunteer placements all add up. To put this participation fee into perspective, think about the costs associated with running a local animal or homeless shelter in your community. Creative funding and the work of volunteers make it all possible. As you begin your search for a volunteer project, keep in mind that you will probably have to pay for many of these basic expenses.

Fees for volunteer projects can start as low as $300 for one- to three-week experiences and can grow to $4,500 or more for programs that take you to places further from the U.S. and that are longer in duration. Many programs offer all-inclusive fees, which include food, lodging, ground transportation, visas, and project materials.

Once you've compiled a list of possible volunteer programs that meet your criteria, your next step is to call the organizations for more information. First impressions are a big deal to me. Talking to a knowledgeable and experienced program coordinator will outweigh any glossy catalog that you receive in the mail. It's also important that you assemble a list of key questions for each organization:

- Are there specific projects you'll be working on, or will you just get involved where help is needed?

- How many volunteers work on a particular project?

- Will you be living with a family in the community or with other volunteers?

- What types of food will be available?

- Does the village have running water?

- How long do the projects last?

- Is there time for additional travel once the project ends?

- What does the program fee include and do you help with fund-raising efforts?

FUNDING YOUR ADVENTURE

For many, one of the biggest obstacles for international volunteering is the financial challenge. However, a lack of funds shouldn't diminish your dreams. With a little planning and hard work, you can definitely succeed in raising nearly all of your needed funds. Steve Rosenthal, the executive director of Cross-Cultural Solutions (see page 361 or visit www.crossculturalsolutions.org), provides these essential fund-raising tips and activities:

WHO DO YOU KNOW?

The cardinal rule of fund-raising is that if you don't ask, you won't get anything. Ask anyone and everyone you know and even those you don't know to contribute to your cause. One of the best places to start is to make a list of everyone you know.

LETTER WRITING

A letter-writing campaign is one of the most simple and effective fund-raising methods you can employ. Send letters to family and friends, employers and coworkers, clubs you belong to, churches or temples, local banks, foundations, and charitable organizations in your area. The Rotary, Lions, and Elks Clubs, Junior League, and the United Way are some larger charitable organizations that may be interested in donating to your cause as well. When writing your fund-raising letter, keep it short and simple and demonstrate the immediate impact of your donor's dollars. Don't forget to mention that all donations are also tax deductible.

ALWAYS FOLLOW UP!

You have to get on the phone with the small businesses, the civic and religious groups, and your friends and relatives to let them know that you really do need their support. One follow-up phone call can make the difference between a donor sending a check or pushing the request to the back burner and never getting to it.

UNIVERSITY FUNDS

If you are a student, a major source of funding is through your own college. Many school clubs are allocated a certain amount of funds through student activities. See if your club is eligible. Many departments also have discretionary funds for projects and programs. If your trip can be integrated into an academic or service learning course there may also be some funds that could be used for your program.

GRANTS

One of the most common ways to raise money is through grant proposals. Though a grant proposal is very simple to write, getting it accepted is difficult. The Ford Foundation receives over one thousand proposals a day requesting money! Also, grants are often time sensitive in that foundations have deadlines and funding cycles. One of the most comprehensive books on foundations is the *Foundation Directory*, which is available at most libraries. The directory lists the board members of all the foundations and the types of projects they fund.

LOCAL BUSINESSES

Local businesses are far more likely to support you than large corporations. The key is to make a link between the owner of the business and you or someone close to you. You may want to approach the business with a letter first. Enclose all relevant material and a pledge form, then follow up with a phone call.

SERVICE CLUBS AND PLACES OF WORSHIP

Service clubs such as Rotary or Kiwanis; fraternal organizations such as the Elk or Moose clubs; and churches and temples are excellent sources for fund-raising. Follow the "Who Do You Know?" principle: is someone you know a member or the friend of a member?

The best course of action is to contact as many clubs in your area as possible and ask to give a presentation to the club. Many clubs have breakfast,

INTERNATIONAL VOLUNTEERING

Most people seek after what they do not possess and are enslaved by the very things they want to acquire. —ANWAR EL-SADAT

363

INTERNATIONAL VOLUNTEERING

lunch, or dinner meetings where you can ask to speak for fifteen minutes to present your request and explain what you will be doing. This is your chance to sell the program while promoting a good cause. Remember, you are not asking for money for your vacation. You are asking for a donation to do volunteer work overseas and to make a difference in the world. Also, let them know that you are willing to come back and show them slides or a video of the program when you return.

After the meeting write a follow-up letter thanking them for letting you speak and reiterating your request for money. Be specific about how much money you are requesting and how it will be used. Be realistic about the amount you are requesting ($200 to $400 is a reasonable amount).

EVENTS

From bake sales to dinner parties, planning an event can be very labor intensive. Be careful how you structure it and be clear about your expectations. One of the traditional ways to raise money is through bake sales, candy sales, garage sales, and so forth. Alternatively, an event, such as a black-tie affair or simple pizza party, might help with your fund-raising efforts. Again, use the "Who Do You Know?" principle. Do

you have a friend in a band? Do you know the owner of a bar or a restaurant? Some simple events include having a band play at a club and you get the cover charge or a percentage of the drink sales. Or perhaps a restaurant will allow you an evening offering an all-you-can-eat-buffet for $15 where you and the restaurant split the proceeds.

MEDIA

Perhaps one of the best ways to promote awareness about your upcoming adventure and to raise funds for it is through the local media. In fact, this is how Cross-Cultural Solutions has attained most of its popularity, having numerous articles published about their programs in major newspapers and magazines across the country. Having a short piece published anywhere can go a long way in your quest for funds.

It is important to remember why you are raising the money. Be persistent. You might get a lot of rejections and become pretty discouraged at times, but there will also be a lot of people who will support and encourage you.

—STEVE ROSENTHAL

RECOMMENDED RESOURCES. . . . .

If you're dreaming about living and volunteering abroad, *How to Live Your Dream of Volunteering Overseas* (Penguin USA, $17) offers all the necessary ingredients for success. The authors—all founders of volunteer organizations—provide a unique insider's perspective on choosing the right program, fund-raising efforts, and how to be an effective volunteer, as well as profile over one hundred volunteer organizations. For further information, turn to the companion website at www.VolunteerOverseas.org.

If there is a program that sends volunteers, interns, or lay missionaries abroad, you'll find it in a searchable database of opportunities through the **International Volunteer Programs Association** (www.volunteerinternational.org). While exploring the IVPA site, be sure to sign up for their bimonthly email newsletter.

THE EXPERIMENT IN INTERNATIONAL LIVING

International Education • Worldwide • Summer
www.usexperiment.org

"HIGH SCHOOL STUDENTS changing the world one friendship at a time"—this is at the core of the Experiment in International Living, where students (known as experimenters) challenge themselves to become immersed in different cultures, learn through adventure travel and language immersion, and celebrate the diversity of life. The Experiment's summer programs feature opportunities in Europe, the Americas, Africa, Oceania, and Asia. For three to five weeks, experimenters focus on themes such as community service, language study, travel, peace studies, ecology, the arts, or outdoor adventure as they enjoy daily life with their host families and participate in activities with their group.

What You'll Be Doing: Each summer, over eighty group leaders spread out all over the world and help facilitate the learning experience for program participants. From program start to finish, leaders guide experimenters in the ongoing acquisition of survival language-skills along with the discussion and reflection of experiences, while conducting group excursions and remaining in close contact with all the host families. At program's end, leaders facilitate the evaluation process—with the realization that each participant's "experiment" has actually just begun.

Commitment: Selected leaders are required to attend a leadership-training workshop in Brattleboro, Vermont, in late June, just prior to program departure.

Perks and Rewards: A bachelor's degree, demonstrated interest in intercultural and experiential learning, in-depth experience living abroad, competency in the language of the host culture, and experience working with young people are essential traits of leaders.

The Essentials: The experience alone is reward enough to most leaders; however, the perks aren't bad: a $100-per-week honorarium, domestic and international airfare, health insurance, and orientation and training.

Your First Move: Call for a leadership application. All materials are due by February 15.

For More Information:
Program Director
The Experiment in International Living
Kipling Road, P.O. Box 676
Brattleboro, VT 05302-0676

(800) 345-2929 • (802) 257-7751 • (802) 258-3428 (fax)
eil@worldlearning.org

FULBRIGHT TEACHER AND ADMINISTRATOR EXCHANGE PROGRAM

Teaching • Worldwide • 6 Weeks–12 Months
www.fulbrightexchanges.org

THE U.S. Department of State promotes national interests through a wide range of overseas information programs. One for teachers in particular is the Fulbright Teacher and Administrator Exchange Program. This program provides opportunities for qualified educators to participate in direct exchanges of positions with colleagues from other countries for six weeks, a semester, or a full academic year. In general, exchange teachers are granted a leave of absence with pay and use their regular salary to cover daily expenses while abroad. A number of country programs provide full or partial transportation awards. Orientation costs, including one-way travel to orientation and two to three days of food and lodging at the orientation site, are paid by the Department of State. There is a deadline of October 15 for all programs that begin the following year.

For More Information:
Director
Fulbright Teacher and Administrator Exchange Program
U.S. Department of State
600 Maryland Ave., SW, Suite 320
Washington, D.C. 20024-2520
(800) 726-0479 • (202) 314-3520 • (202) 479-6806 (fax)
fulbright@grad.usda.gov

GLOBAL CITIZENS NETWORK

Community Service • USA/Guatemala/Kenya/Nepal • 1–3 Weeks
www.globalcitizens.org

GLOBAL CITIZENS NETWORK sends teams of six to twelve people to rural communities around the world, including Guatemala, Kenya, and Nepal as well as Arizona, New Mexico, and South Dakota in the U.S. The teams, led by a trained team leader, spend one to three weeks in their chosen community and become immersed in the daily

Imagination is more important than knowledge. Knowledge is limited. Imagination encircles the world —ALBERT EINSTEIN

Photo Credit: Global Citizens Network

A Global Citizens Network volunteer and a local man from Kenya dig the foundation for a health clinic.

life of the local culture. Community projects are initiated by the local people and may include planting trees, digging irrigation trenches, setting up a schoolroom, or building a health clinic. Each day consists of both work and learning. Volunteers stay in local homes or as a group in a community center, and meals are shared with the host family or communally prepared and shared with project hosts. No special skills or experience are required—only an open mind, open heart, and willingness to experience and accept a new culture. The tax-deductible fee ranges from $600 to $1,650. (Airfare is additional.) Volunteers under eighteen years of age must be accompanied by a parent or guardian.

For More Information:
Kim Schneider, Program Director
Global Citizens Network
130 N. Howell St.
St. Paul, MN 55104
(800) 644-9292 • (651) 644-0960
info@globalcitizens.org

GLOBAL ROUTES

Service Adventures • Worldwide • 1–3 Months
www.globalroutes.org

THROUGH COMMUNITY SERVICE and cross-cultural exchange programs designed by Global Routes, North American high school and college students stretch their minds by living and working with people in small, rural communities throughout the world. Grassroots community development and homestays in Latin America, Africa, Asia, the Caribbean, and North America are at the heart of these experiences. Students work side by side with their host families on projects selected by the community, which might include constructing a community center, teaching local children, or reforesting surrounding areas. Experiential learning covers everything from cultural sensitivity to the history and language of the area.

What You'll Be Doing: Group leaders colead a group of up to eighteen high school students or provide support and coordination for college-level interns who live in pairs in villages. The leader is also responsible for organizing the group's in-country orientation and managing the debriefing process prior to their return. For college programs, preference is given to applicants who are able to lead two or more programs sequentially. The intention of the programs is to place students in an environment radically different from their own where they can reflect on their own life and culture. Leaders must facilitate this process in a fun and creative way in addition to meeting the logistical demands of managing a group in a developing country.

Commitment: Positions are offered year-round and roughly correspond to summer vacation and academic terms. High school leader positions generally involve a four- to six-week commitment, as well as attending a five-day orientation prior to departure. College leader positions involve a three-month commitment.

Perks and Rewards: Group leaders receive $225 per week for four- to seven-week high school programs or $1,800 for three-month college programs. All living expenses and round-trip travel to/from the program destination are covered.

The Essentials: Leader applicants must be at least twenty-four years of age, have extensive experience working with high school and/or college students and travel experience in the region where you wish to lead (preference is given to those who have lived/worked in the region), as well as be certified in first aid and CPR. All Latin American program leaders must be fluent in Spanish, or French for the Guadeloupe program.

Your First Move: Applicants are encouraged to visit their website for more information and application materials.

For More Information:
Jessie Levine, Staffing Coordinator
Global Routes
1814 7th St., Suite A
Berkeley, CA 94710
(510) 848-4800 • (510) 848-4801 (fax)
mail@globalroutes.org

GLOBAL SERVICE CORPS

**Educational Travel • Worldwide •
Weeks–6 Months+
www.globalservicecorps.org**

GLOBAL SERVICE CORPS (GSC), a project of Earth Island Institute (www.earthisland.org), creates opportunities for people, young and old, who want to share their time and experience to help make the world a better place. GSC participants live in developing countries and work on a wide range of projects designed to provide communities with the means to function sustainably. At the same time, participants gain a new perspective on the world we share.

What You'll Be Doing: As a GSC volunteer, you may find yourself harvesting organic food in Tanzania, teaching English to Thai Buddhist monks, or helping Tanzanian

women fight AIDS. The most rewarding aspect of this experience is spending time with the people of the host communities, sharing ideas, and breaking down cultural stereotypes. Many volunteers, in their spare time, visit nearby temples, game parks, hot springs, or volcanic lakes, depending on the country. GSC also offers internships at their headquarters in San Francisco.

Commitment: Short-term (three to four weeks), long-term (two to six months or longer), and student internship programs are available. In general, any length of service over twenty-three days is possible.

Perks and Rewards: Program fees range from $1,895 (for twenty-three days) to $3,305 (for ten weeks), and cover airport pickup, in-country transportation, accommodations (hotel, lodge, or homestay experience), meals, travel excursions, and project administration. Airfare, visas, and inoculations are additional.

The Essentials: Volunteers must be at least twenty years old, flexible, adaptable to the customs and culture of their host country, and willing to perform a valuable service to a community in need.

Your First Move: For application materials, call, email, or visit GSC online. Applications are needed at least two months prior to departure date.

For More Information:
Rick Lathrop, Executive Director
Global Service Corps
300 Broadway, Suite 28
San Francisco, CA 94133-3312
(415) 788-3666 • (415) 788-7324 (fax)
gsc@earthisland.org

The great thing in this world is not so much where we are, but in what direction we are moving. —OLIVER WENDELL HOLMES

FINDING A PLACE IN THE WORLD

Photo Credit: Global Volunteers

Over twenty years ago, Global Volunteers' co-founders Bud Philbrook and Michele Gran discovered their life's work on their honeymoon in Guatemala.

Twenty years ago, we had what my husband, Bud Philbrook, wryly refers to as "a properly balanced honeymoon." We spent five days at theme parks in Orlando, followed by five days in an impoverished Guatemalan village. This curious blending of Disney World and "the real world" was, I believed then, a statement of our commitment to keep our marriage balanced and focused on human values. But more, it was a harbinger of our work to afford others a new perspective on their place in the world.

The first week in Orlando was predictably captivating as we explored all the area attractions. At the week's end, I was eager, but also apprehensive, about the next leg of our journey.

One thought dominated my mind as we embarked on our journey to Conacaste, Guatemala: I was writing a new, significant chapter of my life.

Our act of service would define who we were as individuals and as a couple in a world where humanity struggles to maintain human relationships. Bud's vision was clearer than mine. He believed it was each person's moral responsibility to work for human justice and equality. As a former state legislator, he often challenged me to question my personal role in waging world peace. But I felt ill-equipped to make a real difference outside my immediate area of influence. How would I make sense of the poverty and struggles of a life I knew nothing about?

Our warm welcome into Guatemala assuaged my worries. We were greeted by the American program-directors and the local community leaders. One of my first thoughts was: "They're just like us." While we toured the village, I felt progressively comforted by the openness and hospitality of the villagers.

The little mountain hamlet housed some two hundred families, many descendants of indigenous Indian tribes. They opened their homes to us, welcomed us into their fields, and included us in their friendly conversations, allowing us a glimpse into their daily lives. I was awestruck by how utterly normal—albeit difficult—life here seemed. With minimal electricity, no running water, few books, and no stores for daily necessities, the villagers accepted their formidable challenges not with resignation, but with pride. A nature-dominated flow of daily life seemed to guide their gentle spirits. Life was to be celebrated.

My comfort level in my temporary "home" grew as I became familiar with local residents. We were eager to become as much a part of the community as possible. Bud, with his background in human and economic development, was asked to help write a grant proposal, and I, with my journalism background, began work on a brochure explaining the community's needs to potential benefactors.

Every evening Bud and I joined project leaders to reflect on the day. The goals of their work were explained to us: Conacaste was a "demonstration" village for neighboring communities. The hope was to develop strategies in farming, health care, education, and commerce that other villages could replicate to improve their subsistence-level standard of living. Over several years, several innovations had been developed, including a bread-baking "industry" and basket-weaving center.

The project leaders explained that progress was slow, because as a demonstration project, the construction techniques used must be replicable with locally available resources. The American program-directors knew that the initiative, as well as the strategies, must be the local people's themselves if the community's efforts would remain long term. Therefore, construction practices that to me had first seemed awkward and unnecessarily labor-intensive, gained greater relevance as I began to understand the meaning of "appropriate technology."

As I scanned the village square, I tried to imagine what this place would look like in twenty years. Would one-room, thatched-roofed homes be replaced by more spacious dwellings? Would the village build the educational and medical facilities needed to ensure its children's health and development? Would farmers develop agricultural techniques to raise the families' subsistence-style of life? My heart swelled with hope and optimism.

Now, twenty years later, I have personally witnessed what is possible when local initiative and community self-determination join with catalytic assistance from committed "outsiders."

Like most people, Global Volunteers' team members are at first motivated to make a difference, to "give back" some of what they are grateful for in their own lives, and to know that in a small, personal way, they have altered the course of world history in a positive way. It is upon reflection they often realize, perhaps as they are packing their bags to return home, that they are the ones who have truly benefited from their act of service. Life will never be the same. They have their own story to tell.

—CONTRIBUTED BY MICHELE GRAN,
co-director of Global Volunteers

GLOBAL VOLUNTEERS

Service Adventures • Worldwide • 1–3 Weeks
www.globalvolunteers.org

♥ 🏠 🌍

SINCE 1984, GLOBAL VOLUNTEERS has sent out more than 150 teams of volunteers to live and work with local people on human and economic development projects identified by the community as important to their long-term development. "Travel that feeds the soul" sums up the volunteer experience, where each participant's energy, creativity, and labor are put to use as they gain a genuine, firsthand understanding of how other people live day to day. Development projects are available in twenty countries throughout Africa, the Americas, Asia, the Caribbean, Europe, and the Pacific. Global Volunteers also has special consultative status with the United Nations.

What You'll Be Doing: The work projects encompass six primary categories: English development, caring for children, teaching basic subjects, community infrastructure, health care, and business instruction and consultation. Volunteers might teach conversational English to

To acquire knowledge, one must study; but to acquire wisdom, one must experience. —SUE SCHMID

FINDING A PLACE IN THE WORLD

FINDING A PLACE IN THE WORLD

Photo Credit: Global Volunteers

A Global Volunteers participant walks with children in rural Tanzania.

elementary classrooms in Poland, work with mentally disabled children in Ecuador, assist with building houses or community gardens in Ghana, provide basic health services to communities in the Cook Islands, or teach the principles of business management and free enterprise in China. Volunteers on U.S. service programs have a unique opportunity to experience deeply rooted cultures that lend rich texture to the American fabric.

Commitment: Programs generally last one to three weeks, depending on the destination.

Perks and Rewards: A tax-deductible program fee ranges from $550 to $2,395. Most of this fee supports both the local project and ongoing program costs such as food, lodging, ground transportation, team leader expenses, project materials, volunteer coordination, program development, volunteer materials and communications, and on-site consultants. Airfare, visas, and medical insurance are additional costs. Volunteers find community meals abundant, sometimes adventurous, and a refreshing change for the palate. Lodging is generally double occupancy in hotels, guest houses, community centers, or private homes.

The Essentials: Volunteers typically share common characteristics, such as flexibility, compassion, a sense of adventure, and most important, the desire to work with and learn from local people in the host community. Volunteers are drawn from all occupations and backgrounds, and mostly from throughout the U.S. and Canada (generally between the ages of thirty and seventy-

five). There are no language or professional requirements for participation in most programs.

Your First Move: Call for the most current brochure or visit their website for the latest news. Applicants must complete their application materials one to three months prior to their departure date.

For More Information:
Volunteer Coordinator
Global Volunteers
375 E. Little Canada Rd.
St. Paul, MN 55117-1628
(800) 487-1074 • (651) 407-6100 • (651) 482-0915 (fax)
email@globalvolunteers.org

If our national anthem weren't "The Star-Spangled Banner," it would be an infectious symphony of Tex-Mex polkas, mystical Lakota drumming, Mississippi Delta blues, cowboy soliloquies, and Appalachian reels. You don't need to cross the oceans to explore new worlds. Unique and powerful service opportunities exist within U.S. borders. From coast to coast, we can help as developing communities fight the challenges of high unemployment, substandard living conditions, racism, and low per-capita income.

GLOBAL WORKS, INC.

Service Adventures • Worldwide • Summer
www.globalworksinc.com

GLOBAL WORKS IS an environmental and community service–based travel program (with language immersion and homestay options) for students ages fourteen to eighteen. Leaders and staff provide the backbone for these four-week summer adventures that take participants to places that range from small villages in the mountains of Fiji to castle ruins in Spain. With a work hard, play hard mentality, the program fills the students' days with meaningful projects, travel, and exposure to different cultures. Life-changing community projects may include building a new water system, constructing a playground, educating children about wolves, or rebuilding castles in ruins—all of which hope to positively affect the community. The working conditions are excellent and the pay quite good. Applicants must be at least twenty-three years old and have experience in leading groups and working with kids. Immersion program applicants require a true language proficiency.

For More Information:
Biff Houldin, Director
Global Works, Inc.
R.D. 2, Box 173A
Huntingdon, PA 16652
(814) 667-2411 • (814) 667-3853 (fax)
staffapp@globalworksinc.com

HEALTH VOLUNTEERS OVERSEAS

Medical • Worldwide • 2–4 Weeks
www.hvousa.org

HEALTH VOLUNTEERS OVERSEAS (HVO) sends qualified medical professionals overseas (Africa, Asia, Latin America, and the Caribbean) to train local health-care providers in the following ten specialties: anesthesia, dentistry, hand surgery, internal medicine, nursing, oral and maxillofacial surgery, orthopedics, pediatrics, and physical therapy. Volunteers lecture, conduct ward rounds, and demonstrate various techniques in classrooms, clinics, and operating rooms. In general, there is a two- to four-week minimum commitment; however, longer placements are available. Volunteers pay for

transportation to and from the program site. Most sites provide room, board, and daily transportation for volunteers once they arrive. All volunteers are asked to join HVO; membership fees vary depending on profession (and range from $30 to $125). Highly skilled and experienced professionals from both private practice and university settings, along with a significant number of retirees, volunteer each year.

For More Information:
Nancy Kelly, Executive Director
Health Volunteers Overseas
P.O. Box 65157
Washington, D.C. 20035
(202) 296-0928 • (202) 296-8018 (fax)
n.kelly@hvousa.org

INSTITUTE FOR CENTRAL AMERICAN DEVELOPMENT STUDIES

Language/Social Justice • Costa Rica/Nicaragua • Summer
www.icadscr.com

THE MAIN FOCUS of the Institute for Central American Development Studies (ICADS) is to teach first-world citizens about Central America. This is done by teaching Spanish and by offering academic programs that help students gain insight into current social and economic realities and their effects on women, the poor, and the environment.

What You'll Be Doing: Throughout the year, ICADS offers a four-week Spanish language immersion program; during the spring and fall, a field course in resource management and sustainable development, as well as an internship and research program; and in summer, a ten-week internship/language program. Upon arrival in Costa Rica, participants are introduced to their homestay family and are provided with a rigorous orientation and tour of the San José area. Each program generally begins with four weeks of intensive Spanish training for four-and-a-half hours per day, five days per week (in small classes). Then, depending on the program, students participate in an internship or fieldwork projects in Costa Rica or Nicaragua, emphasizing the environment, agriculture, women's issues, development, human rights, public health, or sustainable development.

Perks and Rewards: Program fees range from $1,500 to $7,900 depending on program, and includes airport pickup, intensive Spanish instruction and internship/ fieldwork placement, room, breakfast and dinner (the main staple in Costa Rica is rice and beans), laundry service, Internet access, and group field trips and activities. (Airfare, health insurance, and visa fees are additional costs.) Students should also budget $350 to $500 per month for local travel, lunches, and other incidental expenses.

The Essentials: High school graduates to working professionals have participated in an ICADS program. Applicants must have a working knowledge of Spanish upon arrival, and those who feel they would like to provide their labor, energy, and expertise to help further the goals of oppressed groups and social justice organizations in Costa Rica and Nicaragua will thrive in the program.

Your First Move: Applications and specific deadlines can be found online. Since applications are considered on a space-available basis, it's best to get materials in by the early deadline date (with decisions announced within two weeks of each deadline).

For More Information:
Program Coordinator
Institute for Central American Development Studies
Dept. 826
P.O. Box 025216
Miami, FL 33102-5216
(011) 506-225-0508 • (011) 506-234-1337 (fax)
icads@netbox.com

INTEREXCHANGE

International Exchange • Worldwide • 1–12 Months
www.interexchange.org

IN ADDITION TO helping to arrange for any necessary work and residence permits, InterExchange prearranges work-abroad experiences for U.S. citizens. The security of a prearranged job and accommodation allows participants to integrate into their new life more easily, without the stress of having to find a position and a place to live. Living and working in another culture enables participants to develop foreign language skills and gain greater insight into another way of life, all while receiving a salary or stipend (or other payment in kind) to help offset living and traveling expenses.

What You'll Be Doing: Have you ever dreamed about ordering a croissant and café au lait in Paris or wanted to become part of a real Spanish family? If so, InterExchange might be the program for you. They have dozens of posi-

tions in dozens of countries worldwide. Typical jobs include picking rhubarb and blackberries, tending livestock, teaching English, being a camp counselor or an au pair, or working at a hotel.

Commitment: Placements vary from one month to one year depending on program: teaching and au pair positions range from six months to a year; farm programs range from two to four months; and internships range from summer positions to yearlong ventures.

Perks and Rewards: Program fees start at $400. Along with a self-sustaining work salary or other payment in kind (not all programs offer salaries), housing is offered with most programs.

The Essentials: Participants must be at least eighteen years of age; some programs have an upper age limit or language and degree requirements. Additionally, all participants must be covered by health and accident insurance.

Your First Move: Applicants are required to submit applications three to four months prior to their desired start dates. After the proper paperwork is completed, most participants receive word of placement anywhere from four to eight weeks before their requested departure date.

For More Information:
Program Manager
InterExchange
Working Abroad Program
161 Sixth Ave.
New York, NY 10013
(212) 924-0446 • (212) 924-0575 (fax)
workabroad@interexchange.org

THE INTERNATIONAL PARTNERSHIP FOR SERVICE-LEARNING

Service Learning • Worldwide • 1–12 Months
www.ipsl.org

THE INTERNATIONAL PARTNERSHIP for Service-Learning, a nonprofit educational consortium of colleges, universities, and service agencies, develops programs that link college-level academic studies with volunteer service in international and intercultural settings. Programs are offered in the Czech Republic, Ecuador, England, France, India, Israel, Jamaica, Mexico, the Philippines, Russia, Scotland, and South Dakota (in the U.S. with Native Americans).

What You'll Be Doing: The International Partnership fully integrates participants into a new culture through service, academics, and living arrangements. Participants work in a community service project up to twenty hours per week in schools and orphanages, health-care and education institutions, recreational centers, or community-development projects. The rest of the week is filled with an academic component, integrating studies and service that range from education and social services to health-care and intercultural studies at a local, accredited university. Finally, living arrangements are provided with a host family or college housing, providing a unique way to interact and learn from the new culture. Also inquire about their master's degree in international service.

Commitment: A variety of terms are available, including a three-week session in India along with summer, semester, and yearlong programs.

Perks and Rewards: Program fees range from $3,000 to $9,200 (depending on location and time frame), and cover tuition, housing and meals, on-site orientation, service placement, field trips, and administrative fees. Students can earn up to eighteen college credits per semester (which are granted from the student's home college).

The Essentials: Applicants from all nations and backgrounds are welcome. The minimum age is eighteen and some programs have language requirements. College students and graduates are encouraged to apply.

Your First Move: Applications must be received at least two months prior to the program start date. Details can be found online or call/email for an information packet.

For More Information:
Howard Berry, President
The International Partnership for Service-Learning
815 Second Ave., Suite 315
New York, NY 10017-4594
(212) 986-0989 • (212) 986-5039 (fax)
pslny@aol.com

INTERNATIONAL VOLUNTEER EXPEDITIONS

Volunteer Service • The Americas • 2–8 Weeks
www.espwa.org

INTERNATIONAL VOLUNTEER EXPEDITIONS conducts short- and medium-term volunteer projects in the Americas. With an emphasis placed on sustainable development, poverty and the environment, and outdoor activities, project work varies, but is primarily physical labor (including painting, construction, trail maintenance, gardening, and reviving agriculture fields). Those with professional skills might plan and prepare educational exhibits, create websites, conduct activities for children, or contribute professional services (from architecture assistance to plumbing). Volunteers usually work six to eight hours per day, five days a week, over a two- to eight-week period. Participants are recruited internationally and all ages are welcome. Curiosity, adaptability, an adventurous spirit, and a sense of humor are indispensable volunteer attributes. Fees range from $450 to $1,500, and include vegetarian meals, simple lodging (ranging from a self-contained tent in the rain forest to dormitory-style facilities), and project materials during the service component. (Airfare is additional.) A $200 nonrefundable registration fee is due with your application (which can be obtained online).

For More Information:
Dawn Moorhead, Executive Director
International Volunteer Expeditions
2001 Vallejo Way
Sacramento, CA 95818
(916) 444-6856 • (510) 496-2740, ext. 4550 (voice mail)
ivexinformation@espwa.org

INTERNATIONAL VOLUNTEER PROGRAM

Learning Adventure • France/U.K. • 8 Weeks
www.ivpsf.com

THE INTERNATIONAL VOLUNTEER Program provides people from North America with the opportunity to work in France or the United Kingdom during the summer months. Volunteers spend six weeks (full-time) with tourism offices, summer camps, hospitals, environmental projects, or local city governments, along with an additional two weeks reserved for travel as an option (at the volunteer's expense). Typical assignments in the past have included reading the newspaper to the elderly, leading a tour of a thirteenth-century museum, working with the disabled, or being a camp counselor at a children's summer camp. Placements are limited and are assigned on a first-come, first-served basis (thus, applicants must be receptive to any assignment). The fee of $1,500 includes round-trip airfare (from San Francisco or New York), housing with host families, dorms, or on-site lodging. Applicants must be at least eighteen years of age (no upper age limit), and for programs in France, a comfortable level of French is required.

For More Information:
Rebecca Jewell, Program Director
International Volunteer Program
210 Post St., Suite 502
San Francisco, CA 94104
(415) 477-3667 • (415) 477-3669 (fax)
rjewell@ivpsf.com

INTERNSHIPS INTERNATIONAL

International Education • Worldwide • 2–3 Months
www.rtpnet.org/intintl

WITH INTERNSHIPS INTERNATIONAL (II), you have the opportunity to add a foreign dimension to your college or graduate degree through carefully chosen internship placements in major international cities. Covering all disciplines and fields, participants are placed in a full-time, volunteer internship for two to three months. Programs are available in Bangkok (Thailand), Budapest (Hungary), Cape Town (South Africa), Dresden (Germany), Dublin (Ireland), Glasgow, (Scotland), London (England), Melbourne (Australia), Paris (France), or Santiago (Chile).

What You'll Be Doing: Think about what you want to do, where you want to go, how long you want to intern, and when you want to start. Don't worry, because you'll get plenty of help. During the application process, the II staff works with you to figure out an internship that best fits your needs and qualifications. Once you've settled on the details, one of II's international partners does all the legwork and finds an internship that meets your criteria. At the same time, you'll also receive a list of possible housing sources. After that, the rest is up to you—time to create, learn, grow, and be exposed to whole new world. (Of course, in an emergency, your program director would be there as a safety net!)

Commitment: A minimum commitment of eight weeks is necessary, with placements up to three months.

Perks and Rewards: There is a placement fee of $800 ($1,000 for London; $1,500 for Dublin) which covers all costs associated with your internship placement. If an appropriate internship is not found based on your qualifications, the fee is fully refundable. All living and travel expenses are additional expenses. Many students have found ways to moonlight to bring in extra money.

The Essentials: The program is geared for college grads or graduate students who want to expand their resume in order to become more competitive in the academic or professional world. Exceptions can definitely be made for mature college seniors who require an internship for graduation. In addition, applicants must be independent and self-sufficient.

Your First Move: Call or send an email to obtain an application packet. In addition to the application form, you will need to provide a statement of purpose in English (and in the language of the country you will work in, if required), two references, your college transcript, a resume, and two photos. Placements generally take three months after your application is complete.

For More Information:
Judy Tilson, Director
Internships International
1612 Oberlin Rd.
Raleigh, NC 27608
(919) 832-1575 • (919) 832-8980 (fax)
intintl@aol.com

JAPAN EXCHANGE AND TEACHING PROGRAM

Teaching • Japan • 1–3 Years
www.embjapan.org/jet

THE JAPAN EXCHANGE and Teaching Program (commonly known as JET) seeks to enhance internationalization in Japan by promoting mutual understanding between Japan and other countries, including the U.S. The program's aims are to intensify foreign language education in Japan and to promote international contacts at the local level by fostering ties between Japanese youth and young foreign college graduates. More than five thousand participants are currently involved in the JET Program, approximately half of whom come from the U.S.

What You'll Be Doing: Assistant Language Teacher (ALT) participants are assigned to local schools and boards of education in various cities, towns, and villages throughout Japan as team teachers, and engage in foreign language instruction. They may also be involved in language clubs, teachers' seminars, and judging speech contests. Coordinator for International Relations (CIR) participants engage in international activities carried out by local governments throughout Japan. These activities include receiving guests from abroad, editing and translating documents, interpreting during international events, assisting with the language instruction of government employees and local residents, assisting with international exchange programs, and various other activities.

Commitment: The duration for an individual contract is one year, beginning in late July. JET contracts are generally renewable for up to three years, upon consent of both the participant and the host institution. Over six thousand people from around the world participate in the JET program each year.

Perks and Rewards: An annual remuneration of ¥3,600,000 (approximately $30,000 per year or check out www.xe.com/ucc for the most current currency exchange) is provided to cover the cost of accommodations, living expenses, and mandatory health insurance. Round-trip airfare is also provided, although only from designated points within the U.S. The host institution in Japan will assist participants with accommodations, which cost about ¥30,000 to ¥60,000 per month.

The Essentials: ALT applicants must have an interest in Japan and excellent English communication skills. Japanese language ability or teaching experience is not required. CIR applicants must have a functional command of Japanese and excellent communication skills. All candidates must have a bachelor's degree, U.S. citizenship, and be under forty years of age. Those outside the U.S. should check out requirements for their country at www.embjapan.org.

Your First Move: Applications for the following year's JET Program will be available beginning in late September. Call 1-800-INFO-JET for an application. Completed application packets must be received by the Japanese Embassy in Washington, D.C., by the first week of December. (Call for exact dates.)

For More Information:
Program Coordinator
Japan Exchange and Teaching Program
Embassy of Japan
2520 Massachusetts Ave., NW
Washington, D.C. 20008
(800) 463-6538 • (202) 238-6772
eojjet@erols.com

KIBBUTZ PROGRAM CENTER

Kibbutz • Israel • 2–12 Months
www.kibbutzprogramcenter.org

THOSE WANTING TO participate in a unique kibbutz way of life have a chance to work, study, and live side by side with Israelis. The Kibbutz "ulpan" program is a combination of language study and strenuous work (generally agricultural) on various kibbutz branches over a five-month period; the Hebrew and work program offers the opportunity to learn Hebrew while living and working within the communal kibbutz environment over a three-month period; and the volunteer program allows participants to live and work on a kibbutz from two to twelve months. Program fees range from $150 to $800 (medical insurance is additional), and include food, lodging, and an educational component. Participants must be between the ages of eighteen and twenty-eight (thirty-two maximum for the volunteer program). Note that there are centers around the world for those who live outside the U.S. and would like to apply to the program.

For More Information:
Tal Lifshitz, Director of Admissions
Kibbutz Program Center
633 Third Ave., 21st Floor
New York, NY 10017
(800) 247-7852 • (212) 318-6118 • (212) 318-6134 (fax)
ulpankad@aol.com

LATIN AMERICAN LANGUAGE CENTER

Language/Community Service • Costa Rica • 1–4 Weeks
www.cal.net/~lalc

AFTER BEING WELCOMED by staff and teachers at Juan Santamaria International Airport, Intensive Spanish Immersion Program participants are transported to their new home in Costa Rica. Host families are typically middle-class professional people and, like most Costa Ricans, are very family oriented. Living with a local family who speaks little or no English is one of the best ways to learn Spanish, make new friends, and begin to understand Costa Rican culture all at the same time. Throughout the week, participants engage in Spanish language classes (of all levels) for four hours per day at the Centro Linguistico

Experience is a hard teacher because she gives the test first, the lesson afterwards. —VERNON SANDERS LAW

Latinoamericano. Teachers provide the two to four students in each class with highly individualized instruction with conversations focused on the student's instructional needs. Beyond learning Spanish, participants also share in Costa Rican dance and cooking classes as well as a three-hour cultural trip once per week. Those who have completed at least two weeks of Spanish immersion classes can also participate in volunteer projects, which may include assisting ESL and computer teachers or spending time with social service projects. The program extends from one to four weeks, with tuition ranging from $345 to $1,380, plus a program fee of $25. Tuition includes a homestay experience (with private room), three meals each day, and laundry service. (Airfare is additional.)

For More Information:
Susan Shores, Registrar
Latin American Language Center
PMB 122
7485 Rush River Dr., Suite 710
Sacramento, CA 95831-5260
(916) 447-0938 • (916) 428-9542 (fax)
lalc@madre.com

MAR DE JADE

Language/Community Service • Mexico • 3 Weeks
www.mardejade.com

SURROUNDED BY A lush tropical forest and palm trees, Mar de Jade is an oceanfront retreat and vacation center in a small fishing village (Chacala, Nayarit) one-and-a-half hours north of Puerto Vallarta on the Pacific Coast of Mexico. Mar de Jade's three-week work/study program provides participants with the opportunity to assist in community health-care, organic gardening, or arts and crafts and teaching projects, along with the chance to study Spanish in small groups with local teachers. The $1,460 fee includes shared housing, meals, nine hours per week of Spanish (plus two hours of medical Spanish for those in health care), and sixteen hours per week of community work. To receive more information, communication by email is preferred.

For More Information:
Work/Study Program Director
Mar de Jade
PMB 078-344
705 Martens Ct.
Laredo, TX 78041-6010

(011) 52-322-222-1171
info@mardejade.com

MONTEVERDE FRIENDS SCHOOL

Teaching • Costa Rica • 2 Years

MONTEVERDE FRIENDS SCHOOL is an English-dominant, bilingual school in Costa Rica's rural mountains. Tuition is kept low for the seventy-five students (in multigrade levels) so that no child will be denied an education. Challenging teaching assignments for a minimum of two years allow North American teachers, who lovingly share their knowledge and skills, to serve as role models for these children. Classes are small (generally eight to twelve students) with a curriculum based on the sciences, math, social studies, history, English, Spanish, and religion, along with special awareness to the environment, community, and peace issues. An interest or experience with bilingual education and conversational Spanish, and a willingness to develop curriculum while living in a rustic tropical setting are required. Benefits include a modest salary, rustic housing, health insurance, and visa costs. Volunteers are also welcome for a minimum stay of six weeks.

For More Information:
Jenny Rowe, Program Coordinator
Monteverde Friends School
Codigo Postal 5655
Monteverde, Puntarenas
Costa Rica
mfschool@racsa.co.cr

OIC INTERNATIONAL

Service Learning/Agriculture •
USA/Africa/Philippines • 3 Weeks–3 Months
www.oicinternational.org

FOUNDED BACK IN THE mid-1960s by Reverend Leon Sullivan (who is known for his significant contribution to ending apartheid in South Africa), Opportunities Industrialization Centers (OIC) International works to improve the lives of the underprivileged in several African nations, Poland, and the Philippines. Thousands of people have become expert farmers, successful business owners, skilled workers, and prominent members of their communities through OIC and its staff, interns, and volunteers.

What You'll Be Doing: Three types of programs encompass OIC volunteer and internship opportunities: FarmServe Africa volunteers are skilled agricultural experts who provide short-term technical assistance to OIC affiliate agricultural programs in West Africa. Assignments range from three to four weeks and volunteers are hosted by local families, assigned to specific projects, and accountable for creating a measurable impact during their visit. International intern assignments vary depending on program and country as well as the intern's skill-set. Interns in the U.S. work in Philadelphia and perform research, support local fund-raising, create public relations material, write reports and proposals, and assist in program administration.

Perks and Rewards: Some positions are paid, while others are strictly volunteer. International volunteers must raise their own funds and support themselves in-country. Domestic positions may include short-term international assignments. The biggest perk is the opportunity to gain practical work experience in response to diverse development challenges in developing regions, especially Africa.

The Essentials: Ideal candidates should be university graduates or candidates for a bachelor's or master's degree in a discipline related to international humanitarian assistance, with excellent writing, communication, research, organization, computer, and interpersonal skills. Proficiency in a second language, preferably French, is a plus.

Your First Move: Call or email for details on current opportunities.

For More Information:
Carla Denizard, Director of Food Security
OIC International
240 W. Tulpehocken St.
Philadelphia, PA 19144-3295
(215) 842-0220, ext. 113 • (215) 849-7033 (fax)
foodsecurity@oici.org

OPERATION CROSSROADS AFRICA

Global Development • Africa/Brazil • Summer
www.igc.org/oca

SINCE OPERATION CROSSROADS Africa's founding in 1957, more than ten thousand volunteers have made contributions to development in thirty-five African and twelve Caribbean countries as well as in Brazil. The late President Kennedy paid special tribute to Crossroads for serving as the example and inspiration for the creation of the Peace Corps.

What You'll Be Doing: After a brief but intense cross-cultural training, Crossroads volunteers are teamed up with eight to ten other men and women and immersed into the culture of their host community (along with a team leader and equal number of local volunteers). All projects are community initiated, and volunteers will live and work with hosts who have designed the project. The project work may entail construction of a school, an inoculation drive, or planting trees—all of which fall under four types of projects: construction of community facilities, community health, agriculture, and education and training. Living conditions only provide the basic amenities and lack many of the modern conveniences many Westerners take for granted (often there is no electricity or running water, and participants eat a modest, high-starch, low-protein diet). Each season Crossroads also hires a handful of team leaders who are responsible for stimulating interest and cooperation among participants and for guiding them in attaining greater contextual understanding of the experience. (Call for the specifics on these positions.)

Commitment: The program runs from mid-June to mid-August and consists of three orientation days in New York City, six weeks of work on a rural project, and one travel week in the host country.

Perks and Rewards: There is a participation fee of $3,500, which covers all program expenses, including round-trip airfare. A majority of volunteers raise all or part of their fee. Crossroads provides fund-raising how-tos, contacts with others who have successfully raised their fee in the past, and consistent encouragement in the process. Scholarships are available for up to fifteen applicants (that will fund 50 to 80 percent of the participation fee).

The Essentials: Though most Crossroaders are college students and young professionals, there are no set age or occupation requirements. Fluency in French or Portuguese is a plus, since these are the main languages of many host countries.

Your First Move: Call for application materials and current deadlines. In general, all applications must be turned in by March 1.

For More Information:
Program Services Director
Operation Crossroads Africa
P.O. Box 5570

Become so wrapped up in something that you forget to be afraid. —LADY BIRD JOHNSON

New York, NY 10027
(212) 289-1949 • (212) 289-2526 (fax)
oca@igc.org

*You will experience Africa from the inside out . . .
this is not an African tour.*

PEACE CORPS

Global Development • Worldwide • 2+ Years
www.peacecorps.gov

SINCE 1961, PEACE CORPS volunteers have been sharing their skills and energies with people in the developing world, helping them learn new ways to fight hunger, disease, poverty, and lack of opportunity.

What You'll Be Doing: As a Peace Corps volunteer, you'll travel overseas and make real differences in the lives of real people. Whether you're helping people stay healthy, expand their businesses, or grow more nutritious food, you will help change and improve the human condition at the grassroots level. There is a particular need for certified teachers, French-language speakers, and those interested in agriculture, environmental education, business development, and teaching English.

Commitment: Assignments last for two years and begin after the successful completion of an intensive language, cultural, and technical training (which lasts from two to three months).

Perks and Rewards: "Two years of service, a lifetime of benefits." It is often said that the Peace Corps is not simply something great; it is the beginning of something great. From practical benefits such as student loan deferment to career benefits like fluency in a foreign language to the intangible benefits that come with making a difference in people's lives, there are a variety of rewards for serving. During this serving time, volunteers receive a monthly allowance to cover housing, food, clothing, and spending money. Medical and dental care, transportation to and from their overseas sites, and twenty-four vacation days a year are also provided. Upon completion of service, volunteers receive a $6,075 readjustment allowance and job-hunting assistance.

The Essentials: Any healthy U.S. citizen of eighteen years or older is eligible for consideration, with most assign-

ments requiring at least a bachelor's degree, or three to five years of substantive work experience. For many assignments, a language other than English is required. Previous knowledge of another language can be very helpful but is not always required. Perseverance, adaptability, creativity in problem solving, and sociability are traits important in volunteers.

Your First Move: For more information, call the toll-free number to locate the recruitment office nearest you. Volunteers will be notified where they'll be serving as much as six months before they get on a plane.

For More Information:
Director
Peace Corps
Volunteer Recruitment and Selection
1111 20th St., NW
Washington, D.C. 20526
(800) 424-8580
webmaster@peacecorps.gov

Not sure if you want to continue with graduate school or become involved with the Peace Corps? Now you can do both by participating in the Master's International Program. Through partnerships with more than thirty schools offering master's-level studies in a variety of subjects, individuals become Peace Corps volunteers as partial fulfillment of a graduate degree.

PEACEWORK

Work Camp • Worldwide • 1–4 Weeks
www.peacework.org

PEACEWORK MANAGES AND organizes short-term international volunteer projects in developing communities around the world—from Zimbabwe to Vietnam. Through volunteer interaction and cooperation, participants learn about the world's cultures, customs, politics, and problems while contributing their skills and interests to a positive process of international development.

What You'll Be Doing: Groups of volunteers learn about the dynamics of global hunger and poverty by working together on housing, health, and other development initiatives. Planned and implemented by leaders in the host community, projects typically involve the construction or renovation of schools, houses, orphanages, and clinics, or work on agricultural, educational, and health-care projects. Group leaders are uniquely experienced in the host country, languages, and working with volunteer groups. Volunteers live and work in sometimes difficult and demanding conditions.

Commitment: Programs vary in length from one to four weeks. The majority of the programs occur during the summer, spring break, or during other holiday seasons; however, dates depend on the sponsoring group.

Perks and Rewards: Fees start at $1,000, plus airfare. Comprehensive orientation materials, planning assistance, in-country arrangements (including housing), visas, supplemental international health insurance, and contributions toward project materials and program administration are included in the program cost. Peacework provides a guide to scholarships and other assistance with fund-raising for those who need additional financial support.

The Essentials: Volunteers range in age from sixteen to seventy-six years old, but in general are college or graduate students. Peacework does not require knowledge of language or construction skills in order to participate in the trips. Acceptance is generally based on one's enthusiasm for international and humanitarian service, academic preparation, volunteer experience or travel, and references that indicate one's ability to work and live in a multicultural and often demanding environment.

Your First Move: Call for further information and application materials.

For More Information:
Program Director
Peacework
305 Washington St., SW
Blacksburg, VA 24060-4575
(800) 272-5519 • (540) 953-1376 • (540) 552-0119 (fax)
mail@peacework.org

PROJECT OTZMA

Kibbutz • Israel • 10 Months
www.projectotzma.org

A GREAT ALTERNATIVE to work or graduate school, Project Otzma is a ten-month leadership development program in which North American young adults (aged twenty to twenty-five, and geared mainly to college

graduates) contribute a year of service to Israel and the Jewish people, and gain an in-depth understanding of the country and their own capacities to lead. Beginning in mid-August, volunteers initially live and work in large groups at immigrant absorption centers, then participate in an "ulpan," a program of intense Hebrew language study. For the next three months, volunteers participate in community-service projects, which range from building playgrounds to coordinating events for youth in the community center. The next phase focuses on a diverse range of service opportunities based on personal interest, and the final two months are dedicated to working and living in groups in youth villages or on a kibbutz. The Otzma year also includes numerous education days, seminars, group trips, and two vacations. Each participant is paired with an Israeli adoptive family with whom to share in holidays and weekends throughout the program. Each participant is responsible for contributing a nominal fee of $1,950 toward the total program cost, along with purchasing his or her own round-trip airplane ticket, food, and incidentals. ($5,250 is already subsidized for each participant.) Candidates submitting their applications by January 15th will receive early notification of their interview status by mail on or before February 15. After January 15, applications will be accepted on a rolling basis, with a final filing date of May 15.

For More Information:
Alison Young, North American Otzma Coordinator
Project Otzma
United Jewish Communities
111 8th Ave.
New York, NY 10011-5201
(877) 466-8962 • (212) 284-6721 • (212) 284-6838 (fax)
otzma@ujc.org

The intensity of my year on Otzma enabled me to grow in ways which far exceeded my expectations. The opportunities that were presented to me, and those that I sought out for myself, led me to have one of the most rewarding adventures of my life.
—BROOKE GARDBERG, participant

SCI-INTERNATIONAL VOLUNTARY SERVICE USA

Work Camp • Worldwide • 2 Weeks–1 Year
www.sci-ivs.org

SCI–INTERNATIONAL VOLUNTARY Service is the U.S. branch of Service Civil International, celebrating over seventy-five years of promoting peace and international understanding through community-service projects. The hallmark of SCI is the annual exchange of thousands of volunteers, who work at short-term community-service projects around the world.

What You'll Be Doing: Eight to fifteen volunteers of various nationalities and backgrounds come together to solve problems, work together in grassroots community-service projects, and have fun throughout the year. Volunteers might help teach solar technology in Denmark, renovate an ancient church in Russia, or work on an organic farm in the Swiss Alps. SCI-sponsored work camps have a local sponsor in more than fifty countries around the globe.

Commitment: Although there are some work-camp opportunities available throughout the year, by far the largest number of camps are offered during the summer months from two to four weeks. Longer opportunities— from three months to one year—are also available.

Perks and Rewards: The application fee for residents of the U.S. and Canada is $65 for domestic programs and $125 for most overseas programs. For work camps in Asia, Africa, Latin America, and Eastern Europe, the fees are higher and vary by location. Participation in more than one camp runs an additional $35 to $80 (with a limit of three camps per year). SCI covers room and board and a supplemental health and accident insurance. (Airfare is additional.) Your fee also pays for a year's membership in SCI.

The Essentials: U.S./Canadian volunteers must be sixteen and older for U.S. camps and eighteen or older for overseas camps. (There is no upper age limit and retirees are welcome.) In general, there is no special experience required, except the ability to work in a team environment.

Your First Move: Information regarding all camps and applications forms are available on the Web. Summer opportunities are generally posted by mid-March. Summer volunteers are placed in work camps of their choice, beginning in mid-April on a first-come, first-served basis. (After June 15, it becomes more difficult to get your first choice.) Have patience, as applications are processed by a small group of volunteer staff across the country.

For More Information:
Volunteer Exchange Coordinator
SCI—International Voluntary Service USA
814 NE 40th St.
Seattle, WA 98105
(206) 545-6585 • (206) 545-6585 (fax)
sciinfo@sci-ivs.org

UNITED NATIONS ASSOCIATION OF THE USA

International Relations • New York • Seasonal
www.unausa.org

THE UNITED NATIONS Association (UNA-USA) is the nation's leading center for research and information on the work and structure of the UN system. Through a unique combination of grassroots activism and high-level policy studies, UNA-USA, through its twenty-three thousand members nationwide, pioneers efforts to involve the American public, government, and business leaders in the discussion of foreign-policy priorities. Intern assignments throughout the year may include researching for publications, identifying new trends and developments, organizing special events, participating in briefings, designing publications, and assisting in outreach to the association's grassroots membership. Internships are unpaid, however interns will undoubtedly gain a valuable experience in the international relations field. In addition, interns will receive invitations to UNA-USA events along with the coveted UN headquarters grounds pass with which they may observe UN meetings and briefings. Candidates must be high school or college students who possess a firm understanding of international affairs and good writing and research skills. Applications are available online or call/write for more information.

For More Information:
Veronica Wayner, Internship Coordinator
United Nations Association of the USA
801 Second Ave.
New York, NY 10017-4706
(212) 907-1326 • (212) 682-9185 (fax)
vwayner@unausa.org

UNIVERSITY RESEARCH EXPEDITIONS PROGRAM

Adventure Education • Worldwide • 1–2 Weeks
www.urep.ucdavis.edu

THE UNIVERSITY OF California Research Expeditions Program (UREP) invites you to join in the challenges and rewards of field research expeditions around the world. These research teams investigate everything from Costa Rican monkeys that use medicinal plants to excavating medieval castles of Ireland. Whether you choose to study archaeological sites to learn about the past or record the biodiversity of fragile environments, your participation will improve our understanding of the planet and help plan for the future. You don't need special training or experience to participate—your curiosity, adaptability, and willingness to share the costs and lend a helping hand are the most important qualifications. The average cost for a two-week expedition runs about $1,500, which includes meals and shared lodging, ground transportation, camping and field gear, and research equipment and supplies. (Airfare and visas are additional.) More than just contributing to a worthy cause, you will have a unique opportunity to learn new skills, make new friends, and gain insights into other cultures in a way that ordinary travelers rarely experience. It's an adventure with a purpose.

For More Information:
Dennis Dutschke, Program Director
University Research Expeditions Program
UC Davis
One Shields Ave.
Davis, CA 95616
(530) 757-3520 • (530) 757-3537 (fax)
urep@ucdavis.edu

VEN-USA

Language • Venezuela • 2 Weeks–10 Months
www.home.earthlink.net/~venusa

VEN-USA, A PRIVATE institute of international studies and modern languages, offers an intensive and highly individualized Spanish language immersion program in the town of Mérida, Venezuela, the principal city of the Venezuelan Andes—a clean, safe university town where the weather and people are always warm and the scenery is breathtaking. Students and professors work together to tailor schedules (four hours of instruction each weekday), teaching styles, and course content to the specific needs of each student. Obtaining room and board with a Venezuelan family is optional but is highly recommended. Program participants and Venezuelan students of English are invited to social events and activities. The immersion program begins every Monday throughout the year. There is an instruction fee of $540 for the first two weeks (each additional week is $180), and room and board is available for a fee of $85 per week. VEN-USA also offer summer, semester, and academic year programs with fees ranging from $3,125 to $6,180, as well as internships and TESL (Teaching English as a Second Language) programs.

For More Information:
Rosa Corley, U.S. Field Coordinator
VEN-USA
6542 Hypoluxo Rd., #324
Lake Worth, FL 33467
(561) 357-8802 • (561) 357-9199 (fax)
venusa@earthlink.com

VIA

Teaching • Asia • 7 Weeks–2 Years
www.viaprograms.org

VIA (FORMERLY VOLUNTEERS in Asia) traces its origins to a 1963 group of Stanford students who saw volunteer work as an appropriate way to enter and better understand the non-Western world. Since its beginnings in the refugee settlements of Hong Kong, VIA has sent more than a thousand volunteers to a wide range of assignments in Asia. Current programs in China, Indonesia, Laos, and Vietnam continue to reflect the organization's original goals: to immerse Americans directly into the workplaces and neighborhoods of contemporary Asia and to provide Asian organizations with volunteer assistance.

What You'll Be Doing: As a small organization with limited resources, VIA focuses its efforts on one skill Americans can offer Asian organizations without displacing Asian workers—native English-language assistance. Thus, most volunteers teach English at the college level or in community organizations such as the YMCA. Others act as English resource volunteers who assist with translation and editing needs. Between thirty and forty volunteers are sent each year.

Commitment: Long-term volunteers participate in a thorough predeparture training program at Stanford beginning in March, which focuses on cross-cultural training, Teaching English as a Foreign Language, and language training. Participants generally depart for Asia in late June.

Perks and Rewards: Participant fees run $1,975 for the summer and one-year program; $950 for two years. This fee represents approximately 10 percent of the cost of sending a volunteer to the field. While on assignment, one- and two-year volunteers receive a monthly housing and living stipend. VIA covers the cost of round-trip transportation, basic health insurance, cross-cultural training, and in-country field support. Living arrangements are provided in guest houses, faculty apartment buildings, or dormitories. Scholarships are available.

The Essentials: Applicants must be mature, responsible, native English speakers, and should hold a bachelor's degree. VIA does not require any specific educational background, prior language training, teaching, or overseas experience. Volunteers range in age from eighteen to eighty and come from many different walks of life.

Your First Move: Applications are available starting in November and are due at the end of January. All prospective applicants are encouraged to attend one of VIA's informational sessions held during this time frame. Staff and former volunteers will be on hand to help you gain a clearer picture of the program and philosophy and whether it meets your needs and interests. Acceptance into the program will be announced in early March.

For More Information:

Ann Le, Recruitment Coordinator
VIA
Haas Center for Public Service, 3rd Floor
P.O. Box 20266
Stanford, CA 94309
(650) 723-3228 • (650) 725-1805 (fax)
info@viaprograms.org

VISIONS IN ACTION

Service Learning • USA/Africa/Mexico • 2–12 Months
www.visionsinaction.org

VISIONS IN ACTION (VIA) is an international nonprofit organization founded in 1988 out of the conviction that there is much that we can learn from and contribute to the developing world by working as part of a community of volunteers committed to social justice in the urban setting.

What You'll Be Doing: VIA programs feature a monthlong orientation, including intensive language study, followed by a five- or eleven-month volunteer placement. Positions are offered in five African countries (Burkina Faso, South Africa, Tanzania, Uganda, and Zimbabwe) and Mexico, with projects that include business and community development, environmental issues, health care, housing and urban planning, human rights, journalism, nonprofit development, scientific research, and women's rights. For those who desire a shorter term, a nine-week summer program is also an option. Intern positions are also available on a continuous basis in the Washington, D.C., office, and range from international administration to recruitment and public relations (with a minimum commitment of three months or more). Although unpaid, an $800 credit toward a VIA overseas program fee is provided.

Perks and Rewards: The total estimated cost for a one-year program is $5,500 to $8,000. Fees include airfare, housing, orientation and language training, medical insurance, overseas support, and all local expenses (food, transport, and entertainment). Volunteers are normally housed in major urban areas in coed group houses, living in a supportive community. All funds donated toward your program are tax-deductible, and Visions in Action will help you with fund-raising ideas once you have been accepted as a volunteer.

The Essentials: Volunteers of all nationalities must be at least twenty years of age (eighteen for the summer program), and have two years of college or equivalent work experience. Most volunteers are university graduates, the average age is twenty-seven, and married couples are encouraged to apply. The French language is required in Burkina Faso; Spanish in Mexico.

Your First Move: Applications are due three months prior to departure, although it's suggested that you apply early so you have time to fund-raise before you go. Materials are available online or call for more information.

For More Information:

Stacy Readal, Program Coordinator
Visions in Action
2710 Ontario Rd., NW
Washington, D.C. 20009
(202) 625-7402 • (202) 588-9344 (fax)
visions@visionsinaction.org

VOLUNTEERS FOR PEACE

Work Camp • Worldwide • 2–3 Weeks
www.vfp.org

♥ 🏕 🌐

International work camps emerged in war-torn Europe back in 1920. More recently, work camps have become an affordable and meaningful way for people of all ages to travel, live, and work in a foreign country. Volunteers for Peace (VFP) coordinates more than fifteen hundred work-camp experiences in seventy countries, including Africa, the Americas, Asia, and Western and Eastern Europe. Hundreds of field volunteers and office staff provide consultation and placement services for work-camp hosts and volunteers.

What You'll Be Doing: As a fully internationalized short-term "Peace Corps," work camps are a way you can respond positively to the challenges we face in our world. Focusing on cooperation, caring, sharing, and group living, you'll have a fun-filled adventure, building bonds with people from diverse cultural backgrounds. Work camps are sponsored by an organization in the host country and coordinated by people in a local community. In general, ten to twenty volunteers from four or more countries arrive at the community sponsoring the work project. Agricultural, archaeological, construction, environmental, and restoration work camps are common.

Commitment: Programs vary as to their start dates and length but generally run two to three weeks from mid-June to mid-October (although others are offered throughout the year). About 20 percent of the people they place abroad every year register for multiple work camps in the same or different countries and spend several months abroad.

Perks and Rewards: Most programs cost $200, with room and meals provided. African, Russian, and Latin American programs may cost $300 to $500. You may be housed in a school, church, private home, or community center. Living arrangements are generally family style, with work campers coordinating and sharing the day-to-day activities, food preparation, work projects, and recreation. Travel expenses will be left up to the volunteer.

The Essentials: You must be at least eighteen years old, (although there are 280 work camps for sixteen- and seventeen-year-olds in France, Germany, Estonia, and many other countries), and there is no upper age limit. (They've placed several folks in their seventies.) The most common age of participants is between twenty and twenty-five. In most areas, foreign language proficiency is not necessary.

Your First Move: Each April the *International Workcamp*

Volunteers for Peace participants restore ancient stairs in the Cinque-Terre of Italy and enjoy views of the Mediterranean stretching as far as the eye can see.

Directory, which lists more than two thousand opportunities, can be obtained for $20. It also contains registration information and VFP's free newsletter. Volunteers are placed on a first-come, first-served basis and are advised to register as soon as possible after receipt of the directory. Most volunteers register between mid-April and mid-May.

For More Information:
Peter Coldwell, International Workcamps Coordinator
Volunteers for Peace
1034 Tiffany Rd.
Belmont, VT 05730-0202
(802) 259-2759 • (802) 259-2922 (fax)
vfp@vfp.org

My work-camp experience was one of the best of my life; in fact it changed my life. It was definitely a good experience to find out how well I function in a foreign environment, and it's definitely good for someone who is thinking of living abroad or joining a longer-term volunteer project. It is an experience which will live within me forever and which no one will understand unless they experience it themselves.
—JILL ZABLOSKI, volunteer in Bolivia

WORLDTEACH

Teaching • Worldwide • 2–12 Months
www.worldteach.org

WORLDTEACH PROVIDES opportunities for individuals who want to make a meaningful contribution to international education by living and working as volunteer teachers in developing countries. Opportunities are available for a full year in Costa Rica, Ecuador, and Namibia; six months in China; or during the summer (for eight weeks) in China, Costa Rica, Ecuador, and Namibia. For those with an interest in the environment, a six-month Nature Guide Training Program in Honduras is also available. Responsibilities include the development and implementation of a curriculum combining English-as-a-foreign-language instruction and natural history, with the goal of training local people for work in nature tourism and environmental education. Program fees range from $3,800 to $5,950, and include housing with a private room and meals (generally with a local host family), a small stipend, round-trip international airfare, health insurance, training, a teaching position, and field support. To help with fund-raising efforts, WorldTeach produces a useful pamphlet called *Fundraising Suggestions*. Candidates must have a bachelor's degree and have a sincere interest in education, international development, and/or cultural exchange. (Summer program applicants must be at least eighteen years of age.) Although the ability to speak a foreign language or teaching experience is not necessary, an open mind, adventurous spirit, and enthusiasm for intercultural learning is essential. Applications are available online.

For More Information:
Ellen Whitman, Admissions Coordinator
WorldTeach
Center for International Development
79 John F. Kennedy St.
Cambridge, MA 02138
(800) 483-2240 • (617) 495-5527 • (617) 495-1599 (fax)
admissions@worldteach.org

This year I have found, more than ever before, that everything always works out as it is supposed to. All of the situations, no matter how scary, surreal, or joyful, have proven to be just what I needed to experience. My coming to Costa Rica was a personal quest, to find a part of myself that I felt was missing. (I needed) to exhibit myself as an independent and resourceful person, able to handle negative situations that may arise. Also, (I needed) to acknowledge positive situations and recognize the special benefits I will receive because of them. I feel I have found a large piece of what I was searching for because I have learned that every experience happens for a specific reason: TO GROW!

—JENNIFER LAMB,
volunteer in Costa Rica

YMCA GO GLOBAL

Work Abroad • Worldwide • 3–12 Months
www.ymcanyc.org/international

THE YMCA GO GLOBAL program provides exciting opportunities for those over the age of eighteen to share their talents, interests, and culture with another country—including fifty YMCA sites throughout the world. Go Global fills a void for U.S. citizens wanting to develop a greater international knowledge and competence along with experiencing a completely different way of thinking, learning, and living. Volunteers typically work up to three months in the summer or winter in a wide variety of YMCA programs, including everything from community development and education to English teaching, teen leadership, and camps. Some overseas YMCAs also look for volunteers who can stay for up to one year. In exchange for your volunteer service, room and board are provided. Volunteers are responsible for their airfare, health insurance, and a $155 application fee, but don't let this discourage you, as scholarships are available.

For More Information:
Jean-Paul Sewavi, Special Programs Director
YMCA Go Global
71 W. 23rd St., Suite 1904
New York, NY 10010
(888) 477-9622 • (212) 727-8800, ext. 130
jpsewavi@ymcanyc.org

RECOMMENDED RESOURCES. . . . .

Would you like to escape to a new country and restart your life? With **EscapeArtist.com**, you can escape from the ordinary with extraordinary ideas. Come explore thousands of resources and links—and be sure to sign up for the free monthly e-zine magazine, *Escape from America.*

Alternatives to the Peace Corps (Food First Books, $9.95) offers many options for those who want to volunteer their time (almost anywhere in the world) for a good cause. The guide provides listings of voluntary service organizations, work brigades, and study tours that work to support development as defined by the local people. A must for anyone dedicated to grassroots work in their own backyard and in the Third World. Food First also offers internships at their headquarters in California, with work dedicated to eliminating the injustices that cause hunger and poverty. For more information contact Marilyn Borchardt, Development Director, Food First, Institute for Food and Development Policy, 398 60th St., Oakland, CA 94618; (510) 654-4400, foodfirst@foodfirst.org, www.foodfirst.org.

For anyone interested in teaching English as a Second Language or working abroad, head to **Dave's ESL Café** (www.eslcafe.com). The café's Job Center provides postings of hundreds of teaching and administration jobs throughout the world, while the ESL Web Guide provides literally thousands of links sorted by category.

Whether you want to intern, volunteer, study, or teach abroad, you'll find plenty of information, programs, and travel resources with the **GoAbroad.com** network.

Written by two seasoned American journalists who lived and worked in Italy, *Living, Studying, and Working in Italy* (Henry Holt, $16) is brimming with candid insider tips and practical advice on experiencing Italy as the locals might. Travis Neighbor and Monica Larner provide information on volunteer opportunities, internship programs, and language schools as well as information about freelance and professional employment opportunities for Americans. Essential for anyone interested in making Italy his or her home—at least for awhile.

Sprechen Sie Deutsch? Parlate Italiano? Parlez-vous Français? A **Middlebury** summer prepares people of all ages for a much more successful study- or work- abroad experience by dramatically improving their language skills, deepening their cultural understanding, and strengthening their confidence and learning strategies. With a formal commitment of "No English Spoken Here," Middlebury students use their target language exclusively—in classes, dining halls, dormitories, and throughout a range of cocurricular activities over a course of seven to nine very full weeks of intensive language learning! Whether studying Arabic, Chinese, French, German, Italian, Japanese, Spanish, or Russian, participants literally live the language at all hours of the day. One summer at Middlebury equals at least one full academic year of conventional language study. Tuition starts at $5,000, which includes room and board, for the seven-week summer program. For more information contact Middlebury College Language Schools, Sunderland Language Center, Middlebury, VT, 05753-6131; (802) 443-5510, languages@middlebury.edu, www.middlebury.edu/~ls.

Published electronically on a biweekly basis, *O-Hayo Sensei: The Newsletter of Teaching Jobs in Japan* (www.ohayosensei.com) provides listings of over one hundred teaching and other language-related positions, writing/editing jobs, and current travel information for Japan. Single issues are free (with one-year subscriptions available for $12). Their website also features more than eighteen hundred Japan-related books, links, and resources.

If you are thinking about joining the Peace Corps, Dillon Banerjee offers an insider perspective of his trials and tribulations before, during, and after his two-year volunteer experience in Cameroon. *So You Want to Join the Peace Corps* (Ten Speed Press, $12.95) is organized around seventy-three questions starting with "What is the application process like?" and ending with "Would you go back and do the Peace Corps all over again?" Extensive information can be found on what programs currently exist, the requirements, and how to strengthen your own application.

StudyAbroad.com provides an online directory of study, language, internship, and volunteer opportunities abroad along with valuable country-specific information.

With over thirty years' worth of experience in Teaching English as a Foreign Language (TEFL), Jeff Mohamed provides detailed information and how-to advice on successfully creating a new teaching lifestyle anywhere in the world. *Teaching English Overseas* (English International, $19.95) contains details of 450 schools and other organizations which hire more than ten thousand teachers every year. For further information and advice on teaching overseas, check out the author's companion website at www.english-international.com.

Anyone making plans to travel abroad should stop in first at **Transitions Abroad** (TA). Along with their companion website (www.transitionsabroad.com), TA publishes a handful of resources and directories that will have you fully engrossed in planning your new adventure. For those who need a constant stream of knowledge throughout the year, you might indulge in their bimonthly magazine, *Transitions Abroad*. Topics include short-term jobs, special interest and language vacations, an overseas travel planner, work abroad, and adventure travel ($28 per year, or $6.45 for a single issue or back issues, which includes shipping). For those who want the whole kit and kaboodle in one book, the *Alternative Travel Directory* focuses on travel, study, and living overseas ($19.95); and their *Work Abroad* guide provides the key contacts on landing an overseas job ($15.95). Stop by their website and sign up for the *Transitions Abroad eNewsletter*, a monthly email newsletter that will keep you updated about new travel websites, programs, recommended publications, and the latest line on their magazine. Visit Transitions Abroad online or call (800) 293-0373 for more information.

Travelers who want to combine a little adventure and personal growth with service to others should include *Volunteer Vacations* by Bill McMillon (Chicago Review Press, $16.95) in their research. This classic profiles more than 250 organizations that need volunteers along with vignettes from previous volunteers.

Get the real scoop on working overseas through the eyes of author Susan Griffith. *Work Your Way around the World* ($17.95), although geared mainly to the U.K. crowd, provides detailed information for the working traveler, with explicit country-by-country overviews that cover everything from picking olives in Greece to working as a tour guide in Peru. And for those who might want to "talk" their way around the world, *Teaching English Abroad* ($17.95) intertwines actual accounts of enjoyable and disappointing experiences by people who have taught abroad. You'll also find specific job vacancy information compiled from language schools from the south of Chile to Iceland. Finally, for a directory of volunteer gigs worldwide, be sure to check out *The International Directory of Voluntary Work* by Louise Whetter ($15.95). All titles are published by Vacation Work in the U.K. (www.vacationwork.co.uk) and distributed by Peterson's in the U.S. (www.petersons.com).

TRAVEL GUIDES

Travel on the cheap and down-to-earth! *Big World* provides such inspiring destination articles that you'll find yourself on the next train to some remote village to celebrate the simple thrill of exploration. Each issue (four per year) includes regular columns on adventuring, biking, cyber-traveling, hosteling, and dozens of budget travel tips ($3.50 per issue). More information can be found at the companion website (www.bigworld.com), which includes everything from pages of travel links to information on becoming a travel writer.

Author Rick Steves takes a lighthearted, personal approach to sharing with you everything you need to know to have a great trip in Europe. *Rick Steves' Europe through the Back Door* ($21.95, Avalon Travel Publishing) is full of practical travel advice—a must for anyone venturing to Europe who desires a more intimate feel for the places that locals patronize rather than hitting the main tourist stops. You can receive a free quarterly travel newsletter or monthly email dispatch, which provides information on the collection of Rick Steves' travel guides as well as tour information, money-saving travel tips, and other great stuff (including the best deals on Eurail passes). Contact Rick at P.O. Box 2009, Edmonds, WA 98020-2009; (425) 771-8303, rick@ricksteves.com, www.ricksteves.com.

Izon's Backpacker Journal (Ten Speed Press, $9.95) is the perfect travel journal, designed to compliment budget travel guidebooks while you trek about the world. The journal includes 160 pages to record your adventures, including three hundred tips and helpful quotes throughout. How else would you know not to blow your nose in public in Japan or not to pick up food with your left hand in Indonesia? With your scintillating entries alongside the author's, you'll have more than just memories of your adventure. *Izon's Backpacker News Wire* at www.izon.com provides the latest line on backpacking around the world.

Researched, written, and produced entirely by students (over 250 of them from Harvard University) who know firsthand how to see the world on the cheap, Let's Go (www.letsgo.com) guidebooks provide information on the hippest backstreet cafes, pristine secluded beaches, the best routes from border to border, off-the-beaten-path cultural sites, and budget-conscious accommodations (starting from the least expensive and working its way up). The classic Europe handbook, *Let's Go Europe* (St. Martin's Press, $23.99), has been the bible for a generation of student travelers; however, over fifty-three in-depth city, regional, and country guidebooks now criss-cross five continents—from the U.S. to China.

Lonely Planet (www.lonelyplanet.com) publishes down-to-earth, comprehensive, and practical guidebooks for independent travelers who "have an interest in things." There are over two hundred books in print, all written in a straightforward, readable style with lots of firsthand tips and recommendations. Upgrades (that document significant changes to current editions) for over sixty guidebooks can be found online as well as a variety of email newsletter subscription options.

For more than two decades, **Moon Travel Handbooks** (www.moon.com) have been guiding independent travelers to the world's best destinations. The guidebooks are adventures in themselves, providing coverage of off-the-beaten-path destinations, fascinating accounts of the region's history and varied cultures, insight into political and environmental issues, street-savvy advice, language glossaries, accommodations and transportation information—everything travelers need for an extraordinary travel experience. Whether you are headed for the Hawaiian surf, the Colorado Rockies, or the streets of Tokyo, Moon probably has the guide to get you there. For U.S. travelers, a must is *Road Trip USA,* (Avalon Travel Publishing, $24), which covers eleven cross-country routes, providing practical information and entertaining sidebars.

Rough Guides (www.roughguides.com) are aimed squarely at independent-minded travelers of all kinds, on all budgets—whether vacationers, business travelers, or backpackers. Thoughtful writing, painstaking research, and conscientiously prepared maps are fundamental to their commitment to provide you with the best possible guides—from Amsterdam to Zimbabwe, with almost two hundred more in between.

Traveling alone need not mean lonely. How about taking a cooking and language workshop in France? What about a three-week cycling tour in the Grand Canyon or hiking the hills of Tuscany? In **Traveling Solo** (Globe Pequot Press, $16.95), Eleanor Berman provides advice and ideas for more than 250 learning adventures for travelers without a companion, along with plenty of advice on how to plan the perfect solo vacation.

RESOURCES

Your diamonds are not in far distant mountains or in yonder seas; they are in your own backyard, if you but dig for them. —RUSSELL H. CONWELL

12

YOUR COMPASS TO THE GUIDE

INDEXES

ALPHABETICAL LISTING OF PROGRAMS . . . .

This index is geared to all the programs and associations located throughout your guide. For a listing of resources, books, publications, and websites, check out the general index on page 418.

The true measure of an individual is how he treats a person who can do him absolutely no good. —ANN LANDERS

Many of life's failures are people who did not realize how close they were to success when they gave up. —THOMAS ALVA EDISON

The game of life is a game of boomerangs. Our thoughts, deeds, and words return to us sooner or later with astounding accuracy. —FLORENCE SCOVEL SHINN

CATEGORY INDEX · · · · · · · · · · · · · · · · · ·

From adventure education to Zen centers (and everything in between), this list provides you with the buzz word associated with each program. Although each has been assigned a particular category, some programs cover such a wide spectrum of opportunities that they could be listed under many categories. So become an explorer while perusing this index.

The shoe that fits one person pinches another; there is no recipe for living that suits all cases. —CARL JUNG

Success is the ability to go from one failure to another with no loss of enthusiasm. —WINSTON CHURCHILL

To live a creative life, we must lose our fear of being wrong. —JOSEPH CHILTON PEARCE

GEOGRAPHICAL LISTING OF PROGRAMS. . . . .

Are you looking for a particular program in a specific locale? This index gives you the tools to narrow your search to a specific state, country, or region. The United States is broken down by state, with the rest of the world grouped by country. You'll also find programs that are offered in more than one state grouped under the heading "USA" and those offered in more than one country grouped under "Worldwide." The programs under these headings are not listed separately by their respective state or country, so you'll have to get the specifics by referring to each listing.

That which we obtain too easily, we esteem too lightly. It is dearness only which gives everything its value. Heaven knows how to put a proper price on its goods. —THOMAS PAINE

History has demonstrated that the most notable winners usually encountered heartbreaking obstacles before they triumphed. They won because they refused to become discouraged by their defeats. —BERTIE C. FORBES

Optimism is the faith that leads to achievement. Nothing can be done without hope and confidence. —HELEN KELLER

409

PROGRAM LENGTH INDEX · · · · · · · · · · · · · · · · ·

Included in this list are programs divided up by program length, with some programs appearing in multiple categories. Seasonal, summer, and winter programs can be found at the end of the index, followed by programs whose length varies.

Whether you think you can do a thing or not, you're right. —HENRY FORD

Summary

Blessed is he who expects nothing, for he shall never be disappointed —JONATHAN SWIFT

To make your ideas work for you, you first have to work for them. —THOMAS ALVA EDISON

GENERAL INDEX . . . .

Consult with this index for general information on career change, general life philosophies, books, publications, resources, or websites. If you want to find a specific program or association—whether by name, category, location, or program length—the previous four indexes will provide you with the information that you need.

If you're not failing every now and again, it's a sign you're not doing anything very innovative. —WOODY ALLEN